TRANSNATIONAL *and* CROSS-BORDER CRIMINAL LAW

TRANSNATIONAL *and* CROSS-BORDER CRIMINAL LAW

Canadian Perspectives

Edited by
ROBERT J. CURRIE

IRWIN LAW

Transnational and Cross-Border Criminal Law

Published in 2023 by

Irwin Law Inc
Suite 206, 14 Duncan Street
Toronto, Ontario M5H 3G8
www.irwinlaw.com

ISBN: 978-1-55221-663-7 | e-book ISBN: 978-1-55221-664-4

Cataloguing in Publication available from Library and Archives Canada

Title: Transnational and cross-border criminal law : Canadian perspectives / edited by Robert J. Currie.
Names: Currie, Robert J., 1970– editor.
Description: Includes bibliographical references and index.
Identifiers: Canadiana (print) 20230518559 | Canadiana (ebook) 20230518710 | ISBN 9781552216637 (softcover) | ISBN 9781552216644 (PDF)
Subjects: LCSH: Transnational crime—Law and legislation—Canada. | LCSH: International law—Canada.
Classification: LCC KE8809 .T73 2023 | LCC KF9219 T73 2023 | DDC 345.71—dc23

Canada | ONTARIO CREATES | ONTARIO CRÉATIF

Cover image: Adobe Stock

Printed and bound by CPI Group (UK) Ltd, Croydon, CR0 4YY.

1 2 3 4 5 27 26 25 24 23

Contents

Foreword

It is a privilege to write the foreword for this new collection of essays that discusses some of the many issues arising in the complex area of transnational and cross-border criminal law—in particular, within the context of Canadian criminal law. Professor Robert Currie, Canada's foremost expert in the field, has gathered an inspired set of papers from a stellar group of legal experts whose work touches crime that transcends borders.

In the book's introductory opening chapter, Professor Currie draws an important distinction between transnational criminal law and cross-border criminal law, although they are intertwined. Transnational criminal law encapsulates the legal regime in which states, agreeing that particular offences are of significant mutual concern, create primarily treaty-based mechanisms with which to cooperate with each other in suppressing those crimes. Cross-border criminal law has more of a domestic flavour; it is a mixed bag of rules and tools that police, prosecutors, defence lawyers, and the courts can (and should) use to deal with offences that involve a foreign state in some way. The two areas are mutually reinforcing. Both have an international law component, but are ultimately geared toward facilitating the prosecution and defence of domestic crimes before domestic courts. Professor Currie convincingly makes the case that the traditional practice of calling all of this "international criminal law" obscures the differences between these bodies of law and that dealing with war crimes, genocide, and the International Criminal Court, and that clarity is preferable to obscurity given the nature of the subject matter.

This book could not be more timely. Criminal activity is increasingly internationalized, but most crimes that engage international law, cross-border law, and transnational law issues are prosecuted domestically; such issues are increasingly part of the mainstream work of the practising criminal lawyer. Issues of jurisdiction, obtaining evidence, and the application of the *Charter of Rights and Freedoms* all come to the forefront in transnational or cross-border investigations and prosecutions. They are interesting and worthy of study, not least because of the increasing need for practical application.

The topics explored in the essay collection include the grievous crimes of human, drug, wildlife, and cultural property trafficking; cybercrime; money-laundering; terrorism; human rights violations; corporate criminality; and extradition. These most heinous crimes are often difficult to investigate because of their transnational nature and the deep involvement of organized crime. This book, with its multidisciplinary approach, will assist those practising in the field of domestic criminal law to identify the importance of the application of international law when faced with it—and perhaps more importantly, when to search for it. It provides sage advice on a broad variety of transnational criminal law matters, and especially identifies that the offences do not exist within silos, but often have related crimes and issues. For example, it is difficult to envision an organized crime offence without the concomitant crime of money-laundering. Extradition and the criminal aspects of refugee law are intertwined with international human rights law. And so on.

This book fills a void on major jurisdictional, human rights, social, and criminal issues that rest under the umbrella of transnational criminal law. There is nothing in the Canadian literature that addresses these topics in a manner that joins the issues and identifies how international law—including domestic legislation that implements various treaties and UN declarations, for example—informs and applies to domestic criminal law, yet is often overlooked, even by the highest Court in the land. This collection addresses how various international legal principles hide in plain sight in our own criminal law and identifies for the reader the importance of being alive to applicable instruments that may have an effect on a prosecution, even if it is solely within the confines of the borders of Canada.

Moreover, the essays often point out the inconsistencies in court decisions, even at the same level of court, including the highest level. While judicial education has come a long way in Canada in the past thirty years, there is a dearth of continuing education courses for judges in the field of international law. This book of essays will therefore be a significantly helpful tool for the judiciary, who often have little experience in the field, in understanding the complexity of competing jurisdictions, laws in relation to evidence, applicable treaties, and other declarations that have been incorporated into domestic law.

I congratulate Professor Currie, and all of the contributors to this book, for their significant contribution to a growing field of law.

Justice Elizabeth Bennett
Court of Appeal for British Columbia
Court of Appeal for Yukon
Court Martial Court of Appeal of Canada
Past-President of the International Society for the Reform of the Criminal Law

Acknowledgments

In 1985, rock artist Sting released his first solo album, *The Dream of the Blue Turtles*. It was an amazing album that changed the course of my life in some ways, but that is another story. In the album's liner notes, Sting wrote:

> Since I started this thing, people have constantly referred to it as my solo album, which of course is ridiculous. It's as if I had done everything myself, well I didn't. The contribution and commitment of all those involved made it far less an indulgent and personal statement than a statement about how well people can work together without diluting or compromising ideas or ideals. We also had a lot of fun.

These are words that I find particularly resonant as this collection is readied for publication. Certainly the idea for the book was my own, the product of a career thus far spent trying to focus attention on transnational and cross-border criminal law, both internationally and in the Canadian context. I was perhaps better placed than most to realize that we have a massive hole in the Canadian legal literature around these topics, and ambitious and cocky enough to think that I could formulate a solid way to close the gap. As self-appointed "Editor" of the collection, I am, in a meaningful way, responsible for its content, including any limitations it may have.

However, like every writing project of any scope, it really takes a "cast of thousands" to make it happen, and this one is no different. In fact, even more so, because in this collection I only wrote one chapter! First off, I am very grateful to my stable of authors, each of whom answered the call to contribute to a somewhat novel project and produced a collection of essays that are hard-hitting, clearly thought out, and just plain interesting. It is not lost on me that virtually all of the discussion, writing, editing, and rewriting went on during the COVID-19 pandemic; this was a time of great strain for us all, and I am humbled that these authors were able to formulate excellent work in such days. The humility I feel about their effort is compounded by the willingness of Justice Elizabeth Bennett to write the foreword, a foreword that modestly omits the important work she has done on transnational and cross-border crime issues, both as lawyer and as jurist.

The Canadian Partnership on International Justice (CPIJ), a collaboration funded by way of a grant from the Social Sciences and Humanities Research Council of Canada (SSHRC), graciously provided funding for me to obtain the wonderful research and editorial skills of Elizabeth Matheson (JD, Schulich School of Law, 2022) and Hannah Loder (JD (anticipated), Schulich School of Law, 2024). I also benefited, as always, from the assistance of Schulich Research Librarian Hannah Steeves, whose cheerfulness and consummate professionalism are so greatly appreciated.

I received advice, help, and hints from a great number of friends and colleagues across the country, including Judge Darin Reeves, Commander Mike Madden (ret'd), Gerald Chan and Stephen Aylward of the Stockwoods firm, Justice Joyce Dewitt-VanOosten, and Justice Jocelyn Speyer. My friend, Professor Emeritus John Currie of the University of Ottawa, was his usual encouraging self. As always, I was privileged to be able to bounce ideas around with Phillip Saunders, Gib van Ert, and Neil Boister, the latter of whose work has been almost as sustaining as his friendship and encouragement over many years.

As I enter the third decade of my academic career, I am more aware than ever of the importance of the shoulders upon which I stand, particularly those from whom I received friendship, education, and encouragement at vital times. In this regard I am especially thankful to Bill Gilmore, Professor of International Criminal Law (ret'd) at the University of Edinburgh, who launched me in the field; Professor Roger Clark, friend and mentor; and for the pioneering work of Professor Jean-Gabriel Castel and the late Professor Sharon Williams, the influence of which can be felt throughout this book.

I am so pleased to have yet another opportunity to work with the wonderful team at Irwin Law, and would like to thank Jeff Miller, Lesley Steeve, and Heather Raven, in particular.

Finally, this book, like all of my work, was greatly enriched by the support of my wife, Donna Davis, MA, LLB (Dalhousie). She is simultaneously a fearless provider of feedback on my legal analysis, a fearsome editor, and an indulgent and gracious receiver of my meandering thoughts and complaints. My daughters, Meg and Katherine, also see fit to put up with me and my writing, and they deserve thanks, too.

March 2023
Halifax, Nova Scotia

List of Abbreviations

CCPCJ	Commission on Crime Prevention and Criminal Justice
CoE	Council of Europe
CRA	Canada Revenue Agency
ECOSOC	United Nations Economic and Social Council
EU	European Union
FATF	Financial Action Task Force
FINTRAC	Financial Transactions and Reports Analysis Centre of Canada
G7	Group of 7 States
G8	Group of 8 States
G20	Group of 20 States
ICC	International Criminal Court
ICJ	International Court of Justice
ICL	International Criminal Law
ICTY	International Criminal Tribunal for the Former Yugoslavia
ILC	International Law Commission
INTERPOL	International Criminal Police Organization
OAS	Organization of American States
OECD	Organization for Economic Cooperation and Development

PCIJ	Permanent Court of International Justice
PPSC	Public Prosecution Service of Canada
RCMP	Royal Canadian Mounted Police
TCL	Transnational Criminal Law
UN	United Nations
UNESCO	Educational, Scientific and Cultural Organization
UNGA	United Nations General Assembly
UNHRC	United Nations Human Rights Council
UNODC	United Nations Office on Drugs and Crime
UNSC	United Nations Security Council
UNTS	United Nations Treaty Series

I

THE BROAD SCOPE *of* TRANSNATIONAL *and* CROSS-BORDER CRIMINAL LAW *in* CANADA

one

Introduction: Locating Transnational and Cross-Border Criminal Law

ROBERT J. CURRIE, KC*

A. THE PURPOSE OF THIS BOOK

As its title indicates, this book deals with a pervasive modern phenomenon — crime that crosses borders — and specifically with the bodies of law that purport to regulate it. It is a subject that is of major and current concern to governments, particularly (but not exclusively) law enforcement authorities, across the world.

And it is no wonder that this is so. In 2022, organized crime gangs threaten the very stability of some states, such as Mexico,[1] and reap untold billions in illicit profit across the world. Human trafficking, cross-border fraud and extortion, and terrorist attacks extract a global-scale toll of human misery that is virtually impossible to measure. The age-old crime of piracy is still a problem.[2] Illegal depletion of natural resources, such as wildlife, timber, and fish, for the purpose of trafficking contributes

* Professor of Law and Distinguished Research Professor, Schulich School of Law, Dalhousie University.

1 Evan Ellis, "Neighbor at Risk: Mexico's Deepening Crisis" *Center for Strategic & International Studies* (4 September 2020), online: www.csis.org/analysis/neighbor-risk-mexicos-deepening-crisis.

2 Andrew Rettman, "EU navies to hunt pirates in West Africa" *euobserver* (19 January 2022), online: https://euobserver.com/world/154120.

to other major worldwide plights, ecosystem destruction, and resultant global warming.[3]

Moreover, even to speak of these brands of criminal conduct under subject-matter labels is to under-emphasize the fact that, like the multinational corporations it most resembles, criminality is increasingly vertically and horizontally integrated on a scale that renders borders somewhat irrelevant. As I have recently written elsewhere,

> [t]his is not just a matter of magnification of "classic" organized crime gangs which diversify their operations through fraud, prostitution, illegal gambling, etc., but rather a massive expansion in fluidity of organization and operational flexibility. The convergence is as startling as it is logical: rebel groups who fund attacks on civilian populations via trafficking in wildlife parts, minerals, and humans, enlisting the assistance of organized gangs; terrorist attacks carried out by specialist cybercrime flotillas; gangland chieftains in one state who use piracy-generated booty to corrupt public officials in a second state, with profits laundered in a third.[4]

For its part, the United Nations Security Council (UNSC) issued a resolution in 2019 that, while nominally focused on the convergence of organized crime and terrorism as a threat to international peace and security, is practically a manifesto calling on states to implement and integrate the inter-state cooperative machinery already in place to address a host of transnational crimes.[5] The United Nations itself has an entire office, the United Nations Office on Drugs and Crime (UNODC), whose remit is largely to help national authorities deal with the scale of the problems and the various barriers to cooperation among themselves. More locally, both Canada and the United States have begun to address a particularly pernicious form of transnational activity, cybercrime, as a national security threat instead of as simply a criminal enforcement problem.[6]

---

3 Pedro Cardoso et al, "Scientists' warning to humanity on illegal or unsustainable wildlife trade" (2021) 263 *Biological Conservation* 109341.

4 Robert J. Currie, review of *Legal Responses to Transnational and International Crimes: Toward an Integrative Approach*, by Harmen van der Wilt & Christophe Paulussen, eds (2018) 16 *New Zealand Yearbook of International Law* 449 at 449.

5 UNSC Res 2482 (19 July 2019).

6 See, for example, Alex Boutilier, "Canadian Spy Agency Targeted Foreign Hackers to 'Impose a Cost' for Cybercrime" *Global News* (6 December 2021), online: https://globalnews.ca/news/8429008/canadian-spy-agency-targets-cybercrime. And for an accessible overview, see John Wilson, "Transnational Crime" in Alexander

Despite all of this, the general public's perception and awareness of these issues tend toward the low side; even the very able students who enter my yearly law school course, International and Transnational Criminal Law, typically have only a vague, piecemeal perception of the overall situation. This is reflected, as well, in media coverage, which, for understandable reasons, tends to leap from issue to issue or from event to event without giving much attention to the broader scope. In Canada, for example, one would search hard to find anyone who was not aware of the extradition case concerning Huawei Chief Financial Officer Meng Wanzhou, which for three years occupied the attention of both the public and those attentive to Canada's place in global diplomatic and security affairs;[7] yet the typical observer would not have become conversant with the most important underlying legal issues, such as how the principle of double criminality operates in extradition cases,[8] or the concern of the international community regarding US jurisdictional overreach in financial crime matters.[9]

A response to the latter point might be that correcting this problem, if it be a problem at all, is the work of legal scholars, and so be it. This is the breach into which I and the various contributors to this book are leaping. The drawing of a distinction between "transnational criminal law" and "cross-border criminal law" is my own doing, and the difference between

---

Lautensach & Sabina Lautensach, *Human Security in World Affairs: Problems and Opportunities*, 2d ed (Victoria, BC: BCcampus & University of Northern British Columbia, 2020), available via a Creative Commons open access license, online: https://opentextbc.ca/humansecurity/.

7 For a timeline see "Contemporary Practice of the United States: Huawei's Meng Wanzhou Released to China After Entering into Deferred Prosecution Agreement with U.S. Justice Department" (2022) 116:1 *American Journal of International Law* 184.

8 The Meng case featured an interesting argument about whether the offence of fraud alleged by the US would have amounted to a crime had it taken place in Canada (thus satisfying the principle of double criminality), given that US sanctions against Iran were squarely at the centre of the supposed financial risk involved, and that Canada does not have such sanctions. The extradition judge ruled that double criminality was nonetheless made out; see *United States v Meng*, 2020 BCSC 785.

9 Among other arguments, Meng's defence team submitted that by asserting jurisdiction over an alleged defrauding of a UK bank, by a Chinese national, at a meeting that took place in Hong Kong, the US was exceeding any jurisdictional claim it might lawfully have had, thus breaching the customary international law of jurisdiction. The ending of the case precluded a judicial decision on the issue, though the defence and Crown briefs are available in the court file.

those two bodies of law is explained below. Broadly speaking, the "fields" of law with which this collection is concerned are criminal law and public international law, but it will be immediately apparent that each chapter is exploring subject matter that exists at some nexus of these. Moreover, the titular flagging of "Canadian perspectives" is deliberate; each paper is written by an author who lives and works in Canada, and who engages with some Canadian angle on the topic about which they have chosen to write. This very specific, perhaps even narrow, approach is also explained below.

B. THE NEED FOR THIS BOOK

1) The Emergence of the Field(s)

In the wake of globalization, it is easy to assume that the internationalization of crime, as with so many other aspects of life, is a modern phenomenon. However, the crossing of borders by both crime and criminals is not new. The earliest example of fugitives fleeing to foreign lands in order to evade government authorities is often said to be traceable to ancient Egypt.[10] Pirates, often associated in the popular imagination with the colonial sea-going era, were in fact a scourge of the ancient world as well.[11] Cross-border mail fraud has existed as long as there has been mail.[12]

Similarly, the formulation by states of legal tools to deal with these phenomena has a long pedigree. Particularly after[13] the genesis of the Westphalian system of sovereign states, there was recognition of one of its essential limitations: a system built on the legal prioritization of territorial sovereignty means that there are limitations on states being able to enforce (and even prescribe) their criminal laws. Simply put, states may

10 Ivan A. Shearer, *Extradition in International Law* (Dobbs Ferry, NY: Oceana Publications, 1971) at 5.

11 References to piracy and its suppression can be found in ancient Greek, Roman, and early European texts; see Alfred Rubin, *The Law of Piracy*, 2d ed (Irvington-on-Hudson, NY: Transnational, 1998) c 1.

12 See Dirk Spennemann, "An Example of Mail Fraud in 19th Century Samoa" (2004) 8:2 *Journal of South Pacific Law* 1, online: www.paclii.org/journals/fJSPL/vol08no2/4.shtml, which examines a case of a European trader who, while living in Samoa, defrauded an Australian wine wholesaler.

13 But not exclusively after this time; see "The Cnidos Text" (1974) 64 *Journal of Roman Studies* 195, cited in Neil Boister, "Treaty-Based Crimes" in Antonio Cassese, ed, *The Oxford Companion to International Criminal Justice* (Oxford: Oxford University Press, 2009) at 540.

have pressing and even valid domestic interest in matters that touch upon or exist in foreign states, but their power to pursue those interests is not unlimited. As I explain it to students, at international law, the RCMP cannot lawfully cross from St. Stephen, New Brunswick into Calais, Maine in order to arrest a fugitive. A US Drug Enforcement Administration agent cannot lawfully question a drug trafficker in Milan, Italy. The Parliament of Canada cannot pass a statute that outlaws smoking on the streets of Paris.[14] The border gets in the way.

This has ramifications at both the international and domestic levels. Internationally, in cases with transnational aspects, states must administer the enforcement of their criminal laws carefully and with attention to the sovereign interests of their counterparts; failure to do so can cause interstate friction, the consequences of which can range from annoying to dire.[15] Cooperation, then, is key, and both legal instruments and informal relationships must be created to facilitate it. Such cooperation has, in fact, existed for centuries, and its history is both colourful and interesting.[16] Domestically, all actors in the criminal justice system may, at some point, be confronted with the need for legal tools that allow them successfully to deal with cases where other states are involved. I will return to this point below, but suffice it to say, again, while the need to deal with these issues has grown in scope in the last several decades, they are neither new nor unknown to the Canadian criminal justice system, nor to those of other states.

---

14 I use this example deliberately, as it is a classic illustration of the point that Parliament is supreme and thus free to pass such a domestic statute even though it breaches international law, but that this would nonetheless open it to responsibility under international law. See Peter W. Hogg, *Constitutional Law of Canada*, student ed (Scarborough, ON: Thomson Carswell, 2003) at 301.

15 My favourite illustration of this point comes from one of the contributors to this book, Chris Ram, who once wrote: "States and intergovernmental organizations act with caution, deliberation and consensus because the consequences of precipitous unilateral actions can be dire. The First World War started, in part, because one State insisted on the right to conduct a criminal investigation into the murder of one of its officials on the sovereign territory of another." Christopher D. Ram, "The Globalization of Crime as a Jurisdictional Challenge," paper delivered at the 2011 Annual Conference of the Canadian Council on International Law, Ottawa, 4–5 November 2011, copy on file with author at 1.

16 See generally Neil Boister et al, eds, *Histories of Transnational Criminal Law* (Oxford: Oxford University Press, 2021).

What is relatively new, however, is the conviction that all of this actually amounts to a legal field or discipline that is worthy of study.[17] To be sure, by the mid-twentieth century there were glimmers of recognition that criminal law, a creature purely of domestic origin, had necessary areas of interface with public international law that were worthy of scholarly study.[18] This stemmed initially from interest in the prospect[19] and eventual realization of international *courts*, in particular, such as the Nuremburg and Tokyo tribunals,[20] and the unsuccessful League of Nations effort toward a terrorism court.[21] Post–World War II, there was also an upsurge in treaties among like-minded states to deal with particular crimes that were felt to affect mutual interests, a development that attracted some scholarly attention.[22]

All of this eventually became reflected in the work of pioneers such as Gerhard Mueller, Edward Wise,[23] Antonio Cassese, Roger Clark, and M. Cherif Bassiouni, who did ground-breaking work on what was eventually described as "the convergence of two disciplines: the penal aspects of international law and the international aspects of national penal law."[24] This convergence was usually lumped into the descriptive label "international criminal law"[25]—and why not? It had international law, it had criminal law, what else was required? Yet this idea of international criminal

17 The criminology field was somewhat quicker out of the gate; for perspective see Phil Williams & Dimitri Vlassis, eds, *Combating Transnational Crime* (London: Frank Cass, 2001).

18 Georg Schwarzenberger, "The Problems of an International Criminal Law" (1950) 3 *Current Legal Problems* 263.

19 James Brierly, "Do We Need an International Criminal Court?" (1927) 8 *British Yearbook of International Law* 81.

20 See, generally, Robert J. Currie & Joseph Rikhof, *International & Transnational Criminal Law*, 3d ed (Toronto: Irwin Law, 2020), c 4.

21 See Sara Wharton & Robert J. Currie, "Transnational Criminal Courts: A Partially-Realized Idea" in Boister et al, eds, above note 16.

22 Roger S. Clark, "Offenses of International Concern: Multilateral State Treaty Practice in the Forty Years Since Nuremberg" (1988) 57 *Nordic Journal of International Law* 49. And see Neil Boister, "The Growth of the Multilateral Suppression Conventions in the First Half of the 20th Century" in Boister et al, eds, above note 16.

23 Gerhard O.W. Mueller & Edward M. Wise, *International Criminal Law* (South Hackensack, NJ: Fred B. Rothman, 1965).

24 Jordan Paust et al, *International Criminal Law: Cases and Materials*, 2d ed (Durham, NC: Carolina Academic Press, 2000) at 3.

25 This brief account is a bit North American-centric, and I would note without exploring it that similar literature existed concurrently in Europe as well.

law as a field obscured unique, complex, and even systemic characteristics that had always been present, as well as divergence that accelerated in the latter part of the twentieth century. Bassiouni went furthest, perhaps, in an effort to produce a rationalized version of the field in the European style,[26] but (at least in my opinion) was bogged down by the complexity of the task.

An innovative 1981 text by Canadian scholars Sharon Williams and Jean-Gabriel Castel was entitled *Canadian Criminal Law: International and Transnational Aspects*,[27] and its content reflected a new state of the art for the field, that: (1) the legal regimes growing up around the core crimes (war crimes, crimes against humanity, genocide, aggression) were different from those under which states were cooperating vis-à-vis other crimes of international concern, from narcotics trafficking and terrorism to counterfeiting and the damaging of undersea cables; and (2) all of this required engagement with international law principles at the level of domestic criminal law (which was not always well-suited to the task). The international law of jurisdiction underpinned all of it, yet it, too, required different interpretation and application depending on which of these contexts it was operating in.

Perhaps even more than Williams and Castel, Professor Clark (to whom colleagues sometimes refer only half-jokingly as "the godfather of transnational criminal law") was uniquely ahead of the game. In a historically grounded and farsighted 1988 article,[28] he fastened upon a remark by Professor A.N. Trainin, writing just before the establishment of the Nuremburg Tribunal, that "conventions are quite possible for combatting individual crimes which are not of an international character ... but which require coordinated methods of struggle."[29] Trainan, Clark wrote,

26 M. Cherif Bassiouni, *Introduction to International Criminal Law* (Ardsley, NY: Transnational, 2003).

27 Sharon A. Williams & Jean-Gabriel Castel, *Canadian Criminal Law: International and Transnational Aspects* (Toronto: Butterworths, 1981). Williams had earlier referred to "two basic branches of international criminal law: *conflict of criminal laws* and *the law of international crimes*. In the first case the basic norm is national in character, whereas in the second it is international." Sharon A. Williams, *International Criminal Law*, 3d rev ed (Toronto: Osgoode Hall Law School, York University, 1978) at i.

28 Clark, above note 22.

29 A.N. Trainin, *Hitlerite Responsibility Under Criminal Law*, trans A. Rothstein (London: Hutchinson, 1945) at 42, quoted in Clark, above note 22 at 84.

was speaking of a reality that was contemporary, but was even more common in the late 1980s: states had long since seen the light of "coordinated measures of struggle" against certain brands of criminals and crime that tended to use state sovereignty to their advantage, and both formal and informal cooperation in suppressing these activities had been in place for well over a century. By the late twentieth century, growth in transportation and telecommunication technology had driven an increase in the ability of criminals to harness the increasing porousness of borders. Also on the rise was the number of cooperative instruments — primarily treaties — and of less formal techniques, which states were compelled to use for crime suppression. Clark identified an expansion of treaty-making around a broader variety of "offenses of international concern"[30] than the usual suspects (genocide, war crimes, etc.), such as narcotics, attacks on UN personnel, and the transnational trade in cultural property.[31]

Writing at around the same time, law and political science scholar Ethan Nadelmann identified these networks of state interaction as "global prohibition regimes."[32] These were reflective of a growing culture of mutual interest-based collaboration among states on crime suppression and, interestingly, criminal law-based norm entrepreneurship, under which powerful states sought to transplant their own criminal law values in the legal frameworks of others.[33] Much of it had to do with illicit drugs, terrorism, jurisdictionally complex areas like airspace and the high seas, and with increasing cooperation of the domestic police forces of different states. Whatever this was, it looked less like "international criminal law."

Clark and Nadelmann's work presaged the true shot heard 'round the world, in the form of Professor Neil Boister's provocatively titled 2003 paper, "'Transnational Criminal Law'?"[34] Taking into account the range

30 Clark, above note 22 at 51.

31 See also Roger S. Clark, "Countering International and Transnational Crime: Defining the Agenda" in Peter J. Cullen & William C. Gilmore, eds, *Crime sans frontières: International and European Legal Approaches* (Edinburgh: Edinburgh University Press, 1998) at 20.

32 Ethan Nadelmann, "Global Prohibition Regimes: The Evolution of Norms in International Society" (1990) 44:4 *International Organization* 479.

33 See also Peter Andreas & Ethan Nadelmann, *Policing the Globe: Criminalization and Crime Control in International Relations* (Oxford: Oxford University Press, 2006) at 228.

34 Neil Boister, "'Transnational Criminal Law'?" (2003) 14:5 *European Journal of International Law* 953.

of developments discussed above, Boister harnessed some of the ideas behind the criminological term "transnational crime" together with Philip Jessup's idea of a "transnational law" to propose a new legal discipline: transnational criminal law (TCL). TCL, Boister wrote, was worth decoupling from international criminal law (ICL) because the two systems had developed differently, asserted and protected different values, and had different features. TCL, in particular, would cover "the indirect suppression by international law through domestic penal law of criminal activities that have actual or potential transboundary effects,"[35] and focus specifically on the network of treaties that Clark was writing about, the "suppression conventions" that have developed since the nineteenth century in order to coordinate inter-state efforts to combat certain types of crime.

Flashing forward to 2010, I waded into these waters with a book that attempted to provide a fully Canadian view on the overall field.[36] While enthusiastically accepting the foundations of TCL as Boister formulated them, I posited that there was another layer that was worthy of attention. Harkening back to Williams and Castel's text and the explicit attention it gave to how this body of international law was dealt with under domestic criminal law, I suggested that the scope of TCL might be under-inclusive. There was a range of criminal cases in which the offences had a domestic origin (i.e., they did not originate in a transnational suppression convention), or at least had no overt "transnational" aspects, but which required engagement with international law issues. For example, the classic case of *Libman v The Queen*[37] dealt with whether Canada had territorial jurisdiction over fraudulent conduct that spanned the territories of three states. It was a criminal case, which required engagement with (customary) international law, yet there was nothing of TCL truly raised by it. Or take a run-of-the-mill US prosecution where a request is made of Canada under the Canada–US *Mutual Legal Assistance Treaty* (*MLAT*)[38] for, say, banking records. This is a criminal case, in which an international law instrument (the treaty) is involved, but is not TCL in the way Boister framed it.

35 *Ibid* at 955.

36 Robert J. Currie, *International & Transnational Criminal Law* (Toronto: Irwin Law, 2010).

37 *Libman v The Queen*, [1985] 2 SCR 178. For engagement on the issues raised by *Libman*, see chapters 6, 7, and 15 of this collection.

38 *Treaty Between the Government of Canada and the Government of the United States of America on Mutual Legal Assistance in Criminal Matters*, (1985) Can TS 1990 No 19.

My proposal was that this was a body of law that dealt with "transnational crimes of domestic concern," and that it was worth distinguishing from TCL, as the latter really dealt with "transnational crimes of international concern."[39] In retrospect, this was a rather clumsy attempt at developing a classification, in no small part because it mingled the nature and characteristics of the crimes themselves with the system(s) of law — procedural, evidentiary, and substantive — that seek to regulate them. What I was truly reaching at was figuring out a way to describe the bundle of legal issues that arise in domestic criminal prosecutions that have cross-border aspects.[40]

Hence, for the purpose of accurately capturing the content of this collection of papers, I have chosen to separate out TCL and "cross-border criminal law" in the title. The distinctions are by no means airtight; any given criminal case that has cross-border aspects to it might very well originate, in some way, from Canada's engagement with the overall TCL regime. Some of the papers engage with the distinction and some do not, nor did I set any editorial requirements of that nature. However, I feel that this approach is more methodologically sound, and in the pandemic-ridden 2020s, we should all do things that make us feel better. It will require some rewriting of chapter 1 of my earlier (and now co-authored) book,[41] but that is a job for another day.

2) Why This Book?

In the years since his original essay, Boister's work has decisively removed the question mark from his title; his own momentous monograph on the field of TCL is now in its second edition,[42] and it is safe to say that a TCL literature has developed.[43] This includes the recently founded *Transnational*

39 Currie, above note 36 at 12–21. The latter phrase was shamelessly lifted from Professor Clark's work.

40 And, to be sure, regulatory/quasi-criminal cases; the distinction is not meaningful for this purpose.

41 Currie & Rikhof, above note 20.

42 Neil Boister, *An Introduction to Transnational Criminal Law*, 2d ed (Oxford: Oxford University Press, 2018).

43 For example, Neil Boister & Robert J. Currie, *Routledge Handbook of Transnational Criminal Law* (Abingdon-on-Thames: Routledge, 2015); Mikkel Jarle Christensen & Neil Boister, eds, *New Perspectives on the Structure of Transnational Criminal Justice* (Leiden: Brill, 2018).

Criminal Law Review, the field's first exclusively TCL-focused law journal.[44] Moreover, the TCL literature is larger than it might appear, since scholarship about its various features and attributes can be safely included under its umbrella, whether or not the phrase "transnational criminal law" is used. There is a large literature about extradition, for example, much of which is based in TCL, as would be scholarship on the major relevant instruments, such as the *United Nations Convention against Transnational Organized Crime (UNTOC)*[45] or *United Nations Convention against Corruption (UNCAC)*.[46]

However, the Canadian literature is decidedly scanty.[47] That is not to say, of course, that there is no or little Canadian legal literature that engages with transnational and cross-border criminal law issues, but that it mostly does not do so in a conscious fashion. Often, its impetus is an engaging issue from a cognate discipline. A comment on extradition to face the death penalty, for example, is certainly cross-border criminal law, but springs from a human rights stable.[48] A wonderful piece on the nationality principle of jurisdiction, which straddles TCL and cross-border criminal law, might be mistaken as simply being public international law.[49] The reasonably substantial terrorism literature is about, well, terrorism.[50] And so on.

The goal of this collection is to assemble essays that have in common their TCL and/or cross-border criminal law content, despite the specific areas of substantive criminal and international law with which they engage. The hope is that this will both plug a hole in the Canadian literature and advance understanding that there is a systemic legal

44 The website for the journal can be found online: https://ojs.uwindsor.ca/index.php/nlj/index.

45 *United Nations Convention against Transnational Organized Crime*, (2000) 2225 UNTS 209.

46 *United Nations Convention against Corruption*, (2003) 2349 UNTS 41.

47 This is not true of ICL, a field choked with literature but where some of the best work is by Canadian scholars such as Professors William Schabas, Darryl Robinson, Payam Akhavan, Frédéric Mégret, and Fannie Lafontaine.

48 William A. Schabas, "*United States v. Burns*" (2001) 95:3 *American Journal of International Law* 666.

49 Frédéric Mégret, "Do Not Do Abroad What You Would Not Do at Home? An Exploration of the Rationales for Extraterritorial Criminal Jurisdiction Over a State's Nationals" (2020) 57 *Canadian Yearbook of International Law* 1.

50 Craig Forcese & Kent Roach, *False Security: The Radicalization of Canadian Anti-Terrorism* (Toronto: Irwin Law, 2015).

umbrella under which these issues can be considered. A criminal case with an international law issue is not simply or only that, but is part of a larger landscape. Engagement with this landscape can increase overall knowledge in a field which, as explained in the introductory section above, is sorely in need of development.

From a scholarly point of view this seems a useful goal. Canada is party to a large number of transnational suppression conventions, but there is little consideration of them outside substantive silos.[51] The terrorism people may talk about the terrorism treaties, the cybercrime people about their respective treaties, and yet my ambition is to show that there is insight that can be gained via TCL analysis across these narrower fields. The substance and interpretation of domestic statutory, common, and constitutional law in the criminal area can be enriched by an understanding of the roles played by international law. Jurisdiction, in its international law sense, underpins nearly everything. The conversations can be richer and more interesting.

I am also strongly of the view that there is a practical need for a collection like this one (and hopefully more to follow). A criminal law course is required in every Canadian law school, but a public international law course is not. Criminal law practitioners and judges in courts of criminal jurisdiction typically do not receive (nor do they even ask for much) in the way of continuing legal education on international matters. There is both caselaw and literature (which I choose not to cite here) showing that the interpolation of domestic criminal law and procedure with international law can produce confusion and suboptimal results. Yet, cases with transnational or cross-border aspects are increasing in number. In the original edition of our textbook, I wrote about the utility of helping criminal and international lawyers to speak each others' languages more fluently,[52] and in my view this is a more important goal than ever. The hope is that this book can help expand the literature to a point where the lawyers and lawmakers involved in TCL will have a greater range of tools to reach better results.

I hasten to add that I am not suggesting these tools are needed because criminal lawyers are too thick to handle international law or

51 An exception is Doug Breithaupt, "The Effect of International Conventional Criminal Law on Domestic Legislative Initiatives Since 1990" in Oonagh Fitzgerald, ed, *The Globalized Rule of Law: Relationships Between International and Domestic Law* (Toronto: Irwin Law, 2006) at 573.

52 Currie, above note 36 at 14.

because international lawyers will not deign to descend to the combat zone of criminal investigations and trials. The simple fact is that the issues raised in cases with transnational and cross-border aspects are outside the ordinary scope of day-to-day domestic criminal law. The issues themselves are as various as they are interesting. A person takes two UN personnel hostage during a conflict in a foreign state: does Canada have jurisdiction to prosecute them?[53] Or over a person who attempts to bribe a foreign government official by making telephone calls from Toronto?[54] Does the *Charter of Rights and Freedoms* bar Canada's assertion of extraterritorial jurisdiction over its nationals?[55] Can a person be extradited to face a sentence of "life without parole" in a foreign state?[56] Is evidence gathered by police in a foreign state admissible at a criminal trial in Canada?[57] Does the *Charter* apply to Canadian police when they are gathering evidence in a foreign state?[58] Does section 12 of the *Canada Evidence Act* permit the cross-examination of a witness on criminal convictions that were imposed in foreign states, or only those from Canada?[59]

As explored in more detail below, the authors of the chapters of this book cover a dazzling variety of issues in the papers they graciously agreed to write. They and their writing are united, I think, by the conviction that transnational and cross-border criminal matters are worthy of examination, and that assembling Canadian perspectives thereon is a worthwhile and even pressing objective.

C. THE CONSTRUCTION OF THIS BOOK

1) Overview

As I was recruiting authors for this collection, I cast my net widely in the Canadian legal and academic communities, and advised each potential contributor that I had a very specific editorial stance. I was open to virtually any topic that involved both crime and international law,

53 *R v Ribic*, 2008 ONCA 790.

54 *R v Karigar*, 2017 ONCA 576.

55 *R v Klassen*, 2008 BCSC 1762.

56 *United States v Muhammad 'Isa*, 2014 ABCA 256.

57 *R v Rajah*, 2020 ONCJ 250.

58 *R v Tan*, 2014 BCCA 9; and see Chapter 8 of this collection.

59 *R v Stratton* (1978), 21 OR (2d) 258 (CA).

that had a Canadian perspective, and that was not concerned with ICL. This admittedly broad approach truly paid off. The authors come from a broad variety of professional backgrounds: academics, Crown prosecutors, defence counsel, lawyers from Justice Canada and the Office of the Judge Advocate General, and leaders of civil society organizations. The topics with which they engage are similarly variegated; also, some provide reasonably broad perspectives on particular brands of crime or procedure, while others focus on extremely specific issues. What shines through is the interest and professional acumen they bring to their subjects of choice.

The book is divided into six sections. Section I is entitled The Broad Scope of Transnational and Cross-Border Criminal Law in Canada, and aside from this chapter it contains Chapter 2, The Internationalization of Canadian Criminal Justice Policy, by Donald K. Piragoff, KC. Piragoff, recently retired from his position as Senior Assistant Deputy Minister of Justice at Justice Canada's Policy Sector, has written something of a capstone piece for this collection. With the perspective of his decades of engagement with the interaction of Canadian criminal law and international law—and law-making—he provides a thorough and textured overview of how our federal government has designed and executed its development of *Canada's* criminal justice policy to respond to *international* criminal justice policy. The chapter descends "into the weeds" of just how Canadian law has been opened and expanded to accommodate international developments, but it is both accessibly written and meticulously sourced in the relevant law, policy writing, and scholarship, as well as being interlaced with the kind of knowledge only available to insiders.

Moreover, without any prompting from me, Piragoff has reflected on one of the major motivations behind this collection. Criminal justice is increasingly internationalized, and Canadian criminal law policy has tilted strongly toward engagement with the global scene. Therefore, Canadian "lawyers and other professionals interested in criminal justice policy will need to be well versed in both domestic and comparative criminal law and procedure," as well as in "the various forms of international law, namely international human rights law, ICL, TCL, international humanitarian law and the interplay between them. They will be asked to translate international to domestic, and domestic to international."[60] This admonition,

60 See page 66.

and the thorough survey which it concludes, provide a sound and fitting backdrop for the rest of the book.

Section II, Implementation and Influence, is a set of chapters that have in common their exploration of how the suppression conventions and related normative instruments have had impacts, both direct and indirect, on Canadian statutory and caselaw. In Chapter 3, Courting Transnational Criminal Law in Canada, Professor Gillian MacNeil of the University of Manitoba's Faculty of Law examines how the Supreme Court of Canada has treated the suppression conventions in its jurisprudence. Through the lens of Canadian law on the implementation of treaties and how they are meant to be used, she concludes that the Court's methodology has been inconsistent in this regard, and that there are good reasons to correct this inconsistency.

In Chapter 4, The Influence of Transnational Criminal Law on Refugee Law, Dr. Joseph Rikhof (recently retired as Manager of the Law at the War Crimes Section of Justice Canada) analyzes how TCL has influenced international and domestic refugee law; specifically, the grounds for exclusion of refugees on the basis of criminality are examined. Based on a comparative review of the caselaw of a number of states, including Canada, he concludes that, while TCL has had an impact, it has overall been misunderstood and underutilized, and that better use could be made.

In Chapter 5, Formalism and Substance in the Domestic Implementation of Transnational Criminal Law in Canada's Anti-terrorism Criminal Regimes, Professor Michael Nesbitt of the University of Calgary's Faculty of Law provides a thorough review of how TCL norms have been utilized by Canada in creating and updating its criminal law and national security regimes regarding terrorism. Reviewing the various touch points where TCL has influenced or been implemented into Canadian anti-terrorism law, he identifies difficulties that have emerged where Canada formalistically adopts international norms, which he contrasts with successes produced where such norms are more substantively implemented into the Canadian domestic framework.

Section III of the book contains essays that squarely address its title subject: The Problems of Jurisdiction. Jurisdiction, in its international law sense, is the heart, or perhaps the engine, of transnational and cross-border criminal law, and the issues are both interesting and immediate. I have taken the unusual step, for a collection of this sort, of including two chapters written by the same author, Christopher Ram, who at the time of writing was senior counsel with the Criminal Law Policy Section of Justice Canada. My reason for this is that, in his years of toiling away in the engine room of Canada's engagement with international criminal justice law and policy, Ram has built up an immense expertise in the field, but regrettably has not been able to contribute to the literature with any frequency. This collection makes a modest effort to address this.

In Chapter 6, Making Sense of Extraterritoriality Jurisprudence: Heuristic Pro-forum Biases and the Need for an Algorithmic Approach, Ram provides a compelling critique of Canadian caselaw dealing with extended territorial and extraterritorial jurisdiction. Arguing that, in considering cases with transnational aspects, Canadian courts have failed to engage sufficiently with international norms that are meant to shape how domestic courts exercise jurisdiction, he posits that the caselaw casts the jurisdictional net too widely. He follows this up in Chapter 7, An Agenda for Jurisdictional Law Reform, which, true to its title, lays out a set of proposals designed to bring Canada's law of criminal jurisdiction in line with international law, particularly focusing on a more cautious approach to infringement on the sovereign interests of other states.

In Chapter 8, Canadian ISIS Fighters and Supporters and the Irony of the *Khadr* Exception, Professor Leah West of Carleton University's Norman Paterson School of International Affairs takes on one of the most pernicious jurisdictional issues of the last thirty years of Canadian jurisprudence: the extraterritorial application of the *Charter*. Focusing on the failure of the Canadian government to investigate the alleged crimes of Canadians who participated in the war in Syria, she contends that its reluctance stems from uncertainty regarding the application of the *Charter* to anything that Canadian investigators might do during any investigation. Placing the blame where it belongs — namely, on the Supreme Court's problematic decisions in *R v Hape*[61] and *Canada v Khadr*[62] — she highlights the irony that "the Court's attempt to vindicate the rights of one citizen interned abroad in deplorable conditions has inadvertently prolonged the detention [in Syria] of more than 40 Canadians."[63]

In Chapter 9, What Side Do You Come From? Borders in *R v Desautel*, criminal defence lawyer and former Justice Canada counsel Robin Parker comments on a uniquely Canadian take on territorial jurisdiction:

61 *R v Hape*, 2007 SCC 26.

62 *Canada (Justice) v Khadr*, 2008 SCC 28.

63 See page 193.

the decision of the Supreme Court of Canada in *R v Desautel*.[64] The American accused was an Indigenous person who was neither a citizen nor resident of Canada, but belonged to an Indigenous community that had historically lived on both sides of what is now the Canada–US border. Prosecuted for illegal hunting in British Columbia, he successfully pleaded an Aboriginal right to hunt in Canadian territory as a complete defence. Parker reflects on how a decision like this necessarily broadens our perspective on territory and territorial jurisdiction, in a manner that will continue to ripple as more Aboriginal rights claims go forward.

Section IV, Corporate, Economic and Financial Crime, Money Laundering, and Proceeds, has the most substantial set of papers in this volume, and with good reason. It is impossible, not to mention short-sighted, to speak of transnational and cross-border crime without some focus on economic crime, particularly white-collar crime and what is increasingly referred to as "illicit financial flows." It has long been recognized that "there are more similarities than differences between organized and white-collar crimes,"[65] and the differences between organized crime gangs and networks of corporate criminals and tax evaders are increasingly irrelevant from a public policy point of view.

The first three papers focus on anti-money laundering (AML) law and policy. This is a topic on which Canada is heavily engaged at the moment, and not for good reasons. Chapter 10, Gatekeepers—The Lawyer Enigma, is written by Dr. Peter M. German, KC, currently President of the International Centre for Criminal Law Reform & Criminal Justice Policy, who also authored a prominent series of reports on money laundering in British Columbia, commissioned by that province's attorney general. He takes on what has been one of the toughest nuts to crack in Canada's approach to suppressing money laundering, which is how and the extent to which lawyers can be regulated so as to prevent their facilitation of these offences. Looking at the legal profession's various relevant roles, he surveys international and comparative domestic developments, concluding that Canada's reluctance to make a serious effort at lawyer regulation will likely need to be revisited in the near future.

In Chapter 11, Tackling Money Laundering in Canada Through Beneficial Ownership Transparency, Transparency International Canada

64 *R v Desautel*, 2021 SCC 17.

65 Jay Albanese, "Organized Crime vs. White-Collar Crime: Which Is the Bigger Problem?" (2021) *Academia Letters* art 310, online: https://doi.org/10.20935/AL310.

Executive Director James Cohen explores an increasingly popular AML tool: beneficial ownership registries. Such registries allow easy access to information about the ownership of shell companies, which are often used as a means of disguising laundered funds, and Cohen makes a powerful case that Canada should have them in place, and in particular that they should be publicly accessible.

In Chapter 12, Harmonious Coexistence: Law and Laundering in Canada, Professor Sanaa Ahmed of the University of Calgary's Faculty of Law critiques Canada's overall approach to the suppression of money laundering, making the (no doubt controversial) claim that Canada's AML laws encourage certain forms of money laundering. She argues that by aligning its law with international AML standards, Canada has also incorporated the under-inclusive scope of those standards, resulting in a narrow approach to defining money laundering and a skewing of enforcement toward cases with predicate offences. A more robust approach, she concludes, would take a broader view of the various contributing factors to illegal financial flows and implant AML measures into contributing areas such as taxation and immigration.

In Chapter 13, Transnational Crime, Tainted Property, and Civil Forfeiture, Professor Michelle Gallant of the University of Manitoba's Faculty of Law puts forward a Canadian viewpoint on a modern but less prominent tool for combatting transnational organized crime: the civil forfeiture of proceeds of crime. Tracing its origin in several currents of TCL, particularly antidrug instruments, she provides a comparative overview of how states have used civil forfeiture, before turning to scrutiny of the Canadian setting (with its various constitutional malcontents). Professor Gallant effectively highlights how civilly based legal regimes have a uniquely effective reach as a means of supplementing criminal enforcement tools in the suppression of transnational organized crime.

Chapter 14, Negotiating Transnational Corporate Criminality, sees Professor Joanna Harrington of the University of Alberta's Faculty of Law taking on the front-burner topic of the criminal liability of corporations for transnational criminal behaviour, particularly bribery and other forms of corruption. Professor Harrington considers the unique aspects of prosecuting corporate persons and examines recent trends in the use of deferred prosecution and other forms of diversion agreements (in Canada and elsewhere), particularly in cases of multi-jurisdictional criminality. She concludes with a persuasive argument in favour of the formulation of international standards for diversion agreements, so that the global public interest is served by such alternatives to prosecution.

Chapter 15, The Long Arm of Canadian Price-Fixing Law? Canadian Jurisdiction Over Foreign Price-Fixing Conspiracies, could just as easily have been placed in Section III, since it deals with Canada's territorial jurisdiction over offences with transnational aspects. Specifically, Michael Osborne, defence counsel at Cozen O'Connor, examines the interesting issue of jurisdiction over price-fixing and similar conspiracies which originate in foreign states, but which affect Canada. The fact that the criminalization of these conspiracies emerges from the *Competition Act* rather than the *Criminal Code* creates some unique attributes, he writes, which in turn affects how jurisdictional analysis should be conducted. He concludes that there has been a tendency for Canadian caselaw to overreach its appropriate jurisdiction, particularly in cases where the effects felt in Canada are only indirect.

Section V, entitled Commodity Crimes, provides Canadian perspectives on two forms of transnational trafficking offences with which Canada has historically been engaged. In Chapter 16, International Trafficking of Cultural Property: An Overview and the Canadian Perspective, recently retired Senior Analyst and Manager of the Department of Canadian Heritage's Policy and Legislation division Kathryn Zedde surveys the international law and policy around this sometimes obscure form of trafficking. She examines the legal regime that Canada has put in place to participate in suppression efforts, and provides first-hand insight into Canada's own participation in the formulation of the overall transnational legal regime.

In Chapter 17, From Opium to Fentanyl: Drug Smuggling, Canada, and Enforcement Challenges, Professor Stephen Schneider of St. Mary's University's Department of Criminology provides a criminological and thorough historical overview of the smuggling of illegal drugs into Canada and consequent criminal law enforcement issues. He explores Canada's unique vulnerability to transnational flows of illegal drugs and notes that, despite Canada's engagement with international suppression efforts, the market in Canada is as strong as ever, and the enforcement challenges just as dire. Highlighting how the "war on drugs" has failed Canada just as thoroughly as it has other states, he calls for alternative measures to address the harm that illegal drugs inflict on Canadian society.

Section VI, the final part of this collection, is entitled Inter-state Cooperation and Enforcement. As the title suggests, these chapters concern what in international law is referred to as enforcement jurisdiction, exploring a fascinating array of somewhat under-the-radar issues that present interesting opportunities and challenges for Canada's participation in transnational criminal law (TCL) regimes.

In Chapter 18, Human Rights Considerations in Extradition, Professor Frédéric Mégret of McGill University's Faculty of Law takes up a knotty topic that has occupied a great deal of my own scholarly energy: What is the role for human rights in the extradition of individuals to face foreign criminal process? Pressing firmly on Canadian extradition law and procedure and the role of the *Charter* therein, Professor Mégret provides a thorough review of human rights issues at both the committal and surrender phases of extradition proceedings. He gives nuanced treatment to the various tensions between two public policy goals that both compete with and complement each other: the protection of human rights and inter-state cooperation in the suppression of crime. He concludes that the symbiotic relationship between these goals is necessary, but that some of the tensions could and should be resolved by careful attention to calibrating areas currently unbalanced.

In Chapter 19, Disguised Extradition Through Deportation as an Abuse of Process, Jeffrey Johnston, General Counsel with the Department of Justice Canada, considers the issue of how to deal with cases where it is alleged that the government is pursuing immigration-based removal of individuals as an alternative to (and avoidance of) the more procedurally protective extradition process. Tracing the lineage of "disguised extradition" through foreign and Canadian caselaw, he tracks the emergence of an approach to such cases that is based in the notion of abuse of process of the jurisdiction of the court. He argues compellingly that the actual threshold for such a finding is and should be high, since there is nothing wrong in principle with a state choosing to employ removal in a situation where the individual will be deported to a state that wishes to criminally prosecute them. Rather, it is only where the immigration proceedings are a sham, initiated solely to accomplish extradition objectives, that an abuse of process should be found.

Chapter 20, Operation CARIBBE: A Case Study in Combatting Drug Trafficking on the High Seas, is authored by Amélie Aubut, who at the time of writing was a Legal Officer in the Office of the Judge

Advocate General of the Canadian Forces. It is an interesting look at a topic that does not often appear in the Canadian literature: Canada's participation in high seas narcotics interdiction operations, predominantly in partnership with the US Coast Guard. Aubut reviews the international and Canadian legal bases for these efforts, and then canvasses a number of thorny legal issues (both actual and prospective) that stem from the jurisdictionally hazy nature of high seas inter-state cooperation. She concludes that Canadian participation in these operations could leave our military personnel open to *Charter* claims regarding alleged abuse or mistreatment.

In Chapter 21, The International Transfer of Sentenced Prisoners to Canada: Procedure and Issues, Professor Adelina Iftene and recent law graduate Olivia Genge, both of the Schulich School of Law at Dalhousie University, shift our focus to the sentencing end of the criminal justice process. They examine Canada's participation in one skein of what might be called "transnational criminal procedure," which is the transfer of convicted offenders from states in which they were convicted to their home states, to have them serve their sentences there. Surveying the positive policy impulses behind this mechanism, they focus on the processes by which Canadians convicted abroad may apply to be transferred back to Canada. Their hard look at Canada's law and practice unearths an unsettlingly discretionary system that is "vulnerable to political influences, benefits from minimal scrutiny, and engages factors that do little to ensure the consistency of the process."[66] There is little Canadian literature on this topic and this paper makes an exceptionally valuable contribution.

The closing chapter, Chapter 22, Canadian Orders Can Compel Production of Data Controlled by US Companies, is authored by Fraser M. Kelly, a senior Crown prosecutor in Ontario. It takes on a front-burner investigational issue that is currently ruffling feathers in Canada and many other states: Can a domestic court compel an individual in a state's territory to produce electronic data that is stored outside that state? Focusing on the unsettled Canadian position, Kelly argues forcefully in the affirmative, outlining how production orders issued under Canada's *Criminal Code* may lawfully issue despite the extraterritorial aspects—and that, in fact, this was precisely Parliament's intention in creating the production order provisions in the first place. He actively refutes arguments to the contrary, noting the dubiousness of separate corporate personalities for

---

66 See page 498.

large transnational data firms. He concludes by expressing skepticism regarding current efforts to create treaty arrangements that would smooth out the situation, proposing Canadian data sovereignty laws and the bolstering of enforcement ability as a better solution.

2) A Word on Style and Editing

For those interested in such matters, some quick notes on editorial considerations. The reader is advised to refer to the List of Abbreviations for the various acronyms that are employed throughout. In terms of citation style, we have used Irwin's standard style guide for legal publications, which puts a reasonable emphasis on brevity. Neutral citations for cases are used wherever possible, and for the most part we did not provide URLs for cases or statutes, since they are easily found online. Much the same approach is taken to treaties and UN documents, which are usually cited by their report/collection series or document numbers. Legal literature is cited only to standard hard copy sources, except where the actual source is virtual in nature, such as an online journal. We did, however, selectively provide URLs for reports or publications that can be slightly more difficult to find online, such as those published by agencies and bodies of the United Nations, European Union, or Council of Europe.

two

The Internationalization of Canadian Criminal Justice Policy

DONALD K. PIRAGOFF, QC*

A. INTRODUCTION

In 1923, in the first edition of the *Canadian Bar Review*, Herbert A. Smith of McGill University questioned Lord Halsbury's 1891 statement that "all crime is local."[1] As Canadians began to feel the impact of drug trafficking, organized crime, and money laundering in the 1980s and 1990s, this historical statement would have appeared too narrowly focused, as these criminal activities do not recognize national boundaries and affect equally and adversely Canada and its inhabitants. Crime has become increasingly transnational in a way that could not have been envisioned in the time of Lord Halsbury, or even in that of Herbert Smith. For instance, the UN Office on Drugs and Crime (UNODC), in its 2010 global threat

* BA, LLB, LLM; and now KC (King's Counsel) as of 8 September 2022. Retired, formerly Senior Assistant Deputy Minister of Justice, Policy Sector, Department of Justice, Canada. The author expresses significant gratitude to Annemieke Holthuis (former Senior Counsel, Department of Justice, Canada) for her major contribution to an earlier unpublished draft manuscript, upon which we worked together a few years ago and of which much is incorporated in this paper. The author also expresses gratitude to former colleagues at the Department of Justice for their peer review of this paper, in particular, Lucie Angers, Erin Mckey, and Paul Saint Denis.

1 *Macleod v New South Wales*, [1891] AC 45, cited in Herbert A. Smith, "Extra-Territorial Legislation" (1923) 1 *Canadian Bar Review* 338 at 342–44, discussing the extent of criminal jurisdiction of colonial legislatures.

assessment and its subsequent regional and thematic assessments, documented the interconnectedness and flows of transnational organized crime from developed to developing economies, and back.[2] The increasing globalization of crime may be attributable to a number of factors. Technological advances in air travel, cargo transport, communications technology, and the development of the internet fuel globalization in all its forms.[3]

To address international aspects of crime, Canada responds by employing international law and principles. As the Supreme Court of Canada noted in *R v Hape*, a case in which the RCMP investigated the money-laundering activities of a Canadian in the Turks and Caicos, the application of domestic criminal law to conduct occurring outside of Canada is premised on international law concepts of state sovereignty, comity and territoriality, and other bases of jurisdiction on which states rely when enacting criminal laws and investigating and prosecuting crime.[4] Concepts of sovereignty and the nation state are, however, being challenged as borders become more porous and the political pressures and priorities of individual states, and various unions of states, demand more coordinated responses within the international community. Non-state actors, such as intergovernmental and international organizations, play an increasing role in this process. In 1973, several noted Canadian legal scholars—Ronald St. John Macdonald, Gerald Morris, and Douglas Johnston—predicted that in the year 2000, the nation state, while still "an important actor in the international policy-making process," would be affected "by trends and institutions that have already changed the substance, if not the form, of sovereignty."[5]

---

2 UNODC, *The Globalization of Crime: A Transnational Organized Crime Threat Assessment, 2010* (2010) at 1, online: www.unodc.org/unodc/data-and-analysis/TOC-threat-assessments.html. Since 2010, the UN has only produced a series of regional and thematic transnational organized crime threat assessments.

3 Parag Khanna, "The Future of Globalization" (Transcript of meeting at Chatham House, London, 15 March 2012) at 3–5, online: www.chathamhouse.org/sites/default/files/public/Meetings/Meeting%20Transcripts/150312khanna.pdf.

4 *R v Hape*, 2007 SCC 26 at paras 35–69.

5 Ronald St. John Macdonald, Gerald L. Morris & Douglas M. Johnston, "International Law and Society in the Year 2000" (1973) 51 *Canadian Bar Review* 316 at 318. Interestingly, Paul Keppner argues that the age of imperialism similarly spread the criminal justice systems of powers like Great Britain, Germany, France, the Netherlands, and Portugal to the farthest corners of the world, resulting in a "homogenisation of crime as an administrative issue across political and natural borders." Paul Knepper, *The Invention of International Crime: A Global Issue in the Making 1881–1914* (Basingstoke, UK: Palgrave Macmillan, 2009) at 43; see also 43–67.

This paper will focus on the manner in which the development of criminal justice policy at the federal level addresses crime with international dimensions, and the impact of international law, standards, and norms (including transnational criminal law (TCL)) on criminal justice policy development and enactment of criminal law in Canada. In the face of global crime, criminal justice policy-making in Canada cannot be undertaken in isolation, but must be considered against the backdrop of international developments and international criminal justice policy-making. This paper considers how international responses by states and international organizations to the changing nature of global crime and security, as well as domestic criminal justice challenges, have led to the internationalization of Canadian criminal justice policies and laws. The paper will also examine the domestic process by which internationalization occurs in Canadian domestic criminal justice policy-making, and internationalization's impact on the ability of the Canadian legal profession to respond.

B. CANADIAN CRIMINAL JUSTICE POLICY ACTORS

Within the Government of Canada, the international criminal justice policy function is shared essentially between the department of global affairs (Global Affairs Canada), the department of justice (Justice Canada), and the department of public safety (Public Safety Canada). Global Affairs Canada, with its general responsibility over Canada's foreign policy and international relations, advances the Government of Canada's positions in multilateral and regional fora, and negotiates multilateral treaties and standards and norms. Its foreign policy coordination function works to ensure consistency between Canada's domestic and international positions.[6] Justice Canada leads on the development of domestic criminal justice policy; leads, advises, or participates in international negotiations pertaining to criminal justice matters; and advises the Government of Canada on implementing, into domestic policy and law, both the international treaties on criminal justice matters which Canada has signed, ratified, or to which it has acceded, and the international standards and norms, developed by international organizations, which Canada has adopted and supports.[7] Public Safety Canada has an interest in transnational crime, as

6 *Department of Foreign Affairs and International Trade Act*, RSC 1985, c E-22.

7 *Department of Justice Act*, RSC 1985, c J-2. The Criminal Law Policy Section, Policy Sector, is primarily responsible for the development of domestic and international

well as in national security, irregular migration, and the sharing of best practices in the areas of crime prevention, emergency management, and corrections policy.[8] This paper will focus primarily on the international criminal justice policy role of Justice Canada.

The Government of Canada as a whole also provides criminal justice related technical assistance to other countries if requested,[9] and assists in evaluating other states' compliance with their international obligations through peer review mechanisms, such as that within the *United Nations Convention Against Corruption* (*UNCAC*),[10] or the *Inter-American Convention Against Corruption* (*IACAC*).[11] As will be discussed below, intra-governmental coordination both horizontally (between departments) and vertically (between the public service and the political level of government) becomes key in delivering desired policy outcomes.

C. THE INTERNATIONALIZATION OF CANADIAN CRIMINAL JUSTICE POLICY

In addition to the values that underlie Canadian foreign policy,[12] foreign policy objectives as they relate to criminal matters may be driven by the nature of the subject-matter priority (cybercrime, money laundering, organized crime, terrorism, victims' rights, protection of women and children, gender equality, etc.) in the domestic agenda of the government of the day, the fora in which the particular issue arises, or the world events that drive policy-making. As a result, international negotiations are often

---

criminal justice policy. The International Assistance Group, Litigation Branch, is responsible for the implementation and administration of Canada's extradition and mutual legal assistance frameworks, but some of its personnel have participated in some international criminal justice policy development.

8 *Public Safety Act, 2002*, SC 2004, c 15. Public Safety's International Affairs Division coordinates the minister's and department's various international activities in furtherance of Canada's security objectives.

9 The International Legal Programs Section, Policy Sector, of Justice Canada generally coordinates the department's work in this area, in cooperation with Global Affairs Canada.

10 *United Nations Convention Against Corruption* (2003) 2349 UNTS 41 [*UNCAC*].

11 *Inter-American Convention Against Corruption* (1996), reprinted (1996) 35 ILM 724 [*IACAC*].

12 For current foreign policy priorities related to crime and security, see: *Global Affairs Departmental Plan 2021–2022*, online: www.international.gc.ca/transparency-transparence/departmental-plan-ministeriel/2021-2022.aspx?lang=eng#a6_1.

conducted bearing in mind not only the objectives of the treaty process or the establishment of a new standard and norm, but also the potential impacts on governmental priorities, domestic law, and programs. With the benefit of public service advice, a political decision is made to sign, and then later to ratify, or accede to, the international instrument in question, or in the case of non-binding standards and norms, to give Canadian government approval to its application.

Internationalization has been described as "building into the domestic structure of law and practice the discipline of meeting universal standards," not simply "having to adhere to an external set of rules."[13] At a minimum, the process of internationalization includes implementing into domestic law the international treaties by which Canada has agreed to be bound, whether through a formal process of signature and ratification or accession, or by aligning Canadian practices, policies, or legislation in a manner consistent with international legal standards and norms. This process is multi-dimensional; at each stage, there are policy, legal, and political aspects to be considered.[14] These considerations must be addressed by the government as a whole, and require coordination amongst departments and between the public service and the political level of government it serves. Before examining these issues further, it will be useful to consider in which international fora criminal justice issues primarily arise, and which have had an impact on Canadian policy and law.

1) Canadian Involvement in International Criminal Justice Policy Fora

The early years of criminal justice policy-making at the international level focused on how states dealt with crime and criminals within the boundaries of the state. In the twentieth century, crime, and in particular transnational forms of crime, such as slavery, trafficking in women and children, the opium trade, and obscene publications, were addressed by means of individual treaties within the League of Nations, the predecessor

13 Lloyd Axworthy, *Navigating a New World, Canada's Global Future* (Canada: Penguin Random House Canada, 2010) at 206.

14 See Harold Hongju Koh, "Twenty-First Century International Lawmaking," (Remarks at Georgetown University), US Department of State, Office of the Legal Adviser (17 October 2012), online: https://2009-2017.state.gov/s/l/releases/remarks/199319.htm2009-2017.state.gov/s/l/releases/remarks/199319.htm.

to the United Nations.[15] For example, the globalization at the end of the nineteenth century that led to the rise of the White slave trade prompted states to address this and other forms of transnational crime in the League of Nations. More comprehensive crime programs, such as the UN Crime Programme, were established within international organizations after World War II to address economic and social welfare of individuals within nation states.[16]

Matti Joutsen analyzed the expansion of the UN Crime Programme from its primary focus on domestic criminal justice issues addressing matters such as juvenile delinquency, correctional treatment, and criminal statistics to, eventually, including crime prevention, restorative justice, and transnational crime. The transition of subject-matter focus was paralleled by a structural progression from an expert-driven committee to a state-driven programme overseen by a UN Commission on Crime Prevention and Criminal Justice (CCPCJ or UN Crime Commission), with corresponding changes in its negotiated products, which, while still primarily involving the development of *soft law* (standards and norms) also included some binding *hard law* (treaty obligations).[17] This paper will focus on Canada's relationship with only a few UN bodies, those being the CCPCJ, UN Congress on the Prevention of Crime and the Treatment of Offenders (UN Crime Congresses), UNODC, and their affiliated supporting institutes.

The UN Crime Commission, established in 1992, is the primary body in which UN Member States debate policy issues relating to criminal justice, and exchange expertise and best practices.[18] Depending on the will of co-sponsors, the subject matter, and other factors, resolutions adopted by consensus by the UN Crime Commission may be brought to the Economic and Social Council of the United Nations (ECOSOC), to inform its work, and more rarely, to the UN General Assembly (UNGA). Canada was significantly involved in the inception of the UN Crime Commission, and

---

15 See Slawomir Marek Redo, *Blue Criminology: The Power of United Nations Ideas to Counter Crime Globally. A Monographic Study* (Helsinki: HEUNI, The European Institute for Crime Prevention and Control, affiliated with the United Nations, 2012) at 48, online: https://heuni.fi/-/report-series-no.-72.

16 *Ibid* at 48–49.

17 Matti Joutsen, *Four Transitions in the United Nations Crime Programme* (Helsinki: HEUNI, The European Institute for Crime Prevention and Control, affiliated with the United Nations 2017), online: https://heuni.fi/-/four-transitions-in-the-united-nations-crime-programme. See also below note 27.

18 On the creation of the Commission, see Redo, above note 15 at 111.

since then has been actively engaged in its work and priorities. These have included addressing transnational crimes such as organized crime, economic fraud and corruption, cybercrime and identity-related crime, human trafficking, and migrant smuggling. As well, protecting vulnerable groups within states from violence, including women and children as victims and witnesses, also figures prominently in Canadian work at the annual UN Crime Commission and the quinquennial UN Crime Congresses.

While performing different functions, the UN Crime Commission and UN Crime Congresses provide states' experts in criminal law policy and practice with opportunities for focused discussion on particular issues. However, the challenge has always been to ensure that delegations to these UN fora include experts in substantive criminal law, as well as diplomatic representatives, so that the negotiated standards and norms are not only representative of the views of states, but also take into account the views of criminal justice experts.[19] The strength of the UN Crime Commission and UN Crime Congresses lies in state representatives who have expert knowledge on the criminal justice policy and operational aspects of the issue under discussion. The development of specialized UN expert groups, such as those on organized crime, cybercrime and identity-related crime, victims, youth, etc., ensure that more in-depth examination of particular forms of transnational and domestic crime informs domestic policy-making.

The UN Crime Commission has been the source of a significant number of soft law standards, such as the *United Nations Rules for the Treatment of Women Prisoners and Non-custodial Measures for Women Offenders*, also called the *Bangkok Rules*,[20] which were drafted taking into account the *Standard Minimum Rules for the Treatment of Prisoners* of 1955,[21] elaborated

---

19 See Redo, above note 15 at 112–13 on questions on the legality of norms elaborated by individual experts at UN Crime Congresses and by the expert committees that preceded the establishment of the UN Crime Commission. Issues around legality were addressed by resolution of the Economic and Social Council, ECOSOC Res 1994/18 (24 July 1994). See also UN Crime Commission, *Compilation on the methods of work of the United Nations Commission on Crime Prevention and Criminal Justice*, UN Doc E/CN.15/2012/CRP.3 (17 April 2012).

20 *United Nations Rules for the Treatment of Women Prisoners and Non-custodial Measures for Women Offenders*, UNGA Res A/RES/65/229 (16 March 2011) [*Bangkok Rules*].

21 *Standard Minimum Rules for the Treatment of Prisoners*, adopted by the First United Nations Congress on the Prevention of Crime and the Treatment of Offenders, held at Geneva in 1955, and approved by ECOSOC Res 663 C (XXIV) (31 July 1957) and

at the first UN Crime Congress, and updated by the UN Crime Commission in 2015 as the *Nelson Mandela Rules*.[22] Much of the work on standards and norms, and reports of UN expert groups, paved the way for multilateral treaties (hard law) like the 2000 *United Nations Convention against Transnational Organized Crime* (*UNTOC*)[23] and the 2003 *UNCAC*.[24] Arguably, the negotiation and ratification of these conventions form part of the era of "great multilateral law" of the international legal framework on human rights, diplomatic protection, law of the sea, and treaty-making.[25] Slawomir Redo suggests that international policy-making on criminal matters, whether in the form of soft law or multilateral treaties, followed developments in criminological thinking. He links the work of the International Penitentiary Commission in the 1870s to the addition of new perspectives, such as victim-oriented and restorative-justice policy elements. As he notes, following the events of 9/11, the UN Crime Programme included within its focus anti-terrorism and other issues relating to the UN's international peace and security objectives.[26]

The UN Crime Congresses find their origins in the criminological congresses held in the mid-1800s by experts interested in child welfare and correctional issues.[27] The early sessions of the UN Crime Commission and UN Crime Congresses focused on how states dealt with crime and criminals within the boundaries of the state, addressing issues such as the accountability of offenders for their criminal conduct, and how the criminal justice processes in Member States dealt with offenders. These issues included standards of detention, rights of the accused, protections for young offenders, victims of crime and abuse of power, codes of

---

Res 2076 (LXII) (13 May 1977). For a comprehensive list of the various standards and norms adopted by the UN Crime Commission and the UN Crime Congresses, see UNODC, *The Compendium* of *United Nations Standards and Norms in Crime Prevention and Criminal Justice* (2006) [*Compendium — UN Standards and Norms*], online: www.unodc.org/unodc/en/justice-and-prison-reform/compendium.html.

22 *United Nations Standard Minimum Rules for the Treatment of Offenders (the Nelson Mandela Rules)*, UNGA Res 70/175 (17 December 2015) Annex [*Nelson Mandela Rules*], online: www.unodc.org/documents/justice-and-prison-reform/Nelson_Mandela_Rules-E-ebook.pdf.

23 *United Nations Convention against Transnational Organized Crime*, (2000) 2225 UNTS 209 [*UNTOC*].

24 *UNCAC*, above note 10.

25 Redo, above note 15 at 49.

26 *Ibid* at 49, 56–63.

27 Redo, above note 15 at 108–9; Joutsen, above note 17.

conduct for law enforcement officials, independence of the judiciary, and protections for those facing the death penalty.[28] As noted by both Redo and Joutsen, above, the subject-matter focus later expanded to include transnational crime and anti-terrorism issues, and improved efficiency in international law enforcement and judicial cooperation.[29]

Every five years, the Congresses provide an intergovernmental forum for the exchange of views among states, intergovernmental organizations, non-governmental organizations and individual experts on criminal justice and crime-prevention issues.[30] Later initiatives added victim-oriented and restorative justice policy elements to the agenda of the UN Crime Commission and the UN Crime Congresses.[31] Many of the products of the UN Crime Congresses also led to the adoption of standards and norms by the UN Crime Commission, as discussed above.[32]

Research institutes, now part of the Crime Prevention and Criminal Justice Programme Network Institutes (PNI), have, since 1962, assisted the UN on crime prevention and criminal justice issues.[33] In 1992, these insti-

---

28 *Ibid.* Some notable instruments include: *Body of Principles for the Protection of All Persons under Any Form of Detention or Imprisonment*, UNGA Res 43/173 (9 December 1988); *United Nations Rules for the Protection of Juveniles Deprived of their Liberty*, UNGA Res 45/113 (14 December 1990); and *Basic Principles for the Treatment of Prisoners*, UNGA Res 45/111 (14 December 1990); and see *Compendium — UN Standards and Norms*, above note 21.

29 See also Matti Joutsen, *The Evolution of the United Nations Congresses on Crime Prevention and Criminal Justice* (Bangkok: Thailand Institute of Justice, 2020) at 108.

30 UNGA Res 46/152 (18 December 1991) Annex art 29. See also UNGA Res 56/119 (19 December 2001), at Preamble, in *Compendium — UN Standards and Norms*, above note 21.

31 Redo, above note 15 at 49 and 56–63. For example, see the *Declaration of Basic Principles of Justice for Victims of Crime and Abuse of Power*, UNGA Res 40/34 (29 November 1985); *Basic Principles and Guidelines on the Right to a Remedy and Reparation for Victims of Gross Violations of International Human Rights Law and Serious Violations of International Humanitarian Law*, UNGA Res 60/147 (16 December 2005); *Basic Principles on the Use of Restorative Justice Programmes in Criminal Matters* (2002) [*Basic Principles Restorative Justice*]: in *Compendium — UN Standards and Norms*, above note 21. See also Yvon Dandurand, "Integrating Restorative Approaches in the Criminal Justice Process: From Slow Progress to Cautious Optimism" in Redo, above note 15 at 88–91.

32 See *Compendium — UN Standards and Norms*, above note 21; Joutsen, above note 29 at 110.

33 Redo, above note 15 at 119, noting the 1962 establishment of the United Nations Asia and Far East Institute on the Prevention of Crime and the Treatment of Offenders, Tokyo, Japan.

tutes (including their centres in Vancouver[34] and Montreal[35]) were specifically mandated to support the UN Crime Commission and UNODC with research, policy advice, and development of technical assistance and training.[36] PNI also organizes practically oriented workshops on the themes debated at annual sessions of the UN Crime Commission, and provide additional expert content to the UN Crime Congresses.[37] In assisting the UNODC and Member States, the PNI has also contributed to the elaboration of various UN standards and norms, in particular, involving the protection of women, such as the *Bangkok Rules*,[38] and *Model Strategies and Practical Measures on the Elimination of Violence against Women in the Field of Crime Prevention and Criminal Justice*.[39] PNI has also consistently contributed at the international level to policy debates relating to victims of crime, particularly to victims of abuses of governmental power.[40] Some commentators have argued that the shift in focus from the offender to the victim is coincident with rising crime rates in the latter quarter of the

34 International Centre for Criminal Justice Policy and Criminal Law Reform, located at the Faulty of Law, University of British Columbia, Vancouver, Canada [ICCLR], online: www.icclr.org.

35 International Centre for the Prevention of Crime, Montreal, Canada, online: https://cipc-icpc.org/en/home.

36 UNGA Res 46/152 (18 December 1991) Annex arts 8 and 35.

37 Redo, above note 15 at 116.

38 *Bangkok Rules*, above note 20. See for example: "Expert Group Meeting on the Standard Minimum Rules for the Treatment of Prisoners" held in Buenos Aires, 11 to 13 December 2012, List of Participants, UN Doc UNODC/CCPCJ/EG.6/2012/INF.5 (6 November 2012); and "Report on the meeting of the expert group to develop supplementary rules specific to the treatment of women in detention and in custodial and non-custodial settings" held in Bangkok, 23 to 26 November 2009, UN Doc UNODC/CCPCJ/EG.3/2009 (17 December 2009).

39 *Model Strategies and Practical Measures on the Elimination of Violence against Women in the Field of Crime Prevention and Criminal Justice*, UNODC (2015), online: www.unodc.org/documents/justice-and-prison-reform/14-08451_Strategy_eBook.pdf.

40 See Matt Matravers, "The Victim, the State and Civil Society" in Anthony Bottoms & Julian V. Roberts, eds, *Hearing the Victim: Adversarial Justice, Crime Victims and the State* (Abingdon-on-Thames, UK: Routledge, 2010) at 1. "I am conscious that the phrase 'rise of the victim' is rather too crude . . . I think the rise of the victim a genuine, if complex, phenomenon that has the potential to alter significantly the shape of (parts of) the criminal justice system." *Ibid* at 1, n 3. Victims have played a greater role in civil law systems, including in certain rights of participation and representation.

twentieth century and with the inability of criminal justice systems to respond adequately.[41]

Development of policies to protect women and victims in the criminal justice system has been a priority for Canadian domestic and international policy development. Development of these policies has been symbiotic, with international and Canadian domestic developments influencing each other. In Canada, for example, work at the federal-provincial-territorial (FPT) levels led, in 1981, to the establishment of the Federal–Provincial Task Force on Justice for Victims of Crime.[42] Its *Report* made a wide-ranging series of recommendations, some of which would later be enacted into the *Criminal Code*, such as the victims' ability to make impact statements,[43] a fine surtax imposed on sentencing, the revenue from which would be earmarked to fund victims' services, and a *Victims Bill of Rights*.[44] This work would also inform the development and adoption in 1985 of the UN *Declaration of Basic Principles of Justice for Victims of Crime and Abuse*

41 Dame Helen Reeves & Peter Dunn, "The Status of Crime Victims and Witnesses in the Twenty-First Century" in Bottoms & Roberts, above note 40 at 47, citing David Garland, *The Culture of Control: Crime and Social Order in Contemporary Society* (Oxford: Oxford University Press, 2001), and Robert Reiner, *The Politics of the Police*, 3d ed (Oxford: Oxford University Press, 2000).

42 A smaller federal-provincial-territorial working group issued a 1981 report, *Justice for Victims of Crime*, which recommended, among other things, the establishment of a broader task force to examine issues such as the needs of victims, legislative options, and raising public awareness about victims' issues: *Canadian Federal–Provincial Task Force on Justice for Victims of Crime Report* (Ottawa: Supply and Services Canada) at v, online: https://publications.gc.ca/site/eng/9.888874/publication.html and www.lareau-law.ca/DigitalLibrary.html.

43 *Ibid*, Recommendation 21 at 157, which was later enacted in *An Act to amend the Criminal Code (sentencing) and other Acts in consequence thereof*, SC 1995, c 22, s 6.

44 *Justice for Victims of Crimes*, above note 42, Recommendations 76–78 at 166. The continuing focus on the protection of victims as a factor in domestic criminal justice policy-making is highlighted by the work of the Policy Centre for Victims within the Department of Justice, particularly in its support for victims affected by federal proceedings under the *Corrections and Conditional Release Act*, SC 1992, c 20; by the establishment of the Office of the Federal Ombudsman for Victims of Crime, in March 2007; by the enactment of a series of victim-oriented legislation, including the *Justice for Victims of Terrorism Act*, SC 2012, c 1 to enable victims of terrorism to sue foreign states that have waived immunity or certain listed entities; the *Increasing Offenders' Accountability for Victims Act*, SC 2013, c 11; and eventually the enactment of the Canadian *Victims Bill of Rights*, SC 2015, c 13, s 2.

of Power (UN *Victims' Declaration*),[45] and both works would influence subsequent Canadian legislative amendments.

Other international standards, whether hard law, such as article 25 of the *UNTOC*[46] or soft law, like UN *Guidelines on Justice in Matters Involving Child Victims and Witnesses of Crime*,[47] and the *Model Strategies and Practical Measures on the Elimination of Violence Against Women*,[48] seek to protect victims in specific contexts.[49] These initiatives, and the UN *Victims' Declaration* at the international level, influenced, reflected, or supported the development of the *Canadian Statement of Basic Principles of Justice for Victims of Crime*, initially issued by FPT ministers of justice in 1988 and reaffirmed in 2003.[50]

Protection of women and victims, as discussed above, is just one example of the symbiotic domestic and international policy-development process; there are other examples[51] that also lead to the following

45 *Declaration of Basic Principles of Justice for Victims of Crime and Abuse of Power*, UNGA Res 40/34 (29 November 1985).

46 *UNTOC*, above note 23.

47 *Guidelines on Justice in Matters Involving Child Victims and Witnesses of Crime*, ECOSOC Res 2005/20, Res 2004/27 (21 July 2004). The Government of Canada supported efforts of the International Bureau for Children's Rights and a later intergovernmental expert group to elaborate these guidelines. Canada earlier sponsored the UN Crime Commission resolution recommending the *Guidelines'* adoption in 2005; International Bureau for Children's Rights, *The UN Guidelines on Justice in Matters Involving Child Victims and Witnesses of Crime* (2005), online: www.ibcr.org/eng/the_un_guidelines_on_child_victims_and_witnesses_of_crime.html.

48 *Model Strategies and Practical Measures on the Elimination of Violence against Women in the Field of Crime Prevention and Criminal Justice*, above note 39.

49 See, for example, *UNTOC*, above note 23, art 25(1) & (2). See also art 24 that applies to protection of witnesses, and David McLean, *Transnational Organized Crime: A Commentary on the UN Convention and Its Protocols* (Oxford: Oxford University Press, 2007) at 266–69. Other UN work to support victims of terrorism includes: a Symposium on Supporting Victims of Terrorism, convened by the UN Secretary General, and ongoing work by the UNODC to frame the criminal justice response to victims of terrorism. See: *Supporting Victims of Terrorism* (New York: United Nations, Executive Office of the Secretary-General, 2009), online: www.un.org/terrorism/pdfs/UN%20Report%20on%20Supporting%20Victims%20of%20Terrorism.pdf; *The Criminal Justice Response to Support Victims of Acts of Terrorism* (New York: UNODC, 2011), online: www.unodc.org/documents/terrorism/Victims_Rights_E-Book_EN.pdf.

50 *Canadian Statement of Basic Principles of Justice for Victims of Crime*, 2003, online: www.justice.gc.ca/eng/rp-pr/cj-jp/victim/03/princ.html.

51 For other examples, see discussion under Section C (3), below.

observation. Internationalization of criminal justice policy is a two-way process. Domestic policies and priorities influence the work and products of international organizations and, in turn, these products influence the development or furtherance of domestic policies and laws.

The means by which criminal justice policy is advanced internationally should also be considered as part of a state's strategy to promote a particular criminal justice policy priority. Treaties are costly, time-consuming, and require a high degree of international consensus. International standards and norms, on the other hand, are standards and best practices that states should strive to meet, but they are not legally obligated to adhere to them. These soft law measures, for example, the *Updated Model Strategies and Practical Measures to Eliminate Violence Against Women in the Field of Crime Prevention and Criminal Justice*,[52] the *Bangkok Rules*,[53] the *Basic Principles on the Use of Restorative Justice Programmes in Criminal Matters*[54] and the *Guidelines for the Prevention of Crime*,[55] remain useful tools in the criminal justice policy toolkit, even if not legally binding. International standards and norms may be easier to negotiate internationally and to internalize into domestic law. Soft law standards may also, in some very limited circumstances, serve as evidence of customary international law principles and norms,[56]

52 *Updated Model Strategies and Practical Measures to Eliminate Violence Against Women in the Field of Crime Prevention and Criminal Justice*, UNGA Res A/RES/65/228 (31 March 2011). An intergovernmental expert group established by the UN Crime Commission assisted with this update of the earlier *Model Strategies and Practical Measures on the Elimination of Violence against Women in the Field of Crime Prevention*, UNGA Res 52/86 (12 December 1997). Representatives of the Government of Canada and the ICCLR participated in the expert group. For more information see ICCLR, "Elimination of Violence Against Women Programme," online: www.icclr.law.ubc.ca/site%20map/programs/VAW.htm, and its briefing note, online: www.icclr.law.ubc.ca/files/2012/ICCLR%20briefing%20note%20-%20Eliminating%20VAW.pdf.

53 *Bangkok Rules*, above note 20.

54 *Basic Principles Restorative Justice*, above note 31.

55 *Guidelines for the Prevention of Crime*, ECOSOC Res 2000/14 (27 July 2000), and see *Compendium — UN Standards and Norms*, above note 21.

56 See, for example, *The Standard Minimum Rules on the Treatment of Prisoners*, above notes 21 & 22. In *Corporation of the Canadian Civil Liberties Association v Her Majesty the Queen*, 2017 ONSC 7491 at para 61, it was held that "the Mandela Rules represent an international consensus of proper principles and practices in the management of prisons and the treatment of those confined." See also *BC Civil Liberties Assn v Canada (Attorney General)*, 2018 BCSC 62 at para 314.

and their importance should not be underestimated.[57] Some international law principles, such as those involving torture, began as a standard and norm, subsequently became a treaty, and eventually became a criminal offence in Canada's *Criminal Code*.[58]

In addition to the UN fora, Canada has participated significantly in the processes of other global, intergovernmental partners like the Commonwealth, by attending meetings of Senior Officials of Law Ministries, and chairing or participating in its various working groups, and attending meetings of Commonwealth Law Ministers. In the criminal justice area, these meetings included negotiating international cooperation schemes involving extradition, mutual legal assistance and transfer of offenders; and model laws, guidelines, and best practices on various subjects such as computer and computer-related crime, corruption, counter-terrorism, prosecution of terrorism, money laundering and terrorist financing, the International Criminal Court (ICC) and prosecution of international crimes, mutual legal assistance, prosecution and disclosure guidelines, victims of crime, violence against women and girls, and juvenile justice systems.[59] Some of these initiatives were led by Canada, such as the work on computer and computer-related crime, electronic evidence and the ICC, and others influenced or reflected Canadian criminal justice policies.[60]

Regional policy-making institutions, such as the Organization of American States (OAS), provide another avenue for Canadian influence and efforts. Meetings of OAS Ministers of Justice or Other Ministers or

---

57 See *Compendium - UN Standards and Norm*, above note 21.

58 See, for example, *Declaration on the Protection of All Persons from Being Subjected to Torture and Other Cruel, Inhuman or Degrading Treatment or Punishment*, UNGA Res 3452 (9 December 1975); *Convention against Torture or Other Cruel, Inhuman or Degrading Treatment or Punishment*, (1984) 1465 UNTS 85; and *Criminal Code*, RSC 1985, c C-46, s 269.1 [*Code*].

59 The international instruments negotiated and adopted at these meetings can be found in: Commonwealth Secretariat, *Commonwealth Schemes for International Cooperation in Criminal Matters* (2017), online: https://thecommonwealth.org/sites/default/files/key_reform_pdfs/P15370_13_ROL_Schemes_Int_Cooperation.pdf; and Commonwealth Secretariat, *Commonwealth Model Laws* (2021), online: https://thecommonwealth.org/commonwealth-model-laws.

60 *Commonwealth Model Laws*, above note 59, see, for example, *Model Law on Computer Related Crime*, *Model Law on Electronic Evidence*, and *Model Law to Implement the Rome Statute of the International Criminal Court*.

Attorneys General of the Americas (REMJA) have been held since 1997.[61] Among Canada's objectives as a participant in the REMJA process has been one to facilitate international cooperation among states and law-enforcement agencies in the Americas.[62] This has included work and funds to develop an information-exchange network to streamline cooperation and information sharing on mutual legal assistance and extradition, which had first been recommended in a meeting of OAS central authorities and other experts held in Ottawa, Canada, in 2003.[63] Canada has also been involved in the negotiation of a number of treaties and other instruments negotiated under the auspices of the OAS, including issues of mutual legal assistance, extradition, corruption, and computer crime, which will be discussed in Section C(3), below.

While not a formal member of the Council of Europe (CoE), Canada has permanent observer status with this regional organization, and participates actively in a number of its expert groups and treaty negotiations involving criminal justice policy issues. These have included issues such as: computer crime, hate crime, transborder access to electronic data, mutual legal assistance, extradition, corruption, terrorism, trafficking in persons, violence against women, and protection of children from sexual exploitation.[64] A significant achievement by Canada was its involvement and leadership in

61 David P. Warner, "Law Enforcement Cooperation in the Organization of American States: A Focus on REMJA (2005–2006)" 37 *University of Miami Inter-American Law Review* 387, for a detailed discussion of the Meetings of Ministers of Justice (known as REMJA in Spanish). See also Organization of American States, Meetings of Ministers of Justice or Other Ministers or Attorneys General of the Americas, "Background," online: www.oas.org/en/sla/dlc/remja/background.asp.

62 Justice Canada represents Canada on OAS working groups that specialize in the areas of cybercrime, mutual legal assistance in criminal matters, transnational organized crime, corruption, hemispheric legal cooperation on family and child law; and Public Safety Canada has participated in areas of penitentiary and prison policies. More broadly, REMJA's agenda also addresses hemispheric legal cooperation and access to justice matters.

63 Warner, above note 61, at 406, 410, and 416. See also the Fifth Meeting of Ministers of Justice or of Ministers or Attorneys General of the Americas, "Recommendations—Meeting of Central Authorities and Other Experts on Mutual Legal Assistance in Criminal Matters," OAS DocOEA/Ser.K/XXXIV.5, REMJA-V/doc.4/04 (15 April 2004), known as the "Ottawa Recommendations," online: www.oas.org/juridico/mla/en/ottawa-recommend.pdf.

64 Council of Europe, *MLA: Council of Europe Standards* (2021), online: www.coe.int/en/web/transnational-criminal-justice-pcoc/MLA-council-of-europe-standards; Council of Europe, *Council of Europe Standards: Extradition* (2021), online:

the CoE's various expert groups on cybercrime and on related investigative procedures over a period of approximately fifteen years, which culminated in the negotiation of the CoE *Convention on Cybercrime*,[65] which Canada signed in 2001 and eventually ratified in 2015.[66] More recently, Canada has been active in CoE studies on cyberviolence,[67] and in the negotiation of the CoE *Second Optional Protocol to the Convention on Cybercrime*.[68]

The mandates of fora, such as those of the G7/G8,[69] the Organisation for Economic Co-operation and Development (OECD)[70] and the Financial Action Task Force (FATF),[71] expanded beyond their original, economic scope, to address issues such as transnational organized crime, corruption, money laundering, and terrorism.[72] Canada played a key role in the mandate expansion. For example, the Berlin Summit (1978) ended with a political declaration on hijacking, followed by similar statements at

---

www.coe.int/en/web/transnational-criminal-justice-pcoc/extradition-council-of-europe-standards.

65 Council of Europe, *Convention on Cybercrime*, (2001 ETS 185) [*Cybercrime Convention*]; and Council of Europe, "Convention on Cybercrime — Explanatory Report" (2001), online: www.oas.org/juridico/english/cyb_pry_explanatory.pdf.

66 Government of Canada, "Canada Completes Ratification of Convention on Cybercrime" (2015), online: www.canada.ca/en/news/archive/2015/07/canada-completes-ratification-convention-cybercrime.html. Only limited amendments were required in order for Canada to ratify, as the bulk of the Convention was consistent with and reflective of Canadian criminal law on cybercrime, *Code*, above note 58, ss 342.1 and 430(1.1).

67 Council of Europe, Cybercrime Convention Committee (T-CY), *Mapping study on cyberviolence* (2018), online: https:// rm.coe.int/t-cy-2017-10-cbg-study-provisional/16808c4914; and see also "Action against Cybercrime," online: www.coe.int/cybercrime.

68 Council of Europe, Cybercrime Convention Committee (T-CY), *Second Optional Protocol to the Convention on Cybercrime on enhanced co-operation and disclosure of electronic evidence, Draft Protocol version 3* (2021) [*Second Protocol to Cybercrime Convention*], online: https://rm.coe.int/0900001680a2aa1c.

69 G7 Information Centre, "What are the G7 and G8?" online: www.g8.utoronto.ca/what_is_g8.html. The G7 was expanded to the G8 in order to include Russia, and then retracted in 2014 to the G7.

70 Government of Canada, "Canada and the Organization for Economic Cooperation and Development" (2021), online: www.international.gc.ca/world-monde/international_relations-relations_internationales/oecd-ocde/index.aspx?lang=eng.

71 Financial Action Task Force, online: www.fatf-gafi.org.

72 On the history of the G7, see, generally, the website of the Margaret Thatcher Foundation, "The G7 Summits: Declassified Records Published for the First Time" [Thatcher], online: www.margaretthatcher.org/archive/g7.asp.

later summits in Tokyo (1979), Venice (1980), Ottawa/Montebello (1981), and Tokyo (1986).[73] Held against the backdrop of a series of terrorist events in Japan, the USA, and Russia, the G7 Heads of State decided, at the 1995 Halifax Summit, to strengthen cooperation against terrorism and to address terrorist financing, and they called for the ratification of existing international conventions against terrorism. They also mandated terrorism experts within G7 states "to report to a ministerial level meeting on specific, cooperative measures to deter, prevent, and investigate terrorist acts."[74] The resulting "Ottawa Ministerial Declaration on Countering Terrorism" called *inter alia* for improved international cooperation and information, for states to ratify the existing international anti-terrorism conventions "by the year 2000," and to take measures to address the financing of terrorism.[75] The subsequent 1996 meeting of G7/P8 ministers responsible for counterterrorism[76] set out a counterterrorism strategy and guidelines for action, consistent with human rights, fundamental freedoms, and the rule of law.[77] Subsequent G8 expert meetings (the Roma Group) were held annually to discuss terrorism-related issues within the G8.[78]

---

73 See, generally, website of the G7 Research Group at the University of Toronto, online: www.g8.utoronto.ca/summit/index.htm, for G7/G8 Summits, Meetings, Official Document under Communiqués, Statements and Documents, and those on terrorism, such as: G7 Summit, "Statement on Air-Hijacking" (Bonn, Germany, 17 July 1978); G7 Summit, Press Release on "Air-hijacking" (Tokyo, 29 June 1979); G7 Summit, "Statement on the Taking of Diplomatic Hostages and Statement on Hijacking" (Venice, 22 June 1980); G7 Summit, "Ottawa Summit Statement on Terrorism" (Ottawa/Montebello, 21 July 1981); G7 Summit, "Declaration on International Terrorism" (London, 9 June 1984); G7 Summit, "Statement on International Terrorism" (Tokyo, 5 May 1986); G7 Summit, "Statement on Terrorism" (Venice, 9 June 1987); G8 Summit, "Political Declaration: Securing Democracy" (Toronto, 20 June 1988); and G7 Economic Summit, "Statement on Transnational Issues" (Houston, 10 July 1990).

74 Thatcher, above note 72; G7 Summit, "Chairman's Statement" (Halifax, 17 June 1995).

75 University of Toronto G8 Information Centre, "Ottawa Ministerial Declaration on Countering Terrorism" (12 December 1995), online: www.g8.utoronto.ca/terrorism/terror96.htm.

76 The P8 meeting included the G7 ministers and Russia's minister responsible for countering terrorism. See also notes 69, 78, and 80 for the relationship between the P8 and the G8.

77 The ministerial meeting concluded in an agreement to undertake twenty-five specified measures; online: www.g8.utoronto.ca/terrorism/terror25.htm.

78 See Thatcher, above note 72 generally, and related meetings of G7/G8 Justice, Interior and Security Ministers, online: www.g8.utoronto.ca/justice/index.html.

The 1995 Halifax Summit, focused, as did its predecessors, on the challenges of transnational crime, including money laundering, and prompted G8 states to convene their experts to examine gaps in international cooperation addressing transnational crime.[79] The P8 Senior Experts Group on Transnational Organized Crime (which later became known as the Lyon Group) met twice in 1995 (in Montebello and Ottawa, Canada) to develop a series of forty recommendations focused on transnational organized crime, which were subsequently presented at the following 1996 Paris Summit.[80] The Lyon Group's subsequent annual meetings produced recommendations to ministers of justice and the interior/home affairs ministers, which resulted in the issuance of statements of shared priorities and best practices, as well as informing the G8 Heads of Government.[81] Subgroups were also established within the Lyon Group to address particular issues dealing with the challenges of transnational crime and particular thematic issues.[82]

Following the events of 9/11, G8 ministers of justice and interior ministers noted "the importance of a coordinated, multidisciplinary approach in order to understand the links between international crime

79 *Ibid*; G7 Summit, "Chairman's Statement" (Halifax, 17 June 1995) at para 10. See also G7 Summit, "Chairman's Statement on Drugs" (Venice, 10 June 1987); G8 Summit, "Political Declaration: Securing Democracy" (Toronto, 20 June 1988); G7 Economic Summit, "Statement on Transnational Issues" (Houston, 10 July 1990); G7 Summit, "Summit Communiqué" (Naples, 9 July 1994) and "Chairman's Statement (Political)" (Naples, 10 July 1994). For G7/G8 Communiqués, Statements and Declarations, see online: www.g8.utoronto.ca/summit/index.htm.

80 G7 Information Centre, "P8 — Senior Experts Group Recommendations to Combat Transnational Organized Crime" (Paris, 12 April 1996), online: www.g8.utoronto.ca/crime/40pts.htm. See also Scherrer, below note 81.

81 See Amandine Scherrer, "The G8 and Transnational Organized Crime: The Evolution of G8 Expertise on the International Stage," Presentation at the Munk Centre for International Studies (Toronto, 21 January 2008) [Scherrer], online: www.library.utoronto.ca/g7/speakers/scherrer2008.htm. As a result of a decision to streamline the work of the G8, these ministerial meetings ceased under the Canadian presidency in 2010, and any significant recommendations were subsequently sent to the leaders' summits, online: www.g8.utoronto.ca/summit/2010muskoka/communique.html.

82 The Subgroups included the Judicial Cooperation Subgroup (later renamed the Criminal Law and Legal Affairs Subgroup), Police Cooperation Subgroup, the High-Tech Crime Subgroup and the Migration Subgroup. After 2001, two additional groups were added, the Law Enforcement Practitioners Subgroup and the Counter Terrorism Action Group, see Scherrer, *ibid.*

and terrorism."[83] Under the Canadian presidency of the G8 in 2002, the two G8 expert groups on terrorism and transnational crime were merged (into the Roma-Lyon Group), in light of the synergies in their two mandates. A review, by Amadine Scherrer, of the work of the Roma-Lyon Group identified several important aspects of its work, namely the ability to coordinate the work of public servants and other experts within G8 states working on criminal justice issues, and the Group's ability to influence the development of treaties, standards, and norms in other fora, such as in the UN Crime Commission.

> This mobility, from one working group to the other, across national boundaries and international bodies, is part of the explanation as to why the fight against transnational organized crime seems to be so consensual on the international stage. G8 experts meet three times a year within the G8 system; some of them gather again within EU delegations, for those who are also members of the EU, in OECD delegations or UN delegations. Throughout our interviews, it was clearly demonstrated that this community of experts dealing with organized crime, was indeed a small world, and that most of these experts know each other very well, since they meet a couple of times a year at international meetings. The multiplication of international meetings favours interactions, and gives roots to a horizontal negotiations space that allows its participants to socialize beyond national bureaucracies. This mobility gives birth to transnationalized public actors. It has certainly allowed the constitution of an international network of experts; such a network facilitates the sharing of understandings of, harmonized approaches to and common perceptions of the appropriate tools to fight organized crime.[84]

This coordinated approach may, however, be critiqued to the extent that alternative approaches and alternative viewpoints were less likely to be included as the basis of consensus.[85] At the same time, it permitted

---

83 G7 Information Centre, G8 Justice and Interior Ministers' Meeting, "Chairpersons' Summary" at paras 12 and 15 (Mont-Tremblant, Quebec, Canada, 13–14 May 2002), online: www.g8.utoronto.ca/adhoc/justice2002chair.htm. See also G8 Foreign Ministers' Meeting, "G8 Foreign Ministers' Progress Report on Counter Terrorism" (Whistler, British Columbia, Canada, 12 June 2002), online: www.g8.utoronto.ca/foreign/fm130602b.htm.

84 Scherrer, above note 81 at 8.

85 *Ibid* at 11.

work achieved in a specialized forum, such as the G7/G8, to be considered and perhaps adopted by other regional or multilateral fora. One example was the development of a G8 guide on mutual legal assistance for regions that historically had difficulty obtaining legal assistance from G8 countries. The guide, which set out their individual legal and procedural requirements and provided contact points in each G8 state, was later published by the UN Crime Commission for use by Member States.[86] Likewise, G8 work on identity-related fraud influenced the development of a UN handbook on identity-related crime, which was funded by Canada.[87]

Another significant example was the G8's influence in the development of the *UNTOC*. Following the call at the 1995 Halifax Summit for G8 experts to consider gaps in the international regime for addressing transnational organized crime, the newly named Lyon Group recommended at the 1996 Paris Summit, *inter alia*, the possibility of adopting new international instruments.[88] The subsequent work of the Lyon Group in response to the Summit's political directive influenced, and closely followed, later developments leading to the *UNTOC*. Likewise, the Lyon Group's sibling, the Roma Group, was active (both before and after the merger of groups) in the development of a number of international standards and norms against terrorism.[89]

Canada also participated in the negotiation of the OECD *Convention on Combating Bribery of Foreign Officials in International Business*,[90] which led to the enactment in Canada of the *Corruption of Foreign Public Officials Act*.[91] Canada was also involved in negotiating the FATF's recommendations on money laundering and terrorist financing, and has taken part

---

86 UN Commission on Crime Prevention and Criminal Justice, *Requesting Mutual Legal Assistance in Criminal Matters from G8 countries: A Step-by-Step Guide*, UN Doc E/CN.15/2011/CRP.6 (12 April 2011) [*Guide to Mutual Legal Assistance*]. As a result, the G20 subsequently engaged in a similar exercise.

87 UNODC, *UN Handbook on Identity-Related Crime* (2011), online: unodc.org/documents/congress/background-information/Corruption/Handbook_on_Identity-related_Crime_ENG.pdf.

88 "P8 — Senior Experts Group Recommendations to combat Transnational Organized Crime," above note 76 at para 29; and see notes 69, 78, and text to note 80.

89 Scherrer, above note 81 at 10–11.

90 *Convention on Combating Bribery of Foreign Public Officials in International Business*, (1997) Can TS 1999 No 23 [*OECD Anti-Bribery Convention*].

91 *Corruption of Foreign Public Officials Act*, SC 1998, c 34.

in a number of its mutual evaluations of members' legal and operational frameworks in these areas.[92]

Other fora were also created that reflect the political necessity of addressing crime at political levels. For example, meetings of the Quintet (a gathering of attorneys general and ministers of justice from Australia, Canada, New Zealand, United Kingdom, and United States of America) were originated at the initiative of the United Kingdom, and Canada (to date) has hosted two of these meetings.[93]

Bilaterally, other policy-related innovations were initiated. For example, the Canada–US Cross-Border Crime Forum began in 1997 with a series of subsequent meetings to address transnational crime,[94] and the

---

92 FATF, "Mutual Evaluations" (2021), online: www.fatf-gafi.org/publications/mutualevaluations/documents/more-about-mutual-evaluations.html. For mutual evaluations of Canada, see FATF, "FATF—Canada" (2021), online: www.fatf-gafi.org/countries/#Canada; Canada participated in mutual evaluations of France, Japan, and Russia (FATF, "Find a Country" FATF (2021), online: www.fatf-gafi.org/countries/#.

93 Canada, Department of Justice, Press Releases, "Attorney General Rob Nicholson Hosts International Quintet Meeting" (15 June 2012), online: www.justice.gc.ca/eng/news-nouv/nr-cp/2012/doc_32752.html. Issues discussed included cybercrime, national security, particularly the use of intelligence and evidence in legal proceedings, and international cooperation, particularly in combating organized crime. Other issues discussed included forced marriages, digital copyright enforcement, data protection, and deferred prosecution agreements; and "Communiqué—The Quintet of Attorneys General Meets to Discuss Shared Priorities" (27 June 2017), online: www.justice.gc.ca/eng/rp-pr/other-autre/priorities-priorites.html. Issues discussed included over-representation of Indigenous Peoples in the criminal justice system, trans-border access to data, intelligence and evidence in legal proceedings, international law of self-defence and imminent threats, and international cooperation between Quintet states and other states.

94 The Forum brings together ministers and senior officials from, *inter alia*, Public Safety Canada, Justice Canada, the US Department of Justice and the US Department of Homeland Security to address transnational crime issues, such as organized crime, counter-terrorism, smuggling, economic crime and other emerging cross-border threats; see the website of Public Safety Canada, online: publicsafety.gc.ca/cnt/brdr-strtgs/bynd-th-brdr/ctn-pln-en.aspx. See also: Government of Canada, Press Releases, "Canada and the United States Discuss Border and Law Enforcement Related Issues at the 12th Cross-Border Crime Forum in Ottawa" (2 March 2012), online: www.publicsafety.gc.ca/media/nr/2012/nr20120302-eng.aspx; and "Canada-United States Cross-Border Crime Forum," online: www.publicsafety.gc.ca/cnt/brdr-strtgs/index-en.aspx. While the Forum has not met since 2012, the two countries announced their intention in 2021 to revive the meeting, see the website of the Office of the Prime Minister, "Roadmap for a Renewed

Beyond the Border Action Plan: A Shared Vision for Perimeter Security and Economic Competitiveness with the United States[95] furthered previous, and led to subsequent, plans for international bilateral cooperation.[96]

Thus, international criminal justice policy is developed in the international fora in which Canada participates, and is influenced by a variety of actors working within them. It also influences and is influenced by and reflective of the development of Canadian criminal justice policy and laws, which occurs in a dynamic, diplomatic, and symbiotic relationship in which international and domestic policy influence each other.

2) Events as Drivers of International Criminal Justice Policy

In the domestic sphere as in the international, specific events also drive criminal justice policy-making.[97] Examples include the events in the former Yugoslavia, and later in Rwanda, that focused the international community's attention on the failure of national systems to protect victims from horrendous acts that are considered international law crimes (genocide, crimes against humanity, and war crimes). *Ad hoc* international tribunals were established by the United Nations Security Council (UNSC) under the authority of Chapter VII of the UN Charter to prosecute those responsible and, in some measure, assist victims of the war crimes, crimes against humanity, and genocide. Through its mutual legal assistance processes, the Government of Canada supported the *ad hoc*

Canada–US Relationship," online: pm.gc.ca/en/news/statements/2021/02/23/roadmap-renewed-us-canada-partnership.

95 A Canada–US action plan, initiated by President Obama and Prime Minister Harper in February 2011, based "on a perimeter approach to security and economic competitiveness," which deals, *inter alia*, with cross-border law enforcement, cybercrime issues and other emergent threats. Public Safety Canada, *Beyond the Border Action Plan* (4 February 2011), online: publicsafety.gc.ca/cnt/brdr-strtgs/bynd-th-brdr/ctn-pln-en.aspx.

96 Previous plans included the "Security and Prosperity Partnership of North America," online: canada.ca/en/news/archive/2005/03/security-prosperity-partnership-north-america-established.html, and the "Smart Border Declaration," online: legislationline.org/documents/id/7543.

97 Theodore Meron makes a similar point in relation to international humanitarian law. "Calamitous events and atrocities have always driven the development of international humanitarian law. The more offensive or painful the suffering, the greater the pressure for adjustment of the law." See Theodore Meron, "The Humanization of International Law" (2000) 94:2 *American Journal of International Law* 239 at 243.

tribunal prosecutions by facilitating the participation and testimony of witnesses, particularly of Canadian peacekeepers who served in the former Yugoslavia. The Government of Canada was also involved in the efforts to establish other international tribunals, namely the Special Court of Sierra Leone, the Extraordinary Chambers for Cambodia and the Special Tribunal for Lebanon. Canada played a significant role in the negotiation and establishment of *The Rome Statute of the International Criminal Court*, chairing several working groups, as well as the final negotiations in both New York and Rome.[98]

Another example of the impact of events on international criminal justice policy-making is the terrorism-related policy-making that began in the early 1970s and 1980s. A series of airplane hijackings, kidnappings, and hostage-taking incidents focused, or perhaps refocused,[99] international and domestic attention on these crimes, and led to the negotiation of a series of international conventions that Canada later signed and ratified.[100]

---

98 *The Rome Statute of the International Criminal Court*, (1998) 2187 UNTS 3 [*Rome Statute*]. For a description of the negotiations, including Canada's roles, see: William Schabas, *The International Criminal Court* (Oxford: Oxford University Press, 2016); and Roy Lee, *The International Criminal Court: The Making of the Rome Statute* (The Hague: Kluwer Law, 1999) at 579–80; and follow references to Canada in the index at 642. See also *Canada and the International Criminal Court* (Government of Canada, 2019), online: www.international.gc.ca/world-monde/international_relations-relations_internationales/icc-cpi/index.aspx?lang=eng. For some examples involving specifically criminal law, see Donald Piragoff, "Procedural Justice Related to Crimes of Sexual Violence" in H. Fischer, C. Kress & S. Luder, eds, *International and National Prosecution of Crimes Under International Law* (Germany: Berlin Verlag, 2001); and Donald Piragoff, "Article 30 — Mental Element," "Article 69 — Evidence," and "Article 70 — Offences Against the Administration of Justice" in Kai Ambos, *Commentary on the Rome Statute of the International Criminal Court*, 4th ed (Munich, Germany: Beck-Hart-Nomos, 2022).

99 Keppner, above note 5 at 128–58, on anarchist bombings, assassinations, and other terrorist acts occurring through Europe, Russia, and the United States between 1880 and 1914; Alain Besançon, "The First European Terrorists" in Benjamin Netanyahu, ed, *Terrorism: How the West Can Win* (USA: The Jonathan Institute, 1986) at 44–47. As well, kidnapping had long been criminalized in the British Colonies, including in Canada's *Criminal Code of 1892*: George H. Crouse, "A Critique of Canadian Criminal Legislation Part Two" (1934) 12 *Canadian Bar Review* 602 at 606–8.

100 The *Convention for the Suppression of Unlawful Seizure of Aircraft*, (1970) 860 UNTS 105; the *Convention for the Suppression of Unlawful Acts against the Safety of Civil Aviation*, (1971) 974 UNTS 177; the *Convention on the Prevention and Punishment of Crimes against Internationally Protected Persons, including Diplomatic Agents*, (1973) 1035 UNTS 167; the *International Convention against the Taking of Hostages*,

The terrorist incidents of 9/11 would lead to an even greater wave of international criminal justice policy-making.

Following the tragic events of 9/11, UNSC Resolution 1373 (2001),[101] issued under Chapter VII of the UN Charter, called on states to prevent and suppress terrorist acts and noted "with concern" the linkages between international terrorism and organized crime and money laundering. Resolution 1373 required states to take measures to prevent terrorist financing, including the freezing of assets of certain listed individuals and entities, and to criminalize various forms of terrorist financing. It also called on states to criminalize all terrorist activities from their planning through to their perpetration, and to impose punishments reflecting the seriousness of terrorist activities. International cooperation in the fight against terrorism was emphasized. Within a matter of months, Parliament enacted the *Anti-terrorism Act*, an omnibus bill that amended or adopted several acts to create an anti-terrorism legislative framework, including new terrorism offences in the *Criminal Code*, measures to detect and deter terrorism financing, new legislation to protect national security information, and a legislative mandate for communications security and intelligence.[102]

Member States were required to report to the UN Counter-Terrorism Committee, established by Resolution 1373, on domestic implementation, within ninety days.[103] Canada's first report to the Counter-Terrorism Committee outlined the steps taken under the *United Nations Act*[104] to freeze, seize, and forfeit assets of persons on UN listings, and outlined the provisions of the *Anti-terrorism Act*, which implemented Resolution 1373 and other international anti-terrorism conventions that Canada had not yet ratified prior to 2001 into domestic law.[105] Since 2001, Canada has sought

---

(1979) 1316 UNTS 205; the *Protocol for the Suppression of Unlawful Acts of Violence at Airports Serving International Civil Aviation*, (1988) 1589 UNTS 474; the *Convention for the Suppression of Unlawful Acts against the Safety of Maritime Navigation*, (1988) 1678 UNTS 221; and the *Protocol for the Suppression of Unlawful Acts against the Safety of Fixed Platforms Located on the Continental Shelf*, (1988) 1678 UNTS 304.

101 UNSC Res 1373, UN Doc S/RES/1373 (2001) [*Resolution 1373*] at operative para 4.

102 *Anti-terrorism Act*, SC 2001, c 41; and see Government of Canada, "About the Anti-terrorism Act" (2017), online: www.justice.gc.ca/eng/cj-jp/ns-sn/act-loi.html. See also Chapter 5 in this volume.

103 *Resolution 1373*, above note 101, at operative para 1.

104 *United Nations Act*, RSC 1985, c U-2.

105 When the events of 9/11 took place, Canada had not yet ratified the *International Convention for the Suppression of Terrorist Bombings*, (1997) 2149 UNTS 256, Can TS

to advance the objectives of the UN Global Anti-terrorism Strategy by participating in the negotiation of new international instruments, such as those addressing nuclear terrorism and the protection of nuclear materials; seizing and forfeiture of assets linked to terrorist activities; conducting Canadian investigations and prosecutions of persons suspected of terrorist activities; and enacting legislation to assist these investigations, and to protect the ability of victims of state-sponsored terrorism to obtain legal remedies.[106] The anti-terrorism offences in the *Criminal Code* and other Canadian activities would influence the anti-terrorism work of various international organizations, as noted and discussed in Section C(1), above.

3) The Domestic Process of Internationalization of Criminal Justice Policy

As noted above, international fora, actors, and events all shape how international criminal justice policy is developed. Once a treaty is ready for Canada to consider signing, ratifying, or acceding, or once an international standard and norm is adopted by an international organization, a domestic process is initiated. The Government of Canada must assess whether the international treaty is one that it wishes to implement in domestic policy and law. This may require amending Canadian law to meet a particular standard, or deciding that the international standard, even if lower, will apply in Canada. A somewhat similar, but more flexible, process exists for non-binding soft law standards and norms. In essence, the question becomes to what extent Canada wishes to harmonize its policies and laws with the legal or normative standards of the international community, and

---

2002 No 8, the *International Convention for the Suppression of the Financing of Terrorism*, (1999) 2178 UNTS 197, Can TS 2002 No 9 [*Terrorism Financing Convention*], or the *International Convention for the Protection of UN and Associated Personnel*, (1994) Can TS 2002 No 7.

106 Office of the High Commissioner for Human Rights, "UN Global Counter-Terrorism Strategy" (2021), online: www.ohchr.org/EN/Issues/Terrorism/Pages/Strategy.aspx. For discussion of Canada's response to terrorism, see Stanley Cohen, *Privacy, Crime and Terror: Legal Rights and Security in a Time of Peace* (Canada: LexisNexis, 2004); Kent Roach, *September 11: Consequences for Canada* (Canada: McGill-Queen's University Press, 2003); *The Views of Canadian Scholars on the Impact of the Anti-terrorism Act* (Canada: Department of Justice, 2005), online: www.justice.gc.ca/eng/rp-pr/cj-jp/antiter/rr05_1/index.html; and "About the Anti-terrorism Act," above note 102.

in what instances the government wishes, or is constitutionally required, to adhere to particular, alternative Canadian values and norms.[107] This process, whether described as one of "convergence, approximation, or harmonization,"[108] forms part of the internationalization of Canadian criminal law.

The assessment process engages various domestic actors within government, and may be influenced by public perception of the international initiative. Depending on the nature of the initiative, public opinion may be gauged in a variety of ways: public-opinion polling, analysis of social media data, online consultation, or more formal meetings with stakeholders. Regarding treaties, Government of Canada policy requires the minister of foreign affairs, subject to limited exceptions, to table treaties and other "instruments governed by international law" concluded directly with foreign states or within international organizations, in the House of Commons, following signature or adoption, and before Canada formally notifies that it considers itself bound by that treaty or instrument.[109]

Internationalization can also occur at the other end of the policy-making spectrum should the Government of Canada find itself scrutinized by international bodies and found wanting through an individual complaint mechanism of the United Nations High Commissioner for Refugee (UNHRC),[110] or the reporting mechanisms of the Human Rights Council's Universal Periodic Review, or other treaty-body processes. Although the views or concluding observations of international

---

107 Constitutional requirements are considered at the stage of both negotiation of international treaties and at the time of Canadian ratification. In rare instances, reservations to a treaty are required.

108 Chris Reed, *Making Laws for Cyberspace* (Oxford: Oxford University Press, 2012) at 47. See also Macdonald, Morris & Johnston, above note 5 at 331.

109 Canada, Department of Foreign Affairs, Treaty Law Division, "Policy on Tabling of Treaties in Parliament," online: www.treaty-accord.gc.ca/procedures.aspx?lang=eng. Note the exceptions in s 6.3 of the Policy.

110 See *Michel Dumont v Canada*, UN Doc No CCPR/C/98/D/1467/2006 (21 May 2010), concluding that Mr. Dumont's rights under art 2(3), read in conjunction with art 14(6) of the *ICCPR* (below note 114), had been infringed as he did not receive compensation under the applicable federal guidelines on compensation for miscarriages of justice. Following the Human Rights Committee's concluding observations, Mr. Dumont appealed his civil suit against the Government of Quebec for compensation to the Supreme Court of Canada, which dismissed his request for leave to appeal, with costs. *Michel Dumont, et al v Attorney General of Quebec, et al*, SCC File #35168, 16 May 2013.

rights bodies are not legally binding, Canada takes them into consideration in its policy development.[111]

a) Assessment of International Requirements Against Constitutional Standards

The implementation of an international treaty, or standard and norm, into domestic policy and law requires an assessment of the international requirements in light of the constitutional division of powers and of the *Canadian Charter of Rights and Freedoms.*[112] The intricacies of Canadian federalism are often difficult to understand for foreign delegations that are involved in international negotiations, particularly as some areas of implementation could require action by provincial or territorial, not federal, governments. In the criminal law area, the exclusivity of federal responsibility over the enactment of criminal law makes this issue somewhat less difficult. However, the views of the provinces and territories are important, as potential criminal law reforms will necessarily have an impact on the administration of justice in their jurisdictions.

A treaty may set out particular criminalization requirements; it may dictate the type of conduct that must be criminalized and often may specify elements of the offences. While the standards in the *Universal Declaration of Human Rights*[113] and in the UN *Covenant on Civil and Political Rights* (*ICCPR*)[114] inform international negotiations and treaty-making (as well as the issuance of binding UNSC resolutions), it is up to

111 For example, s 76(2) of the *Youth Criminal Justice Act*, enacted as part of *Safe Streets and Communities Act*, SC 2012, c 1, s 186, provides that no young person under eighteen shall serve their *sentence* in an adult institution. The obligation to *detain* children separately from adults is enshrined in art 37(c) of the *Convention on the Rights of the Child*, (1989) 1577 UNTS 3, to which Canada entered a reservation upon ratification. As a result of the reservation, domestic criminal law and practice regarding detention is aligned legally with its human rights obligations under the Convention. See Human Rights Council, 24th Sess, *Report of the Working Group on the Universal Periodic Review — Canada*, A/HRC/24/11 (28 June 2013) at para 128, recommendation 128; United Nations, Human Rights Council, Working Group on the Universal Periodic Review, *National Report Submitted in Accordance with Paragraph 5 of the Annex to Human Rights Council Resolution 16/21 — Canada*, UN Doc A/HRC/WG.6/16/CAN/1 (8 February 2013) at paras 9 and 23.

112 *Canadian Charter of Rights and Freedoms*, Part I of the *Constitution Act, 1982*, being Schedule B to the *Canada Act 1982* (UK), 1982, c 11 [*Charter*].

113 *Universal Declaration of Human Rights*, UNGA Res 217A(III) (1948).

114 *ICCPR* (1966) 999 UNTS 171.

each state to determine how best to characterize the offence or offences in specific drafting language when implementing the treaty in a manner consistent with its constitutional requirements.

Issues that might be problematic for Canada from a constitutional perspective can be raised during the negotiations of a particular treaty or instrument dealing with international, transnational, or domestic crime.[115] A reservation would be necessary in the event of direct inconsistency with constitutional requirements, although depending on the nature of the obligation, statements of understanding or declarations may suffice. Generally, the Government of Canada makes its best effort not to enter a reservation to treaties, and some treaties do not permit reservations. Addressing constitutionally related issues during a negotiation process is thus preferable; otherwise, ratification may not be possible.[116]

Treaties may also contain standards that may be best described as "the agreed-upon minimum" in terms of human rights protections, thus permitting states to exceed the standard. When implementing the treaty into domestic law, consistency with the *Charter* or other criminal law policy objectives may require adding procedural or other substantive protections in certain circumstances. The additional protections incorporated into the

115 See, for example, UNSC resolutions issued under Chapter VII of the UN Charter, and binding on Canada, may need to be considered from a *Charter* perspective, as was necessary for SC Resolutions 1373 and 1540. Another example, the offence of illicit enrichment under art 20 of the *UNCAC*, above note 10, may be problematic for certain states and, therefore, the Convention requires states only to consider criminalizing it, subject to their constitution and fundamental principles of their legal system.

116 For example, a proposed provision in the *Inter-American Convention Against Corruption*, reprinted (1996) 35 ILM 724, would have created a reverse onus by requiring public officials to disclose any increase in wealth of assets and presuming corruption if no accounting could be given for the increase in wealth. Some delegations, including Canada's, took the position that as it would not have been possible to make a reservation under the Convention, and had the provision been adopted, these states would not have been able to ratify for constitutional reasons. Eventually, as a compromise, Article IX recognized that while states may not establish such measures, they must continue to provide assistance to other states in accord with the Convention. On the other hand, despite some accommodations being made during the negotiation process to the CoE, *Additional Optional Protocol to the Convention on Cybercrime, concerning the criminalisation of acts of a racist and xenophobic nature committed through computer systems*, (2003) ETS 189, it is unlikely that Canada would be able to ratify the protocol, without making a number of reservations/declarations.

Criminal Code process for the listing of terrorist entities, including ministerial review of the listing process, is one example.[117]

b) Treaty Requirements to Criminalize Certain Conduct

International treaties dealing with transnational crime (including domestic manifestations), like the *UNTOC*, *UNCAC*, and CoE *Convention on Cybercrime* require states to criminalize certain conduct in domestic law. The *UNTOC* and *UNCAC* contain both mandatory and permissive obligations to criminalize conduct.[118] Treaties that require criminalization into domestic law are often signed and ratified when domestic law already meets the international law standard, or if there is a political decision that domestic priorities include taking the necessary measures to meet the international standard. For example, by the time that the intergovernmental Ad Hoc Committee on the Elaboration of a Convention against Transnational Organized Crime was established in 1999,[119] the Government of Canada had already enacted legislation to amend the *Criminal Code* to include a criminal organization offence and to counter organized crime.[120] A few years later, in 2001, Bill C-24 addressed domestic concerns that the earlier enacted definition of "organized crime group" was too narrow, as it did not sufficiently encompass the range of activities in which criminal organizations engage.[121] Bill C-24 incorporated three amendments which were consistent with the *UNTOC* definitions of organized crime and serious offences.[122] As amended, the definition more closely

117 *Code*, above note 58, s 83.05(1).

118 See, for example, *UNTOC*, above note 23, arts 5, 6, 8(1), and 23, requires States Parties to criminalize participation in an organized criminal group, laundering the proceeds of crime, corruption, and obstruction of justice in relation to Convention offences, while for other offences the treaty is permissive (for example, art 8(2) & (3) regarding foreign public officials, and accomplices, respectively). The three additional Protocols to the Convention also require the criminalization of trafficking in persons, migrant smuggling, and the illicit manufacture and trafficking of firearms. Canada has ratified and implemented the first two Protocols and signed the third; for example, *An Act to amend the Criminal Code (trafficking in persons)*, SC 2005, c 43.

119 UNGA Res 53/111 (9 December 1998).

120 *An Act to Amend the Criminal Code (Criminal Organizations) and to Amend Other Acts in Consequence*, SC 1997, c 23, s 11.

121 See Canada, Parliament, House of Commons, *Proceedings of the House of Commons Standing Committee on Justice and Human Rights*, 8 May 2001 and 15 May 2001.

122 *An Act to amend the Criminal Code (organized crime and law enforcement) and to make consequential amendments to other Acts*, SC 2001, c 32, s 27. The amendments

reflects the *UNTOC* definition.[123] Bill C-24 also included provisions to protect justice system participants, amendments to the *Immigration and Refugee Protection Act*[124] that criminalized migrant smuggling and human trafficking in a manner consistent with the Protocols to the *UNTOC*, and other measures.

Existing *Criminal Code* and other federal offences are sometimes broad enough to encompass a significant amount of the criminal conduct sought to be criminalized under a new international instrument. Bribery and offences such as breach of trust, theft, and fraud have long addressed corrupt activities.[125] However, in order to align with international obligations, the legislative framework to address corrupt activities was supplemented during subsequent revisions of the *Criminal Code*,[126] and by enactment in 1998 of the *Corruption of Foreign Public Officials Act*.[127] Corruption and its associations with organized crime have been the subject of a series of domestic inquiries, such as the Charbonneau Commission in Quebec,[128] as well as of international work and negotiation amongst states,

---

reduced the number of people required to constitute a criminal organization from five to three, removed the requirement that offences be committed within the past five years, and broadened the scope of the offences to all serious offences.

123 Article 2 of *UNTOC*, above note 23, refers to "a structured group of three or more persons," "existing for a period of time" and acting together to commit "one or more serious crimes or offences established in accordance with this Convention" and "to obtain, directly or indirectly, a financial or other material benefit."

124 *Immigration and Refugee Protection Act*, SC 2001, c 27.

125 Lisette Lafontaine, "Canada's Experience with the Implementation of International Conventions Against Corruption" (Paper prepared for the China Programmes of the International Centre for Criminal Law Reform and Criminal Justice Policy, Vancouver, March 2006), online: https://icclr.org/publications/canadas-experience-with-the-implementation-of-international-conventions-against-corruption at 3–4. For information on the China Programsme, see ICCLR, *Annual Report 2006–2007 & Programme of Work 2007–2008*, online: www.publicsafety.gc.ca/lbrr/archives/cnmcs-plcng/icclr-ar-2006-2007-eng.pdf; and see above note 34 regarding ICCLR.

126 See, in particular, *An Act to amend the Criminal Code in order to implement the United Nations Convention Against Corruption*, SC 2007, c 13 [Bill C-48].

127 *Corruption of Foreign Public Officials Act*, SC 1998, c 34.

128 These include the Cliche Commission, the Oliphant Inquiry, the Gomery Inquiry, the Mississauga Judicial Inquiry, and the Charbonneau Commission investigating the management of public contracts in the Quebec construction industry, Quebec, Charbonneau Commission, *La Commission d'enquête sur l'octroi et la gestion des contrats publics dans l'industrie de la construction* (established 9 November 2011), online: https://numerique.banq.qc.ca/patrimoine/details/52327/2502593?docref=mflwEhK5XXkMeXiXXXDVgA. See Eileen Skinnider, "Corruption in Canada:

including Canada, that resulted in other conventions to which Canada is a state party. These include the 1996 *Inter-American Convention Against Corruption*,[129] the OECD *Anti-Bribery Convention*,[130] and the corruption-related provisions of the *UNTOC*.[131] In 2007, Bill C-48, which was enacted to implement the *UNCAC*, required few amendments to existing *Code* offences and proceeds-of-crime provisions, as most of the framework already existed to address corruption as envisaged in the *UNCAC*.[132]

Criminalization in accordance with a treaty or convention is not just an end in itself. First, it is important to criminalize and prosecute certain conduct in order to protect public safety and individuals within a state, and a convention provides an international consensus of the definition of such criminality. Second, harmonized criminalization furthers international cooperation to the extent it ensures dual criminality for purposes of extradition or surrender.[133]

If a treaty is concluded, treaty implementation properly becomes the focus, and states are required to meet standards of accountability. For

---

Reviewing Practices from Abroad to Improve Our Response," ICCLR (March 2012) at 3, online: www.icclr.law.ubc.ca/files/2012/Final%20Paper%20Corruption-09%20May%202012.pdf.

129 *IACAC*, above note 11.

130 *OECD Anti-Bribery Convention*, above note 90.

131 Douglas R. Breithaupt, "Implementation Issues and Procedures Related to the Recovery and Return of Assets Under both the UN Convention Against Transnational Organized Crime and the UN Convention Against Corruption" Paper, Workshop on the UN Convention Against Transnational Organized Crime and the UN Convention Against Corruption, ICCLR (Beijing China, 27–28 October 2006) at 2–3, n 2; and see above note 125 regarding the ICCLR China Programme. Although a non-member, but with official observer status of the Council of Europe, Canada has not signed or ratified its *Criminal Law Convention on Corruption.*

132 Bill C-48, enacted by SC 2007, c 13, see also above note 126. The framework to address corruption includes a wide variety of legislative and administrative measures; for analysis of the current framework, see: Peter McKay, Lisa Douglas & Christopher Burkett, "Anti-corruption in Canada" *Global Compliance News* (2021), online: www.globalcompliancenews.com/anti-corruption/handbook/anti-corruption-in-canada/; Tudor Carsten, "Canada — Global Bribery Offences Guide" (DLA Piper, 2019), online: www.dlapiper.com/en/us/insights/publications/2019/09/bribery-offenses-guide/canada; Benjamin Bathgate et al, "Anti-Corruption" (McMillan LLP, 2021), online: mcmillan.ca/wp-content/uploads/2020/07/Anti-Corruption-CANADA-LP.pdf; and Mark Morrison & Michael Dixon, "The Anti-Bribery and Anti-Corruption Review: Canada" *The Law Review* (30 November 2020), online: thelawreviews.co.uk/title/the-anti-bribery-and-anti-corruption-review/canada.

133 See, for example, *Extradition Act*, SC 1999, c 18, s 3 [*Extradition Act*].

example, States Parties have established a peer-review mechanism under the *UNCAC*, whereby states engage in a state-to-state process of assessing and monitoring the degree to which its obligations are adhered.[134] A similar mechanism is being established under the *UNTOC*.[135] As noted earlier, the FATF established a mutual-evaluation review process to assess implementation of its recommendations, and the OECD has undertaken an evaluation of its *OECD Anti-Bribery Convention*.[136] Such accountability mechanisms can produce measurable results for Member States, although they would need to be assessed against the costs associated with implementing such peer-review mechanisms.

c) Consider the Scope of the Implementation Measures Required

The extent of the obligations created within a treaty on transnational crime (including domestic manifestations) may dictate whether its implementation will require a comprehensive change to domestic criminal law or not. As noted above, Bill C-48 made only targeted amendments to implement the *UNCAC*. Likewise, only minor amendments were required to implement the CoE *Convention on Cybercrime*, as the negotiated treaty provisions significantly reflected existent Canadian law.[137]

In contrast, the *Crimes Against Humanity and War Crimes Act* implemented the *Rome Statute of the International Criminal Court*[138] in a comprehensive manner.[139] Amendments to mutual legal assistance, extradition,

134 *UNCAC*, above note 10, arts 63(5), (6) & (7). See UNODC, "Implementation Review Mechanism" (2021), online: www.unodc.org/unodc/en/corruption/implementation-review-mechanism.htm.

135 *UNTOC*, above note 23, art 32(4) & (5). See UNODC, "Mechanism for the Review of the Implementation of the United Nations Convention Against Transnational Organized Crime and the Protocols Thereto" (2021), online: www.unodc.org/unodc/en/organized-crime/intro/review-mechanism-untoc/home.html.

136 FATF, above note 92; *OECD Anti-Bribery Convention*, above note 90; OECD, "2019 Enforcement of the Anti-Bribery Convention" (2020), online: oecd.org/daf/anti-bribery/OECD-Anti-Bribery-Convention-Enforcement-Data-2020.pdf.

137 *Protecting Canadians from Online Crime* Act, SC 2014, c 31, and see above note 65.

138 *Rome Statute*, above note 98, online: www.icc-cpi.int/resource-library/documents/rs-eng.pdf.

139 *Crimes Against Humanity and War Crimes Act*, SC 2000, c 24 [*CAHWCA*], online: laws-lois.justice.gc.ca/eng/acts/C-45.9/page-5.html#h-114895. These included amendments to the *Criminal Code*, the *Citizenship Act*, the *Corrections and Conditional Release Act*, the *Extradition Act*, the *Mutual Legal Assistance in Criminal*

and proceeds-of-crime regimes were necessary in order for Canada to cooperate with the ICC and other international criminal tribunals, and to assist victims of these serious international crimes through the direct enforcement of ICC orders for reparation. In enacting the *CAHWCA*, Canada also advanced a number of domestic and international objectives that went beyond the strict implementation of the *Rome Statute*, such as adjusting domestic law relating to war crimes prosecutions,[140] and creating domestic offences that aligned with those in the treaty, even if such enactment is not required by the treaty.[141]

d) Consider Whether to Extend Jurisdiction to Prosecute

The question of jurisdiction lies at the heart of state sovereignty: How far and for what purposes will a state extend its jurisdiction, and subject to what limitations? Territoriality is the foundation of international law. However, as crime began to extend beyond the boundaries of the nation-state, states or their domestic courts began to re-examine the concept of territorial jurisdiction. For example, the Supreme Court of Canada's decision in *Libman v The Queen* extended territorial jurisdiction to include transborder activities in which a significant portion of the activities took

---

Matters Act, the *State Immunity Act*, the *Witness Protection Program Act*, the *Application of the Proceeds of Crime provisions of the Criminal Code* and the *Seized Property Management Act*; see Annemieke Holthuis, "Ratification and Implementation of the Rome Statute: The Canadian Experience" in *Commonwealth Meeting on the International Criminal Court*, Marlborough House, 5–7 October 2010 (London: International Criminal Court & Commonwealth Secretariat, 2011) at 43ff, online: asp.icc-cpi.int/iccdocs/asp_docs/Publications/ASP-PUB-Cmw-Sem2009-ENG.pdf.

140 The *CAHWCA* addressed a number of deficiencies/difficulties in conducting a war crime prosecution as a result of the decision in *R v Finta*, [1994] SCR 701, addressing the need to prove both the domestic offence (for example, murder) and the international crime, the historical status of customary international law, and the definition of the defence of superior orders.

141 Under the *Rome Statute*, the ICC's exercise of jurisdiction is *complementary* and subject to any valid and *bona fide* exercise of jurisdiction by a state, such that the ICC will not exercise its jurisdiction if a state is *bona fide* investigating or prosecuting the offence. Enacting offences in the *CAHWCA*, in alignment with the ICC treaty crimes, would enable Canada to assert better the primacy of its own jurisdiction in any future Canadian *bona fide* investigation/prosecution of the same case brought before the ICC. See William Schabas & Mohamed Zeidy, "Article 17—Issues of Admissibility" in Kai Ambos, 4th ed, *Rome Statute of the International Criminal Court* (Munich, Germany: Beck-Hart-Nomos 2022) at 957ff.

place in Canada, such that there is "a real and substantial link" between the offence and Canada.[142]

In the context of transnational crime, states have considered the potential of extraterritorial jurisdiction to address the gaps in the prosecution of crimes, particularly as some states cannot, or will not, extradite their nationals to a third state or prosecute them for crimes committed in another state. In the 1988 *UN Drug Convention*[143] and the *UNTOC*, states agreed to extend their jurisdiction in certain circumstances. Under the *UNTOC*, states are required to extend jurisdiction when they do not, for constitutional or other reasons, extradite their own nationals, and may consider extending jurisdiction when persons present in their territories are alleged to have committed transnational offences within the scope of the Convention.[144] Article 15 of the *UNTOC* also adverts to the problem of overlapping or competing jurisdictions amongst states to investigate and prosecute such offences, and envisages consultations and coordination of action.

Parliament may enact extraterritorial jurisdiction by expressly extending its prescriptive jurisdiction over conduct occurring completely outside of Canada. When it does, Canadian courts have taken the position that they have adjudicative jurisdiction, subject to the interests of the sovereignty of other states and comity.[145] Generally, when Parliament decides to use its prescriptive jurisdiction to criminalize extraterritorial conduct and extend adjudicative jurisdiction, it does so in a manner required by, or consistent with, an international obligation. Unilateral extensions of jurisdiction otherwise are rare, and generally justified on the basis of an international law. For example, Parliament enacted an extraterritorial provision to deal with sex tourism, which was consistent with the *Optional Protocol to the Convention on the Rights of the Child on the Sale of Children, Child Prostitution and Child Pornography*,[146] but which was not legally mandated by it.[147]

142 *Libman v The Queen*, [1985] 2 SCR 178 at para 74. See also chapters 6, 7, and 15 in this volume.

143 *United Nations Convention against Illicit Traffic in Narcotic Drugs and Psychotropic Substances*, 20 December 1988, 1582 UNTS 95 [*UN Drug Convention*]; *UNTOC*, above note 23, art 15.

144 *UNTOC*, above note 23, art 15.

145 *Hape*, above note 4.

146 *Optional Protocol to the Convention on the Rights of the Child on the Sale of Children, Child Prostitution and Child Pornography*, UN Doc A/RES/54/263 (2000), art 4.

147 *Code*, above note 58, s 7(4.1). The extension of jurisdiction was upheld in *R v Klassen*, 2008 BCSC 1762 at para 58.

An exception under customary international law relates to jurisdiction that applies to serious international crimes, such as piracy,[148] and those in the *Rome Statute* that are implemented domestically in the *CAHWCA*. Although not required by the *Rome Statute*, the *CAHWCA* extended Canadian jurisdiction on the basis of nationality, territoriality, passive personality, the protective principle, and universal jurisdiction provided that the accused is physically present in Canada.[149] The foreign-policy implications of exercising, by way of prosecution, such extraterritorial extensions of jurisdiction are recognized by the fact that the attorney general or deputy attorney general of Canada must personally consent in writing to the initiation of the prosecution.[150]

e) Facilitating International Cooperation

Cooperation between states for the investigation and prosecution of crime is not novel. However, the impetus for improving mutual legal assistance, extradition, and proceeds-of-crime regimes has been renewed as crime becomes increasingly globalized. Canada's *Mutual Legal Assistance in Criminal Matters Act*[151] and *Extradition Act*[152] enable Canada to assist in the investigation and prosecution of transnational crimes, such as those in the 1988 *UN Drug Convention*,[153] *UNTOC*,[154] *UNCAC*,[155] and CoE *Cybercrime Convention*.[156] There are also provisions in these acts allowing for cooperation with the ICC in regard to serious international crimes.[157]

The *UNTOC* and the *UNCAC* also directly address international cooperation. For example, where States Parties to the Conventions do not have existing bilateral treaties, the Conventions' provisions can serve as a basis for extradition and mutual legal assistance in respect of Convention

148 *Ibid*, s 74.

149 *CAHWCA*, above note 139, s 8. These extensions of extraterritorial jurisdiction would strengthen any claim by Canada of the primacy of its own jurisdiction over a case brought before the ICC.

150 *Ibid*, s 9(3); *Code*, above note 58, s 7(4.3).

151 *Mutual Legal Assistance in Criminal Matters Act*, RSC 1985, c 30 (4th Supp) [*MLACMA*].

152 *Extradition Act*, above note 133.

153 *UN Drug Convention*, above note 143, arts 6 (extradition) and 7 (mutual legal assistance).

154 *UNTOC*, above note 23.

155 *UNCAC*, above note 10.

156 *Cybercrime Convention*, above note 65.

157 *Extradition Act*, above note 133, s 47.1; *MLACMA*, above note 151, ss 9.1 & 9.2.

offences.[158] Canada has also ratified regional treaties in the area of extradition and mutual legal assistance, including the 1992 *Inter-American Convention on Mutual Assistance in Criminal Matters*.[159] The *Cybercrime Convention* contains extensive provisions concerning both extradition and specific forms of mutual legal assistance. States Parties are obligated to provide assistance under their own legal frameworks and cooperation treaties, but the Convention's mutual legal assistance framework can be employed in the absence of other applicable treaties. The *Second Additional Protocol* contains extensive provisions on enhanced cooperation and disclosure of electronic evidence, including expedited or direct enforcement of orders in some situations.[160]

Treaty provisions are but one aspect of furthering international cooperation. At its most basic, improving cooperation through mutual legal assistance requests, extradition requests, and police-to-police cooperation depends on improving officials' understanding of the domestic requirements of other states' criminal justice systems, and on knowing who to contact for various types of assistance. The G7/G8 mutual legal assistance guide and the OAS information portal, mentioned earlier, are examples of policy and operational initiatives to improve assistance.[161] Another example is the creation of networks of contact persons to improve international cooperation in cybercrime investigations which, given the transitory nature of internet communications, are often time-sensitive and fit uneasily within the formal requirements of applicable mutual legal assistance regimes. While these networks greatly facilitate communications, generally the formal requirements of mutual legal assistance still apply unless domestic law provides otherwise.[162]

158 *Ibid*; *UNTOC*, above note 23, arts 16 and 18, and *UNCAC*, above note 10, arts 44 and 46.

159 *Inter-American Convention on Mutual Assistance in Criminal Matters*, Organization of American States (1992) OAS Treaty Series No 75.

160 *Cybercrime Convention*, above note 65, art 23–34; *Second Protocol to Cybercrime Convention*, above note 68, art 5–14.

161 See Warner, above note 61; *Guide to Mutual Legal Assistance*, above note 86.

162 Sergio Staro, Member of the Italian delegation at the G8 Rome/Lyon Group (Subgroup on High Tech Crime), Presentation, "The G8 24/7 Network" (Tblisi, 13 May 2010) at slide 6, online: www.coe.int/t/dghl/cooperation/economiccrime/cybercrime/cy_project_in_georgia/Presentations/Regional%20Ws%20on%20Cybercrime_13May10/2215_The_G8_24-7%20Network_SStaro.pdf.

In 1997, the G8 High Tech Crime Subgroup established a network of points of contact (including Canada) to assist with cybercrime investigations that has since expanded to more than seventy countries.[163] A further network emanates from the *Cybercrime Convention* that requires States Parties (including Canada) to designate points of contact available every day, all day, for immediate assistance, to provide technical advice, and to preserve data and collect evidence in accordance with domestic law.[164] These networks have received consistent political support. For example, in April 2013, G8 foreign ministers meeting in the United Kingdom emphasized the importance of training and capacity building for fighting cybercrime generally, and for the 24/7 Network in particular, highlighting the participation of governments, the private sector, and civil society in countering cybercrime internationally "in a way which promotes openness, trust and security, stability, and the rule of law in the digital realm."[165]

International cooperation is also key to addressing the proceeds of crime and crime-related property issues. The *UNTOC* provided internationally accepted definitions of "property" and "proceeds of crime," and required states to criminalize the laundering of the proceeds of crime relating to "the widest range possible of predicate offences,"[166] including all serious crime in accordance with the *UNTOC* definition or, at a minimum, those offences associated with organized crime. Canada had previously relied upon the method of listing particular predicate offences, but amended the *Criminal Code* proceeds-of-crime provisions to apply effectively to all federally enacted indictable offences, and conspiracies or attempts to commit such offences.[167] Similarly, the *UNTOC*, as well as the 1988 *UN Drug Convention*, encouraged states to facilitate the freezing, seizure, and confiscation of proceeds of crime, including property derived

163 *Ibid.* See CoE, "G7 24/7 Cybercrime Network," online: rm.coe.int/16803o3ce2; OAS, "G7 High Tech Crime Network," online: www.oas.org/juridico/english/cyb20_network_en.pdf; and Chris Ott, "What You Should Know About the 24/7 Cybercrime Network (28 June 2018), online: www.dwt.com/files/uploads/documents/publications/What%20You%20Should%20Know%20About%20The%2024.pdf.

164 *Cybercrime Convention*, above note 65, art 35.

165 G7 Information Centre, "G8 Foreign Ministers Statement" (Aylesbury, UK, 11 April 2013), online: www.g8.utoronto.ca/foreign/formin130411.html.

166 *UNTOC*, above note 23, art 6.

167 Bill C-24, SC 2001, c 32, s 12(3). See definition of "designated offence" in s 462.3(1) of the *Criminal Code*, above note 58.

indirectly from the commission of Convention offences.[168] The *UNTOC* sets out the additional requirements for international cooperation, when seeking to seize or forfeit property as proceeds of crime, consistently with domestic mutual legal assistance regimes and can, in certain circumstances, serve as a treaty basis for such requests.[169] The *UNCAC* further addresses the recovery of assets by recommending the establishment of financial intelligence units, consistent with recommendations of the FATF to establish such units.[170] By the time that the *UNCAC* was concluded in 2003, Canada had already established, in 2000, the Financial Transaction and Reports Analysis Centre of Canada (FINTRAC).[171] Other treaties, such as the *Rome Statute*, also envisage the restraint, forfeiture, and recovery of assets in regard to international crimes.[172]

f) New Means of Preventing and Investigating Crime

The internationalization of Canadian criminal justice policy is also visible in crime prevention and investigation in Canada. Crime prevention is reflected at the international level in the mandate and focus of the UN Crime Commission.[173] Since the 1990s, the Government of Canada has sought to integrate crime prevention initiatives into its response to crime.[174] Crime-prevention efforts can have a broader societal focus and can include measures to alleviate economic and other impacts of crime, and to reduce harm to potential victims. Measures to educate people about the costs and risks of crime, and technical measures that make crime harder to commit and easier to detect, may also be more cost effective than investigation and prosecution responses to crime *ex post facto*.

168 *UNTOC*, above note 23, art 12; *UN Drug Convention*, above note 143, art 5.

169 *UNTOC*, above note 23, arts 13, 13(6), and 18.

170 *UNCAC*, above note 10, art 58.

171 *Proceeds of Crime (Money Laundering) and Terrorist Financing Act*, SC 2000, c 17. Regarding the mandate of FINTRAC, see online: www.fintrac-canafe.gc.ca/intro-eng.

172 *MLACMA*, above note 151, ss 9.1, 9.2, 10 & 11*ff*.

173 UNODC, "Commission on Crime Prevention and Criminal Justice," online: unodc.org/unodc/en/commissions/CCPCJ/index.html; for example, see *Updated Model Strategies and Practical Measures to Eliminate Violence Against Women in the Field of Crime Prevention and Criminal Justice*, above note 52.

174 Public Safety Canada, "Crime Prevention" (2021), online: www.publicsafety.gc.ca/cnt/cntrng-crm/crm-prvntn/index-en.aspx.

As to investigation, policy and operational initiatives like the European Arrest Warrant, the establishment of Joint Investigation Teams, and the European Investigation Order, which reduce barriers for requesting states, and require executing states to use various investigative means on their behalf, have gained traction at the regional level as they seek to facilitate cooperation amongst states with comparatively similar legal systems and legal norms.[175] Nevertheless, even in these cases, concerns and challenges are posed regarding how rights will be safeguarded and a certain measure of national sovereignty preserved.[176] The *UNTOC* also encourages joint investigations and law enforcement cooperation.[177] Similarly, pilot projects involving joint US and Canadian investigative teams operating along the international maritime boundary to combat smuggling, organized drug crime, firearms trafficking, and other criminal activity have been followed by the enactment of legislation to implement the *Canada–US Shiprider Framework Agreement*.[178] These international joint investigative teams between the two states complement efforts in Canada to incorporate federal–provincial investigative teams, for example, the integrated

175 See European Commission, "Types of Cooperation," online: ec.europa.eu/info/law/cross-border-cases/judicial-cooperation/types-judicial-cooperation_en; and Council of the European Union, "Council Conclusions on the Eurojust Annual Report 2012" (15 November 2013) at paras 5–6 and 8, online: www.consilium.europa.eu/uedocs/cms_data/docs/pressdata/en/jha/139608.pdf.

176 European Parliament, "Cross-Border Crime: Make Investigations Easier, But Protect Suspects' Rights," Press Release (27 February 2014), online: www.europarl.europa.eu/news/en/news-room/content/20140221IPR36647/html/Cross-border-crime-make-investigations-easier-but-protect-suspects%E2%80%99-rights; European Union Agency for Fundamental Rights, "Opinion of the European Union Agency for Fundamental Rights on the Draft Directive Regarding the European Investigation Order" (2011), online: fra.europa.eu/en/publication/2011/fra-opinion-draft-directive-regarding-european-investigation-order-eio; and Regina Garcimartín Montero, "The European Investigative Order and Report for Fundamental Rights in Criminal Investigations" (2017) 1 EUCRIM 45, online: eucrim.eu/articles/european-investigation-order-respect-fundamental-rights/.

177 *UNTOC*, above note 23, art 19.

178 Public Safety Canada, "Integrated Cross-Border Maritime Law Enforcement Operations (Shiprider)" (2015), online: www.publicsafety.gc.ca/cnt/brdr-strtgs/brdr-lw-nfrcmnt/ntgrtd-crss-brdr-mrtm-en.aspx; *Integrated Cross-Border Law Enforcement Operations Act*, SC 2012, c 19.

border enforcement teams (IBET)[179] and integrated proceeds-of-crime teams (IPOCS),[180] which seek to coordinate the resources of differing departments and agencies when investigating crimes.

Canada–USA initiatives like the Cross-Border Crime Forum[181] and the *Beyond the Border Action Plan*,[182] as well as international meetings like the Quintet,[183] similarly furthered the *UNTOC* objective of information sharing and the sharing of best practices relating to investigations, prosecutions, and protecting victims and witnesses.

In summary, the previous sections have attempted to demonstrate that it is futile to view crime as exclusively local in terms of both commission and jurisdiction. Rather, crime is prevented, investigated, and prosecuted more effectively when policy-makers, both internationally and domestically, consider crime in its global context.

D. INTERNATIONALIZATION: IMPACT ON THE LEGAL PROFESSION IN CANADA

The internationalization of criminal justice has also had an impact on the legal profession and its ability to respond. In 1955, Maxwell Cohen[184] wrote a prescient article addressing some public and private international law problems that were, or should be, of interest and relevance to Canadian lawyers and their practice. At that time, only a few pages addressed issues of extradition and public policy regarding criminal justice issues.[185] Since then, as discussed above, issues of domestic and transborder criminal justice have become matters of international concern, and international criminal justice has become of concern to domestic legal systems.

179 Department of Homeland Security, "Fact Sheet: Beyond the Border United States—Canada Law Enforcement Cooperation" (6 December 2011), online: www.dhs.gov/news/2011/12/06/fact-sheet-beyond-border-united-states-canada-law-enforcement-cooperation.

180 Public Safety Canada, "Integrated Proceeds of Crime" (2015), online: publicsafety.gc.ca/cnt/cntrng-crm/rgnzd-crm/ntgrtd-prcds-crm-en.aspx.

181 See above note 94.

182 See above note 95.

183 See above note 93.

184 *The Canadian Encyclopedia* (2021), s v "Maxwell Cohen," online: www.thecanadianencyclopedia.ca/en/article/maxwell-cohen.

185 Maxwell Cohen, "Some International Law Problems of Interest to Canada and to Canadian Lawyers" (1955) 4 *Canadian Bar Review* 389 at 417 & 418–20.

In 1983, Cohen also predicted the impact that the *Charter* would produce by implanting international human rights doctrines in Canadian law, particularly in criminal law. There is hardly a clause in the *Charter* that does not have some connection with two historical influences, "the Anglo-American constitutional and criminal justice tradition, and the modern international law of human rights, treaties, and principles."[186] His prediction has come true, and this has had a significant impact, not only on Canadian law but on the legal profession. "No Canadian lawyer, pleading the *Charter*, is likely to find it possible to avoid the temptation of resorting to these once exotic footnotes of international principles, conventions, and treaties that only a few years ago would have seemed remote for practical and daily use in a busy firm."[187]

For the legal profession, and for government lawyers in particular, addressing the requirements of global crime has brought forth a greater number and specialization of lawyers with knowledge of international law principles, as well as of ICL and TCL. This is particularly so within Justice Canada and Global Affairs Canada, which deal with criminal law, ICL, and transnational criminal and security matters.

A related development is the importance of relationships that Canadian policy advisors and policy-makers have with counterparts of other states, and intergovernmental and regional organizations, many of whom face similar policy dilemmas when dealing with transnational and domestic crime. As discussed above, the proliferation of organizations that address criminal justice issues has resulted in an international network of officials whose mandate includes developing options, implementing international obligations, and working to operationalize these at the domestic level.[188] Networking, at the individual level and between states and international and intergovernmental organizations, permits officials to exchange ideas,

186 Maxwell Cohen, "The Canadian Legal Profession and International Law" (1983) 13 *Manitoba Law Journal* 201 at 204.

187 *Ibid.*

188 Macdonald, Morris & Johnston, above note 5 at 321–22. The authors predicted in 1973 that this development would be of a competitive nature. By the year 2000, they said, the erosion of the state as an international actor would be accompanied by the rise of "elite" intergovernmental organizations "locked in contest" with one another for knowledge, data, and technology, advised by "similarly trained experts, including international lawyers with highly specialized knowledge and techniques of particular utility to the super-elite."

policy options, and best practices.[189] While the tendency remains for Canadian criminal law lawyers to turn to traditional allies in the common law world as comparators for initiatives, broader aspects involving civil law and TCL, which address both substantive and procedural criminal law issues, are increasingly considered in policy-making. Participation in the various multilateral, regional, and other organizations not only provides the Canadian policy advisor and policy-maker with opportunities to learn of international and other states' national developments, but also to contribute to the development of international treaties and criminal justice standards and norms. This requires a greater level of coordination within government to ensure that Canadian interests in the global crime agenda are adequately identified and asserted on a consistent basis.

The trend toward specialization in the legal profession also affects the educational and professional development needs, and the career aspirations of Canadian lawyers and other professionals interested in international criminal justice, whether in government, private practice, or non-governmental or intergovernmental organizations.[190] To deal with global crime, it will be increasingly important to have a diverse profession. The educational requirements for criminal lawyers and other professionals means that while many have previous degrees in arts, humanities, social sciences, or other fields, criminal justice policy-making in the future will need to rely on a wider array of disciplines than it does presently. Knowledge of specialized areas of international law, including TCL, ICL, and comparative criminal law systems will continue to be important for the legal profession and, in particular, criminal justice policy advisors and policy-makers in Canada.

To engage in this work, lawyers and other professionals interested in criminal justice policy will need to be well versed in both domestic and comparative criminal law and procedure. Crown counsel and criminal defence lawyers will increasingly face questions relating to extradition and mutual legal assistance, jurisdiction, immigration, and other matters that require a knowledge of international law. Similarly, government lawyers and officials will require a greater knowledge of the various forms of

189 Scherrer, above note 81.

190 Canadians have been, and are, embedded in varying levels of international legal fora, for example, as judges, prosecutors, or defence counsel at international criminal tribunals, as well as officials in international organizations. Canadians are also clearly involved in domestic cases of extradition, mutual legal assistance, and immigration.

international law, namely, international human rights law, ICL, TCL, and international humanitarian law, and of the interplay among them. They will be asked to translate international to domestic, and domestic to international, in a process that Harold Koh describes as "a swirling interactive process whereby norms get 'uploaded' from one country into the international system, and then 'downloaded' elsewhere into another country's laws or even a private actor's internal rules."[191] Ideally, these individuals will be good communicators who recognize the importance of information sharing, international cooperation, and working through partnerships with various layers of government, the private sector, and civil society. These qualities will be needed to enable criminal justice policy advisors and policy-makers to demonstrate to Canadians the practical results of involvement at the international level.

"International law has been described as the 'cutting edge' of global legal systems because so often it touches areas not yet legally well-defined while its naked exposure of the relation of 'law' to 'power' renders its claims to jural effectiveness — compliance — debatable."[192] This statement is particularly relevant in the areas of ICL and TCL which balance, on one hand, the power of the state to impose and enforce societal norms with force and penal sanctions, and the human rights, freedoms, and dignity of persons on the other. It applies also in the area of domestic criminal justice policy-making, which tends to address cutting-edge issues of law, politics, sociology, and human rights. It is the engagement with the challenges resulting from the international and domestic developments discussed in this paper upon which this writer, whose professional career has been spent in criminal justice policy-making, both domestically and internationally, reflects. It is a professional career that is worthy of pursuit by others.

191 See Koh, above note 14.

192 Cohen, above note 185 at 207.

II

IMPLEMENTATION *and* INFLUENCE

three

Courting Transnational Criminal Law in Canada

GILLIAN MACNEIL*

A. INTRODUCTION

Criminal law has long been closely tied to state sovereignty.[1] However, states have increasingly agreed, by treaty, to implement a large amount of non-domestic criminal law. This has given international law a growing influence over this core area of sovereign power. In this chapter, I examine the way Canadian courts engage with a specific subset of criminal law treaties: those aimed at creating inter-state cooperation to suppress transnational crimes, usually referred to as the "suppression conventions."

The Supreme Court of Canada has determined that Canadian courts should use international law (including the suppression conventions) in a comprehensive manner when interpreting domesticating law. The reality differs. Sometimes the engagement is significant.[2] In some cases, reference

* Assistant Professor, Faculty of Law, University of Manitoba.

1 There is a strain of scholarship that questions whether there can be a criminal law without a sovereign. See Kai Ambos, "Punishment Without a Sovereign? The *Ius Puniendi* Issue of International Criminal Law: A First Contribution Towards a Consistent Theory of International Criminal Law" (2013) 33:2 *Oxford Journal of Legal Studies* 293 at 298–301.

2 For a clear example, see the Supreme Court of Canada decision in *B010 v Canada (Citizenship and Immigration)*, 2015 SCC 58 [*B010*].

is perfunctory.[3] In some cases, courts give cogent reasons for not relying on underlying treaty norms.[4] At other times, the reasons given are less cogent.[5] In some cases, relevant treaties are not mentioned at all.[6] The disconnect is not simply between the Supreme Court and other Canadian courts. Supreme Court practice is internally inconsistent.

This chapter is not simply a survey of court practice; rather, I take this opportunity to consider the reasons for the varying approaches. This is a necessary step to understanding why the inconsistency is a problem. Canada's legal system provides part of the explanation.[7] However, the cases equally contain hints that the suppression conventions are themselves a factor in their non-use. While there are identifiable reasons for the inconsistent ways Canadian courts use the suppression conventions, I will argue that this inconsistency is neither inevitable, nor is it desirable. It is not inevitable because, at a formal level, Canadian caselaw provides clear directions as to the appropriate use of international legal sources. When the conventions are brought to the attention of Canadian courts, they have

---

3 See, for example, the Supreme Court of Canada decision in *R v Malmo-Levine; R v Caine*, 2003 SCC 74.

4 In some cases, the courts have referenced international instruments only to conclude that they are not relevant. See for example: *Wang v Canada (Public Safety and Emergency Preparedness)*, 2021 FC 226 at para 58; *Canada (Public Safety and Emergency Preparedness) v JP*, 2013 FCA 262 at para 81 (rev'd in *B010*, above note 2); *Sittampalam v Canada (Minister of Citizenship and Immigration)*, 2006 FCA 326 at para 40. The cases suggest at least three reasons for which courts find treaties are not relevant: (1) the court does not consider the international instrument addresses the particular issue (*R v Orr*, 2013 BCSC 1883); (2) the international instruments provide less guidance than Parliament's implementation (*R v D'Souza*, 2016 ONSC 2749 at para 147 [*D'Souza*]); (3) Parliament has chosen to go beyond what is required by a treaty (*R v Tejani*, 1999 CanLII 3765 (Ont CA)).

5 See, for example, *Canada (Citizenship and Immigration) v Singh Dhillon*, 2012 FC 726 at para 58, where the court found (wrongly) that certain treaty obligations had not been domesticated in Canadian law.

6 *R v Craig*, 2009 SCC 23 [*Craig 2009*] (which interprets the offence-related property provisions of the *Controlled Drugs and Substances Act*, SC 1996, c 19); *R v Ouellette*, 2009 SCC 24 [*Ouellette*]; *R v Nguyen*, 2009 SCC 25 [*Nguyen*].

7 This does not mean that Canadian courts have no resort to non-Canadian sources when approaching problems of criminal law. Canadian criminal law is rooted in the English common law and consideration of how common law jurisdictions address problems of criminal law is a familiar part of the Canadian approach. What I argue here is twofold: that resort to international law in a criminal context is still not reflexive, and that doctrines of Canadian law may limit the applicability of international law.

generally proved willing to acknowledge the provisions.[8] It is not desirable because Canada's legal system is based on precedent: inconsistency injects unnecessary confusion into the law, undermining legal certainty. The inconsistent engagement also means that courts may be prevented from playing their role in ensuring that Canada respects its treaty obligations to suppress transnational criminal activities. Before considering these issues, I begin with a brief description of transnational criminal law.

Neil Boister has usefully divided the criminal laws that states have agreed to implement as falling into one of two categories: international criminal laws (ICL) or transnational criminal laws (TCL).[9] The former are crimes that threaten "international order or international values."[10] They are addressed through direct mechanisms that limit state sovereignty.[11] Transnational crimes undermine values that are shared but that are not international,[12] and are addressed through means that reinforce state sovereignty.[13] The treaties, which establish states' obligations to combat transnational crimes (the suppression conventions), position states as the essential actors in the system. These treaties impose obligations on states to criminalize certain conduct, to assert jurisdiction over the offences, and to cooperate (through mutual legal assistance and extradition) in

8 I say generally because in some cases, as will be discussed below, courts have not engaged with international law even when it is referenced by the parties. In some cases, courts have found that the international law raised by the parties is not relevant (see, for example, the cases referenced above note 4).

9 See Neil Boister, "Transnational Criminal Law?" (2003) 14:5 *European Journal of International Law* 953 [Boister 2003]. There are, of course, other divisions possible. However, the distinction between international and transnational criminal laws is the most helpful. States have proved more willing to harmonize crimes than other areas of criminal law. See, for example, James G. Stewart, "Ten Reasons for Adopting a Universal Concept of Participation in Atrocity" in Elies van Sliedregt & Sergey Vasiliev, eds, *Pluralism in International Criminal Law* (Oxford: Oxford University Press, 2014) 320 at 324, noting the lack of convergence in modes of attribution. The distinction between international and transnational criminal laws best captures the differences in substantive law.

10 Boister 2003, above note 9 at 966.

11 Neil Boister, "Further Reflections on the Concept of Transnational Criminal Law" (2015) 6:1 *Transnational Legal Theory* 9 at 10 [Boister 2015].

12 Boister 2003, above note 9 at 968 refers to "shared national interests or cosmopolitan values."

13 *Ibid* at 956; Boister states that in transnational criminal law "sovereignty is still a dominant value." He explores the different typologies in Boister 2003, above note 9 at 968–74, and Boister 2015, above note 11.

the suppression of transnational crimes. However, the treaties leave considerable discretion to states parties in deciding both what to implement and how. Not all offences identified in each treaty must be criminalized: beyond a core minimum, states have a choice.[14] Not every head of jurisdiction recognized in the treaties is mandatory: some are permissive.[15] The treaties generally avoid prescriptive language.[16] Even when states must implement obligations, it is left to each state to determine the appropriate legislative language.[17] Finally, some of the treaties expressly subject the obligations to the fundamental laws or principles of domestic legal orders.[18] The effectiveness of the suppression conventions depends upon the widest possible adherence. The treaty drafters chose flexibility as a

14 See, for example, the *United Nations Convention against Corruption*, (2003) 2349 UNTS 41 [*UNCAC*]. While states are required to criminalize the intentional bribery of domestic public officials and the solicitation or acceptance of a bribe by a public official (art 15), the intentional bribery of a foreign public official or official of a public international organization (art 16(1)), the embezzlement or misappropriation of funds by a domestic public official (art 17) and money laundering (art 23), parties are only required to consider criminalizing the solicitation or acceptance of a bribe by a foreign public official or official of an international organization (art 16(2)), trading in influence (art 18), abuse of functions by a public official (art 19), obstruction of justice (art 25), and private sector bribery (art 21) and embezzlement (art 22).

15 For example, the *International Convention for the Suppression of the Financing of Terrorism*, (1999) 2178 UNTS 197 [*Terrorist Financing Convention*] provides that States Parties must enact measures to enable them to take territorial, flag-state, and nationality jurisdiction over terrorist financing offences. Parties may take jurisdiction on the basis of protective and security jurisdiction as well as being permitted (but not required) to assert jurisdiction over stateless offenders who are habitually resident in the state and over cases in which the offence is committed on board a government-operated aircraft (art 7).

16 I will engage with this in more detail below. For some key examples, see the *United Nations Convention against Illicit Traffic in Narcotic Drugs and Psychotropic Substances*, (1988) 1582 UNTS 95 [*1988 Narcotic Drugs Convention*]; *United Nations Convention against Transnational Organized Crime*, (2000) 2225 UNTS 209 [*UNTOC*] and the *UNCAC*, above note 14. Although the conventions do sometimes include definitions which may be domesticated.

17 See, for example, the *1988 Narcotic Drugs Convention*, above note 16; "Nothing contained in this article shall affect the principle that the description of the offences to which it refers and of legal defences thereto is reserved to the domestic law of a Party and that such offences shall be prosecuted and punished in conformity with that law." *Ibid*, art 3.11.

18 See for example the *UNTOC*, above note 16, art 12(9).

practical means to encourage states to ratify the treaties.[19] The decision to embed choice in how to domesticate the treaty obligations may also have had an unintended consequence: inconsistent application within legal orders like Canada's.

I start the main part of this chapter by providing some legal background that details how the Supreme Court, when directly considering the issue, has held that international treaties are to be used when a court is considering domesticating legislation. This provides the baseline against which we can assess what Canadian courts are in fact doing; I do this in the second part of this chapter. I next consider possible factors that explain the inconsistent approaches. Finally, I will argue that there are important reasons for courts to consistently incorporate meaningful analysis of the underlying suppression conventions in their consideration of the domesticating statutes. In a chapter of this length, it is not possible to delve deeply into every Canadian court decision that does, or should, reference one of the suppression conventions. For this reason, most of my analysis will focus on decisions of the Supreme Court of Canada.

B. BACKGROUND

1) Domesticating International Law

Treaties are not self-executing in the Canadian legal order. To be enforceable before a Canadian court, treaties must be domesticated either through incorporating legislation or implementing legislation.[20] Incorporating

---

19 In critiquing the TCL system, Boister pointed out that "States have shown themselves unwilling to harmonize their penal systems to a greater degree than absolutely necessary due to domestic resistance to the application of unfamiliar penal principles." Boister 2003, above note 9 at 958.

20 Treaty obligations may also be given force through the *Canadian Charter of Rights and Freedoms*, Part I of the *Constitution Act, 1982*, being Schedule B to the *Canada Act 1982* (UK), 1982, c 11 [*Charter*]. The Supreme Court has, with relative consistency, held that the provisions of the *Charter*, which have parallels to international human rights norms binding on Canada, should generally give protection at least equal to those international norms. See, for example, *Reference Re Public Service Employee Relations Act (Alta)*, [1987] 1 SCR 313 at para 59, Dickson CJ; *Quebec (Attorney General) v 9147-0732 Québec inc*, 2020 SCC 32 at para 31, Brown and Rowe JJ [*Quebec (Attorney General)*]. In addition, Parliament has, in one instance, domesticated the obligations in human rights treaties that Canada has signed through an interpretive directive in legislation: the Act "is to be construed and applied in a manner that …

legislation is easy to identify; while there might be minor variations in the language used,[21] the relevant provisions of incorporating legislation are readily identifiable by reference to the underlying treaties.[22] The language used, if not identical, will be substantially similar. Implementing legislation is often harder to spot. The language is chosen by the legislature to implement a treaty obligation but may differ considerably from the treaty language. Implementing legislation may follow or precede the ratification of a treaty.[23]

2) Principles of Interpretation

The interpretive approach to domesticating legislation derives from the Canadian constitutional order. While it is the federal executive that has the power to enter into treaties, the legislatures are the primary lawmakers. The role of the courts as the third branch of government is (mostly) to interpret and apply the law.[24] By interpreting incorporating legislation in accordance with international law, the courts are respecting the separation of powers: they are respecting the legislative decision to adopt the terms

complies with international human rights instruments to which Canada is signatory." *Immigration and Refugee Protection Act*, SC 2001 c 27, s 3(3)(f) [*IRPA*].

21 For example, the language in s 96 of the *IRPA*, *ibid*, differs from that in art 1 of the *Convention Relating to the Status of Refugees*, (1951) 189 UNTS 137 [*Refugee Convention*], but has been consistently understood as incorporating rather than implementing the definition of refugee found in art 1 of the *Refugee Convention*.

22 See, for example, the *Foreign Missions and International Organizations Act*, SC 1991, c 41 which expressly incorporates a number of treaty provisions in four Schedules to the Act.

23 On the changing approach to implementing legislation and its complexity, see, for example, Hugh M. Kindred, "The Use and Abuse of International Legal Sources by Canadian Courts" in Oonagh E. Fitzgerald, ed, *The Globalized Rule of Law: Relationships between International and Domestic Law* (Toronto: Irwin Law, 2006) 5 at 10–17. Gib van Ert also makes the point that domesticating legislation may precede the ratification of a treaty. Gib van Ert, "Domestic Reception of International Law" in Phillip M. Saunders & Robert J. Currie, eds, *Kindred's International Law: Chiefly as Interpreted and Applied in Canada*, 9th ed (Toronto: Emond Publishing, 2019) 153 at 207 (addressing human rights treaties specifically); see also his more general discussion of domestication at 212–16.

24 Because Canada is largely a common law system, there is a nuance to this. The common law remains judge-made law. For current purposes, it is statutory law that is of more importance because it is the means of domesticating treaties.

as used and understood in international law, and are respecting the federal executive's power to enter into treaties.[25] By interpreting implementing legislation in a way that gives greater effect to the language of the domestic instrument, the courts are respecting the principle of parliamentary sovereignty, embodied in the legislator's choice to depart from the treaty terms.[26]

While incorporating and implementing legislation do the same job of domesticating treaty obligations, they are not the same thing and are not interpreted in the same way. When legislation incorporates a treaty provision, the interpretation is done according to the rules found in articles 31 and 32 of the *Vienna Convention on the Law of Treaties*.[27] That interpretation is determinative of the incorporating text.[28] The interpretation of implementing legislation requires use of the modern approach to statutory interpretation familiar in Canadian law generally.[29] The underlying

25 *B010*, above note 2 at para 47.

26 This can of course be problematic from the perspective of international law. Article 32 of the International Law Commission's "Draft Articles on Responsibility of States for Internationally Wrongful Acts" in the "Report of the Commission to the General Assembly on the Work of Its Fifty-Third Session" (UN Doc A/56/10) in *Yearbook of the International Law Commission 2001*, vol 2, part 2 (New York: UN, 2007) at 26. A/CN.4/SER.A/2001/Add.1 (Part 2) provides that "The responsible State may not rely on the provisions of its internal law as justification for failure to comply with its obligations." My focus here is internal to Canada's legal system.

27 *Vienna Convention on the Law of Treaties*, (1969) 1155 UNTS 331. On the correct approach see *Febles v Canada (Citizenship and Immigration)*, 2014 SCC 68 at para 11 [*Febles*]. The decision in *Febles* on this point simply reiterated prior holdings of the Court in cases including: *Pushpanathan v Canada (Minister of Citizenship and Immigration)*, [1998] 1 SCR 982 at para 51 [*Pushpanathan SCC*]; *Thomson v Thomson*, [1994] 3 SCR 551; *Canada (Attorney General) v Ward*, [1993] 2 SCR 689.

28 *Febles*, above note 27 at paras 11 and 66. As noted, there has been some inconsistency. One inconsistency is terminological. In *Office of the Children's Lawyer v Balev*, 2018 SCC 16, the Supreme Court referred to the legislation in issue as implementing the relevant international treaty; in fact, the legislation incorporated it. More troublingly, the Court has also been occasionally inconsistent in the proper approach to international law. To some extent, this inconsistency is actually evidence of an evolution in the Court's approach (see Kindred, above note 23). To some extent, the inconsistency appears to be the product of continuing disagreement regarding the proper approach: see *Quebec (Attorney General)*, above note 20.

29 *B010*, above note 2 at para 29. Acceptance of the modern approach by the Supreme Court of Canada is often traced to the decision in *Rizzo & Rizzo Shoes Ltd (Re)*, [1988] 1 SCR 27.

treaty forms part of the context for interpreting the statutory language.[30] It also gives rise to an interpretive presumption: "legislation is presumed to comply with Canada's international obligations."[31] However, if the statutory language makes it clear that the domestic legislator intended to depart from the terms of the treaty, it is the language of the statute to which courts must give effect.[32]

There are two additional wrinkles.[33] First, courts may use TCL instruments to help inform terms which are (1) defined in international conventions, and (2) found in non-domesticating Canadian legislation.[34] Second, non-binding instruments which nonetheless "inspired" Canadian legislation may also be used to inform the interpretation of the legislative provisions.[35]

The vast majority of the legislation domesticating Canada's TCL obligations is implementing legislation. In other words, according to the accepted approach to interpretation, it is the meaning of the domestic text that predominates.

3) Constitutional Litigation

When treaties underpin Canadian legislation, they are also relevant to assessing the constitutionality of that legislation. Courts may refer to treaties to help identify the legislative purpose. This helps inform whether legislation is overbroad and so infringes section 7 of the *Charter*.[36] It is

30 *BO10*, above note 2 at paras 47–50.

31 *R v Appulonappa*, 2015 SCC 59 at para 40 [*Appulonappa SCC*].

32 *Kazemi Estate v Islamic Republic of Iran*, 2014 SCC 62 at paras 60–63.

33 These are identified by considering how the Supreme Court has used international sources in situations where it is not directing a particular approach.

34 *Suresh v Canada (Minister of Citizenship and Immigration)*, 2002 SCC 1 at para 96. In *Pushpanathan SCC*, above note 27, the dissent (without comment by the majority on this point) used transnational criminal law instruments, including the *1988 Narcotic Drugs Convention* to help inform what was then the *Immigration Act*, RSC 1985, c I-2 provisions, which implemented Canada's obligations under the *Refugee Convention*, above note 21. See also *Pushpanathan v Canada (Minister of Citizenship and Immigration)*, 2002 FCT 867 at paras 46–47 for a case in which the Federal Court used the *Terrorist Financing Convention*, above note 15, to inform what complicity in terrorism meant for the purpose of exclusion from refugee status.

35 *Németh v Canada (Justice)*, 2010 SCC 56 at paras 79–81.

36 *Charter*, above note 20. Section 7 provides that "[e]veryone has the right to life, liberty and security of the person and the right not to be deprived thereof except in

equally relevant for establishing whether the legislation has a pressing and substantial objective(s): the first step to justifying the limitation of rights under section 1 of the *Charter*.[37]

C. A CLOSER LOOK AT THE CASES

1) Inconsistency in Application

a) Overview

While the Supreme Court of Canada has provided direction on how the suppression conventions (indeed, treaties generally) must and may be used, an examination of relevant cases reveals that even at the Supreme Court, practice is inconsistent. The Supreme Court has sometimes engaged deeply with a relevant TCL convention.[38] In some cases, the relevant convention has received a bare mention or is used only to confirm a result already arrived at.[39] In some cases, relevant obligations are not referenced at all.[40] While the decisions do not expressly address why the Court sometimes engages with the relevant international law and sometimes does not, a consideration of Canada's judicial system, of the cases and of the conventions, suggests three possibilities:

1) That parties do not direct the Court to relevant treaties.
2) That there has only recently been a Supreme Court decision directing the required engagement.
3) That the discretion granted by the treaties acts as a disincentive to their use.

---

accordance with the principles of fundamental justice." The suppression conventions have been used this way in, for example, *R v Appulonappa*, 2014 BCCA 163 rev'd on other grounds 2015 SCC 59, above note 31.

37 Section 1 of the *Charter*, above note 20 states: "The *Canadian Charter of Rights and Freedoms* guarantees the rights and freedoms set out in it subject only to such reasonable limits prescribed by law as can be demonstrably justified in a free and democratic society." International conventions were used this way in *R v Oakes*, [1986] 1 SCR 103, the case which gave its name to the proportionality analysis under *Charter* s 1.

38 See *B010*, above note 2. The analysis in *B010* was applied to its companion case, *Appulonappa SCC*, above note 31.

39 *Application under s 83.28 of the Criminal Code (Re)*, 2004 SCC 42 [*Re Criminal Code*]; *R v Venneri*, 2012 SCC 33 at paras 32–33.

40 *Craig 2009*, above note 6.

b) The Role of the Parties

Canada's judicial system is, of course, largely adversarial in nature. It is primarily for the parties to frame the issues, present evidence, and inform the courts of the relevant law. The *Canada Evidence Act* states that judges must take judicial notice of domestic laws: Acts of Parliament must be judicially noticed, even if not raised by the parties.[41] There is a more limited legislative direction with respect to certain treaties.[42] There appears to be no authority, legislative, or common law, that courts must otherwise take judicial notice of international law that has not been raised by the parties. Absent notice by the parties, courts may simply not be aware of the international obligations underlying a legislative provision.[43]

While this may be a partial explanation for the inconsistent use of the suppression conventions, it is clear that this cannot be the only explanation. There are cases in which the Court does not address underlying treaty obligations even when those obligations are raised by a party. In *R v Rafilovich*,[44] a case engaging the proceeds of crime provisions of the *Criminal Code*,[45] the Crown's factum before the Supreme Court referenced

---

41 *Canada Evidence Act*, RSC 1985, c C-5, ss 17–18. Section 18 directs that "Acts of Parliament" must be judicially noticed "without being specially pleaded."

42 Of relevance to the current topic, the *Extradition Act*, SC 1999, c 18, s 8 provides that extradition agreements must be published in either the *Canada Gazette* or the *Canada Treaty Series* within 60 days of entering into force. Once an agreement, or the provisions of a multilateral extradition agreement respecting extradition are published, they must be "judicially noticed." Section 5 of the *Mutual Legal Assistance in Criminal Matters Act*, RSC 1985, c 30 (4th Supp) enshrines the same direction for mutual legal assistance agreements or provisions respecting mutual legal assistance. In *Nevsun Resources Ltd v Araya*, 2020 SCC 5 [*Nevsun*], a majority of the Supreme Court confirmed that "established norms of customary international law are law, to be judicially noticed" at para 97. The Supreme Court was distinguishing customary international law from foreign law, which must be proved as a matter of fact (paras 96 –97). It is not clear that the Supreme Court was directing that courts had to take judicial notice of customary law not raised by the parties. The Supreme Court judgment makes no similar reference to international treaties.

43 For example, in *Canada (Attorney General) v Federation of Law Societies of Canada*, 2015 SCC 7 [*Federation of Law Societies of Canada*], the *facta* of the various parties and intervenors (available on the Supreme Court of Canada's website, online: www.scc-csc.ca/case-dossier/info/af-ma-eng.aspx?cas=35399 last accessed 28 June 2021) do not reference any of the suppression conventions that impose obligations to combat money laundering.

44 *R v Rafilovich*, 2019 SCC 51 [*Rafilovich*].

45 *Criminal Code*, RSC 1985, c C-46.

the *1988 Narcotic Drugs Convention*,[46] the *UNCAC*,[47] the *UNTOC* and its three Protocols.[48] None of these instruments was mentioned by the Court in its judgment. It is clear that non-notice by parties may be *a* factor in the failure of courts to rely on relevant treaty provisions, but it is not the *only* factor: it does not provide a complete explanation for the inconsistency. The nature of Canada's system suggests another possibility.

c) The Role of Precedent

Canada's judicial system operates on the basis of precedent and *stare decisis*. Because of this, another possible reason for inconsistent approaches to the suppression conventions may simply be a matter of timing. The Supreme Court's most detailed consideration of a suppression convention came in its 2015 decision in *B010*.[49] In that case, the Court also articulated how courts should approach international treaties when interpreting domesticating legislation. As a matter of Canada's system of precedent, we might expect that cases decided after the decision in *B010* would display greater engagement than those decided before *B010*. However, there are two problems with this hypothesis. In some of the cases decided after *B010*, there is no evident engagement with relevant international obligations.[50] If *B010* were a determinative factor, we would expect to see consistently detailed engagement following that judgment. There is simply no evidence of that. Perhaps more importantly, while the Court in *B010* engaged with the relevant international instruments in a remarkably comprehensive manner,[51] as a matter of legal principle, it did not break new ground.

46 *1988 Narcotic Drugs Convention*, above note 16. The Crown *factum* is available on the Supreme Court of Canada's website, online: www.scc-csc.ca/case-dossier/info/af-ma-eng.aspx?cas=37791 last accessed 28 June 2021.

47 *UNCAC*, above note 14.

48 *UNTOC*, above note 16. The Protocols are the *Protocol to Prevent, Suppress and Punish Trafficking in Persons, Especially Women and Children, supplementing the United Nations Convention against Transnational Organized Crime*, (2000) 2237 UNTS 319; the *Protocol against the Smuggling of Migrants by Land, Sea and Air, supplementing the United Nations Convention against Transnational Organized Crime*, (2000) 2241 UNTS 507 [*Migrant Smuggling Protocol*]; the *Protocol against the Illicit Manufacturing of and Trafficking in Firearms, Their Parts and Components and Ammunition, supplementing the United Nations Convention against Transnational Organized Crime*, (2001) 2326 UNTS 208.

49 *B010*, above note 2.

50 See for example *Rafilovich*, above note 44.

51 *B010*, above note 2.

In *B010*, the Court reiterated long-standing directions concerning the use of international treaties to aid in the interpretation of domesticating legislation.[52] In other words, even before the decision in *B010*, we should have consistently seen the type of engagement which the Supreme Court had already said was required. The actual practice both before and after *B010* shows inconsistency instead.

These obvious possibilities, based in the adversarial and precedential nature of Canada's legal system, do not entirely account for the inconsistent use of the suppression conventions. To provide a more complete explanation, it is helpful to consider another possibility: that the conventions act as a disincentive to their use. As I noted in the introduction, the suppression conventions reinforce state sovereignty. They largely avoid prescriptive language. The conventions deliberately reserve the choice of implementing language to states. The corresponding Canadian interpretive approach prioritizes the intentions of the domestic legislator. These elements may discourage Canadian courts from engaging with the substance of the conventions. This is, of course, hard to measure, but there are some cases that suggest the non-prescriptive nature of the conventions is having this impact.

2) Going Deeper

I want to start with a consideration of the *B010* case because, as I noted above, it is a case in which the Supreme Court affirmed the use courts should be making of international treaties. It is also a case in which the Supreme Court comprehensively used international treaties in its interpretation of the domesticating law.[53]

---

52 *National Corn Growers Assn v Canada (Import Tribunal)*, [1990] 2 SCR 1324 at 1371–72 [*National Corn Growers*] though the language used by the Court in *B010*, above, note 2 admittedly differs from that of the earlier decision. While the change in language may suggest a greater openness to international law, the decision in *National Corn Growers* clearly accepted the relevance of international treaties to the interpretation of domesticating legislation.

53 In Lon L. Fuller, *The Morality of the Law*, rev ed (New Haven: Yale University Press, 1969) at 81–91, the author identified a potential threat to law-making: a disconnect between the law as stated and the law as applied by public authorities. This, I think, also provides a useful frame to understand cases: looking both at what a court formally states the law is, and at what the court actually does when it is applying the law. In *B010*, above note 2, there was a congruence between what the Court said

At issue in *B010* was whether asylum seekers were inadmissible to Canada for engaging in people smuggling in the context of transnational crime.[54] In order to settle this, the Supreme Court identified three sub-questions that needed to be addressed: (1) whether "people smuggling" requires that those engaged in the smuggling received a material benefit; (2) what limits the term "organized criminality," which appears in section 37(1) *IRPA*, places on the scope of inadmissibility; and (3) what the requirement that the people smuggling be done "in the context of transnational crime" means.[55] The terms in issue make it easy to understand why the Court considered the *UNTOC* and *Migrant Smuggling Protocol* to be relevant. Put simply, the statutory language in issue closely parallels language found in those instruments.[56]

The Court noted that section 37(1)(b) of the *IRPA* was one of the provisions enacted in order to give domestic effect to the obligations Canada was about to undertake in becoming party to the *UNTOC* and the *Migrant Smuggling Protocol*.[57] The Court's recognition that section 37(1)(b) of the *IRPA* was rooted in international law[58] was sufficient to establish the relevance of the instruments to the interpretive exercise. As the Supreme Court observed:

> In interpreting legislation which has been enacted with a view towards implementing international obligations, as is the case here, it is reasonable for a tribunal to examine the domestic law in the context of the relevant agreement to clarify any uncertainty. Indeed where the text of the domestic law lends itself to it, one should also strive to expound an interpretation which is consonant with the relevant international obligations.[59]

International law provides relevant context if legislation is intended to implement the obligations: similar language is not a prerequisite. However,

---

the law was (in terms of the use to be made of international treaties) and the way it in fact used the treaties in its analysis.

54 Section 37(1)(b) of the *IRPA*, above note 20.

55 *B010*, above note 2 at para 19.

56 The similarities between people smuggling and migrant smuggling are obvious. The *UNTOC*, above note 16, art 2(a) contains a definition of the terms "organized criminal group" which is similar to the term "organized criminality." It also contains directions as to when crime is considered to be transnational (art 3(2)).

57 *B010*, above note 2 at para 43.

58 *Ibid* at para 51.

59 *National Corn Growers*, above note 52 at 1371.

a reading of the decision in *B010* makes it clear that the similarity of the terms used in the *IRPA* to the terms of the international instruments influenced the Court's extensive reliance on the international law.[60]

3) The Contrary Evidence

In a relatively short span of time before and after the decision in *B010* was given, the Supreme Court issued major decisions dealing with money laundering,[61] proceeds of crime,[62] forfeiture of offence-related property,[63] and terrorism,[64] without engaging with (or, in many cases, mentioning) the underlying international obligations. It released decisions in which it had to assess the constitutionality of legislation that domesticates Canada's money laundering obligations[65] and anti-terror obligations,[66] again without mentioning or analyzing the relevance of the underlying international obligations. A consideration of the questions at issue in those cases and the nature of the conventions suggests why.

In the *Federation of Law Societies of Canada* case,[67] the issue was the constitutionality of federal money laundering legislation that imposed certain client-identification and verification requirements, and reporting

60 *B010*, above note 2 at paras 55 and 64–66.

61 *Federation of Law Societies of Canada*, above note 43.

62 *Quebec (Attorney General) v Laroche*, 2002 SCC 72 [*Laroche*]; *R v Lavigne*, 2006 SCC 10 [*Lavigne*]; *Rafilovich*, above note 44. *Lavigne* was the only one of these decisions in which the international roots of the provisions were mentioned.

63 *Craig 2009*, *Ouellette*, and *Nguyen*, above note 6.

64 *R v Khawaja*, 2012 SCC 69 [*Khawaja*]; the Court was clearly aware of the international context. In the judgment, the Court noticed that the relevant provisions of the *Criminal Code* were enacted after the 11 September 2001 attacks on New York and the Pentagon. The Court also referenced UNSC Res 1373 (2001). In addition, the *Criminal Code* provisions defining terrorism specifically refer to a number of the suppression conventions. *Criminal Code*, above note 45, s 83.01(1). In *Khawaja*, those Conventions were not directly relevant: the Court had to address the interpretation and constitutionality of the more general definition of terrorism which Parliament added to the *Criminal Code*.

65 *Federation of Law Societies of Canada*, above note 43.

66 *Re Criminal Code*, above note 39; *Khawaja*, above note 64. In *Re Criminal Code*, the majority recognized that the anti-terror legislation in issue had been passed to implement Canada's obligations under two anti-terror conventions (para 37). However, the majority did not refer to those international treaties either in interpreting the implementing legislation or in assessing its constitutionality.

67 *Federation of Law Societies of Canada*, above note 43.

obligations on legal professionals. In *Rafilovich*,[68] the question was whether an accused, who had been authorized to use money that had been frozen as proceeds of crime to fund his defence against criminal charges (which was accordingly not available for forfeit), could then be fined for an equivalent amount. In *Laroche*,[69] the validity of a series of restraint orders and special warrants was at issue. In *Lavigne*,[70] the Court was concerned with whether the ability of an accused to pay a fine was a factor a Canadian court should consider in deciding whether to impose a fine or in determining the amount. The decision in *Craig 2009*[71] required the Court to decide whether partial forfeiture of offence-related property was possible. In *Khawaja*,[72] the Court had to interpret the prescriptive part of the definition of terrorism in the *Criminal Code* and assess its constitutionality.

The major obligations concerning money laundering, proceeds of crime, and offence-related property are sourced in the *1988 Narcotic Drugs Convention*,[73] the *UNTOC*,[74] and the *UNCAC*.[75] In the cases noted above, it is the first two conventions that were the most relevant (none of the cases involved allegations of corruption). There are now no fewer than nineteen anti-terror conventions. Canada is not party to all the relevant treaties and protocols, but is party to key instruments, including the *Terrorist Financing Convention*.[76] A brief consideration of the terms of these treaties suggests why the Court may not have relied on them in the above cases.

The *1988 Narcotic Drugs Convention* requires the criminalization of a number of drug-related offences and money laundering related to those drug offences.[77] States are not required to criminalize all the conduct listed; some obligations are subject to the constitutional principles and basic concepts of each party's legal system.[78] All the obligations to criminalize are without prejudice to "the principle that the description of the offences … is reserved to the domestic law of a Party and that such

68 *Rafilovich*, above note 44.
69 *Laroche*, above note 62.
70 *Lavigne*, above note 62.
71 *Craig 2009*, above note 6.
72 *Khawaja*, above note 64.
73 *1988 Narcotic Drugs Convention*, above note 16.
74 *UNTOC*, above note 16.
75 *UNCAC*, above note 14.
76 *Terrorist Financing Convention*, above note 15.
77 *1988 Narcotic Drugs Convention*, above note 16, art 3(1)(b)(i)(ii).
78 *Ibid*, art 3(1)(c)(i).

offences shall be prosecuted and punished in conformity with that law."[79] Similarly, although parties are required to adopt measures that permit the confiscation (including forfeiture) of proceeds of drug-related crimes, fines in lieu of confiscation, and confiscation of offence-related property,[80] these obligations are not prescriptive. That is, although the *1988 Narcotic Drugs Convention* tells States Parties they must do these things, the Convention does not specify how. The article requiring parties to enable confiscation or fines provides expressly that the measures are to "be defined and implemented in accordance with and subject to the provisions of the domestic law of a Party."[81] Finally, the Convention provides that a State "may adopt more strict or severe measures than those provided in this Convention."[82]

The *UNTOC* imposes a similar obligation to criminalize money laundering, though in relation to a wider range of offences.[83] Like the *1988 Narcotic Drugs Convention*, the UNTOC is not prescriptive: it is up to each Party to choose how to describe the offences.[84] States must enact measures to confiscate the proceeds of crime and offence-related property "to the greatest extent possible within their domestic legal systems."[85] All the measures are again "defined and implemented in accordance with and subject to the provisions of" each State Party's domestic law.[86] All the obligations in the *UNTOC* are subject to the "fundamental principles of [each State Party's] domestic law."[87] Additionally, States Parties are free to adopt stricter or more severe measures.[88]

The anti-terror conventions are, in general, sectoral: they lack prescriptive definitions of terrorism of the type seen in section 83.01(1)(b) of the *Criminal Code*, which was in issue in *Khawaja*.[89] Efforts to finalize a comprehensive anti-terror convention have been unsuccessful because

79 *Ibid*, art 3(11).
80 *Ibid*, art 5.
81 *Ibid*, art 6(9).
82 *Ibid*, art 24.
83 *UNTOC*, above note 16, art 6.
84 *Ibid*, art 11(6).
85 *Ibid*, art 12(1).
86 *Ibid*, art 12(9).
87 *Ibid*, art 34(1).
88 *Ibid*, art 34(3).
89 *Khawaja*, above note 64.

of an inability to agree on a prescriptive definition and its limits.[90] The only anti-terror convention to which Canada is a party that contains a (partially) prescriptive definition of terrorism is the *Terrorist Financing Convention*.[91] That definition has some similarities to the Canadian definition, but is less complex.

In addition to the broad choice the treaties give to states in how they implement the relevant obligations, review of the relevant treaties reveals a second factor which may impact a Canadian court's willingness to reference the treaties. Nothing in the *1988 Narcotic Drugs Convention* or the *UNTOC* expressly answers the questions the Supreme Court had to decide in *Federation of Law Societies of Canada*,[92] *Rafilovich*,[93] *Lavigne*,[94] *Laroche*,[95] or *Craig 2009*.[96]

This review suggests two apparent reasons not to resort to the relevant suppression conventions. First, it was the language of Canadian legislation that was in issue, language that had no clear parallel in the international instruments. Second, the conventions did not include provisions directly answering the questions in issue. While these circumstances help to explain the lack of resort to the suppression conventions, in my view, the approach used in *B010* could, and should, have been used.

---

90 See, for example, Mahmoud Hmoud, "Negotiating the Draft Comprehensive Convention on International Terrorism: Major Bones of Contention" (2006) 4:5 *Journal of International Criminal Justice* 1031.

91 *Terrorist Financing Convention*, above note 15. Article 2 provides in part that

> 1. Any person commits an offence within the meaning of this Convention if that person by any means, directly or indirectly, unlawfully and wilfully, provides or collects funds with the intention that they should be used or in the knowledge that they are to be used, in full or in part, in order to carry out:
>
> . . .
>
> b. Any other act intended to cause death or serious bodily injury to a civilian, or to any other person not taking an active part in the hostilities in a situation of armed conflict, when the purpose of such act, by its nature or context, is to intimidate a population, or to compel a government or an international organization to do or to abstain from doing any act.

See also Chapter 5 by Michael Nesbitt in this volume.

92 *Federation of Law Societies of Canada*, above note 43.

93 *Rafilovich*, above note 44.

94 *Lavigne*, above note 62.

95 *Laroche*, above note 62.

96 *Craig 2009*, above note 6.

The suppression conventions eschew prescriptive language but nonetheless impose obligations on the parties to criminalize certain conduct, assert jurisdiction over that conduct, and cooperate in its suppression.[97] As I noted above, the relevance of these instruments to interpreting domesticating Canadian legislation does not depend on linguistic similarities. To reiterate: the Supreme Court has directed that international obligations are relevant to interpreting domesticating legislation.[98] What matters is that the legislation is intended to domesticate an international obligation. Linguistic similarity is immaterial.

The second factor which seems to have an impact is that the suppression conventions do not obviously answer the issues the Court had to decide in these cases. This again should not inevitably result in a conclusion that the conventions are irrelevant. The Supreme Court has directed that Canada's international obligations are part of the context in which legislation is enacted.[99] That context may include (1) an understanding of the harms a convention (and its implementing legislation) is intended to address, (2) the scope of the problem and the seriousness with which the international community views the offences, and (3) the seriousness with which the international community views the need to suppress and deter the commission of the offences. These factors may be relevant to the interpretation of an implementing statute or the determination of whether that statute is constitutional. The fact that a treaty does not, in express terms, answer a narrow, specific question is not determinative. The treaty may still be part of the answer; it is relevant context for interpreting legislative meaning.[100]

---

97 See generally Neil Boister, *An Introduction to Transnational Criminal Law*, 2d ed (Oxford: Oxford University Press, 2018) c 2.

98 *National Corn Growers*, above note 52. In *B010*, the Court said in part:

> This Court has previously explained that the values and principles of customary and conventional international law form part of the context in which Canadian laws are enacted. . . . This follows from the fact that to interpret a Canadian law in a way that conflicts with Canada's international obligations risks incursion by the courts in the executive's conduct of foreign affairs and censure under international law. The contextual significance of international law is all the more clear where the provision to be construed "has been enacted with a view towards implementing international obligations."

B010 above note 2.

99 *Ibid.*

100 This is the way the *UNTOC*, above note 16, *Migrant Smuggling Protocol*, above note 48, and *Refugee Convention*, above note 21 were used in *B010*, above note 2 at paras 42–66.

Because neither similarity in language nor obvious answers to specific questions are required to trigger the use of international law, the inconsistent approach evident in the cases reviewed was not inevitable. As I will argue in the next section, it is also not desirable.

D. THE IMPORTANCE OF CONSISTENT ENGAGEMENT: THE GOOD AND THE BAD

1) Overview

The lack of consistent engagement with the suppression conventions is both contrary to precedent and inconsistent with the role of the courts. To demonstrate this, I will start by discussing the importance of consistently engaging with the suppression conventions. I will then address two institutional problems that arise from a failure to engage.

2) The Good

Even when the conventions do not seem obviously applicable, there are good reasons for courts to engage with their terms. As argued above, conventions are a relevant part of the legislative context. They can, at a minimum, help in identifying the purpose of the legislation — an essential element in interpreting provisions. The purpose is an equally essential factor to assessing the constitutionality of domesticating legislation, where that is at issue.[101] The first step of the *Charter* section 1 analysis requires

---

The specific provisions of the *UNTOC*, *Migrant Smuggling Protocol*, and *Refugee Convention* were obviously relevant to the issues in *B010* (particularly the meaning of "to engage in people smuggling" in the context of transnational crime according to s 37(1)(b) of the *IRPA*) but, as argued, facial similarity is not determinative.

101 *R v Carson*, 2017 ONCA 142 at paras 28–31, aff'd 2018 SCC 12. The majority of the ONCA referenced the *UNCAC*, above note 14, to inform the purpose of s 121(1)(d) of the *Criminal Code*, above note 45 (influence peddling), which resulted in finding that the trial judge in the case had adopted an unnecessarily narrow interpretation of the language of the provision. Neither the majority nor the dissenting judges at the Supreme Court referenced the *UNCAC*. The majority did not entirely agree with the decision made by the majority of the ONCA (para 26, Karakatsanis J) but affirmed Carson's conviction. On the use of international conventions to inform the purpose of a legislative provision to help assess its constitutionality, see for example *D'Souza*, above note 4 at para 162. In *R v Parker* (2000), 188 DLR (4th) 385, [2000] OJ No 2787 (CA) at paras 140–42, the Court used both the international

a court to identify the purposes (objectives) underlying challenged legislation and determine whether those legislative objectives are pressing and substantial. The objectives drive the section 1 analysis and may be determinative of the outcome. Engaging with the conventions will mean much more robust and accurate legislative interpretations and constitutional determinations.

There is also a purely formal concern: adherence to precedent. The Supreme Court has been clear that international obligations are relevant to interpreting domestic legislation. Absent consistent, and overt, engagement with relevant international obligations, it is difficult to know if courts are giving effect to that binding direction. This is closely related to a potentially problematic outcome: lack of confidence in precedent.

3) The Bad

The common law is based on the principle of certainty.[102] There are limited situations in which courts will overturn precedents.[103] A key reason to overturn a prior judgment is to correct an error.[104] The *per incuriam* exception to *stare decisis* applies if, in an earlier case, (1) a court "did not advert" to binding statutory or judicial authority, and (2) the case would have been decided differently had that authority been considered.[105] While some descriptions of the exception refer only to binding domestic authorities, the Supreme Court's decision in *Bedford* refers to laws more generally.[106] In light of the Supreme Court decisions directing how treaty obligations should be used,[107] the reference to laws in *Bedford* should be

instruments and a comparative approach in support of its finding that Canada's then prohibition on the medical use of marijuana was a violation of s 7 of the *Charter*, above note 20.

102 *Canada (Attorney General) v Bedford*, 2013 SCC 72 at para 38 [*Bedford*].

103 See for example *Canada v Craig*, 2012 SCC 43 [*Craig 2012*]; *Bedford*, above note 102; *Teva Canada Ltd v TD Canada Trust*, 2017 SCC 51; *R v Sullivan*, 2022 SCC 19 [*Sullivan*].

104 *Craig 2012*, *ibid* at para 27, *Bedford*, above note 102 at para 42, *Sullivan*, *ibid* at paras 73–80.

105 See *Royal Bank of Canada v Trang*, 2014 ONCA 883 at para 38, Laskin JA, rev'd 2016 SCC 50. The Supreme Court did not comment on the ONCA majority's description of the *per incuriam* exception.

106 *Bedford*, above note 102 at para 42.

107 *B010*, above note 2; *Febles*, above note 27.

understood as encompassing international laws. A failure to incorporate relevant international laws into a decision may undermine confidence that a court has taken all relevant laws into account in reaching a conclusion. This leaves the legal conclusions open to challenge in a later case engaging the same issues.

Finally, there is an important institutional reason for Canadian courts to consistently engage with relevant international conventions. Courts play an essential role in ensuring that Canada satisfies its international obligations. As the Supreme Court has observed:

> This Court has previously explained that the values and principles of customary and conventional international law form part of the context in which Canadian laws are enacted: *R. v. Hape*, 2007 SCC 26, [2007] 2 S.C.R. 292, at para. 53. This follows from the fact that to interpret a Canadian law in a way that conflicts with Canada's international obligations risks incursion by the courts in the executive's conduct of foreign affairs and censure under international law.[108]

Courts must engage with relevant treaties if they are to play this role. In spite of the fact that the suppression conventions leave considerable discretion to states parties, the treaties impose legal obligations. Domestic courts need to engage with those obligations if they are to help ensure the obligations are fulfilled.[109]

E. CONCLUSION

The Supreme Court has, as a matter of formal law, given clear direction as to the use Canadian courts must make of international treaties which underlie Canadian legislation. The practice of the courts, and the Supreme Court itself, has been inconsistent. In this chapter, I have suggested three reasons which help to explain that inconsistency. An important factor is the level of discretion that the suppression conventions leave to states. This combines with a Canadian interpretive approach requiring courts to give effect to the language chosen by the legislator. Together, these may

---

108 *B010*, above note 2 at para 47.

109 Anthea Roberts, "Comparative International Law? The Role of National Courts in Creating and Enforcing International Law" (2011) 60 *International & Comparative Law Quarterly* 57 at 58; *Nevsun*, above note 42 at para 71, Abella J.

help to explain the lack of consistent engagement with relevant TCL conventions. These factors enable the accidental, or deliberate, minimization of relevant international law. The inconsistency is, as I have argued, neither inevitable nor desirable. We have the tools to enable more consistent engagement; we need only put them to use.

four

The Influence of Transnational Criminal Law on Refugee Law

JOSEPH RIKHOF*

A. INTRODUCTION

It is generally accepted that there are synergies between transnational criminal law (TCL) and other disciplines of public international law which touch on individual criminality, such as international criminal law (ICL) and international humanitarian law (IHL). It is also generally thought that areas of public international law that address the rights of victims of such crimes, such as international human rights law or refugee law, are less suited to benefit from TCL notions and concepts. However, TCL has had influence on some areas of refugee law and this chapter will discuss the interaction between the two fields.

* Adjunct Professor, University of Ottawa, Faculty of Common Law. He is recognized internationally as an expert in the area of refugee criminality and has sixty-five publications in this and related areas, including the books *The Criminal Refugee: The Treatment of Asylum Seekers with a Criminal Background in International and Domestic Law* (Dordrecht: Republic of Letters Publishers, 2012, with a second edition now called *Exclusion and* Refoulement*: Criminality in International and Domestic Refugee Law*, Toronto: Irwin Law, forthcoming in 2023); as co-author with Robert J. Currie, *International and Transnational Criminal Law*, 2d ed (Toronto: Irwin Law, 2013) and 3d ed (Toronto: Irwin Law, 2020); and as co-author with Terje Einarsen, *International Criminal Law: A Theory of Punishable Participation in Universal Crimes* (Oslo: Torkel Opsahl Epublisher, 2018).

B. OVERVIEW OF BASIC REFUGEE LAW CONCEPTS

Refugee law is based on two pillars. The first one is that an asylum seeker who fulfills the requirements of being a refugee will be granted asylum. The second one is that a person who has received refugee status cannot be removed from the state of refuge, which has granted this status against the state of origin from which asylum was claimed; the latter is called protection against *refoulement*. Upon receiving refugee status, a person is entitled to basic rights according to the *Refugee Convention*, such as the right of association (article 15), employment (articles 17–19), housing (article 21), education (article 22), social security (article 24), and freedom of movement (article 26).[1]

In order to receive refugee status, a person has to show a "well-founded fear of being persecuted for reasons of race, religion, nationality, membership of a particular social group or political opinion, is outside the country of his nationality and is unable or, owing to such fear, is unwilling to avail himself of the protection of that country."[2] Such an assessment is based on both past and future fear of persecution. Since this concept of persecution was framed immediately after World War II, and since not all issues arising out of situations of turmoil causing refugee movements are covered by the *Refugee Convention*, new concepts such as complementary, temporary, and subsidiary protection have been developed at the global, regional, and national levels to fill the gap between new realities and the existing convention's legal regime.[3] Similarly, the notion of r*efoulement* has also undergone changes over the last decades.

The *Refugee Convention* contains exceptions against *refoulement*,[4] which is based on the same grounds as contained in the definition of refugee, namely persecution. To avoid situations whereby a person could be expelled who might be exposed to other human rights abuses, or who falls outside the groups mentioned in this provision, regional and national

1 *Convention Relating to the Status of Refugees*, (1951), 189 UNTS 137 [*Refugee Convention*].

2 *Ibid*, art 1A(2).

3 For details see Joseph Rikhof, *Exclusion and Refoulement: Criminality in International and Domestic Refugee Law* (Toronto: Irwin Law, forthcoming in 2023) at 18–26.

4 They can be found in arts 32(1) and 33(2) of the *Refugee Convention*; the exceptions based on the commission of very serious criminal offences or on grounds of national security or public order, usually when occurring in the country of refuge; for a detailed study of these exceptions see *ibid* at 589–706.

legislative instruments have supplemented the concepts of the *Refugee Convention*. This is done in two ways, either by providing a different form of protection, such as subsidiary protection at the front end of the refugee process, or by expanding the reasons for prohibiting *refoulement* at the back end. These expanded forms of protection have been borrowed from other human rights instruments,[5] and typically include protection against killing, torture, or other cruel, inhuman, or degrading treatment or punishment.[6]

While the *Refugee Convention*, regional refugee treaties, and national legislation primarily regulate aspects of obtaining refugee status and their associated rights, they do contain exceptions to these general tenets whereby in certain circumstances refugee status will not be bestowed, can be revoked, or will not be an impediment to removing a refugee from a state of refuge.[7] This chapter will only discuss exceptions related to criminality, of which the one employed at the front end of the process — called exclusion — is the most important.[8] Article 1F, the exclusion clause in the *Refugee Convention*, reads as follows:

> The provisions of this Convention shall not apply to any person with respect to whom there are serious reasons for considering that:
> (a) he has committed a crime against peace, a war crime, or a crime against humanity, as defined in the international instruments drawn up to make provision in respect of such crimes;
> (b) he has committed a serious non-political crime outside the country of refuge prior to his admission to that country as a refugee;
> (c) he has been guilty of acts contrary to the purposes and principles of the United Nations.[9]

5 Such as the *International Covenant on Civil and Political Rights*, (1966) 999 UNTS 171, the *United Nations Convention against Torture and other Cruel, Inhuman and Degrading Treatment or Punishment*, (1984) 1465 UNTS 85, Can TS 1987 No 36 [*CAT*], and the *International Convention for the Protection of All Persons from Enforced Disappearance*, (2006) 2716 UNTS 3 [*Enforced Disappearance Convention*], while at the regional level the *European Convention on Human Rights*, (1950) ETS 5, has been utilized.

6 See Rikhof, above note 3 at 17–21.

7 *Ibid* at 21–22.

8 See *ibid* at 22–26 with respect to criminality at the back end.

9 *Refugee Convention*, above note 1, art 1F.

C. TRANSNATIONAL CRIMINAL LAW AND EXCLUSION GROUND 1F(a)

The parameters of exclusion ground 1F(a) are circumscribed by the words "as defined in the international instruments drawn up to make provision in respect of such crimes." These words have been clarified by indicating that "international instruments" is now equivalent to international criminal law,[10] while "as defined" does not only apply to the parameters of the three crimes mentioned in this exclusion ground, but also to the word "committed," incorporating international criminal law for concepts related to individual responsibility.[11]

As a result, any influence of TCL on 1F(a) can only be assessed in an indirect way by determining the relationship between TCL and ICL.[12] At the international level, there have been and are still a number of points where ICL utilized TCL concepts to either clarify or introduce concepts

---

10 The most influential international source of interpretation for exclusion, the 2003 *Background Note on the Application of the Exclusion Clauses: Article 1F of the 1951 Convention Relating to the Status of Refugees*, refers to the *Rome Statute of the International Criminal Court*, (1998) 2187 UNTS 3, Can TS 2002 No 13, UN Doc A/CONF.183/9 [*Rome Statute*], as the most important reference for 1F(a) crimes. The debate in academic circles has been whether the term "instruments" can only refer to treaties or also to non-binding instruments, with the trend leaning toward the latter. See Yao Li, *Exclusion from Protection as a Refugee; An Approach to a Harmonizing Interpretation in International Law* (Leiden/Boston: Brill Nijhoff, 2017) at 306–7; for a more general comment regarding international instruments, see International Law Commission, *Draft Articles on Prevention and Punishment of Crimes Against Humanity, with Commentaries 2019*, UN Doc A/74/10 at 47, para 44.

11 The parameters of the term "committed" have been addressed in common law states at the highest judicial level between 2010 and 2013 in Canada (*Ezokola v Canada (Citizenship and Immigration)*, 2013 SCC 40), New Zealand (*The Attorney-General (Minister of Immigration) v Tamil X and the RSAA*, [2010] NZSC 107) and the United Kingdom (*R (on the application of JS) (Sri Lanka) (Respondent) v Secretary of State for the Home Department (Appellant)*, [2010] UKSC 15); all three courts sought a connection between this term and international criminal law, which was best set out in the analysis by the Supreme Court of Canada in *Ezokola* when it made an inquiry as to which are the broadest forms of extended liability both under the ICTY/ICTR statutes (Annexed to UN Doc S/RES/827 (1993) and Annexed to UN Doc S/RES/955, 33 ILM 1598, 1600 (1994)) and the *Rome Statute* on the understanding that Canadian exclusion law should not go beyond these forms of liability in international law (paras 42–46).

12 The conceptual difference between international criminal law and transnational criminal law is discussed in the introductory chapter of this book.

related to both the parameters of crime and extended liability. In this context, it is useful to point out that two of the four ICL crimes started out as transnational crimes, as they were originally contained in treaties addressing these crimes before they became embedded in ICL, namely, the 1948 *Genocide Convention*[13] (for genocide) and the enforcement provisions in the 1949 Geneva Conventions[14] (for war crimes).[15]

This general connection between ICL and TCL remained important during the discussions for the establishment of the International Criminal Court (ICC). The impetus for this discussion was initially exclusively TCL-based, as Trinidad and Tobago, leading a group of like-minded states, wanted such an institution to prosecute major narcotics producers and traffickers.[16] The first draft statute produced by the International Law Commission (ILC) in 1994, which followed this initiative, contained a combination of the core international crimes of aggression, war crimes, crimes against humanity and genocide, and a number of crimes based on TCL treaties.[17] However, a year later, these references to TCL had disappeared in the ILC's next draft,[18] but another TCL crime, namely, crimes against the United Nations and associated personnel, was included

---

13 *Convention for the Prevention and Punishment of the Crime of Genocide*, (1948) 78 UNTS 277, Can TS 1949 No 27 [*Genocide Convention*].

14 *Geneva Convention for the Amelioration of the Condition of the Wounded and Sick in Armed Forces in the Field*, (1950) 75 UNTS 31 [*GC* I], *Geneva Convention for the Amelioration of the Condition of Wounded, Sick and Shipwrecked Members of Armed Forces at Sea*, (1950) 75 UNTS 85 [*GC* II], *Geneva Convention Relative to the Treatment of Prisoners of War*, (1950) 75 UNTS 135 [*GC* III], and *Geneva Convention Relative to the Protection of Civilian Persons in Times of War*, (1950) 75 UNTS 287 [*GC* IV]; the articles in question re war crimes are art 50 in *GC* I, art 51 in *GC* II, art 130 in *GC* III and art 147 in *GC* IV. More war crimes were identified in *Additional Protocol 1 to the Geneva Conventions*, (1977) 1125 UNTS 3 arts 11 and 85; see for more details Robert J. Currie & Joseph Rikhof, *International & Transnational Law*, 3d ed (Toronto: Irwin Law, 2020) at 146–49 and 155–64.

15 For more details, see Terje Einarsen & Joseph Rikhof, *A Theory of Punishable Participation in Universal Crimes* (Brussels, Oslo: Torkel Opsahl Academic EPublisher, 2018) at 263–65 and 270.

16 See Currie & Rikhof, above note 14 at 211.

17 *Draft Code of Crimes against the Peace and Security of Mankind*, UN Doc A/49/10 (1994) art 20(e) at 38 and the Annex at 67–68, with the relevant articles at 71–73; the eight TLC treaties in question were related to terrorist activities (5), torture, apartheid, and drug trafficking.

18 *Report of the International Law Commission on the Work of its 47th Session*, UNGAOR, 50th Sess, Supp No 10, UN Doc A/50/10 (1995) [*Report of the ILC 47th Sess*].

as a separate crime in the 1996 version of this ILC document.[19] The final version of the *Rome Statute* included this crime as a war crime,[20] while apartheid became part of the enumeration of crimes against humanity.[21] This was also the case for the crimes of enforced disappearance[22] and enslavement,[23] both of which have their genesis in TCL.

In addition to the connection between ICL and TCL in the *Rome Statute* with respect to crimes, the clearest example as part of extended liability was the concept of common purpose, which is contained in article 25(3)(d) and which was inspired by the 1997 *Terrorist Bombing Convention* in using the same wording.[24]

It is unclear how far this trend will continue. In the ICC context, the *Rome Statute* can only be amended through the procedure laid down in article 121(3), which requires a meeting of the Assembly of States Parties (ASP) or a Review Conference of the Rome Statute. The first review conference in Kampala in 2010 resulted in the adoption of a definition of the crime of aggression[25] while ASP meetings so far have added only

---

19 *Report of the International Law Commission on the Work of its 48th Session*, UNGAOR, 51st Sess, Supp No 10, UN Doc A/51/10 (1996) art 19 at 50–53.

20 *Rome Statute*, above note 10, arts 8(2)(b)(iii) and 8(2)(e)(iii); for more details, see Currie & Rikhof, above note 14 at 180–82. The *Rome Statute* also contains a provision, which was not discussed by the ILC, namely the war crime of child recruitment, which can be found in arts 8(2)(b)(xxvi) and 8(2)(e)(vii) and which was inspired by art 77(2) of the *Additional Protocol I to the 1949 Geneva Conventions* as well as art 38(3) of the *Convention on the Rights of the Child*, (1989) 1577 UNTS 3; for more details, see Currie & Rikhof, above note 14 at 182–84.

21 *Rome Statute*, above note 10, art 7(1)(j); see for the transnational aspects Currie & Rikhof, above note 14 at 353–55. Footnote 11 of the ICC *Elements of Crimes* document indicates that "[i]t is also understood that the conduct described in this element includes trafficking in persons, in particular women and children." (International Criminal Court, *Elements of Crimes* (2011), online: www.icc-cpi.int/NR/rdonlyres/336923D8-A6AD-40EC-AD7B-45BF9DE73D56/0/ElementsOfCrimesEng.pdf)

22 *Rome Statute*, above note 10, art 7(1)(h); see for the transnational aspects the *Enforced Disappearance Convention*, above note 5.

23 *Rome Statute*, above note 10, art 7(1)(c); see for the transnational aspects Currie & Rikhof, above note 14 at 347–52.

24 *International Convention for the Suppression of Terrorist Bombing*, (1998) 37 ILM 249 art 2(3); the language between these two articles is very similar while this notion of common purpose was used for the first time in a TCL treaty. See Einarsen & Rikhof, above note 15 at 273–82.

25 See Currie & Rikhof, above note 14 at 188–90.

new war crimes,[26] which had their source in IHL.[27] However, there have been proposals in the ASP to add provisions for crimes which had their basis in TCL: by Mexico in 2009, to add employing nuclear weapons as a war crime;[28] by Trinidad and Tobago and Belize, to include the crime of international drug trafficking as a stand-alone crime;[29] and by the Netherlands, to include the crime of terrorism as a stand-alone crime.[30] As well, academics have suggested that although the *Elements of Crimes* document of the ICC indicates that trafficking in persons is part of the crime against humanity of enslavement,[31] the slave trade by itself should be considered an international crime.[32]

When war crimes became entrenched in ICL, the connection with TCL became of less importance, as the International Criminal Tribunal for the former Yugoslavia (ICTY) and the International Criminal Tribunal for Rwanda (ICTR) developed a methodology for identifying possible new

---

26 Some amendments added war crimes, which were already contained in art 8(2)(b), which pertains to international armed conflicts, to art 8(2)(e), which is related to non-international armed conflicts, namely arts 8(2)(e)(xiii)–(xv) and (xix), all dealing with prohibited weapons.

27 In 2017, the following crimes were added in art 8(2)(b): (xxvii) employing weapons, which use microbial or other biological agents, or toxins, whatever their origin or method of production; (xxviii) employing weapons the primary effect of which is to injure by fragments which in the human body escape detection by X-rays; and (xxix) employing laser weapons specifically designed, as their sole combat function or as one of their combat functions, to cause permanent blindness to unenhanced vision, that is to the naked eye or to the eye with corrective eyesight devices. (They are repeated in art 8(2)(e)(xvi)–xviii.) The sources for these provisions were art I(1) of the *Biological Weapons Convention*, (1972) 1015 UNTS 163, *Protocol I* of the *Convention on Certain Conventional Weapons*, (1980) 1342 UNTS 137 and Article 1 of *Protocol IV* of the *Convention on Certain Conventional Weapons*, (1998) 1380 UNTS 370.

28 *Report on the Working Group on Amendments*, 9 December 2011, UN Doc ICC-ASP/10/32 at 13–16.

29 *Ibid* at 19–20.

30 *Ibid* at 17–18.

31 See above note 23.

32 Patricia Viseur Sellers & Jocelyn Getgen Kestenbaum, "Missing in Action: The International Crime of the Slave Trade" (2020) 18 *Journal of International Criminal Justice* 517 at 533–37. It has also been suggested (though without a reference to TCL) that ecocide should be a distinct crime under the *Rome Statute*; see the Independent Expert Panel for the Legal Definition of Ecocide, *Commentary and Core Text*, June 2021, online: https://static1.squarespace.com/static/5ca2608ab914493c64ef1f6d/t/60d1e6e604fae2201d03407f/1624368879048/SE+Foundation+Commentary+and+core+text+rev+6.pdf.

war crimes, based entirely on international humanitarian law.[33] With respect to genocide, it is unlikely, as well, that TCL will be used as a source, since the interpretation of this crime has been developed for the most part in *sui generis* fashion, by relying on the *travaux preparatoires* of the *Genocide Convention* for interpretation, while at times reference is made to international human rights law.[34]

The same can be said for crimes against humanity where, due to their affinity to human rights, the interpretation of such crimes was initially sought in international human rights law[35] or in a comparative domestic analysis,[36] after which further judicial developments were based on this initial interpretation. However, occasionally there is a direct reference to TCL concepts, as can be seen in a recent decision by the ICC Appeals Chamber (AC), where the *United Nations Convention against Transnational Organized Crime* (*UNTOC*) definition of an organized criminal group was given in the context of crimes against humanity in the *Rome Statute*:[37]

> Considering that the Court is a criminal court and given the international crimes under its jurisdiction, which generally involve organised criminality, guidance can be sought from other international treaties addressing similar types of criminality. In this regard, the United Nations Convention against Transnational Organised Crime defines an "organised criminal group" in article 2(a) as "a structured group of three or more persons, existing for a period of time and acting in concert with the aim of committing one or more serious crimes or offences [. . .]." Similarly, article 2(c) defines a structured group as "a group that is not

33 *Tadić* (IT-94-1), Appeals Chamber, Decision on the Defence Motion for Interlocutory Appeal on Jurisdiction, 2 October 1995 at para 94; *Kunarac et al* (IT-96-23/IT-96-23/1), Appeals Chamber Judgment, 12 June 2002 at para 66; *Aleksovski* (IT-95-14/1-A), Judgment, Appeals Chamber, 24 March 2000 at para 20; and *Mladić* (MICT-13-56-A), Appeals Chamber Judgment, 8 June 2021 at para 285.

34 See for instance *Krstić* (IT-98-33-T), Trial Chamber Judgment, 2 August 2001 at para 555 and *Report of the ILC 47th Sess*, above note 18 at 45–46.

35 See for instance for the crime of torture, *Mucić et al (Čelebići Camp)* (IT-96-21), Trial Chamber Judgment, 16 November 1998 at paras 461–67; for the crime of inhumane acts, see for instance *Brđanin* (IT-99-36), Trial Chamber Judgment, 1 September 2004 at para 1005.

36 *Kunarac et al* (IT-96-23/IT-96-23/1), Appeals Chamber Judgment, 12 June 2002 at paras 129–30 for the crime of rape.

37 *Rome Statute*, above note 10, art 7(2)(a).

> randomly formed for the immediate commission of an offence and that does not need to have formally defined roles for its members, continuity of its membership or a developed structure." The interpretative note to this provision indicates that "the term 'structured group' is to be used in a broad sense so as to include both groups with hierarchical or other elaborate structure and non-hierarchical groups where the roles of the members of the group need not be formally defined."[38]

This approach can also be detected in the recent work by the ILC, where the commentaries on the *Draft Articles on Prevention and Punishment of Crimes Against Humanity*[39] are replete with references to TCL, for both substantive aspects of crimes against humanity and procedural issues. Examples are the general obligation to not engage in crimes against humanity,[40] the obligation to prevent crimes against humanity,[41] criminalization under national law,[42] the defence of superior orders,[43] statute of limitations,[44] liability of legal persons,[45] obligation to prosecute or

---

38 *Ntaganda*, (ICC-01/04-02/06-2666-Anx3 30-03-2021 1/163 SL A A2), Judgment Appeals Chamber, Separate Opinion of Judge Luz Del Carmen Ibáñez Carranza on Mr. Ntaganda's appeal, 30 March 2021 at para 47. For the implementation of this requirement into Canadian immigration law, see *Canada (Public Safety and Emergency Preparedness) v Verbanov*, 2021 FC 507.

39 *Draft report of the International Law Commission on the work of its seventy-first session*, ILC, Chapter IV, Crimes against Humanity, Text of the draft articles and commentaries thereto, UN Doc A/CN.4/L.928/Add.1 (19 June 2019).

40 *Ibid*, art 3(1) with a reference to the *Enforced Disappearance Convention*, above note 5 at 52, para 21.

41 *Ibid*, art 4 with references to sixteen TCL treaties at 55–56, para 3.

42 *Ibid*, art 6 with a reference to provisions dealing with extended liability in the 2006 Convention at 71, para 15; for a critical assessment, see Joseph Rikhof, "The International Law Commission's Draft Articles on the Prevention and Punishment of Crimes Against Humanity: Incitement/Conspiracy as Missing Modes of Liability" (2020) 6 *African Journal of International Criminal Justice* 239 at 240–53.

43 *Ibid*, art 6 with a reference to the *Enforced Disappearance Convention*, above note 5 at 75, para 27.

44 *Ibid*, art 6 with a reference to the *Enforced Disappearance Convention*, above note 5 at 79, para 36.

45 *Ibid*, art 6 with references to six TCL treaties at 80–81, para 44.

extradite,[46] amnesties,[47] rights of victims,[48] and the political offence exception to extradition.[49] It is unlikely, however, that this brief foray into TCL in the area of international crimes will be followed at the national level, as any recent reference in exclusion jurisprudence has been to the ICC statute and its caselaw.

D. TRANSNATIONAL CRIMINAL LAW AND EXCLUSION GROUND 1F(b)

Unlike in exclusion ground 1F(a), one would expect a more direct utilization of TCL in exclusion ground 1F(b), which stands to reason given its wording. Specifically, the notion of "serious non-political crime," has to be found outside ICL, since 1F(b) contains no reference to that body of international law, as is the case with 1F(a).

A definition of serious crimes can be found in the *UNTOC*,[50] which states: "'Serious crime' shall mean conduct constituting an offence punishable by a maximum deprivation of liberty of at least four years or a more serious penalty."[51] The United Nations High Commissioner for Refugees (UNHCR), the foremost international authority in refugee law, indicated that "the gravity of the crime should be judged against international standards, not simply by its characterisation in the host State or country of origin."[52] While there is no further clarification on this statement, it is pos-

46 *Ibid*, art 10 with references to *Convention for the Suppression of Unlawful Seizure of Aircraft*, (1970) 860 UNTS 105 at 92–93, para 3, with also a large number of TCL treaties at the same page, footnote 457 and the *CAT*, above note 5 at 93, para 4.

47 *Ibid*, art 10 with a reference to the *Enforced Disappearance Convention*, above note 5 at 96, para 12.

48 *Ibid*, art 12 with a reference to the *Enforced Disappearance Convention*, above note 5 at 103, para 3 and the *CAT* at 103, para 4 with also references to a number of other TCL treaties at 102, footnotes 501–4 (with further modalities of such rights and references to TCL treaties at 105, para 7 and para 10; at 107, para 17; at 108, para 19).

49 *Ibid*, art 13 with a reference to *Enforced Disappearance Convention*, above note 5 at 114, paras 11–12 with references to a large number of TCL treaties at 113–14, footnote 567.

50 *Convention against Transnational Organized Crime*, (2000) 2225 UNTS 209 [*UNTOC*]; for details see Currie & Rikhof, above note 14 at 379–83.

51 *Ibid*, art 2(b).

52 See *Background Note on the Application of the Exclusion Clauses: Article 1F of the 1951 Convention Relating to the Status of Refugees*, UNHCR (4 September 2003) at 14, para 38 [*Background Note*]; this document provides more detail to the *Guidelines*

sible that the drafters had TCL in mind. Similarly, while a direct reference to the *UNTOC* has been absent from national exclusion jurisprudence, the methodology whereby the seriousness of the crime is expressed by a maximum penalty has been used in the past in Canada, as well as in France. In Canada, it was said in the early jurisprudence that a serious crime is a capital crime or very grave punishable act with a presumption that any crime with maximum penalty of more than ten years in the country of refuge would fall within those descriptions,[53] while in France the reference was vaguer, only referring to crimes with a lengthy maximum penalty.[54] In some countries, such as Australia,[55] Germany,[56] and more recently France,[57] the judiciary have stated that, in general, article 1F(b) applies to capital or grave crimes, but without using a more detailed methodology. In other countries, judges have issued more specific instructions by assessing what penalty would likely be imposed if a person were to be tried criminally; for instance, in New Zealand, a tribunal came to the conclusion that this sentence should be, at a minimum, between eighteen months and two years,[58] while in the United Kingdom a two-year minimum is set out in the legislation.[59]

However, at times, the national jurisprudence[60] has followed the guidance of the UNHCR and has indicated that national legislation needs to

---

on International Protection: Application of the Exclusion Clauses: Article 1F of the 1951 Convention relating to the Status of Refugees, UNHCR, HCR/GIP/03/05 (4 September 2003), which is the most recent and most authoritative international document re exclusion.

53 *Chan v Canada (Minister of Citizenship and Immigration)*, [2000] 4 FC 390 (FCA) [*Chan*].

54 Frédéric Tiberghien, *La Protection des Refugies en France*, 2e ed (Paris: Presses Universitaires D'Aix-En-Marseille, 1988) at 103–4 and 468–69.

55 *Minister for Immigration and Multicultural Affairs v Singh*, [2002] HCA 7; *SZJRI v Minister for Immigration & Citizenship*, [2008] FCA 1090; *Ballibay and Minister for Immigration and Multicultural Affairs*, [2000] AATA 1147; *SRLLL and Minister for Immigration Multicultural and Indigenous Affairs*, [2002] AATA 795 [*SRLLL*].

56 BverwG 10 C 7.09, 10 February 2010, para 47; BverwG 10 C 24.08, 24 November 2009, para 41 and BverwG 10 C 48.07, 14 October 2008 at para 19.

57 CNDA, 27 October 2014, 14016605, M. E. and CNDA, 3 November 2015, 10013998, M. B.

58 RSAA Appeal No. 76157, 26 June 2008 at paras 196–200.

59 *Polat, R v SSHD*, [2011] EWHC 3445 (Admin) at para 73; *R (ABC a minor) v Home Secretary*, [2011] EWHC 2937 (Admin) at para 35.

60 For specific examples of the crimes that fall within the parameters of "serious," see Joseph Rikhof, "The Interpretation of Exclusion 1F(b) of the 1951 Refugee

be reflective of international criminality in that particular area of the law. This principle was applied in the Netherlands[61] in a case regarding drug trafficking, where reference was made to the *Vienna Narcotics Convention*,[62] and also in Canada,[63] where a reference to this Convention was made, as well as to two other treaties, namely, the *Single Convention on Narcotic Drugs*[64] and the *Convention Against Psychotropic Substances*.[65] In two cases in the Netherlands, references were made to the *United Nations Convention on the Law of the Sea*[66] in a situation of piracy.[67]

In another Canadian case,[68] reference was made not to TCL, but to the treaty regarding the civil law subject of child abduction,[69] where the court said "the Board also considered the existence of the Hague Convention as a demonstration of the international community's view of international kidnapping as a serious matter. I see no error in the Board's use of the *Chan* decision or its analysis of whether international kidnapping of a child constitutes a serious non-political crime."[70]

However, this reference to international criminality was also used in a puzzling manner in the Netherlands, in that the court made it a requirement to show criminality (of rape) at the international level, even though such criminality exists in both the country of origin (Libya, where the rape had been committed), and in the country of refuge.[71] Rather astonishingly, this requirement to show international criminality was also applied to the crime of practising female genital mutilation (FGM). While it is a

Convention Internationally and in Canada" in Idil Atak & James C. Simeon, eds, *The Criminalization of Migration, Context and Consequences* (Montreal and Kingston: McGill-Queen's University Press, 2018) at 171.

61 AbRS, 201202758/1 (27 September 2013).

62 *United Nations Convention against Illicit Traffic in Narcotic Drugs and Psychotropic Substances*, (1988) 1582 UNTS 95 [*Vienna Narcotics Convention*].

63 *Jayasekara v Canada (Citizenship and Immigration)*, 2008 FCA 404 at para 49 [*Jayasekara*].

64 *Single Convention on Narcotic Drugs*, (1961) 976 UNTS 105.

65 *Convention Against Psychotropic Substances*, (1971) 1019 UNTS 175.

66 *United Nations Convention on the Law of the Sea*, (1982) 1833 UNTS 3, 21 ILM 1261 art 101; for more details, see Currie & Rikhof, above note 14 at 340–46.

67 Rb, The Hague, Awb 14/9363, 1 July 2014 and Rb, The Hague, Awb 14/12590, 10 July 2014.

68 *Kovacs v Canada (Minister of Citizenship and Immigration)*, 2005 FC 1473 [*Kovacs*].

69 *Convention on the Civil Aspects of International Child Abduction*, (1980) Hague XXVIII.

70 *Kovacs*, above note 68 at para 27.

71 Rb, The Hague, Awb 13/12113, 17 September 2013.

crime in the Netherlands, it was not in the country of origin, Sierra Leone, and although there have been a number of international instruments prohibiting this practice, the court found FGM did not amount to a serious crime, as there was no international treaty criminalizing it.[72]

However, more recently, these more superficial approaches for assessing whether a crime is serious have been replaced by a more functional method, which looks at a number of mitigating and aggravating factors. This method has been advocated by the UNHCR[73] and used in Australia,[74] Belgium,[75] Canada,[76] New Zealand,[77] the United States,[78] and, in some respects, in France.[79]

In Canada, this was expressed by Létourneau J as follows:

> I believe there is a consensus among the courts that the interpretation of the exclusion clause in Article 1F(*b*) of the Convention, as regards the seriousness of a crime, requires an evaluation of the elements of the crime, the mode of prosecution, the penalty prescribed, the facts and the mitigating and aggravating circumstances underlying the conviction.... In other words, whatever presumption of seriousness may attach to a crime internationally or under the legislation of the receiving state, that presumption may be rebutted by reference to the above factors.[80]

72 AbRS, 201208875/1/V1 (10 February 2014); incidentally, a French tribunal without mentioning international instruments was of the view that FGM is a crime, see CNDA, 19007358, Mme T., 12 November 2019.

73 *Background Note*, above note 52 at 14, para 39, which refers to the nature of the act, the actual harm inflicted, the form of procedure used to prosecute the crime, the nature of the penalty for such a crime, and whether most jurisdictions would consider the act in question as a serious crime.

74 *FTZK v MIBP*, [2014] HCA 26; *JSDW and Minister for Immigration and Border Protection (Migration)*, [2017] AATA 2420.

75 CCE, No 239.570, 11 August 2020.

76 *Jayasekara*, above note 63; *Febles v Canada*, 2014 SCC 68 [*Febles*]; *Hasani v Canada*, 2020 FC 125.

77 *AF (Mexico)* [2018] NZIPT 801315; *AY (Malaysia)* [2019] NZIPT 801143; *AH (Mexico)* [2020] NZIPT 801631.

78 *Mahini v INS*, 779 F.2d 1419 (9th Circuit, 1986).

79 CRR, 26 May 2005, 459358, V.; CRR, 28 January 2005, 448119, C.; CRR, 4 April 2005, 487639, N.; CNDA, 15 January 2009, 594649, R.

80 *Jayasekara*, above note 63 at para 44. This approach was confirmed by the Supreme Court in *Febles*, above note 76; for Canadian jurisprudence regarding these factors, see Rikhof, above note 60 at 177–78.

This approach has also found favour with the Court of Justice of the European Union (CJEU), which refers to factors such as the nature of the act at issue, the consequences of that act, the form of procedure used to prosecute the crime, the nature of the penalty provided, and the taking into account of whether most jurisdictions also classify the act at issue as a serious crime.[81] Accordingly, it might very well be that this has become the prevalent method of determining the seriousness of a crime. This will also mean that there might be less opportunity for TCL to directly play a role in such an assessment, even though in Canada it is acknowledged that international law may play a role in assessing seriousness. However, since all national exclusion jurisprudence will use its own criminal law as a starting point for the analysis of seriousness, and since TCL crimes have found their way into those laws, TCL can still play an indirect role when a 1F(b) exclusion decision will deal with the subject matter of TCL treaties.

There is one crime with a stronger connection to TCL, namely terrorism. All national exclusion decision makers have faced the issue of terrorist activities in the context of 1F(b). TCL has addressed this phenomenon with an incremental approach by criminalizing certain aspects of terrorism,[82] as an overarching definition for the notion of terrorism has been elusive.[83] However, the exclusion jurisprudence in general has eschewed using the decentralized approach of TCL, but instead has attempted to exclude persons for terrorist activities in general. This approach is certainly acceptable, as there are several indicators which show a growing international consensus regarding the essential elements of the crime of terrorism. The first of these indicators is set out in the *Draft United Nations Comprehensive Convention on International Terrorism*, which states in article 2:

> 1. Any person commits an offence within the meaning of the present Convention if that person, by any means, unlawfully and intentionally, causes:
> (a) Death or serious bodily injury to any person; or
> (b) Serious damage to public or private property, including a place of public use, a State or government facility, a public transportation system, an infrastructure facility or to the environment; or

81 *Shajin Ahmed v Bevándorlási és Menekültügyi Hivatal*, Case C369/17, [2008] ECR I-8403 at I-8410 (13 September 2018) at para 56.

82 See Currie & Rikhof, above note 14 at 408–34.

83 *Ibid* at 355–61.

> (c) Damage to property, places, facilities or systems referred to in paragraph 1 (b) of the present article resulting or likely to result in major economic loss,
>
> when the purpose of the conduct, by its nature or context, is to intimidate a population, or to compel a Government or an international organization to do or to abstain from doing any act.[84]

A definition with similar core elements was arrived at by the Special Tribunal for Lebanon, an international tribunal that conducted a survey of the legislation of more than fifty countries to determine the common traits with respect to terrorism.[85] The same can be found in a more recent review of the legislation of fifty-five countries done by the Organization for Security and Co-operation in Europe (OSCE).[86] On the African continent, the African Union has adopted two instruments with these core elements, namely the *Convention on the Prevention and Combating of Terrorism*,[87] and the *Malabo Protocol*.[88]

In sum, while the connection between TCL and exclusion 1F(b) regarding crimes was rather strong in the past, TCL's influence has weakened over the recent years. However, there is another area of 1F(b) where TCL could play a more helpful role, namely with respect to extended liability, which is captured by the word "committed" in exclusion ground 1F(b). While in most cases 1F(b) was applied to persons personally involved in serious crimes, there has been little hesitation by the judiciary to extend the reach of this clause to persons who carried out such activities in an indirect fashion. The contours of complicity have been specifically

---

84 *Draft United Nations Comprehensive Convention on International Terrorism*, UN Doc A/C.6/65/L.10 (3 November 2010) Appendix I.

85 Special Tribunal for Lebanon, Interlocutory Decision on the Applicable Law: Terrorism, Conspiracy, Homicide, Perpetration, Cumulative charging, STL-II-OI/I/AC/RI76bis, Appeals Chamber, 16 February 2011, at paras 83–113.

86 See Legislationline.org under "Counter-Terrorism"; in addition, in the EU there is the *Council Framework Decision of 13 June 2002 on combating terrorism*, art 1.

87 *Organization of African Unity Convention on the Prevention and Combating of Terrorism*, UNTS Registration Number I-39464 (adopted 14 June 1999 in Algiers, in force 6 December 2002), art 1(3).

88 2014 Annex to the *Protocol on Amendments to the Protocol on the Statute of the African Court of Justice and Human Rights*, art 28G(A) [*Malabo Protocol*]; the Protocol is not in force yet.

addressed in Australia,[89] Belgium,[90] Canada,[91] Germany,[92] the Netherlands,[93] New Zealand,[94] the United Kingdom[95] and the United States.[96] Some of these decisions state that the same principles that apply to article 1F(a) should be used for article 1F(b) as well. Specifically, in Belgium and the Netherlands, the decisions make a reference to article 25 of the *Rome Statute*. However, at times the caveat has been added that where an individual was a member of an organization that has been placed on a prohibited list, this by itself does not absolve the government from the obligation to show that a member supported the organization, implying that membership alone is not sufficient to attract article 1F(b) liability.[97]

This interplay between articles 1F(a) and 1F(b) regarding extended liability poses a conceptual dilemma. The same word "committed" is used in both provisions, but exclusion 1F(a) has a specific reference to international instruments. It has been suggested that "committed" in 1F(b) has the capacity to be broader than the same term used in 1F(a), but that any distinction in terms of meaning should be kept to a minimum given the use of the same word. A solution to this dilemma could be that all modes of extended liability applicable to 1F(a) are also applicable to 1F(b), but that 1F(b), *in addition*, can also contain other modes of liability if there is a credible source for them. This would mean that the entire body of ICL regarding present modes of liability can be imported into 1F(b). In terms of credible sources of extended liability for 1F(b), TCL would be a very good candidate. Based on these two observations, it would mean

89 *Minister for Immigration and Multicultural Affairs v Singh*, [2002] HCA 7.

90 CPPR No 99-0164/W5686, 17 September 1999; CCE No 118.284, 31 January 2014.

91 *Gregorio v Canada*, IMM-1447-98; *Zrig v Canada*, 2003 FCA 178; *Jaouadi v Canada*, 2005 FC 1256; and *Rudyak v Canada*, 2006 FC 1141.

92 Bundesverwaltungsgericht, BVerwG 10 C 48.07, 14 October 2008 at para 21; Bundesverwaltungsgericht, BVerwG 1 C 19.09, 26 October 2010 at para 23.

93 Rb, The Hague, Awb 05/54643, 15 September 2006.

94 RSAA Appeal No. 74273, 10 May 2006; RSAA Appeal No. 71335, 12 September 2000; RSAA Appeal No. 71398, 10 February 2000; RSAA Appeal No. 70001, 30 April 1997.

95 *Polat, R v SSHD*, above note 59.

96 *Singh-Kaur v Ashcroft*, 385 F.3d 293 (3d Circuit, 2004); *Perinpanathan v INS*, 310 F.3d 594 (8th Circuit, 2002); *Khan v Holder*, 584 F.3d 773 (9th Circuit, 2009); *Raghunathan v Holder*, Docket No. 08-2475, 08-3147 (2d Circuit, 2010); *Haile v Holder*, 658 F.3d 1122 (9th Circuit, 2011); *Jiang Guan v Barr*, 925 F.3d 1022 (9th Circuit, 2019).

97 At the CJEU level see *Bundesrepublik Deutschland v B and D*, C-57/09 and C-101/09 (9 November 2010) at paras 87–99 and *Commissaire général aux réfugiés et aux apatrides v Mostafa Lounani*, Case C573/14 (31 January 2017) at para 79 [*Lounani*].

that 1F(b) would contain modes of liability from ICL that are not used in TCL or used sparingly, such as superior responsibility, but also that modes of liability in TCL, which do not exist in ICL, are possible; threats come to mind,[98] as do financial operations in connection with offences,[99] cooperation,[100] and facilitating.[101]

E. TRANSNATIONAL CRIMINAL LAW AND EXCLUSION GROUND 1F(c)

While the Dutch[102] and UK judiciaries[103] mentioned the use of 1F(c) for human rights abuses in passing, Australia,[104] Belgium[105] (specifically mentioning genocide),[106] France,[107] and Germany[108] have used this provision for that purpose regularly in cases before their tribunals and courts. In

98 Joseph Rikhof, "Complicity in Exclusion for Terrorist Crimes" in James C. Simeon, ed, *Terrorism and Asylum* (Leiden/Boston: Brill Nijhoff, 2020) at 147–56.

99 See Einarsen & Rikhof, above note 15 at 279.

100 *Ibid* at 280.

101 *Ibid* at 282.

102 Rb, The Hague, Awb 04/36169, 30 June 2006; Rb, The Hague, Awb 03/46645, 21 February 2006; see also its Aliens Manual (*Vreemdelingencirculaire* 2000 (C), art C2/7.10.2.3).

103 *KJ (Sri Lanka) v Secretary of State for the Home Department*, [2009] EWCA Civ 292; *SS v SSHD* (SC/56/2009) (SIAC); KK (Article 1F(c), Turkey) [2004] UKIAT 00101; AA (Exclusion clause) Palestine [2005] UKIAT 00104; BE (Disobedience to orders, landmines) Iran [2007] UKAIT 00035; SS (Libya) v DDHD [2011] Civ 1547.

104 N96/12101 [1996] RRTA 3349; *SRLLL*, above note 55.

105 CPRR No 03-3331/W10302, 5 December 2005; CCE No 18.307, 3 November 2008; CPRR No 02-2607/F2192, 19 October 2005; CCE No 27.479, 18 May 2009; CCE No 64.356, 1 July 2011.

106 CE No 39.015 (Bennai c Etat Belge), 17 March 1992; CPPR No 95/1917/F390, 28 March 1995

107 CE, 25 March 1998, 170172, Mahboub; CRR, 21 February 1996, 293625, Singh; CRR, 5 June 2000, 338011, Dembe Nyobanga; CRR, 2 November 2000, 336285, Matumba; CRR, 23 June 2003, 418091, Ndebo; CRR and CRR, 21 November 2003, 432770, Voungbo Ndebo; CRR, 18 December 2006, 540733, Mme Soaline; CRR, 23 May 2007, 577110, A.; CNDA, 3 December 2008, 629222, B.; CNDA, 13 February 2009, 629208, A.; CNDA, 13 February 2009, 629207, C.; CNDA, 7 July 2009, 643451/09002255, D.; CNDA, 30 November 2011, 11005411, M. S.; CNDA, 17 October 2011, 10005838, M. A.; CNDA, 21 April 2011, 10014066, M. R. alias H.; CNDA, 6 September 2011, 10005808, M. E.

108 BverwG 10 C 48.07, 14 October 2008; BverwG 10 C 46.07, 25 November 2008; BverwG 10 C 2.10, 31 March 2011; BverwG 10 C 26.12, 19 November 2013.

Canada, the Supreme Court provided detailed reasoning setting out the circumstances in which article 1F(c) could apply.[109]

In addition to its use in human rights abuse cases, 1F(c) has become increasingly important to address the issue of terrorism, which provides a connection to TCL. The connection between terrorism and article 1F(c) was made by the UN Security Council in Resolution 1373 in 2001,[110] and this instrument provided the major impetus to bring terrorism activities under article 1F(c) (in addition to using article 1F(b) for this purpose). All states which use this provision to exclude persons for terrorism activities refer to this Resolution, while in Belgium and Germany, the judiciary also mentioned European instruments, such as the Qualification Directive, making the same connection.[111]

The Supreme Court of Canada cited torture, hostage taking, apartheid, forced disappearance, and terrorism as 1F(c) activities while relying on predecessor international instruments to TCL treaties, such as declarations of the UN General Assembly (in the case of torture, forced disappearance, and terrorism) and on judgments of the International Court of Justice (ICJ) (for hostage taking and apartheid), as they all specifically designate acts that are contrary to the purposes and principles of the United Nations.[112] In the United Kingdom, attacks on UN personnel were also found to be included within the parameters of this exclusion ground,[113] while France included tampering with witnesses testifying before the ICC[114] (though without reference to TCL). On the other hand, judges have rebuffed attempts by their governments to broaden the range of

109 *Pushpanathan v Canada*, [1998] 1 SCR 982 [*Pushpanathan*].

110 UN Doc S/RES/1373 (2001) art 5.

111 *Directive 2011/95/EU of the European Parliament and of the Council of 13 December 2011 on standards for the qualification of third-country nationals or stateless persons as beneficiaries of international protection, for a uniform status for refugees or for persons eligible for subsidiary protection, and for the content of the protection granted (recast)*, preambular paragraph 31.

112 *Pushpanathan*, above note 109.

113 *Al-Sirri v SSHD and DD v SSHD*, [2012] UKSC 54 at paras 63-68 [*Al-Sirri*].

114 CNDA, 17 January 2020, No. 18035545.

crimes, namely, drug trafficking in Canada,[115] violations of UN sanctions in the Netherlands,[116] and pimping in France.[117]

Article 1F(c) was intended by the drafters of the *Refugee Convention* to be a residual clause in relation to the other two exclusion clauses. While such a role could have been usefully fulfilled in the past, it would appear that with the strong development of ICL in the last few decades and its effect on article 1F(a), fewer activities formerly identified as exclusively falling within article 1F(c) still maintain this status. For instance, of four specific non-terrorist offences mentioned by the Supreme Court of Canada (torture, apartheid, forced disappearance, and hostage taking), three are now included in the *Rome Statute* as crimes against humanity, while the fourth, hostage taking, is a war crime in the same instrument, and would likely also fall under the crime against humanity of inhumane acts.

Similarly, the overarching test for 1F(c), namely, human rights violations carried out in a non-war crimes context, can now be seen as crimes against humanity, since a connection to an armed conflict is no longer a requirement in ICL.[118] The same can be said for the UK Supreme Court decision with respect to attacks against UN personnel, since such activities are now included in the *Rome Statute* as war crimes.[119] Because of this lacuna, and the fact that especially in the *Pushpanathan* case recourse had already been had to TCL, it has been suggested that TCL would be an excellent source for the identification of other crimes under 1F(c), as long as the crimes in TCL treaties meet the gravity requirement implicit in this exclusion ground—namely, serious implications for international peace and security, such as terrorist acts with an international dimension,[120] a

115 *Pushpanathan* above note 109; this was the case even though there were a number of TCL treaties in this area but none fit (yet) within the overarching approach developed by the court.

116 Rb, The Hague, Awb 03/46645, 21 February 2006.

117 CE, 14 October 2020, 428361.

118 See Currie & Rikhof, above note 14 at 123–24.

119 *Rome Statute*, above note 10 at arts 8(2)(c)(iii) and 8.2(e)(iii); this is acknowledged in para 63.

120 Sandesh Sivakumaran, "Exclusion from Refugee Status: The Purposes and Principles of the United Nations and Article 1F(c) of the Refugee Convention" (2014) 26:3 *International Journal of Refugee Law* 350 at 375–79. It has also been suggested that ethnic cleansing could be a 1F(c) crime; see Joseph Rikhof, "Ethnic Cleansing and Exclusion, in Serious International Crimes" in James C. Simeon, ed, *Serious International Crimes, Human Rights and Forced Migration* (London: Routledge Publishers, 2022).

sentiment already expressed in the United Kingdom in the *Al-Sirri* case,[121] and by the UNHCR.[122]

Although the wording in article 1F(c) with respect to individual responsibility differs from articles 1F(a) and (b) in that it refers to "guilty" rather than "committed," this has so far had no discernible impact on the application of this clause, as all countries have applied it to persons who had indirect involvement. This is made clear in Canada,[123] France,[124] Germany,[125] and the United Kingdom,[126] while the CJEU has said the following:

> Individual responsibility must be assessed in the light of both objective and subjective criteria. To that end, the competent authority must, inter alia, assess the true role played by the person concerned in the perpetration of the acts in question; his position within the organisation; the extent of the knowledge he had, or was deemed to have, of its activities; any pressure to which he was exposed; or other factors likely to have influenced his conduct.[127]

However, given the wording in UNSC Resolution 1373[128] and in articles 12(3) and 17(2) of the *Qualification Directive* (which use the word "incite"),[129]

---

121 *Al-Sirri*, above note 113 at paras 39–40.

122 Above note 52 at 18, para 47; the same was said in France and Germany, above notes 107 & 108.

123 *Pushpanathan* above note 109.

124 CRR, 7 October 2006, 585731, Tebourski; CNDA, 27 June 2008, 611731, M.; CNDA, 30 November 2011, 11005411, M. S.; CNDA, 17 October 2011, 10005838, M.A.; CNDA, 21 April 2011, 10014066, M. R. alias H.

125 BverwG 10 C 26.12, 19 November 2013.

126 *Al-Sirri* above note 113.

127 *B and D*, above note 97 at paras 96–97; the court makes it clear that this also applies to exclusion ground 1F(b).

128 Above note 110. Recital 5 states: "Declares that acts, methods, and practices of terrorism are contrary to the purposes and principles of the United Nations and that knowingly financing, planning and *inciting* terrorist acts are also contrary to the purposes and principles of the United Nations" [emphasis added].

129 See *Lounani* above note 97 at para 81, which says: "Mr Lounani has not committed, *nor attempted to commit, nor threatened to commit terrorist offences*, within the meaning of Article 1(1) of Framework Decision 2002/475" (emphasis added). Article 1(1) of the Framework Decision has been replaced with *Directive (EU) 2017/541 of the European Parliament and of the Council* of 15 March 2017, which states in article 14(3): "Member States shall take the necessary measures to ensure that *attempting* to commit an offence referred ... is punishable" [emphasis added].

it is also possible that certain inchoate offences,[130] such as incitement and attempt,[131] could be included within the parameters of the word "guilty," as it would appear that this notion could be broader than the notion of "committed" in 1F(a) and (b).[132] If TCL can be a valuable source for crimes as indicated above, there should be no reason not to extend this approach to forms of complicity, namely the ones mentioned above under 1F(b), as well as all inchoate offences, including conspiracy.[133]

F. CONCLUSION

The influence of TCL on exclusion law has been persistent but not consistent. For 1F(a), with its indirect application through ICL, there have been references to TCL on a regular basis both in terms of extended liability and the characterization of the crimes. However, only crimes against humanity law lends itself to possible further reliance on TCL, but in spite of some recent interest in TCL (by the ICC Appeals Chamber and the ILC), there does not seem to be too much opportunity for further development.

On the other hand, 1F(b) and (c) are more promising. While the possibility of a general application of TCL in the development of the notion of "serious crimes" in 1F(b) has passed, an indirect application of TCL by using the subject matter of TCL treaties as contained in domestic criminal law is certainly appropriate. Decision makers on domestic refugee cases could also make use of TCL in considering modes of liability, as the word "committed" in 1F(b) can be considered as broader than in 1F(a),

130 While traditionally inchoate offences used to be more prevalent in common law countries than in civil law countries, this distinction is becoming less clear, see Einarsen & Rikhof, above note 15 at 501 and 512–13.

131 *Conspiracy* has been discussed for 1F(c) in the UK in *KJ (Sri Lanka) v Secretary of State for the Home Department*, [2009] EWCA Civ 292, para 35 while the Supreme Court in *Al-Sirri*, above note 113 refers to commission, organization, *incitement or threat of serious acts of violence* as forms of extended liability in para 39.

132 Both in international criminal law and in national legislation the word "committed" does not include inchoate offences, which are typically set out and defined separately; see for instance at the ICL level, the *Rome Statute*, above note 10, art 25(3)(e) for incitement and art 25(3)(f) for attempt, while the same can be seen in the documents mentioned in above note 130.

133 These offences are mentioned regularly in TCL treaties; see Einarsen & Rikhof, above note 15 at 285.

due to the absence of the restrictive terms "international instruments"; and types of complicity, which are known in TCL but not in ICL, could be used for 1F(b).

Interestingly, exclusion ground 1F(c), which was traditionally seen as the most restrictive of the three exclusion grounds, offers the most opportunity for TCL to play a role, both in the types of crimes that could fall within its parameters, and for extended liability via the term "guilty." Regarding the latter, it is already clear that inchoate offences are part of 1F(c), due to the influence of TCL treaties in terrorism, and this could be further developed for other TCL crimes. With respect to types of crimes, it has been suggested that TCL could be a good source, but only to the extent that the crimes are committed with an international dimension. This last restriction for 1F(c) would make this exclusion ground narrower as compared to 1F(b), in terms of which, crimes could fall under either provision. On the other hand 1F(c) has a wider reach due to absence of the requirement that the crime has to be committed for a non-political purpose.[134]

In conclusion, TCL has been misunderstood and underutilized in exclusion law, and it is hoped that, in the future, refugee case decision makers will take a better look at TCL to remedy this situation.

134 Regarding the notion of non-political crimes, see Rikhof, above note 60 at 172–74.

five

Formalism and Substance in the Domestic Implementation of Transnational Criminal Law in Canada's Anti-terrorism Criminal Regimes

MICHAEL NESBITT*

A. INTRODUCTION

On 16 October 1970, Canada enacted the (now replaced) *War Measures Act* in response to the FLQ crisis and specifically to the kidnappings of British diplomat James Cross and Quebec politician Pierre LaPorte, the latter of whom was tragically killed by his kidnappers. On 23 June 1985, Air India Flight 182 exploded mid-air on its way from Montreal to London, killing all 329 persons on board. Both incidents were treated publicly as terrorism and are often seen as such today—the politically motivated killing of innocents to advance a group or organization's aims. Yet, in neither case did Canada respond with criminal terrorism charges under domestic law. The reason for this was simple: applicable terrorism offences did not exist at the time.

The events of 9/11 and the domestic and international reaction thereto changed that dynamic for Canada. On 12 September 2001, Canada began drafting legislation that would quickly become the *Anti-terrorism Act, 2001*.[1]

---

* Associate Professor, University of Calgary, Faculty of Law; Senior Research Affiliate with *The Canadian Network for Research on Terrorism, Security and Society (TSAS)*; and Fellow with the *Canadian Global Affairs Institute*. The author wishes to thank Dalal Souraya for her truly exceptional research assistance and for her impressive capacity to maintain such a professional, positive, can-do attitude while her final year of law school was interrupted by COVID-19. All errors are solely those of the author.

1 *Anti-terrorism Act*, SC 2001, c 41 [*ATA, 2001*].

Indeed, by 24 December 2001, the *ATA, 2001* was enacted. In so doing, Canada was able to claim that it had met the end-of-December deadline imposed by UNSC Resolution 1373[2] to report back on the measures Canada had taken to fight terrorism.[3] The *ATA, 2001* introduced Part II.1 of the *Criminal Code*,[4] which included what we now know as the *Code*'s anti-terrorism criminal offences; it also created the power to promulgate by way of regulation what is now known as the *Code*'s terrorist entity listing regime.[5]

Meanwhile, as Canada was working toward enacting the *ATA, 2001*, it also took the opportunity to enact the *Suppression of Terrorism Regulations*[6] under the *United Nations Act*,[7] also in response to Resolution 1373. Like the *Criminal Code*'s anti-terrorism provisions, the *Terrorism Regulations* allowed for the unilateral (Canadian) listing of terrorist entities and individuals, while similarly seeking to combat terrorist financing. In subsequent years, Canada also worked to renovate the *Taliban, ISIL (Da'esh) and Al-Qaida Regulations*,[8] which were first enacted as the *Taliban Regulations* in 1999, also under the *UN Act*.[9] Thus completed the trilogy that is now, in essence, both Canada's anti-terrorism criminal regime and its three-pronged regime for listing terrorist groups and/or individuals. Today this regime is many things, but first and foremost it was a direct response to international pressures and legal obligations to respond to al-Qaida and the attacks of 9/11 with concrete action.[10]

In Section B of this chapter, I take a broad look at the *ATA, 2001* and the criminal offences regime it created, with a specific focus on the

---

2 *Threats to International Peace and Security Caused by Terrorist Acts*, SC Res 1373, UNSCOR, 56th Year, UN Doc S/INF/57 (2001) [*Res 1373*].

3 See generally Kent Roach, *September 11: Consequences for Canada* (Toronto: University of Toronto Press, 2002) at 21 [Roach, *Consequences for Canada*].

4 *Criminal Code*, RSC 1985, c C-46.

5 See *Regulations Establishing a List of Entities*, SOR/2002-284 [*Criminal Code Listings*].

6 *Regulations Implementing the United Nations Resolutions on the Suppression of Terrorism*, SOR/2001-360 [*Suppression of Terrorism Regs*].

7 *United Nations Act*, RSC 1985, c U-2 [*UN Act*].

8 *Regulations Implementing the United Nations Resolutions on Taliban, ISIL (Da'esh) and Al-Qaida*, SOR/99-444 [*ISIL Regs*].

9 See *Report of the Government of Canada to the Counter-Terrorism Committee of the United Nations Security Council on Measures Taken to Implement Resolution 1373* (2001) [*Canada's 1373 Report*].

10 For a compelling analysis demonstrating this point, see Roach, *Consequences for Canada*, above note 3 at 22–23.

areas most directly influenced by transnational criminal law (TCL), those being how Canada does (or does not) define terrorism as well as the financing offences, and more generally the priority given under the *ATA, 2001* to criminalizing inchoate acts (those being acts in the latent or planning stage, in contrast to completed acts). In Section C, I then consider the three terrorist group listing regimes, those being the *Criminal Code*'s regime, the *ISIL Regulations*, and the *Terrorism Regulations*.

In examining the *ATA, 2001*'s focus on inchoate and financing offences as well as these three listing regimes, I revisit the cross-fertilization of ideas and practices between TCL tools and the domestic criminal anti-terrorism regime. We see through this analysis how TCL has pressured Canada to take action to counter terrorism with criminal offences. But we also see how due process and effectiveness concerns have arisen to a greater degree the more Canada has tried to copy the form of the TCL tools (what I call a more formalistic approach to domestic implementation), as opposed to finding unique Canadian methods to implement the spirit of TCL obligations (what I call a more substantive approach). This chapter adopts the book's overall approach to analyzing TCL, including *inter alia* consideration of how states have used international *tools* to cooperate in suppressing transnational crimes,[11] in this case being terrorism.

B. DRAFTING THE *ANTI-TERRORISM ACT, 2001* AND THE CREATION OF CANADA'S *CRIMINAL CODE* TERRORISM REGIME

As outlined above, Canada did not have an anti-terrorism *Criminal Code* regime as of 11 September 2001. That all began to change when Canada commenced work drafting the *ATA, 2001*, which, according to the government at the time, was a direct response[12] to Resolution 1373,[13] which mandated state updates (reporting) on steps taken to prevent and punish terrorism at a national level. As Canadian national security experts Craig Forcese and Kent Roach have stated, Canada saw Resolution 1373 as "a

11 See Chapter 1.

12 See *Canada's 1373 Report*, above note 9.

13 *Res 1373*, above note 2.

mandate to enact new legislation by the end of 2001 even when other countries did not."[14]

In drafting the *ATA, 2001*, the first, and perhaps most vexing, problem for Canada was: should it define terrorism and, in so doing, explicitly create offences such as committing and planning terrorism (or even committing and/or planning terrorist activity)? Or should Canada follow another path? Canada searched transnationally for guidance, looking for a consensus definition of terrorism, or at least one that might satisfy the need to be rigorous and broadly applicable across various types of acts widely understood as terrorism. It found no such consensus definition. As the Supreme Court of Canada would later note in *Suresh v Canada*, "One searches in vain for an authoritative definition of 'terrorism' ... [but] there is no single definition that is accepted internationally."[15] Thus, the *ATA, 2001* does not define terrorism. Instead, Canada took its own unique approach to constructing an anti-terrorism criminal offences regime; however, in so doing it borrowed heavily from the United Kingdom's criminal regime and from the documents containing Canada's international obligations related to criminalizing terrorism.[16]

So rather than criminalizing terrorism—because it could not define terrorism—Canada's *Criminal Code* regime creates a series of offences based largely off of two predicates, those being "terrorist activity" and "terrorist group". Put simply, Canada's terrorism offences are largely linked either to proving an association with terrorist activities or between the accused's actions and a terrorist group.

Terrorist groups are then understood in two discrete ways. First, groups may be listed under the *Criminal Code*,[17] as discussed in greater detail below, which describes the *Criminal Code*'s terrorist listing regime. Second, a terrorist group is defined as one, "that has as one of its purposes

---

14 Craig Forcese & Kent Roach, *False Security: The Radicalization of Canadian Anti-terrorism* (Toronto: Irwin Law, 2015) at 56. The deputy prime minister said as much at the time: "the [*ATA, 2001*] ... brings Canada into full compliance with ... Resolution 1373." Canada, Parliament, House of Commons, Sub-Committee on National Security of the Standing Committee of Justice and Human Rights, *Evidence*, 37th Parl, 1st Sess (10 April 2002).

15 *Suresh v Canada (Minister of Citizenship and Immigration)*, 2002 SCC 1 at para 94 [*Suresh*].

16 See Roach, *Consequences for Canada*, above note 3 at 32.

17 *Criminal Code*, above note 4 at s 83.01(1), which defines "terrorist group."

or activities facilitating or carrying out any terrorist activity,"[18] which brings us back to the definition of terrorist activity as the key ingredient.

The concept of terrorist activity is likewise conceived of in two general ways. First, it is defined as "an act or omission that is committed in or outside Canada and that, if committed in Canada" would constitute an offence under section 7 of the *Criminal Code*, which implements Canada's obligations under ten international terrorism treaties.[19] Put simply, this definition incorporates as criminal offences various international terrorism treaty obligations. Second, the concept of terrorist activity is given a precise definition, which generally requires the proof of three (further) predicates or what I have previously called "clauses": a *motive clause*, which requires proof that an act was committed "in whole or in part for a political, religious or ideological purpose, objective or cause"; a *consequence clause*, which requires proof that the implicated act resulted in a serious consequence like death, serious bodily harm, endangering a person's life, or substantial property damage or interference with an essential service likely to result in such a serious harm; and, a *purpose clause*, which demands that the act (or omission) be committed "with the intention of intimidating the public ... with regard to its security ... or compelling a person, a government or ... an organization to do or to refrain from doing any act."[20]

Putting aside the section 7 offences (treaty offences), the remainder of Canada's *Criminal Code* terrorism offences are found in sections 83.02–83.04 and 83.18–83.23 and, as noted, rely on a connection to either a terrorist group or activity.[21] So, for example, it is a crime to participate in a terrorist group (section 83.18), or to facilitate terrorist activity (section 83.19), to finance a terrorist group or finance a terrorist activity (sections 83.02–83.04), to commit an offence for a terrorist group (section 83.20), to instruct someone to carry out an activity for a terrorist group (section 83.21), and so on.

Two general comments are apt here regarding the creation of these offences. First, as should be apparent, is that the majority of these offences are inchoate insofar as they seek to pre-empt violent criminal (terrorist)

18 *Ibid.*

19 *Ibid.*

20 *Ibid.* The three clauses are discussed in greater detail at: Michael Nesbitt, "Violent Crime, Hate Speech or Terrorism? How Canada Views and Prosecutes Far-Right Extremism (2001–2019)" (2021) 50:1 *Common Law World Review* 38 at 40.

21 The *Criminal Code*, above note 4, s 2 defines "terrorism offence."

acts before they take place—they allow for arrests while terrorist acts are still in the planning and financing stages. This approach is no accident. As then Justice Minister Anne McLellan asserted at the time of drafting:

> Perhaps the greatest gap in the current laws is created by the necessity of preventing terrorist acts from taking place. Our laws must reflect fully our intention to prevent terrorist activity, and currently they do not.... I think we all agree that Canadians have a right to expect their government to do everything it can to prevent such horrific acts as those of September 11 from happening in the first place.[22]

Second, of these inchoate offences, the financing ones were viewed with particular importance, in no small part because they were thought to implement directly mandates under both Resolution 1373[23] and the *International Convention for the Suppression of the Financing of Terrorism*.[24] Such offences filled holes in the Canadian law and were thought crucial to combatting terrorism; having said that, the role of TCL in shaping the Canadian focus should not be downplayed.[25]

In drafting the *ATA, 2001* Canada acknowledged that it had the tools to respond to mass attacks after the fact[26]—perpetrators could simply be

---

22 Canada, Parliament, House of Commons, Standing Committee on Justice and Human Rights, *Evidence*, 37th Parl, 1st Sess, No 49 (20 November 2001) at 1220 (Hon Anne McLellan).

23 *Res 1373*, above note 2 obliges states to punish "any person who participates in the financing, planning, preparation or perpetration of terrorist acts."

24 *International Convention for the Suppression of the Financing of Terrorism*, (1999) 2178 UNTS 197 [*Terrorist Financing Convention*]. For example, as Minister McLellan said at the time of drafting: "large parts of this legislation implement our obligations in relation to the UN conventions in relation to the suppression of terrorist bombings and the suppression of terrorist financing. Those two conventions were signed and we have to implement them." Section 83.02 is, in fact, essentially taken directly from the terrorism financing convention. See Canada, Parliament, Special Senate Committee on Bill C-36, *Evidence*, 37th Parl, 1st Sess (22 October 2001), online: https://sencanada.ca/en/Content/Sen/committee/371/sm36/01evb-e.

25 For an analysis of the transnational legal and political pressures on terrorist financing regime, as well as early insight into the regime more broadly, see Kevin E. Davis, "Cutting off the Flow of Funds to Terrorists: Whose Funds? Which Funds? Who Decides?" in Ronald J. Daniels, Patrick Macklem & Kent Roach, eds, *The Security of Freedom: Essays on Canada's Anti-Terrorism Bill* (Toronto: University of Toronto Press, 2002) at 299.

26 Kent Roach first persuasively made this argument in 2002. See Roach, *Consequences for Canada*, above note 3 at 21.

charged with murder, for example, which continues to attract Canada's most serious penalty of life in jail with no possibility of parole for twenty-five years—but what it lacked was a robust capacity to pre-empt such events and lay criminal charges against individuals that were still in the planning stages.

That said, a heretofore unrecognized trend has begun to emerge with respect to Canada's anti-terrorism criminal regime. Canada criminalized acts by direct reference to its international treaty obligations via section 7 of the *Criminal Code*, yet this direct incorporation of treaty crimes as terrorism offences in Canada has led to zero terrorism prosecutions. This is particularly surprising because Canada has arguably had the opportunity to target hostage taking, in particular, as terrorism,[27] but failed to do so.[28] In the case of *R v Ader*,[29] the prosecution did not seem even to mention that the section 279.1 charge of hostage taking seemingly met the *Criminal Code*'s definition of a terrorism offence as incorporated via section 7, thus requiring an aggravated sentence by virtue of section 718.2. By contrast, where Canada adopted what I will call "the spirit of its international obligations"—for example prioritizing the more vague and ephemeral obligation to prevent and punish terrorism—it has created and enforced a regime that has performed very well: Participation in a terrorist group (section 83.18 of the *Criminal Code*) remains Canada's most prosecuted terrorism offence (facilitation of a terrorist offence in section 83.19 is the third);[30] the prosecution record in terms of convictions has likewise been very strong;[31] and, the commitment to due process has been consistent with Canada's criminal regime more generally.

---

27 See *R v Ader*, 2017 ONSC 7052 [*Ader*].

28 For further discussion of this point and the *Ader* case, see Michael Nesbitt & Harman Nijjar, "Counting Terrorism Charges and Prosecutions in Canada Part I: What Does the Data Say?" *Intrepid Podcast* (17 June 2021), online: www.intrepidpodcast.com/blog/2021/6/15/counting-terrorism-charges-amp-prosecutions-in-canada-part-1-what-does-the-data-say.

29 *Ader*, above note 27.

30 See Michael Nesbitt & Dana Hagg, "An Empirical Study of Terrorism in Canada: Elucidating the Elements of the Offence" (2020) 57:3 *University of Alberta Law Review* 595 at 605.

31 See Michael Nesbitt, "An Empirical Study of Terrorism Charges and Terrorism Trials in Canada Between September 2001 and September 2018" (2019) 67 *Criminal Law Quarterly* 95 at 112 [Nesbitt, "Empirical Study"]. For an updated evaluation of the prosecution success rate in terrorism trials as of June 2021, see Michael Nesbitt & Harman Nijjar, "Counting Terrorism Charges and Prosecutions in Canada

What remains perplexing is Canada's approach to terrorist financing, which, as we saw, was amongst the most important set of offences. Yet the enforcement rate of the three terrorist financing offences remains abysmal by almost any measure,[32] with only two completed prosecutions as of the date of writing. One offender received one of the very lowest terrorism sentences for an adult in Canadian history,[33] and the other amounted to little more than an add-on final charge in *R v Khawaja*, Canada's first terrorism trial.[34] Ironically, both the *ISIL Regulations* and *Terrorism Regulations*, below, also primarily target financing activities, so Canada has most certainly — across three legal regimes — taken its transnational obligations to criminalize terrorist financing extremely, perhaps even uniquely, seriously. But the flip side of the coin is that Canada has been extremely underwhelming when it comes to enforcing such offences.[35] Why Canada has had so few prosecutions, despite ample evidence to suggest that terrorist financing is fairly widespread,[36] remains a mystery, one very much worthy of further study.

C. CANADA'S ANTI-TERRORISM LISTING REGIMES

As outlined in the Introduction, Canada's anti-terrorism listing regimes are located across three different regulations:[37] there is the *Criminal Code*

Part II: Trends in Terrorism Charges" *Intrepid Podcast* (24 June 2021), online: www.intrepidpodcast.com/blog/2021/6/24/counting-terrorism-charges-and-prosecutions-in-canada-part-2.

32 Nesbitt, "Empirical Study," above note 31 at 117–19.

33 *R v Thambaithurai*, 2010 BCSC 1949, aff'd 2011 BCCA 137.

34 *R v Khawaja*, 2012 SCC 69.

35 For an excellent evaluation of the terrorist financing that might have been charged in the Toronto 18 trials but never was, see Jessica Davis, "Financing the Toronto 18" (2021) 44:1 *Manitoba Law Journal* 197 at 197.

36 Nesbitt, "Empirical Study," above note 31 at 117–19; Canada, Parliament, Senate, Standing Committee on Banking, Trade and Commerce, *Follow the Money: Is Canada Making Progress in Combatting Money Laundering and Terrorist Financing? Not Really*, 41st Parl, 1st Sess (March 2013), online: https://sencanada.ca/content/sen/Committee/411/BANC/rep/rep10mar13-e.pdf.

37 The Government of Canada also subscribes to this three-part taxonomy for the criminal terrorism listing regimes: Global Affairs Canada, "Canadian Sanctions Relating to Terrorist Entities including Al-Qaida and the Taliban," online: www.international.gc.ca/world-monde/international_relations-relations_internationales/sanctions/terrorists-terroristes.aspx?lang=eng.

listing regime first created by the *ATA, 2001*, and then two so-called *UN Act* regulations, or listing regimes, those being the *ISIL Regulations* and the *Terrorism Regulations*. The former listing regime is created via regulation as authorized by the *Criminal Code*;[38] the latter two regulations are issued under authority of the *UN Act*, and maintained by Global Affairs Canada, though the regulatory (criminal, really) offences thereunder are prosecuted by the Public Prosecution Service of Canada just as with the *Criminal Code* regime. Each of these three regimes lists various entities[39] and criminalizes not the listed individuals or groups, but how others deal with them. In other words, the listing regimes do not criminalize mere membership; rather, they each place constraints on how others may engage with the groups or individuals, including restricting the transfer of funds to listed entities.

All three listing regimes will now be discussed in detail, below, starting with the *Criminal Code* regime.[40]

1) *Criminal Code* Listing Regime

As noted above, because Canada does not define terrorism and/or make it a discrete offence, it has a series of terrorism offences based on two general predicates, those being terrorist activity and terrorist group. What exactly constitutes a terrorist group (entity in the words of the *Criminal Code*) is then once again definitionally split in two. The first refers to what Forcese and West have aptly called "self-nominating" groups,[41] defined in the *Criminal Code* as "an entity that has as one or more of its purposes or activities facilitating or carrying out any terrorist activity."[42] Self-nominating groups must be proven in court to be terrorist groups, i.e., the prosecutor must prove beyond a reasonable doubt (BARD) that the self-nominating group has engaged in or facilitated terrorist activity, or is associated with other groups that have facilitated terrorism. Likely the best-known example of a self-nominating group in Canada is the

38 *Criminal Code Listings*, above note 5.

39 *Criminal Code*, above note 4, s 83.05. An entity is defined in the *Criminal Code* as: a person, group, trust, partnership or fund or an unincorporated association or organization.

40 For an excellent introduction into Canada's anti-terrorism listing regimes, see Craig Forcese & Leah West, *National Security Law*, 2d ed (Toronto: Irwin Law, 2021) at 184–203 and 216–24.

41 *Ibid* at 216.

42 *Criminal Code*, above note 4, s 83.05.

so-called Toronto 18, a group that came together to plan, broadly speaking, two sets of terrorist attacks in Toronto and Ottawa in early 2006.[43] The group — or by then two splinter groups — were disrupted in June 2006, and eleven individuals were eventually convicted of various terrorism offences associated with their actions in support of the self-nominating Toronto 18 group.[44]

The second manner in which the *Criminal Code* defines a terrorist group is as "a listed entity, and includes an association of such entities."[45] The listing of such groups draws heavily on the UN Security Council practice of doing the same, which was particularly prevalent at the time of enacting the *ATA, 2001*; indeed, for a time at least the *Criminal Code*'s listing regime was used to implement Canada's obligations under Resolution 1373 (as discussed in more detail, below). Such groups include widely recognized entities like ISIS (sometimes called ISIL), al-Qaida, the Taliban, and Hezbollah. Section 83.05 of the *Criminal Code* provides for the process of listing such entities.

The listing process begins with federal bureaucrats collecting and receiving from allies abroad both publicly available and secretly held information on such groups.[46] To justify a listing, such public and secret intelligence must demonstrate that there are "reasonable grounds to believe" that the entity has knowingly carried out, attempted to carry out, participated in, or facilitated a terrorist activity or that the entity has knowingly acted on behalf of, at the direction of, or in association with, an entity who commits any of the former.[47] Based on that information, the minister of public safety will make a recommendation to Cabinet, which in turn makes the ultimate listing decision, all on the "reasonable grounds" standard. The government has tended to provide an extremely

43 For a detailed assessment of the Toronto 18, see, generally, "Canadian Terror: Multi-Disciplinary Perspectives on the Toronto 18 Terrorism Trials" (2021) 44:1 *Manitoba Law Journal*, a special issue edited by Michael Nesbitt, Kent Roach & David C. Hofmann.

44 See Michael Nesbitt et al, "Introduction to Canadian Terror" in *ibid* at xx–xxi.

45 *Criminal Code*, above note 4, s 83.05(1).

46 The Government of Canada provides a nice overview of the listing process. See Public Safety Canada, "About the Listing Process," online: www.publicsafety.gc.ca/cnt/ntnl-scrt/cntr-trrrsm/lstd-ntts/bt-lstng-prcss-en.aspx.

47 *Criminal Code*, above note 4, s 83.05(1).

brief description of some—though presumably far from all—of the evidence it has considered to support a listing.[48]

Once the listing is on the books,[49] it is important to remember that being a member of a listed entity is not a crime; however, any non-trivial support for a listed entity may be a terrorism offence. All listed entities have the right to appeal the listing by way of requesting that the minister of public safety re-evaluate the listing. The group then has the right to appeal to the Federal Court if either the minister denies the listed group's request or ninety days elapse without a response.[50] All listings are reviewed after five years and every five years hence.[51] There is a further provision in the *Criminal Code* for "mistaken identities," which allows the minister to issue a certificate to an entity, clarifying any mistakes or misunderstandings (for instance, that a group in Canada is not, in fact, the one listed).[52]

Procedurally, the first problem with this listing regime is the lack of notice and opportunity to respond given to a listed group in advance of the public listing. Kent Roach has argued that such listing without notice "may be too late for a group ..." because of both the stigma of a listing and the fact that the listing will cut off funding and support for an organization, even if they were wrongly listed and can show that to be the case.[53] More fundamentally, Forcese and West have made the case that because of the lack of a notice requirement—and/or without some sort of procedure to give notice as a matter of practice—and because of Supreme Court jurisprudence that finds notice and comment obligations under section 7 of the *Charter*,[54] "[t]here is reason to believe ... that the listing process in section 83.05 is constitutionally suspect."[55]

48 For a complete schedule of listed groups and the government-provided justifications therefor, see: Public Safety Canada, "Currently Listed Entities," online: www.publicsafety.gc.ca/cnt/ntnl-scrt/cntr-trrrsm/lstd-ntts/crrnt-lstd-ntts-en.aspx.

49 See *ibid.*

50 *Criminal Code*, above note 4, s 83.05(2) & (3).

51 *Ibid*, s 83.05(8.1).

52 *Ibid*, s 83.07.

53 For a critique of the lack of notice to affected groups, see Roach, *Consequences for Canada*, above note 3 at 37; Craig Forcese & Kent Roach, "Yesterday's Law: Terrorist Group Listing in Canada" (2018) 30:2 *Terrorism and Political Violence* 259 especially at 271–73 [Forcese & Roach, "Yesterday's Law"].

54 See *Suresh*, above note 15 at paras 122–23.

55 Forcese & West, above note 40 at 220–21.

The due process problems extend to the process of challenging a delisting. The government releases very little information on the basis for and evidence upon which the listing is justified. As such, listed entities may not know much about the case to meet—the evidence and intelligence to which they must respond to justify a delisting. That concern is rectified somewhat by the fact that listed entities may subsequently appeal for delisting[56] to a designated (security-cleared) judge of the Federal Court, where Crown disclosure obligations will kick in and there will be more information given to the applicant about the case to meet. But this right of appeal is attenuated by the *Criminal Code*, which sets out the procedures by which the judge is to review the listing decision. In particular, the judge is first to

> examine, in private, any security or criminal intelligence reports considered in the making of the decision … and may … hear all or part of that evidence or information in the absence of the applicant and any counsel representing the applicant, if the judge is of the opinion that the disclosure of the information would injure national security or endanger the safety of any person.[57]

Moreover, the judge may also "receive into evidence anything that, in the opinion of the judge, is reliable and appropriate, even if it would not otherwise be admissible under Canadian law, and may base his or her decision on that evidence."[58] The applicant then has a right to "a statement summarizing the information available to the judge," though of course that will be sanitized to exclude any information that would "in the judge's opinion, injure national security or endanger the safety of any person."[59]

Perhaps more fundamentally for an aggrieved entity, even before one gets to the court challenge, gathering the funding and support necessary to legally challenge a listing will likely be quite difficult.[60] Once an entity is listed, the *Criminal Code* requires that financial institutions and other Canadian actors or actors in Canada must disclose property believed to

56 *Criminal Code*, above note 4 at s 83.05(5).

57 *Ibid*, s 83.05(6).

58 *Ibid*, s 83.05(6.1).

59 *Ibid*, s 83.05(6).

60 For a pointed critique of the lack of notice to affected groups, see Roach, *Consequences for Canada*, above note 3 at 37.

be owned by a terrorist group,[61] continually self-audit to determine if they are in possession or control of such property,[62] and institute asset freezes, property seizures, and the like.[63] These obligations can lead and have led to what is called debanking, where access to the financial markets is cut off, and other denials of services occur. As Jessica Davis has noted, "these individuals [associated with a listed group] would find it difficult, if not impossible, to obtain a bank account, conduct financial transactions (including purchasing a house), both in Canada and abroad."[64] While this is a serious consequence, at least as concerns a legal challenge to a listing there is a provision in the *Criminal Code* that provides for the freeing of funds for a court challenge.[65] However, there are no concomitant obligations on financial institutions, for example, to release property and funds. In any event, how such an administrative public authorization would be received by a private lawyer, bank, etc., and how quickly and easily the authorization would come and the money would be released, is extremely opaque: it depends almost wholly on what private actors not overseen by government choose to do.

This concern is not purely theoretical: the only delisting appeal to date appears to have fallen apart when the government refused to unfreeze the applicant group's property to pay its legal fees.[66] Though some of the group's lawyers agreed to act *pro bono*, which meant that the Court did not address the Catch-22 in which the applicant found itself,[67] the delisting application nevertheless dissolved at this time, meaning the entity remained listed without court challenge at least in part due to an inability to access funds.[68]

61 *Criminal Code*, above note 4, s 83.10.

62 *Ibid*, s 83.11.

63 *Ibid*, ss 83.08, 83.13 & 83.14.

64 See Jessica Davis, "Canada Can't Continue to Give the Proud Boys and Other Extremist Groups a Free Pass" *Globe and Mail* (11 January 2021), online: www.theglobeandmail.com/opinion/article-canada-cant-continue-to-give-the-proud-boys-and-other-extremist-groups.

65 *Criminal Code*, above note 4, s 83.09.

66 See Darryl Greer, "Canadian Charity Fights to Remove 'Terrorist' Label" *Courthouse News Service* (9 March 2017), online: www.courthousenews.com/canadian-charity-fights-remove-terrorist-label/; *International Relief Fund for the Afflicted and Needy (Canada) v Canada*, 2015 FC 435 [*IRFAN*].

67 See *IRFAN*, *ibid* at para 4.

68 For a brief discussion of this point see Forcese & West, above note 40 at 222.

Independent of the due process concerns, it is not evident that the *Criminal Code* listing regime is terribly effective in practice, at least in terms of supporting criminal enforcement/prosecutions.[69] These effectiveness concerns start with the very foundation of the listing regime, that the government must collect evidence to support a listing on a reasonable grounds standard.[70] The practical problem is that, if someone is charged with an offence that relies on the terrorist group predicate, then proving that one funded or participated in a terrorist group theoretically becomes an element of the offence. In Canadian criminal law, all elements of the offence must be proven on a BARD standard—a standard distinctly more onerous than reasonable grounds. So, the prosecutor will have to prove the existence of a terrorist group on a BARD standard, but the listing is completed on the reasonable grounds standard.

In practice, the Ontario Superior Court of Justice rejected this standard of proof concern in *R v Hersi*, though in so doing the court found that it could reject the complaint precisely because the Crown still had to prove in court that the group has or will engage in terrorist activity.[71] Thus, the reality is that when cases go to trial (as opposed to being resolved by guilty pleas), prosecutors do not rely on listings *per se*. Instead, they furnish proof sufficient to justify BARD that a group meets the necessary grounds of being a terrorist entity, independent of the list. In this way, it is difficult to see how the terrorist listing provides much legal assistance when it comes to supporting criminal prosecutions.

Of course, the listings will still have a potentially significant effect. As noted above, listings will lead to debanking, asset, property, and service freezes, and make everyday life (and certainly funding) much more difficult for listed entities and associated individuals. However, the effectiveness of these elements of the regime must be balanced with associated due process concerns, namely, that listed groups have never been proven in

69 For an evaluation of the history and use of Canada's listing regimes, see generally Forcese & Roach, "Yesterday's Law," above note 53.

70 For a seminal and thorough critique of the standard of proof, see (now Justice) David Paciocco's article, "Constitutional Casualties of September 11: Limiting the Legacy of the *Anti-terrorism Act*" (2002) 16 *Supreme Court Law Review* (2d) 185.

71 *R v Hersi*, 2014 ONSC 1217 at paras 22–24.

court to be terrorist groups, are suspected to be so on secret evidence on a reasonable grounds basis never publicly articulated, and court challenges of the listings will be extremely difficult and rare at best. As a result, the effectiveness of the regime stems from private-sector operators working in the shadow of the law—without much in the way of legal guidance or supervision—implementing on their terms little-understood obligations related to asset freezes, processes that are unlikely ever to be litigated. I say "in the shadow of the law" because although banks, for example, will be implementing what they see as their legal obligations in debanking a "Charles Smith," there is no oversight or review of that process; if the government does not provide much in the way of identifying details about which "Charles Smith" is listed, then all individuals named Charles Smith could be debanked, and the process for unravelling that without serious economic damage is unknown. Put simply, the whole process is implemented because of law, but is executed and operates in its shadows, ungoverned and unsupervised.

We are left here with due process concerns regarding the listing and delisting challenge regime, as well as efficacy concerns, at least as concerns how listings can and should support criminal prosecutions (keeping in mind this whole regime is under the *Criminal Code*, and thus primarily criminal in intent). Where the listing regime seems to be efficacious—with respect to cutting off access to funds for listed groups—due process concerns are heightened, because while the obligations are legal, the implementation is taking place in the shadow of the law. The response to any such criticism may well be that hard choices must be made in national security and that, in this case, Canada must not forget that this *Criminal Code* listing regime is a direct outgrowth of international legal obligations. But the relationship between domestic law and transnational tools is an uneasy one; it is not obvious that Canada must implement its international obligations in a way that demands such a list, even if it would seem that the list—and the private-sector asset freezes and property seizures that flow from it—are the most efficacious aspect of Canada's anti-terrorism "criminal" regime. In the end, Canada has taken a rather formalistic approach to implementing its transnational obligations—where the UNSC created a list to criminalize groups and fight terrorist financing, so did Canada—but it is the formal letter-of-the-law copying of the transnational approach that has bred both due process and, in terms of prosecutions, efficacy concerns.

2) The (Two) *UN Act* Regulations

Both *UN Act* regulations, those being the *ISIL Regulations* and the *Suppression of Terrorism Regulations*, were formally issued—and are updated—under the authority of Canada's *UN Act*, which explains why we call them the *UN Act* regulations.[72] Canada's *UN Act* is, *inter alia*, the vehicle that both requires and allows Canada to enact UNSC decisions into domestic law (though Canada may comply with UN obligations in other ways, or through other legislation as well). As succinctly described by Forcese and West, the *UN Act* "empowers the Governor in Council ... to make orders and regulations that appear to it 'to be necessary or expedient' to implement a measure called for by the UN Security Council.... Under the *United Nations Act* itself, a violation of these regulations is a crime, attracting a substantial penalty of up to ten years' imprisonment."[73]

Canada actually has a host of regulations issued under the *UN Act*. Most such *UN Act* regulations sanction geographically defined areas (for example, a country like Iran). However, the *ISIL Regulations* and *Terrorism Regulations* differ from the others in that they both sanction transnational groups as well as individuals, and that they focus on terrorism or terrorist groups rather than nation-state wrongdoing.

a) *ISIL Regulations*

Canada's *ISIL Regulations* date to 1999 and are the first of the three terrorism listing regimes to be created. In its original incarnation it was simply called the *Afghanistan Regulations* because it was issued in response to UNSC Resolution 1267, which targeted the Taliban (the *de facto* government in Afghanistan at the time) for harbouring "international terrorists" including Osama Bin Laden and his associates, who had shortly before been indicted by the United States for the 7 August 1998 bombings of US Embassies in Nairobi, Kenya, and Dar es Salaam, Tanzania.[74] Under Resolution 1267, the Security Council had created a listing subcommittee of the UNSC,[75] which then recommended individuals for listing, and in turn *required* governments to do the same.[76] The *Taliban Regulations* were

72 *UN Act*, above note 7.

73 Forcese & West, above note 40 at 199.

74 UN Doc S/RES/1267 (1999) [*Res 1267*].

75 See *ibid.*

76 Forcese & West, above note 40 at 185.

then amended in 2001 to include al-Qaida after the Security Council had done the same the previous calendar year, courtesy of UNSC Resolution 1333.[77] By 2011, the UNSC updated the Sanctions Committee via Resolution 1988,[78] which both targeted Taliban affiliates (though not the Taliban) and ensured that a "Consolidated List" was subject to review of listing, delisting, and other procedures by Member States.

However, over time the Canadian regulations failed to keep pace with the Listing Committee. As Forcese and West assert with respect to the law as it was in late 2019 or early 2020, "the regulations seem now to persist as a means of listing persons and entities named by the UN committees, but not covered by Canada's terrorist group *Criminal Code* listing system.... It would be awkward and potentially confusing to double-list entities under two sanctions regimes."[79] Put another way, the *Criminal Code* regime became the predominant forum for listing terrorist groups in Canada; those that were not listed under the *Criminal Code* but by the UN Committee "blacklists" were then reserved for the *UN Act* regimes.

However, this explanation is arguably incomplete and in any event leaves open many questions, a situation that was only exacerbated in 2020 when the Canadian regulations were again updated to become, finally, the *Regulations Implementing UN Resolutions on Taliban, ISIL (Da'esh) and Al-Qaida*.[80] Thus was born Canada's *ISIL Regulations* in direct response to—and in implementation of—a series of UNSC resolutions wherein the body acted under Chapter VII of the UN Charter. This most recent update, along with another in 2019, seems to have accomplished three major tasks.

First, ISIL was added to the regulations, belatedly reflecting domestically changes that had already been made to the international listings. As such, proscribed behaviour historically associated with the Taliban, Taliban affiliates, and al-Qaida—proscriptions on supporting or financing these groups, for example—were extended to ISIL.

Second, Canada removed its own schedule of listed entities and individuals and now simply refers generically to the Taliban, ISIL, and al-Qaida, thus ensuring that Canada's list would not again become out of date, i.e., ensuring that there was no need to add names or entities each

77 UN Doc S/RES/1333 (2000) [*Res 1333*].
78 UN Doc S/RES/1988 (2011) [*Res 1988*].
79 Forcese & West, above note 40 at 200.
80 See *ISIL Regs*, above note 8.

time the United Nations did so. Again, just as with the listed individuals and entities, the regime does not criminalize the groups *per se*.

Instead, for example, the *ISIL Regulations* now: contemplate a duty to determine whether one is dealing in property associated with or held by the Taliban, ISIL, or al-Qaida; impose disclosure obligations for those dealing with property associated with or held by the three terrorist groups whereby they must inform CSIS and/or the RCMP;[81] require Canadians or those on its territory not to deal in such property (or supply it) in the first place,[82] or to supply, deal in, ship, or assist in the transport of arms or related materials to these groups;[83] and so on. Put more simply, the regime puts a ban on engaging in certain prescribed ways with individuals within these groups and holds those individuals criminally responsible for their support.

In essence, we are left with a blanket ban on certain activities associated with supporting these three international terrorist groups just as exists in the *Criminal Code*—and, to be clear, just as is almost certainly already covered by the participation, facilitation, or financing offences in the *Criminal Code*. Having said that, the *ISIL Regulation*'s historical connection to the UN blacklists—and of course the update to bring Canada's regulations into greater conformity with these lists—suggests the possibility of a sort of list by proxy, or at least intention to wave vaguely at the UN lists, even if Canada has formally moved away from individual listings in this regime.

Third, evidently because Canada is not officially listing individuals and entities under this updated *ISIL Regulation*, certain due process protections that were added in 2006 to allow for and govern legal challenges of listings were removed.[84] So, individuals may still apply for special exemptions, whereby a "person that wishes to engage in any activity that is prohibited under these Regulations must, before doing so, apply to the Minister in writing for a certificate to exempt the activity from the application of the Regulations."[85] The minister may then approve a certificate to engage in the behaviour, so long as they are satisfied that "the Security

81 *Ibid*, s 8(1).

82 *Ibid*, s 2.

83 See *ibid* at ss 3 and 5.

84 For a previous version of the regulations, see for example, *UN Al-Qaida and Taliban Regulations*, SOR/99-444, ss 5.3 and 5.4.

85 *ISIL Regs*, above note 8, s 9(1).

Council did not intend that the activity be prohibited" or that it otherwise has approved the activity.[86] However, because no specific subgroups or individuals are listed by Canada, there are no longer procedures for the challenge of improperly listed individuals other than in cases of mistaken identity;[87] the procedures associated with judicial review of such challenges, which had been similar to the *Criminal Code*'s procedures, have similarly been removed.

Returning to the assertion by Forcese and West that it would be "awkward" and "confusing" to list entities across two regulations—*ISIL* and the *Criminal Code*—these most recent updates seem to bring this concern into stark relief: now, the *ISIL Regulations* proscribe conduct associated with "a person associated with the Taliban"[88] or ISIL or al-Qaida,[89] and the *Criminal Code* list includes the Taliban, al-Qaida, and ISIL. Plus, both regimes prohibit similar or the same activities associated with these groups—in particular they bar financing activities associated with them, as well as similar activities that would likely fall under the section 83.18 "participation in a terrorist group" offence under the *Criminal Code*. The *Criminal Code* regime, of course, is much broader than the participation and financing associated with terrorist group offences, and thus its criminal proscriptions extend well beyond the *ISIL Regulations*, though again how any activity captured under the *ISIL Regulations* is not also captured under the *Criminal Code* is unclear.

In the end, we must ask why the groups (or perhaps associates thereof) are essentially listed twice across two legal documents. What would cause the government to choose to pursue criminal (enforcement) proceedings using one and not the other, and particularly to choose the lesser-known and narrower *ISIL Regulations*? (This cross-listing is a long-standing problem for the *UN Act* regime more broadly: Canada has "Iran Regulations" under its domestic sanctions legislation, the *Special Economics Measures Act*, as well as under the *UN Act* regime, for example.)

It is also confusing why the government thought it necessary to include provisions in the *Criminal Code* for the admission of foreign intelligence to support prosecutions, freezing as well as seizure and restraint of

86 *Ibid*, s 9(2).

87 *Ibid*, s 11.

88 *Ibid*, ss 2(a)(i) and 7(a)(i).

89 *Ibid*, ss 2(a)(ii) and 7(a)(ii).

property, a broader ministerial exemption for activities, one that is not tied to the Security Council,[90] and so on, but not under the *ISIL Regulations*.

Put simply, the *Criminal Code*'s regime is far more robust and comprehensive in terms of both due process and the quality and quantity of the procedural enforcement mechanisms available to a prosecutor. In the end, Canadians are surely left to wonder why we have two regimes to accomplish similar tasks and more pointedly why the government would ever enforce the *ISIL Regulations* when a more robust, more legally sound option with better due process protections and more enforcement options is available under the *Criminal Code*. The question and result may indeed be distinctly "awkward" and "confusing," but the answer is fairly clear: it makes little sense to enforce the *ISIL Regulations* as opposed to the *Criminal Code* regime. Perhaps for this very reason the *ISIL Regulations* have never been enforced in Canada—there are zero attempted prosecutions to date.

In practice then, the *ISIL Regulations* serve only as a direct, if crude and formalistic, implementation of Canada's international obligations,[91] one that is unlikely ever to be (successfully) enforced; as such, even though they represent a formal implementation of international obligations, they fail to implement the substance, or spirit, of those international obligations, that being to actually take action to deter and enforce against terrorist financing and similar behaviour. The irony, of course, is that the spirit of these international obligations is already arguably being met in substance by a *Criminal Code* offences regime that is both enforceable and has been enforced—that has targeted those inspired by or associated with ISIL and al-Qaida.

b) The *Suppression of Terrorism Regulations*

The 9/11 attacks and the UNSC response thereto was likewise the impetus for the *UN Suppression of Terrorism Regulations*. Its origin dates to

90 *Criminal Code*, above note 4, s 83.06 for admission of foreign intelligence; s 83.12 for freezing of assets; s 83.013 for seizure and restraint; s 83.09 for ministerial exemption.

91 As Global Affairs Canada says on its website explaining the *UN Act* terrorism regimes, "These regulations, as amended, implement in Canadian domestic law the binding elements of United Nations Security Council Resolution 1267 (1999) and its successor resolutions." See online: www.international.gc.ca/world-monde/international_relations-relations_internationales/sanctions/terrorists-terroristes.aspx?lang=eng.

Resolution 1373 of 28 September 2001, which imposed, via chapter VII of the UN Charter, the obligations of the *Terrorist Financing Convention*.[92] The idea was once again to create a list of individuals associated with terrorism broadly, and then to proscribe the financing of said individuals (just as the *Criminal Code* subsequently did).

The instrument allows for either the unilateral listing of an individual, or the domestic listing based on UNSC Resolutions. In either case, a minister must first have "reasonable grounds to believe" that the person:

> (a) has carried out, attempted to carry out, participated in or facilitated the carrying out of a terrorist activity;
> (b) is controlled directly or indirectly by any person conducting any of the activities set out in paragraph (a); or
> (c) is acting on behalf of, or at the direction of, or in association with any person conducting any of the activities set out in paragraph (a).[93]

The *Terrorism Regulations* then criminalize financial transactions—including providing or collecting funds,[94] dealing in property, or facilitating financial transactions[95]—between Canadians or persons in Canada and listed individuals; thus, the list is used as a mechanism to attach to criminal offences, much as it is used in the *Criminal Code* (and as was used in the *ISIL Regulations* before individuals were removed and replaced with three groups). As with each of the other listing regimes, banks and other financial institutions have an ongoing duty to monitor and report on whether they are in possession of property owned or held by a listed person or associate of a group,[96] and to report to CSIS and/or the RCMP if they find themselves in control of such property.[97]

Likely because Canada continues to maintain a list associated with the *Terrorism Regulations*,[98] the instrument also includes several due process protections similar to those that were discussed above with respect to the *Criminal Code* listing regime (and similar again to what used to

92 *Terrorist Financing Convention*, above note 24.

93 *Suppression of Terrorism Regs*, above note 6, s 2(1).

94 *Ibid*, s 3.

95 *Ibid*, ss 4 and 6.

96 *Ibid*, s 7.

97 *Ibid*, s 8.

98 Though the list is moribund, not having been updated since 2006; see Forcese & West, above note 40 at 201.

be associated with the *ISIL Regulations* prior to recent updates and particularly the removal of the list of entities). For example, the *Terrorism Regulations* offer a mechanism to appeal listings and for judicial review[99] similar to that which exists under the *Criminal Code* as well as a similar procedure for the admission of secret evidence.[100] As with the *ISIL Regulations* and *Criminal Code* regimes, there are also mechanisms to appeal based on mistaken identity or that an activity was never intended to be prohibited by the Security Council (the latter of which is not, of course, included in the *Criminal Code* regime).[101]

In any event, the reality is that within months of promulgation, the *Suppression of Terrorism Regulations* was largely overtaken — and duplicated — by the *ATA, 2001*'s new *Criminal Code* financing and listing provisions. Once again, we must ask what the *Terrorism Regulations* provide that the others do not, and why in particular one would ever choose to use them as the basis of an enforcement action as opposed to the arguably broader and more robust — and better understood — *Criminal Code* regime. It seems the answer is again clear: there has never been a prosecution under this regulation[102] and there likely never will be. It seems to exist to comply with a rather rigid and formalistic understanding of how obligations "legislated" by the UNSC must be domestically implemented in a format similar to that used by the Council.[103] As Global Affairs describes the regulations on its website, "The Suppression of Terrorism Regulations,

99 *Suppression of Terrorism Regs*, above note 6, ss 2.1 & 2.2.

100 *Ibid*, s 2.3.

101 *Ibid*, s 11.

102 One minor caveat of sorts is worth noting: in the case of Liban Hussein, an Ottawa resident indicted in Massachusetts for purportedly operating an unlicensed money transfer operation, the Canadian government used the *Suppression of Terrorism Regulations* to show so-called double criminality — that a similar crime existed in both the United States and Canada — to allow for the extradition of Hussein. The case eventually collapsed, Mr. Hussein's name was removed from the Canadian list, and an undisclosed amount of compensation was paid to Mr. Hussein. See Forcese & West, above note 40 at 202–3 referring to Jake Rupert, "Government Pays Off Victim of Terror Smear: Ottawa Man Was Arrested, His Business Ruined" *The Ottawa Citizen* (2 October 2003) A1.

103 As Global Affairs Canada describes on its website, the *Terrorism Regulations* exist to "implement in Canadian domestic law the binding elements of the United Nations Security Council Resolution 1373 (2001)." See online: www.international.gc.ca/world-monde/international_relations-relations_internationales/sanctions/terrorists-terroristes.aspx?lang=eng.

as amended, implement in Canadian domestic law the binding elements of United Nations Security Council Resolution 1373 (2001)." Little more needs be said. The irony again is that the spirit of these international obligations has largely or completely been met in substance by more robust (and enforceable) domestic criminal law provisions in the *Criminal Code*, the prosecution of which needs neither the *Terrorism Regulations* list nor the *Criminal Code* list.

c) Due Process and Efficacy under the *ISIL* and *Terrorism Regulations*

The UNSC Resolution 1267 and 1373 regimes differ from traditional sanctions regimes—whether those be Canadian or UN sanctions mandated by the Security Council—in that they target listed individuals and/or groups as opposed to state targets that were traditionally identified due to, for example, their involvement with the shipment of illicit weapons. By contrast, the Resolution 1267 regime instead "required that governments ... bar financial transactions by their nationals or those within their territories with the listed persons,"[104] freeze the assets of listed persons, and bar cross-border travel of such persons (in practice, no fly lists), etc.[105]

From the beginning, this put Canada in a rather peculiar and arguably difficult position. On the one hand, Canada's obligation under international and domestic law was to implement the UNSC resolutions, and so it did. At one level, regardless of the flaws with the international regime, Canada's choice to issue *UN Act* regulations was a matter of respect for both international law and for Canada's obligations thereunder. Canada's domestic implementation also signalled its commitment to engaging in good faith with the international system through the United Nations and its most powerful body, the Security Council, and to tackling transnational terrorism in a multilateral, cooperative fashion. It is not every state that takes the time to directly, clearly, and transparently implement its obligations under international law in such a deliberate and formal fashion.

On the other hand, under Resolutions 1267 and later 1333[106] (and then later still under 1988[107]) as well as through 1373, the UN was acting in a quasi-judicial way by, essentially, blacklisting individuals associated with

104 Forcese & West, above note 40 at 185.

105 See *Res 1267*, above note 74; *Res 1333*, above note 77.

106 *Res 1333*, *ibid.*

107 *Res 1988*, above note 78.

various international terrorist groups and then requiring the domestic criminalization of support for these same (internationally) listed individuals. The result was a series of conspicuous due process concerns that arose almost immediately after the Security Council passed its resolutions: the basis for listings under domestic law was handed down from the Security Council, yet that basis was often unknown to implementing states, meaning for example that asset freezes (for example, on mortgage payments) were implemented with nothing more than a name appearing on an international (and in Canada, Canadian) list.[108] Because the private sector would be responsible for implementing asset freezes such as those to bank accounts or risk criminal sanction themselves, they would bear the majority of the cost of implementing a regime with little information or assistance from the government as to whom, precisely, they were targeting. And, because countries like Canada offered little more than a name on a list, the lists risked targeting (and debanking, and preventing from flying) everyone who shared a name with (or had a similar name to) one listed. There was (and is) the risk of serious individual reputation damage, not only for being on the list, but for sharing the name of someone on the list.[109] Moreover, the criteria for listing were unclear,[110] meaning that the basis for the listing—and the accusations to which the individual might respond—were likewise opaque, even after efforts at the Security Council to add greater due process to listing and delisting procedures.[111] Finally, how one would, in practice, afford and mount a challenge to a listing has become only slightly less unclear over time.[112]

108 For an evaluation of these concerns in the Canadian context, see *Abdelrazik v Canada (Minister of Foreign Affairs)*, 2009 FC 580 [*Abdelrazik*].

109 See the International Helsinki Federation for Human Rights report, *Anti-terrorism Measures, Security and Human Rights: Developments in Europe, Central Asia and North America in the Aftermath of September 11* (April 2003) at 130.

110 For more on this and associated due process concerns, see *ibid* especially at 130.

111 Perhaps most famously, this became a point of criticism by the European Court of Justice (ECJ) in the case of *Yassin Abdullah Kadi and Al Barakaat International Foundation v Council of the EU and Commission of the EC* (ECJ Judgement), Cases Joined C-402/5 and C-415/05, 3 September 2008 [*Kadi*]. In that case, the ECJ found serious due process shortcomings, starting with the impossibility of knowing the case against a listed individual. See paras 345–47. In Canada, see also *Abdelrazik*, above note 108 at para 43.

112 This was a pointed criticism early on by the UN High Level Panel, *A More Secure World*, UN Doc A/59/565 (2004) at para 152. See also *Abdelrazik*, above note 108 at paras 51–53.

The due process concerns, coupled with the very real threat that EU states could not participate in the regimes after the European Court of Justice's now-famous decision in *Kadi* in 2008,[113] led to a series of real changes in the listing regimes, including the appointment of an Ombudsperson under Resolution 1267 for complaints and to review delistings, new standards for listings, and greater due process in delistings.[114] But in a way all of this mattered less for Canada for two reasons. First, by June 2006 Canada had created an appeal mechanism for listed individuals under each of its regimes; of course, by 2020, this appeal mechanism was absent from the *Taliban, ISIL (Da'esh) and Al-Qaida Regulations*, but so was the listing of particular individuals or entities (though again how Canada was incorporating international lists remains unclear). Second, the overlap between the regulations and the *Criminal Code* regime, which has existed since the beginning, makes it difficult to figure how the regulations would ever be enforced and, even if they were, whether their more lax due process guarantees and more limited enforcement options would ever make them attractive alternatives. Third, and perhaps flowing from point two, Canada has never enforced the regulations, so there has never been much need—or, due to their esoteric nature, much pressure—to question their substantive value.

The end result is that Canada continues to be a good actor in meeting its international obligations in form and letter of the law, but does not provide the legal architecture including due process protections seemingly necessary to enforce said obligations. In the result, we see that Canada's commitment to transnational terrorism listing regimes—and its peculiar national approach to implementing many international legal obligations—is a tangled web of transnational law and domestic law, of specific international obligations and pressures coupled with complexities around enacting and enforcing them, of good intentions alongside formalistic solutions and, in the end, very little in the way of enforcement.

113 *Kadi*, above note 111.

114 For a clear, general overview of the updated process, see Forcese & West, above note 40 at 189–90.

D. CONCLUSIONS

There is little doubt that TCL has had a profound effect on Canada's anti-terrorism criminal regime. It was Canada's transnational obligations that pressured it to act legislatively and decisively to criminalize terrorism in a variety of ways. These obligations likewise influenced how Canada chose to define terrorist activity rather than terrorism in general; they caused Canada to focus first and foremost on financing and inchoate offences; and, this transnational pressure was the spark that ignited all three of Canada's terrorist listing regimes.

But whereas TCL has greatly contributed to legislative enactments, which together create a robust criminal anti-terrorism regime in Canada, much of that regime remains largely or completely unenforced. Ironically, the more formalistic the implementation of international obligations—the more Canada seems to have copied the approach or directly implemented the scheme from the transnational to the domestic—the greater the concerns we see with the substance, both in terms of questionable due process protections and how the formal terms of the scheme can be enforced within the bounds of the broader Canadian legal and enforcement context.

Overall, it would seem that Canada is better served by focusing on the spirit of its TCL obligations in creating a substantively robust domestic regime, rather than focusing on the specifics of an international legal regime and a direct line to a Canadian replica, as it did with the *Terrorism Regulations*. In still other cases, including in the example of terrorist financing, perhaps Canada would be well served simply by demonstrating the same commitment to enforcement as it did to ensuring that said offences were formally on the books.

III

THE PROBLEMS *of* JURISDICTION

six

Making Sense of Extraterritoriality Jurisprudence: Heuristic Pro-forum Biases and the Need for an Algorithmic Approach

CHRISTOPHER RAM*

A. INTRODUCTION

This chapter, the first of two by me, seeks to point out a problem in Canadian jurisprudence concerning the limits of jurisdiction in cases with transnational and extraterritorial aspects. The following chapter discusses possible statutory and judicial responses that might address this problem.

Legal reasoning usually combines *algorithmic* reasoning, in which the selection and application of principles and rules is itself rule based, with *heuristic* reasoning. Heuristics, sometimes described as "common sense," "mental shortcuts," or "rules of thumb," generate assumptions, which are applied, often unconsciously, to reach conclusions in complex scenarios where information is incomplete or uncertain.[1] Heuristics are essential to complex legal reasoning and decision-making, but they become unreliable when the assumptions extend beyond the factual contexts in which they were developed, which frequently occurs when heuristics based on the

---

* The author was, at the time of writing, Legal Counsel with Justice Canada. Views expressed herein are those of the author personally and are not intended to reflect the views or positions of the Government of Canada or any department or agency thereof.

1 See Cass Sunstein, "Moral Heuristics and Moral Framing" (2004) 88 *Minnesota Law Review* 1556, and Jeffrey Rachlinski, "Heuristics, Biases and Philosophy" (2008) 43:4 *Tulsa Law Review* 865.

laws and legal cultures of one state are applied to parties or events that arise in another.

Over time, conscious and unconscious heuristics that predominantly favour forum state law and jurisdiction produce cumulative pro-forum biases in jurisprudence. These then clash with algorithmic heuristic interpretive principles intended to preserve parliamentary supremacy and limit judicial discretion in extraterritorial matters. Judges are required to presume that domestic law is intended to conform with international law[2] and not to have extraterritorial application unless the legislature itself clearly says otherwise,[3] but pro-forum biases produce inconsistent cases that apply the presumption, create arbitrary exceptions, or on occasion, simply ignore it. This is a problem because it shifts both the exclusive authority of Parliament to make extraterritorial laws and the executive authority of ministers over foreign policy into the hands of independent judges.

The solutions proposed in the next chapter include judicial and statutory changes to reinforce the presumption against extraterritoriality as a fairly hard limit on judicial discretion, to allow less discretion for heuristic "common sense" reasoning, and choosing among rules based on pro-forum biases. Drafting conventions should require clear and consistent language whenever extraterritorial application is intended and silence when it is not. Reliance on clear language would also ensure that international law and foreign policy implications and safeguards were duly considered and documented during the legislative process. Apart from reinforcing judicial independence and the superior roles of Parliament and ministers over extraterritorial matters, this would distinguish between substantive jurisprudence that evolves differently for constitutional, criminal, and other domestic substantive questions, and jurisdictional cases that should apply the same territorial limits to all Canadian laws.

B. JURISDICTION AND ITS DISCONTENTS

Questions of jurisdiction[4] are fundamentally different from other issues of domestic law. Domestic reasoning, principles of law, and heuristic

---

2 *R v Hape*, 2007 SCC 26 at paras 53–54 [*Hape*].

3 See cases listed in note 14 below.

4 "Jurisdiction" creates other limits on domestic law and judicial authority, but references herein are only to limits based on national sovereignty and territoriality at international law.

assumptions are unreliable in extraterritoriality cases, where they consistently favour extending forum jurisdiction and law. Extensions may occasionally be justified, but in most cases subjective heuristic reasoning creates risks and rule of law problems.

Risks of conflict with foreign law and sovereignty are magnified by the fact that forum judges assert sovereign-state authority, but do so in strict isolation from legislative and executive accountability and everyday carriage of the state's broader diplomacy and foreign policy interests. Judicial independence, forum-based litigation structures, and case-by-case decision-making are also ill-suited to extraterritoriality scenarios, where the interests affected and implications can be much broader. In foreign policy terms, the efforts of private parties to use the courts of one state to impose national or international standards on another will also often be counterproductive to diplomatic, development aid, and other state-based efforts to the same end. Extraterritorial judgments also weaken the rule of law both in forum and territorial states. In the former, they exceed not just enforcement capacity, but the legitimacy and policy capacity of its legislature. In the latter, they attempt to apply laws that were not enacted or published by sovereign territorial-state authorities.

This is not a universal view. The alternative is that states with robust domestic laws, courts, and rule-of-law principles ought to extend these to fill perceived gaps in the states where they are weaker, both to address whatever immediate issues are at hand, and to construct a patchwork international rule-of-law framework from the bottom up.[5] Which approach is taken often depends on the assumptions of the advocates involved, the way they frame questions, and whether heuristic or algorithmic reasoning is applied. This matters because the heuristic biases of most domestic lawyers, academics, and judges favour the application of the rules and reasoning in which they were trained, and underestimate the less accessible and unfamiliar ones of comity and foreign and international law. Over time, systemic biases produce accumulating legislation and jurisprudence tending both to expand local discretion and to extend local jurisdiction, and to avoid algorithmic approaches more likely to limit both jurisdiction and the discretion to extend it. Judges *want* to decide cases on the merits,

5 See the following chapter and Uta Kohl, "Corporate Human Rights Accountability: The Objections of Western Governments to the *Alien Tort Statute*" (2014) 63:3 *International and Comparative Law Quarterly* 665; and Natalie Davidson, "Human Rights Realism" (2021) 54:1 *Vanderbilt Journal of Transnational Law* 31 as examples.

and even when they decide against their own jurisdiction, they try to avoid limiting their discretion in future cases.

The importance of jurisdictional law as a boundary limit and buffer between different territorial rule-of-law structures tends to be underestimated in domestic law because lawmakers, judges, and civil society advocates instinctively resort to domestic assumptions. These assumptions then become embedded in written and unwritten procedures and practices, and as this accumulates, pro-forum decisions become self-propagating. They also tend to become ambiguous and inconsistent because underlying conflicts among domestic, transboundary, and foreign principles remain unresolved. For example, customary international law and domestic jurisprudence often differ on what "extraterritorial enforcement" means and why.

Judicial independence and limits on litigation evidence and argument are designed to ensure that domestic cases are decided fairly, and that domestic law is applied consistently, but they also systematically exclude broader state interests of foreign policy and the interests of foreign states. This leads to the problems above, but can also create constitutional and rule-of-law conflicts within the forum state between judicial independence, executive domestic and foreign policy mandates, and the exclusive powers of the legislature to make extraterritorial law on the advice of political and executive authorities. Such conflicts are critical with respect to jurisdiction because they can produce friction between states with very different ideas about the rule of law and separation of executive and judicial authority.

The resulting inconsistencies range from case-specific questions of *how* local law applies (for example, the elements or *situs* of a crime or tort) to jurisdictional threshold questions of *whether* local laws and jurisdiction apply at all, and to more fundamental jurisdictional and constitutional questions about *whether courts should have the authority to extend their own jurisdiction*. Judges have generally tried either to reconcile or blend substantive and jurisdictional paradigms, or to choose principles from one or the other in an effort to reach a desired outcome, which is usually the extension of the forum state's jurisdiction and law. Over the past 150 years, commentators and judges have described such efforts as: a choice between jurisdictional legislation and the "exigency of the case"; "a tendency to arrive, if possible, at the application of local law"; a source of "doctrinal confusion"; "far from satisfactory"; and "an unprincipled mess of *ad hoc* decisions with no sound theoretical underpinnings and containing no overarching or principled justifications beyond the expediency of the moment."[6]

The jurisprudence also reflects long-term and cyclic trends. Nineteenth- and twentieth-century globalization generated pressures to globalize rule of law, human rights, environmental, and other standards. Armed conflict, cold war ideologies, diplomacy, and scholarship have also influenced customary law principles of sovereignty, territoriality, and non-interference. Pro-forum biases have produced lines of jurisprudence that gradually extended forum law and jurisdiction until some tipping point of retrenchment was reached, notable examples being the line of US *Alien Tort Statute* cases from 1980–2013, and Canadian *Charter* jurisprudence from 1985–2010.

C. THE CANADIAN *CHARTER* JURISPRUDENCE AND ITS PROBLEMS

Examinations of jurisdictional biases are necessarily qualitative and not quantitative assessments, focusing not on statistical outcomes, but on the principles and reasoning applied, and Canadian caseloads are small. The examinations are also subjective, in the case of the *Charter*, depending on whether one reasons from a substantive human rights perspective or a more structural and international jurisdictional perspective. From the author's jurisdictional perspective, erroneous decisions extending jurisdiction are more common than those against extending it, whereas most human rights advocates are critical of the reasoning in *R v Hape* that the *Charter* cannot apply extraterritorially. Both cite internal inconsistencies, which in the author's view arise from heuristic judicial reasoning backward from a desired outcome rather than starting from an algorithmic extension of existing rules. Whether or not one accepts this as a structural bias problem, the incongruities and contradictions in the *Charter* cases

---

6 In order: *R v Keyn* (1876), 2 Ex Div 63 at 231, Cockburn CJ [*Keyn*]; Michael Akehurst, "Jurisdiction in International Law" (1972–73) 46 *British Yearbook of International Law* 145 at 185; *Libman v The Queen*, [1985] 2 SCR 178 at 186, La Forest J [*Libman*]; *Treacy v DPP*, [1971] AC 537, 55 Cr App R 113 at 125, Reid LJ [*Treacy*]; *Lipohar and Winfield v The Queen*, [1999] HCA 65 at paras 133–35, Kirby J; and Matthew Goode, "The Tortured Tale of Criminal Jurisdiction" (1997) 21 *Melbourne University Law Review* 411 at 411.

clearly exist, and make it difficult to develop a reliable base line for assessment from the limited jurisprudence that does exist.

Of the eleven Supreme Court cases considering extraterritorial *Charter* application, only three actually applied it, one of those was reversed, and the eventual result was that it should almost never apply.[7] But the justices consistently reasoned from the assumption that the *Charter* ought to apply, struggling to avoid jurisdictional constraints and apply it without conflicting with foreign law and sovereignty, and producing twenty-five separate opinions as a result.

Pro-forum bias includes direct heuristic preferences for forum law and jurisdiction, more general preferences for forum-style approaches to legal reasoning and argument, and indirect preferences, such as in the choice of interpretive rules, that produce those results. In the *Charter* cases, these included a focus on substantive interests and effects ahead of rules of application and on domestic law reasoning over international and foreign law considerations. Also evident is a preference for consistency with domestic values: extraterritorial *Charter* application was seen as necessary to apply consistent controls on official activities inside and outside of Canada, and to avoid the perceived unfairness of treating only some litigants as "rights holders," depending on where cases had arisen and which rights were in issue. A further pattern can be seen in the preference for developing principles incrementally and avoiding reasoning that would limit discretion to deal with future cases.[8]

Biases are also evident in rule selection. Until *Hape*, most questions of extraterritoriality were characterized as exercises of prescriptive

---

7 *Spencer v The Queen*, [1985] 2 SCR 278; *Canada v Schmidt*, [1987] 1 SCR 500; *Argentina v Mellino*, [1987] 1 SCR 536; *United States v Allard*, [1987] 1 SCR 564; *R v Harrer*, [1995] 3 SCR 562; *R v Terry*, [1996] 2 SCR 207; *Schreiber v Canada*, [1998] 1 SCR 841 [*Schreiber*]; *R v Cook*, [1998] 2 SCR 597 [*Cook*]; *Hape*, above note 2; *Canada (Minister of Justice) v Khadr*, 2008 SCC 28; and *Canada (Prime Minister) v Khadr*, 2010 SCC 3. *Cook* relied on a balancing of comity interests to extend *Charter* rights, *Hape* held that any extension offended comity, and *Khadr* applied the *Charter* in exceptional circumstances despite comity.

8 See, for example, *Schreiber*, *ibid*, at paras 32 and 42 (whether privacy rights based on location), *Cook*, *ibid*, at paras 84–91 (rights holders), *Hape*, above note 2 at paras 160–61 (different application of *Charter* and investigative law inside and outside of Canada "unprincipled"), *Hape* at paras 91 and 177 (disagreement over the difference between applying s 8 rights extraterritorially and ss 7 and 11(d) rights to fairness of Canadian proceedings), and *Hape*, at paras 175 and 182–91 (incremental reasoning and future discretion).

jurisdiction, mindful of the customary law limits on enforcement jurisdiction. The presumption against extraterritoriality was also avoided, probably because the sort of clear expression of legislative intent needed to rebut the presumption does not appear in section 32 of the *Charter*.[9] The "broad, generous and purposive" rule for interpreting *Charter* rights was also applied to the very different question of whether section 32 allowed extraterritorial application, and other interpretive rules were relied on to fill the gap created by the absence of clear extraterritoriality language.[10] Most of the cases, including *Hape*, also did not distinguish between the clear constitutional authority of Parliament to enact extraterritorial law, and the much more limited powers of courts to apply enacted laws extraterritorially.[11]

The over-arching focus was on the exceptionality of the *Charter* as a Canadian constitutional human rights instrument, and not on the foreign and international law perspective, that stresses territorial limits on application and treats all domestic law the same regardless of substance. Substantive exigencies also led to reasoning that considered the implications of applying the *Charter* as a control on a range of domestic, foreign, and cooperative officials and processes, forgetting that it actually operates indirectly, by codifying rights and applying them to third parties, not

9 When the presumption eventually was raised Gonthier and Bastarache JJ fell back to *Charter* exceptionality, and argued that it should not apply: *Cook*, above note 7 at paras 129 and 147–48.

10 *Hape*, above note 2 at paras 158–61, Bastarache, Abella and Rothstein JJ.

11 In *Hape*, above note 2, both sides did this, with different results. The majority held (paras 94 and 104-5) that extraterritorial enforcement was beyond s 32 because extraterritorial enforcement was *ultra vires* Parliament, even though there is actually no constitutional limit on what Parliament may enact, and a number of valid extraterritorial enforcement powers can be found in Canadian statutes. The dissent (paras 162-66) took the silence of s 32 on territorial limits as a basis for applying provisions extraterritorially, effectively reversing the presumption. Both interpreted s 32 as a basis for applying the *Charter* out to the theoretical limits of what Parliament could enact if it chose to disregard the customary international law constraints, rather than distinguishing between the text of the *Charter* as an exercise in prescription and their own authority to interpret s 32 and apply *Charter* rights and remedies extraterritorially as an exercise in enforcement. Had s 32 of the *Charter* expressly required extraterritorial application the Court would have been obliged to so apply it despite the countervailing comity and customary international law concerns. See *Daniels v White and The Queen*, [1968] SCR 517 at 541 (Pigeon J) (see also *Cook*, above note 7 at para 129).

officials.[12] And critically for the state of other jurisprudence, none of the judgments considered whether principles thought applicable to the *Charter* ought also to apply to other laws.

This produced *R v Greco*, which relied on *Cook* to enforce Canadian court orders extraterritorially, by applying both a probation order and breach offence to an aggravated assault in Cuba.[13] The characterization of this as prescriptive rather than enforcement jurisdiction was later reversed in *Hape*, but *Greco* is still being applied, with the surprising result that while extending *Charter* rights is impermissible extraterritorial enforcement, applying *Criminal Code* probation orders and breach-of-probation offences extraterritorially is not. Of particular concern is the erosion of the presumption against extraterritoriality, which has operated, sometimes unevenly, as a critical limit on both jurisdiction and judicial discretion since *Keyn* in 1876.[14]

Several patterns can be seen in the cases:

- Less restrictive principles developed for private international law are extended into public law scenarios, forum states treating as

---

12 See for example, *Schreiber*, above note 7 at para 16, Lamer CJ. Justice L'Heureux-Dubé did call attention to this question in *Cook* (above note 7 at para 87) but chose not to decide the case on it, as did LeBel J in *Hape* (above note 2 at para 81). In *Hape* (para 161), Bastarache J makes the argument expressly: "s.32(1) . . . defines *who* acts, not *where* they act." Effectively, this allocated status as "rights-holders" based on the desire to regulate interactions with Canadian law enforcement rather than on countervailing jurisdictional and sovereignty considerations based on territorial *situs*.

13 *R v Greco* (2001), 159 CCC (3d) 146 (Ont CA) [*Greco*], leave denied (presumably based on *Cook*) at [2001] SCCA No 656. Post-*Hape* citations of *Greco* include *R v Gillingham* (2004), 184 CCC (3d) 97 (BCCA) (application of US order in Canada); *R v Karaalp*, 2010 ONCJ 545 (assessing Canadian and US comity interests in breach of Canadian custody order); and *R v Rattray*, 2008 ONCA 74 (conviction for breaching Canadian firearms order by acquiring a firearm in the US rather than for illegal importation and possession of the weapon in Canada).

14 See *Keyn*, above note 6; *R v Jameson*, [1896] 2 QB 425 at 435; *Arcadi v The King*, [1932] SCR 158 at 159; *Daniels*, above note 11 at 541; *Treacy*, above note 6 at 124–25, Reid LJ; *Air India v Wiggins*, [1980] 2 All ER 593 at 597, Scarman LJ [*Wiggins*]; *Hape*, above note 2 at para 53; and *Society of Composers, Authors and Music Publishers of Canada v Canadian Association of Internet Providers*, 2004 SCC 45 [*SOCAN*] at paras 54–55, Binnie J and 141–44, LeBel J. US cases include *Chicago & Southern Air Lines, Inc v Waterman Steamship Corp* (1948), 333 US 103 at 111; *Morrison v National Australia Bank*, 130 S Ct 2869 (2010) at 2881 [*Morrison*]; and *Kiobel v Royal Dutch Petroleum Co*, 133 S Ct 1659 (2013) at 1669 [*Kiobel*].

private civil actions cases that territorial states see as having public law and sovereignty implications.[15]

- Subjective heuristic tests of common-sense reasoning have been preferred to more objective algorithmic approaches.[16]
- Comity-balancing tests allowing judges to assess foreign interests directly, generally without evidence or foreign representation, have been preferred over fact-based *situs* tests.[17]
- In Canada, the Supreme Court's decision in *Libman* provided for the extension of territorial jurisdiction in cases with territorial and extraterritorial elements, but this has been replaced by open-ended consideration of "real and substantial links" in cases with no territorial activities.[18]

---

15 See, for example, *Equustek Solutions Inc v Google Inc*, 2015 BCCA 265 and *Google Inc v Equustek Solutions Inc*, 2017 SCC 34; *British Columbia (Attorney General) v Brecknell*, 2017 BCSC 460 and 2018 BCCA 5; and *Google LLC v Equustek Solutions Inc*, 2017 WL 5000834 (ND Cal Nov 2, 2017). *Equustek* upheld a private law injunction seen as public law (*First Amendment* and internet regulation) in the United States, and in Canada was extended to criminal evidence orders in *Brecknell.*

16 See following note and also *Greco*, above note 13 at paras 26 and 29 ("common sense" inference and concern that probation orders and offences would be "light-bulbs that can be switched on and off" — as do all offences — when the subjects cross borders).

17 Most of the *Charter* arguments were based on comity-balancing; for example, *Cook*, above note 7 at paras 133–38. In *Libman*, La Forest J quoted Diplock LJ in *Treacy* (both above note 6) arguing, *obiter*, that the presumption against extraterritorial application should be replaced by a presumption that Parliament did not intend to offend comity, which would have replaced strict statutory interpretation limits both on extraterritoriality and judicial discretion with subjective judicial assessments of comity. This was not followed in either country, but is often cited in Canada to interpret *Libman* as support for comity-balancing. In *Libman* itself, La Forest J actually clarified that territorial jurisdiction extended to transnational scenarios if there were "substantial . . . activities" in Canada and stated that the limits of this jurisdiction, which was concurrent with other territorial states, would be "coterminous with the requirements of international comity" (at 212–14). This was at best *obiter dicta* and did not, at least in the author's view, create a separate and parallel comity test for jurisdictional extensions based on interests other than partly-territorial facts. See also Section B(6) and (7) of the following chapter on this point. The only case reviewed in which evidence of foreign interests was tendered was *R c Ouellette* (1998), 126 CCC (3d) 219 at paras 16–21 (CSQ).

18 For discussion of *Libman* and replacement of the requirement of territorial activities with open-ended comity-balancing based on the dissent of Diplock LJ in *Treacy*, see Section B(7) of Chapter 7. The idea has been criticized as excessive even at private law. See Joost Blom & Elizabeth Edinger, "The Chimera of the Real and Substantial Connection Test" (2005) 38:2 *University of British Colombia Law*

- Until *Hape* reversed *Cook* on this point in 2007, cases characterized extraterritorial rulings as prescriptive, and not enforcement jurisdiction, to avoid the customary international law requirement of territorial state consent. At customary law, the enactment of a law is *prescription* and its direct application by any judicial or executive authority is *enforcement*, at least to the extent that this usurps the affected territorial state's plenary sovereign prerogatives. In comity terms, infringement on sovereignty of enforcement also depends more on territorial state perception than on forum-state courts' characterization.[19]
- Faced with a choice of rules or principles, courts tend to choose those that favour extending jurisdiction and that allow greater discretion over rules that limit either or both. Rules that limit jurisdiction and discretion have also been reformulated to reduce those limits. Cases on the presumption against extraterritoriality have extended the "clear language" requirement to include broad versions of necessary implication, for example.[20]

Review 373. Fully extraterritorial cases include *Greco*, above note 13; *Rakuten Kobo Inc v Canada (Commissioner of Competition)*, 2018 FC 64 (effects-based jurisdiction to extend anti-competition orders) and *R v Oler*, 2018 BCCA 323 [*Oler*] (link based on offence provision rather than transnational facts). Similar wording was used in the 2012 *Justice for Victims of Terrorism Act*, SC 2012, c 1, s 2. In *Re (X)*, 2014 FCA 249, it was suggested without deciding that national security interests might have a "real and substantial link" to Canada as a basis for extraterritorial CSIS investigative warrants.

19 See Akehurst, above note 6 at 145–51; "Predictability and Comity: Toward Common Principles of Extraterritorial Jurisdiction" (comment) (1985) 98 *Harvard Law Review* 1310 at 1322–23; Alex Mills, "Rethinking Jurisdiction in International Law" (2014) 84:1 *British Yearbook of International Law* 187 at 194–200; and *Hape*, above note 2 at paras 64–65.

20 See, for example, *Oler*, above note 18 at paras 35 and 41–46. Rebuttal by necessary implication applies where the law cannot be given effect to any other way, not where it is thought necessary to apply it to a specific accused or location. This was applied in *Wiggins* (above note 14 at 196, Widgery LJ) and in Canada, to the presumption that legislation does not bind the Crown. See *Friends of the Oldman River Society v Canada (Minister of Transport)*, [1992] 1 SCR 3 at 50–53 ("the statute cannot operate with reasonable efficiency unless the Crown is bound"), *Sparling v Quebec*, [1988] 2 SCR 1015 at 1022–23, and *Alberta Government Telephones v Canada (CRTC)*, [1989] 2 SCR 225 at 281 (either clear intention to bind the Crown must appear, or the purpose of the statute must be "wholly frustrated" if not so applied).

D. THE BASIS AND NATURE OF STRUCTURAL AND INDIVIDUAL PRO-FORUM BIASES

The phrase "pro-forum bias" originated in a 1987 judgment expressing concern about judicial balancing of US and foreign extraterritorial civil discovery interests,[21] but the basic tension between the external pressures and constraints of international law and comity and the desire to follow domestic heuristic reasoning and address the "exigency of the case" dates back to the nineteenth century and even earlier.[22] Citing a 1943 source in 1972, Dr. Akehurst described "the tendency of courts to follow a 'homeward trend,' a tendency to arrive, if possible, at the application of domestic law."[23] US cases applying the 1987 *Aérospatiale* test demonstrated that the concerns were justified. Subsequent extraterritorial discovery orders extended to demanding breaches of foreign privilege, banking, or privacy laws, based on domestic assumptions about foreign comity interests, in some cases even ignoring or rejecting express foreign submissions. The bias against litigants and systems was stronger for those more different from the US in legal and cultural terms, and the rejection of foreign objections caused predictable harm to commercial and diplomatic relations.[24] Similar patterns can be seen in Canadian cases, as above, often following the *obiter dicta* discussions of comity in *Treacy* and *Libman* to over-extend the "real and substantial link" test, or engaging in exercises of statutory interpretation that confuse policy justifications of extraterritoriality with the need for express parliamentary intent.

In fairness to the lawyers and judges involved, many of the biases appear to arise from structural factors over which they have little control. Litigation processes within national rule-of-law systems isolate judges, courts, evidence, and argument from extrinsic factors in order to produce

---

21 *Société Nationale Industrielle Aérospatiale v US District Court for the Southern District of Iowa*, 482 US 522, at 553 (1987), Blackmun J [*Aérospatiale*].

22 In the US, *Murray v Schooner Charming Betsy*, 6 US (2 Cranch) 64, 118 (1804) [*Charming Betsy*]; *Schooner Exchange v M'Faddon*, 11 US 116 (1812); and in the UK, *Keyn*, above note 6, which cited the US cases and English precedents back to the late thirteenth century.

23 Akehurst, above note 6 at 185.

24 See Geoffrey Sant, "Court-Ordered Law-Breaking: U.S. Courts Increasingly Order the Violation of Foreign Law" (2015) 81:1 *Brooklyn Law Review* 181, and "Courts Increasingly Demand that Businesses Break the Law" (2018) 52:1 *Akron Law Review* 121.

fair, unbiased, and consistent decisions, but this filters out the broader domestic policy issues and foreign and international interests that arise when international comity and foreign laws and territorial sovereignty are engaged. Individual heuristic biases then tend to: apply reasoning that is valid in domestic, but not in extraterritorial scenarios; prefer the more familiar and accessible principles of domestic law; and weigh the known factors of domestic law and adjudication against the unknown and uncertain results if jurisdiction is declined. These are usually unconscious until attention is called to them.

Bias factors overlap and tend to be mutually reinforcing, which amplifies the effects, both in court and over time. In common law systems, jurisprudence from past efforts straining to extend jurisdiction accumulates, and is then used to support future extensions. Other heuristic biases vary, which randomizes the effects over time. But pro-forum biases are more consistent, contributing to what have been described as "widespread and self-reinforcing" patterns, and causing "not just a snowball effect, but an avalanche of bad law."[25]

1) Structural, Systemic, and Statutory Biases

Individual bias factors tend to create systemic and structural biases over time, and most of the heuristic thinking of lawyers and judges accumulated in professional education and practice is valid for domestic cases, but less so for transnational and extraterritorial ones. And this does not just apply to lawyers and judges: it also extends to domestic political dynamics and policy mechanisms that govern legislative drafting and enactment, and to the media, academic, and public perceptions of the law and domestic justice systems. Dismissing a case for want of jurisdiction instead of considering the substantive merits is often described as dismissal on a "technicality," for example. The 2007 decision in *Hape* against extraterritorial *Charter* application drew extensive media and academic criticism,[26] as

25 Sant, 2018, *ibid*, at 193, quoting in part, James Chalmers, "The Hague Evidence Convention and Discovery *Inter Partes*: Trial Court Decisions Post-*Aérospatiale*" (2000) 8 *Tulane Journal of International and Comparative Law* 189 at 201.

26 See, for example, Kent Roach, "*R v Hape* Creates Charter-Free Zones for Canadian Officials Abroad" (2007) 53 *Criminal Law Quarterly* 1; and John Currie, "*Khadr*'s Twist on *Hape*: Tortured Determinations of the Extraterritorial Reach of the Canadian *Charter*" (2008) 46 *Canadian Yearbook of International Law* 307.

did the 2013 US decision in *Kiobel* rejecting extraterritorial human rights tort jurisdiction.[27]

States with common law systems rely on equality before the law, judicial independence, and strict limits on the scope of evidence and argument to ensure judicial impartiality, fairness, and consistency in decision making, and they separate judicial functions from legislative and executive ones as a constitutional safeguard. This works well internally, but less well where outside interests are engaged. Foreign states rarely seek standing or input into foreign proceedings;[28] consideration of broader foreign policy interests would be seen as irrelevant or prejudicial in court; and contact with executive or foreign officials outside of court violates judicial independence. This protects the integrity of litigation, but the extrinsic interests in extraterritoriality cases can often be far more sweeping and important than any of the immediate issues at bar. Judicial recognition of this fact was the basis of deference to parliamentary supremacy in *Keyn* and US cases deferring to the "political branches" on separation of powers grounds.

Legislative drafting can also create, amplify, or fall prey to pro-forum biases. Section 6(2) of the *Criminal Code*[29] is sometimes described as codifying the presumption against extraterritoriality, but it applies only to federal offences, and limits only conviction, not adjudicative jurisdiction. It was enacted before transnational offences became common, and before *Libman* established concurrent jurisdiction over offences committed both inside and outside of Canada. It was applied in *Greco* as a bar to convicting

27 See, for example, Austen Parrish, "*Kiobel*, Unilateralism, and the Retreat from Extraterritoriality" (2013) 28 *Maryland Journal of International Law* 208; and Sarah Cleveland, "The *Kiobel* Presumption and Extraterritoriality" (2013) 52 *Columbia Journal of Transnational Law* 8.

28 The US Supreme Court considers *amicus curiae* briefs submitted by foreign states, but this rarely occurs in Canada. In *Kazemi Estate v Islamic Republic of Iran*, 2014 SCC 62, Iran did not appear and *amicus curiae* counsel were appointed. It did appear in later cases, but only after US and Canadian legislation established extraterritorial tort jurisdiction and stripped away its sovereign immunities, effectively displacing diplomatic settlement mechanisms. See Karinne Coombes, "The Quest for Justice for Victims of Terrorism: International Law and the Immunity of States in Canada and the United States" (2018) 69 *University of New Brunswick Law Journal* 251; and *Tracy v Iranian Minister of Information and Security*, 2016 ONSC 3759; *Tracy v Iran (Information and Security)*, 2017 ONCA 549.

29 *Criminal Code*, RSC 1985, c C-46, s 6(2): "Subject to this Act or any other Act of Parliament, no person shall be convicted or discharged … of an offence committed outside Canada."

the accused for an aggravated assault committed outside Canada but not to the breach of probation offence, even though there was either no offence (if the Canadian probation order did not apply extraterritorially) or a wholly-extraterritorial offence (if the order did apply).[30]

In *R v Blackmore and Oler* (2017–18),[31] an unfortunate combination of drafting and interpretation led the BC Supreme Court not to extend jurisdiction where it could have done so based on *Libman*, and the Court of Appeal to correct this, but for the wrong reason. The Blackmores and Oler had participated in a scheme that removed three underage victims from Canada to the United States for arranged marriages that involved illicit sexual activities, and the Blackmores, who took the girls out of Canada, were convicted of this. But the offence consisted of "doing anything" for the purpose of removal, and Oler, who had acted on both sides of the border, was acquitted based on section 6(2), citing a reasonable doubt that he knew the purpose of the scheme until after he arrived in the United States. The scheme was clearly "both here and there" as envisaged by *Libman*, which establishes concurrent territorial jurisdiction based on "substantial activities," which need not all be elements of the offences.[32]

Oler's knowing participation after he crossed into the United States triggered *Libman* jurisdiction based on a "substantial portion" of the scheme in Canada, in the same way as it does for complex transnational fraud and drug-trafficking scenarios, but the use of the words "does anything" in the provision led the court to construct a separate and exclusive *situs* for each co-accused. Instead of relying on the extended territorial reasoning of *Libman*, the Court of Appeal then cited *Libman* and necessary implication to rebut the presumption that the offence did not

30 *Greco*, above note 13.

31 *R v Blackmore (sub nom R v Oler)*, 2017 BCSC 192 and *Oler*, above note 18, considering an offence under s 273.3(1)(b) of the *Criminal Code*.

32 This was *obiter* in *Libman* itself because elements of the frauds had been committed from Toronto, but La Forest J mentions (at 211) that planning and the receipt of proceeds "while not in strictness part of the offence" were still relevant, and arguments that *situs* required "elements" rather than "activities" have since been rejected: *R v Roblin and Rowbotham* (1992), 76 CCC (3d) 542 (Ont CA) (jurisdiction based on location of activities not part of the *actus reus*); and *R v Karigar*, 2017 ONCA 576 and *R v Barra*, 2021 ONCA 568 (jurisdiction over the same complex transnational bribery scheme based on "activities" in Canada that were not elements of the actual bribery, and used to extradite Barra and Govindia, who participated from outside of Canada).

apply extraterritorially, and ordered a retrial on the basis that it did. This overextended the meaning of necessary implication, and used *Libman* to create new, fully-extraterritorial, jurisdiction. It may have been necessary to apply the offence to Mr. Oler in policy terms, but it was clearly not necessary to give effect to the offence at all, as the Blackmores had already been convicted of it.

A combination of structural and cognitive heuristic bias elements also arises when factual bases of substantive and jurisdictional questions overlap. Requiring separate legal and conceptual determinations would greatly reduce conscious and unconscious biases, and Canadian law treats jurisdiction as a separate question of law to be decided on a balance of probabilities. But the practice, based on *Finta*, is to hear the entire case before deciding on jurisdiction.[33] In *Finta*, both statutory extraterritoriality and moral culpability turned on factual and *mens rea* differences between crimes against humanity and the underlying conventional offences, but the need to put both to the jury was questionable in *Finta*, and should not extend to more conventional cases.[34]

Distinguishing between substantive and jurisdictional matters is important in both legal and cognitive terms. Hearing substantive evidence before deciding threshold questions of jurisdiction is likely to trigger several of the cognitive heuristic pro-forum biases discussed below, and also to result in structural pressures from parties and observers to have the case decided on substantive merits rather than refused on a jurisdictional "technicality." A better approach would be to apply *Balcombe*, and require courts to decide jurisdiction at the outset without the jury, based on factual allegations or proof to a balance of probabilities, then hear the case and apply a final decision on jurisdiction based on its factual conclusions.

---

33 See *Balcombe v The Queen*, [1954] SCR 303 at 305–6 (jurisdiction as a question of law determined by the judge on a balance of probabilities), and *R v Finta* (1992), 92 DLR (4th) 1 (Ont CA) [*Finta* Ont CA] and [1994] 1 SCR 701 [*Finta* SCC].

34 In *Finta* SCC, *ibid*, the majority held that additional questions of fact and *mens rea* needed to establish that the offences had been war crimes and crimes against humanity as a basis of jurisdiction were for the jury. These are distinct questions from whether the accused had committed them. Some of the factual determinations were the same, but, while the accused's individual actions and knowing participation were questions of fact requiring proof beyond a reasonable doubt, the nature of the broader scheme was a question of law and the lower burden of proof. See the decisions of Tarnopolsky JA in *Finta* Ont CA, above note 33, and of La Forest, L'Heureux-Dubé and McLachlin JJ.

Courts in *Oler* and other cases have also incorrectly acquitted accused persons based on jurisdictional assessments. Lack of jurisdiction is not a criminal defence; it does not just preclude conviction, but any verdict. If the court has no jurisdiction, it can only discharge the accused, still presumed innocent, or dismiss the case without decision.[35] A judicial determination of *Libman* jurisdiction on a balance of probabilities is also not inconsistent with an eventual acquittal based on a reasonable doubt about other factors, and the accused is not (or should not be) entitled to a criminal presumption against jurisdiction. The trier of fact is concerned with whether the accused actually committed the offence, not where, and *Libman* jurisdiction depends on the location of the offence or "substantial activities," and not the location of the accused at the time it was committed.

2) Individual Heuristic Pro-forum Biases

Both conscious and unconscious biases are based on heuristics, which have been described as evolutionary "cognitive short cuts" or "rules of thumb" that conserve limited cognitive resources and allow decisions based on incomplete information in complex cases.[36] Snap decisions that "all lions are dangerous" were important for human evolution, but stereotyping people who look, speak, or act differently is now problematic, especially because heuristic biases tend to be negative and risk-averse. This is why we have concerns about unconscious biases based on visible differences of gender, race, sexual orientation, and gender identity.[37]

---

35 The difference matters: an acquittal bars a retrial under *Charter* s 11(h), but without jurisdiction, the accused is never in jeopardy and no "acquittal" is possible. See, for example, *R c Ibeagha*, 2019 QCCA 1534. In *Chowdhury v Canada*, 2014 ONSC 2635 the Court confused jurisdiction over the accused and *Libman* jurisdiction over the transnational bribery scheme, but it did stay the charge with leave to resume should the accused be extradited.

36 See Amos Tversky & Daniel Kahneman, "Judgment Under Uncertainty: Heuristics and Biases" (1974) 185:4157 *Science* 1124; and Christine Jolls, Cass Sunstein & Richard Thaler, "A Behavioral Approach to Law and Economics" (1998) 50 *Stanford Law Review* 1471.

37 See Anthony Greenwald & Mahzarin Banaji, "Implicit Social Cognition: Attitudes, Self-esteem, and Stereotypes" (1995) 102:1 *Psychological Review* 4; and Anthony Greenwald & Linda Krieger, "Implicit Bias: Scientific Foundations" (2006) 94:4 *California Law Review* 945. For critical comment see Samuel Bagenstos, "Implicit Bias and Antidiscrimination Law" (2007) 1 *Harvard Law and Policy Review* 477; and "Implicit Bias's Failure" (2018) 39:1 *Berkley Journal of Employment and Labour Law* 37.

Social cognition and the neuropsychology of judicial decision making are beyond the scope of the present chapter, but all humans—including lawyers and judges—have heuristic biases.[38] Heuristics are essential to legal argument and judicial reasoning: we use them to formulate arguments, propositions, and principles, apply precedents, and make necessary assumptions to fill factual gaps, but this becomes problematic when the assumptions go beyond what the actual facts will support. This is usually done unconsciously, creating cognitive distortions that can obscure or diminish facts that conflict with the assumptions. Not much attention has been paid to this as a source of pro-forum bias, but there is clearly a distortion that puts factual and emotional considerations ahead of jurisdictional ones in which "courts are weighing the value of their own work as courts."[39]

The most common heuristics, representativeness, availability, and anchoring, all seem likely to generate pro-forum biases, bearing in mind that general heuristics evolve along specific lines based on legal education and practice.[40] Domestic laws and reasoning that reflect a judge's personal and professional experience are more easily understood (availability), tend to be substituted for less familiar foreign and international ones (representativeness), and are more clearly remembered (anchoring). Other heuristics may also produce pro-forum effects. The fairness heuristic, for example, creates biases for perceived fairness and against perceived unfairness.[41] Fairness in judges is important, but it can also create a preference to "do justice" on the merits, rather than be "unfair" to everyone by not asserting jurisdiction. The fairness bias also prefers the interest of the parties in court over more remote foreign policy and sovereignty interests.

38 See Chris Guthrie, Jeffery Rachlinski & Andrew Wistrich, "Inside the Judicial Mind" (2000) 86:4 *Cornell Law Review* 777; and "Judging by Heuristic: Cognitive Illusions in Judicial Decision Making" (2002) 86:1 *Judicature* 44; Anuj Shah & Daniel Oppenheimer, "Heuristics Made Easy: An Effort-Reduction Framework" (2008) 134:2 *Psychological Bulletin* 207; Anna Spain Bradley, "The Disruptive Neuroscience of Judicial Choice" (2018) 9:1 *University of California Irving Law Review* 1 at 13–16 and 25–29; and Eyal Peer & Eyal Gamliel, "Heuristics and Biases in Judicial Decisions" (2013) 49 *Court Review: The Journal of the American Judges Association* 114.

39 Sant 2018, above note 24 at 146.

40 See, for example, Morell Mullins, "Tools, Not Rules: The Heuristic Nature of Statutory Interpretation" (2003) 30:1 *Journal of Legislation* 1 at 47–55.

41 See Jolls et al, above note 36 at 1493–97 and 1495–96; Cass Sunstein, "Some Effects of Moral Indignation on Law" (2009) 33 *Vermont Law Review* 405; and "Hazardous Heuristics" (2003) 70:2 *University of Chicago Law Review* 751.

Hindsight biases, which make events seem more predictable after they have occurred than they were beforehand, are also likely to create pressures to decide on the merits when the evidence is heard before jurisdiction is decided.

Heuristic biases also extend to emotional reasoning. Officials (and voters) put crimes with immediate and identifiable harms ahead of events that are more serious but also more distant in time, space, or magnitude. In *Greco*, the courts focused on the victim's injuries and the accused as a local threat as more important than the abstract comity implications of extraterritorial court orders. The "more seasoned practitioners" described in *Libman* understand this very well: transnational fraud and cybercrime offenders usually avoid targeting victims in their own jurisdictions.

E. REBALANCING JURISDICTIONAL DECISIONS: OBJECTIVE PRINCIPLES AND ALGORITHMIC REASONING

International law creates inherent inconsistencies between the plenary nature of state sovereignty and the countervailing limits of sovereign equality and non-interference with other states.[42] This does not translate easily into domestic adjudication, the integrity of which depends on rules, rights, and procedures involving more specific questions and parties, all framed within the sovereign jurisdiction of the forum state. Domestic proceedings ask what the law means, and apply specific offences and rights to specific facts and parties, whereas extraterritorial cases are not concerned with purposive meanings, instead asking whether the law applies at all and whether the courts have any authority at all beyond threshold determinations of their own jurisdiction.

This created a dilemma for the English, American, and European courts confronted with the first extraterritoriality cases in the nineteenth century. Judgments that ignored foreign-state interests in ships, citizens, or territory risked judicial intrusion into other essential interests of both the forum, and any affected territorial states, while judgments that considered them compromised domestic interests in judicial independence and neutrality between the parties. Merely assuming jurisdiction could

42 Edward Morgan, "Criminal Process, International Law, and Extraterritorial Crime" (1988) 38:3 *University of Toronto Law Journal* 245 at 250 *et seq.*

be a breach of sovereignty and non-interference, and it was clear that the underlying issues were not just beyond the legal authority of the courts, but beyond both the scope of cases and litigation processes, and the expertise of judges.

The perceived risks were (and still are) real and significant. The early cases unfolded against a background of European, Anglo-American, and colonial conflicts highlighting the serious risks of jurisdictional overreach, and during the time of gradual emergence of customary international law to reduce those risks, including by providing clearer jurisdictional limits that linked sovereignty to territory.[43] *Charming Betsy* upheld Danish sovereignty and property rights in a case dealing with a vessel seized first by French privateers and then by a US warship.[44] In *M'Faddon*, a vessel was refused restoration to its US owner after it had been seized and converted to a warship by France, [45] during a period in which the United States was attempting to stay neutral in the Napoleonic wars, only to be drawn into the 1812 war with Britain instead. The *Keyn* decision, which engaged German maritime interests, came five years after a series of wars in which Bismarck consolidated what would become modern Germany, and was creating peaceful alliances between the new superstate and its European neighbours, many of whom had been at war with Britain two decades earlier in Crimea.

All three courts considered not just limits on forum sovereignty and jurisdiction, but constitutional and functional limits on their own powers. They resolved the underlying conflicts and risks by deferring to foreign sovereignty interests implicitly at bar, and by selectively applying emerging customary law principles to limit their own powers and "outsource" the fundamental underlying problems to legislative and executive bodies. *Keyn* relied on the supremacy of Parliament, and the US cases relied upon the separation of powers doctrine, but the constitutional result and

43 This mostly worked, but failed spectacularly in August 1914, when Austrian diplomatic officials intentionally breached the emerging framework by demanding the right to conduct a criminal investigation in Serbia, knowing that this would be refused based on customary law principles and start a conflict. Which it did, redrawing the map of Europe, ending at least ten monarchies, and killing more than 15 million people, including 60,000 Canadians. See Holger Herwig, *The First World War: Germany and Austria-Hungary, 1914–1918* (London, UK: Arnold, 1997) at 16–18; and John Keegan, *The First World War* (London, UK: Hutchinson, 1998) at 62–65.

44 *Charming Betsy*, above note 22.

45 *Ibid.*

underlying logic were the same. The attempt was to resolve the inconsistencies of sovereignty by distinguishing between the plenary powers allocated to the state itself by international law and the constitutional allocation of powers among courts and other entities within the state, by vesting extraterritorial powers that might infringe foreign sovereignty in legislative and executive authorities and by limiting the authority of independent judges as arbiters of their own extraterritorial powers. What the US cases call the "political branches" were seen as inheriting this sovereign state power in the absence of any concrete constitutional or legislative decision to the contrary and because these branches were seen as much better equipped to consider questions of foreign policy, international comity, and then-emerging customary international law.

In *Keyn*, the court rejected arguments that it should assume jurisdiction over the offshore acts of a German captain based on either English common law or emerging customary law concepts of "territorial waters" that were at the time based on the three-mile range of nineteenth century artillery fire. And it did not just decline to assert jurisdiction, but held that it had no authority to decide its own jurisdiction in the absence of clear legislation. It cited *M'Faddon* and subsequent US cases that also opted for Congressional enactments over *ad hoc* extensions based on "the reach of a cannon-shot."[46] No doubt mindful of Bismarckian diplomatic interests and the implications of punishing German sailors in English courts, Cockburn CJ wisely pointed out that if the territorial waters in question had become British territory at customary law:

> it follows that Parliament can legislate in respect of it. Parliament has only to do so, and the judges of the land will, of course, as in duty bound, give full effect to the law which Parliament shall so create. The question is, whether legislative action shall be applied to meet the exigency of the case, or judicial authority shall be strained and misapplied in order to overcome the difficulty. Every such usurped exercise of judicial power is, in my opinion, a violation of fundamental principles, and in the highest degree unconstitutional. The responsibility is with the legislature, and there it must rest.[47]

46 *Keyn*, above note 6 at 72–74 and 77–79, Phillimore J (citing *United States v Kessler* (1829), 1 *Baldwin's Rep* 15).

47 *Ibid* at 231, Cockburn CJ. See also Lush J at 238–39: "[T]he dominion is the dominion of Parliament, not the dominion of the common law."

The UK and US approach was not followed immediately in other common law states, but only because it was assumed at the time that dominion legislatures had not inherited extraterritorial competence to begin with. Legislatures do not normally make extraterritorial laws, and the common law presumption to that effect was also seen as needed to provide what the US Supreme Court has since called "a stable background against which Congress can legislate with predictable effects."[48] In the dominions, emerging sovereign independence put extraterritoriality into contention from 1900–31, and when it became clear that those legislatures actually could make extraterritorial laws, *Keyn* was quickly taken up.[49]

The presumption has sometimes been applied unevenly based on the tension between pro-forum biases and jurisdictional concerns. English, Canadian, and US courts have all flirted with Diplock-style comity assessments and other forms of discretion to weaken or avoid the presumption, but eventually the fact that domestic litigation processes and courts are neither mandated nor well equipped to deal with the issues this raises usually prevails, as it did in *Kiobel* and *Hape*. US cases mention both mandates and competence in deferring to the political branches of government:

> [T]he very nature of executive decisions as to foreign policy is political, not judicial.... They are decisions of a kind for which the Judiciary has neither aptitude, facilities nor responsibility and . . . in the domain of political power not subject to judicial intrusion or inquiry.[50]

> The presumption against extraterritoriality guards against our courts triggering such serious foreign policy consequences, and instead defers such decisions, quite appropriately, to the political branches.[51]

---

48 *Morrison*, above note 14 at 261.

49 An *obiter* comment by Halsbury LJ in *McLeod v AG of New South Wales*, [1891] AC 455 suggested that dominion parliaments could not make extraterritorial laws, and the question was not settled until 1931 by s 3 of the *Statute of Westminster* and *Croft v Dunphy*, [1932] All ER 154, [1933] 1 DLR 225. See also Walter Johnson "Extra-Territorial Criminal Legislation" (1935) 13:3 *Canadian Bar Review* 127; Charles Doherty (Rt Hon), "Extraterritorial Bigamy" (1930) 8 *Canadian Bar Review* 25; Herbert Smith, "Extraterritorial Legislation" (1923) 1 *Canadian Bar Review* 338; Thomas Mohr, "The Foundations of Irish Extra-Territorial Legislation" (2005) 40 *Irish Jurist* 86; and Morgan, above note 42. Australia responded to *McLeod* by codifying the presumption in 1901. See Chapter 7 for discussion.

50 *Chicago & S Air Lines, Inc v Waterman SS Corp* (1948), above note 14 at 111, Jackson J.

51 *Kiobel*, above note 14 at 1669, Roberts CJ.

> The question is not whether we think Congress would have wanted a statute to apply to foreign conduct if it had thought of the situation before the court, but whether Congress has affirmatively and unmistakably instructed that the statute will do so.[52]

Similar principles appear in Canadian jurisprudence:

> [T]o interpret a Canadian law in a way that conflicts with Canada's international obligations risks incursion by the courts in the executive's conduct of foreign affairs and censure under international law.... In keeping with the international context in which Canadian legislation is enacted, this Court has repeatedly endorsed and applied the interpretive presumption that legislation conforms with the state's international obligations.... This interpretive presumption is not peculiar to Canada. It is a feature of legal interpretation around the world.[53]

> It is a common law presumption that Parliament does not intend legislation to apply extraterritorially. But this presumption is rebuttable where the contrary intention is expressly stated or implied by the legislation.... This presumption flows from the principle of territoriality, a tenet of international law. Because each State is sovereign in its own territory, it is presumed that States hesitate to exercise jurisdiction over matters that may take place in the territory of other States.[54]

F. CONCLUSION

The emergence of both the general presumption of conformity with international law and the specific presumption against extraterritoriality reflected a general understanding of the need to push domestic law in the direction of conformity, and to avoid inconsistencies and conflicts. But it

52 *RJR Nabisco v European Community et al*, 136 S Ct 2090 at 2100 (2016), Alito J, citing also *Morrison*, above note 14. See also *Sosa v Alvarez-Machain*, 542 US 692 at 739–49, Scalia and Thomas JJ, and Roberts CJ.

53 *B010 v Canada (Citizenship and Immigration)*, 2015 SCC 58 at paras 47–48, McLachlin CJC.

54 *SOCAN*, above note 14 at para 144, LeBel J. The presumption against extraterritoriality is mentioned in at least sixteen Supreme Court decisions since 1896, including *Libman*, above note 6, in which it was not applied because the offence had been committed partly in Canada, *Cook*, above note 7, and *Hape*, above note 2, both of which struggled to avoid applying it to the *Charter*.

also demonstrated an understanding of the need for extrinsic limits on judicial discretion and that the inherent risks of pressures created by the heuristic reasoning by lawyers, judges, parties, and observers were best dealt with by establishing a more algorithmic approach both in common law jurisprudence and, it was hoped, in statutory provisions creating and tailoring such extraterritorial jurisdiction as might be needed. The presumptions operate by encouraging and allowing courts to consider and apply international law principles to domestic law where consistency is possible, but also by precluding interpretations that are inconsistent with the customary law principle of deference and non-interference with foreign territorial sovereignty.

If extraterritorial intent is clearly expressed, there is a superior constitutional obligation on judges to give effect to it, but this is an exception that departs from international law. Its use should be limited to legislative and executive authorities that speak for the state itself and not judges who are fully independent of it. Clear language is preferred, but any sort of extraterritorial interpretation or necessary implication should only be resorted to where no other interpretation is possible, as in *Wiggins* and *Oldman River*, and not where the court deems it necessary to give effect to a policy or do justice in the case at bar. This returns the onus to drafters and Parliament to decide whether extraterritoriality is justified, and if so to enact the necessary language. This approach reflects an important constitutional and rule of law safeguard and must logically apply to all domestic law, including statutes and constitutional conventions establishing the courts themselves, and in Canada, to the *Charter of Rights*.

If the power to make extraterritorial law attaches to Parliament alone, and the presumption is a safeguard against judicial overreach, it follows that there can also be no common law or inherent jurisdiction to make an end run around it with the sort of extraterritorial orders suggested by *Greco* and subsequent cases. Inherent jurisdiction is important, but can only exist within constitutional and territorial limits.[55] There is a quantum difference between the territorial powers of a court to make and enforce orders, and those required to extend application and enforcement beyond the territorial sovereignty of the state which established the court. And as a usurpation of foreign sovereignty, extraterritorial court orders are likely to be seen as enforcement by territorial states wherever compliance

55 *Ontario v Criminal Lawyers' Association of Ontario*, 2013 SCC 43.

is expected and non-compliance is threatened, even if forum state courts choose to characterize such orders as extraterritorial prescription.

In the *Charter* cases, the "exigencies" of human rights values and the need to regulate Canadian officials abroad led courts to assume the *Charter* would apply, but without clear language and the sort of legislative tailoring needed to reconcile sweeping *Charter* rights and domestic jurisprudence with foreign laws and sovereignty, and to deal with the rule of law problems when laws developed by and for one jurisdiction are unilaterally applied by its courts to people and events in another. In so doing, they eventually found themselves in much the same position that led Cockburn CJ to call for a clearer legislative mandate based on something better than the range of a cannon shot.

seven

An Agenda for Jurisdictional Law Reform

CHRISTOPHER RAM*

A. THE NEED FOR CONSENSUS ON THE NATURE AND PURPOSE OF JURISDICTIONAL LAW

The previous chapter[1] argued that relying on forum courts to decide when to extend forum law and assert their own jurisdiction in transnational or extraterritorial cases inevitably gives rise to pro-forum bias effects that accumulate over time in the jurisprudence.[2] It further argued that a more algorithmic framework is needed to rebalance the law and assure that broader foreign policy and foreign legal and comity factors are better reflected. This chapter discusses different perspectives on the nature and function of jurisdictional law and the need for basic policy consensus, and then considers some specific law reform proposals.

* The author was, at the time of writing, Legal Counsel with Justice Canada. The views expressed herein are those of the author personally and are not intended to reflect the views or positions of the Government of Canada or any department or agency thereof.

1 See Chapter 6 in this volume.

2 As in Chapter 6, references to jurisdiction are only to those based on national sovereignty and territoriality, not internal powers or limits.

1) Is Jurisdictional Law Different?

Views differ on whether jurisdictional law is exceptional and how this interacts with other axes of exceptionality, especially when principles of constitutional and human rights law are engaged.[3] When exceptionalities collide, discussions tend to be dominated by substantive arguments, rather than reconciliation of underlying principles. Constitutional, rule-of-law, and human rights principles operate across substantive laws and processes to regulate domestic governance structures and ensure values are applied consistently. Jurisdictional rules must operate as an outer boundary on all of these, limiting all of the domestic laws and powers of each state, including judicial powers, based on the territorial sovereignty of other states.

The substantive and jurisdictional paradigms are not inconsistent, and one thesis of this chapter is that each should be interpreted and applied with this in mind. Human rights principles influence the meaning of substantive and procedural laws, jurisdictional principles set outer limits on the application of domestic laws and powers of domestic institutions, and constitutional rule of law principles provide a structure by which they inter-operate. This logically requires not only that human rights principles be given the constitutional supremacy and generous application of the *Charter* and its jurisprudence, but also that limits of territorial jurisdiction be given supremacy over both. Section 52(1) of the *Constitution Act, 1982*,[4] of which the *Charter* is a part, expressly makes the *Act* the "supreme law *of Canada*," not the world. By the same logic, the purposive and generous interpretation needed to construe and apply specific rights within Canada should not be applied to section 32 of the *Charter* to extend those rights into the sovereign territory of another country.

Kiobel and *Hape* both distinguished substantive rights from jurisdictional limits.[5] *Hape* notes that the *Charter* is supreme within Canada, but still subject to the same jurisdictional limits as any Canadian law, and *Kiobel* restated the idea that US law "governs domestically but does not rule the world."[6] This is not always the view in official, legal, or popular

3 Zachary Clopton, "Replacing the Presumption against Extraterritoriality" (2014) 94:1 *Boston University Law Review* 1.

4 Schedule B to the *Canada Act, 1982* (UK), 1982, c 11.

5 *Kiobel v Royal Dutch Petroleum Co et al*, 133 S Ct 1659 (2013) [*Kiobel*], and *R v Hape*, 2007 SCC 26 [*Hape*].

6 *Hape*, *ibid* at para 69, and *Kiobel*, *ibid* at 1664 quoting *Microsoft Corp v AT&T Corp*, 550 US 437 (2007) at 454.

discourse, however. In light of that, the second thesis of this chapter is that a robust discussion about what jurisdictional law is actually *for* is needed as a basis for law reform. Such a discussion must reflect jurisdictional comity and sovereignty concerns to a much greater extent than is usually seen.

The *Charter* cases before *Hape* applied the same supremacy and purposive and generous approach to both substantive rights and extraterritorial application, whereas a customary and common law jurisdictional approach would presume against extraterritorial application without looking at the content of the rights. This was further complicated by arguments that human rights are supra-national, creating an apparent inconsistency that was resolved in *Hape* by distinguishing between the existence of rights at international law and any direct application of the *Charter* itself as a form of extraterritorial enforcement of Canadian law, on which the dissenting justices disagreed.[7]

The alternative applied in *Cook* and some European jurisprudence seeks to extend domestic rights and remedies based on balancing comity interests, the objective being to construct a sort of bottom-up global rule-of-law and human rights infrastructure, in which extraterritorial application of rights and remedies by states where they are robust is seen as filling rule-of-law and human rights gaps in states or regions where they are weak.[8] This can be seen in *Cook* and *Khadr* (2008),[9] the extraterritorial US *Alien Tort Statute* jurisprudence from *Filartiga* (1980) to *Kiobel* (2013), and in arguments that the *European Convention on Human Rights* should apply beyond the combined territories of its States Parties.[10] As discussed in Chapter 6, in

7 See *R v Cook*, [1998] 2 SCR 597 at paras 147–48, Bastarache J [*Cook*] and *Hape* above note 5 at paras 53–56 (LeBel J), para 125 (Bastarache J), and para 186 (Binnie J).

8 See, for example, Uta Kohl, "Corporate Human Rights Accountability: The Objections of Western Governments to the *Alien Tort Statute*" (2014) 63:3 *International and Comparative Law Quarterly* 665, and Natalie Davidson, "Human Rights Realism" (2021) 54:1 *Vanderbilt Journal of Transnational Law* 31, arguing for a compromise between sovereignty and human rights.

9 *Cook*, above note 7; *Canada (Justice) v Khadr*, 2008 SCC 28.

10 *Filartiga v Pena-Irala*, 630 F2d 876 (2d Cir 1980) and *Kiobel*, above note 5, discussed below, Hugh King, "The Extraterritorial Human Rights Obligations of States" (2009) 9:4 *Human Rights Law Review* 521; Pierre Leval, "Beyond *Kiobel*: The Future of Human Rights Litigation in US Courts" (2015) 19 *UCLA Journal of International Law and Foreign Affairs* 1; and Michael Kearney, "Extraterritorial Jurisdiction of the *European Convention on Human Rights*" (2002) 5 *Trinity College Law Review* 126. The ECtHR cases are similar to *Amnesty International*, note 28, below, arguing that human rights should be based on military control over individual

Canada the human rights reasoning was then extended to non-human rights cases by courts extending local laws to fill gaps and provide remedies, and to extend their own powers to make enforcement orders.[11]

For law reform, this raises important preliminary questions as to the basic nature and purpose of jurisdictional law; how and by whom the basic purpose should be determined; and how the law can be maintained and applied in the dynamic environment generated by pressures from globalization, transnational organized crime and cybercrime, terrorism, and other such developments. Judge-made law is an important element of law reform, but the extent of judicial competence to make jurisdictional law raises both practical and constitutional issues. In practical terms, judges are independent of foreign policy interests, and questions of foreign sovereignty and international comity are usually outside the scope of litigation cases. In constitutional terms, any judicial creation of extraterritorial law or authority is inconsistent with the separation of powers or supremacy of Parliament and the exclusive powers of legislatures and executive authorities over extraterritorial law and diplomacy.

2) What Is Jurisdictional Law For?

In extraterritoriality cases, jurisdictional law has several different legal and constitutional functions.

It should structure law and adjudication to ensure that some of the legal and non-legal interests that arise with respect to foreign sovereignty and comity are factored into domestic litigation without risking international conflicts of sovereignty or law, on one hand, and without compromising the independence and fairness of domestic proceedings, on the other. It also has an important domestic constitutional function in protecting executive control over foreign relations, while at the same

rights-holders rather than territorial sovereignty or control. See *Banković et al v Belgium et al*, [2001] ECHR 890, (2007), 44 EHRR SE5, reprinted at 41 ILM 517 (Balkans), *Al Skeini v United Kingdom* (2011) 53 EHRR 18 (Iraq) and most recently *Hanan v Germany* (2021) (Afghanistan) (ECHR case no 4871/16 of 16 February 2021).

11 *Equustek Solutions Inc v Google Inc*, 2015 BCCA 265, aff'd 2017 SCC 34 (copyright remedy injunction), applied in *BC (Attorney General) v Brecknell*, 2018 BCCA 5 [*Brecknell*] (*Criminal Code* production order). See also *AT v Globe 24h.com*, 2017 FC 114 at paras 81–86 [*Globe 24h*] (need for extraterritorial privacy remedies) and *R v Greco* (2001), 159 CCC (3d) 146 at paras 22–32 (Ont CA) (extension of power to make probation orders) [*Greco*].

time protecting judicial independence against case-extrinsic influences by domestic foreign policy officials and foreign governments. Like comity, it is both a barrier and a bridge, balancing national and international interests and the interoperation of legislative, executive, and judicial processes, protecting each from encroachment or undue influence from the others.

A second, often-overlooked function is protecting the rule of law in both forum and foreign territorial states. Applying laws made by and for one state in another erodes legitimacy and functional effectiveness of laws in both jurisdictions. It exceeds the policy, legitimacy, and enforcement capacity of one, circumvents the normal policy and legislative process of the other, and can generate the sort of conflicting and inconsistent rules that prevented *Charter* application in the cases before *Cook*.

A third function is to limit the discretion of judges to extend their own jurisdiction beyond the territorial limits of the court itself and of the sovereignty of the state which established it. Customary law and most national constitutions make it clear that the national legislature may make extraterritorial laws as an attribute of sovereignty, but the presumption against extraterritoriality was developed to prevent independent courts from doing the same thing by interpreting legislation as extraterritorial without clear language establishing the necessary legislative intent.[12]

A fourth function relates to the relationship between legislatures, the courts, and the way legislation is drafted as a basis for certainty in the law. US jurisprudence describes the presumption as creating "a stable background against which Congress can legislate with predictable effects."[13] If courts apply the presumption strictly, legislative drafters will understand that each provision must include clearly extraterritorial language if such application is intended, and courts can safely assume that silence expresses the intention that the provision not apply extraterritorially.

US sources have suggested that silence is as likely to result from Congressional oversight as any specific legislative intent,[14] but this is not the

12 See below note 15 and *Society of Composers, Authors and Music Publishers of Canada v Canadian Association of Internet Providers*, 2004 SCC 45 at paras 54–55 [*SOCAN v CAIP*], Binnie J and paras 141–44, LeBel J; Ruth Sullivan & Elmer A. Driedger, *Driedger on the Construction of Statutes*, 4th ed (Toronto: Butterworths, 2003) at 591–601.

13 *Morrison v National Australia Bank*, 130 S Ct 2869 (2010) at 2881 [*Morrison*].

14 Eric Posner & Cass Sunstein, "*Chevron*izing Foreign Relations Law" (2007) 116:6 *Yale Law Journal* 1170 at 1182–84. The US Congress provides professional support and advice, but the wording of legislation originates with political staff members and is negotiated among partisan interests.

case in Canada, where government legislation is drafted by independent professional drafters on ministerial and parliamentary policy direction. The difference is significant. Canadian reliance on non-partisan professional drafters produces greater consistency of statutory language and ensures that extraterritoriality issues are identified and actively considered by ministers and legislators, creating legislative records of what was intended. But the drafting convention only works if both drafters and the courts actually rely on one another, and the uncertainty created by efforts to apply *Charter* reasoning to other cases such as *Greco* create the prospect of having to either codify the presumption as a general rule or deal expressly with extraterritoriality in each individual enactment.

As discussed in the previous chapter, jurisdictional cases have grappled with constitutional questions because they had to consider the outer limits of forum sovereignty and their implications for entities within the state, and because those implications are different for legislative, executive, and judicial authorities. Extraterritorial actions must be attributable to the state itself and not to specific institutions within it. This is why nineteenth-century cases translated emerging customary law principles of sovereignty and non-interference into common law interpretive tools: judges should interpret ambiguous domestic law as consistent with international law whenever possible; statutes are presumed not to apply extraterritorially; and in cases where the intention to depart from customary law was clear and not ambiguous, that the intention of the legislature must prevail and be applied.[15]

But while the principles are clear, the resulting jurisprudence is another matter. It displays conflicts, inconsistences, and an ebb and flow between pro-forum pressures on judges to assert jurisdiction on one hand, and the constitutional limits on judicial discretion and allocation

15 UK and Canadian sources include *R v Keyn* (1876), 2 Ex Div 63; *R v Jameson*, [1896] 2 QB 425; *Arcadi v The King*, [1932] SCR 158; *Cox v Army Council*, [1963] AC 48; *Daniels v White and The Queen*, [1968] SCR 517; *Treacy v DPP*, [1971] AC 537, 55 Cr App R 113, at 551 [*Treacy*]; *Air India v Wiggins*, [1980] 2 All ER 593 at 597; *Hape*, above note 5 at para 53; *SOCAN v CAIP*, above note 12 at paras 54–55, Binnie J and 144, LeBel J; and *Kazemi Estate v Islamic Republic of Iran*, 2014 SCC 62, para 60, LeBel J. In the US, see *Murray v Schooner Charming Betsy*, 6 US (2 Cranch) 64, 118 (1804); *Schooner Exchange v M'Faddon*, 11 US 116 (1812); *United States v Kessler* (1829), 1 *Baldwin's Rep* 15; *Chicago & Southern Air Lines, Inc v Waterman Steamship Corp*, (1948) 333 US 103 at 111 (functional limits on judicial decision making); *Morrison*, above note 13; and *Kiobel*, above note 5 at 1669 (judicial avoidance of political questions).

of extraterritorial competence to the legislature on the other, returning periodically to a strict presumption because the underlying sovereignty-equality-territoriality construct on which all domestic legal systems are based does not change. Cases have variously ignored the presumptions entirely, reversed them by reading statutory silence as extraterritorial permission, or crafted exceptions based on "necessary implication," "real and substantial links," or on whether the subject matter sufficiently "touched and concerned" forum interests.

When the judicial pendulum swings too far and a correction is needed, in cases such as *Hape* and *Kiobel*, the public, media, and academic commentary is dominated by dismay and criticism,[16] often based on arguments that perceived gaps should be filled by domestic laws and reasoning. Following *Hape*, the perceived gap lay in not extending domestic rights as a control on extraterritorial official activities,[17] and following *Kiobel* it was in the perceived loss of the US justice system and tort law as a default mechanism for creating and enforcing extraterritorial human rights standards. The rejection of US jurisdiction over torts committed by Nigerian officials and employees of a Dutch company entirely in Nigeria in *Kiobel* prompted suggestions that Canadian courts might be resorted to instead.[18] One source described *Kiobel* as having lost

> a core truth that is difficult to deny—the idea that if the domestic forum with the greatest relationship to the claim is unavailable, perpetrators of gross human rights violations should be able to be held accountable, and their victims should be able to secure a remedy—*somewhere*.[19]

---

16 See Eleni Kannis, "Pulling (Apart) the Triggers of Extraterritorial Jurisdiction" (2014) 40:1 *University of Western Australia Law Review* 221; King 2009, above note 10; Sarah Cleveland, "After *Kiobel*" (2014) 12:3 *Journal of International Criminal Justice* 551; and Stuart Hendin "Extraterritorial Application of Human Rights: The Differing Decisions of Canadian and U.K. Courts" (2010) 28 *Windsor Review of Legal and Social Issues* 57.

17 See, for example, Kent Roach, "*R v Hape* Creates *Charter*-free Zones for Canadian Officials Abroad" (2007) 53 *Criminal Law Quarterly* 1.

18 Sean Fairhurst & Zöe Thoms, "Post-*Kiobel v Royal Dutch Petroleum Co*: Is Canada Poised to Become an Alternative Jurisdiction for Extraterritorial Human Rights Litigation?" (2014) 52:2 *Alberta Law Review* 389; and Chilenye Nwapi, "Accountability for Canadian Mining Corporations for Their Overseas Conduct: Can Extraterritorial Criminal Prosecution Come to the Rescue?" (2016) 54 *Canadian Yearbook of International Law* 227.

19 Cleveland 2014, above note 16 at 577.

Territorial courts must adjudicate transnational and extraterritorial cases, and the collective results are an important source of customary law, especially as foreign jurisprudence is considered and a more modern, globalized, sense of judicial comity emerges.[20] But as domestic rule-of-law constructs whose functions depend on the independence of judges and the isolation of case-based adjudication, there are important legal and functional limitations on what domestic courts can be expected to accomplish, and on what they should be permitted to decide with respect to their own jurisdiction. A shift away from reliance on heuristics in the direction of more algorithmic reasoning is needed to balance the influences of sustained pro-forum bias pressures, which suggests using a more legislative approach to jurisdictional limits. In constitutional terms, it is important to reaffirm that Parliament alone has the authority to create extraterritorial law and jurisdiction, and to separate judicial functions from executive ones in ways that protect judicial independence and executive policy prerogatives from each other.

B. SPECIFIC LAW REFORM ISSUES AND OPTIONS

1) Should the Presumption Against Extraterritorial Application Be Codified?

The presumption first arose from nineteenth-century judicial decisions refusing to extend adjudication without clear legislative authority. Responding to a suggestion by Halsbury LJ that dominion legislatures had no extraterritorial competence at all, Australia codified it in 1901.[21] Other common law states left it to the courts, but Canada (1953) and New Zealand (1961) found it necessary to prohibit extraterritorial

20 Anne-Marie Slaughter, "Judicial Globalization" (2000) 40 *Virginia Journal of International Law* 1103, and "A Global Community of Courts" (2003) 44 *Harvard International Law Journal* 191.

21 Stuart Dutson, "The Conflict of Laws and Statutes: International Operation of Legislation Dealing with Matters of Civil Law in the United Kingdom and Australia" (1997) 60 *Modern Law Review* 668 at 674–76 (discussing para 21(b) of the Australian *Acts Interpretation Act 1901* and an 1897 predecessor). Halsbury LJ questioned whether Westminster had bestowed or retained extraterritorial competence in *McLeod v AG of New South Wales*, [1891] AC 455, an issue resisted in dominion states and not settled until the 1931 *Statute of Westminster* and *Croft v Dunphy*, [1932] All ER 154, [1933] 1 DLR 225. See also Thomas Mohr, "The Foundations of Irish Extra-Territorial Legislation" (2005) 40 *Irish Jurist* 86.

criminal convictions. As noted above, the Canadian presumption has been reinforced by reliance on professional drafters and clear language, but also weakened by efforts to avoid applying it in the *Charter* cases and in subsequent non-*Charter* applications such as *Greco*. The enactment of limits in specific provisions could also backfire, by suggesting that other provisions without limits might be applied extraterritorially.[22]

Libman described section 6(2) of the *Criminal Code* as having codified the presumption, but that provision is not drafted as a rule of statutory interpretation or a limit on extraterritoriality, and it does not address the "both here and there" complexities of modern transnational crime. This proved problematic in *Oler*,[23] when applying it to the offence in section 273.3(1) led the trial court to acquit one of the three persons accused of a transnational offence for lack of evidence that he had been inside Canada when it was committed. The court established a different *situs* for each accused based on their locations, rather than applying *Libman situs* to assume jurisdiction over the entire scheme of removing underage girls from Canada to the United States. Section 6(2) was also not applied in *Greco*, which convicted the accused of breaching an Ontario probation order by assaulting his partner in Cuba, disregarding the presumption that neither the assault nor the breach offence applies extraterritorially.

Libman alleviated some of the pressure. It did not extend to fully extraterritorial cases (see below), but it did extend concurrent territorial jurisdiction to transnational cases with territorial elements, for which the interests in asserting jurisdiction are usually the most compelling. The idea of concurrent territorial jurisdiction originally arose from nineteenth century applications of customary law territoriality to transnational activities. It appears in a dissenting judgment in the 1971 UK decision in *Treacy* and 1965 and 1972 papers all cited in *Libman*,[24] and a 1984 Canadian Law Reform Commission paper suggested both concurrent jurisdiction and

22 See, for example, *Libman v the Queen*, [1985] 2 SCR 178 at 209 (*obiter*) [*Libman*].

23 *R v Oler*, 2018 BCCA 323.

24 Glanville Willams, "Venue and the Ambit of Criminal Law" (1965) 81 *Law Quarterly Review* 276, 395 and 421 at 518 and 526–29 (quoting an 1879 UK Criminal Law Commission proposal similar to the later New Zealand and Australian provisions at 527); Lynden Hall, "'Territorial Jurisdiction' and the Criminal Law" (1972) *Criminal Law Review* 276 at 280 (citing the 1826 *Criminal Law Act*); and *Treacy*, above note 15. The significance of these in *Libman* is discussed below.

codifying the presumption itself.[25] Concurrency provisions were enacted by New Zealand in 1961 and in Australia in 2001,[26] and eventually adopted by the UK courts in 2004.[27]

The general presumption of conformity with international law has been widely accepted because it encompasses broad principles, especially in human rights, which expand judicial discretion to limit what states may do, while the presumption against extraterritoriality is often avoided because it incorporates more specific customary law principles—those requiring deference to foreign territorial sovereignty—that limit what the judges themselves may do. Efforts to avoid it have included treating fully extraterritorial scenarios as transnational, characterizing enforcement orders as prescriptive, replacing it with judicial comity-balancing, ignoring or reversing it without explanation, and over-extensions of the necessary implication exception. Assuming that the specific presumption is indeed intended to limit not just extraterritorial application, but judicial discretion, it should be codified as a general rule of statutory interpretation, with *prima facie* application to all federal legislation.

Codification would probably render some existing jurisdictional provisions redundant. These should be reviewed, some could be repealed, and others clarified to deal with cases such as *Oler*, where the locations of offences and offenders were not the same, and other possible multiple-*situs* scenarios. It is argued in Chapter 6 that the same basic

25 Law Reform Commission of Canada, *Working Paper No 37: Extraterritorial Jurisdiction* (1984), c 1 at 12–14 and c 18 at 159–66, relying in part on an unpublished 1980 paper by La Forest J, before he was appointed to the bench and five years before he wrote the unanimous decision in *Libman*. The draft legislation (s 4) refers to the need for "a real and substantial link" based on territorial elements, but the scheme also suggested other statutory extensions, including over some offences by Canadian nationals based on Crown allegiance and some effects-based jurisdiction.

26 Sections 5–7 of the New Zealand *Crimes Act, 1961* both limit the extraterritorial application of offences and clarify the *situs* of offences in transnational scenarios along lines similar to *Libman*. Part 2.7 of the Australian *Criminal Code Act 1995* was added in 2001 to clarify principles that included the application of federal law to offences involving "conduct ... [occurring] wholly or partly within Australia."

27 *R v Smith (Wallace Duncan) (No 4)*, [2004] QB 1418 (leave to appeal to the House of Lords denied) [*Smith (Wallace Duncan)*]. For discussion of the interval see Geoff Gilbert, "Crimes *Sans Frontières*: Jurisdictional Problems in English Law" (1992) 63:1 *British Yearbook of International Law* 414 at 424–36. A similar rule was applied in Australia in *Lipohar and Winfield v The Queen*, [1999] HCA 65 but not described as a "real and substantial link." See Matthew Goode, "The Tortured Tale of Criminal Jurisdiction" (1997) 21 *Melbourne University Law Review* 411 and below for discussion.

presumption against extraterritoriality should apply to the common law and constitutional law mandates of courts themselves, so that inherent powers or jurisdiction could not be used to extend judicial orders or other measures where statutes are silent. Extraterritorial orders should only be possible where expressly authorized by statute, either in the general mandate of the court or the specific provision on which an order is based.

2) Extraterritorial Application of *Charter* rights or Controls to Canadian Officials Abroad

Hape concluded that the *Charter* cannot apply extraterritorially unless the territorial state consents or there is Canadian participation in some extraterritorial violation of international human rights that make *Charter* remedies more important than foreign comity interests. Apart from *Khadr* (2008), the courts have wisely resisted efforts to expand the exception,[28] but have also not applied the common law presumption, resulting in non-*Charter* cases such as *Greco*. Statutory attempts to either extend or limit application could be seen as constitutional amendments, and the courts are unlikely to fully apply the common law, but this does not end the matter.

Most of the criticism has not been about extending affirmative rights to what L'Heureux-Dubé J described in *Cook* as "rights holders," but extending controls to Canadian officials abroad. The customary law and comity problem is not with the *Charter* as a control, but the fact that it operates indirectly by extending rights, a sovereign prerogative of the territorial state. Extending either rights or controls is extraterritorial enforcement, but extraterritorial controls are *intra vires* Parliament and a common exception to the customary law limits. A broad, *Charter*-based, and whole-of-government approach would avoid gaps,[29] set clearer general standards, better reflect overarching values and ethics, and permit

28 See *R v Tan*, 2014 BCCA 9 [*Tan*], *Amnesty International Canada v Canada (Chief of the Defence Staff)*, 2008 FC 336, aff'd 2008 FCA 401, leave denied [2009] SCCA No 63 (both rejecting broad or implicit foreign consent arguments), and *Slahi v Canada (Minister of Justice)*, 2009 FC 160, aff'd 2009 FCA 259 (holding that the exceptional application of the *Charter* in *Khadr* does not apply to non-Canadians).

29 Examples include gaps in the extension of jurisdiction by *Criminal Code*, RSC 1985, c C-46 at s 7(4) and ensuring that Canadian nationals or residents who enjoy functional immunities abroad can be prosecuted in Canada.

the sort of tailoring needed to avoid the concerns raised by any direct application of the *Charter* and its jurisprudence.[30]

3) Statutory Extensions to Extraterritorial Scenarios Based on Representative or Consent-Based Jurisdiction

There will always be jurisdictional gaps, but some of the pressures seen in cases such as *Greco* and *Ouellette*[31] could be relieved by actually extending jurisdiction, where this was justified in policy terms and countervailing customary law and comity concerns can be addressed. The idea of relying on the consent of a foreign state is not new in Canadian law,[32] and would require different approaches to transnational and extraterritorial cases.

In transnational cases concurrent territorial jurisdiction already exists based on *Libman*. No clear statutory language is needed, and foreign consent is limited to comity-based discussions of the sort envisaged in *Libman*, usually between executive officials considering extradition, mutual assistance, and prosecutorial discretion.[33]

If the facts are purely extraterritorial, comity requires deference to the primary jurisdiction of the territorial state, and domestic law requires — and should require — clear statutory jurisdiction that displaces the presumption. If consent-based jurisdiction was enacted, it would relieve judicial pressure to avoid the presumption and reduce the risks created by speculative comity assessments. Consent would probably be given in cases such as *Greco* and *Oullette*, in which travelling Canadians

---

30 One example would be the *National Defence Act*'s Code of Service Discipline, RSC 1985, c N-5, Part III, which already extends prescriptive, adjudicative, and enforcement to military personnel outside of Canada and is the subject of long-term discussions and jurisprudence considering how to apply the *Charter* in such matters. See *R v Généreux*, [1992] 1 SCR 259; *R v Moriarity*, 2015 SCC 55; and *R v Stillman*, 2019 SCC 40 (application of *Charter* to personnel and proceedings) and *R v Wehmeier*, 2012 CM 1005, 2014 CMAC 5 (accompanying civilians).

31 *R c Ouellette* (1998), 126 CCC (3d) 219 (CSQ) [*Ouellette*].

32 See *Criminal Code*, above note 29, s 7(4.2), enacted by SC 1997, c 16, s 1, repealed by SC 2002, c 13, s 3(2) (territorial consent to prosecute "sex tourism" offences); Council of Europe, "Extraterritorial Criminal Jurisdiction" (1992) 3:3 *Criminal Law Forum* 441 at 452; and Gilbert 1992, above note 27 at 423.

33 See *United States of America v Cotroni; United States of America v El Zein*, [1989] 1 SCR 1469 (prosecution declined in favour of extradition on public interest grounds) [*Cotroni*].

committed offences against other Canadians,[34] and might also be an option for accusations against Canadian officials or aid workers in places where local investigative and rule-of-law capacity is lacking, discussed below. Jurisdiction based on a Canadian request and no response from the territorial state would also allow foreign states to accede to Canadian proceedings without diplomatic concerns about giving consent in open court. Post-*Hape* cases such as *Tan* set a high sovereign consent standard for *Charter* application, but there is no reason why Parliament or the courts should apply this to individual prosecutions. None of this would address the common evidentiary challenges, the need to gain custody of the accused, or the exercise of normal prosecutorial discretion.

4) Extraterritorial Jurisdiction Over Canadians Employed Outside of Canada by Intergovernmental and International Non-governmental Organizations

The lack of effective accountability and criminal jurisdiction over intergovernmental, governmental, and non-governmental aid workers is a long-standing problem.[35] Peacekeeping forces are usually subject to extraterritorial military jurisdiction, but civilian intergovernmental organizations have no criminal jurisdiction and limited disciplinary recourse, and international non-governmental organizations have none at all. Past scenarios of international concern have usually involved either sexual exploitation and abuse[36] or the corrupt diversion of aid resources,[37] but a range of other offences is possible.

---

34 See also *R v B(O)* (1997), 116 CCC (3d) 189 (Ont CA).

35 Anthony Miller, "Legal Aspects of Sexual Exploitation and Abuse in UN Peacekeeping Operations" (2006) 39 *Cornell Law Journal* 71; and Zuszsanna Deen-Racsmány, "Towards a Convention on the Criminal Accountability of UN Personnel, Including UN Military Experts on Mission and Police Officers" (2015) 54 *Military Law and the Law of War Review* 195.

36 Note of the Secretary General to the General Assembly, Report of the Special Advisor, *A comprehensive strategy to eliminate future sexual exploitation and abuse in United Nations peacekeeping operations*, UNGA, 59th Sess, UN doc A/59/710 (24 March 2005) Annex.

37 Corrupt abuses of the 1996–2003 Iraq Oil-for-Food Programme are thought to represent the largest economic crime in modern history. See "Corruption at the Heart of the United Nations" *The Economist* (9 August 2005), online: www.economist.com/unknown/2005/08/09/corruption-at-the-heart-of-the-united-nations; "Iraq Scandal Taints 2000 Firms" *BBC News* (27 October 2005), online: news.bbc.co.uk/2/hi/

Customary international law and UN policy have a strong preference for local territorial law and jurisdiction, but many of the incidents, especially those involving sexual misconduct, tend to arise in post-conflict, refugee, and disaster-relief scenarios where the lack of local enforcement and rule of law capacity creates *de facto* impunity, and local populations are vulnerable to exploitation. Procurement fraud and corruption offences tend to be multi-jurisdictional and to involve combinations of officials and outsiders. In the case of the United Nations, such offences have sometimes been prosecuted by the US attorney for the South District of New York based on territorial jurisdiction over UN headquarters and its financial centre,[38] but this places a significant burden on US resources and is problematic in that it vests a significant aspect of UN disciplinary enforcement in the prosecutors and courts of a single Member State. Reliance on the accused's nationality state to assume jurisdiction is problematic in other ways, but would at least represent an improvement. Some intergovernmental officials have functional immunities held by the organization, not their own state, but waiver can be impossible in jurisdictions where rule of law and human rights protections are weak, and moot in those where enforcement and prosecution capacities are limited.[39]

---

americas/4382820.stm; "Timeline: Oil-for-Food Scandal" *BBC News* (7 September 2005), online: news.bbc.co.uk/2/hi/middle_east/4445609.stm.

38 US authorities conducted a series or prosecutions based on a joint UN-US investigation of the Iraq programme. Its head, Benon Sevan, was indicted and could not be extradited from Cyprus, but a series of other US convictions and guilty pleas resulted. A few other countries whose companies were implicated pursued criminal cases based on concurrent jurisdiction, but most did not. See *United States v Kuznetsov*, 442 F Supp 2d 102 (SDNY, 2006) [*Kuznetsov*]; and *United States v Behal*, 662 F 3d 610 (2011), "Former UN Procurement Officer Pleads Guilty to Taking Bribes from Contractors" [*United States v Alexander Yakovlev*, unreported] (8 August 2005) *New York Times* and "Rolling up the Culprits" (13 March 2008) *The Economist*. In May 2022, the USAO SDNY concluded proceedings against a UN employee involving at least eighteen incidents of extraterritorial sexual assault by obtaining guilty pleas to the two offences over which the US had jurisdiction: making false statements to the FBI inside the US, and the sexual assault of the one victim who was an internationally protected person, making the offence subject to treaty-based statutory extraterritorial jurisdiction under 18 US Code § 1116 (c). See US Department of Justice Release 22-175, 24 May 2022.

39 See UNGA, *Report of the Group of Legal Experts on ensuring the accountability of United Nations staff and experts on mission with respect to criminal acts committed in peacekeeping operations*, UN Doc A/60/980 (16 August 2006) at paras 20–22

Such offences create strong international policy justifications to extend jurisdiction. They can have serious effects on vulnerable populations, damage the trust and credibility needed to deliver on international mandates, and divert or waste scarce development and relief resources. The UN Secretary General, General Assembly, and Security Council have all attempted to persuade Member States to put extraterritorial jurisdiction on a customary international law footing, or to elaborate an international legal instrument to deal with the problem. But somebody must take the first step.

Nationality-based extraterritorial jurisdiction would still be subject to immunity waivers and either the consent or silence of the territorial state. Consideration would have to be given to whether Canadian jurisdiction would extend only to Canadian nationals or also include residents and others present in Canada where comity and practical considerations supported a Canadian prosecution. Practical considerations with respect to things like investigative capacity and jurisdiction and the status of non-governmental aid workers as offenders or victims would have to be addressed, but these are manageable and case-volumes would probably be small. The UN would certainly welcome such an initiative, not least as a precedent that Member States which contribute UN officials and experts also contribute the same sort of accountability they extend to their own officials abroad.

5) Default Jurisdiction Where Extradition Impossible

A further possibility might be to enact extraterritorial extensions of Canadian law and jurisdiction over persons in Canada who could not be extradited for rule-of-law or human rights reasons, for serious offences with dual-criminality. In such cases comity concerns do arise, but from the refusal to extradite before any prosecution, and this might be preferable to allowing the accused to be at large in Canada.

(immunities) and 44 (jurisdiction). The immunity is that of the organization, not the worker or their nationality state: see *Kuznetsov*, *ibid*, accepting UN immunity waiver and rejecting Russian claims of diplomatic status.

6) Clarify *Libman*: Does It Extend Territorial Jurisdiction Over Transnational "Activities"? Or Create Extraterritorial Jurisdiction to the Limits of International Comity?

Libman sought to address "doctrinal confusion," and established two important principles: that the *situs* of a transnational offence should be concurrent, not exclusive, based on the location(s) of any "significant portion of the activities" rather than any single element; and that when an offence was factually "both here and there," concurrent territorial jurisdiction could vest in more than one state. The oft-quoted lines are:

> I might summarize my approach to the limits of territoriality this way. As I see it, all that is necessary to make an offence subject to the jurisdiction of our courts is that a significant portion of the activities constituting that offence took place in Canada. As it is put by modern academics, it is sufficient that there be a "real and substantial link" between an offence and this country, a test well-known in public and private international law .... As Professor Hall notes ... this does not require legislation....
>
> Just what may constitute a real and substantial link in a particular case, I need not explore. There were ample links here. The outer limits of the test may, however, well be coterminous with the requirements of international comity.[40]

Libman clearly addressed only extended territorial jurisdiction based on substantial territorial activities, not extraterritorial jurisdiction, but has since been interpreted as creating two alternative "real and substantial link" assessments. One of these requires Canadian territorial elements, but the other constructs links based on open-ended comity balancing assessments, even where the facts themselves are wholly extraterritorial. *Libman* itself refers only to "the limits of territoriality," and its analysis and its sources were all based on pre-existing territorial *situs* concepts of jurisdiction.[41]

Justice La Forest and Professor Hall said that legislation was not required because territorial "activities" established territorial *situs* and jurisdiction, avoiding the presumption triggered if the offences had been wholly extraterritorial. Hall also referred to a proposal of Diplock LJ in *Treacy* a

40 *Libman*, above note 22 at 212–13, paras 74 and 76.

41 See Goode 1997, above note 27 at 441–42 discussing the broader test and its rejection by Australian courts in *R v Thompson* (1989), 1 CLR 1, as not requiring proof of locality.

year earlier and suggested the idea of a "real and substantial link" as a way of creating a narrower jurisdictional test, not a broader one.[42] Subsequent Canadian jurists and commentators, especially in the *Charter* cases, have instead expanded the idea to allow the sort of open-ended comity-balancing that Diplock LJ had in mind, which is not supported by the actual text of *Libman*. That refers to comity as the "outer limits of the test" that had just been created and not the outer limits of jurisdiction itself. A better interpretation is probably that La Forest J was distinguishing between the *existence* of concurrent territorial jurisdiction based on "significant" territorial activities, and limiting the *exercise* of this jurisdiction based on an assessment of the comity interests of other states that might assert their own concurrent jurisdiction. Canada might have deferred to extradition requests from the US jurisdictions where victims were defrauded, for example.[43]

In *Treacy*, Diplock LJ had suggested, *obiter*, that the presumption against extraterritorial intent should be replaced with a presumption that Parliament had not intended to offend comity.[44] This would have had the fairly radical effect of replacing a strict test of statutory interpretation that restricts judicial discretion with a much broader extension of judicial discretion to assess Parliament's past or present intent regarding comity. Whether or not the implications were clear to Lord Diplock at the time, his idea was overbroad for Professor Hall, and not taken up by the UK courts[45] or by Diplock himself in subsequent cases.[46]

42 See Hall 1972, above note 24 at 276–78 and 283–86 (cited in *Libman*, above note 22 at 213, para 74).

43 For a recent discussion of this difference (in military-law scenarios) see *Stillman* 2019, above note 30 at paras 103–7. In *Cotroni*, above note 33, Canadian prosecutors did defer to a US prosecution for comity reasons.

44 *Treacy*, above note 15 at 140–41 and 144–45, Diplock LJ, discussed in *Libman*, above note 22 at 195, para 37 *et seq*.

45 *Libman* and Diplock LJ's *Treacy* dissent were partially followed on concurrency in *Liangsiriprasert v United States of America*, [1991] 1 AC 225 (applying a rule similar to s 465(4) of Canada's *Criminal Code* to a conspiracy case), and more broadly in *Smith (Wallace Duncan)*, above note 27, resolving the longstanding conflict between exclusivity and concurrency in favour of the latter). Some of the cases describe Diplock's dissent as a comity approach, but in contexts that suggest only concurrency is referred to.

46 See Michael Hirst, *Jurisdiction and the Ambit of the Criminal Law* (Oxford: Oxford University Press, 2003) at 8–9, citing the decision of Lord Diplock in *Secretary of State for Trade v Markus*, [1976] AC 35; Gilbert, above note 27 at 424–36; and Julian Lew "The Extraterritorial Jurisdiction of English Courts" (1978) 27 *International & Comparative Law Quarterly* 168 at 175–79.

The idea of comity balancing without any territorial element is constitutionally problematic because it shifts control from Parliament to the courts. It vastly increases judicial discretion, shifts the focus from factual *situs* to comity assessments that courts are ill equipped to conduct, and allows judges to create fully extraterritorial jurisdiction without any statutory support. The resulting test is simultaneously circular and open-ended, allowing courts to extend their own jurisdictions based on any link thought sufficiently real and substantial to warrant the extension.[47] This produces jurisprudence that tends to be consistent only in its preference of forum jurisdiction. For example, the combined effect of *Cook*, *Greco*, and *Hape* is that while *Hape* found the extension of *Charter* rights to be impermissible extraterritorial enforcement, *Greco* and subsequent cases hold the extraterritorial application of coercive probation orders and related breach offences to be either not extraterritorial or not enforcement — depending on which cases one reads.

Unfettered comity balancing might be intuitively attractive, but the vague nature of comity and the compelling nature of both domestic and foreign policy, political, and comity interests combine to make it significant risk. Following the *Charter* cases, Canadian judges have relied upon *Libman* comity-balancing interpretations to make and enforce their own orders extraterritorially,[48] to reverse the presumption and create extraterritorial application based on statutory silence,[49] and to hold that legislation has no extraterritorial effects if a Canadian court finds a real and substantial link.[50] In *Re: X*, following a tortured series of efforts to find authority for extraterritorial investigative warrants under the *CSIS Act*, the Federal Court of Appeal suggested, without deciding, that national

47 This has been criticized as unhelpful even in private law. See Joost Blom & Elizabeth Edinger, "The Chimera of the Real and Substantial Connection Test" (2005) 38:2 *University of British Colombia Law Review* 373.

48 *R v Rattray*, 2008 ONCA 74, and *Greco*, 2001, *Brecknell*, 2018, and *Globe 24h*, 2017, all above note 11; and *Rakuten Kobo Inc v Canada (Commissioner of Competition)*, 2018 FC 64.

49 Several of the *Charter* cases, and most of those in the previous note, starting with *Greco*, expressly reverse the presumption. Regarding inferences made from statutory silence see, for example, *Cook*, above note 7 at paras 24, 26, 46, and 48, *Hape*, above note 5 at paras 160–61 and *Greco*, above note 11 at para 31.

50 See *Rakuten Kobo*, above note 48 at para 94.

security interests, which raise major comity concerns on all sides, might somehow constitute the necessary real and substantial link:

> [T]he stronger the real and substantial link between Canada and the extraterritorial enforcement of its law, the less such enforcement offends the principle of comity.[51]

7) Clarify What Comity Actually Means and How Courts Should Assess It

Comity originated as international courtesy and prudent deference to foreign sovereignty based on uncertainty, risks, and the desire to avoid conflict. It has since been described (and used) as a "sword," a "shield," a "bridge," a "wall," as "permissive and preclusive," as "more than a courtesy but less than a duty," as being both non-legal and a "synonym for international law" and as "a mess, because courts do not know when it applies."[52] These reflect the need to treat comity as a buffer among divergent domestic and foreign interests. There are also underlying existential conflicts, which is what led the courts in early cases to defer to the political and legislative bodies, and later US commentators to cite separation of powers concerns.[53] Judges do need to assess comity in cases such as *Libman*, but its vague and non-legal nature is inconsistent with the litigation standards of evidence and common law precedent. Foreign states usually have no

51 *Re (X)*, 2014 FCA 249 at para 95 (quote) and 96. Extraterritorial intelligence gathering occurs despite comity, not based on it. The same factors that increase the extraterritorial interests of the forum state usually increase the countervailing comity concerns of other states. The decision was never appealed, the government deciding to give up on litigation and amend the statute instead. See SC 2015, c 9, amending the *Canadian Security Intelligence Service Act*, RSC 1985, c C-23, s 21(1) and (3.1).

52 In order, Joel R. Paul, "Comity in International Law" (1991) 32:1 *Harvard International Law Journal* at 1–80; William S. Dodge, "International Comity in American Law" (2015) 115:8 *Columbia Law Re*view 2071; Kerry Sun, "International Comity and the Construction of the *Charter*'s Limits: *Hape* Revisited" (2019) 45:1 *Queen's Law Journal* 115; Michael Akehurst, "Jurisdiction in International Law" (1972–73) 46 *British Yearbook of International* Law 145 at 214–16; and Donald E. Childress III, "Comity as Conflict: Resituating International Comity as Conflict of Laws" (2010) 44 *University of California (Davis) Law Review* 11 at 59.

53 See Posner & Sunstein, 2007, above note 14 (arguing that comity assessments should be executive matters) and William S. Dodge, "International Comity in American Law" (2015) 115:8 *Columbia Law Review* 2071 at 2132–40 (arguing for a more functional approach).

standing or representation, and direct evidence of their interests is rarely available to the court. As discussed in Chapter 6, this often results in forum courts filling in the gap with domestic assumptions about foreign interests, often with one eye fixed, consciously or not, on their own desire to adjudicate the case.

Comity assessments should be avoided or reduced where possible and generally made more fact-based and algorithmic in nature when they are needed.[54] Where possible, comity should be considered by executive authorities in advance, before case-specific interests and judicial independence issues arise. Provision should be made to allow foreign states to file pleadings or *amicus curiae* briefs raising their concerns directly, which is common with US Supreme Court extraterritoriality cases, but not elsewhere.[55]

More fundamentally, comity arose out of the idea that judging foreign sovereign interests could be challenging, and that misjudging them could have serious consequences, making it necessary to err on the side of caution and prudent deference:

> [I]nternational comity is not just recognition but *deference—a* word that captures comity's use both as a principle of recognition and as a principle of restraint.[56]
>
> If comity among nations is to have any meaning, a doctrine of extraterritoriality must err on the side of restraint....
>
> Only by placing the burden of proof on those who would subject foreign activity to jurisdiction ... can courts ensure that foreign sovereigns are accorded the deference they deserve.[57]

This suggests that the most fundamental and important algorithmic element for assessing comity would involve, with due respect to Lord Diplock, the replacement of comity-balancing with deference and a robust presumption that extraterritorial extensions do engage foreign comity interests, rebuttable only by actual evidence and not judicial conjecture.

---

54 See, for example, Childress 2010, above note 52 at 65–71.

55 Kristen Eichensehr, "Foreign Sovereigns as Friends of the Court" (2016) 102:2 *Virginia Law Review* 289.

56 Dodge 2015, above note 52, at 2078.

57 Note, "Predictability and Comity: Toward Common Approaches to Extraterritorial Jurisdiction" (1985) 98 *Harvard Law Review* 1310 at 1323.

C. CONCLUSION

This chapter has argued that jurisdictional law should be seen as quasi-constitutional, based on what it does and the differences of interpretation and application needed for it to work effectively. It arises from territorial sovereignty, establishing limits of the legal jurisdiction of each state, while at the same time serving as a buffer and a bridge when interests overlap and different systems must interact. To do this, it must have a degree of supremacy over other law and set fairly prescriptive and algorithmic rules governing the situations in which it must be applied. Human rights are given constitutional status as fundamental values, but also because they require entrenchment and prescriptive application to all other laws; the same is true for jurisdictional limits on both extraterritoriality and the powers of independent courts.

This has important implications for both cumulative jurisprudence and episodic law reform, as evidenced by the inconsistencies that can be seen when domestic lawyers and courts attempt to develop jurisdictional law reasoning upward from substantive principles of human rights, criminal law, environmental law, and the sorts of public-private law issues raised in cases like *Kiobel*, *Equustek*, and *Nevsun Resources Ltd v Araya*.[58] Judge-made law is an important source of law reform, but it is also problematic for jurisdictional law reform because the majority of heuristic and structural biases that arise in litigation consistently push it in a pro-forum direction.

The reasoning of *Keyn*, *M'Fadden*, and other early cases reflected not only the importance of common law jurisprudence in conventional and common law constitutional structures, but also the judges' understanding of the boundary nature of jurisdictional law, the risks of extraterritorial decisions, and the limits of their own powers and capabilities. Those cases stand out not just as judicial decisions to decline jurisdiction but as illustrating that courts could not constitutionally create their own jurisdiction. As Cockburn LJ put it in *Keyn*, "The responsibility is with the legislature, and there it must rest."[59] Jurisprudence thus has a part to play, but also has clear and important limits and courts should defer to Parliament for both constitutional and practical reasons.

58 2020 SCC 5.

59 *Keyn*, above note 15 at 231.

This is not to suggest that there is no place for extraterritorial law, especially in a globalized world, and those same constitutional and pragmatic factors make it incumbent on governments and parliaments to enact such measures as are needed to keep pace with dynamic pressures. This may require periodic interventions to reinforce the principles that limit ambit and jurisdiction, but another approach is the extension of laws to alleviate some of the pressures that confront judges in cases like *Greco* and *Khadr* (2008). There is considerable room for such an approach within existing customary international law, especially if consent options are included, and enacting clearly extraterritorial provisions where they are possible would also reinforce the territorial limits that apply in all other scenarios. All of this requires a conservative approach, careful deliberation, due regard for foreign sovereignty and comity, and the recognition that the sort of *ad hoc* jurisdictional extensions rejected in *Keyn* but created in cases like *Cook*, *Greco*, and *Khadr* could well do more harm than good.

eight

Canadian ISIS Fighters and Supporters and the Irony of the *Khadr* Exception

LEAH WEST*

A. INTRODUCTION

There are between forty and fifty Canadians currently held by the Syrian Defence Forces (SDF) in Northeast Syria. The majority of the Canadians are under the age of twelve, children whose parents are alleged members or supporters of ISIS. They and between fifteen to twenty adult women are detained in one of two overcrowded detention camps: Al Roj and Al Hol. Public reporting also confirms that four Canadian men are currently imprisoned by the SDF, Canada's ally in the fight against ISIS, for their alleged membership in ISIS and the crimes they committed as part of the brutal terrorist organization: Jack Letts, Mohammed Ali, Aboubakr Siddique, and a fourth man whose name has never been published. Mohammed Khalifa, a Saudi-born Canadian citizen was detained from March 2019 until he was transferred to the United States in October 2021, where he was charged and pleaded guilty to conspiring to provide material support to a terrorist organization resulting in death.[1] While in custody,

* SJD, Assistant Professor, Norman Paterson School of International Affairs, Carleton University. Many thanks to Jake Norris for his fantastic research assistance with this piece.

1 US, Justice Department, "Leading ISIS Media Figure and Foreign Fighter Pleads Guilty to Conspiring to Provide Material Support to a Terrorist Organization, Resulting in Death" (10 December 2021), online: www.justice.gov/usao-edva/pr/leading-isis-media-figure-and-foreign-fighter-pleads-guilty-conspiring-provide-material.

Khalifa, Ali, and Letts spoke to reporters about their actions in Syria and claim to have spoken with foreign investigators since their detention in the spring of 2018.[2]

To date, nine Canadian men have been charged *in absentia* for terrorism offences under the *Criminal Code*, five of them for their activities with ISIS in Syria.[3] To date, no women have been charged *in absentia*, but three women have been charged with attempting to leave Canada to participate in the activity of a terrorist group (ISIS).[4] Thus, there is a precedent for charging Canadian adults who travelled from Canada to Syria to join ISIS with criminal offences. However, none of the adult Canadians currently detained by the SDF for their alleged participation in, or support for, ISIS has been charged with a single crime.[5]

When pressed as to why these Canadians—along with others who have already returned to Canada—are not facing charges for terrorist activity, Prime Minister Trudeau and former Public Safety Minister Ralph Goodale made clear that the government's intent is to prosecute them.[6]

---

2 Stewart Bell, "As Fate of ISIS Prisoners in Syria Grows More Unpredictable, RCMP Has Still Not Charged Any of the Canadians" *Global News* (15 October 2019), online: globalnews.ca/news/6027248/kurdish-forces-rcmp-canadians; Maryam Shah, "U.K. Citizenship Stripped from 'Jihadi Jack,' Leaving Him with Only Canadian Citizenship" *Global News* (18 August 2019), online: globalnews.ca/news/5780603/jihadi-jack-citizenship-revoked/; Kelly McEvers, "How It Ends: The Brother" *Embedded*, NPR podcast (5 April 2019), online: www.npr.org/transcripts/710489192.

3 John Maguire, Khadar Khalib, Farah Mohamed Shirdon, Hasibullah Yusufzai, Ahmad Waseem, Maiwand Yar, Ferid Ahmed Imam, Mokhtar Belmokhtar, and Omar Ould Hamaha. Maguire, Yusufzai, Shirdon, Khalib, and Imam are reportedly deceased, although Maguire and Imam are still wanted by the RCMP. See RCMP, "Wanted by the RCMP," online: www.rcmp-grc.gc.ca/en/wanted. For a discussion on this point see Michael Nesbitt & Dana Haag, "An Empirical Study of Terrorism Prosecutions in Canada: Elucidating the Elements of the Offences" (2020) 57:3 *Alberta Law Review* 595 at 600.

4 At the time of writing, only Rehab Dughmosh has been convicted of this offence. See *R v Dughmosh*, 2019 ONSC 1036. Haleema Mustafa's trial was pending and Sabrine Djermane was acquitted at trial. See Katie Nicholson, "Ontario Woman Facing Terror-Related Charges Granted Bail" *CBC News* (31 March 2021), online: www.cbc.ca/news/canada/haleema-mustafa-bail-1.5970940; *R c Jamali*, 2017 QCCS 6078. See Addendum for update.

5 See Addendum for update.

6 Canada, Parliament, *House of Commons Debates*, 42th Parl, 1st Sess, No 234 (20 November 2017) at 15314 (Hon Ralph Goodale); Rachel Gilmore, "Canada Struggling to Prosecute Returned ISIS Fighters" *iPolitics* (26 November 2017), online: http://

However, Goodale repeatedly remarked that prosecuting Canadians for their activities on the battlefield in Syria would be difficult, noting, "[t]his is an issue that is bedevilling countries around the world in terms of how you actually move from intelligence to evidence and make a case stick."[7]

The intelligence to evidence dilemma, as I have written elsewhere, is unquestionably a major hurdle in successfully prosecuting terrorism cases, especially in Canada.[8] To be used at trial, the collection of evidence must comply with constitutional and legislated standards, and law enforcement's adherence to these standards is often the subject of litigation. This is extremely challenging when the information available to law enforcement about criminal activity is derived from intelligence agencies that vehemently defend against the public disclosure of operational information for fear that it will reveal their sources and methods. This challenge is further exacerbated when evidence of criminal activity is produced and often destroyed on a foreign battlefield, and eyewitnesses are either deceased or resettled following conflict.[9]

The intelligence to evidence dilemma, however, does not explain why law enforcement would not investigate Canadians for the perpetration of, or participation in, the horrific crimes of ISIS where they occurred. Indeed, the dilemma makes the need for law enforcement to investigate and interview witnesses and suspects in the region even more acute. Yet, no reporting suggests that the RCMP or officials from the Canadian Security Intelligence Service (CSIS) have travelled to the region to investigate Canadian involvement with ISIS. In the more than three years that they have been detained by the SDF, no Canadians have been interviewed by the RCMP.

---

ipolitics.ca/2017/11/26/canada-struggling-prosecute-returned-daesh-fighters; Rachel D'Amore, "Jihadi Jack hopes Canada Will Take Him as Trudeau Says Laws Will Be Enforced" *Global News* (19 August 2019), online: globalnews.ca/news/5784253/jihadi-jack-trudeau-canada-laws/.

7 Gilmore, above note 6.

8 Leah West, "The Problem of 'Relevance': Intelligence to Evidence Lessons from UK Terrorism Prosecutions" (2018) 41:4 *Manitoba Law Journal* 57.

9 For detailed discussions on this point see, for example, Christophe Paulussen & Kate Pitcher, "Prosecuting (Potential) Foreign Fighters: Legislative and Practical Challenges" (2018) ICCT Research Paper at 26–30; Adam Hoffman & Marta Furlan, "Challenges Posed by Returning Foreign Fighters" Occasional Paper, Program on Extremism, George Washington University (2020) at 11–14; Kenneth Watkin, "The Search for Justice: Military Collection of Evidence on the Battlefield" (2020) 4 PKI *Global Justice Journal* 27.

If these detained Canadians are willing to share their stories publicly with the media, researchers (like me), and foreign law and intelligence agencies, certainly sending RCMP officers to conduct interviews would be an effective means of gathering evidence to support the laying of criminal charges, and ultimately ensure their secure repatriation to Canada to face prosecution.

So why has the RCMP never interviewed them?

While Global Affairs Canada has repeatedly stated that the situation in the region is "too dangerous" to send diplomatic officials to Syria to provide consular services, the reality on the ground does not support this claim, and there has been no explanation why the same risk holds true for security officials.[10] Moreover, Canadian officials safely travelled to Syria in October 2020 to facilitate the repatriation of a five-year-old orphaned girl.[11] These facts, considered alongside the frequency with which diplomatic and security officials from allied states have travelled safely in and out of the region in recent years, belies the notion that "safety concerns" are the basis for inaction by the RCMP.

Why, then? This chapter argues that Canada has failed to investigate, charge, and prosecute Canadian ISIS fighters and supporters detained in Northeast Syria, at least in part, because of uncertainty surrounding the extraterritorial reach of the *Canadian Charter of Rights and Freedoms*.[12]

The argument will proceed in two parts. Part B of this chapter begins by describing the Supreme Court of Canada's jurisprudence on the

---

10 Paul Workman & Christy Somos, "'Too Dangerous' to Pull 4-Year-Old Canadian Orphan Out of ISIS Camp, Trudeau Says" *CTV News* (16 December 2019), online: www.ctvnews.ca/canada/too-dangerous-to-pull-4-year-old-canadian-orphan-out-of-isis-camp-trudeau-says-1.4732977; Alex Boutilier, "Ottawa Says It Has No 'Obligation' to Help Canadian Children Trapped in Syrian Detention Camp" *Toronto Star* (5 June 2020), online: www.thestar.com/politics/federal/2020/06/05/ottawa-says-it-has-no-obligation-to-help-canadian-children-trapped-in-syrian-detention-camp.html; Ashley Burke, "American Who Freed Canadian Girl Calls on World to Repatriate Children Stranded in Syrian Camps" *CBC News* (16 March 2021), online: www.cbc.ca/news/politics/former-us-diplomat-wants-children-freed-syria-detention-camps-1.5951716.

11 Janice Dickson, "Ottawa Repatriates Canadian Orphan Detained in Syria, But Has No Plan to Help Others" *The Globe and Mail* (5 October 2020), online: www.theglobeandmail.com/politics/article-ottawa-repatriates-canadian-orphan-detained-in-syria-but-has-no-plan. See Addendum for update.

12 *Canadian Charter of Rights and Freedoms*, Part I of the *Constitution Act, 1982*, being Schedule B to the *Canada Act 1982* (UK), 1982, c 11 [*Charter*].

extraterritorial application of the *Charter*. This review starts with an examination of the leading case on the matter, *R v Hape*,[13] which found that, barring host-state consent, international law precludes the application of the *Charter* outside of Canada in partnered transnational criminal investigations. Next, this chapter examines the development of the so-called international human rights exception to the *Hape* rule, established by the Court in *Canada v Khadr*,[14] and affirmed two years later in *Canada v Khadr*.[15] In short, the *Khadr* exception holds that participation by Canadian officials in a foreign process that violates Canada's international obligations triggers the *Charter*'s protections.

In Part C, I consider the Supreme Court's precedent in light of the current situation in Northeast Syria and demonstrate how the Court's "guidance" in *Hape* and both *Khadr* cases is nearly impossible to apply with any level of confidence. I contend that legal uncertainty about whether the *Charter* would apply to a Canadian investigation reliant on assistance from the SDF and, if it did, the total lack of clarity as to what the *Charter* requires of investigators, disincentivizes action by the RCMP. In turn, the Court's attempt to vindicate the rights of one citizen interned abroad in deplorable conditions has inadvertently prolonged the detention of more than forty Canadians.

B. THE EXTRATERRITORIAL APPLICATION OF THE *CHARTER*

Hape, the leading case on the extraterritorial application of the *Charter*, has long been condemned by human rights and international law scholars. *Hape* involved a criminal investigation of a Canadian businessman accused of laundering money through his investment company in the Turks and Caicos. At trial in the Ontario Superior Court of Justice, Juriansz J (as he then was) found that the RCMP engaged in a cooperative investigation with Turks and Caicos authorities.[16] He based this ruling on several findings

13 *R v Hape*, 2007 SCC 26 [*Hape*].

14 *Canada (Justice) v Khadr*, 2008 SCC 28 [*Khadr I*].

15 *Canada (Prime Minister) v Khadr*, 2010 SCC 3 [*Khadr II*].

16 *R v Hape*, [2002] OJ No 3714 at para 26 (QL) [*Hape SCJ*]. The following section is largely reproduced from portions of my article "'Within or Outside Canada': The *Charter*'s Application to the Extraterritorial Activities of the Canadian Security Intelligence Service" (2023) 73:1 *University of Toronto Law Journal* 1.

of fact, most notably that the RCMP sought and received permission from local officials to conduct their investigation, and that RCMP officers acted under the authority of local Detective Superintendent Lessemun (who was outranked only by the Commissioner and Deputy Commissioner of Turks and Caicos police).[17] The trial judge found that Lessemun "was adamant he was going to be in charge, and that the RCMP would be working under his authority,"[18] and that he played an active role in the investigation.[19] On the island, the RCMP carried out covert entries of Mr. Hape's office on two occasions, and conducted another search during which they seized more than 100 banker's boxes of records. Canadian officers testified that they understood that local warrants were in place for each search.[20] The fact that Turks and Caicos authorities prevented the RCMP from transporting evidence collected from the search of Mr. Hape's offices back to Canada, and that the RCMP complied with this directive, also strongly supported the finding that the RCMP was operating under local authority.[21]

After making these findings, Juriansz J applied the test set out by the Supreme Court of Canada in *R v Cook*, which at that point had been the leading case on the issue of the *Charter*'s extraterritorial application for almost ten years.[22] In that case, Mr. Cook, an American citizen, was accused of murdering a taxi-cab driver in Vancouver and fleeing to the United States. Canadian authorities asked US law enforcement to arrest Mr. Cook for his extradition. Once in custody, *Miranda* rights were provided by US officials, but American authorities explicitly avoided questioning him. Two days later, Vancouver police arrived in New Orleans and interviewed Mr. Cook. The officers did not provide rights to counsel before questioning the accused, and when his rights were described, the officer's explanation was so confusing that the trial judge found that it deprived Mr. Cook of the ability to make an informed decision about seeking legal advice.[23] The issue before the Court was whether the *Charter* applied to the Vancouver Police Department's investigatory activities

17 *Ibid* at para 4.
18 *Ibid.*
19 *Ibid* at para 25.
20 *Ibid* at paras 10–13.
21 *Ibid.*
22 *R v Cook*, [1998] 2 SCR 597.
23 *Ibid* at 612.

in the United States, and, if so, whether its conduct violated Mr. Cook's *Charter* rights under section 10(b). In other words, did the conduct of Canadian officials outside of Canada trigger section 32 of the *Charter?*

The five-judge majority found that the actions of the Vancouver police fell within section 32(1) of the *Charter* and that, in that specific circumstance, the application of Canadian constitutional law to Canadian agents abroad did not create an objectionable extraterritorial effect.[24] The Court reasoned that territoriality was not the only basis upon which a state may assert jurisdiction; international law permits states to assert extraterritorial jurisdiction on other grounds, most notably nationality.[25]

At trial in *Hape*, Juriansz J applied the test from *Cook* and determined that the application of the *Charter* to this cooperative investigation would have an objectionable extraterritorial effect because it would impose Canadian criminal law standards on foreign officials and procedures.[26] As such, the *Charter* did not apply. In just three short paragraphs, the Ontario Court of Appeal addressed and affirmed Juriansz J's conclusions.[27]

The single ground of appeal to the Supreme Court of Canada was whether the *Charter* ought to apply to the actions of the RCMP officers, thus necessitating compliance with section 8 when searching Mr. Hape's office and seizing his business records. Before analyzing this issue, the majority in *Hape* felt it necessary to explain how "international law assists in the interpretation of s. 32(1)" of the *Charter*.[28] In the course of their explanation, the majority made two significant findings regarding questions of law that were never addressed by the parties in their submissions.

First, the Court explicitly endorsed the adoptionist approach to the reception of customary international law into the law of Canada.[29] That is to say, the Court concluded that prohibitive rules of customary international law are automatically incorporated into Canadian law unless those rules conflict with domestic legislation.[30] Under this approach, direct

---

24 *Ibid* at 616.

25 *Ibid* at 618.

26 *Hape SCJ*, above note 16 at paras 29–31.

27 *R v Hape*, [2005] OJ No 3188 (QL) at paras 7–9.

28 *Hape*, above note 13 at para 34.

29 *Ibid* at paras 39 and 46.

30 Scott Fairley, "International Law Comes of Age: *Hape v. The Queen*" (2008) 87:1 *Canadian Bar Review* 229 at 232.

intervention by Parliament is unnecessary to transform these international legal rules into the law of Canada.[31]

Second, the majority affirmed that Canadian legislation is presumed to comply with international law, be it treaty or customary law, unless the language of the relevant act cannot support such an interpretation.[32] That is, Parliament is not only presumed to act in compliance with Canada's international legal obligations, but international law is presumed to form part of the context in which lawmakers create legislation.[33] In this, notes Scott Fairley, the majority did not break new ground but merely enriched "the existing turf of the established doctrine."[34]

As a result of these findings, the Court affirmed that the development of Canadian law includes the international legal principle of sovereign equality and the correlative principle of non-intervention.[35] Citing Luzius Wildhaber, LeBel J explained that sovereignty is "the power of each state freely and autonomously to determine its tasks, to organize itself, and to exercise within its territory a 'monopoly' of legitimate physical coercion."[36] Tied to sovereignty is the concept of comity among nations, based on the premise that states should act courteously with one another and show deference and respect for the actions of states within their sovereign territories. While respect for comity is not a binding obligation, the majority affirmed it as a principle of interpretation. This finding was not controversial.[37]

However, the majority went further, finding that conformity with international law and the principle of comity not only guides our understanding of legislation but that our interpretation of the Constitution must also comply with customary international law. "In interpreting the

---

31 Despite widespread acceptance of this finding, there was some early critique. See, for example, John H. Currie, "Weaving a Tangled Web: *Hape* and the Obfuscation of Canadian Reception Law" (2007) 45 *Canadian Yearbook of International Law* 55 at 59. (Currie's criticism is that the majority's choice of language actually dilutes and confuses the doctrine of adoption.)

32 *Hape*, above note 13 at paras 53–56.

33 *Ibid.*

34 Fairley, above note 30 at 236.

35 *Hape*, above note 13 at paras 40–46.

36 *Ibid* at para 42; Luzius Wildhaber, "Sovereignty and International Law" in Ronald St. John Macdonald & Douglas M. Johnston, eds, *The Structure and Process of International Law: Essays in Legal Philosophy, Doctrine and Theory* (The Hague: Martinus Nijhoff, 1983) 425 at 436.

37 *Hape*, above note 13 at para 47.

scope of application of the *Charter*," wrote LeBel J, "the courts should seek to ensure compliance with Canada's binding obligations under international law where the express words are capable of supporting such a construction."[38]

Before *Hape*, the Supreme Court of Canada had relied on international human rights law to assist in identifying the content of constitutional protections afforded by the *Charter*. Former Chief Justice Dickson notoriously held in *Slaight Communications Inc v Davidson*, that

> the content of Canada's international human rights obligations is, in my view, an important indicia of the meaning of the "full benefit of the *Charter*'s protection." I believe that the *Charter* should generally be presumed to provide protection at least as great as that afforded by similar provisions in international human rights documents which Canada has ratified.[39]

This passage explained that *human rights* protections afforded by international law are a baseline, or as Currie wrote, "a 'floor' of human rights protection below which *Charter* interpretation should not 'generally'— absent 'exceptional circumstances'— drop."[40] Without explanation, LeBel J cited this precise quotation in support of an entirely different conclusion: courts must interpret the application and reach of the Canadian Constitution in a manner that conforms not only with human rights law but with Canada's various international treaty obligations and customary international law.[41] Ultimately, the perverse impact of this finding (and the Court's emphasis on sovereignty) is the curtailment of human rights protections owed by Canadian officials when acting abroad.

In brief, LeBel J concluded that without consent from the host state, the sovereign equality of nations prevents Canada from enforcing its laws in a foreign territory. "As the supreme law of Canada," finds LeBel J, "the *Charter* is subject to the same jurisdictional limits as the country's other laws or rules. Simply put, Canadian law, whether statutory or constitutional, *cannot* be enforced in another state's territory without the other state's consent."[42] From here, LeBel J leapt without explanation or

38 *Ibid* at para 56.
39 *Slaight Communications Inc v Davidson*, [1989] 1 SCR 1038 at 1056.
40 Currie, above note 31 at 75.
41 *Hape*, above note 13 at para 56.
42 *Ibid* at para 69 [emphasis added].

citation to find that, because the Government of Canada may not exercise enforcement jurisdiction over matters in a foreign state, those matters fall beyond the authority of Parliament. As extraterritorial matters (including the actions of Canadian officials overseas) are not within the authority of Parliament, they do not trigger section 32 of the *Charter*.[43]

While this finding is problematic for several reasons, that discussion is beyond the scope of this chapter.[44] However, what remains important in the context of ISIS detainees is that the majority carved out two exceptions to their sweeping conclusion that "the *Charter* cannot apply" in a foreign state.[45]

1) Exception 1: Consent

The first exception is consent. Justice LeBel found that the "*Charter* can apply to the activities of Canadian officers in foreign investigations where the host state consents. In such a case, the investigation would be a matter within the authority of Parliament and would fall within the scope of s. 32(1)."[46]

What evidence triggers this exception? At the time of writing, no court has ever found sufficient evidence to trigger the consent exception. The first case to consider whether Canada received consent to apply the *Charter* was *Amnesty International Canada v Canada (Canadian Forces)*.[47]

At issue in that application for judicial review was whether the *Charter* applied to individuals detained by Canadian Armed Forces personnel participating in the armed conflict in Afghanistan. In assessing the issue of consent, MacTavish J found that while the Government of Afghanistan consented to the presence of Canada and other NATO allies within its territory, this consent was subject to an agreement, and Canada was not an occupying force. She also found that the framework and scope of the agreement between Afghanistan and Canada was set out in the 2006 *Afghanistan Compact*, and the *Technical Arrangements between*

---

43 *Ibid.*

44 For further discussion on why the decision is problematic, see Robert J. Currie & Joseph Rikhof, *International and Transnational Criminal Law*, 3d ed (Toronto: Irwin Law, 2020) at 610–23.

45 *Hape*, above note 13 at para 105.

46 *Ibid* at para 106.

47 *Amnesty International Canada v Canada (Canadian Forces)*, 2008 FC 336 [*Amnesty*].

the Government of Canada and the Government of the Islamic Republic of Afghanistan, dated 18 December 2005.[48]

Justice MacTavish found that nothing in the *Afghanistan Compact* suggested that Afghanistan consented to the application of Canadian law within its territory, and that there was "no consent by the Government of Afghanistan to having Canadian *Charter* rights conferred on its citizens, within its territory."[49] Rather, the *Afghanistan Compact* was explicit that the Afghan Constitution, along with international human rights covenants and instruments, governed the actions of the international community operating in Afghanistan.[50] Under the technical agreement, the two states also agreed that international humanitarian law governed the treatment of Afghan detainees in Canadian custody, and required that they were to be afforded prisoner of war status.[51] Ultimately, MacTavish J found that, per the Supreme Court of Canada's ruling in *Hape*, the *Charter* did not apply to the Canadian Forces in Afghanistan.[52] The Court of Appeal concurred,[53] and the Supreme Court refused to hear the case.[54]

More recently, in *R v Tan*, the British Columbia Court of Appeal considered the question of consent in a case involving the investigation and prosecution of Mr. Tan for second-degree murder.[55] After the murder, Mr. Tan fled to Malaysia, where the RCMP eventually interviewed him with the assistance of local authorities. During the interview, with local officials present and translating, Mr. Tan agreed to be fingerprinted by the Canadians. His prints matched those found at the crime scene and were admitted as evidence at trial. Mr. Tan sought to have them excluded on appeal on the basis that his *Charter* rights were violated. The issue before the Court of Appeal was whether there had been "positive,

48 *Ibid* at paras 41–44.

49 *Ibid* at paras 160, 172, and 182–84.

50 *Ibid* at paras 161, 167, and 178–79.

51 *Ibid* at para 162.

52 *Ibid* at para 184.

53 *Amnesty International Canada v Canada (Chief of the Defence Staff)*, 2008 FCA 401 at para 36: "I conclude that the motions Judge made no errors in answering the way she did the two questions that were before her. The *Charter* has no application to the situations therein described. There is no legal vacuum, considering that the applicable law is international humanitarian law."

54 *Amnesty International Canada v Canada (Canadian Forces)*, [2009] SCCA No 63.

55 *R v Tan*, 2014 BCCA 9.

authoritative and effective consent by the foreign state to the application of the *Charter*."[56]

Writing for the Court of Appeal, Bennett JA reviewed both *Hape* and *Amnesty* before concluding "that evidence of consent of a foreign state requires an expression of sovereign authority, often in the form of a bilateral agreement."[57] Only "officials with the authority to bind the state in question, or an expression of that state's sovereign will, can establish consent."[58]

Relying on international law doctrine governing state responsibility[59] and the Federal Court's decision in *Amnesty* for guidance, the Court of Appeal set out general principles for determining when a state consents to the application of Canadian constitutional law.[60] The *Tan* principles, taken together, set an incredibly high bar—so high that the Court of Appeal suggested that this threshold would likely only ever be established through a treaty or binding international agreement.[61]

2) Exception 2: Fundamental Human Rights

The second exception permitting the *Charter*'s extraterritorial application is sometimes referred to as the "fundamental human rights exception," although it is broader than this title implies. This exception arises when Canadian officials partner or participate in activities of a foreign state where "clear violations of international law and fundamental human

56 *Ibid* at para 72.

57 *Ibid* at para 58.

58 *Ibid.*

59 The doctrine of state responsibility is set out in the ILC's *Articles on State Responsibility*, UN Doc A/RES/56/83 (2001). These articles are generally considered a restatement of customary international law. Article 20 describes the issue of consent for state action that would otherwise constitute a violation of state sovereignty: "Valid consent by a State to the commission of a given act by another State precludes the wrongfulness of that act in relation to the former State to the extent that the act remains within the limits of that consent."

60 *Tan*, above note 55 at para 64.

61 *Ibid* at para 66. The Supreme Court is expected to revisit the consent exception to the *Charter*'s extraterritorial application in an appeal of the Court Martial Appeal Court decision in *R v McGregor*, 2020 CMAC 8, leave granted 2021 CanLII 98081—in particular, how this exception applies to investigations of members of the Canadian Armed Forces who are deployed abroad.

rights" occur.[62] The *Hape* majority wrote in *obiter dicta* that while the principle of sovereignty typically bars Canada from exercising its jurisdiction in a foreign state, "comity does not offer a rationale for condoning another state's breach of international law."[63] In other words: "*deference ends where clear violations of international law and fundamental human rights begin*," and in such circumstances the *Charter* will govern the conduct of Canadian officials.[64]

Comity, however, is not a rule of customary law; it is a non-binding principle of mutual respect that does not have legal effect under international law. Violating the principle of comity has no legal consequence. Thus, what remains unclear from the majority's comments about deference is how or why a violation of international law by a host state gives Canada license to violate the principle of *sovereignty*. After all, it was respect for another state's sovereignty, not comity, that led the majority to conclude that the extraterritorial application of the *Charter* was impossible.[65]

Justice MacTavish raised this precise question in *Amnesty*, decided before the Supreme Court of Canada's decision in *Khadr*.[66] The applicants in *Amnesty* argued that in handing over detainees to Afghanistan where they faced the possibility of torture, Canada was participating in a process that violated fundamental human rights, thereby triggering the *Hape* exception. Justice MacTavish disagreed. She opined that the *Charter* either applies to Afghan detainees, or it does not. She rejected the idea that the nature or quality of a *Charter* breach could serve as the trigger for its extraterritorial application, calling it "a completely unprincipled approach to the exercise of extraterritorial jurisdiction."[67] She also noted that this kind of approach would "surely lead to tremendous uncertainty on the part of Canadian state actors 'on the ground' in foreign countries."[68]

---

62 *Hape*, above note 13 at para 52. See also Kent Roach, "*R. v. Hape* Creates *Charter*-Free Zones for Canadian Officials Abroad" (2007) 53 *Criminal Law Quarterly* 1.

63 *Ibid* at para 51.

64 *Ibid* at para 52 (emphasis added).

65 For more on this see John Currie, "*Khadr*'s Twist on *Hape*: Tortured Determinations of the Extraterritorial Reach of the Canadian *Charter*" (2008) 46 *Canadian Yearbook of International Law* 307 at 321–23.

66 *Khadr I*, above note 14.

67 *Amnesty*, above note 47 at paras 310–13.

68 *Ibid* at para 314.

Unfortunately, the Supreme Court adopted this precise approach in *Khadr*.

Omar Khadr, a fifteen-year-old Canadian citizen, was detained in 2002 by US forces in Afghanistan for allegedly throwing a grenade that killed an American soldier.[69] US personnel transferred him to the military detention centre at Guantanamo Bay, where he was mistreated. In detention, Canadian officials from the Department of Foreign Affairs and International Trade (DFAIT) and CSIS interviewed Mr. Khadr on several occasions and subsequently shared the product of those interviews with the Americans.[70] In 2005, Mr. Khadr was charged under US law with war crimes. He subsequently brought an application in Canadian Federal Court for disclosure of the information stemming from his interviews with the DFAIT and CSIS.[71] Mr. Khadr argued that under section 7 of the *Charter*, he was entitled to the disclosure of all documents in the possession of the Canadian government relevant to the charges he faced. The Crown appealed the order of the Federal Court of Appeal that mandated disclosure of the requested material to Mr. Khadr. The Crown argued that, according to the Supreme Court of Canada's decision in *Hape*, the *Charter* did not apply to the actions of the DFAIT or CSIS at Guantanamo Bay.[72]

In brief but unanimous reasons, the Court dismissed the Crown's appeal by relying on the "important exception to the principle of comity" set out in *Hape*, and reaffirmed that "the principles of international law and comity of nations, which normally require that Canadian officials operating abroad comply with local law, do not extend to participation in *processes that violate Canada's international human rights obligations*."[73] As such, if by interviewing Mr. Khadr in Cuba, "Canada was participating in a process that was violative of Canada's *binding obligations under international law*, the *Charter* applies to the extent of that participation."[74]

Referring to *Hape*, the Court noted, "While not unanimous on all the principles governing extra-territorial application of the Charter, the Court was united on the principle that comity cannot be used to justify

69 *Khadr I*, above note 14 at para 5.
70 *Ibid* at para 7.
71 *Ibid* at para 8.
72 *Ibid* at para 17.
73 *Ibid* at para 2.
74 *Ibid* at para 19 (emphasis added).

Canadian participation in activities of a foreign state or its agents that are contrary to Canada's international obligations."[75] The Court added:

> If the Guantanamo Bay process under which Mr. Khadr was being held was in conformity with Canada's international obligations, the *Charter* has no application and Mr. Khadr's application for disclosure cannot succeed: *Hape*. However, if Canada was participating in a process that was violative of Canada's binding obligations under international law, the *Charter* applies to the extent of that participation.
>
> At this point, the question becomes whether the process at Guantanamo Bay at the time that CSIS handed the products of its interviews over to U.S. officials was a process that violated Canada's binding obligations under international law.[76]

The Supreme Court of Canada, however, did not analyze the extent of Canada's participation or examine whether the conduct of the DFAIT or CSIS violated Canada's binding obligations under international law. Instead, the Court relied on the US Supreme Court's finding that the process that detainees like Mr. Khadr were subjected to *by American authorities* violated Common Article 3 of the *Geneva Conventions*.[77] As Canada is a signatory to the *Geneva Conventions*, the Court held that "participation in the Guantanamo Bay process" was contrary to "Canada's binding international obligations."[78] Of course, the *Geneva Conventions* are binding instruments of international humanitarian law, not international human rights law (the basis for the exception identified by the majority in *Hape*). Importantly, Common Article 3 applies to "conflicts not of an international character," or what is known as a non-international armed conflict, "occurring in the territory of one of the High Contracting Parties."[79]

From here the Court jumped to a conclusion seemingly premised on the notion that two wrongs make a right: "We conclude that the principles

75 *Ibid* at para 18 [emphasis added].

76 *Ibid* at paras 18–20.

77 *Ibid* at para 23.

78 *Ibid* at para 25. The Court made clear (at para 27) that it was not the fact that Mr. Khadr was interviewed that violated international law, as this may be necessary to provide consular assistance etc., but the fact that Canadian authorities shared the product of their interviews with the Americans.

79 See, for example, *Geneva Convention for the Amelioration of the Condition of the Wounded and Sick in Armed Forces in the Field*, (1949) 75 UNTS 31, Can TS 1965 No 20, Article 3.

of international law and comity that might otherwise preclude application of the *Charter* to Canadian officials acting abroad do not apply to the assistance they gave to U.S. authorities at Guantanamo Bay."[80] In other words, because Canada participated in an unlawful American process by handing over the product of its interviews to US authorities, Canada no longer needed to respect US sovereignty (which the majority in *Hape* determined would otherwise preclude the extraterritorial application of the *Charter*.)

Having concluded that the *Charter* governed the actions of DFAIT and CSIS as soon as they participated in a process that violated international law, the Court ultimately ordered the requested disclosure. The Court found that disclosure was required under section 7 of the *Charter*, as a remedy to mitigate the effect of Canada's "breach of a constitutional duty that arose when Canadian agents *became participants in a process that violates Canada's international obligations*."[81]

The Court's invocation of the *Hape* exception in *Khadr* not only confirmed its existence but made clear that the actions of Canadian officials themselves need not violate international law or human rights for the exception to apply. Mere participation in a foreign process that violates international law is enough to extend the application of the *Charter* overseas.

However, what "participation" entails remains entirely unclear outside of the specific facts of Mr. Khadr's case. Rather than clarify what a finding of participation requires, the Court remarked that "merely conducting interviews with a Canadian citizen held abroad under a violative process may not constitute participation in that process. Indeed, it may often be essential that Canadian officials interview citizens being held by violative regimes to provide assistance to them." The Court went on to find that it was not "necessary to conclude that handing over the fruits of the interviews in this case to U.S. officials constituted a breach of Mr. Khadr's s. 7 rights."[82]

What are we to take from this statement? Interviewing Canadians detained abroad may or may not constitute participation in a foreign process, thus triggering the *Charter*. Arguably, participation depends on the intent of the Canadian officials conducting the interview or what is done with the information obtained in the interview, or both. If, for example,

80 *Ibid* at para 26.

81 *Ibid* at paras 34, 36 & 37 [emphasis added].

82 *Khadr I*, above note 14 at para 27.

the interview is meant merely to provide consular assistance, it would be difficult to assert that this constitutes participation. However, if the aim of the interview is to obtain intelligence or evidence of a criminal offence, it is unclear whether it would trigger the *Charter* if the information obtained is not subsequently shared with the foreign entity detaining a Canadian in conditions that contravene the *Geneva Conventions*.

Of course, if the *Charter* does not apply, this leads us back to the absurd result of *Hape*: Canadian law enforcement can engage in conduct abroad unencumbered by the *Charter* for the ultimate purpose of enforcing Canadian law against a Canadian within Canada. Wholly absent from the judgment is any legal justification to explain why or how Canadian participation in a foreign process triggers the *Charter*.[83]

Of course, the Supreme Court's 2008 decision was not the end of the Khadr saga. In 2010, the Supreme Court once again considered Canada's *Charter* obligations vis-à-vis Mr. Khadr's detention in Guantanamo. There were two issues before the Court: first, whether the provision of CSIS and DFAIT's interview records to US officials contributed to Mr. Khadr's continued detention, thus engaging his section 7 *Charter* rights, in a manner that did not accord with the principles of fundamental justice; and second, whether an order mandating the Government of Canada to ask the United States to repatriate Mr. Khadr was an appropriate remedy under section 24(1).[84]

Citing *Suresh v Canada*, the Court strained to find that the actions of Canadian officials engaged Mr. Khadr's security and liberty interests because there was a sufficient causal connection between their conduct and his continued detention in Guantanamo to engage section 7.[85] The Supreme Court also found that the statements taken by CSIS and DFAIT were obtained by participating "in a regime which was known at the time to have refused detainees the right to challenge the legality of detention

83 John Currie, "*Khadr* (2008) and Extraterritorial Applicability of the Charter: Deepening the Morass" *The Court* (4 November 2009), online: www.thecourt.ca/khadr-2008-and-extraterritorial-applicability-of-the-charter-deepening-the-morass.

84 *Khadr II*, above note 15

85 *Ibid* at para 19, citing *Suresh v Canada (Minister of Citizenship and Immigration)*, 2002 SCC 1. For a discussion on why this conclusion is a strained application of the causal connection test set out in *Suresh* see Audrey Macklin, "Comment on *Canada (Prime Minister) v. Khadr* (2010)" (2010) 51 *Supreme Court Law Review* (2d) 295 at 309.

by way of habeas corpus," and without access to counsel.[86] These findings established Canada's "participation in state conduct that violates the principles of fundamental justice."[87] As Audrey Macklin points out, the Court never addressed whether the manner in which Canadian officials interrogated Mr. Khadr violated his section 7 rights.[88] Instead, the Court "regards the United States as the sole violator of his right to liberty and security of the person."[89] Therefore, "*section 7 is violated for the same reason that the Charter applies*,"[90] and it applies because of American action.

Having found an infringement of Mr. Khadr's section 7 rights, the Court turned to the question of remedy. The Crown argued that the Court lacked the constitutional authority to require the executive branch of government to take a specific foreign policy action, as such matters fall under the Crown prerogative over foreign affairs.[91] The Supreme Court held otherwise, finding that when exercising those powers, if the executive refuses to "abide by constitutional constraints, courts are empowered to make orders ensuring that the government's foreign affairs prerogative is exercised in accordance with the constitution."[92] Nevertheless, in this case, because whether the United States would comply with the request was unclear, the impact of the request on Canada's relations with the United States could not be properly assessed by the Court, and as the Court was unaware of any ongoing diplomatic negotiations, it was inappropriate to order such a specific remedy.[93] In short, the Court could, but would not, order the government to make the request.[94] Rather, the prudent remedy was declaratory relief.[95]

On the basis of this declaration, Mr. Khadr subsequently brought a civil lawsuit against the Government of Canada.[96] The Trudeau government

86 *Ibid* at para 24.
87 *Ibid* at para 25.
88 Macklin, above note 85 at 305.
89 *Ibid.*
90 *Ibid* at 309 [emphasis added].
91 *Khadr II*, above note 15 at para 35.
92 *Ibid* at para 37.
93 *Ibid* at 43–44.
94 Macklin, above note 85 at 307.
95 *Khadr II*, above note 15 at para 46.
96 *Khadr v Canada*, 2014 FC 1001.

ultimately settled the lawsuit in 2017 for $10.5 million and offered Mr. Khadr an apology.[97]

Taken together, the totality of the Supreme Court's direction on the extraterritorial application of the *Charter* amounts to the following:

- the principles of international law and comity prevent the *Charter*'s extraterritorial application; however,
- it may apply if the host state consents to its application; and
- comity will not prevent the *Charter*'s application to the extraterritorial conduct of Canadian state actors if they participate in a foreign process that violates Canada's international obligations; yet,
- not all participation in a foreign process that violates Canada's international obligations will trigger the *Charter*; and
- if the *Charter* is triggered by Canada's participation in a foreign process, the foreign process will likely violate the section 7 rights of a Canadian caught in the process.

Trying to apply this seemingly contradictory guidance to new or different factual scenarios would be a challenge on its own. However, without any discussion or explanation of the international or domestic legal principles the Court relied on to justify the *Khadr* exception, it is nearly impossible to determine when the *Charter* applies extraterritorially. Moreover, the Supreme Court provides no guidance on what the *Charter* requires of *Canadian* actors operating abroad once it is triggered by a foreign process. On top of all of that, it is completely unknown if the *Khadr* exception can be triggered if the foreign actor in question is either (1) a non-state actor, or (2) not governed by the same international obligations as Canada.

C. APPLYING *HAPE* AND *KHADR* IN NORTHEAST SYRIA

As noted above, there remain at least four Canadian men in the custody of the SDF in a region governed, not by the Syrian state, but by the Autonomous Administration of Northeastern Syria. These men have not been charged with criminal offences under Kurdish, Syrian, or international law. In the more than two years they have been in custody, they have not

97 John Paul Tasker, "Government Formally Apologizes to Omar Khadr, as Andrew Scheer Condemns 'Disgusting' Payout" *CBC News* (7 July 2017), online: www.cbc.ca/news/politics/cabinet-explain-omar-khadr-settlement-1.4194467.

been given access to lawyers. They have never been to court, and there is no plan to bring these men before a judge to review the basis for their continued and indefinite detention. The facilities in which they are held are overcrowded and filthy.[98] Kurdish officials admit that the makeshift prison facilities do not meet the UNGA's *Standard Minimum Rules for the Treatment of Prisoners*.[99]

Two of the Canadian men left in detention have admitted publicly to leaving Canada to join ISIS, to participating in, and contributing to, the activities of ISIS, and to facilitating the activities of ISIS.[100] All of these constitute offences under provisions of the *Criminal Code* that have extraterritorial reach. The two other men are, by virtue of their ongoing detention, allegedly affiliated with ISIS, a designated terrorist entity under the *Criminal Code*.

We should expect that the RCMP wants to send officers to interview the Canadians in Kurdish detention, in support of a Canadian criminal investigation into their activities in Syria and into the activities of other Canadians who travelled abroad to join ISIS. Indeed, many other states have done just that with the support of Kurdish officials.[101] In order to proceed, however, the RCMP would need to ascertain and understand their legal authorities and limits when conducting their investigation in Northeast Syria; most importantly, does the *Charter* apply?

---

98 Human Rights Watch, "Thousands of Foreigners Unlawfully Held in NE Syria" (23 March 2021), online: www.hrw.org/news/2021/03/23/thousands-foreigners-unlawfully-held-ne-syria.

99 *United Nations Standard Minimum Rules for the Treatment of Prisoners*, GA Res 70/175, UNGAOR, 70th Sess, UN Doc A/RES/70/175 (2016) (referred to as the Nelson Mandela Rules).

100 *Criminal Code*, RSC 1985, c C-46, ss 83.181, 83.191, 83.201, & 83.202.

101 The author travelled to Northeast Syria in 2019 to interview Canadians in Kurdish custody. In those interviews, Canadian detainees repeatedly stated that they had been interviewed by foreign officials including officers from the US Federal Bureau of Investigation. It has also been reported that one Canadian woman in detention cooperated with the Federal Bureau of Investigation; that cooperation was used to support her release from detention in Syria. While she was awaiting Canadian travel documents in Erbil, Iraq, five RCMP officers travelled there to interview her before her return to Canada. See Paul Workman, "Exile in Erbil: Ottawa Accused of Abandoning Canadian Woman Stranded in Iraq" *CTV News* (5 November 2021) online: www.ctvnews.ca/world/exile-in-erbil-ottawa-accused-of-abandoning-canadian-woman-stranded-in-iraq-1.5654086.

Regrettably, the existing precedent offers no clear answer to this question. The starting presumption, based on *Hape*, is that the *Charter* would not govern the actions of Canadian officials carrying out an investigation in Northeast Syria unless one of two exceptions arise.

First, the *Charter* could apply if Canada sought and received consent from the host state. According to *Tan*, this probably requires the establishment of a bilateral agreement between Canada and Syria. Obviously, given the current diplomatic relationship between these two states, and the fact that the Syrian regime does not govern the region, consent is not only unlikely, but it would also be meaningless.

Second, the *Charter* will apply if Canada participates in a process that is violative of Canada's international obligations. As in *Khadr*, Common Article 3 of the *Geneva Conventions* establishes the basic legal protections for prisoners of war in a non-international armed conflict. Both Canada and Syria are parties to the *Geneva Conventions*, and Article 3 applies to all parties in a "conflict not of an international character occurring in the territory" of a contracting party. As such, the SDF are also bound by the Article and must, at a minimum, ensure that all prisoners are treated humanely.

Canada's international legal obligations also include customary international law, which contains rules against arbitrary deprivation of liberty in both international and non-international armed conflicts.[102] Canada is also party to the *International Covenant on Civil and Political Rights*, which stipulates that no one may be subjected to arbitrary arrest or detention.[103] These prohibitions include obligations to bring detained persons promptly before a judge, and provide them an opportunity to challenge the lawfulness of their detention.[104]

Whether the detention regime in Northeast Syria does in fact violate the SDF's obligations under Common Article 3, or would violate Canada's obligations under international law, is beyond the scope of this chapter. The point of this discussion is to demonstrate that there is a

---

102 ICRC, IHL Database: Customary IHL, "Rule 99: Deprivation of Liberty," online: ihl-databases.icrc.org/customary-ihl/eng/docs/v1_rul_rule99#Fn_EC41E6AF_00030.

103 *International Covenant on Civil and Political Rights*, (1966) 999 UNTS 171, art 9; UN Human Rights Committee, *General Comment No 8 (Article 9 of the International Covenant on Civil and Political Rights)*, U.N. Doc. HRI/GEN/1/Rev.6 at 131 (30 June 1982) § 2644.

104 See, for example, *General Comment No 8*, *ibid* § 2735.

significant risk that indefinite detention of alleged ISIS fighters in Syria could run afoul of these legal rules, and if so, Canadian "participation" in that regime by interviewing Canadians in SDF custody for the purpose of a criminal investigation would not only trigger the *Charter*, but it would also violate those prisoner's rights under section 7. The violation would arise not because of any particular rights infringement or impairing action taken by Canada, but by the sheer fact that Canada took action.

The irony is that because of the *Khadr* exception, there may be no way for Canadian officials to prevent the application and violation of the *Charter* should they conduct interviews in Syria, and those Canadians will continue to languish in makeshift prisons. Without enough evidence to confidently prosecute Canadians for their conduct in Syria, the government is incentivized to delay the laying of charges and their repatriation for as long as the SDF is willing and able to keep them locked up. Thus, the Supreme Court's exception, designed to vindicate the rights of those detained in human rights violative conditions, will ultimately lead to the prolonged detention of Canadians in those conditions.

D. CONCLUSION

In his dissent in *Hape*, Binnie J quoted from *Hamlet*: "There are more things in heaven and earth, Horatio, Than are dreamt of in your philosophy."[105] Using the immortal words of Shakespeare, Binnie J warned the majority that common law courts traditionally avoid making "far-reaching pronouncements before being required by the facts before them to do so."[106] He advised his brother and sister judges that the participation of Canadians in foreign terrorist groups like the Taliban and al-Qaida, and the role Canadian security officials may play overseas in preventing and investigating terrorism, would likely raise new and difficult legal issues about the *Charter*'s reach and the extraterritorial treatment of Canadians. He cautioned against making sweeping pronouncements about the *Charter*'s extraterritorial application without the benefit of extensive legal and scholarly arguments.

Less than a year later, Binnie J's warning came true. The Court relied on a single *obiter* sentence from *Hape* regarding deference to a foreign

105 *Hape*, above note 13 at para 184.
106 *Ibid.*

state's sovereignty to carve out an exception to the rule that the *Charter* does not apply abroad. Unfortunately, in so doing, the Court did not assess or judge the actions of Canadian officials in finding a violation of Mr. Khadr's section 7 rights. Instead, they based their findings on the conclusions of a foreign court, examining the actions of foreign state officials, in light of Canada's international legal obligations.

The consequence is that whether the *Charter* applies abroad is not necessarily tied to the actions of Canadian officials. No matter what steps law enforcement takes to ensure compliance with the *Charter*, merely participating in a foreign process that violates any number of Canada's international obligations may not only trigger, but also breach, the *Charter* rights of a subject of investigation. The perverse result is that the only sure way to avoid any such violation (and the resulting costs) is to refuse to participate.

Failure to heed Binnie J's advice has, in part, brought us to where we are today: Canadians who have publicly admitted to joining and supporting ISIS have not been charged for their crimes, their victims are denied justice, and the Government of Canada is indirectly complicit in their continued mistreatment.

ADDENDUM

Since the time of writing, there have been several developments. The Government of Canada (GoC) has repatriated or facilitated the return of seven Canadians.[107] The first, a five-year-old orphan known as Amira, was repatriated in October 2020. In March 2021, a four-year-old girl was escorted out of a Syrian Democratic Forces (SDF) detention camp into Canadian custody in Iraq by a former US diplomat. Her mother followed a similar path back to Canada in November 2021. Subsequently, in October 2022, Kimberly Polman, Oumaima Choua, and Choua's two children, were repatriated by Canadian officials. RCMP arrested each adult woman upon their arrival in Canada. Choua was charged with four terrorism offences including leaving Canada to participate in the activity

---

107 For details on the repatriations and the Judicial Review application see Leah West, "Shortsighted Security: Canada's Policy on Repatriating Canadians Detained in North East Syria" in *PKI Global Justice Journal* (2023), online: https://globaljustice.queenslaw.ca/news/human-rights-and-citizenship-abandoned-in-ne-syria-a-special-issue-of-the-global-justice-journal#Shortsighted.

of a terrorist group and participation in the activity of ISIS. The other two women consented to a terrorism peace bond.

On 19 January 2023, the lawyers representing twenty-three Canadians (four men, six women, and thirteen children) in a judicial review proceeding before the Federal Court of Canada announced that a deal had been reached with the GoC to repatriate the nineteen women and children. A day later, the Federal Court ordered that to ensure the section 6 *Charter* rights of the applicants, the GoC must ask the Autonomous Administration of North East Syria to release the four men into the custody of a Canadian representative or delegate for their repatriation. However, the Federal Court of Appeal overturned that decision on 31 May 2023.[108] To date, no RCMP officers have interviewed Canadians in SDF custody.

Finally, on 17 February 2023, the Supreme Court of Canada released its long-awaited decision in *McGregor*.[109] For those hoping that the *Hape* methodology would be revisited, it was mostly disappointing; the majority decided that the issue of extraterritorial application of the *Charter* was not actually before it (despite this having been the issue on which most of the interveners were granted leave to participate) and decided the case on an application of search and seizure law. In joint concurring reasons, Karakatsanis and Martin JJ explored the issue in some depth and signalled their own view that a revision was needed. However, it appears that this will have to wait for another case.

108 *Canada v Boloh 1(a)*, 2023 FCA 120..

109 *R v McGregor*, 2023 SCC 4. Disclaimer: I was co-counsel for the intervener Canadian Civil Liberties Association.

nine

What Side Do You Come From? Borders in *R v Desautel*

ROBIN PARKER*

A. INTRODUCTION

Like any good hunters, Richard and Linda Desautel set out early from the camp in their traditional Sinixt territory in the West Kootenays. By the time they reached their hunting ground on the steep hillsides near Valhalla Provincial Park, the fog had started to lift, but it was cold, and the ground was slick with frost. Just before 7 a.m., Richard Desautel shot and killed a large cow elk he spotted below them on the embankment. He and his wife dressed the elk, returned to camp and hung the meat.[1] Then, they got in their truck and drove until they found good cell reception. Desautel called the British Columbia conservation office, reported what he had done, and provided directions to the camp. Still, it took the wardens a few days to find him.[2] When they did, they charged Desautel with hunting

* Robin Parker, BA (Toronto), LLB (Dalhousie), MSt (International Human Rights Law) (Oxon) (Dist), practises criminal, public, and Aboriginal law in Ontario and the Northwest Territories. Thank you to Professor Rob Currie for his mentorship with this article.

1 Anna V. Smith, "How an Arrow Lakes Elk Hunt Became a Case of Tribal Recognition" *High Country News* (28 October 2018), online: www.hcn.org/issues/51.18/indigenous-affairs-a-hunt-for-tribal-recognition-at-the-us-canada-border-sinixt-desautel.

2 Adrian Humphreys, "Rights Beyond Borders: Big Questions Were Triggered When an Indigenous American Shot an Elk in Canada" *National Post* (1 May 2021)

without a licence,[3] and hunting big game while not being a resident of Canada or British Columbia.[4] Everything was going according to plan.

Desautel's hunting trip was an act of planned civil disobedience. The elk meat was bound for his home community, but Desautel was headed for court. There, he joined a long line of Indigenous people[5] in Canada who have advanced their rights in the context of alleged illegal acts. Like Ronald Sparrow, Dorothy Van Der Peet, and Donald Marshall Jr., Desautel argued he was in his traditional territory, exercising an Aboriginal right to hunt protected by section 35 of the *Constitution Act*.[6] What made his case unique is that Desautel is not a Canadian citizen, or even a resident of Canada. He is a US citizen who has lived his whole life on the Colville Indian Reservation in Washington State.

There was little doubt that Canadian courts had jurisdiction to prosecute Desautel. As La Forest J explained in *R v Libman*:

> The primary basis of criminal jurisdiction is territorial. The reasons for this are obvious. States ordinarily have little interest in prohibiting activities that occur abroad and they are, as well, hesitant to incur the displeasure of other states by indiscriminate attempts to control activities that take place wholly within the boundaries of those other countries.[7]

---

online: www.nationalpost.com/news/rights-beyond-borders-big-questions-were-triggered-when-an-indigenous-american-shot-an-elk-in-canada.

3 *Wildlife Act*, RSBC 1996, c 488, s 11(1).

4 *Ibid*, s 47(a).

5 In this paper the term "Indigenous people" is used to refer to First Nations, Inuit, and Métis people in Canada collectively. The term "Aboriginal" is used to refer to specific legal rights recognized in s 25 of the *Canadian Charter of Rights and Freedoms*, Part I of the *Constitution Act, 1982*, being Schedule B to the *Canada Act 1982* (UK), 1982, c 11 [*Charter*] and s 35 of the *Constitution Act*, *ibid.* See Gregory Younging, *Elements of Indigenous Style: A Guide for Writing By and About Indigenous Peoples* (Edmonton: Brush Education, 2018) at 62–64. Please note that when quoting s 35, I have not capitalized "Aboriginal" as it is not capitalized in the document itself.

6 *R v Sparrow*, [1990] 1 SCR 1075 (fishing with a drift net longer than permitted); *R v Van Der Peet*, [1996] 2 SCR 507 (selling salmon harvested pursuant to an Indian food-fishing licence) [*Van Der Peet*]; *R v Marshall*, [1999] 3 SCR 456, (selling eels without a licence). See also *R v Morris*, [2006] 2 SCR 915 (hunting at night); *R v Bernard*, 2003 NBCA 55, and *R v Sappier*, 2006 SCC 54 (harvesting timber on Crown land).

7 *Libman v The Queen*, [1985] 2 SCR 178 at para 11.

It seemed like a straightforward case. Desautel killed an elk while hunting in Canada. Charging him with hunting without a licence was easy, and prosecuting him should have been even easier, because there was no open season on cow elk in the area.[8] The more complex question, one that would take more than a decade to wend its way to the Supreme Court of Canada, was whether a US citizen could claim the rights of "the aboriginal peoples of Canada" recognized and affirmed in section 35 of Canada's Constitution as a defence. The Supreme Court ultimately answered this question in the affirmative. This remarkable ruling — that a person who is not a citizen or resident of Canada can successfully plead an Aboriginal rights defence in a Canadian prosecution — is explored here, against the backdrop of Canada's Indigenous rights litigation.

B. THE SINIXT AND THE ARROW LAKES

Richard Desautel is a member of the Lakes Tribe, one of the twelve bands that comprise the Confederated Tribes of the Colville Reservation. The northern boundary of the Colville Reservation, Desautel's home, is about sixty kilometres south of the Canada–US border. The Arrow Lakes area where Desautel shot the elk, on the other hand, is nestled between the Monashee and Selkirk Mountains in British Columbia, and extends from the Kettle River north to Revelstoke.[9] The entire area is unceded territory.

The historical and archaeological record is clear that the Lakes people, also known as the Sinixt, lived in the Arrow Lakes region for approximately 3,500 years before first contact with European explorers and settlers.[10] The profound relationship between the Sinixt and the Arrow Lakes is reflected in both the Sinixt and settler's language. Sinixt means "people of the spotted fish place,"[11] or "Dolly Varden people," Dolly Varden being a spotted fish found in the Arrow Lakes. Settlers simply called them "Lakes" people,[12] and called the lakes "Arrow" because they are near a bluff

8 *R v Desautel*, Agreed Statement of Facts, SCC File No 38734, Appeal Record of Appellant.

9 *R v Desautel*, 2017 BCPC 84 at para 20 [*Desautel PC*].

10 *Campbell v British Columbia (Forest and Range)*, 2011 BCSC 448 at para 15 [*Campbell* BCSC].

11 *R v Desautel*, Evidence of Elder Shelly Boyd, SCC File No 38734, Appeal Record of Respondent, Vol 2 at 6.

12 *Desautel PC*, above note 9 at para 22.

where the Sinixt, renowned hunters,[13] practised archery for millennia.[14] Desautel's trial judge stated: "Each of the names by which the Sinixt identified themselves or were identified by others serve as evidence of a clear and ancient link between the Sinixt and the Arrow Lakes region."[15]

The Sinixt population at the time of contact in 1811[16] was estimated to be about 500. After smallpox ravaged the community, only 200 were left.[17] Up to, and well after, the time of contact, the Sinixt travelled seasonally throughout the area, heading as far south as what used to be Kettle Falls, which is now submerged beneath the Grand Coulee Dam in Washington state.[18] In 1846, the Canada–US border was extended west along the 49th parallel to the Strait of Georgia, bisecting Sinixt territory.[19] For reasons that are not entirely clear, the Sinixt began a gradual migration south, into the area where the United States later established the Colville Reservation in 1872. It is likely that smallpox, what the Sinixt describe as a campaign of harassment north of the border, the willingness of US government to treat with them when British Columbia would not,[20] and the establishment of Hudson's Bay trading posts in the United States, influenced their decision.[21] However, they continued to hunt near the Arrow Lakes, so consistently that in 1896, British Columbia passed a law making it "unlawful for Indians not resident of this Province to kill game at any time of year."[22]

---

13 *Ibid* at paras 80–83.

14 *Ibid* at para 29.

15 *Ibid* at para 23.

16 *Ibid* at para 33. The time of first contact between settlers and Indigenous people is significant in Aboriginal rights cases because the person claiming the right must show it was widely practised before contact. *Van Der Peet*, above note 6. It is obviously a problematic concept that has been subject to extensive scholarly and social commentary, nowhere better than in blues musician Murray Porter's song, "1492 Who Found Who."

17 *Campbell* BCSC, above note 10 at para 23; *Desautel PC*, above note 9 at paras 17–19.

18 They followed the animals and fish seasonally to harvest. *Desautel PC*, above note 9 at paras 25 and 37.

19 The border was extended by the Oregon Treaty: *Campbell v British Columbia (Forest and Range)*, 2012 BCCA 274 at para 2 [*Campbell* BCCA].

20 Andrea Geiger, "Crossed By the Border: The US–Canada Border and Canada's 'Extinction' of the Arrow Lake Band, 1890–1956" (2010) 23 *Western Legal History* 121 at 126.

21 *Desautel PC*, above note 9 at paras 33 and 41–44.

22 *An Act to Amend the Game Protection Act, 1895*, SBC 1896, Vict 59, c 22, s 6.

Despite these obstacles, members of what was then called the Lakes Tribe continued to hunt in British Columbia until the 1930s.[23]

In 1902, Canada finally set aside a reserve for what it called the "Arrow Lake Band," but by then the census showed only twenty-one Sinixt living north of the border.[24] By the 1930s, there was no evidence of Sinixt entering Canada to hunt. In 1956, the last remaining member of the band, Annie Joseph, died. This was of great importance to the BC government, whose efforts to sell timber from the land had been hampered by Ms. Joseph's presence.[25] Canada promptly declared the band extinct. The reserve lands reverted to the BC government, which immediately started resource exploitation.[26] In the years that followed, the entire area was submerged by flooding behind the High Arrow Dam at Castelgar.[27]

C. CONTEMPORARY SINIXT ACTIVISM

Although the Sinixt no longer hunted in the Arrow Lakes, the record is also clear that they never forgot their traditional territory. Anthropologist Dr. Dorothy Kennedy testified at Desautel's trial that in 1972, Charlie Quintasket, whom she described as "a Lakes Indian from the Colville Reservation," walked into her office asking why the Lakes people did not have a reserve in Canada.[28]

Over time, the Sinixt began to engage in activism aimed at self-determination. In 1989, hearing that road construction near Vallican, British Columbia, would affect Sinixt graves, a group of Lakes people, including Linda and Rick Desautel and their children, headed into Canada and blocked the road. The burial ground was designated an archaeological site, and the road diverted.[29] In 1990, the Colville Confederacy authorized Sinixt

23 *Desautel PC*, above note 9 at para 49.

24 Likely further influencing Sinixt migration south, the reserve land was on a steep hillside, inaccessible by road. Geiger, above note 20 at 138.

25 *Ibid* at 140–47.

26 *Desautel PC*, above note 9 at para 43–48; *Campbell* BCSC above note 10 at para 34; *Campbell* BCCA, above note 19 at para 2.

27 Geiger, above note 20 at 147.

28 *Desautel PC*, above note 9 at para 49.

29 Smith, above note 1. And see Justus Caudell, "Remembering the 1989 Blockade in the Vallican," *Tribal Tribune* (24 October 2016), online: www.tribaltribune.com/news/article_21baa988-99f7-11e6-8a0e-dbd7d3695e79.html. Caudell writes, "There they stood ... the extinct Sinixt."

Elders to petition a BC museum to remove Sinixt remains from their collection and bury them properly.[30] In 2008, a representative group of petitioners commenced a land claim against British Columbia,[31] and in 2010 brought an injunction to try and stop logging in their traditional territory.[32]

It was also in 2010 that the Fish and Wildlife Director of the Colville Confederacy asked Desautel to secure ceremonial meat from their territory north of the border to share with other members of the community. Desautel was acknowledged as a ceremonial hunter in his community. One of the tasks of that role, as the trial evidence showed had been the case for millennia, was to provide ceremonial meat for funerals, celebrations, and weddings.[33]

Desautel gladly obliged the request. At his trial he described how it felt to be by the ancient lakes, deep in the heart of his unceded traditional territory: "When I come up here, I'm walking with the ancestors. . . . And it just runs chills up and down me that I can be where my ancestors were at one time and do the things that they did."[34]

D. THE PRACTICAL CONSIDERATIONS OF PLEADING ABORIGINAL RIGHTS AS A DEFENCE

Section 35 of the *Constitution Act* recognizes and affirms the "existing aboriginal and treaty rights of the aboriginal peoples of Canada." "Aboriginal peoples" is not defined, but section 35(2) states that it "includes the Indian, Inuit and Métis people of Canada."

To determine the existence of a section 35 right, the claimant must show that the practice claimed today as a section 35 right (1) was exercised by the group prior to contact; (2) was integral to the distinctive culture of the group claiming the right;[35] and (3) continues to the present day.[36] In *Van Der Peet*, Dickson J explained that the purpose of framing the test this

30 *Campbell* (BCSC), above note 10 at para 38.

31 *Ibid* at para 4.

32 *Ibid.* The injunction was dismissed when the court found the petitioners had failed to properly define whom it was they claimed to represent. By the time the case was heard in the BCCA, the issue was moot because the logging had been completed. *Campbell* (BCCA), above note 19.

33 *Desautel PC*, above note 9 at paras 116–17.

34 *Ibid* at para 124.

35 *Van Der Peet*, above note 6 at paras 44, 46, and 55.

36 *Ibid* at paras 63–65.

way was "reconciling pre-existing [A]boriginal societies with the assertion of Crown sovereignty over Canada."[37]

The evidentiary burden of this legal test for the claimant is immense. It involves testimony about conditions at the time of contact from historians, ethnographers, and anthropologists, based on what is often a sparse, anecdotal, and biased record. Some claimants flesh this out with evidence from the community's oral history, but this has become increasingly difficult with the passage of time as communities lose Elders with these living memories.

Because of the difficulties associated with proving history "across a gulf of centuries and without a written record," courts have been instructed to approach the rules of evidence bearing in mind these issues, as well as the "special nature of [A]boriginal claims."[38] Despite that, oral history evidence is often given less weight. For example, at Desautel's trial, Elders testified to being told some Sinixt had been forced to leave Canada at gunpoint. The trial judge determined that the most she could do with this evidence was make a finding that the Sinixt "felt unwelcome" in British Columbia at the end of the nineteenth century. She noted that if this had happened, "a record of the event would have survived."[39] This reasoning is flawed. Most interactions between settlers and the Sinixt would have been unrecorded, but as the judge's finding illustrates, even the absence of the written word has more weight than oral history in our legal system.

The claimants' burden does not end with proving the historical record. As the Supreme Court noted in its decision in Desautel's case, to prove an exercise of "Aboriginal rights held by ... modern-day successors within the Canadian legal order,"[40] the claimants must also lead detailed genealogical evidence to prove they are related to the people who historically exercised the rights claimed in the same geographical area.

This detailed, technical, and specialized evidence is expensive and time-consuming to amass and tender. Desautel was charged in 2010, but it took the parties until 2016 to be ready to proceed to trial. Of course, the trial was not the end of the proceeding. The case was appealed three times and finally decided by the Supreme Court of Canada eleven years later in 2021. These test cases require tremendous commitment and financial

37 *Ibid* at para 57.

38 *Mitchell v MNR*, 2001 SCC 33 at paras 27 and 30–34 [*Mitchell*].

39 *Desautel PC*, above note 9 at paras 100–2.

40 *R v Desautel*, 2021 SCC 17 at para 22 [*Desautel SCC*].

resources. Still, Rowe J commented in *obiter* that criminal and regulatory proceedings are not the best context in which to resolve these issues, because the nature of the proceeding means the evidence is less extensive. It is an opinion judges have been expressing for some time; in *R v Marshall; R v Bernard*, LeBel J wrote, "[I]t is clear to me that we should re-think the appropriateness of litigating [A]boriginal treaty rights and title issues in the context of criminal trials."[41] The courts would clearly prefer these cases to proceed by civil claims, applications for declaration, or better still, not to be in court at all, and resolved through negotiations.[42]

It is true that in a criminal trial, only the parties directly affected are permitted to tender evidence and make argument. In Desautel's case this meant that other Indigenous communities in British Columbia (some with Sinixt descendants) did not have the opportunity to lead evidence about the impact the case could have on their own claims of Indigenous rights.[43] Civil proceedings would have generated the more fulsome evidentiary record Rowe J was looking for. But Rowe J's commentary is unfair. It is unlikely that Desautel could have started a civil action in British Columbia because the BC Court of Appeal has ruled civil claims of Aboriginal rights or title are not justiciable in the absence of a "violation of or threat to" the right claimed.[44] Furthermore, while the evidentiary burden of a claim of Aboriginal rights in a criminal or regulatory prosecution is immense, it is still more manageable than in a civil claim. Courts need to accept that these test cases will continue unless governments make reasonable steps toward timely, well-funded negotiations. And if negotiations are too slow, Indigenous rights claimants, like

41 *R v Marshall; R v Bernard*, 2005 SCC 43 at para 142. And see *R v Marshall*, [1999] 3 SCR 533 at para 22. The Court repeated this plea in *Lax Kw'alaams Indian Band v Canada (Attorney General)*, 2011 SCC 56 at para 11.

42 *Desautel SCC*, above note 40 at paras 87–92.

43 The Okanagan Nation Alliance and Métis Nation of British Columbia intervened at the SCC on this issue and specifically asked the Court not to make findings that would prejudice their interests.

44 *Cheslatta Carrier Nation v British Columbia*, 2000 BCCA 539 at paras 15 and 19, leave to appeal refused [2000] SCCA No 625. In addition, the SCC has further limited access in non-criminal proceedings by holding that Aboriginal claims in the context of judicial review proceedings are not permitted: *Ktunaxa Nation v British Columbia (Forests, Lands and Natural Resource Operations)*, 2017 SCC 54 at para 84. Please see Kent McNeil & Kerry Wilkins, "Welcome Home: Aboriginal Rights After Desautel" (2001) *All Papers* 333, online: https://digitalcommons.osgoode.yorku.ca/all_papers/333/ at p 18-22 for a detailed discussion of this issue.

any other claimant, should be able to access the courts through test cases without being scolded for exercising their rights.

E. WHO ARE THE "ABORIGINAL PEOPLES OF CANADA"?

The fact that Desautel's people hunted in the Arrow Lakes area prior to contact was not in dispute at his trial. Nor was the fact that hunting was, and remains, integral to Sinixt culture. Relying on a presumption of territoriality, the Crown argued that section 35 only protects the rights of Aboriginal peoples living and exercising traditional rights in Canada *continuously from the time of contact to the present day*.[45] Because Desautel could not prove the existence of a present-day collective in the area where his people had historically exercised their rights, he was not one of the "aboriginal peoples of Canada," and therefore had no rights under section 35.[46]

The Supreme Court (and every court below) disagreed with the Crown, and found that groups physically located outside Canada can be "aboriginal peoples of Canada" with section 35 rights. Justice Rowe affirmed that the purpose of section 35 was to "recognize the prior occupation of Canada by organized, autonomous societies, and to reconcile their modern-day existence with the Crown's assertion of sovereignty over them."[47] He carefully examined Aboriginal rights doctrine, and found that it looks back to the practices of groups in what is now Canadian territory, and then expresses those practices as constitutional rights held by modern-day successor groups, and recognized in the Canadian legal order. On this interpretation he found that "aboriginal peoples of Canada" meant "modern-day successors of Aboriginal societies that occupied Canadian territory at the time of contact."[48] In other words, people like Richard Desautel. Justice Rowe continued:

> I would add that an interpretation of "aboriginal peoples of Canada" in s. 35(1) that includes Aboriginal peoples who were here when the Europeans arrived and later moved or were forced to move elsewhere, or on whom international boundaries were imposed, reflects the purpose

45 *R v Desautel*, Factum of the Appellant, Her Majesty the Queen (29 January 2020), online: www.scc-csc.ca/WebDocuments-DocumentsWeb/38734/FM010_Appellant_Her-Majesty-the-Queen.pdf.

46 *Desautel SCC*, above note 40 at para 16.

47 *Ibid* at para 22.

48 *Ibid* at para 23.

> of reconciliation. The displacement of Aboriginal peoples as a result of colonization is well acknowledged. . . . By contrast, an interpretation that excludes Aboriginal peoples who were forced to move out of Canada would risk "perpetuating the historical injustice suffered by aboriginal peoples at the hands of colonizers."[49]

He stressed that section 35 did not *create* rights but *affirmed* rights already in existence long before 1982. An interpretation of section 35 that limited its scope to people located in Canada would fail to give effect to that fact by incorrectly treating section 35 as the source of rights.[50] Justice Rowe rejected the Crown's reliance on the presumption of territoriality because, while groups outside Canada may have section 35 rights, they can only exercise them while they are in Canada.[51]

Having found that the members of the Lakes Tribe were Aboriginal peoples of Canada, Rowe J upheld the trial judge's finding that Desautel was exercising a traditional right to hunt as a continuation of a pre-contact practice of his people. He rejected the Crown's argument that "continuation" required an "on-going presence in the lands over which an Aboriginal right is asserted," noting that an unbroken chain of continuity was not required.[52]

F. CONCLUSION: WHAT SIDE DO YOU COME FROM?

In the short story "Borders," by Thomas King, a Blackfoot boy and his mom try to enter the United States from Alberta, on their way to Salt Lake City. When asked by a US border guard to declare her citizenship, the boy's mom answers, "Blackfoot." The guard replies, "Now I know that we got Blackfeet on the American side and the Canadians got Blackfeet on their side. Just so we can keep our records straight, what side do you come from?" The mom replies, "Blackfoot side."[53]

The notion of a territorial nation state is so deeply entrenched in modern political and economic structures that it is rarely, if ever, questioned.

49 *Ibid* at paras 33–34, citing *R v Coté*, [1996] 3 SCR 139 at para 53.

50 *Ibid* at para 34.

51 *Ibid* at para 43.

52 *Ibid* at para 63, though he specifically left for another day whether a right could be lost or abandoned by non-use.

53 "Borders," in Thomas King, *One Good Story, That One* (Toronto: Harper Collins, 1993) at 137–38.

States grant political, social, and economic rights to citizens, and citizenship is defined or granted in relation to territory.[54] In criminal law, this concept is expressed as territorial jurisdiction, which largely (with some exceptions[55]) ends at the border. The facts of *Desautel* might seem unusual, and it would be easy to say that Desautel's assertion of being from the "Sinixt side," is *sui generis.* But it is not.

As the Crown noted in its argument in the Supreme Court, there are examples of Indigenous peoples and territories that cross modern boundaries all along the Canada–US border, including, as Thomas King points out, the Blackfoot nation, but also the Ktunaxa, Kinbasket, Okanagan, Nl;aka'pamux, Sto:lo, Quwutsun' and Haida nations,[56] as well as the Tsmishian at Canada's border with Alaska, and the far north.[57] Kanien'kehá'ka territory at Akwesasne straddles the Ontario–Quebec and US–Canada borders, which led to an unsuccessful challenge of the imposition of Canadian duty on goods brought across the border by Grand Chief Michael Mitchell.[58] The territories of the Passamaquoddy in New Brunswick and the White River First Nation in Yukon are also bisected by the borders with the United States.

In 2016, the federal minister of Crown–Indigenous Relations and Northern Affairs commissioned a report on First Nations border-crossing issues. The report states that imposition of the Canada–US border has been, "in the eyes of First Nations, destructive of family, cultural, governance and other connections with US Tribes which are of great importance to their identity as well as to their cultural survival."[59] None of the recommendations in the report appear to have been implemented,

54 Harald Bauder, "The Possibilities of Open and No Borders" (2014) 39:4 *Social Justice* 76 at 81.

55 Canada exercises limited extraterritorial criminal jurisdiction over Canadian citizens abroad in some limited circumstances for some serious crimes related to Canada's treaty obligations (for example, sexual crimes against children) and over public officials acting in the course of their duties abroad. For a detailed analysis see Robert J. Currie & Joseph Rikhof, *International and Transnational Criminal Law*, 3d ed (Toronto: Irwin Law, 2020) c 2, 5, and 8.

56 Factum of the Appellant, Her Majesty the Queen, above note 45 at para 34.

57 *Reference as to whether "Indians" in s. 91 (24) of the B.N.A. Act includes Eskimo in habitants of the Province of Quebec*, [1939] SCR 104 at 107.

58 *Mitchell*, above note 38.

59 Fred Caron, "Report on First Nations Border Crossing Issues" (31 August 2017), online: https://caid.ca/RepFirNatBorCro2017.pdf.

though Canadian Border Services Agency has installed trilingual signage at Akwesasne.[60]

Issues like Desautel's continue to arise. For example, in 2018, Mique'l Dangeli, a Tsimshian woman who left a tenure-track position at the University of Alaska to teach the Sm'algyax language to students in Kitsumkalum, northern British Columbia, was forced to return to the United States after her visa expired even though, like Desautel, her Tsimshian traditional territory spans the border.[61] Desautel's case is not unique, and the ruling will ground other, similar claims.

When considering the possible future impact of *Desautel*, it is important to note that while the Court recognized the right of the Sinixt peoples to use the land, it did not recognize a right to the land itself, which will have to be decided either through negotiations, or litigation of the Sinixt land claim. The Court did find, however, that once the Crown is aware of the existence of rights-claiming Indigenous groups outside Canada, it may have a duty to consult, if it has been put on notice of their claims.[62] This is obviously significant to the Lakes, who have clearly put the Crown on notice. They may now have to be consulted on logging, hydro-electrical developments, or on other similar activities in their traditional territory. Justice Rowe may not have favoured the use of a regulatory trial to advance the Sinixt rights' claim, but it is a significant victory for the Lakes people.[63] It will go down in history as the only case in which an "extinct"[64] people fought the Canadian government all the way to the Supreme Court, and won.

---

60 Canadian Border Services Agency, "Blueprint 2020 Report" (December 2018), online: www.cbsa-asfc.gc.ca/agency-agence/reports-rapports/bp2020/2018/ias-saa-eng.html.

61 Amy Smart, "Indigenous Woman Fights to Stay in Canada, Saying Traditional Territory Is B.C." *CBC News* (30 June 2019) online: www.cbc.ca/news/canada/british-columbia/indigenous-woman-fights-to-stay-in-canada-saying-traditional-territory-is-b-c-1.4729876.

62 *Desautel SCC*, above note 40 at paras 72–76.

63 "I'm very, very, very happy," Desautel told the *Washington Post*. "I don't know how to express the joy and relief." Amanda Colette, "Canada's Supreme Court Says Some Native Americans Can Hunt in British Columbia," *Washington Post* (23 April 2021), online: www.washingtonpost.com/world/2021/04/23/canada-sinixit-supreme-court-british-columbia.

64 I would be remiss in ending this paper without referring the reader to Marilyn James & Taress Alexi, *Not Extinct: Keeping the Sinixt Way* (New Denver, BC: Maa Press, 2021), and the beautiful related interactive website: https://keepingthesinixtway.ca/#sinixt.

IV

CORPORATE, ECONOMIC *and* FINANCIAL CRIME, MONEY LAUNDERING *and* PROCEEDS

ten

Gatekeepers — The Lawyer Enigma

PETER M. GERMAN, KC*

A. THE PROFESSION OF LAW

The quintessential Englishman of the eighteenth century would have little difficulty defining a professional to be a learned person in the fields of divinity, law, or medicine, who practices his skills in churches, offices, or hospitals. Over time, this rarified collective grew to include a few other occupations, but only a few. All of that has changed, however. It can now be argued that society no longer draws a distinction between the "traditional" professions and all other trades and occupations, be they house cleaners, retail salespersons, firefighters, or machinists. We glibly assert that any person can be viewed as a professional if they approach work with pride, expertise, and care.

But is this really the case? Is this nuanced approach not simply a sop to our liberal and egalitarian perspective on life in the new millennium? Is it not true that the traditional professions have, in fact, retained their elevated status in society, despite admitting new members to the club? Arguably this is precisely what has occurred, and the law itself has facilitated this evolution. We now refer to the club members as "self-regulated professions," occupations that have been granted a status not accorded to others.

* PhD, Barrister and Solicitor of the British Columbia and Ontario Bars, President of the International Centre for Criminal Law Reform, Vancouver, BC.

As we shall see in the pages that follow, this is extremely relevant to our discussion of organized crime, money laundering, and the role of lawyers.

In this chapter, we examine the pivotal role played by lawyers and others with "lawyer-like" authority who control entry, not only to their profession, but who also serve as gatekeepers, or keepers of the keys to modern commerce and the global flow of money. It is a privileged and oftentimes lucrative role, but one that can be burdened by onerous responsibility and is susceptible to numerous external threats. We examine the role of the legal profession in the context of transnational organized crime by considering first, the risks that lawyers face in their daily work, then, how organized crime seeks to leverage lawyers to its benefit, and finally, what Parliament, the bureaucracy of government, and lawyers are doing or not doing to deal with the issue. A brief look at comparative developments will drive a conclusion that Canada will need to look more closely at the regulation of lawyers in this arena than it has done to date.

B. MONEY LAUNDERING

There was a time, not too many decades ago, and certainly within the memory of many legal practitioners, when *laundering* was simply viewed as the process of washing and starching the wing-tipped collars of barristers' shirts. Today, those shirts still require a good clean and press, but the descriptor has now found its own place in Canada's *Criminal Code*.[1]

Because most crime is committed for financial gain, obvious exceptions being sexual and public order offences, those who steal or plunder require that their illicit proceeds be laundered to a level of sophistication which varies from basic to complex, and from local to international, but always involves the well-known stages of placement, layering, and integration.[2] Skilled practitioners wash, spin, and dry this money until its origin is obfuscated and the forensic paper trail is sufficiently complex that law enforcement either cannot unravel it, or has not the time, resources, or inclination to do so. Often referred to as the "back office" of organized crime, laundering is a serious offence.

1 *Criminal Code*, RSC 1985, c C-46, s 462.31 [*Code*].

2 Peter German, *Proceeds of Crime and Money Laundering* (Toronto: Thomson Reuters Canada, 2021) s 2.2.

The three stages of laundering are of equal importance and key to the success of a sophisticated illegal enterprise. Placing the proceeds, generally in the form of cash, into the financial system is the initial entry point. For most criminal activity, however, placement is just a staging point. Layering is where the fun begins, and money starts to spin locally, nationally, or around the world, oftentimes as digital representations of cash, and in different financial vehicles. These transactions may occur with lightning speed. Repatriation in the final, integration stage, represents the return of the money to the criminal organization, but sufficiently washed to disguise its sordid trail.

However simple these stages may sound in the abstract, they can be incredibly complex. The moment that money crosses borders, it requires a safe landing spot, which is likely a financial institution and an offshore company account. If the destination state has weak transparency laws, there is a strong likelihood that the funds will be lost to regulatory oversight, and from there can transit to other offshore states, or be placed in different vehicles, ranging from real property to short-term investments, online trading accounts, online gaming accounts, or a wide range of businesses. Almost all require the engagement of lawyers, accountants, company formation agents, or similar occupations.

Money returning to the state of origin may be repatriated in digital form, directly to an account or by a more circuitous route. Probably the most desirous penultimate stop is a lawyer's trust account.

C. GATEKEEPERS

As life becomes increasingly complex, it is beyond the ability of mere mortals to know all that there is to know, even in one's own job. In the eons before recorded history, hunters and gatherers lived a basic life, following herds, fishing the waters, and picking berries and fruit. Knowledge was passed down through generations and reflected the basics of food and shelter. That simple existence continues in many countries but has long since disappeared in the industrialized world.

Today, as space tourism is no longer the thing of science fiction, as money can be virtual, as planes criss-cross the skies, and satellites have replaced road maps, as the world of knowledge is an internet search away, and as conversations can be virtual, life has changed. The global community has shrunk with advances in transportation and technology which bring us, or at least the virtual we, closer together.

The complexity of life makes it essential that specialists be available to help navigate the road ahead and unlock the mysteries of life. Gatekeepers are those people. In the parlance of transnational organized crime and money laundering, "gatekeepers" and "facilitators" are often used synonymously. They may, however, possess a slightly different constituency of occupations and professions. Quite simply, gatekeepers are needed for certain activity to occur. They hold the keys. Facilitators, on the other hand, make things happen through the open gates.

Membership in either category is not finite. It really depends on what must be accomplished and who is best able to accomplish it within the legal structure that exists in a jurisdiction. For example, if you require a company to be created in a Caribbean state, you may turn to an accountant, a lawyer, or a company formation agent. Likewise, if your intent is to purchase property in a Central American state, you will engage a person or entity that can effect the transfer on your behalf.

In this highly regulated world, in which laws have largely supplanted customs and traditions, and normative behaviour is now the subject of copious regulations, gatekeepers and facilitators increasingly oversee the intersections between legal entities. In both the legal and the illegal worlds of commerce, that role often rests with lawyers.

D. THE PRACTICE OF LAW

For decades, a law degree served as a door opener to a wide range of work in business, government, non-profits, and politics. There are many lawyers, however, who continue in the traditional practice of law, alone or in combination with others. They are the artisans of the trade, and in Canada are referred to as barristers and solicitors. The former are the denizens of the courtroom, the latter are the purveyors of legal documents. Most lawyers toil in obscurity and seldom, if ever, brush shoulders with organized crime or money launderers. But some do, and some are more likely than others to do so because of their specialty.

Corporate and commercial lawyers face a laundry list of client-centric and transactional risks in the practice of their profession. They handle business and real estate purchases and sales, create trust agreements, undertake corporate restructures, provide tax advice, act as nominees, coordinate international transactions, and so much more. However, one cannot forget that all lawyers receive fees for service and deal with a wide assortment of clients. Some, and they are fortunately only a few, cross the line of what is legal, and willingly participate in criminal activity.

It has been said to lawyers that "[n]o matter what kind of law you practice, you are potentially a money launderer's facilitator – and his victim."[3] In the words of the late Kenneth Young, this translates into how lawyers relate to their clients:

> [W]hat inquiries we make as to the origin/source of our clients [*sic*] funds and property; what transactions we will or will not undertake on behalf of our clients; and how, in context, we will … come to handle funds and property entrusted to us as counsel.[4]

To better understand the pivotal role of lawyers and the risks that they face in their daily work, the Federation of Law Societies of Canada (Federation) has published case studies and recognized red flags regarding risks that lawyers face in their practices.[5] These risks may be client-centric, transaction-centric, specific to a particular field of practice, or more broadly based. Five key areas of practice outlined by the Federation are the use of trust accounts, real estate transactions, the creation and management of trusts and companies, managing client affairs and making introductions, and disputes and litigation.[6]

The susceptibility of lawyers to being witting or unwitting accomplices to crime occurs principally at three stages: the representation decision, obtaining a retainer, and the use of trust accounts. Let us briefly examine each.

---

3 Derek Lundy, "It's a Law Firm, not a Laundry" *Canadian Lawyer* (January 1997) at 35.

4 Kenneth Young, "Proceeds of Crime" in David L. Greenbank & Selwyn Romilly, eds, *The Drug Case* (Vancouver: Continuing Legal Education Society, 1990) at 2.1.04.12.

5 Federation of Law Societies of Canada, Anti-Money Laundering and Terrorist Financing Working Group, *Risk Assessment Case Studies for the Legal Profession* (February 2020), online: https://flsc.ca/wp-content/uploads/2020/02/CasestudiesENv5.pdf.

6 *Ibid* at 2.

1) Representation

It is fundamental that a lawyer must know who the client is. That sounds like a remarkably basic and self-evident statement, but it is an issue fraught with complexity, and can easily be overlooked in the bountiful excitement that accompanies attracting a new and paying client. In a recent publication, the Federation stated:

> The practice of law exposes members of the legal profession to unique risks and vulnerabilities in relation to money laundering. Criminals may target legal advisors to lend legitimacy to their illicit operations or make use of trust accounts to launder proceeds of crime activity. Legal advisors are also necessary to complete real estate transactions and set up trusts, both common vehicles for cleaning dirty money.[7]

In a commentary that once accompanied its *Rules of Professional Conduct*, the Law Society of Ontario stated:

> To obtain information about the client and about the subject matter and objectives of the retainer, the lawyer may, for example, need to verify who are the legal or beneficial owners of property and business entities, verify who has the control of business entities, and clarify the nature and purpose of a complex or unusual transaction where the purpose is not clear. The lawyer should make a record of the results of these inquiries. It is especially important to obtain this information where a lawyer has suspicions or doubts about whether he or she might be assisting a client or any other person in dishonesty, fraud, crime or illegal conduct.[8]

Knowing Your Client (KYC) is a term that is well known around the world. It reflects the onus on a person or entity that provides goods or services to know with whom they are transacting business. For a lawyer, this means knowing who the person sitting across the desk is, confirming that person's identity, and ensuring that the client is, in fact, the individual in the office. If one is dealing with an agent or nominee, it is critical to know who the principal is, in order to avoid a conflict of interest and being a pawn in fraud or other illegal conduct.

---

7 *Ibid* at 1.

8 The Law Society of Ontario, *Rules of Professional Conduct* (Toronto: Law Society of Ontario, 2000) sub-rule 2.02(5).

2) Financial Retainer

Closely allied to the issue of knowing one's client is that of receiving a retainer for services. It is typical in the legal profession to obtain funds in advance of performing work on behalf of a client. The reason is obvious: holding payment until completion of work ensures no receivables for non-payment of invoices.

In days of old, receiving money was unfettered by external considerations. Not so today. Lawyers are now faced with the reality that by receiving money that happens to be the product of illegal activity, they become the recipients of proceeds of crime. What obligation is there on lawyers to inquire into this possibility? If there is an obligation, does it increase if the client is unemployed, has a criminal record, or is charged with a crime that typically gives rise to proceeds of crime? Should cash be treated differently than electronic transfers or digital currency?

In the case of seized or restrained funds, the *Criminal Code* permits the release of a portion of these monies to fund an accused's defence.[9] In this manner, a financial retainer can be obtained out of property that is allegedly the proceeds of crime, a fictional cleansing sometimes referred to as *judicial laundering* but more properly *statutorily approved laundering*. The underlying theory, of course, is that a judicial finding has not been made that the property is the proceeds of crime and therefore, it would be inappropriate to restrict access to the funds for a *bona fide* purpose, such as payment of legal counsel.

3) Trust Accounts

Trust accounts are the lifeblood of a lawyer's practice. In most provinces, the great majority of real estate transactions engage lawyers at both ends of the purchase and sale. The purchase monies are typically transferred from the purchaser's bank or credit union to the trust account of the purchaser's lawyer, where they reside until the property is registered, at which time they transit to the trust account of the seller's lawyer and are then sent to the seller's bank or credit union account. Along the way, funds are deducted in accordance with statements of adjustments, including for real estate fees, taxes, legal fees, and other expenses. A similar scenario plays

9 *Code*, above note 1, s 462.34(4).

out with the purchase and sale of businesses, and in many other commercial transactions, both domestic and international.

The key to a trust account is that it is only to be used for work related to the giving of legal advice. A trust account can never be confused with a personal account, and the money in a trust account, although commingled with that of other clients, must never be used for a purpose other than that for which it was deposited in the first instance.[10] Trust accounts are not Ponzi accounts! Unfortunately, in the past, some lawyers have abused these accounts. As a result, law societies tend to be extremely vigilant in monitoring trust accounts. What is new, however, is an emphasis on marrying legal advice to the contents of a trust account. In other words, ensuring that the funds are on deposit for a purpose related to the giving of legal advice.

E. LAWYERS BEHAVING BADLY

Canada's best-known Mafioso was likely Vito Rizzuto. He had a certain aura about him that was reminiscent of the godfather of New York's five mob families, John Gotti.[11] The similarities in behaviour reflected a much broader connection, as Canada's mob was inextricably linked to the New York and Buffalo mob families for many decades. The Marseilles to New York transportation route for heroin grown in Asia, immortalized on the big screen as *The French Connection*, transited through Montreal.[12] As the FBI and other agencies increased the pressure on the mob in the United States, and eventually brought its house of cards tumbling down by dismantling its upper echelon in the Commission case of 1986,[13] pressure also mounted on Canadian police to act.

In Montreal, Toronto, and Vancouver, RCMP officers developed elaborate reverse-sting operations in which they created and operated covert

10 See *Gellert (Re)*, 2013 LSBC 22 at paras 71–73; *Gurney (Re)*, 2017 LSBC 15 at paras 79–80.

11 I use the term "mob" loosely to describe what is commonly referred to as the Mafia or Cosa Nostra.

12 Discussed in Alexandre Marchant, "The French Connection: Between Myth and Reality" (2012) 115:3 *Vingtième Siècle: Revue d'Histoire* 89. See also Robin Moore, *The French Connection: A True Account of Cops, Narcotics, and International Conspiracy* (Boston: Little, Brown, and Company, 1969).

13 *United States v Anthony Salerno, et al*, described in Selwyn Raab, *Five Families: The Rise, Decline, and Resurgence of America's Most Powerful Mafia Empires* (New York: Thomas Dunne Books, 2006) at 273, 291–92.

currency exchange houses and an undercover financial investment business, aimed at servicing the criminal element. The operation in Montreal, dubbed Project Compote, was so successful that it led to many offshoot investigations, including huge drug importation cases, with links to the Colombian cocaine cartels, the Hells Angels, and the Rizzuto family.[14]

Giuseppe (Joe) Lagana was Vito Rizzuto's personal lawyer. His office in downtown Montreal overlooked the Montreal International Currency Centre, a busy operation that just happened to be the RCMP's covert currency exchange. Police surveillance revealed that Lagana also played a significant role in the mob's money laundering activities. He coordinated the exchange of large sums of money, some lugged across the street by two fellow lawyers. He even met with undercover officers in the Netherlands.[15]

Lagana went to prison, as did many members of the Montreal mob. Rizzuto was later extradited and convicted of murder-related charges in the United States and died in 2013, a year after his release from a US federal penitentiary. The mob scene in Montreal changed dramatically as traditional organized crime crumbled under the weight of numerous police actions and convictions, and was quickly replaced by other, more disparate criminal organizations. The role of Joe Lagana and his privileged status as a lawyer had provided the mob with a form of protection that money could not normally buy.

Lagana was by no means the only lawyer to run afoul of the law. There is a long list, despite that list representing a minuscule percentage of lawyers practising in Canada. However, the damage to the profession caused by a "dirty" lawyer who hides behind the confidentiality and privilege accorded to the profession can be quite profound.

Simon Rosenfeld was a senior lawyer in Toronto who fell upon hard times financially, resulting in personal bankruptcy.[16] He was not entirely blameless for his financial woes, apparently living a lavish lifestyle and choosing not to pay debts or taxes.[17] An undercover RCMP officer was referred to Rosenfeld by a Caribbean money launderer, who indicated that Rosenfeld could launder large sums of money. Posing as a money

---

14 Margaret E. Beare & Stephen Schneider, *Money Laundering in Canada: Chasing Dirty and Dangerous Dollars* (Toronto: University of Toronto Press, 2007) at 167.

15 *Ibid* at 169. See also André Cédilot & André Noël, *Mafia Inc.: The Long, Bloody Reign of Canada's Sicilian Clan* (Toronto: Vintage Canada, 2011) ch 9.

16 *R v Rosenfeld*, 2009 ONCA 307.

17 *Ibid* at para 37.

man for a Colombian cartel, the officer contacted Rosenfeld, who was quite happy to launder funds for an 8 percent fee. They met in Florida, and the officer gave Rosenfeld one dollar to secure his services as a lawyer. Rosenfeld encouraged the officer to launder funds in Canada because, according to him, there was little police enforcement. Two transactions totalling $440,000 ensued, for which Rosenfeld received $43,000. He acted as a classic gatekeeper and facilitator, by establishing bank accounts for corporate shells which he controlled in different jurisdictions. These structures facilitated the layering process.[18]

Rosenfeld was convicted by a jury and sentenced to three years in prison, which was increased to five years by the Ontario Court of Appeal. The appeals court pointed to aggravating factors, including Rosenfeld's belief that he was laundering the proceeds of a Colombian cartel's international cocaine trade, his operation's size and sophistication, his motivation of greed, his status as a lawyer, and his apparent experience in money laundering.[19] The Court of Appeal did not mince its words when addressing the culpability of the accused:

> The appellant thought he was playing a crucial role in the successful operation of the international cocaine trade. That trade kills countless people and destroys the lives of even more. The appellant's conduct was designed to give the appearance of legitimacy to the profits reaped from one of the most nefarious and socially harmful of all criminal activities. His culpability is properly analogized to others who perform services to assist those who control and reap the profits of the international cocaine trade.[20]

The Court of Appeal also described two significant aggravating factors related to Rosenfeld being a lawyer. The first was his breach of public trust and failure to protect the due administration of justice. By abusing the privileges accorded to the legal profession, Rosenfeld brought discredit on the profession and fed public cynicism toward lawyers, which ultimately serves to undermine confidence in the justice system. The second factor was that Rosenfeld took advantage of lawyers not being subject to financial reporting conditions, while benefitting from the privilege covering solicitor–client communications. The Court of Appeal referred to this as

18 *Ibid* at para 4.

19 *Ibid* at paras 37–39.

20 *Ibid* at para 37.

the offender's "willingness to prostitute his legal services and abuse the special privileges associated with them."[21]

Lagana and Rosenfeld are but two of many who have willingly crossed the line. Most, however, do so quite unwittingly. Separating the former from the later is a matter for the police and the courts; however, educating and monitoring those who are oblivious to the pivotal and valuable position in which they find themselves is likely a more difficult task. Professors Beare and Schneider wrote about the problem:

> In many of the police cases in our research, lawyers appear to have been unaware of the criminal source of funds provided by an offender and were unknowingly used to facilitate money laundering. However the research also identified cases where a lawyer should have become suspicious of the circumstances surrounding a particular transaction. . . . Moreover, some lawyers appeared to offer services that were tailored expressly to satisfy the objectives of money laundering.[22]

In a 2004 study of 149 RCMP proceeds-of-crime cases, Professor Schneider found that lawyers were involved in 49.7 percent of the cases, second only to deposit institution staff at 67.8 percent. The great majority involved the use of trust accounts in real estate transactions.[23]

Canada is obviously not alone. In the United States, there have been many high-profile cases in which lawyers unwittingly became involved in money laundering schemes.[24] In one transaction, a Malaysian financier, alleged to have misappropriated more than $3.5 billion from a state investment fund, wired $148 million from a Swiss bank account to the pooled trust account of a US law firm. The funds were then used to fund several real estate transactions.[25] In another case, the son of the president of Equatorial Guinea was able to move more than $100 million into the

21 *Ibid* at paras 40–41.

22 Beare & Schneider, above note 14 at 233.

23 Stephen Schneider, *Money Laundering in Canada: An Analysis of RCMP Cases* (Toronto: Nathanson Centre for the Study of Organized Crime and Corruption, 2004) at 3–4, 68, and 70.

24 Rachel Louise Ensign & Serena Ng, "Law Firms' Accounts Pose Money-Laundering Risk" *Wall Street Journal* (26 December 2016), online: www.wsj.com/articles/law-firms-accounts-pose-money-laundering-risk-1482765003.

25 *Ibid.*

United States through his lawyer's trust account at Bank of America, even though his own account at the same bank had already been shut down.[26]

In 2016, *60 Minutes* broadcast the story of a Global Witness sting in which an actor met with sixteen lawyers and posed as an African government official seeking to move millions of dollars in potentially illicit funds into the United States to buy a townhouse, jet, and yacht. Film footage of the meetings showed that fifteen of the sixteen lawyers were receptive to representing the would-be client.[27]

F. INTERNATIONAL NORMS

To prevent lawyers becoming the witting or unwitting facilitators of crime, supranational bodies, most notably the Financial Action Task Force (FATF), have developed guidelines for states to follow when regulating the legal profession. Almost without exception, these guidelines, which have evolved into international rules of engagement, target the back office of organized crime, where the proceeds of its activities meet the legitimate financial system.

The FATF was never intended to be a permanent body, but it is unlikely that it will disappear anytime soon. Its mandate, originally to help coalesce the world community's fight against money laundering, quickly expanded after 9/11 to include the financing of terrorism. The starting point for the FATF is its 40 Recommendations, intended to capture best practices in dealing with money laundering. The *FAFT Recommendations* have evolved over time, seeking to remain abreast of technological change and the machinations of organized crime.[28]

Building on its Recommendations, the FATF has developed a peer-review mechanism with which states evaluate each other for compliance with the Recommendations. Regional FATF bodies undertake much of this work. Those states that do not perform at a basic level of compliance

---

26 *Ibid.*

27 Steve Kroft, "Anonymous, Inc." *CBS News* (31 January 2016), online: www.cbsnews.com/news/anonymous-inc-60-minutes-steve-kroft-investigation.

28 FATF, *The FATF Recommendations — International Standards on Combating Money Laundering and the Financing of Terrorism & Proliferation* (2012), as amended, online: www.fatf-gafi.org/media/fatf/documents/recommendations/pdfs/FATF%20Recommendations%202012.pdf.

may be "grey listed," which has serious implications for the banking and financial sector of a country.

The *FATF Recommendations* place lawyers under the rubric of Designated Non-Financial Businesses and Professions (DNFBP). Recommendation 22 makes the customer due-diligence and record-keeping requirements applicable to DNFBPs. With respect to lawyers, notaries, and other independent legal professionals, Recommendation 22 applies to a specified, yet broad range of activities:

- buying and selling real estate
- managing client money, securities, or other assets
- managing bank, savings, or securities accounts
- organizing corporate finances
- creating, operating, or managing legal persons or arrangements
- buying and selling business entities

Recommendation 23 requires that the same subset of DNFBPs report suspicious transactions that they encounter in the above situations. The interpretive note to Recommendation 23 provides that suspicious transaction reports (STR) are not required "if the relevant information was obtained in circumstances where they are subject to professional secrecy or legal professional privilege, the ambit of which is for each country to determine." The note also permits reporting of suspicious transactions to the applicable "self-regulatory organisations, provided that there are appropriate forms of cooperation between these organisations and the FIU [Financial Intelligence Unit]."[29]

Peer reviews have consistently criticized countries, including Canada, for failing to require lawyers to comply with the *FATF Recommendations*. The reason for non-compliance is simple. Reporting is often viewed as a direct assault on the inviolable communication between lawyer and client. Without a trained and trusted confidant, an individual is often lost amid myriad laws that control human and corporate behaviour. Lawyers help to navigate this morass, resolving legal problems, making deals, and transacting business. It is not surprising that this privilege is closely guarded by the profession.

---

29 *Ibid.*

National responses to the *FATF Recommendations* affecting lawyers cover the gamut from non-compliance to partial and full compliance. Some states are challenged by unique constitutional or other legal impediments that make compliance difficult. Others are simply dragging their heels on reform, or under pressure from law societies to maintain the status quo. History tells us, however, that idiosyncratic behaviour by nation states will eventually give way to the global tidal wave of change. Even if governments and politicians do not, the international banking system and the world's interdependent securities markets inevitably will force the adoption of policies and regulations, which on paper, if not in practice, reflect international standards.

Attacking a problem head on with brute force seldom succeeds over the long term. Seeking to impose restrictions or reporting requirements on the legal profession is no different. To comply with the *FATF Recommendations* while not restricting the legal privilege accorded to lawyers and their clients will almost invariably require a workaround. Regulation tends, therefore, to concentrate on the margins of the professional engagement, on entry and exit points, and on third-party solutions.

G. THE CANADIAN FEDERAL LANDSCAPE

Canada's first foray into money laundering compliance and prevention occurred in 1991, with passage of the *Proceeds of Crime (money laundering) Act*.[30] It was a lame piece of legislation which, in many ways, confirmed existing practices at established financial institutions. It required the recording and retention of records and little else of substance.

Criticism ensued from the FATF, and in 2000, the *Proceeds of Crime (Money Laundering) and Terrorist Financing Act* (*POCMLTFA*) became law.[31] Not only did it engage the emerging issue of terrorist financing, but it overhauled the existing legislation by requiring the reporting of numerous types of transactions to a newly formed Financial Intelligence Unit (FIU), FINTRAC. This included reporting cross-border transactions and most importantly, suspicious transactions. Canada emerged from its near-pariah status among G7 countries and joined the fight against money laundering.

30 *Proceeds of Crime (money laundering) Act*, SC 1991, c 26.

31 *Proceeds of Crime (Money Laundering) and Terrorist Financing Act*, SC 2000, c 17. The original title was amended to include "terrorist financing" by SC 2001, c 41.

The compliance and reporting provisions of the *POCMLTFA* do not target all businesses, only those that fit into certain categories. For example, banks, co-ops and credit unions, life insurance companies, brokers and agents, securities dealers, foreign exchange dealers, money service businesses, real estate brokers, casinos, and more, must comply with its terms. This can be a costly endeavour. Others, such as car and truck dealers, boat dealers, antique shops, and most vendors of luxury goods, are curiously exempt.

Included in the original iteration of the legislation and its subordinate regulations was the legal profession, which became subject to regulatory oversight by FINTRAC, and was required to adhere to client identification rules and suspicious transaction reporting. The triggering events for reporting included the giving of instructions or performing any of the following:

- receiving or paying funds, other than those received or paid in respect of professional fees, disbursements, expenses, or bail
- purchasing or selling securities, real property, or business assets or entities
- transferring funds or securities by any means

Lawyers were not required, however, to report any information that was the subject of solicitor–client privilege, although the scope of that privilege was not defined. Lawyers could not disclose having submitted suspicious transaction reports (STR), or the contents of those reports, to their clients, on pain of criminal sanction.

From its inception on the parliamentary order paper, the legal community expressed vehement opposition to the legislation, and a form of righteous indignation at what was seen as an attempt by Parliament to invade the sanctity of solicitor–client privilege and client confidentiality.

On 8 November 2001, the day that the suspicious transaction regulations came into force, the Federation and the Law Society of British Columbia jointly filed a petition in the British Columbia Supreme Court, challenging the constitutionality of the new legislation, seeking both interim and permanent relief for lawyers from its provisions. Justice Allen granted the interim relief, observing that the legislation "authorizes an unprecedented intrusion into the traditional solicitor–client relationship."[32]

32 *Law Society (British Columbia) v Canada (Attorney General)*, 2001 BCSC 1593 at para 108.

Upheld on appeal[33] and buttressed by similar decisions in other jurisdictions, the Federation and the Office of the Attorney General of Canada agreed in 2002 that lawyers would be exempted from the provisions of the *POCMLTFA* pending a full hearing of the challenge. In 2003, the federal government removed lawyers from the recording and reporting regime, promising to introduce a new regime that better reflected the duties of legal counsel. Four years later, in 2007, a new regulatory regime was proposed. The federal government hoped that this rework would pass constitutional muster.[34] It took another eight years to learn that it did not.

On 13 February 2015, the Supreme Court of Canada released its judgment in *Canada (Attorney General) v Federation of Law Societies of Canada*,[35] finding that certain provisions of the *POCMLTFA* did not provide the constitutionally required protection for solicitor–client privilege and, as a result, infringed the right to be free from unreasonable search and seizure found in section 8 of the *Charter of Rights and Freedoms*.[36] Furthermore, the provisions limited the right of lawyers not to be deprived of liberty other than in accordance with the principles of fundamental justice under section 7 of the *Charter*.

According to the highest court, these limitations could not be demonstrably justified in a free and democratic society and were therefore not saved by section 1 of the *Charter*. The effect of the ruling was to exempt lawyers from the client identification, record keeping, and search and seizure requirements of the *POCMLTFA*, effectively removing them from the regime.

In September 2016, the FATF published its mutual evaluation report on Canada's compliance with its recommendations, as well as an assessment of the level of effectiveness of Canada's efforts at combatting money laundering.[37] The FATF found that the non-application of the *POCMLTFA* regime to the legal profession constituted a "significant loophole"

33 *Law Society (British Columbia) v Canada (Attorney General)*, 2002 BCCA 49.

34 *Regulations Amending Certain Regulations Made Under the Proceeds of Crime (Money Laundering) and Terrorist Financing Act* (2007-2), SOR 2007/-293.

35 *Canada (Attorney General) v Federation of Law Societies of Canada*, 2015 SCC 7 [*Federation Case*].

36 *Canadian Charter of Rights and Freedoms*, s 8, Part I of the *Constitution Act, 1982*, being Schedule B to the *Canada Act 1982* (UK), 1982, c 11 [*Charter*].

37 FATF, *Anti-Money Laundering and Counter-Terrorist Financing Measures: Canada* (September 2016), online: www.fatfgafi.org/publications/mutualevaluations/documents/mer-canada-2016.html.

and a "serious impediment" to Canada's efforts to fight these scourges.[38] It noted that the legal profession in Canada was "especially vulnerable" because of its involvement in activities considered to be of high risk, including real estate transactions, the formation of corporations and trusts, and the use of trust accounts.[39]

H. SUSPENDED ANIMATION

As the Supreme Court of Canada's ruling effectively removed lawyers from Canada's money laundering regime, the federal government was left to find a new route that did not offend the *Charter*. That process continues to the present. By default, the issue has landed squarely in the laps of provincial law societies, which may have received more than they bargained for when challenging the application of the *POCMLTFA* to lawyers.

The Federation developed model rules for lawyers and notaries, intended to reflect the legislative objectives of the *POCMLTFA*, but in the context of lawyer–client confidentiality and privilege. These include rules dealing with cash transactions, client identification and verification, and trust accounting.[40]

Over the past number of years, the law societies have individually taken action to bolster lawyer regulation, along the lines recommended by the Federation. Numerous cases have reached disciplinary bodies, and lawyers are generally much more aware today of the risks they face than they were a decade ago. Rules have also been implemented to restrict the amount of cash that lawyers can accept, usually a maximum of $7,500, although exceptions have been made for the payment of fees and bail.

Law enforcement is also affected by the status quo. In addition to the absence of actionable intelligence being submitted to FINTRAC, law enforcement has no means to see into a lawyer's trust account, save through a search warrant. It matters not that there has been reporting by a bank to FINTRAC of a wire transfer into a lawyer's trust account, as the bank will likely have no knowledge of the ultimate source or destination

38 *Ibid* at 3 and para 27.

39 *Ibid* at paras 50 and 217.

40 Federation of Law Societies of Canada, *Model Rules to Fight Money Laundering and Terrorist Financing*, online: https://flsc.ca/national-initiatives/model-rules-to-fight-money-laundering-and-terrorist-financing.

of the funds, or whether the transfer is anything other than part of a routine real estate or other transaction.

The *Federation Case* leaves Canada, a G7 country, non-compliant or only partially compliant with various FATF Recommendations, including Recommendations 22 and 23. Although there does not appear to be a groundswell movement for change in Canada, that impetus may yet arrive from south of the border.

In the United States, which is also not compliant with Recommendations 22 and 23, gatekeepers are viewed by many in government and civil society as an untouched and almost sacrosanct group of professions that have avoided the regulation that has been an integral part of business for most financial institutions and many other entities for decades. The Biden Administration has launched numerous high-profile initiatives to attack kleptocracy and corruption on a global scale.[41] Pressure is mounting within the country to deal with its own backyard, and the gatekeepers.

I. A CANADIAN SOLUTION

In the *Federation Case*, the Supreme Court of Canada made it clear that a lawyer's duty to its client does not conflict with the need to ensure that legal services are not co-opted for illegal purposes.[42] Writing for the majority, Cromwell J observed:

> The information gathering and record retention provisions of this scheme serve important public purposes. They help to ensure that lawyers take significant steps so that when they act as financial intermediaries, they are not assisting money laundering or terrorist financing.... In order to pursue these objectives, *Parliament is entitled, within proper limits which I have outlined, to impose obligations beyond those which the legal profession considers essential* to effective and ethical representation.[43]

41 Transparency International, "House Approves Half Dozen Measures to Fight Foreign Corruption Via Defense Bill" Press statement from the US office, 24 September 2021, online: https://us.transparency.org/news/house-approves-half-dozen-measures-to-fight-foreign-corruption-via-defense-bill/.

42 *Federation Case*, above note 35 at para 93.

43 *Ibid* at para 113 [emphasis added].

Justice Cromwell also expressed the view that the applicable provisions of the *POCMLTFA* could be recrafted in a way that would bring the legal profession under its ambit, in a manner that is *Charter* compliant:

> Given that *there are a number of ways in which the scheme could be made compliant with s. 8*, I do not want to venture into speculation about how a modified scheme could appropriately respond to the requirements of s. 7. However, it seems to me that if, for example, the scheme were to *provide the required constitutional protections for solicitor-client privilege as well as meaningful derivative use immunity of the required records* for the purposes of prosecuting clients, it would be much harder to see how it would interfere with the lawyer's duty of commitment to the client's cause.[44]

In response to this suggestion, the federal Department of Finance stated that it intends "to develop constitutionally compliant legislative and regulatory provisions that would subject legal counsel and legal firms to the *POCMLTFA*."[45]

Other states impose requirements on lawyers, ensuring transparency of financial dealings while preserving client confidentiality and privilege. This includes common law jurisdictions, not the least being the mother church of the common law, the United Kingdom, as well as New Zealand. However, despite their common legal tradition, the law has evolved differently in other former colonies, including Australia, the United States, and Canada. Among states which follow the civilian system of justice, the European Union has been a leader. Below are brief overviews.

1) United Kingdom

In the United Kingdom, lawyers must submit suspicious activity reports to the FIU within the National Crime Agency, if they know or suspect that a person is engaged in money laundering.[46] Provision is made to

44 *Ibid* at paras 112–13 [emphasis added].

45 Canada, Department of Finance, *Reviewing Canada's Anti-Money Laundering and Anti-Terrorist Financing Regime* (7 February 2018) at 21, online: www.canada.ca/en/department-finance/programs/consultations/2018/canadas-anti-money-laundering-anti-terrorist-financing-regime.html.

46 *Proceeds of Crime Act 2002* (UK), c 29; National Crime Agency, UK Financial Intelligence Unit, *Suspicious Activity Reports – Annual Report 2020*, online: www.nationalcrimeagency.gov.uk/who-we-are/publications/480-sars-annual-report-2020/file.

protect privileged communications. The Law Society is the designated supervisory authority responsible for overseeing members' compliance with anti-money laundering rules.[47]

In turn, the Office for Professional Body Anti-Money Laundering Supervision (OPBAS) oversees the compliance of twenty-five professional bodies, referred to as professional body supervisors. This includes nine entities representing lawyers and lawyer-like occupations. The agency is funded by fees paid by the professional associations, and is housed within the Financial Conduct Authority (FCA). Although the OPBAS does not directly supervise law firms, it has authority to gather information, review, and issue directions to the self-regulatory professions. If the self-regulator does not comply or provides misleading information, the FCA can recommend to government that its authorities be removed.[48]

A 2018 survey of lawyers from several firms found a "general consensus" that the *Proceeds of Crime Act* had not undermined their professional duty to clients. One lawyer noted that the firm was "very rarely in a situation" where they could not claim privilege. Others either accepted the policy shift requiring lawyers to act with "broader public interests in mind," or reported no impact on their practice because money launderers were savvy enough to find dodgy lawyers elsewhere.[49]

2) New Zealand

New Zealand also requires lawyers to report suspicious transactions to its financial intelligence unit, contained within the national police force. Lawyers must "know your customer," perform a risk assessment of client matters, undertake appropriate customer due diligence, maintain records,

47 The Law Society (UK), *Suspicious Activity Reports* (3 June 2021), online: www.lawsociety.org.uk/en/topics/anti-money-laundering/suspicious-activity-reports.

48 Financial Conduct Authority (UK), Office for Professional Body Anti-Money Laundering Supervision (OPBAS), last modified 20 September 2021, online: www.fca.org.uk/opbas.

49 Hilary Hurd, "Applying Anti-Money Laundering Reporting Obligations on Lawyers: The UK Experience" *GAB, The Global Anticorruption Blog*, 8 June 2018, online: https://globalanticorruptionblog.com/2018/06/08/applying-anti-money-laundering-reporting-obligations-on-lawyers-the-uk-experience/.

and submit suspicious activity reports to the FIU, subject to legal professional privilege.[50]

3) Australia

In Australia, while lawyers are presently not included as reporting entities under the state's *Anti-Money Laundering and Counter-Terrorism Financing Act 2006*,[51] they are subject to the *Financial Transaction Reports Act 1988*,[52] which requires solicitors to report "significant cash transactions" (defined as AUD$10,000 or more) to its FIU.[53] The Australian government's stated intention is to expand this reporting requirement in the future, to include suspicious transactions.[54] It has faced significant criticism for repeatedly delaying this planned expansion.[55]

4) United States

As in Canada, the legal profession in the United States is exempt from anti-money laundering reporting. In addition, attorney trust accounts are exempt from federal rules requiring financial institutions to know the beneficial owners of accounts opened in the names of legal entities.[56] The

---

50 *Anti-Money Laundering and Countering Financing of Terrorism Act 2009* (NZ), 2009/35. See also New Zealand Law Society, *AML/CFT Compliance: Emerging Practical Issues* (30 November 2018), online: www.lawsociety.org.nz/news/lawtalk/issue-924/amlcft-compliance-emerging-practical-issues/.

51 *Anti-Money Laundering and Counter-Terrorism Financing Act 2006* (Austl), 2006/169.

52 *Financial Transaction Reports Act 1988* (Austl), 1988/64.

53 *Ibid*, s 15A.

54 Law Council of Australia, *Anti-Money Laundering Guide for Legal Practitioners* (2009, updated January 2016) at 16–17, online: www.lawcouncil.asn.au/publicassets/0d21289c-e1d6-e611-80d2-005056be66b1/1601-Policy-Guideline-Anti-Money-Laundering-Guide-for-Legal-Practitioners.pdf.

55 Nathan Lynch, "Government Flip-Flops Again on Money-Laundering, Counter-Terror Finance Laws" *Michael West Media* (17 October 2018), online: www.michaelwest.com.au/government-flip-flops-again-on-money-laundering-counter-terror-finance-laws.

56 American Bar Association, *Gatekeeper Regulations on Attorneys*, online: www.americanbar.org/advocacy/governmental_legislative_work/priorities_policy/independence_of_the_legal_profession/bank_secrecy_act.

American Bar Association has nonetheless developed voluntary practice guidelines to assist lawyers in combatting money laundering.[57]

Lawyers in the United States are required, however, to file reports with its FIU for any transaction in which they receive more than $10,000 in cash. These reports must contain the name and address of the person from whom the cash was received, the amount of cash, and the date and nature of the transaction.[58] US lawyers are also subject to sanction regulations, which prohibit transactions with specified persons, entities, and countries.[59]

Notwithstanding the absence of specific anti-money laundering legislation or professional rules, a 2013 report by the FATF cited the United States as one of only three countries that reported double-digit numbers of disciplinary cases and criminal prosecutions of lawyers for money laundering or terrorist financing in the preceding five-year period.[60]

5) European Union

In 2001, the European Union (EU) amended its 1991 AML Directive to require Member States to adopt legislation imposing anti-money laundering obligations and suspicious transaction reporting on lawyers and other non-financial professionals.[61] By 2006, all EU Member States had adopted legislation which complied with the Directive.[62]

An EU staff working document noted that the reporting obligation represented a "radical change to the principle of confidentiality that the

57 American College of Trust and Estate Counsel (ACTEC), *Voluntary Good Practices Guidance for Lawyers to Detect and Combat Money Laundering and Terrorist Financing*, online: www.actec.org/resources/voluntary-detect-and-combat-money-laundering.

58 *Reports Relating to Coins and Currency Received in Nonfinancial Trade or Business*, 31 USC § 5331.

59 ACTEC, above note 57.

60 FATF, *Money Laundering and Terrorist Financing Vulnerabilities of Legal Professionals* (June 2013) at 30, online: www.fatf-gafi.org/media/fatf/documents/reports/ML%20and%20TF%20vulnerabilities%20legal%20professionals.pdf.

61 European Communities, *Council Directive 91/308/EEC of 10 June 1991 on prevention of the use of the financial system for the purpose of money laundering*, [1991] OJ, L 166/28.6.

62 Commission of the European Communities, *The Application to the Legal Profession of Directive 91/308/EEC on the Prevention of the Use of the Financial System for the Purpose of Money Laundering* (19 December 2006) at paras 7–8, online: https://aei.pitt.edu/43082/1/SEC_(2006)_1793.pdf.

legal profession has traditionally observed."[63] Several states and national bar associations filed legal challenges, arguing a violation of the right of professional secrecy as guaranteed by the EU *Charter of Fundamental Rights*.[64] Those challenges were not successful.

The exquisite difference between Canada and most other states is our *Charter of Rights and Freedoms*, a shield intended to prevent unjust incursions into the liberties of Canadians. The EU's *Charter of Fundamental Rights* may be the closest in terms of a constitutional instrument. Regardless, there are likely only two options at this point if Canada is to require financial recording and reporting by lawyers. The options are supervision and reporting to either the law societies, or to a third-party professional oversight agency. Neither solution is without inherent complexities.

J. CONCLUSION

Clearly, lawyers are an at-risk profession by the very nature of their work with real estate, trusts, and other financial vehicles, and most of all because they can hold funds in trust. Organized crime, corrupt politicians, dictators, fraudsters, and cheats require the same assistance to navigate legal processes as do the rest of us. They must invest their ill-gotten gains, purchase real estate, and hide their investments. Lawyers cannot, however, be the agents of crime. They, as do all citizens, have a public duty. *Where* their duty to the client meets the broader public interest is the issue.

Despite dire pronouncements of impending doom and a desecration of client rights, the experience to date in those jurisdictions which do require reporting by lawyers has tipped toward the positive. The roof has not fallen, the clients keep coming, and the authorities have one more tool in their toolbox to deal with organized crime, drug trafficking, and other nefarious business.

Finding the sweet spot is key to effective regulation that respects the time-tested protections which lawyers and clients enjoy. This requires an understanding of the reality that lawyers are integral to the conduct of business and life, which in turn requires that the profession jealously guards its privileges, but do so in a manner that contributes to the greater good.

---

63 *Ibid* at para 19.

64 *Ibid* at para 21.

Lawyers will continue to be the gatekeepers, the facilitators, the interconnective tissue that brokers in-person and virtual deals, mediates disputes, advances causes, pays reparations, and makes laws. This is obviously good news for lawyers, but it should also serve as a reminder of the risks they face in the best of times, and how those risks are increasing during times of change.

eleven

Tackling Money Laundering in Canada Through Beneficial Ownership Transparency

JAMES COHEN*

A. INTRODUCTION

Anonymous companies are often referred to as the "getaway cars" of crime. Whether illicit funds are obtained through theft, fraud, bribery, tax evasion, trafficking, sanctions busting, or kleptocracy, eventually the people who commit those crimes would like to enjoy their spoils in the legitimate economy. However, taking a bag full of cash into a bank, or trying to make a major purchase like property, can raise suspicions from a bank teller or real estate agent, leading them to report the transaction to authorities. If a flag is not immediately raised by the financial or commercial sector, then at a minimum the crook has left a paper trail.

Enter the anonymous company or *shell company*. While there is nothing inherently illegal about someone establishing an anonymous company, the legal mechanism, along with other tools like trusts and nominee directors and shareholders, are lynchpins in facilitating a global network of illicit financial flows. These tools hide the true legal owner, or the ultimate beneficial owners (UBO), of a company. Through a practice known as *layering*, whereby one shell company owns another shell company, a

* Executive Director, Transparency International Canada. The author holds a Master of International Studies degree from the Graduate Institute of International Studies, Geneva.

criminal can create a maze for law enforcement trying to trace the origins of dirty money. This is particularly the case if shell companies are spread across different jurisdictions.

With the reporting of a number of data leaks since 2016, notably the Panama Papers in 2016, Paradise Papers in 2017, and the Pandora Papers in 2021, the public has gained direct insight into how anonymous companies are abused in a global network of illicit financial flows. These revelations have subsequently put pressure on governments and international organizations to stop the exploitation of anonymous beneficial ownership through companies and trusts. While some states moved quickly in recent years to increase beneficial ownership transparency, Canada addressed the issue slowly at first, but by 2021 was beginning to gain momentum.

In this chapter, I will (1) profile the international norms and standards around beneficial ownership transparency and Canada's performance in upholding them; (2) review Canada's laws relating to beneficial ownership and anti-money laundering and what changes these laws have gone through; (3) discuss the idea of a transparent beneficial ownership registry as means to fighting money laundering; and (4) outline how Canada could adopt a publicly accessible beneficial ownership registry to fight money laundering.

B. INTERNATIONAL NORMS AND STANDARDS OF BENEFICIAL OWNERSHIP TRANSPARENCY

The *FATF Recommendations*,[1] the main global standards used to guide anti-money laundering and terrorist financing, include recommendations on beneficial ownership transparency. However, the recommendations on beneficial ownership transparency concerning corporations and trusts have not been updated since 2012. While the recommendations are undergoing review in 2021, a number of global standards have emerged that increase the threshold for transparency on beneficial ownership beyond requirements set out by the Financial Action Task Force (FATF).

1 FATF, *International Standards on Combatting Money Laundering and the Financing of Terrorism & Proliferation: The FATF Recommendations* (2012, as amended 2022) at 22, online: www.fatf-gafi.org/publications/fatfrecommendations/documents/fatf-recommendations.html [*FATF Recommendations*].

1) The Financial Action Task Force

The establishment of the FATF was agreed upon by the G7 through the 1989 Economic Declaration.[2] The call for the FATF appears in the Declaration's section on drug issues, where members claimed the issue had reached "devastating proportions" and required both national and international actions, explicitly including addressing laundering the proceeds of drug trafficking.[3]

The FATF established its first set of standards for its members' legal and regulatory systems in 1990, and they were endorsed by 180 states. These standards were eventually updated in 2012, adding recommendations specifically on countering terrorist financing.

The FATF's guidance for beneficial ownership transparency is in Recommendations 24 and 25. Recommendation 24 on the transparency and beneficial ownership of legal persons states:

> Countries should assess the risks of misuse of legal persons for money laundering or terrorist financing, and take measures to prevent their misuse. Countries should ensure that there is adequate, accurate and up-to-date information on the beneficial ownership and control of legal persons that can be obtained or accessed rapidly and efficiently by competent authorities, through either a register of beneficial ownership or an alternative mechanism. Countries should not permit legal persons to issue new bearer shares or bearer share warrants, and take measures to prevent the misuse of existing bearer shares and bearer share warrants. Countries should take effective measures to ensure that nominee shareholders and directors are not misused for money laundering or terrorist financing. Countries should consider facilitating access to beneficial ownership and control information by financial institutions and DNFBPs undertaking the requirements set out in Recommendations 10 and 22.[4]

Recommendation 24 was updated in February 2022. Prior to this, establishing a beneficial ownership registry was not a specific recommendation. Recommendation 25 on the transparency and beneficial ownership of legal arrangements states:

---

2 G7 Information Centre, *Economic Declaration* (Paris, 16 July 1989), online: www.g8.utoronto.ca/summit/1989paris/communique/index.html.

3 *Ibid* at paras 52–53.

4 *FATF Recommendations*, above note 1.

> Countries should take measures to prevent the misuse of legal arrangements for money laundering or terrorist financing. In particular, countries should ensure that there is adequate, accurate and timely information on express trusts, including information on the settlor, trustee and beneficiaries, that can be obtained or accessed in a timely fashion by competent authorities. Countries should consider measures to facilitate access to beneficial ownership and control by financial institutions and DNFPBs undertaking the requirements set out in Recommendations 10 and 22.[5]

The FATF elaborates on its recommendations in interpretive notes. Regarding Recommendation 24, the FATF separates the responsibility of entities that should hold basic corporate information[6] and should house beneficial ownership information. Specifically, a state's corporate registry should hold basic descriptive information about a company, but a company itself should hold basic shareholder information.[7] The FATF recommends that a multi-pronged approach to beneficial ownership information access by competent authorities be used, which includes the following components:

> a) Countries should require companies to obtain and hold adequate, accurate and up-to-date information on the company's own beneficial ownership; to co-operate with competent authorities to the fullest extent possible in determining the beneficial owner, including making the information available to competent authorities in a timely manner; and to co-operate with financial institutions/DNFBPs to provide adequate, accurate and up-to-date information on the company's beneficial ownership information.
>
> b) (i) Countries should require adequate, accurate and up-to-date information on the beneficial ownership of legal persons to be held by a public authority or body (for example a tax authority, FIU, company registry, or beneficial ownership registry). Information need not be held by a single body only.

---

5 *Ibid.*

6 *Ibid* at 92. The FATF lists basic corporate information as "company name, proof of incorporation, legal form and status, the address of the registered office, basic regulating power (e.g., memorandum and articles of association), a list of directors, and unique identifier such as a tax identification number or equivalent" in addition to shareholder information.

7 *Ibid.*

b) (ii) Countries may decide to use an alternative mechanism instead of (b)(i) if it also provides authorities with efficient access to adequate, accurate and up-to-date BO information. For these purposes reliance on basic information or existing information alone is insufficient, but there must be some specific mechanism that provides efficient access to the information.

c) Countries should use any additional supplementary measures that are necessary to ensure the beneficial ownership of a company can be determined; including for example information held by regulators or stock exchanges; or obtained by financial institutions and/or DNFBPs in accordance with Recommendations 10 and 22.[8]

The FATF does not provide examples of what an alternative might be to beneficial ownership information being held by a public authority or body. While the FATF does recommend that counties use a risk based approach as well as assessing context and materiality to determine choosing between b)(i) and b)(ii), it does not set any kind of threshold to determine if a country made a legitimate choice.

The interpretive note for Recommendation 25 on legal arrangements does not offer as stringent guidance on how beneficial ownership information should be stored. Trustees are meant to "disclose their status to financial institutions and DNFBPs when, as a trustee, forming a business relationship or carrying out an occasional transaction above the threshold."[9] In terms of holding pertinent information like beneficial ownership on trusts, trustees, and trust assets, the FATF recommends sources including:

(a) Registries (for example, a central registry of trusts or trust assets), or asset registries for land, property, vehicles, shares or other assets

(b) Other competent authorities that hold information on trusts and trustees (for example, tax authorities which collect information on assets and income relating to trusts)

(c) Other agents and service providers to the trust, including investment advisors or managers, lawyers, or trust and company service providers[10]

8 *Ibid* at 93.

9 *Ibid* at 96.

10 *Ibid.*

To ensure members implement and uphold its recommendations, the FATF regularly coordinates mutual evaluations amongst peers. The FATF published its mutual evaluation for Canada in 2016. While receiving an overall adequate review, Canada received dismal scores for compliance with Recommendations 24 and 25, receiving "partially compliant"[11] and "non-compliant"[12] scores respectively. Specifically, at the time of the report, beneficial ownership information was only collected by Canada's financial institutions (FIs). This leaves a large gap in Canada's economy for a number of businesses that are vulnerable to money laundering, such as accounting, real estate, money services business, and luxury goods. As a whole, these sectors are known as designated non-financial businesses and professions (DNFBPs). While DNFBPs are required to conduct customer due diligence, in 2016 they were not required to collect beneficial ownership information. The mutual evaluation report stated that Canada's anti-money laundering regime's reliance on the commercial sector, and FIs in particular had "deficiencies with regards to the collection and availability of full and updated beneficial ownership information" and that "timely access by law enforcement authorities to such information is not guaranteed in all cases."[13]

The legal profession is also considered a DNFBP. However, in a 2015 case *Canada (Attorney General) v Federation of Law Societies of Canada*,[14] the Supreme Court ruled that due to solicitor–client privilege, legal professionals do not have to provide suspicious transaction reports (STRs). While provincial and territorial law societies do require "know your customer" due diligence by lawyers and Quebec notaries, the FATF cited this exemption as a "significant loophole" for potential money laundering.[15] The Department of Justice has been in ongoing deliberations with the Federation of Law Societies of Canada on how to rectify this issue. In the meantime, some law societies have updated their due diligence requirements.

---

11 FATF, *Anti-Money Laundering and Counter-Terrorist Financing Measure: Canada, Fourth Round Mutual Evaluation Report* (2016) at 168 [*Mutual Evaluation Report*].

12 *Ibid* at 170.

13 *Ibid* at 165.

14 *Canada (Attorney General) v Federation of Law Societies of Canada*, 2015 SCC 7.

15 *Mutual Evaluation Report*, above note 11 at 5. See also Chapter 10 in this volume.

The priority actions identified in Canada's mutual evaluation report contained two recommendations specifically on beneficial ownership. First, the report states that Canada should "[i]ncrease timeliness of access by competent authorities to accurate and up-to-date beneficial ownership information ... [and] consider additional measures to supplement the current framework."[16] Second, the report states that Canada should "[r]equire DNFBPs to identify and verify the identity of beneficial owners and PEPs."[17]

2) G7 and G20

Beyond establishing the FATF, the G7 continued to play an important role in highlighting the importance of beneficial ownership transparency. The G7's expanded counterpart, the G20, with a specific Anti-Corruption Working Group, has also taken up the cause of beneficial ownership by establishing its own principles. In 2013, in St. Petersburg, Russia, the G20 recognized opaque legal ownership information as a key issue related to money laundering, stating in the *Leaders' Declaration*: "We encourage all countries to tackle the risks raised by opacity of legal persons and legal arrangements."[18] In the declaration, the G20 leaders tasked their finance ministers to provide an update on their own progress implementing FATF standards.

In 2014, ahead of the G20 Summit in Australia, the Anti-Corruption Working Group proposed to finance ministers that the G20 "will lead by

16 *Ibid* at 9.

17 *Ibid.* PEPs stands for "politically exposed person." The FATF defines a PEP as "an individual who is or has been entrusted with a prominent public function." See FATF, *FATF Guidance: Politically Exposed Persons* (2013) (Recommendations 12 and 22) at 3. The Government of Canada defines a PEP as a head of an international organization (HIO), as well as "a person entrusted with a prominent position that typically comes with the opportunity to influence decision and the ability to control resources." See FINTRAC, "Politically Exposed Persons and Heads of International Organizations — Securities Dealers" (2017), online: www.fintrac-canafe.gc.ca/guidance-directives/client-clientele/Guide13/13-eng.

18 OECD, G20, *G20 Leaders' Declaration* (2013) at para 7, online: www.oecd.org/g20/summits/saint-petersburg/Saint-Petersburg-Declaration.pdf.

example."[19] This statement led to the development and adoption of the *G20 High-Level Principles on Beneficial Ownership Transparency*.[20]

The principles build on the FATF recommendations but are shorter—ten principles compared to forty recommendations—as well as being flexible enough to be adaptable by different legal systems. On the establishment of beneficial ownership registries for legal persons, Principle 4 of the *G20 Principles* states:

> Countries should ensure that competent authorities (including law enforcement and prosecutorial authorities, supervisory authorities, tax authorities and financial intelligence units) have timely access to adequate, accurate and current information regarding the beneficial ownership of legal persons. Countries could implement this, for example, through central registries of beneficial ownership of legal persons or other appropriate mechanisms.[21]

In regard to legal arrangements, Principle 6 makes the same recommendation about timely access for competent authorities, but does not recommend a registry.[22]

The *G20 Principles* are not stricter on documenting beneficial ownership information than the *FATF Recommendations*; however, they specified a registry of beneficial ownership information as a mechanism for transparency before the FATF.

Since 2015, Transparency International has conducted two reviews of how well G20 members have implemented the *G20 Principles*. In the first (2015) review, Canada received the second-lowest categorization of "weak" for its beneficial ownership framework. Canada shared this distinction with Australia, Brazil, China, South Korea, and the United States.[23] This might not be surprising, given that the review was conducted after the

19 Stolen Asset Recovery Initiative (StAR), G20, *2015–16 G20 Anti-Corruption Action Plan* (2014), online: https://star.worldbank.org/sites/star/files/g20_2015-2016_anti-corruption_action_plan_australia_2014.pdf.

20 G20 Information Centre, *G20 High-Level Principles on Beneficial Ownership Transparency* (2014) [*G20 Principles*], online: www.g20.utoronto.ca/2014/g20_high-level_principles_beneficial_ownership_transparency.pdf.

21 *Ibid.*

22 *Ibid.*

23 Transparency International, "Just for Show: Reviewing G20 Promises on Beneficial Ownership" (12 November 2015) at 8, online: www.transparency.org/en/publications/just-for-show-g20-promises# .

G20 Principles were established. However, in the 2017 follow up review, Canada fared no better, remaining in a "weak framework" rank with only South Korea.[24] Notably on Principles 4 and 6, Canada received ratings of 18 percent and 33 percent.[25]

Ahead of the 2021 UK Summit, a meeting of G7 finance ministers included beneficial ownership transparency in the agenda. The finance ministers' final communiqué stated:

> We agree that beneficial ownership registries are an effective tool to tackle illicit finance. We are implementing and strengthening registries of company beneficial ownership information to provide timely, direct and efficient access for law enforcement and competent authorities to adequate, accurate and up-to-date information, including through central registries. We further note the benefits of making beneficial ownership information publicly available where possible. We call on all countries to fully implement the Financial Action Task Force (FATF) Standards and strengthen them.[26]

Given the role of the G7 in establishing the FATF, this public stance may have led to diplomacy within the FATF to create a more rigorous standard on beneficial ownership transparency through registries.

3) OGP & EITI

There are a number of other international initiatives of which Canada is part that either set out priorities or emphasize beneficial ownership

---

24 The study that the report is based on employed volunteer researchers in each country profiled who used an assessment framework of fifty-nine questions across the ten G20 Principles. See Transparency International, "G20 Leaders or Laggards: Reviewing G20 Promises on Ending Anonymous Companies" (2018) at 11, online: www.transparency.org/en/publications/g20-leaders-or-laggards.

25 *Ibid* at 56. Transparency International summarizes the methodology for scoring principles as follows "Questions were designed to capture and measure the necessary components that should be in place for a G20 member to have an adequate beneficial ownership transparency legal framework according to each of the 10 G20 principles. The assessment framework is based on *Technical Guide: Implementing the G20 Beneficial Ownership Principles* (Transparency International, 2015). The number of questions per principle dictates the number of points available. The total points available varies according to the complexity and number of issues covered in each original principle." *Ibid* at 20.

26 G7 Information Centre, *G7 Finance Ministers Communiqué* (5 June 2021) at 2.

transparency. Formed in 2011, the Open Government Partnership (OGP) is a coalition of national and local governments, as well as civil society organizations, working together to increase the accessibility of government data with the goal of making government more responsive to the public. Canada is one of seventy-eight state members as of 2021, and Ontario and Quebec are also local members.[27] In 2019, to address beneficial ownership transparency, OGP members established the Beneficial Ownership Leadership Group. Members of the group agree to uphold a set of principles, chief among these being to publish "company beneficial ownership data that is free, downloadable, searchable, and reusable by the public, without a fee, proprietary software, or the need for registration."[28] As of writing, Canada had yet to join the group.

However, OGP members are required to develop a national action plan (NAP) every two years. Canada's 2018–20 NAP set the following commitment on beneficial ownership transparency:

> 1.1 Implement legislative amendments to require federal corporations to hold accurate and up-to-date beneficial ownership information, and eliminate use-of-bearer shares
>
> 1.2 Work with provincial and territorial governments and key stakeholders representing various perspectives on possible options to improve timely access to beneficial ownership information, including retention and disclosure obligations relating to such information and the exploration of a public registry option
>
> 1.3 Continue to work with provincial and territorial governments to support coordinated implementation of the Agreement to Strengthen Beneficial Ownership Transparency[29]

Canada is also a founder of the Extractive Industry Transparency Initiative (EITI), another standard-setting body, focused on extractive industry good governance. While a founder and a funder of the EITI Secretariat,

---

27 Open Government Partnership, "Members" (2021), online: www.opengovpartnership.org/our-members.

28 Open Government Partnership, "Beneficial Ownership Leadership Group" (undated), online: www.opengovpartnership.org/beneficial-ownership-leadership-group.

29 Government of Canada, "Canada's 2018–2020 National Action Plan on Open Government" (2018) at 23, online: https://open.canada.ca/en/content/canadas-2018-2020-national-action-plan-open-government.

Canada is not a signatory to EITI standards. One standard set by the EITI is on beneficial ownership disclosure. Under the EITI Standard 2019, requirement 2.5 recommends the following for Member States:

> a) It is recommended that implementing countries maintain a publicly available register of the beneficial owners of the corporate entity-(ies) that apply for or hold a participating interest in an exploration or production oil, gas or mining license or contract, including the identity(ies) of their beneficial owner(s), the level of ownership and details about how ownership or control is exerted. Where possible, beneficial ownership information should be incorporated in existing filings by companies to corporate regulators, stock exchanges or agencies regulating extractive industry licensing. Where this information is already publicly available, the EITI Report should include guidance on how to access this information.[30]

In summary, through the initiatives of the FATF, G20 and G7, the OGP, and EITI, as of May 2022 there were 117 states that are fully or partially committed to beneficial ownership transparency, according to the civil society organization Open Ownership.[31] Each state including Canada, has different legal and technical arrangements to amend and construct in order to achieve beneficial ownership transparency. In the next section I will review Canada's laws and the steps that have been taken in recent years on beneficial ownership transparency.

C. CANADIAN LAWS REGULATING ANTI-MONEY LAUNDERING AND BENEFICIAL OWNERSHIP TRANSPARENCY

Canada's regulation of beneficial ownership transparency is governed by the *Proceeds of Crime (Money Laundering) and Terrorist Financing Act*.[32] The *PCMLTFA* is intended to set measures for detection and deterrence

30 EITI, *The EITI Standard 2019: The Global Standard for the Good Governance of Oil, Gas and Mineral Resources* (17 June 2019) at 18, online: https://eiti.org/sites/default/files/2022-03/EITI%20Standard%202019%20EN.pdf.

31 Open Ownership, *Worldwide Commitments and Actions* (undated), online: www.openownership.org/map.

32 *Proceeds of Crime (Money Laundering) and Terrorist Financing Act*, SC 2000, c 17 [*PCMLTFA*].

of potential money laundering and terrorist financing, provide tools to law enforcement, fulfill Canada's international obligations on anti-money laundering and terrorist financing, and protect Canada's financial system from exploitation by nefarious actors.[33]

Among those measures, a large emphasis is placed on Canadian companies to conduct "know your customer" due diligence as a first line of defence in preventing individuals' and organizations' illicit funds from gaining entry into Canada's financial system and licit economy. Until recently, though, only FIs had to include beneficial ownership information as part of their customer due diligence, which was critiqued by the FATF. Beneficial ownership due diligence was expanded to DFNBPs as of 21 June 2021.[34]

While there are regulations under the *PCMLTFA* regarding beneficial ownership transparency, the definition of a beneficial owner is contained in the *Canada Business Corporations Act*.[35] The ultimate beneficial owner of a company cannot be another company, trust, or entity. It must be an individual who has significant control or ownership. The *CBCA* defines significant control and ownership as follows:

> **Individual with significant control**
> **2.1** (1) For the purposes of this Act, any of the following individuals is an individual with significant control over a corporation:
> (a) an individual who has any of the following interests or rights, or any combination of them, in respect of a significant number of shares of the corporation:
> (i) the individual is the registered holder of them,
> (ii) the individual is the beneficial owner of them, or
> (iii) the individual has direct or indirect control or direction over them;
> (b) an individual who has any direct or indirect influence that, if exercised, would result in control in fact of the corporation; or
> (c) an individual to whom prescribed circumstances apply.

---

33 *Ibid*, s 3.

34 *Regulations Amending the Regulations Amending Certain Regulations Made Under the Proceeds of Crime (Money Laundering) and Terrorist Financing Act*, SOR/2020-112.

35 *Canada Business Corporations Act*, RSC 1985, c C-44 [*CBCA*].

Joint ownership or control

(2) Two or more individuals are each considered to be an individual with significant control over a corporation if, in respect of a significant number of shares of the corporation,

(a) an interest or right, or a combination of interests or rights, referred to in paragraph (1)(a) is held jointly by those individuals; or

(b) a right, or combination of rights, referred to in paragraph (1)(a) is subject to any agreement or arrangement under which the right or rights are to be exercised jointly or in concert by those individuals.

Significant number of shares

(3) For the purposes of this section, a significant number of shares of a corporation is

(a) any number of shares that carry 25 percent or more of the voting rights attached to all of the corporation's outstanding voting shares; or

(b) any number of shares that is equal to 25 percent or more of all of the corporation's outstanding shares measured by fair market value.[36]

In 2019, as part of the federal budget, the Canadian government made amendments to the *CBCA* as a measure to increase transparency and accountability, as well as to follow guidance from the FATF on increasing accessibility of UBO information.

As a first measure, the amendments require federally incorporated corporations to record the information of individuals with significant control and to keep it in an internal register.[37] The company is required to take "reasonable measures" to update the information at least once a year, or inside fifteen days from a change of which the corporation would be aware.[38] Directors and officers are liable for fulfilling requirements.[39] This

36 *Ibid*, s 2.1(1)-(3).

37 The information of individuals with significant control that corporations are required to record includes their name, date of birth, address (residential or service), country or countries of residence for tax purposes, the date when significant control began, when significant control ended, and a description of that significant control. See Innovation, Science and Economic Development Canada, *Individuals with Significant Control* (2020), online: www.ic.gc.ca/eic/site/cd-dgc.nsf/eng/cs08216.html.

38 *Ibid.*

39 *Ibid.*

provision does not apply to public companies.[40] The information is not publicly accessible, but can be requested by shareholders and creditors.[41]

This leads to the second amendment, which is that investigative bodies may request the register of significant control. Investigative bodies include the CRA and any entity that can conduct criminal investigations, like the RCMP. Investigative bodies may only request this information when there are reasonable grounds to suspect that the information in the registry would be pertinent to an investigation.[42] This process is different from that required to obtain a warrant, in that investigative bodies can immediately access a corporation's registry. The investigative body must either deliver or send notice to the corporation's registered address, at which point the corporation is required to comply with the request "as soon as feasible."[43] The fine for lack of compliance is C$5,000.[44]

While the *CBCA* amendments may work toward meeting FATF recommendations, they create what could be considered a minimal tactic toward fighting money laundering. If criminals are using a shell company to conduct illicit activities, and receive a notice from investigative bodies to provide their register, there is ample time to make changes to the register to hide UBOs. Even if the criminals took too long to make those amendments, a C$5,000 fine could be viewed as a minor business expense for many criminals and kleptocrats.

While the *PCMLTFA* applies across Canada, the *CBCA* only applies to federal companies. A Transparency International Canada review identified the federal corporate registry as only the fourth largest in the country, smaller than those of Ontario, Quebec, and Alberta.[45] In other words, for transparent UBO information to be an effective tool against money laundering in Canada, all the provinces and territories must also follow suit in the efforts carried out by the federal government.

In December 2017, finance ministers at the federal, provincial, and territorial levels signed an agreement to increase beneficial ownership

---

40 *Ibid.*

41 *Ibid.*

42 *CBCA*, above note 35, s 21.31(3).

43 *Ibid*, s 21.31(1).

44 *Ibid*, s 21.31(5).

45 Transparency International Canada, "No Reason to Hide: Unmasking the Anonymous Owners of Canadian Companies and Trusts" (2016) at 17, online: https://transparencycanada.ca/beneficial-ownership-transparency/our-work.

transparency. To this end, they all agreed to carry out appropriate amendments to their business laws to require companies to hold beneficial ownership information in a registry and make it available to authorities. The ministers also agreed to try to make these amendments by 1 July 2019.[46] As of January 2023, British Columbia, Quebec, Saskatchewan, Manitoba, Prince Edward Island, Ontario, New Brunswick, and Nova Scotia have made the necessary amendments. Alberta , Yukon, Northwest Territories, and Nunavut have not introduced legislation.

Pressure for the government to address money laundering also grew out of provincial scandals. Between 2011 and 2015, the *Commission d'enquête sur l'octroi et la gestion des contrats publics dans l'industrie de la construction* (Charbonneau Commission) in Quebec detailed corruption in the construction industry, largely centred around Montreal.[47] During hearings, the public learned how criminal organizations infiltrated legitimate companies, essentially turning them into shell companies to launder the proceeds of crime. A number of recommendations came about in Quebec to address corruption and money laundering;[48] however, the Charbonneau Commission did not create urgency on addressing money laundering at the national level.

Regional money laundering problems worked their way into headlines once again in 2017 in British Columbia. Following the 2017 election of the NDP, David Eby was appointed the BC minister of justice. One of his early and consistent points of advocacy was on suspected money laundering in BC casinos. Describing the context in British Columbia, Eby testified to the federal House of Commons Finance Committee that

---

46 Canada, Department of Finance, "Agreement to Strengthen Beneficial Ownership Transparency" (undated), online: www.canada.ca/en/department-finance/programs/agreements/strengthen-beneficial-ownership-transparency.html.

47 France Charbonneau & Renaud Lachance, *Tome 3 du rapport de la Commission d'enquête sur l'octroi et la gestion des contrats publics dans l'industrie de la construction: Stratagèmes, causes, conséquences et recommandations* (2015), English translation online: www.scribd.com/document/342552195/Volume-3-of-the-Charbonneau-Commission-report-in-English#from_embed.

48 *Ibid* at 135–36. Relevant recommendations include: Recommendation 6 (requiring non-profit organizations to be subject to the same contractual obligations as corporations); Recommendation 8 (to improve whistleblower protection); Recommendation 10 (making offences money laundering and corruption as grounds for non-issuance of a licence by the Régie du bâtiment du Québec); and Recommendation 12 (reducing shareholder control from 20 percent to 10 percent in order to be considered a director and thus part of contract review).

during his first briefing with BC casino regulators, they said, "I think we are going to blow your mind.[49]" The regulators were alluding to what is referred to as the "Vancouver Model"[50] of money laundering. During the time that Eby was conducting public advocacy, civil society groups and journalists were publishing reports about alleged connections between money laundering and Vancouver's rising real estate prices, as well as connections to organized crime.[51] Minister Eby eventually commissioned retired RCMP Deputy Commissioner Dr. Peter German to conduct a study on the extent of money laundering in British Columbia.[52] Finance Minister Carol James further commissioned an expert panel to explicitly review the impact of money laundering on BC real estate.[53] In 2019, BC Premier Brian Horgan commissioned retired judge Alan Cullen to

49 Canada, Parliament, House of Commons, Standing Committee on Finance, *Evidence* (17 March 2018), online: www.ourcommons.ca/DocumentViewer/en/42-1/fina/meeting-140/evidence.

50 The term "Vancouver Model" was coined by Professor John Langdale of Macquarie University in Australia. The model describes the flow of funds from China to British Columbia. In summary, the model alleges that Chinese individuals move money outside of China, bypassing Chinese currency export caps of US$10,000 with assistance of illegal banks that are operated by organized crime groups. The groups have counterparts in British Columbia who provide funds to those Chinese nationals to gamble in BC casinos, where upon cashing out casino chips, patrons will receive clean currency. Minister Eby has presented video evidence and testimony that, to bring the funds to gamblers, hockey bags of cash were exchanged in casino parking lots. To keep that currency in Canada, the Chinese nationals are alleged to have invested the funds in Canada in luxury goods like real estate. Funds for the Canadian illegal banks are also obtained through domestic criminal activity such as the fentanyl trade. See Sam Cooper, "How Chinese Gangs Are Laundering Drug Money Through Vancouver Real Estate" *Global News* (5 June 2018), online: https://globalnews.ca/news/4149818/vancouver-cautionary-tale-money-laundering-drugs.

51 See, for example, Kathy Tomlinson & Xaio Xu, "B.C. Vows Crackdown after Globe Investigation Reveals Money-Laundering Scheme" *Globe & Mail* (16 February 2018), online: www.theglobeandmail.com/news/investigations/real-estate-money-laundering-and-drugs/article38004840.

52 Peter German, *Dirty Money—Part 2: Turning the Tide—An Independent Review of Money Laundering in B.C. Real Estate, Luxury Vehicle Sales & Horse Racing* (2019), online: https://icclr.org/wp-content/uploads/2019/06/Dirty_Money_Report_Part_2.pdf?x96127.

53 Maureen Maloney, Tsur Somerville & Brigitte Unger, *Combatting Money Laundering in BC Real Estate: [Report of the] Expert Panel on Money Laundering in BC Real Estate* (2019), online: www2.gov.bc.ca/assets/gov/housing-and-tenancy/real-estate-in-bc/combatting-money-laundering-report.pdf.

oversee the Inquiry into Money Laundering in British Columbia. Justice Cullen submitted his final report to Minister Eby on 3 June 2022 and it was released to the public on 15 June 2022.[54]

By 2019, Prime Minister Justin Trudeau acknowledged money laundering as a national problem, commenting: "This is a real and pressing problem for Canadians and it's a problem around the world."[55] Anti-money laundering also gained some prominence during and after the 2019 federal election. Three of the federal parties had an anti-money laundering initiative in their electoral platform.[56] After the Liberal Party won a minority government, Prime Minister Trudeau's mandate letters for his Cabinet directed the minister of finance and the minister of innovation, science and industry (ISI), to hold consultations on the possibility of establishing a beneficial ownership registry in Canada.[57]

The federal government, led by ISI—now ISED[58]—with support from Finance Canada, held a public consultation, from 13 February to 30 May 2020, regarding a publicly accessible beneficial ownership registry.

54 British Columbia, Commission of Inquiry into Money Laundering in British Columbia, *Cullen Commission Final Report* (15 June 2022) [Cullen], online: https://cullencommission.ca/com-rep.

55 The Canadian Press, "Trudeau Calls B.C. Money Laundering Report 'Extremely Alarming'" *CTV News* (10 May 2019), online: https://bc.ctvnews.ca/trudeau-calls-b-c-money-laundering-report-extremely-alarming-1.4417600.

56 The Liberal Party of Canada platform called for more resources for the RCMP to specifically address money laundering and for working with provinces and territories on beneficial ownership transparency. See Liberal Party of Canada, *Forward: A Real Plan for the Middle Class* (2019) at 8, 39, online: https://2019.liberal.ca/wp-content/uploads/sites/292/2019/09/Forward-A-real-plan-for-the-middle-class.pdf. The Conservative Party of Canada proposed a public inquiry into money laundering in the real estate sector. See Conservative Party of Canada, *Andrew Scheer's Plan for You to Get Ahead* (2019), online: https://cpc-platform.s3.ca-central-1.amazonaws.com/CPC_Platform_8.5x11_FINAL_EN_OCT11_web.pdf. The New Democratic Party proposed a dedicated anti-money laundering law enforcement unit, a national inquiry into money laundering, and a national real estate beneficial ownership registry. See Sam Cooper, "NDP Promises New RCMP Money Laundering Unit, Transparency Ownership Registry" *Global News* (25 September 2019), online: https://globalnews.ca/news/5949342/ndp-rcmp-money-laundering-unit.

57 Office of the Prime Minister of Canada, "Minister of Finance Mandate Letter" (2019), online: https://pm.gc.ca/en/mandate-letters/2019/12/13/minister-finance-mandate-letter; Office of the Prime Minister of Canada, "Minister of Innovation, Science and Industry Mandate Letter" (2019), online: https://pm.gc.ca/en/mandate-letters/2019/12/13/minister-innovation-science-and-industry-mandate-letter.

58 Ministry of Innovation, Science and Economic Development Canada.

The results of the consultation were released on 6 April 2021. The consultation took in the perspective of a range of stakeholders, including the private sector, law enforcement, professional societies, and civil society organizations. In its *What We Heard* report, ISED reported that "nearly all parties agreed that there is a legitimate public policy rationale for housing beneficial ownership data within a central government repository."[59] On whether a beneficial ownership registry should be publicly accessible, the report claimed that stakeholders were divided, with the majority not desiring public access. ISED claims in the report that the majority of respondents were in favour of tiered access, whereby public authorities could have access to all information in the register, and some stakeholders, such as "private sector companies with anti-money laundering obligations," could have access to a restricted amount of information.[60]

Despite this conclusion, two weeks later in the federal budget announcement Finance Minister Chrystia Freeland proposed that ISED receive C$2.1 million to study how a publicly accessible registry of beneficial ownership could be established, with the goal of establishing such a registry by 2025.[61] In testimony before the Senate Standing Committee on National Finance, Minister Freeland said the registry was a "personal priority" of hers, and that the registry would be "public" and "transparent."[62]

Global events potentially played a hand in expediting the implementation of the registry. On 24 February 2022, Russia conducted an illegal invasion of Ukraine, building on Russia's annexation of the Crimean Peninsula and occupation of the Donbas region of Ukraine in 2014. Canada and allies extended sanctions that were already in place on Russia,[63] however they soon realized that they were having difficulties tracking assets of sanctioned Russians.

---

59 Innovation, Science and Economic Development Canada, *Public Consultation on Strengthening Corporate Beneficial Ownership Transparency in Canada: What We Heard* (2021), online: www.ic.gc.ca/eic/site/142.nsf/eng/00002.html.

60 *Ibid.*

61 Canada, Department of Finance, *Budget 2021: A Recovery Plan for Jobs, Growth, and Resilience* (2021) at 309, online: www.budget.gc.ca/2021/home-accueil-en.html.

62 Canada, Parliament, Senate, Standing Committee on National Finance, *Evidence*, 43-2 (27 May 2021).

63 Canada, Global Affairs Canada, Canadian Sanctions Related to Russia (7 June 2022), online: www.international.gc.ca/world-monde/international_relations-relations_internationales/sanctions/russia-russie.aspx?lang=eng

In the 2022 federal budget, the federal government cited Russia among hostile global actors and tied anti-money laundering to promoting global democracy and the rules-based international order. To this end the government proposed expediting implementation of the beneficial ownership registry to 2023.[64]

The registry will be a federal registry with the aim of being scalable for provinces and territories to integrate their own registries. While some provinces have so far only non-committal or cautious greeting to the federal government's proposal,[65] the two provinces that have directly investigated money laundering in their jurisdictions, British Columbia and Quebec, were already taking their own steps beyond *CBCA* amendments to address beneficial ownership transparency.

In British Columbia, in addition to the Cullen Commission, the province implemented a first-of-its-kind Land Ownership Transparency Registry (LOTR), which was fully functional online in April 2021. The registry provides beneficial ownership information on land titles. British Columbia was able to begin taking this step in 2019 as real property is under provincial jurisdiction.

While the spirit of the initiative was applauded, the implementation has received criticism. Kevin Comeau argues that LOTR is missing some key elements for it to be a useful anti-money laundering tool, including proactive identity verification, usable search functionality, a confidential tip line, and tough enough sanctions.[66] Despite these technical deficiencies, British Columbia's establishment of the LOTR and the Cullen Commission show promise that the government will likely coordinate with the federal government on a corporate beneficial ownership registry. Dr. German[67] and the Expert Group on Housing[68] in their

---

64 Canada, Department of Finance, Budget 2022: A Plan to Grow Our Economy and Make Life More Affordable (2022) at 141, online: https://budget.gc.ca/2022/home-accueil-en.html.

65 Ivan Angelovski & Zach Dubinsky, "Federal Pledge to Publicly Disclose Who Owns Some Private Companies Catches Provinces Off-Guard" *CBC News* (28 April 2021), online: www.cbc.ca/news/canada/federal-private-ownership-registry-1.6004004.

66 Kevin Comeau, "C.D. Howe Institute Commentary No. 583: BC's Public Registry to Combat Money Laundering: Broken on Arrival" (2020), online: www.cdhowe.org/sites/default/files/attachments/research_papers/mixed/Commentary_583.pdf.

67 German, above note 52 at 19.

68 Maloney et al, above note 53 at 4.

government-commissioned reports recommend beneficial ownership transparency. In response to the federal government proposal, the BC finance ministry commented, "[T]he establishment of this type of registry is a key tool for combatting financial crime."[69] Commissioner Cullen concurred with these views, recommending in his final report that British Columbia "work with its federal, provincial, and territorial partners to ensure that, before the end of 2023, a publicly accessible pan-Canadian corporate beneficial ownership registry is in place."[70]

In June 2021, the Government of Quebec took even bolder action than British Columbia or the federal government, passing Bill 78, which requires the collection and public disclosure of ultimate beneficial ownership information in the provincial *Registraire des entreprises* (REQ).[71]

D. BENEFITS OF A PUBLICLY ACCESSIBLE BENEFICIAL OWNERSHIP REGISTRY

In discussing the establishment of a beneficial ownership registry, it is important to understand why a publicly accessible registry is better suited to combat illicit financial flows than a closed registry. A publicly accessible registry would require no account registration, have no fees for searches, and would make all but the most sensitive beneficial ownership information available to all users. Those entities that would have access to the most sensitive information would include law enforcement, and competent authorities such as the CRA and FINTRAC. While one could hope that making a beneficial ownership registry available only to these entities would be sufficient, in practice, the measure would face shortcomings.

First, opening up a registry with no barriers to access acts as an initial deterrent to those actors who have viewed Canada as an easy target to deposit their illicit funds. The example of Scottish Limited Partnerships (SLP) demonstrates the effectiveness of open access to a registry. SLPs had gained notoriety as a legal mechanism for facilitating illicit financial flows in the 2010s due to their association with large "laundromat" money laundering schemes in Russia and Azerbaijan.[72] From 2011 through 2016,

69 Angelovski & Dubinsky, above note 65.

70 Cullen, above note 54 at 39.

71 *An Act Mainly to Improve the Transparency of Enterprises*, SLQ 2021, c 19 [Bill 78].

72 Global Witness, "The Companies We Keep: What the UK's Open Data Register Actually Tells Us About Company Ownership" (2018), online:

SLPs saw an incorporation rate of roughly 200 filings in a quarter, to more than 1,600. In 2017, the UK people with significant control (PSC) register started to include SLPs as part of their oversight, resulting in a more than 70 percent drop in incorporation in one quarter.[73]

Those criminals who would hope to remain undetected in a beneficial ownership registry have a better chance with a closed registry. Law enforcement resources are limited for financial crimes in Canada. At the federal level, Dr. German found in his report that "the RCMP's money laundering team is more than three-quarters unstaffed."[74] Since that assessment, the federal government has dedicated more funds to RCMP financial crime capacity,[75] but building up expertise will take time, and it could be reduced again in the future. In an open registry, in addition to law enforcement and competent authorities reviewing data, journalists and civil society would also analyze information. States from which illicit finances originate would also provide "extra eyes." Law enforcement from foreign states would also have access to the registry. In turn, Canada would have more credibility in international forums, like the FATF, to call on other states to open up their beneficial ownership information in order to aid Canadian investigations.

Finally, businesses with beneficial ownership reporting obligations, including financial institutions and DNFBPs, will have access to the data. A central registry would both provide the data that the government is requiring businesses to collect, and carry the responsibility for verifying that data. This would create greater transparency and reliability in Canada's business environment and cut costs for businesses conducting due diligence.

In Canada, advocates and experts have put forward the following of beneficial ownership information for a registrar to collect and either make public or restrict.[76]

---

www.globalwitness.org/en/campaigns/corruption-and-money-laundering/anonymous-company-owners/companies-we-keep/?accessible=true.

73 *Ibid.*

74 "No Federally Funded RCMP Officers Dedicated to Money Laundering in B.C., Report Reveals" *CBC News* (8 April 2019), online: www.cbc.ca/news/canada/british-columbia/peter-german-money-laundering-report-2019-1.5089036.

75 Government of Canada, *Investing in the Middle Class: Budget 2019* (2019) at 185, online: www.budget.gc.ca/2019/docs/plan/toc-tdm-en.html.

76 Chart drawn from Transparency International Canada, "Implementing a Publicly Accessible Pan-Canadian Registry of Beneficial Ownership: Legislative and Technical Option" (2020) at 13 [Pan-Canadian Registry], online: https://static1.squarespace.com/static/5df7c3de2e4d3d3fce16c185/t/5f59467c6b42946483da7d78/1599686271536/BOT-Implementation-Report+FINAL+200819.pdf.

TABLE II.1 PROPOSED BENEFICIAL OWNERSHIP REGISTRY FIELDS

Data Field	Public or Private Disclosure	Rationale for Collection and/or Disclosure
A unique identifier or number that shows ties to other business entities over which the individual has significant control (generated by the database itself)	Public	• Avoids confusion between registered persons of the same name
Full legal name	Public	• Needed for identification • Assists whistleblowers
All other names commonly known by	Public	• Needed to identify persons who do not use their exact legal name
Date of birth	Partial (M/Y) — Public Full (D/M/Y) — Private	• Improves positive identification • Assists whistleblowers
Usual residential address and service address	Public	• Improves identification and allows for correspondence
Country of principal tax residency	Private	• Important for financial institutions and allows CRA and other tax agencies to identify taxpayer information
Country of usual residence	Public	• Improves positive identification • Assists whistleblowers
Citizenship(s)	Private	• Helps establish identity • Law enforcement requires this information for international cooperation
Nature and extent of beneficial interest held	Public	• Clarifies whether the person owns or controls a company and to what extent

Data Field	Public or Private Disclosure	Rationale for Collection and/or Disclosure
Day on which the individual became or ceased to be a beneficial owner	Public	• Establishes a time frame for the purchase or sale of shares, etc.
Politically exposed person status and/or Head of International Organization Standard	Public	• Helps reporting entities to meet their obligations under the *PCMLTFA* • Assists whistleblowers

A number of these data fields are already available for public companies in different registries, and therefore carry a low expectation of privacy.[77] And while the precedence of data availability helps make the case for the disclosure of this information, the mandate of the registry being broad enough and in the public interest can help justify making the information public.[78] In the case of the beneficial ownership registry, the mandate would include deterring and detecting crime, as well as helping to facilitate business transparency.

Looking forward, while the Canadian government has committed to a publicly accessible registry on paper, and one province has already legislated corporate beneficial ownership information to be public, there are still critical technical issues for the federal government and its provincial and territorial partners to consider about how a publicly accessible registry is established in a federated state like Canada.

E. LEGISLATIVE AND TECHNICAL DESIGN OF A REGISTRY

When considering the legislative and technical mechanisms for establishing a beneficial ownership registry in Canada, there are decisions to be made about where to house a registry and how to share information across jurisdictions.

77 Publish What You Pay Canada, Transparency International Canada & Canadians for Tax Fairness, "A Public Beneficial Ownership Registry and the Canadian Privacy Regime: A Legal Analysis" (2019) at 29, online: https://static1.squarespace.com/static/5c8938b492441bf93fdbc536/t/5eac6df826b8946d37f7e4f1/1588358649136/endsnowwashing-public-beneficial-ownership-registry-summary.pdf.

78 *Ibid* at 9.

A natural way to build a scalable registry is that each jurisdiction's government ministry responsible for business incorporation requires companies to submit beneficial ownership information as part of routine business filings. This has been the path taken so far, through amendments to the *CBCA* at the federal level and through mirroring legislation in the provinces and territories, which requires businesses to hold beneficial ownership information in-house. Quebec then continued this trajectory through Bill 78 to bring beneficial ownership transparency to the REQ.[79] While it is likely that the federal government will continue to make amendments to the *CBCA*, it could take another legislative path and establish an independent beneficial ownership registry under the *PCMLTFA*. The Department of Finance Canada would then be solely responsible for beneficial ownership information. Not only would the department work independently at the federal level through such a registry, but less coordination between federal, provincial, and territorial governments would be needed. Corporate beneficial ownership information could be collected through tax filing information or through stand-alone data filings.

A review of technical considerations for a Canadian registry cites the money services business (MSB) registry as a precedent for a stand-alone system at the federal level under FINTRAC jurisdiction.[80] It further notes that the UK PSC Register is also a stand-alone entity, in which the Canadian government has expressed interest.[81]

However, if the Canadian government ultimately incorporates beneficial ownership transparency in corporate registries, then all governments must decide if and how information can be shared. A centralized or harmonized registry will be much more effective for anti-money laundering and general business conduct than fourteen fully independent corporate registries that share no information. Every jurisdiction going it alone on a registry will create inconsistencies in data and enforcement. Smaller jurisdictions may not have the resources to update their registries or conduct monitoring. In order to minimize the burden on business to comply with registry requirements, a single point of filing beneficial ownership information that is consistently used across Canada, and potentially globally, is

79 Bill 78, above note 71.
80 Pan-Canadian Registry, above note 76 at 12.
81 *Ibid* at 11.

also desirable. Without unified enforcement and data, Canada will have weak-link jurisdictions that illicit actors can still exploit.

Two models of a federal registry—a federated, distributed architecture and a centralized architecture—are feasible. In the federated, distributed architecture, provinces and territories would independently gather beneficial ownership information, and then feed that information to a central registry.[82] In the centralized model, the federal government would first collect beneficial ownership data, and then provinces and territories would access the information.[83] The centralized model provides greater assurance of data quality and enforcement compared to the federated, distributed model, which could have a central interface, but still relies on all jurisdictions to manage data. A compromise could also be reached whereby provinces and territories agree to collect beneficial ownership data and submit it directly to a federal registry, bypassing their own.[84]

In order to provide maximum deterrence and enforcement of illicit finances, a fully functional registrar should also have adequate staff with a pro-active mandate for investigations, adequate sanctions capabilities for non-compliance, and an anonymous tip line.

F. CONCLUSION

Canada is moving toward greater beneficial ownership transparency at a crucial time. It is scheduled to undergo another FATF peer-evaluation in 2023, where a beneficial ownership registry will now be a requirement. Beyond reputational damage control, Canada's inability to credibly back up its sanctions against Russia demonstrates the importance of fixing the national gaps in beneficial ownership transparency. Many Western democracies had turned a blind eye to the illicit financial flows entering their economies for years despite the security risks this posed domestically and geo-politically. From both a reputational and security perspective, Canada cannot stop at just corporate beneficial ownership transparency. Just as it pledged to establish a publicly accessible registry before such a measure was required by the FATF, Canada also needs to increase transparency for trusts and nominees. Further, the federal government needs to make sure

82 *Ibid* at 18.

83 *Ibid* at 20.

84 *Ibid* at 18–21.

that all provinces come onboard to its registry so that there are no secrecy haven hold outs. Even a lack of alignment on data and verification standards amongst Canada's fourteen jurisdictions could create blind spots that can continue to be exploited by nefarious actors.

twelve

Harmonious Coexistence: Law and Laundering in Canada

SANAA AHMED*

A. INTRODUCTION

Canada's growing reputation as a premier onshore destination for laundered monies[1] from across the globe is now a matter of public record. Despite an ostensibly well-regulated financial sector, strict anti-money laundering (AML) compliance rules for many sectors of the economy[2] and an adherence to global AML regulation, Canada frequently makes

* Assistant Professor of Law, Faculty of Law, University of Calgary. This chapter stems from research conducted as a Killam postdoctoral fellow at the Schulich School of Law, Dalhousie University, from 2019 to 2021. The author wishes to acknowledge the generosity of the Killam Foundation in funding this project.

1 In this chapter, "money laundering" and "illicit financial flows" are used interchangeably, unless otherwise suggested by the context.

2 Entities bound to report suspicions of laundering include financial institutions, money service businesses, real estate dealers, securities dealers, accountants, agents of the Crown, British Columbia notaries, casinos, dealers in precious metals and stones, as well as life insurance. However, lawyers and notaries are exempt from reporting due to a Supreme Court judgment that held that the practice would breach client-attorney privilege. See *Canada (Attorney General) v Federation of Law Societies of Canada*, 2015 SCC 7. Car dealerships, private mortgage and lending businesses, and auction houses are some others that are similarly exempt. See Peter M. German, *Dirty Money—Part 2: Turning the Tide—An Independent Review of Money Laundering in B.C. Real Estate, Luxury Vehicle Sales & Horse Racing* (2019), online: https://cullencommission.ca/files/Dirty_Money_Report_Part_2.pdf.

headlines for money laundering.[3] Most of these headlines focus on the link between laundering and predicate crimes: drug trafficking (especially in opioids), organized crime and, more recently, fraudulent applications under pandemic benefits programs.[4] Occasionally, however, big business has also been linked with laundering. In 2015, for example, a government-initiated inquiry into corruption within the construction industry in Quebec showed the intimate linkages between Mafia-type criminal organizations and domestic politicians, big business, and service industry professionals (lawyers, accountants, etc.).[5] In the same year, SNC Lavalin was charged with the bribery of foreign officials under the *Corruption of Foreign Public Officials Act*.[6]

However, the real game changers were the Panama and Paradise Papers revelations between 2016 and 2017. Till then, the government as well as the media had characterised laundering as the preserve of career criminals and the odd corporate actor. The latter, particularly, were thought of as delinquents who infrequently engaged in one-off laundering events. In sharp contrast, then, both the Panama and Paradise data leaks showed the *systemic* nature of money laundering in Canada: neither was laundering

3 Marco Chown Oved, "Corporate Secrecy Makes Canada a Haven for White-Collar Crime, Says Report" *Toronto Star* (7 December 2016), online: www.thestar.com/news/world/2016/12/07/report-corporate-secrecy-makes-canada-a-haven-for-white-collar-crime.html.

4 Catharine Tunney, "Organized Crime 'Knowingly and Actively' Exploited Federal Pandemic Benefits: Intelligence Reports" *CBC News* (12 November 2021), online: www.cbc.ca/news/politics/cerb-organized-crime-1.6241211.

5 The Charbonneau Commission, officially called the Commission of Inquiry on the Awarding and Management of Public Contracts in the Construction Industry, was a public inquiry into corruption in the management of public construction contracts in Quebec. For critical reads on the report, see Margaret E. Beare, "Shadow Boxing Against the Crimes of the Powerful" in Steve Bittle et al, eds, *Revisiting Crimes of the Powerful: Marxism, Crime & Deviance* (New York: Routledge Press, 2018); Denis St. Martin, "Systemic Corruption in an Advanced Welfare State: Lessons from the Québec Charbonneau Inquiry" (2015) 11:8 Osgoode Legal Studies Research Paper No. 39; online: https://digitalcommons.osgoode.yorku.ca/cgi/viewcontent.cgi?article=1114&context=olsrps.

6 The charges were brought by the RCMP and the Public Prosecution Service of Canada (PPSC) for SNC Lavalin's activities in Libya between 2001 and 2011. The case ended in a plea deal. See Peter Zimonjic, "After Year of Political Turmoil, SNC-Lavalin Gets Most of What It Wanted in Plea Deal" *CBC* (18 December 2019), online: www.cbc.ca/news/politics/canada-wilson-raybould-snc-lavalin-1.5401353. *Corruption of Foreign Public Officials Act*, SC 1998, c 34.

limited to career criminals nor were the "errant" corporate actors exceptions to the rule. Instead, the data showed a vibrant, Canadian-made money laundering operation, poetically referred to as "snow washing," that had at its heart weak corporate transparency and beneficial ownership rules.[7]

The systemic argument gained traction with the emergence of the "Vancouver Model" in 2017: casinos in British Columbia were found running laundering operations sophisticated enough to merit their own name, while the ongoing opioids (especially fentanyl) crisis was also producing a steady stream of illicit monies. In the background, there were reports of C$10 billion having been laundered in Alberta in 2015,[8] as well as a scandal about a Canadian bank being involved in money laundering.[9]

With the International Consortium of Journalists' FinCEN (Financial Crimes Enforcement Network) Files investigation in September 2020, six more banks were flagged for having conducted suspicious transactions and omitting beneficial ownership details. The FinCEN Files showed that a total of US$15.6 million came in and US$16.9 million went out of Canada, including a wire transfer for a drug dealer operating in a Canadian jail, through CIBC, RBC, TD, Bank of Montreal, UBS, and HSBC Canada.[10] In October 2021, the Pandora Papers offered details about the offshore holdings of at least 500 prominent Canadian citizens or residents.[11] While Fred Sharp's prolific Vancouver-based consultancy Corporate House had

7 The term "snow washing" varies the original "laundering" phrase with a nod both to the pristine reputations of Canada and its financial regulators and to the Canadian winter. See Robert Cribb & Marco Chown Oved, "Snow Washing: Canada Is the World's Newest Tax Haven" *Toronto Star* (25 January 2017), online: projects.thestar.com/panama-papers/canada-is-the-worlds-newest-tax-haven.

8 Diego Romero, "Alberta Tops Provinces in Money Laundering: Report" *CTV News* (10 May 2019), online: https://edmonton.ctvnews.ca/alberta-tops-provinces-in-money-laundering-report-1.4418173.

9 The bank was eventually identified as Manulife, but was only fined for laundering money. Dave Seglins, "Manulife Revealed as Bank Fined $1.15m for Violating Anti-money Laundering Reporting Rules" *CBC News* (27 February 2017), online: www.cbc.ca/news/business/fintrac-fine-name-secret-1.3999156.

10 Canadians for Tax Fairness, Media Release, "Coalition Calls to End Snow-Washing and Urges Feds for Improved Transparency in Wake of FinCEN Files" (25 September 2020), online: www.taxfairness.ca/en/press_release/2020-09/media-release-coalition-calls-end-snow-washing-and-urges-feds-improved.

11 Zach Dubinsky, "Huge 'Pandora Papers' Leak Exposes Secret Offshore Accounts of Politicians, Celebrities and Billionaires" *CBC News* (3 October 2021), online: www.cbc.ca/news/pandora-papers-offshore-tax-avoidance-1.6197303.

come into the limelight due to the Panama Papers leaks,[12] other reports of similar agencies across Canada, including one in Halifax, surfaced subsequently.[13]

Interestingly, the multiple incidents of laundering cut across professional and even industry-specific boundaries. Besides the drug traffickers and organized crime networks that occupied the popular imaginary, businesses such as banks, engineering firms, casinos, real estate and construction industry players, public figures, and financial consultants were all found equally invested in laundering. To disinterested observers outside Canada, it was apparent that laundering in Canada was not a few-bad-eggs endeavour; it had seeped into the fabric of the political economy.[14]

Within Canada, however, laundering mostly remains a siloed activity to be examined within the context of certain industries and businesses only. In British Columbia, for example, discovery of the Vancouver Model pushed the provincial government to commission a series of reports and inquiries into laundering.[15] Unfortunately, most reports suffered from extreme myopia: laundering was unfailingly presented as a weakness of the individual industry or business and was seldom located within the broader economic context or political landscape.[16] Instead of investigating

12 Natalie Clancy & Yvette Brend, "Panama Papers Reveal Canada's Top Offshore Middleman, Fred Sharp of Vancouver, Linked to Fraudster" *CBC News* (9 May 2016), online: www.cbc.ca/news/canada/british-columbia/panama-papers-fred-sharp-1.3567174.

13 Tax Justice Network, "Financial Secrecy Index 2020: Narrative Report on Canada" (2020) at 3 ["Narrative"], online: https://fsi.taxjustice.net/PDF/Canada.pdf.

14 For a more detailed discussion of how laundering plugs into the Canadian political economy, see Sanaa Ahmed, "Locating the Centre: State, Capital and the Political Economy of Money Laundering in Canada" in Tonita Murray, ed, *Big Crime, Big Policing: All about the Money?* (Toronto: University of Toronto Press, forthcoming) [Ahmed, "Locating the Centre"].

15 These include the Commission of Inquiry into Money Laundering in British Columbia (the Cullen Commission, discussed below) as well as several commissioned reports.

16 German makes a commendable effort to do so in the executive summary of the report, but the bulk of the report is consumed by the usual suspects: real estate, luxury vehicles, and horse racing. See German, above note 2. The Cullen Commission is the rare exception in that its mandate actually includes "financial institutions, and the corporate and professional sectors" in addition to real estate and gaming. Its final report was released in June 2022, too late for consideration here. See Commission of Inquiry into Money Laundering in British Columbia, "Commission Reports," online: https://cullencommission.ca/com-rep.

why Canada was so attractive to launderers or analysing *why so many* businesses and industries were prone to laundering, the reports focused on the businesses and industries themselves and what the authors saw as the "human costs" of money laundering: the worsening opioid crisis, the meteoric rise of real estate markets in Toronto and Vancouver,[17] and its implications for housing affordability.[18] As I have discussed elsewhere, such an approach discounts the very real economic *advantages* of laundering for businesses, industries, states, and citizens alike.[19]

New data, meanwhile, kept offering tantalising but unsubstantiated guesstimates regarding the scale of Canada's money laundering problem. Some suggested the volume laundered across Canada in 2018 was some C$47 billion,[20] others cited "official reports" showing it was between C$5 billion and C$100 billion,[21] while yet others contended the volume was between C$100 billion and C$130 billion.[22] The more scrupulous insisted that all these figures were estimates only, and the sole known quantity was the C$100 million-plus laundered in Lower Mainland casinos in British Columbia.[23] On the other hand, Tax Justice Network (TJN) data for 2021 showed that Canada lost some US$5 billion in tax revenues due to global corporate tax abuse by multinationals (US$3 billion) and global private tax evasion by private individuals (US$2 billion).

17 See Maureen Maloney, Tsur Somerville & Brigitte Unger, "Combatting Money Laundering in BC Real Estate" (2019) ["BC Real Estate"], online: www2.gov.bc.ca/assets/gov/housing-and-tenancy/real-estate-in-bc/combatting-money-laundering-report.pdf; Dan Perrin, "Real Estate Regulatory Structure Review" (2018), online: cullencommission.ca/files/Real_Estate_Regulatory_Structure_Review_Report_2018.pdf.

18 "BC Real Estate," *ibid.*

19 Ahmed, "Locating the Centre," above note 14.

20 "BC Real Estate," above note 17 at 47.

21 Denis Meunier, "Hidden Beneficial Ownership and Control: Canada as a Pawn in the Global Game of Money Laundering" (September 2018), online: www.cdhowe.org/sites/default/files/attachments/research_papers/mixed/Final%20for%20advance%20release%20Commentary_519_0.pdf.

22 C.D. Howe Institute, Intelligence Memo, "Kevin Comeau — Closing the Biggest Money Laundering Loophole" (30 May 2019), online: www.cdhowe.org/intelligence-memos/kevin-comeau-closing-biggest-money-laundering-loophole.

23 German, above note 2 at 31–32. The report does not state over what period of time, only that the C$100 million-plus figure held true at the time of publication of the report.

However, these figures pale in comparison to the tax losses Canada has caused other jurisdictions: US$19 billion by facilitating global tax abuse.[24] (It is unclear from the TJN data whether this figure also includes money lost through capital flight from other economies to Canada.) The data found Canada responsible for 3.87 percent of global tax losses. In its 2020 Financial Secrecy Index report, TJN ranked Canada at nineteenth of 133 jurisdictions due to its secretiveness *and* large-scale weighting; while Canada's reputation as a haven has only recently come to the fore, the country accounts for "1.6 percent of the global market in offshore financial services."[25] That Canada is no stranger to laundering is obvious but, far more interesting, it seems to have no real desire to change the status quo: Transparency International data showed Canada at the bottom of the pack of G20 states in meeting G20 commitments on beneficial ownership and transparency.[26]

This chapter contends that this bottom-of-the-pack ranking is no accident. While Canada has a seemingly robust anti-laundering regime (discussed below), transparency and beneficial ownership rules are low on its list of priorities. Since its last FATF-mandated Mutual Evaluation in 2016, Canada has improved, maintained, or is in the process of improving its performance on FATF's 40 Recommendations. The sole exception is the recommendation regarding transparency and beneficial ownership.[27]

Given the foregoing, it is evident that Canada's ostensible endorsement of global conventions against money laundering has a negligible impact on suppressing illicit financial flows (IFFs) both to and from Canada. This is because, first, the definition of "money laundering" espoused

---

24 This amount includes global corporate tax abuse (worth US$18 billion) and global private tax evasion. See Tax Justice Network, Illicit Financial Flows Vulnerability Tracker, "Canada 2021," [Vulnerability Tracker], online: https://iff.taxjustice.net/#/profile/CAN.

25 "Narrative," above note 13 at 1.

26 Transparency International, "G20 Leaders or Laggards: Reviewing G20 Promises on Ending Anonymous Companies" (2018), online: https://images.transparencycdn.org/images/2018_G20_Leaders_or_Laggards_EN.pdf. Canada and South Korea were the two countries in the Report with an overall "weak" legal framework (at 12, see also 14).

27 FATF, "Anti-Money Laundering and Counter-Terrorist Financing Measures — Canada: 4th Enhanced Follow-up Report & Technical Compliance Re-Rating" (October 2021) ["Canada Anti-Money Laundering Re-Rating"], online: www.fatf-gafi.org/media/fatf/documents/reports/fur/Follow-Up-Report-Canada-2021.pdf.

by the global regulators expressly excludes many of the activities and practices that contribute to IFFs. Second, Ottawa relies on this inherently flawed definition to circumscribe the ambit of what it considers—and prosecutes—as money laundering. While the Canada Revenue Agency (CRA) has begun investigating some instances of tax avoidance in the wake of the Panama Papers,[28] Canada mostly pursues—and prosecutes—laundering cases with causal connections to predicate offences. Third—and most significant, perhaps—is the fact these ineffectual regulations and their skewed enforcement are no match for well-considered and effective public policy in areas such as immigration and taxation. This chapter contends that Canada's laws actively encourage certain forms of laundering, despite Ottawa's avowedly anti-laundering stance.

B. GLOBAL REGULATORY FRAMEWORK

"One finds the crime one looks for" holds as true for money laundering as for any other crime. Even so, the truism relies on how crime is defined. While the politics of the use of the term "money laundering" is beyond the scope of this chapter,[29] a quick overview of its usage is necessary.

As defined in 1920, the term "money laundering" originally referred to the sluicing of money derived from criminal enterprises (drugs trafficking, smuggling, etc.) through legitimate businesses with a view to obliterating the causal link with crime. More than a hundred years later, the global regulator for money laundering—the Financial Action Task Force or FATF—continues to define laundering as the processing of the proceeds of criminal acts to disguise their illegal origin so that "criminals" may enjoy these profits without jeopardizing their source.[30] Indeed, until the 2021 OECD-backed convention on global tax reform, FATF was adamant that only drugs and arms trafficking, smuggling, sex work, embezzlement, insider trading, bribery, and computer fraud schemes qualified as

28 Zach Dubinsky, "CRA Battling Attempt to Halt Its Probe of Offshore 'Mastermind' and His Clients" *CBC News* (17 November 2021), online: www.cbc.ca/news/canada/cra-fred-sharp-court-of-appeal-offshore-1.6251729.

29 For lucid accounts, see, generally, the scholarship of Petrus van Duyne, Rainer Hullse, Nicholas Shaxson, and John Christensen. For historical overviews of the development of AML regulation, see John Braithwaite & Peter Drahos, *Global Business Regulation* (Cambridge: Cambridge University Press, 2000) and, generally, Peter Alldridge and Michael Levi, among others.

30 FATF, "Money Laundering," online: www.fatf-gafi.org/faq/moneylaundering.

crimes proper, and all tax-related issues were specifically outside its purview. However, once 136 jurisdictions agreed to reform the international tax system at the 2021 Rome convention,[31] FATF reluctantly agreed to re-examine its recommendations regarding beneficial ownership by canvassing stakeholders.[32]

The re-examination has been long awaited. FATF's original definition of money laundering was roundly criticised by academics, intergovernmental organizations, and think tanks. While the list of specific criticisms is extensive,[33] three are particularly germane. First, defining money laundering as a proceeds-of-crime issue explicitly or implicitly excludes several highly problematic activities from the ambit of laundering. Tax abuse is the most obvious exclusion, but so is capital flight—a serious concern for China and swathes of Africa—as well as the proceeds from informal economies. Trade-related malpractices—particularly transfer pricing, Base Erosion Profit Shifting, as well as instances of capital flight effected through dodgy trade—are another pressing concern for scores of states. In 2018, global trade data show a gap of US$835 billion between 134 developing states and thirty-six advanced economies.[34] That

31 OECD, "International Community Strikes a Ground-Breaking Tax Deal for the Digital Age" (10 August 2021), online: www.oecd.org/tax/international-community-strikes-a-ground-breaking-tax-deal-for-the-digital-age.htm.

32 FATF, "Revisions to Recommendation 24 and Its Interpretive Note—Public Consultation," online: www.fatf-gafi.org/publications/fatfrecommendations/documents/public-consultation-r24.html.

33 These include methodological challenges to FATF's estimates regarding the volume of laundering, ideological challenges to FATF's crime–laundering causality, and even its claims about laundering being a globalized endeavour. The most strident criticism, however, is targeted at FATF's claims regarding the purported impact of laundering on business and the global economy. See, for example, R.T. Naylor, *Wages of Crime: Black Markets, Illegal Finance and the Underworld Economy* (Montreal: McGill-Queen's University Press, 2004); Vincenzo Ruggiero, *Dirty Money: On Financial Delinquency* (Oxford: Oxford University Press, 2017); Eleni Tsingou, "Global Financial Governance and the Developing Anti-Money Laundering Regime: What Lessons for International Political Economy?" (2010) 47:6 *International Politics* 617.

34 Global Financial Integrity (GFI), "Trade-Related Illicit Financial Flows in 134 Developing Countries 2009–2018" (2021) [GFI 2021], online: https://secureservercdn.net/50.62.198.97/34n.8bd.myftpupload.com/wp-content/uploads/2021/12/IFFs-Report-2021.pdf?time=1639811244. Relying exclusively on official data submitted by governments to the UN, this December 2021 report focuses on dodgy trade alone. GFI uses the term "trade misinvoicing" to describe the practice of deliberately over- or under-pricing the declared value of imports

is, US$835 billion were transferred from developing states to the advanced economies through trade misinvoicing alone.[35] However, FATF again insists on defining trade-based money laundering only in relation to "criminal organisations and terrorist financiers."[36]

Many of the critics thus advocate the substitution of "money laundering" with the far more expansive term illicit financial flows, which encapsulates methods, practices, and crimes aiming to transfer money or capital from one country to another, in contravention of national or international laws or their spirit. Thus conceived, the term covers a range of practices including tax abuse (evasion and avoidance), trade-related malpractices, white-collar crime (including political, corporate, and criminal corruption), capital flight, as well as the proceeds of informal economies.

The expanded definition, argue the critics, will have a material bearing on what gets prosecuted as money laundering. FATF's single-minded pursuit of the crime-laundering causality, critics say, defangs its recommendations with respect to the issues that matter to many developing states. The issue becomes even more significant when one considers that the destination states for these monies are overwhelmingly those of the global North. Yet FATF regulations ignore or overlook the global patterns of money laundering and, instead, focus on laundering within individual jurisdictions. That illicit capital from China and Russia, for example, often ends up in Canada and the United Kingdom *because of their investment and taxation policies* is often disregarded. Instead, AML regulations focus on—among others—the role of bankers, real estate brokers, jewellers, and casinos in flagging so-called suspicious transactions within individual jurisdictions. This, of course, ignores the fact that businesses are in the

---

or exports submitted to customs authorities, in order to "transfer money across international borders, evade tax and/or customs duties, launder the proceeds of criminal activity, circumvent currency controls, and hide profits in offshore bank accounts." For excellent overviews and critiques of trade-based money laundering, see, generally, Nikos Passas; for a more credulous view, see John A. Cassara, *Trade-Based Money Laundering: The Next Frontier in International Money Laundering Enforcement* (Hoboken, NJ: John Wiley & Sons, 2016).

35 GFI 2021, *ibid* at 1. The figure jumps up to US$1.6 trillion when the trade data for developing countries and all their trading partners is considered.

36 FATF, "Trade-Based Money Laundering" (2006), online: www.fatf-gafi.org/publications/methodsandtrends/documents/trade-basedmoneylaundering.html.

business of making money,[37] and not policing moral turpitude, which is why there is little political or corporate will to combat laundering and investigate white-collar crime, particularly once the story disappears from news cycles.[38]

Second, FATF's definitional error does not exist in isolation: it is reinforced and perpetuated by other global agencies and networks in their own work. While the Basel Committee on Banking Supervision, for example, devises prudential regulations regarding laundering and trade agreements, and regional treaty arrangements, such as the European Union, have their own harmonised standards for money laundering, the FATF definition permeates and influences much of this "independent" regulation also.[39] Similarly, while the task of coordinating among the standard-setting bodies has been given to the G20-endorsed Financial Stability Board (FSB), FATF's 40 Recommendations are among the "key standards for sound financial systems" the FSB endorses,[40] and both organizations have many members in common.[41] The deployment of the *same* standards by *different* organizations gives FATF's standards resonance and heft beyond its immediate membership.

This effect is further enhanced by AML enforcement by the Toronto-based Egmont Group of Financial Intelligence Units,[42] as well as by the

37 Margaret E. Beare, "Case Study—'Voluntary' Ethical Conduct: Anti-Money Laundering Compliance and the Financial Sector" in W. Craig, ed, *Ethics Codes: The Regulatory Norms of a Global Society* (Aldershot, UK: Edward Elgar, 2005) at 30–31.

38 Beare 2018, above note 5 at 514. She contends that street crimes and crimes involving visible signs of violence have always been accorded greater political priority than what she scathingly refers to as "*so-called* 'victim-less' [emphasis added]" crimes, such as corruption or white-collar crime.

39 Kern Alexander, Rahul Dhumale & John Eatwell, *Global Governance of Financial Systems: The Legal and Economic Regulation of Systemic Risk* (Oxford: Oxford University Press, 2005) at 9–10 [Alexander et al].

40 Financial Stability Board, "Key Standards for Sound Financial Systems" (last modified 7 January 2021), online: www.fsb.org/work-of-the-fsb/about-the-compendium-of-standards/key_standards/.

41 The FSB now brings together central banks, finance ministries, supervisory, and regulatory authorities for the G20 as well as Hong Kong, Singapore, Spain, and Switzerland. FATF's current membership, meanwhile, is even broader. See FSB, "Work of the FSB," online: www.fsb.org/work-of-the-fsb/.

42 Egmont Group, "About" [Egmont Group], online: www.egmontgroup.org/en/content/about. The group is meant to facilitate international cooperation and the secure exchange of expertise and financial intelligence to combat money laundering and terrorist financing.

activities of the International Monetary Fund and World Bank.[43] With the IMF's active involvement, the standards and codes work their way into the fabric of all international economic transactions and relationships.[44] As such, FATF's view of what constitutes laundering has a material impact on how the rest of the world views laundering. For example, after the IMF added the FATF Recommendations to its list of standards and codes in 2002, the World Bank and the IMF "substantially increased" technical assistance available to those states looking to strengthen financial, regulatory, and supervisory frameworks for anti-money laundering and the combatting of terrorism (AML-CTF).[45] In the last ten years alone, some forty states have availed themselves of AML-CTF capacity building funded by IMF partners.[46]

Further, a study of enforcement practices at the level of the market shows how the global market also functions as an IMF and World Bank *amplifier* and thus, indirectly, adds to the legitimacy of FATF 40 Recommendations. Some commercial banks, for example, insist on IMF conditionality as a precondition to lending to states.[47] The debt "clubs" usually

---

43 International Monetary Fund, "About the IMF," online: www.imf.org/external/work.htm. The IMF describes its core activities as surveillance, providing technical assistance, lending, economic research and statistics, development of standards and codes, and "the fight against money laundering and terrorism financing." However, when it comes to AML-CTF regulation, the IMF chooses to rubberstamp the standards developed by other private-sector agencies such as the Basel Committee, FATF, and the OECD instead of devising its own.

44 Robert P. Delonis, "International Financial Standards and Codes: Mandatory Regulation Without Representation" (2004) 36:2-3 *New York University Journal of International Law & Politics* 563 at 623–24. The IMF usually works almost all of its officially supported standards and codes into its loan agreements with states; see *ibid* at 597; Alexander et al, above note 39 at 89; Joseph E. Stiglitz, *Globalisation and Its Discontents* (New York: W.W. Norton & Company, 2002). Further, compliance with standards such as those of the Basel Committee is a prequalification for IMF loans; Alexander et al, above note 39 at 39. Compliance is also a guarantee of better terms on the next loan. Delonis, *ibid* at 612. The standards and codes are also at the heart of IMF surveillance operations: International Monetary Fund, "Factsheet" (1 March 2021), online: www.imf.org/en/About/Factsheets/IMF-Surveillance.

45 International Monetary Fund, "The IMF and the Fight Against Money Laundering and the Financing of Terrorism" (14 July 2021), online: www.imf.org/en/About/Factsheets/Sheets/2016/08/01/16/31/Fight-Against-Money-Laundering-the-Financing-of-Terrorism.

46 *Ibid.*

47 Stiglitz, above note 44 at 44.

insist on an IMF clause in their agreements with countries.[48] Many private financial institutions and investors base investment decisions on IMF surveillance data.[49] As a result, the publication of AML-CTF compliance data brings to bear an inordinate amount of pressure on the non-compliant state[50] looking to the international financial markets for funds. Not only do states with better compliance have lower debt-risk premia and better sovereign credit ratings,[51] but states use compliance as a "signalling device" to potential trading partners and international investors in order to attract trade and investment.[52] As Brummer argues, non-compliance with key international standards (such as AML-CTF regulation) poses significant reputational risks: not only does it cause counterparties in international financial agreements to re-evaluate their expectations regarding a regulator's future conduct, it also undermines incentives to cooperate with such a regulator in the future.[53] Even market players, he says, generally perceive adherence to major international standards as a mark of good regulatory practice.[54]

Third, and perhaps the most crucial criticism, is that this network of influences[55] results in the import of the FATF's flawed definition of money laundering into domestic legislation and regulations. This fatal flaw rests at the heart of a jurisdiction's anti-laundering model; questions of what constitutes laundering and who should be prosecuted — choices that ostensibly belong to the state — are not determined by the legislature or even the bureaucracy. Use of the FATF definition ensures that these decisions mirror, essentially, FATF's choices.

---

48 Sundhya Pahuja, "Technologies of Empire: IMF Conditionality and the Reinscription of the North/South Divide" (2000) 13:4 *Leiden Journal of International Law* 749 at 765

49 Delonis, above note 44 at 609. He cites the specific examples of Pricewaterhouse-Coopers and the California Public Employees Retirement System.

50 *Ibid* at 596–96. In a similar vein, see Braithwaite & Drahos, above note 29 at 132.

51 Delonis, above note 44 at 610–11.

52 Rhys Bollen, "The International Financial System and Future Global Regulation" (2008) 23:9 *Journal of International Banking Law and Regulation* 458 at 468.

53 Chris Brummer, "Why Soft Law Dominates International Finance — and Not Trade" (2010) 13:3 *Journal of International Economic Law* 623.

54 *Ibid.*

55 I owe the phrase to Braithwaite & Drahos. See above note 29.

C. FAULT IN OUR STARS? CANADA'S ANTI-MONEY LAUNDERING FRAMEWORK

On the face of it, Canada boasts a strong, independent AML regime that is simultaneously plugged into global networks. Ottawa was among the founding members of FATF in 1989 and is a member of the Asia Pacific Group on Money Laundering (APG).[56] Ottawa also has ringside seats at many of the global organizations tasked with devising AML-CTF regulations. Further, Canada hosts the Egmont Group,[57] and its own financial intelligence unit, FINTRAC, sees part of its work as contributing to other multilateral fora such as FATF, the APG, and the Caribbean FATF, besides participating in international policy making and the provision of technical assistance to other FIUs.[58]

The perception of a strong AML-CTF regime is further reinforced by a gamut of laws and regulations. Within Canada, money laundering is currently governed by fifteen different laws and regulatory instruments,[59] with responsibility for their implementation and enforcement assigned to various organs and institutions of the state. Twelve federal agencies are tasked with AML enforcement and prosecution, while approximately fourteen agencies operate within each province.[60] As per FATF requirements,

---

56 FATF, "Asia/Pacific Group on Money Laundering," online: www.fatf-gafi.org/pages/asiapacificgrouponmoneylaunderingapg.html. While the list of APG members includes several states seen as recalcitrant, and thus in need of such assistance, presumably the same does not apply to states such as Canada, the US, Australia, and New Zealand, which are also FATF members, and can be reliably presumed to be the ones *providing* assistance.

57 Egmont Group, above note 42.

58 FINTRAC, "Who We Are" (last modified 5 May 2021), online: www.fintrac-canafe.gc.ca/fintrac-canafe/1-eng.

59 Primarily the *Criminal Code*, RSC 1985, c C-46, and the *Proceeds of Crime (Money Laundering) and Terrorist Financing Act*, SC 2000, c 17. For comprehensive treatment see Department of Finance Canada, *Reviewing Canada's Anti-Money Laundering and Anti-Terrorist Financing Regime* (7 February 2018), online: https://www.canada.ca/content/dam/fin/migration/activty/consult/amlatfr-rpcfa-eng.pdf.

60 The federal agencies include the CBSA, the CRA, CSIS, Department of Finance, Department of Justice, FINTRAC, Public Prosecution Service of Canada, RCMP, Stats Canada, Canada Mortgage and Housing Corporation, Bank of Canada, and the Office of the Superintendent of Financial Institutions. The provincial agencies include the RCMP (except in Ontario and Quebec), municipal police, Crown counsel (for example, BC Crown Counsel), Civil Forfeiture Office, MoF Revenue Division, Office of the Chief Information Officer (British Columbia), Land Title

Canada has legislated extensive reporting requirements for a number of entities, such as accountants, Crown agents, British Columbia notaries, casinos, dealers in precious metals and stones, financial institutions, life insurance, money services businesses, real estate, securities dealers, and virtual currency dealers.[61] In its last FATF Mutual Evaluation Report in 2016,[62] Canada was commended by FATF for the overall strength of its AML-CTF regime,[63] and more kudos followed in October 2021.[64]

That said, the extent of money laundering in Canada raises significant questions about the purported efficacy of these laws, regulations, and agencies in impeding or preventing laundering. Some of the problems are obvious: first, the definition of laundering in the *Criminal Code* hews closely to the one used by FATF and sets up a crime–laundering causality that reduces the scope of what can be prosecuted as a laundering offence.[65] For example, the tax-abuse issues unearthed by the Panama, Paradise, and Pandora Papers would not qualify as laundering.

Second, and overarching as an issue, is that of jurisdiction. Given that crime enforcement — including financial crime — is a provincial responsibility, much turns on the individual province's response to laundering, as well as its willingness to call in the federal agencies.[66] Third, the paucity of investigative ability, both provincially and nationally, further reduces

---

and Survey Authority (British Columbia), BC Assessment, real estate regulators, financial sector regulators, securities regulators, Financial Institutions Commission (British Columbia), professional regulators (for example, Law Society of Ontario, Notaries Public, Chartered Professional Accountants, etc.) as well as lottery and gambling regulators.

61 FINTRAC, "Transaction Reporting Requirements" (last modified 4 November 2021), online: www.fintrac-canafe.gc.ca/guidance-directives/transaction-operation/1-eng.

62 See FATF, "High-Risk and Other Monitored Jurisdictions," online: www.fatf-gafi.org/publications/high-riskandnon-cooperativejurisdictions/more/more-on-high-risk-and-non-cooperative-jurisdictions.html; FATF, "Procedures for the FATF Fourth Round of AML/CFT Mutual Evaluations," online: www.fatf-gafi.org/publications/mutualevaluations/documents/4th-round-procedures.html. FATF regularly conducts peer reviews of each member to assess levels of implementation of the FATF Recommendations.

63 FATF, "Canada," online: www.fatf-gafi.org/countries/#Canada.

64 "Canada Anti-Money Laundering Re-Rating," above note 27.

65 See *Code*, above note 59, s 462.31, and the *Proceeds of Crime (money laundering) and Terrorist Financing Act*, s 2(1).

66 Anti-Corruption Law Program, "Anti-Corruption Law Program: Financial Crime Law Enforcement in Canada" (18 November 2021) ["Anti-Corruption"], online: www.youtube.com/watch?v=cgWDvKRXMuc&t=1078s at 12:15.

the number of successful laundering prosecutions. In 2013, the Harper government shut down a dozen specialized proceeds-of-crime units and scattered the experts across the country.[67] By 2018, the RCMP had publicly confessed it lacked institutional expertise to conduct sophisticated financial or corporate investigations.[68] While the federal government has been talking about a federal, multi-agency anti-money laundering unit since 2019[69]—including in the run up to the 2021 election—the details are still fuzzy, which does not bode well for the future of the unit.[70] In the meantime, early in 2020, the RCMP disbanded its Financial Crimes Unit

---

67 Mike Hager, "RCMP's Dismal Record on Investigating Money Laundering in B.C. Is Improving, Cullen Commission Hearing" *Globe and Mail* (2 May 2021), online: www.theglobeandmail.com/canada/british-columbia/article-investigating-money-laundering-in-bc-an-issue-for-rcmp.

68 Grant Robertson & Tom Cardoso, "RCMP Aims to Use Outside Experts to Crack Down on White-Collar Crime" *Globe and Mail* (11 April 2018), online: www.theglobeandmail.com/business/article-rcmp-aims-to-use-outside-experts-to-crack-down-on-white-collar-crime.

69 Sam Cooper, "Canada Proposes National Money Laundering Task Force in Budget 2019" *Global News* (19 March 2019), online: https://globalnews.ca/news/5069141/2019-budget-money-laundering.

70 Late in 2020, for example, Public Safety Canada (PSC) said it had been allocated C$24 million over five years to set up the Anti-Money Laundering Action, Coordination and Enforcement team to coordinate interagency efforts to address money laundering. The PSC announcement also spoke of C$28 million in funding over a five-year period for the Canada Border Security Agency (CBSA) to set up a unit specializing in trade-based laundering. See Public Safety Canada, "Combatting Money Laundering" (last modified 10 September 2020), online: www.publicsafety.gc.ca/cnt/trnsprnc/brfng-mtrls/prlmntry-bndrs/20200621/041/index-en.aspx. Shortly after, the RCMP announced the constitution of new "Integrated Money Laundering Investigative Teams" or IMLITs in British Columbia, Ontario, Alberta, and Quebec. Expecting C$98.9 million from the government over five years, the teams were meant to comprise personnel from the RCMP, the CBSA, the Forensic Account Management Group, and the PPSC. See RCMP, "Government of Canada Invests $98.9M over Five Years to Modernize the RCMP and Strengthen Its Foundations to Help Fight Money Laundering and Identify Proceeds of Crime" *Newswire* (17 December 2020), online: www.newswire.ca/news-releases/government-of-canada-invests-98-9m-over-five-years-to-modernize-the-rcmp-and-strengthen-its-foundations-to-help-fight-money-laundering-and-identify-proceeds-of-crime-826272067.html. Meanwhile, a pre-election proposal by the Liberal Party website for a new national financial crime agency has not materialized. See Liberal Party of Canada, "Canada Financial Crimes Agency," online: https://liberal.ca/our-platform/canada-financial-crimes-agency.

in Ontario since the "new" priorities were national security, transnational serious and organized crime, and cybercrime.[71]

That said, those close to law enforcement circles also point to what they see as an inhospitable environment that breeds a general reluctance to investigate. Onerous criminal disclosure obligations, a slow process for obtaining search warrants, lack of investigative subpoena powers, court-imposed time limits on prosecution post–*R v Jordan*,[72] lack of reporting requirements for some laundering-prone industries (such as car dealerships and auction houses), the reporting exemption for lawyers, as well as the lack of minimum sentencing guidelines are held up as significant impediments to investigative zeal. Why would the police spend five to six years investigating and building a solid case of fraud, so the argument goes, when the non-violent offender can "get off" with just house arrest?[73]

Fourth, while watertight investigations are critical to the chances of successful prosecutions, Canadian prosecutors lack the appetite for prosecuting laundering that involves corporations.[74] This has primarily to do with domestic legislation that makes it difficult to prosecute corporate criminality. Unlike the common law in the United Kingdom or the *respondeat superior* rule in the United States, Canada relies on the modified identification doctrine first identified by the Supreme Court in *Canadian Dredge and Dock v The Queen* in 1985.[75] To secure a conviction, a would-be prosecutor thus needs strong evidence and proof of subjective fault on part of a senior officer of the company, but neither are easily available. Further

71 Marco Chown Oved, "The RCMP Is Shutting Down Its Financial Crimes Unit in Ontario. Here's Why Former Top Mountie Says It's a Mistake" *Toronto Star* (15 January 2020), online: www.thestar.com/news/investigations/2020/01/15/the-rcmp-is-shutting-down-its-financial-crimes-unit-in-ontario-heres-why-former-top-mounties-says-its-a-mistake.html.

72 *R v Jordan*, 2016 SCC 27.

73 "Anti-Corruption," above note 66.

74 *Ibid*, Jennifer Quaid's perspective.

75 *Canadian Dredge & Dock Co v The Queen*, [1985] 1 SCR 662 at para 34. Taking a restrictive approach to the idea of vicarious liability in criminal law, the Court held that a corporation would be responsible for the acts of an employee only if three successive conditions were met: (1) that the employee be in a policy-making role such that they could be considered the "directing mind" of the corporation, (2) that they be acting within the scope of their employment, and (3) that they not have been acting in breach of instructions or for their own benefit or with a view to defrauding the employer.

compounding this problem is that Canadian courts are also seen as less friendly to prosecutors than in the United States.[76]

Given the lack of a coordinated, coherent strategy to combat laundering[77]—or even a consistent understanding of what it entails—it is unsurprising that there is not clear data about prosecutions and convictions. In a 2019 report, Maloney et al stated that there had been fewer than fifty laundering convictions in Canada in the preceding ten years.[78] A *Global News* investigation, on the other hand, claimed that between 2000 and 2016, there were 321 convictions in a total of 1,130 laundering cases while 72 percent of cases were stayed, withdrawn, or dismissed.[79] Yet another report, in the *Toronto Star*, cited Statistics Canada data as showing that 86 percent of money laundering charges filed between 2012 and 2017 never made it to trial because they were withdrawn or stayed.[80]

Finally, regulatory and legislative missteps have not helped the state's anti-laundering cause. In 2019, once the extent of snow-washing through shell companies was established, then Finance Minister Bill Morneau initially refused to institute a public register containing ownership details of corporations, and subsequently instituted one at the federal level that was meant to have persons with more than 25 percent beneficial interest disclose the same.[81] But not only did the initiative ignore the fact that 90 percent of corporations are registered provincially, not federally,[82] it

76 "Anti-Corruption," above note 66. Anthony Cole believes specialized courts for financial crime are essential to navigating this impasse.

77 See, for example, the interaction between Peter German, Jennifer Quaid, Anthony Cole, and Mary Inman in "Anti-Corruption," above note 66.

78 "BC Real Estate," above note 17. Interestingly, the authors say that while terrorism financing is generally prioritised over laundering, even the police see civil forfeiture as an easy alternative to criminal prosecution for money laundering.

79 Cooper, above note 69.

80 Marco Chown Oved, "In Canada, Nearly All Accused Money Launderers Get Their Charges Dropped" *Toronto Star* (26 December 2019), online: www.thestar.com/news/investigations/2019/12/26/in-canada-nearly-all-accused-money-launderers-get-their-charges-dropped.html.

81 See Government of Canada, "Individuals with Significant Control" (last modified 14 October 2020), online: www.ic.gc.ca/eic/site/cd-dgc.nsf/eng/cs08216.html. After the 2019 amendments to the *Canada Business Corporations Act*, RSC 1985, c C-44, companies must disclose true ownership to both shareholders and creditors. However, this information is (1) only provided about individuals who own more than 25 percent of voting or all shares outstanding, and (2) is not available publicly.

82 Marco Chown Oved & Robert Cribb, "Ottawa Vows to Lift Corporate Secrecy in Bid to Stop Tax Evasion and Money Laundering" *Toronto Star* (18 July 2017),

further ignored that 25 percent is too high a limit to catch anything worthwhile.[83] In the same year, the BC government also came up with legislation mandating transparency in land ownership[84] and, subsequently, corporate ownership.[85] However, the laws as they stand are unlikely to have the kind of impact on either housing prices or corporate transparency that champions of transparency would have hoped for.[86]

As the foregoing demonstrates, the multiplicity of ineffectual anti-laundering laws and regulations would have been sufficient to sink this ship on its own. However, the addition of whimsically conceived additional regulation and legislation, lacklustre law enforcement, and patchy prosecution have torpedoed the ship while at harbour. The big question is why.

D. MIXED SIGNALS? AML AND CANADIAN PUBLIC POLICY

Tempting though it is, it would be facile to conclude that Canada's response to laundering stems from gross incompetence and utter mismanagement. Equally lazy would be the conclusion that Canadians do not care about

---

online: www.thestar.com/news/canada/2017/07/18/corporate-secrecy-to-be-lifted-to-help-stop-tax-evasion-and-money-laundering.html. The ratio of federally registered companies to provincially registered ones is 1:9.

83 *Ibid.*

84 This is the *Land Ownership Transparency Act*, SBC 2019, c 23. Meanwhile, in its 2019 budget, Quebec promised to begin consultations regarding the setting up of a public beneficial ownership registry and was followed by British Columbia in early 2020. See Jen St. Denis, "Fight Against 'Nefarious' Money Laundering Gets $10 million Federal Boost for RCMP" *Toronto Star* (13 June 2019), online: www.thestar.com/vancouver/2019/06/13/fight-against-nefarious-money-laundering-gets-10-million-federal-boost-for-rcmp.html.

85 In 2019, the BC legislature amended the British Columbia *Business Corporations Act*, SBC 2002, c 57 and *Business Corporations Regulation*, BC Reg 65/2004, OC 201/2004 to mandate greater transparency in corporate ownership. The amendments took effect in October 2020. See OIC 169/2020.

86 *Ibid.* Space constraints preclude a detailed discussion of the reasons here, but the primary problems with the laws are that the additional information about ownership is, first, required only about individuals who own more than 25 percent of the interest in a property or more than 25 percent of the voting shares or all shares outstanding, and second, this information is not available publicly. Additionally, the law does not set out specifically what happens in cases where individuals control corporations through legal entities and/or other individuals.

economic crime, since no election has turned on such issues. While some commentators have correctly recognized Ottawa's lack of a consistent, coordinated AML strategy, the inference that Canada *lacks* a "permanent, strategic vision"[87] or policy on laundering is to miss the forest for the trees.

Several influential theorists have discussed the centrality of invisibility to the construction of an edifice of power.[88] Althusser makes the crucial point that invisibility, too, is constructed; the invisible becomes so *because* it is "repressed from the field of the visible." It goes unperceived because the *function* of the field of knowledge "is not to see them, to forbid any sighting of them." As such, he contends the invisible does not exist *outside* the visible but is "the *inner darkness of exclusion*, inside the visible itself [emphasis in original]."[89] Similarly, Canada's actual, unarticulated AML policy exists *within its visible non-policy, within its seeming lack of a permanent strategic vision*. More simply: to understand why Canada's ostensibly robust AML framework produces the outcomes it does, the framework must necessarily be situated within the broader public policy framework. The state's *articulated* response to laundering events is only ever a starting point; to understand how the state truly approaches laundering, one must look to governmental policy in areas that have an *unstated or understated but equally muscular nexus with laundering*. Two worthy contenders in Canada are immigration and corporate taxation policy.

In the last decade, every revelation about Canada's laundering problem — the casinos, the data leaks, etc. — has been met with Ottawa's *visible, articulated AML policy*: public outrage and calls for greater regulatory oversight. But the linkages between the laundering events have not been

87 Anthony Cole in "Anti-Corruption," above note 66.

88 These include *Max Weber on Law in Economy and Society*, ed and trans Max Rheinstein (Cambridge, Harvard University Press, 1966); Pierre Bourdieu, *Language and Symbolic Power*, ed John B. Thompson, trans Gino Raymond & Matthew Adamson (Cambridge, Harvard University Press, 1991); generally, Michel Foucault & Steven Lukes, *Power: A Radical View* (Basingstoke, Palgrave Macmillan, 2005). In more recent scholarship, David Kennedy speaks of this invisibility where he argues that expertise provides plausible deniability regarding the agency of individual decision makers and again, in the context of war and law, where he contends that the process of abstraction allows actors to make decisions without having to assume responsibility for the same. See David Kennedy, *A World of Struggle: How Power, Law and Expertise Shape Global Political Economy* (Princeton: Princeton University Press, 2016) at 111, 275.

89 Louis Althusser et al, *Reading Capital*, trans Ben Brewster & David Fernbach (London: Verso, 2015) at 24–25 [emphasis in original].

mounted into a more nuanced discussion of money laundering in Canada. Public discourse on laundering remained mired in regulatory minutiae regarding casinos, housing, and drugs even as the state trotted out a slew of seemingly ambitious but essentially unquantifiable policy responses: "rooting out" corruption, tax fairness, "tackling" the opioids crisis, and making housing "affordable" for "ordinary Canadians." Subsumed by this grandstanding were the more prosaic questions that get to the heart of the *invisible, unarticulated AML policy*. How, for example, is corruption in the Quebec construction industry to be rooted out when rigged bidding is an industry feature known to both government officials and politicians? Or, how is tax abuse to be checked if beneficial ownership rules are not tightened? Is the sizeable financial crime policing apparatus ineffective because of its systemic design flaws, its operational inefficiencies, or both?

While critics of Canada's AML policy have long argued there is little political or corporate will to combat laundering and investigate white-collar crime,[90] the policy flaws are mostly read as a lack: lack of political will, lack of effective regulation, lack of trained investigators. But this lack, this absence is a *deliberate assertion of power* that traverses the distance between the visible and the invisible policy. *Failure* to exercise political will is as much an act of power as the exercise of said will: the *seeming* lack of will to combat laundering is not *external* to the body politic but is *a passionate will to particular action* (for example, defunding financial crime investigation units) or *inaction*[91] (for example, choosing not to prosecute corporate actors). This passionate will is expressed more in institutional arrangements than in political statements and, ultimately, reflects state policy more accurately than the articulated policy.

Canada's immigration system is a good example. Business immigration has been a feature of Canadian immigration since the 1952 *Immigration Act*,[92] and since the 1990s, the federal government and Quebec have concurrently been running immigration programs specifically designed to

90 Beare 2018, above note 5 at 514.

91 The inaction refers to the fact that governments act *even when they choose not to act*, that inaction is as valid a policy response as action. See, generally, Frank Pearce, *Crimes of the Powerful: Marxism, Crime and Deviance* (London: Pluto Press Limited, 1976), who develops the idea of an "imaginary social order" to explain why the behaviour of police, state, and corporation diverges from their stated priorities.

92 Canada, Citizenship and Immigration, "Evaluation of the Federal Business Immigration Program" (June 2014) ["Evaluation"], online: www.canada.ca/content/dam/ircc/migration/ircc/english/pdf/pub/e2-2013_fbip.pdf at 17.

draw foreign capital into Canada. The program logic was to have foreign investors make up for the lack of Canadian capital by financing industries and businesses that would both generate income and provide employment.[93] While there appears to be little or no data about the volume of monies Canada has attracted under its business investor program, the 2016 census data shows the number of economic migrants to Canada between 1980 and 2016 was 2,994,135,[94] of which 9.5 percent were applicants under business programs while 11 percent had applied under provincial and territorial nominee programs.[95] Investors made a one-time capital contribution of either C$400,000 (pre-2010) or C$800,000 (post-2010) to the Canadian economy in the form of a five-year interest-free loan. While bringing funds from their home states to Canada was a precondition for business immigration, even the economic migrants who were workers (78.7 percent[96]) or provincial or territorial nominees brought funds for their resettlement costs, their savings, etc. Between 2007 and 2011 alone, Canada attracted C$6.42 billion under just its federal and Quebec immigrant investor programs.[97] Significantly, the economic migration program does not seem to have had any significant stipulations regarding the source or origin of funds in the home state.[98] This clearly indicates that the cleanliness of the money was not a priority. Indeed, TJN data shows Canada's

93 *Ibid* at 2, 73. In its program logic model for the Business Immigration Program (Appendix A), the report specifically sees the investor immigrants category as providing "low-cost capital for provincial investment."

94 Statistics Canada, "Data Tables, 2016 Census" (last modified 17 June 2019), online: https://tinyurl.com/435va2ft.

95 Statistics Canada, "Immigrant Population by Selected Places of Birth, Admission Category and Period of Immigration, Canada, Provinces and Territories, Census Metropolitan Areas and Areas Outside of Census Metropolitan Areas" (27 October 2017), online: www12.statcan.gc.ca/census-recensement/2016/dp-pd/dv-vd/imm/index-eng.cfm.

96 *Ibid.*

97 "Evaluation," above note 92 at 47. The other two categories available under the Business Immigration Program are entrepreneurs and self-employed persons.

98 *Ibid* at 3–4. Interestingly, the replication of the Canadian immigration strategy more recently by EU countries such as Cyprus, Portugal, and Malta have drawn vehement criticism by developed countries for selling citizenship in exchange for wads of dirty money. See Simon Goodley & David Pegg, "Malta Still Selling Golden Passports to Rich Stay-Away 'Residents'" *Guardian* (23 April 2021), online: www.theguardian.com/world/2021/apr/23/malta-still-selling-golden-passports-to-rich-stay-away-residents.

greatest vulnerability to illicit financial flows is posed by inward Foreign Direct Investment (debt).[99]

This is not to imply that *all* economic migrants to Canada were kleptocrats, corrupt government officials, or drugs traffickers who brought in pools of filthy lucre from their states of origin. But the *absence* of stipulations clearly indicates that the cleanliness of the money was *not* a pressing concern for the Canadian state. While the idea appears controversial initially, it makes imminent sense: once in the system, dirty money behaves just like clean money. Banks and casinos profit off even "laundered monies," pay their employees and use this money to grow their businesses, and make more jobs. The lawyers, accountants, and government officials who deal with this money—to conduct real estate transactions or set up shell companies—plough this money back into the economy, through both their own consumption and by paying federal and provincial taxes on this income. The federal and provincial governments also reap corporate taxes and fees for many of these transactions. The money that is funnelled into the Canadian economy increases the production of goods, services, and tax revenues. Why would *any* government—let alone a cash-strapped government that expects its net debt to double to C$1.5 trillion by 2025–26[100]—worry about the *origins* of this money?

Even though the federal investor program was discontinued in 2014, provinces continue to have their own investor and entrepreneurial streams. Further, in a bid to stimulate the lacklustre pandemic economy, the federal government has announced ambitious new immigration targets. Whether the government imposes a "cleanliness" requirement on funds being brought in by the new immigrants—beyond the routine screening by banks transferring the funds from the home countries to Canada—remains to be seen. This is a scenario worth watching as most indicators—especially the Panama, Paradise, and Pandora Papers findings, as well as the 2020 Tax Justice Network figures—suggest that Canada is still not unduly worried about the cleanliness of inflows, whether from immigration or from investment. The paucity of domestic savings and tax revenue have rendered the state dependent on external monies and by all accounts, the state is not looking this gift horse in the mouth.

99 Vulnerability Tracker, above note 24.

100 Canadians for Tax Fairness, "Platform for Tax Fairness 2021," online: www.taxfairness.ca/sites/default/files/pdf/c4tf_platform_for_tax_fairness_2021.pdf.

Similarly, Canada's corporate taxation policy coupled with its beneficial ownership rules have long rendered the country an attractive onshore haven. A 2018 Transparency International review of beneficial ownership rules in the G20 countries found that only Canada and South Korea had a "weak framework."[101] Significantly, Canada and South Korea were also the only two states (of six) that did not improve the quality of the framework after scoring the same ranking in the 2015 review.[102] In the six years since, Canada has done little to improve the situation, barring a few cosmetic measures.[103] In the October 2021 follow-up to its 2016 Mutual Evaluation with FATF, for example, Canada remained non-compliant on just *one* of FATF's forty recommendations: Recommendation 22, which mandates transparency and information regarding beneficial ownership of legal arrangements.[104] Meanwhile, KPMG's 2016 *Focus on Tax* report on international global competitiveness, for example, ranked Toronto, Vancouver, and Montreal among the top ten tax-competitive cities, while Canada was overall first in lowest total effective tax rate. Further, Canada also ranked first in an industry-wide survey of research and development, digital services, corporate services, and manufacturing.[105] Canada still offers a very low effective tax rate for businesses, and is widely seen as a regulatory haven for the world's extractive industries.[106]

101 Transparency International, "Six Things to Know: New G20 Beneficial Ownership Principles" (17 November 2014), online: www.transparency.org/en/news/six-things-to-know-new-g20-beneficial-ownership-principles. The G20 countries adopted the High-Level Beneficial Ownership Principles at the G20 Brisbane summit in November 2014, a year after the G8 adopted the principles in 2013.

102 Maíra Martini & Maggie Murphy, "G20 Leaders or Laggards? Reviewing G20 Promises on Ending Anonymous Companies" (2018) at 10–11, online: https://images.transparencycdn.org/images/2018_G20_Leaders_or_Laggards_EN.pdf.

103 For example, the institution of the public registry at the federal level and a public consultation by the Ministry of Innovation, Science and Economic Development in the winter of 2020 on whether a public registry can prevent laundering in Canada. The results of the consultation have yet to be made public. See Canadians for Tax Fairness, Media Release, "Civil Society Calls for Results of Federal Consultation on Public Registry One Year Later" (4 March 2021), online: www.taxfairness.ca/en/press_release/2021-03/media-release-civil-society-calls-results-federal-consultation-public-registry.

104 "Canada Anti-Money Laundering Re-rating," above note 27.

105 KPMG, "Focus on Tax: KPMG's Guide to International Tax Competitiveness" (2016), online: https://mmkconsulting.com/compalts/reports/compalt2016_report_tax_en.pdf.

106 "Narrative," above note 13 at 1.

While domestic tax-focused institutions and non-profits have made much of Ottawa's progressive slashing of the effective tax rate for businesses and the wealthy over the last few decades,[107] there is little discussion of Ottawa's role in *propagating* tax abuse, both within its borders and abroad. TJN's Financial Secrecy Index report on Canada for 2020, for example, highlights Ottawa's role in the development of tax havens in the Caribbean, particularly in the Bahamas and the Cayman Islands, through the development of business districts and legislative initiatives that provided tax benefits for banks, businesses, and wealthy clients. While the report notes that trade relations between Canada and the Caribbean date to the seventeenth century, it cites a 2013 IMF report as saying, "Foreign banks, primarily Canadian, play a leading role throughout the Caribbean, accounting for about 60 per cent of banking system assets."[108]

Further, Canada has also executed a series of controversial non-double taxation treaties (while characterising them as Tax Information Exchange Agreements) with a series of tax havens. These agreements were signed by the government "without consulting Parliament in any way" and include several renowned tax havens.[109] Under the terms of these tax treaties, Canadian corporations can register assets in, for example, Barbados and then transfer them back to Canada, with income that has been realised in Barbados being almost completely untaxed. The report cites Statistics Canada data to show that by the end of 2018, Canadian corporations reported C$353 billion in so-called foreign direct investments in the top twelve tax havens, including Luxembourg, Barbados, Bermuda, Cayman Islands, and the British Virgin Islands.[110] Interestingly, the report notes that after the 2016 Panama Papers leak, the amount officially reported by Canadian

107 These include Publish What You Pay Canada, Canadians for Tax Fairness and Transparency International Canada. See, for example, Toby Sanger, "Tax the Rich: How Tax Fairness Will Make a Better Canada" (19 October 2021), online: www.taxfairness.ca/en/resources/presentations/tax-rich-how-tax-fairness-will-make-better-canada.

108 "Narrative," above note 13 at 1–2.

109 *Ibid* at 2. According to a CBC report, the tax treaty with Barbados was presented as Bill S-2 in December 1980. Bob Rae, then the NDP's finance critic, pointed out the potential consequences for the Canadian economy, but was unable to persuade MPs of either party, who proceeded to sign it into law: Zach Dubinsky, "How Canada Got into Bed with Tax Havens" *CBC News* (18 June 2016), online: www.cbc.ca/news/business/canada-offshore-treaties-barbados-tax-avoidance-1.3641278.

110 "Narrative," above note 13 at 2.

corporations in Panama increased by 9 percent while in the BVI, it increased by 50 percent.[111] According to the TJN's calculations, assuming a 5 percent return, and an effective tax rate of 20 percent for these corporations, Canadian governments are losing a minimum of US$3.5 billion annually from corporate profit and tax shifting to these tax havens.

That said, the governments do not appear to be too worried about such potential "losses." Punishments for both tax avoidance and evasion are a rarity and penalties remain low.[112] A 2018 report conducted by the Office of the Auditor General of Canada showed that not only does the CRA assess compliance by different categories of taxpayers differently, it also applies and waives penalties inconsistently.[113] This is, of course, in addition to secret out-of-court settlements with wealthy and well-connected taxpayers.[114]

However, the revenue losses to Canadian governments do not detract from the country's own significant role as an onshore haven itself. Despite a 2018 amendment in the *Canadian Business Corporations Act* mandating self-reporting of beneficial ownership interest beyond 25 percent,[115] Canada remains a very lax jurisdiction when it comes to establishing shell companies. Besides the data leaks in the Panama, Paradise, and Pandora Papers, FinCEN data also linked front companies in Alberta and New

111 *Ibid.* The authors do add the caveat that the reported figures are likely to be on the lower end as they are officially reported figures by corporations.

112 *Ibid* at 4–5.

113 Canada, Office of the Auditor General, "Report 7—Compliance Activities—Canada Revenue Agency" (2018), online: www.oag-bvg.gc.ca/internet/English/parl_oag_201811_07_e_43205.html.

114 A CBC News investigation in May 2019 showed that the CRA had reached an out-of-court settlement with wealthy KPMG clients over their involvement in an offshore scam. The CRA maintained that the settlement represented "substantial savings to the public and a benefit to the justice system." Harvey Cashore, "CRA Signs Secret Settlement with Wealthy KPMG Clients Involved in Offshore Tax Scheme" *CBC News* (30 May 2019), online: www.cbc.ca/news/business/cra-kmpg-settlement-taxes-1.5154610.

115 Via the *Budget Implementation Act, 2018, No 2*, SC 2018, c 27, s 182. The 25 percent requirement was also mirrored in the amendments to the *Proceeds of Crime (Money Laundering) and Terrorist Financing Regulations* in 2019; online: www.gazette.gc.ca/rp-pr/p2/2019/2019-07-10/html/sor-dors240-eng.html.

Brunswick with businesses in Russia that were allegedly involved in illegal fishing activities as well as insurance fraud.[116]

E. CONCLUSION

In the popular imagination, money laundering is often classified as a crime of opportunity where criminals exploit "loopholes" in regulations and laws. As the above shows, these "loopholes" are not accidental or inadvertent mistakes; they reflect the deliberated yet unarticulated policy of the state on money laundering. As with other vibrant onshore havens (including the United States and the United Kingdom), Canada relies on a strategic mix of active and torpid public policy to facilitate laundering while making appropriate noises about cracking down on launderers. Current Canadian immigration and taxation policies thus continue to encourage the influx of illicit funds even as Ottawa signs up for tighter global regulation and various provincial governments commission reports and surveys to check laundering. As I have argued elsewhere in more detail, the laundering industry does not flourish because laundering regulation is weak; regulation is weak *because* the industry is strong.[117] The political and economic benefits accruing from laundering obviate state desire to extinguish the phenomenon. And so, while laundering regulation is ostensibly strengthened in line with global trends, its efficacy is undercut by, first, what the state chooses to see as laundering, and second, by the network of other laws and regulations within the jurisdiction. For the Canadians hoping otherwise, the bad news is that snow washing is as Canadian as Beaver Tails and poutine, and as likely to persist.

---

116 Karissa Donkin & Frédéric Zalac, "Top-Secret Records Show New Brunswick, Alberta Companies Received Millions in Suspicious Transfers" *CBC News* (25 September 2020), online: www.cbc.ca/news/canada/new-brunswick/fincen-files-icij-nb-1.5734110?cmp=rss.

117 Sanaa Ahmed, "Running with the Hare, Hunting with the Hounds: The Canadian State and Money Laundering" in Christian Leuprecht, ed, *Canada: The State of the Federation 2022* (Montreal: McGill-Queen's University Press, forthcoming).

thirteen

Transnational Crime, Tainted Property, and Civil Forfeiture

MICHELLE GALLANT*

A. INTRODUCTION

Two related developments shape the modern control of transnational criminal phenomena. The first is the late twentieth, early twenty-first century forging of a transnational strategy centred on finance and the financial dimensions of crime. This strategy, embedded in modern treaties and other instruments of international reach, strives to disrupt connections between crime and financial activity. The second development, tied to the first, is the migration of civil processes, or of civil devices, onto this crime control terrain. Some migrations appear in transnational mechanisms; others in domestic regimes.[1]

Within these, a peculiar device, commonly identified as civil forfeiture, has received some degree of recognition. When the migration of regulation first gained traction, this device was virtually non-existent in transnational dialogues. It has latterly come to feature prominently in tackling criminal finance, and took root in Canada in 2001. This device is peculiar

* Professor of Law, University of Manitoba. A note of thanks to Steven Dressler for research assistance, to the Legal Research Institute, Manitoba, and to Robert Currie.

1 For example, the *United Nations Convention against Corruption*, (2003) 2349 UNTS 41, art 54(2) [*UNCAC*]; domestic models are discussed in Section C, below.

because it targets property, rather than people. Part of that peculiarity, too, is that it is a civil device imported into the domain of the criminal law.

This essay explores civil forfeiture and its centrality to combatting transnational crime. It charts the innovative transnational finance-centric approach, and considers civil forfeiture's location within global fora. It sketches the development of the use of civil forfeiture in other states and canvasses the central issues this kind of tool provokes. Shifting to the Canadian context, it delineates the generic architecture of provincial civil forfeiture regimes and discusses an intriguing aspect — the use of *in rem* proceedings — that serves, in particular, transnational ambitions. It concludes with an examination of the congruency of the provincial mechanisms with domestic constitutional ordering.

B. CONFRONTING TRANSNATIONAL CRIME: A MODERN MODEL

Finance has played a critical role in agitating and abetting crime for centuries. Few species of crime are bereft of some financial dimension — whether ancient piracy or contemporary insider trading and fraud on the financial markets. Nor is it novel to exercise circumspection in matters tainted by crime. Only a fool openly brandishes illicitly acquired wares, announces where the stolen treasure lies or shouts that the contents of a bank account are to secure the purchase of nuclear weaponry.

Within global circles, what was new in the twentieth century was the fashioning of strategic control initiatives centred on relationships between crime and finance. From the 1980s onwards, acknowledgement that finance agitates (and that secret finance abets) transnational crime has become a lynchpin of modern control. Contemporary commentary usually identifies this strategic intervention as the anti-money laundering strategy. More aptly, it could be described as a finance-centric approach to suppressing transnational criminal activity — whether proliferation, corruption, organized crime, terrorism, or drug trafficking. The strategy specifically attends to the financial aspects of crime, to the money derived therefrom, and to the financial activity associated therewith. The appeal to civil devices, and to civil forfeiture, emanates from this contemporary approach to criminal phenomena.

1) The Finance-Centric Model

Toxic correlations between finance and crime began to smoulder in World War II, as revelations about secret finance and the atrocities of Hitler's wartime Germany came to light.[2] Decades later, the purging of financial secrecy became a central plank of transnational initiatives. In the 1960s and the 1970s, the term *money laundering* became frequent in America and shaped the adoption of rules designed to pierce bank secrecy.[3] Global tax flight, secrecy, and crime started to generate some noise by the early 1980s.[4]

The formal foundation of finance-centric transnational governance happened in 1988, born out of a burgeoning and unrepentant global trade in illegal drugs. Up to that point, transnational intervention had principally sought to define the boundaries between the lawful and the unlawful trade in drugs, and to subject the latter to prohibitions and serious criminal sanctions.[5] Throughout the 1970s and 1980s, policy makers realized that this methodology had failed. Attention shifted to the profits of the drug trade—often measured in billion-dollar sums—and the belief that much of the drug money was hidden, or otherwise escaped capture.[6] In response to the toxicity of this money, the 1988 *United Nations Convention Against Illicit Traffic in Narcotic Drugs and Psychotropic Substances* ushered in a modern finance-centric approach to fighting the trade in illegal drugs.[7]

---

2 International Committee of Eminent Persons, *Report on Dormant Accounts of Victims of Nazi Persecutions in Swiss Banks* (1999), online: www.icep-iaep.org/press.-releases/980916sr.htm; Independent Commission of Experts Switzerland—Second World War, *Switzerland, National Socialism and the Second World War* (2002), online: www.uek.ch/en/.

3 One of the earliest efforts to deal with crime, criminal finance, and secrecy was the United States *Bank Secrecy Act* of 1970; see generally, US Treasury, "History of Anti-Money Laundering Laws," online: www.fincen.gov/history-anti-money-laundering-laws.

4 OECD, Committee on Fiscal Affairs, *Taxation and the Abuse of Bank Secrecy* (Paris: OECD, 1985); OECD, Committee on Fiscal Affairs, *International Tax Avoidance and Evasion: Four Related Studies* (Paris: OECD, 1987).

5 See generally, Syamal Kumar Chatterjee, *Legal Aspects of International Drug Control* (London: Martinus Nijhoff, 1981).

6 See generally, William C. Gilmore, "International Efforts to Combat Money Laundering" (1992) 18:3 *Commonwealth Law Bulletin* 1129.

7 *United Nations Convention Against Illicit Traffic in Narcotic Drugs and Psychotropic Substances*, (1988) 1582 UNTS 95, Can TS 1990 No 42.

Focused almost exclusively on the financial dimensions of crime, the 1988 convention mandated the criminalization of laundering the proceeds of drug offences and the confiscation, or forfeiture, of property connected to drug offences.[8] It also mandated machinery to detect and prevent the circulation of resources linked to drug crimes.[9] Once instituted, in the context of the global trade in illegal drugs, a finance-centric approach to transnational criminal phenomenon quickly became the norm. From 1988, a series of treaties expanded the finance-centric strategy. A 1999 convention on terrorism applied the strategy to terrorist financing.[10] A 2000 convention applied it to transnational organized crime.[11] A 2003 convention applied the strategy to corruption.[12]

Somewhat unorthodoxly, pieces of transnational finance-centric governance also came out of a series of United Nations Security Council resolutions.[13] In the immediate wake of September 2001, UNSC Resolution 1373 endorsed an assault on terrorist financing.[14] In the wake of news about an errant entrepreneur engaged in the development and sale of weapons of mass destruction, another series of UNSC resolutions mandated the finance-centric starving of proliferation.[15]

8 *Ibid*, art 5.

9 *Ibid*, art 19, s 2(b).

10 *International Convention on the Suppression of the Financing of Terrorism*, (1999) 2178 UNTS 197, Can TS 2002 No 9.

11 *United Nations Convention against Transnational Organized Crime*, (2000) 2225 UNTS 209 [*UNTOC*].

12 *UNCAC*, above note 1.

13 The unorthodoxy, in particular, relates to the focus on individuals, rather than on the state. Security Council resolutions conventionally speak to states, and of state conduct. Some of the content of these resolutions, by contrast, applies to individuals and appears to prescribe the content of state laws applicable to individuals. In some respects, the resolutions denote an exercise of unilateral international law making; see generally, Daniel H. Joyner, "Non-Proliferations Law and the United Nations System: Resolution 1540 and the Limits of the Security Council" (2007) 20:1 *Leiden Journal of International Law* 489; Bardo Fassbender, "Targeted Sanctions and Due Process" (20 March 2006) study commissioned by the UN Office of Legal Affairs, online: www.un.org/law/counsel/Fassbender_study.pdf; Andrea Bianchi, "Assessing the Effectiveness of the UN Security Council's Anti-Terrorism Measures: The Quest for Legitimacy and Cohesion" (2006) 17:5 *European Journal of International Law* 881.

14 *Threats to International Peace and Security Caused by Terrorist Acts*, UNSC Res 1373 (2001).

15 UNSC Res 1540 (2004); UNSC Res 1696 (2006). See also UNSC Res 1737 (2006); UNSC Res 1747 (2007); UNSC Res 1803 (2008); UNSC Res 1835 (2008); UNSC Res 1929 (2010); UNSC Res 2224 (2015).

The treaties and the UNSC actions established a strategy to combat transnational money laundering and terrorist financing. Patterned on their finance-centric thrust, copious initiatives—global, regional, governmental, and non-governmental—came to populate the modern crime discourse.[16] Broad and pervasive, this innovative modern finance-centric approach to criminal financing rests loosely on three primary pillars. The first is the criminalization of money laundering and the enactment of confiscation, or forfeiture, laws. Criminalization denotes the creation of offences related to the management, handling, or concealment of property derived from, or linked to, an underlying crime. Confiscation, or forfeiture, anticipates the taking or removal of property, principally described as proceeds, connected to crime. The second pillar consists of transnational norms attentive to money laundering prevention and detection. This is, by far, the most extensive aspect of the modern model, and is discussed elsewhere in this volume. It entails imposing obligations on financial institutions, financial actors, and industries to detect the presence of money and financial activity linked to crime as well as to prevent money laundering. The third pillar of the strategy countenances enhanced international coordination and the sharing of information related to the financial aspects of transnational crime.

2) Forfeiture Within the Transnational Strategy

Although this finance-centric strategy has evolved significantly since its initial inception in the context of the global drug trade, there is no consensus that civil forfeiture is, or ought to be, a part of the plan. The kind of confiscation, or forfeiture, of property generally contemplated under transnational norms is tightly tied to the criminal process. There is wide agreement that confiscation is triggered by a criminal conviction: the post-conviction, or conviction-related, seizure of criminal property.[17]

16 Examples of these initiatives include the work of the FATF and its creation of a set of money laundering, terrorist financing, and proliferation standards, online: www.fatf-gafi.org; the establishment of the Egmont Group composed of members of the financial investigative units of individual states, online: https://egmontgroup.org; and in connection with banks, money laundering governance initiatives mediated through the Basel Institute on Governance, online: https://baselgovernance.org/basel-aml-index.

17 Council of Europe, *Impact Study on Civil Forfeiture* (2013) at 12–13 [*Impact Study on Civil Forfeiture*].

However, there is a civil flavour, or a civil ingredient that can be added. In a post-conviction context, states can consider adopting requirements that an offender must demonstrate the lawful origins of property, rather than placing that burden on the state.[18] The civil piece, or the non-criminal piece, is the anticipation that once a crime is proven, a civil burden of proof shifts to an offender to demonstrate lawful provenance in order to preclude the confiscation of criminal resources.

While they do not often make it obligatory, transnational instruments do signal some approval of a civil approach to criminal property. In the context of the transnational dimensions of corruption, there is clear encouragement to consider permitting non-conviction based confiscation in discrete circumstances.[19] Some collective projects sanction, or tentatively sanction, these kinds of civil processes.[20] An authoritative set of international money laundering, terrorist financing, and proliferation standards invites states to consider adopting laws which enable resources linked to transnational crime to be confiscated without any related criminal conviction.[21] Tellingly perhaps, a 2016 review of Canadian compliance with the transnational finance-centric approach commented favourably on the existence of non-conviction based provincial civil forfeiture regimes.[22]

The posture of gentle encouragement, short of an obligatory element of regulation, ought not to surprise. To be sure, the complex fabric that underlies the making of transnational norms tends to preclude civil mechanisms. There is a shared global sense that while tools can be sharpened to deal with the financial element of crime, those tools ought to be drawn from the criminal law. Civil forfeiture, or any other non-conviction-based

18 *UNTOC*, above note 11, art 12(7).

19 *UNCAC*, above note 1, art 54(1).

20 *Impact Study on Civil Forfeiture*, above note 17 at 27–29.

21 See FATF, *International Standards on Combating Money Laundering and the Financing of Terrorism & Proliferation* (2012, as amended), Recommendation 4, online: www.fatf-gafi.org/en/publications/Fatfrecommendations/Fatf-recommendations.html.

22 FATF, "Anti-Money Laundering and Counter-Terrorist Financing Measures — Canada" (September 2016), online: www.fatf-gafi.org/en/publications/Mutualevaluations/Mer-canada-2016.html. Recently, however, the Cullen Commission's final report pointedly said that efforts under British Columbia's forfeiture regime were inadequate, noting that the number and value of the assets seized were "shockingly low" (Commission of Inquiry into Money Laundering in British Columbia, *Cullen Commission Final Report: Executive Summary* (2022), online: https://cullencommission.ca/com-rep.

mechanism, is not a criminal mechanism. It is different: it permits forfeitures completely outside of a criminal process. Notably, even within jurisdictions that have implemented a civil method, those methods cause tension because of their application to criminal contexts.

Rather than being a feature in transnational frameworks, civil regulation tends to emerge from domestic legal orders. Canada's embrace of civil devices in 2001 is part of an amplifying global movement. Many states have decided that civil devices are simply good policy.

C. A TERSE CANVASSING OF CIVIL MECHANISMS IN DOMESTIC LAW

When transnational finance-centric developments began to emerge in the late 1980s, few states apart from the United States had laws that authorized the taking of property connected to crime through a civil device.[23] Although there has not been a groundswell since then, there has been some proliferation, particularly in western democracies. Ireland, prompted in part by the strange murder of a journalist whose investigations centred on organized crime and the drug trade, adopted a civil approach to criminal money in the mid-1990s.[24] A few years later, the United Kingdom created civil approaches for its internal jurisdictions.[25] South Africa endorsed civil regulation in 1998.[26] Malaysia, as part of a comprehensive money laundering and terrorist finance law, opted for a similar path.[27] New Zealand has created civil processes.[28] Australia has both federal and state level non-conviction-based takings.[29]

---

23 Civil forfeiture has long been a part of US law. Legislators began to craft modern regimes centred on the civil taking of property in the 1980s. Caleb Nelson, "The Constitutionality of Civil Forfeiture" (2016) 125:8 *Yale Law Journal* 2446 at 2457–82; Daniel Reed, "The Next Step in Civil Asset Forfeiture Reform: Passing the Civil Asset Forfeiture Reform Act of 2014" (2016) 66:4 *Catholic University Law Review* 933 at 935–41.

24 *Proceeds of Crime Act* (Ireland), 1996, No 30.

25 *Proceeds of Crime Act 2002* (UK), c 29.

26 *Prevention of Organised Crime Act* (S Afr), No 121 of 1998.

27 *Anti-Money Laundering, Anti-Terrorism Financing and Proceeds of Unlawful Activities Act* (Malaysia), 2001, Act A1208. For discussion see Anusha Aurasu & Aspalella A. Rahman, "Money Laundering and Civil Forfeiture Regime: Malaysian Experience" (2016) 19:4 *Journal of Money Laundering Control* 337.

28 *Criminal Proceeds (Recovery) Act 2009* (NZ), 2009/8.

29 *Proceeds of Crime Act* (Cth), 2002; *Criminal Assets Recovery Act 1990* (NSW).

Without investigating the multiple permutations of this crescive cluster, there are some themes that, regardless of geographic location, tend to be common in narratives about civil mechanisms in the context of criminal finance. An obvious generic one, consistent with transnational developments and prevalent in all jurisdictions, is the imperative to find new ways to deal more effectively with the prosperity of crime.[30] While conviction-based apparatuses have their place, more potent tools are needed. Drug trafficking and corruption, with concomitant flow of proceeds into money laundering, lend themselves to the use of civil tools.

A second theme can be seen in the explanations and justifications that are given for choosing to depart from, or add to, a classic approach that is based on prosecutions and the securing of a criminal conviction. One recurrent explanation is clearly instrumental; that it is difficult to secure convictions of the principal orchestrators of crime and of those who receive the bulk of the profits.[31] They are too far removed from the crimes, and prosecutions only capture the criminal minions. A civil approach, focused on tainted property, is a more direct way of attacking the principal financial beneficiaries of criminal conduct.

A second justification alludes to compensation for the victims of crime. This victim-related rationale contends that civil regimes assert the collective rights of the victims of crime to be compensated for injuries

---

30 The 2021 proposals to introduce new powers in Northern Ireland reflect this theme. See "Long: Removing Profits an Important Tool in the Fight Against Organized Crime" (8 June 2021) Department of Justice (Northern Ireland), Press Office release, online: www.justice-ni.gov.uk/news/long-removing-profits-important-tool-fight-against-organised-crime.

31 Colin King, "Civil Forfeiture and Article 6 of the ECHR: Due Process Implications for England & Wales and Ireland" (2014) 34:3 *Legal Studies* 371 at 372–73 [King]. A 2009 Australian report makes this plain: "The committee acknowledges that unexplained wealth orders are a departure from the traditional approach to the proceeds of crime which requires a person to be convicted of a criminal offence before the proceeds may be confiscated. However, the committee heard throughout this inquiry about the increasing sophistication and transnational nature of serious and organized crime groups. The directors of modern organized crime have sophisticated and dynamic methods of avoiding the law. They are well-informed and well-resourced. The committee is therefore convinced that such a departure from traditional approaches to confiscating the proceeds of crime is necessary and defensible." Australia, Commonwealth, Parliamentary Joint Committee on Australian Crime Commission, *Inquiry into Legislative Arrangements to Outlaw Serious and Organized Crime Groups* (2009), ch 5, para 5.138.

occasioned by criminality. This is sometimes framed in reference to reparative justice, in that the civil takings promise, not to punish crime, but to fix the damages that crime causes.[32] A third common explanation for using civil devices is a broad plaintive appeal to the idea that law ought not to protect entitlements to criminal earnings or that a person ought not be able to profit from crime.[33]

Perhaps the most important theme is that constitutional and rights-based challenges to civil mechanisms do not generally appear to achieve much success. The mechanisms usually attract controversy for the fusion of a civil process with allegations of crime. Most complaints related to legality and the rule of law urge that civil mechanisms targeting criminal behaviour ought to comply with the rules of criminal engagement. Although the particularities differ in the various jurisdictions, all jurisdictions acknowledge differences between criminal actions and civil, or administrative, actions. Challenges to civil machinery centre on the presumption of innocence and the tantamount protection of a higher standard of proof in criminal proceedings, or the protection against double jeopardy, or the re-litigation of the same matter in a civil action previously litigated (and favourably determined for a defendant) in a criminal prosecution. The lines of contention revolve around distinctions between criminal sanctions and penal or punitive matters, and civil process and civil matters. Generally, in entertaining complaints of this ilk, the courts in the various states have held that civil tools align with constitutional, or rights-based, protections.[34] The overall stance is that, while allegations of

---

32 King, *ibid* at 374.

33 *Ibid* at 375.

34 *Gale and another v Serious Organized Crime Agency*, [2011] UKSC 49 (a prior acquittal on criminal charges did not preclude a civil action); *Gilligan v Criminal Assets Bureau*, 2001, IESC; *Gilligan v Ireland* (2001), ECHR 095 (2021) (a lengthy delay in proceedings did not violate art 6 right to be tried within a reasonable time); *United States v Ursery*, 116 S Ct. 2135 (1996) [*Ursery*] (double jeopardy does not bar a subsequent civil forfeiture action); *National Director of Public Prosecutions v Phillips and Others*, [2002] 4 SA 60 (W) (a civil taking is not a criminal proceeding so as to attract the right to a fair trial); *National Director of Public Prosecutions v Botha*, [2020] ZACC 6 (Constitutional Court of South Africa) (property rights are not violated); *Marwood v Commissioner of Police*, [2016] NZSC 139 (evidence excluded by an unlawful search from criminal proceedings could be considered in a civil forfeiture action). But see, *Austin v United States*, 509 US 602 (1993) [*Austin*] (civil forfeiture subject to the constitutional constraint against excessive fines) and *GIEM SRL and Others v Italy* (2018), ECHR June 2018 (no violation of art 7, punishment

criminal wrongdoing underpin the actions to recover property, that is not by itself sufficient to require the application of criminal legal rights or to cast doubt on the legitimacy of the civil forfeiture instruments.

Of course, as noted above, civil tools, or civil forfeiture-like regimes, are relatively novel. They are a newer method of tackling the financial aspects of crime. Aspects of their legitimacy continue to be vetted. Still, the civil approach is popular and generally—although tentatively—perceived to cohere with constitutional, or rights-based, protections.

D. CIVIL FORFEITURE IN CANADA

In integrating the finance-centric transnational approach, Canadian federal criminal law provides for the post-conviction forfeiture of criminal property.[35] Additionally, in a non-criminal context pertaining to criminal offences, federal law envisions a non-conviction-based taking. Here, the forfeiture relates to the failure to comply with federal laws that require the declaration of the export of property in excess of certain thresholds.[36] The failure to declare is not itself a crime.

Where civil forfeiture finds a home in Canada in connection with criminal finance is in provincial law. In 2001, Ontario introduced civil forfeiture regulation.[37] Many provincial legislators followed suit: Alberta

---

without law, but breaches of art 6, right to fair trial, and art 1 of Protocol 1 to the EHRC, property rights. This case involved land development rather than drugs, organized crime, or corruption). Campbell points out that the best that might be promised would be the recognition of some middle ground which encompasses some rights, but still operates in the civil sphere. See Liz Campbell, "The Recovery of 'Criminal' Assets in New Zealand, Ireland, and England: Fighting Organized and Serious Crime in the Civil Realm" (2010) 41:1 *Victoria University of Wellington Law Review* 15. See also *Komisia za protivodeystvie v BP and ors*, C-234/18, [2020] Judgement of the Court of Justice of the European Union (holding that EU conviction-based confiscation law did not preclude Member States from enacting civil, or non-conviction-based, regimes).

35 *Criminal Code*, RSC 1985, c C-46, s 462.37 [*Code*]. An exception is federal non-conviction taking in regard to absconders. See *Code*, s 462.38 (although the standard that applies is proof beyond a reasonable doubt that the property was obtained through crime).

36 *Proceeds of Crime (Money Laundering) and Terrorist Financing Act*, SC 2000, c 17, ss 18, 25. See generally, *Tourki v Canada (Minister of Public Safety and Emergency Preparedness)*, 2006 FC 50.

37 *Civil Remedies Act*, SO 2001, c 28 [*CRA*].

in 2001; British Columbia in 2005; Manitoba in 2004; New Brunswick in 2010; Nova Scotia in 2007; Quebec in 2007; and the province of Saskatchewan in 2009.[38] In Yukon, vociferous debate shuttered explorations of a civil mechanism.[39] The other provinces, and the other Canadian territories, have not adopted civil devices.

1) Provincial Instruments

There is no pan-Canadian civil forfeiture model. In terms of constitutional interplay and other aspects of the domestic rule of law, distinctions amongst discrete regimes can obviously matter greatly. However, the provincial regimes are, in species, substantively similar. They share a number of central attributes, five of which are discussed here.

First, the provincial statutes typically enable two actions: (1) the forfeiture of the proceeds of unlawful activity, and (2) the forfeiture of instruments of unlawful activity.[40] *Unlawful activity* denotes offences under both federal law and provincial enactments, as well as offences occurring in foreign jurisdictions when Canadian law recognizes the same.[41] *Proceeds* generally refers to property acquired, directly or indirectly, from unlawful activity.[42] *Instruments* generally denotes property that has been used, or is likely to be used, to engage in unlawful activity that, in turn (1) resulted in, or was likely to result in, the acquisition of property; or (2) caused, or was likely to cause, serious bodily harm to a person.[43] This action is sometimes called the instrumentalities provision.

Second, the civil standard of proof, the balance of probabilities standard, governs the forfeiture process.[44] The commission of some offence

---

38 *Civil Forfeiture Act*, SA 2001, C-15.2 (Alberta); *Civil Forfeiture Act*, SBC 2005, c 29 [*CFA*, BC]; *Criminal Property Forfeiture Act*, SM 2004, CCSM c C306 (Manitoba); *Civil Forfeiture Act*, SNB 2010, c C-4.5 (New Brunswick); *Civil Forfeiture Act*, SNS 2007, c 27 (Nova Scotia); *Act respecting the forfeiture, administration and appropriation of the proceeds and instruments of unlawful activity*, CQLR c C-52.2 (Quebec); *Seizure of Criminal Property Act*, SS 2009, c S-46.002 (Saskatchewan).

39 "Yukon Shelves Civil Forfeiture Act" *CBC News* (26 October 2010), online: www.cbc.ca/news/canada/north/yukon-shelves-civil-forfeiture-act-1.902180.

40 See, for example, *CRA*, above note 37, s 1.1.

41 *Ibid.*

42 *Ibid.*

43 *Ibid.*

44 *Ibid*, s 16.

relating to property (usually not a specific offence) must be proven in accordance with the civil standard. Axiomatically, no offence in relation to the property need be proven beyond a reasonable doubt, which is the conventional criminal legal standard of proof.

Third, the nature of the proceedings is identified as *in rem*.[45] It is unusual for any legal regime to specifically identify a particular nature. *In personam* proceedings, or an *in personam* nature is the standard character of legal process. It is assumed, rather than stated, that legal process, whether civil or criminal, anticipates the determination of the liability of the individual, the person. In the common law tradition, *in rem* is a legal fiction that connotes the liability of the thing, the *res*, the property. Commensurately, under provincial forfeiture law, it is the criminal property that is the subject of the action. The standard of proof and the specific nature formally imprint forfeiture as a civil legal mechanism. The idea that property can be held criminally liable is an anathema; it cannot be jailed, can suffer no criminal ignominy, and cannot be punished. Rather, it can only be forfeited, through a legal process.

A fourth shared component is the provision of some relief against forfeiture. Once a link to an offence is proven, the court must order forfeiture of the property.[46] One element of relief is judicial discretion to refuse forfeiture if it is not in the "interests of justice."[47] Relief is also typically offered in connection with "innocent" property owners.[48] This generally anticipates situations where the owners of the relevant property may not have any connection with underlying crime or who have positively sought to prevent any misuse of their property.

The fifth common feature is the designation that property secured under the regime be deployed, in part, to serve the interests of the victims

---

45 *Ibid*, s 15.01.

46 *CFA*, BC, above note 38, s 5.

47 *Ibid*, s 6(1).

48 *Ibid*, s 6(2). These provisions generally protect persons who owned property that someone else used in the commission of a crime, or persons who paid fair value for property, not having knowledge of its connection to criminal activity. In the context of a forfeiture of the instruments of crime, Ontario law imposes a positive duty on property owners. To preclude forfeiture, a "responsible owner" must have done all one reasonably could to prevent property being used to engage in unlawful activity. See *CRA*, above note 37, s 7(1).

of crime.[49] The provincial machinery typically contemplates the creation of a pool of resources to compensate the victims and to defray the social and other consequences of criminal activity. In this, forfeit property is kept separate and apart from provincial treasuries.

There are granular differences amongst the provincial forfeiture devices, as well as other commonalities. These five elements form the bedrock of provincial civil forfeiture law.

Again, and similarly to foreign mechanisms, provincial law permits property tainted by crime to be taken without a criminal conviction. Dispensing with convictions dispenses with the exigencies of a prosecutorial process. This averts the application of any higher order of rights, or entitlements, to procedural or substantive justice that a criminal prosecution would import. As elsewhere, dispensing with criminal convictions provokes complaints that mechanisms of this type violate constitutional norms.

Before canvassing the status of domestic law, some account needs to be taken of the explicit provincial countenancing of the proceedings having an *in rem* nature. That designation, a reflection of the focus on property rather than individuals, points to a particular transnational lineage. In a sense, it makes the provincial device an acutely barbed global weapon in the context of transnational crime.

2) The Relevance of *in rem* to Transnational Regulation

The transnational finance-centric approach accounts for the fact that crime, particularly serious crime, can defy state control. Crime—whether trade in destructive weaponry, trade in illegal drugs, or corruption—thrives on money and property that travels the globe. Modern law seeks to confront the property-based aspects of transnational crime on its own terrain, the porous global environment. Local regimes ordinarily have difficulty

49 Ontario law, for instance, creates a special purpose account from which payments may be made to compensate the victims of crime. See *CRA*, above note 37, s 1.9. Manitoba, which recently announced plans to expand its Criminal Property Forfeiture unit, sequesters assets seized into a fund for victims of crime, crime prevention generally, and purchase of law enforcement equipment, *inter alia*; see Katrina Eñano, "Manitoba expands Criminal Property Forfeiture unit to combat money laundering," *Canadian Lawyer* (18 August 2022), online: www.canadianlawyermag.com/practice-areas/criminal/manitoba-expands-criminal-property-forfeiture-unit-to-combat-money-laundering/369119.

coping. Switzerland's post–World War II posture on financial matters impeded external efforts to recover property linked to Germany. America cannot seize drug revenues, derived from US purchasers, once they settle in Colombian bank accounts. Once the profits of one corrupt regime flee state boundaries, they lie beyond the reach of an ascendant political order interested in their recovery.

In tackling criminal finance, the property-based piece of transnational crime, *in rem*, or the provincial reference to an *in rem* nature, incorporates an ancestry of transnational governance in the context of the high seas. In that context, legal genealogy acknowledges its functional utility within that early international environment. Reliance on *in rem* was practical, a means of asserting authority in order to hold foreign property owners to account before local admiralty courts.

The grounding of legal authority on the seizure of ships, the *res* (i.e., the property) has historically served as a practical approach to governance in maritime law. Seizing and holding vessels upon their arrival at domestic ports has long secured the exercise of authority in relation to events occurring on the high seas. The attaching of jurisdiction to, and attaching of liability to, vessels is part of the canon, with *in rem* precisely serving transnational governance.[50] It continues to exist as a cornerstone of domestic authority.[51]

In rem copes with foreign dimensions. Vessels arriving at domestic ports of entry were often under foreign ownership, the particular parties responsible for some incident or breach of customs law neither resident, nor present, within the state. *In rem* jurisdiction, or the concomitant concept of *in rem* liability, secures the delivery of justice in a setting fraught with foreign complications. Short of attaching governance to vessels, or to cargo off-loaded from vessels, foreign owners would otherwise enjoy immunity from local law. Provincial forfeiture law draws upon this lineage, putting an old concept into a modern project.

Notably, the statutory regimes define unlawful activity, not only in relation to domestic law, but as inclusive of foreign offences that have domestic parallels. Developments seek to capture criminal property, regardless of where the offences happen. Under the provincial regimes,

50 *An Act for increase of Shipping and Encouragement of the Navigation of this Nation 1651* (UK), 2 Cha II; *An Act for the Encouraging and increasing of Shipping and Navigation 1660* (UK), 12 Cha II, c 18.

51 See *Federal Courts Act*, RSC 1985, c F-7, s 22.

the only piece of any transnational crime that need settle in the province is the property, the *res*. This makes it an extremely effective device in the borderless world of crime.

Anchorage within this admiralty and customs law tradition shapes US analysis of modern civil forfeiture regulation. Tracts of jurisprudence held that admiralty- and customs-related forfeiture was a civil, not a criminal, proceeding.[52] Reliance on this established body of law influenced Supreme Court decisions about the nature of modern regimes, and whether they attracted constitutional protections aligned with criminal matters.[53] Part of the United States' interpretive pattern involved consideration of the "legal property fiction," the idea that civil forfeiture, focusing on the *res*, relied upon some fictitious notions that property could commit a wrong.[54]

Canadian jurisprudence, for its part, does not insist that the idea of *in rem* denotes some fictitious sense that property was responsible for any species of wrongdoing. Maritime law maintains that any responsibility for wrongdoing lies not with the property itself, but with the property owners.[55] *In rem* liability, or the *in rem* jurisdiction of the courts, was a functional method of securing justice, of holding foreign owners, or foreign orchestrators of some wrong, legally responsible. It does not displace the responsibility of the owners of that property.

This lineage demonstrates *in rem*'s central utility in governing transnational phenomenon. Property-based regulation has a history of service to transnational governance. Within that setting, it is an extremely useful tool.

3) Civil Forfeiture and the Canadian Constitution

In *Chatterjee v The Attorney General of Canada*, the Supreme Court of Canada considered the constitutionality of provincial civil forfeiture when a property claimant alleged that the statutory machinery encroached on federal competence over the criminal law and was *ultra vires* provincial

52 *Austin*, above note 34 at 613–19; *Ursery*, above note 34 at 274–78.

53 See, for example, *Calero-Toledo v Pearson Yacht Leasing Co*, 416 US 663 (1974); *United States v One Assortment of 89 Firearms*, 465 US 354 (1984); *Austin*, above note 34; *Ursery*, above note 34.

54 *Austin*, above note 34 at 615.

55 *Goodwin Johnson Limited v The Ship, et al*, [1954] SCR 513.

powers.[56] Under Canada's Constitution, the boundaries between the civil and criminal law are important, from the perspective of federalism, and in connection with the application of *Charter* rights, particularly section 11 criminal legal rights. The decision validated the provincial mechanism as a legitimate *intra vires* exercise of authority in relation to property and civil rights.

In *Chatterjee*, the Court was asked whether Ontario's civil forfeiture regime, the *Civil Remedies Act*, lay within provincial constitutional jurisdiction.[57] Ontario police stopped and searched a vehicle on a suspected traffic violation. The search disclosed cash and drug-related paraphernalia. The cash, some C$29,000, was seized and forfeited. A claimant, Chatterjee, alleged that the Ontario Act infringed the federal government's exclusive constitutional jurisdiction to make criminal law, particularly in relation to forfeiture and federal offences.

Applying established analytic methodology, the Court investigated the substance and dominant purpose of the provincial statute, in order to assign it to a discrete constitutional category. Both levels of government have responsibilities to deter and suppress criminal activity. Crime imposes significant costs on society, many of which are borne by the provinces. The dominant purpose of civil forfeiture is to allay the costs of crime, to render crime unprofitable, and to compensate the victims of crime. However, nothing in the law, according to the Court, went beyond "the redistribution of property tainted by crime" nor did forfeiture "result in the conviction of anyone for any offence."[58] The regime fell within provincial competence with respect to property and civil rights. The underlying provincial concern was the "deleterious effects of crime in general rather than a colourable way to tack a penalty onto the federal sentencing process."[59]

Throughout its analysis, the Court recognized the duality of certain constitutional matters, the presence of both federal and provincial aspects. While acknowledging some overlap between provincial civil forfeiture and federal criminal law powers, it accepted that the regime in relation

56 *Chatterjee v Ontario (Attorney General)*, 2009 SCC 19 [*Chatterjee*]. Arguments regarding the *Canadian Charter of Rights and Freedoms*, Part 1 of the *Constitution Act, 1982*, being Schedule B to the *Canada Act 1982* (UK), 1982, c 11 [*Charter*] were raised in the lower court but abandoned on appeal.

57 *Ibid.*

58 *Ibid* at 640.

59 *Ibid* at 641.

to property and civil rights could function without "doing violence to the division of powers."[60] Provided a measure designed to mitigate the effects of criminality and criminal finance did not compromise the functioning of the criminal law, the overlap did not rend constitutional boundaries. More directly, in the context of the specific case at issue, the civil forfeiture of the proceeds of crime did not interfere with the federal sentencing process. Other remedies might avail in a different context, perhaps a civil forfeiture action brought subsequent to a failed federal criminal forfeiture action. But that was not the case in this instance.

Although discussed within the rubric of federalism rather than in consonance with rights-based norms, the Supreme Court decision reflects the general disposition of comparative foreign jurisprudence. It confirms that the provincial power to forfeit the proceeds of crime is not sufficiently criminal in character to usurp federal competence in matters of criminal law. This anointing, however, ought to be approached with some caution. *Chatterjee* addressed the constitutionality of the provincial power to forfeit the proceeds of crime. It did not deal at all with the provincial power to forfeit the instruments of crime.

Transnational and local dialogues on criminal finance speak powerfully of the need to confront the profitability of crime, to capture the money derived from criminal pursuits. Seizing profits resonates with elementary justice ideals: no one ought to rest comfortably with property derived from crime. The Supreme Court decision speaks of the proceeds of unlawful activity, in an action brought against C$29,000 allegedly derived from crime.

Constitutional infringements may, however, be found with respect to the instruments provision of the provincial schemes. A lower court decision recently held that the power to forfeit the instruments of crime on the basis of their prospective use was unconstitutional.[61] This particular case formed part of protracted battles with organized crime and the attempt to capture a clubhouse allegedly used to orchestrate criminal activity. The court determined that the "future use" provisions were based on an individual's propensity to commit crime.[62] In this, the provision either created a new offence based on a "propensity to commit crime" or penalized an

60 *Ibid* at 645.

61 *British Columbia (Director of Civil Forfeiture) v Angel Acres Recreation and Festival Property Ltd*, 2020 BCSC 880.

62 *Ibid* at paras 1487–97.

act that had been previously punished, either of which intruded onto the exclusive jurisdiction of the federal legislature over the criminal law.

Relatedly, a difficulty with the instrument provisions of provincial forfeiture mechanisms is that they are not tailored to the proceeds of crime. British Columbia law, for example, defines the instruments of unlawful activity to include property that has been used to engage in unlawful activity that, in turn, caused, or was likely to cause, serious bodily harm.[63] Nothing therein correlates with an assault on criminal finance. Part of what shapes the tenability of the assault on criminal financing is the idea that it is a proportionate response. The taking of the proceeds of crime, or in provincial language, the proceeds of unlawful activity, is inherently proportionate to any underlying crime; it equates to the very sum of criminal earnings.[64]

Disturbingly, an action brought to forfeit the instruments of crime could produce vast disproportionality. An expensive house could be the location of a serious assault, the *situs* of the crime constituting an "instrument" of unlawful activity. The forfeiture of that house would not necessarily be, in any way, shape, or form, proportionate to the underlying offence. Again, the *Chatterjee* decision examined an action to forfeit the proceeds of unlawful activity, not the instrumentalities provision of the Ontario Act. A disproportionate taking is apt to trigger a challenge to compliance with section 11 *Charter* rights. Regardless of what a particular proceeding might be formally called—whether civil, administrative, or disciplinary—it can, in substance, invoke the section 11 rights applicable to someone charged with a criminal offence.[65] It is misleading to say that *in rem* property-based actions do not implicate the rights of individuals. The provincial regimes admit as much by proffering relief for innocent property owners. No one seriously countenances the argument that the forfeiture of property does not affect individuals. Gross disproportionality

---

63 *CFA*, BC, above note 38, s 1(1).

64 There are debates about whether the proceeds of crime are the same as the profits of crime, and whether there is any need to acknowledge or draw distinctions. See *United States v Santos*, 553 US 507 (2008).

65 See *R v Wigglesworth*, [1987] 2 SCR 541.

between the value of an instrumentality and any underlying crime would likely prompt a different response from the Supreme Court of Canada.[66]

E. CONCLUSION

The transnational finance-centric strategy represents a new model of crime suppression. The need to counter the financial elements of crime is acknowledged. New tools are, for the most part, tools of the criminal law: they are firmly rooted in conventional understandings of the procedural and substantive protections that govern criminal proceedings.

However, civil mechanisms are not disavowed by transnational discourse: they have a place within the modern financially focused strategy. They are increasingly popular, in domestic law, as devices with which to tackle criminal property. While such civil tools must obviously align with constitutional and rights-based protections, they play a critical role in confronting the financial products that undergird transnational crime.

66 The courts appear to be using the discretionary relief under the "interests of justice" provision of provincial laws to refuse forfeiture when it is disproportionate, or not substantively or significantly connected, to an underlying offence. See, for example, *Ontario (Attorney General) v 1140 Aubin Road, Windsor and 3142 Halpin Road, Windsor (In Rem)*, 2011 ONCA 363; *Ontario (Attorney General) v 20 Strike Avenue*, 2014 ONCA 395; *British Columbia (Director of Civil Forfeiture) v Rai*, 2011 BCSC 186; *British Columbia (Director of Civil Forfeiture) v Wolff*, 2012 BCCA 473.

fourteen

Negotiating Transnational Corporate Criminality

JOANNA HARRINGTON*

A. INTRODUCTION

In today's world of global economic interdependence, corporate activity easily crosses national borders, as may the corporate commission of serious crime. In theory, a body corporate, whether a partnership, firm, or company, can commit all sorts of crimes, with the legal fiction that a corporation is a person having long attracted support.[1] In practice, there is a focus on crimes of a financial or economic nature that have a connection to business, such as fraud and false accounting, or tax evasion, price fixing, and insider trading. Corruption is also a key concern, with bribery having become the standard criminal charge for addressing corruption through the offering of an undue reward to influence the behaviour of a public

---

* Professor and Eldon Foote Chair in International Business and Law, Faculty of Law, University of Alberta.

1 In Canada, s 2 of the *Criminal Code*, RSC 1985, c C-46, as amended, defines "every one, person and owner" to "include ... an organization," which is defined to include "a body corporate," "firm," and "company." See also Bryant Smith, "Legal Personality" (1928) 37:3 *Yale Law Journal* 283 at 289: "Whenever society, in the administration of justice sees fit to disregard the individual members of an organization for a particular purpose, and for that purpose to look upon the organization as a unit, the organization to that extent or for that purpose becomes a legal person. This is true even where the group is organized as a partnership or other unincorporated association."

office holder.[2] As business transactions crossed borders, so too did crimes such as bribery, leading to the adoption first of US legislation,[3] and then of international treaties, to stimulate a shared transnational effort to criminalize and suppress the bribery of foreign public officials.[4] So successful has this effort been to include the commission of corruption and foreign bribery within the corpus of transnational criminal law that the leading treaty now attracts 189 states parties.[5] This treaty also covers embezzlement, the misappropriation of public funds, and trading in influence.

A corporation, however, is not your usual criminal defendant, with this truism necessitating different expectations of the criminal justice process. One obvious reality is that a corporation cannot go to jail. This means that the main punishment option for an organizational offender is a financial sanction, which may be comprised of fines or penalties, orders for confiscation and the disgorgement of profits, and possibly a compensation order for victims, or a requirement to pay the investigation and prosecution costs. To serve as a deterrent, the financial sanction must be of a degree that has an economic consequence, with past practice indicating that the fines can be steep, particularly in the foreign corruption context, where corporate defendants have been required to pay fines of many millions of dollars. Such fines do not, however, guarantee that there will be individual criminal accountability, prompting criticism that corporate criminal accountability can serve to shield the individuals involved from prosecution.

With a monetary penalty as the means for securing corporate criminal accountability, pragmatism would suggest that most corporate criminal

2 See further Monty Raphael, *Bribery: Law and Practice* (Oxford: Oxford University Press, 2016) at 2.15–2.27. See also Kevin E. Davis, *Between Impunity and Imperialism: The Regulation of Transnational Bribery* (Oxford: Oxford University Press, 2019).

3 *Foreign Corrupt Practices Act* (United States), 15 USC §§78dd-1 *et seq*. See further, Mike Koehler, "The Story of the Foreign Corrupt Practices Act" (2012) 73:5 *Ohio State Law Journal* 929.

4 See, for example, the *Convention on Combating Bribery of Foreign Public Officials in International Business Transactions*, 17 December 1997, OECD Doc DAFFE/IME/BR(97)20 (1997), 37 ILM 1 (1998), Can TS 1999 No 23 (entered into force 15 February 1999, ratified by Canada 7 December 1998) [*OECD Anti-Bribery Convention*]. On Canada's implementation efforts, see Joanna Harrington, "Addressing the Corruption of Foreign Public Officials: Developments and Challenges within the Canadian Legal Landscape" (2018) 56 *The Canadian Yearbook of International Law* 98 [Harrington 2018].

5 *United Nations Convention Against Corruption*, (2003) 2349 UNTS 41, Can TS 2007 No 7 (entered into force 14 December 2005, ratified by Canada 2 October 2007).

cases should be resolved by way of a deal. Indeed, research undertaken for the International Bar Association from 2016–18 indicates a global trend toward the enforcement of corruption cases using means outside the traditional criminal trial process, even in jurisdictions where settlements are ostensibly not allowed.[6] A subsequent study of the practices of twenty-seven countries (including Canada) under the *OECD Anti-Bribery Convention*[7] further confirms that settlement agreements have become the main means for resolving foreign bribery cases, with 78 percent of prosecutions in the past twenty years resolved without a full trial on the merits.[8] The complexity of corporate crime, and the difficulties faced by prosecutors in obtaining evidence of acts intended to be kept secret, further favours the use of settlements, with negotiations as to the amount of the financial penalty providing an opportunity (or leverage) to incentivize a company to cooperate with law enforcement authorities. This cooperation may also assist with the bringing of criminal proceedings against the company's officers, directors, or employees for the same criminal conduct.

But unlike with human defendants, a prosecutor may also need to consider a corporation's value to the economy and wider society, particularly where a prosecution would have significant repercussions for third parties, such as employees and suppliers, and where a conviction would debar a company from securing future work.[9] To this end, a negotiated settlement need not involve a guilty plea, nor a trial, with prosecutors developing ways to allow a company to avoid a conviction in return for a robust cleaning of house and the internal reform of its business practices. The business community also appears supportive of this shift in approach; many Canadians are likely aware that the engineering and construction giant, the SNC-Lavalin Group, was a vocal supporter for the creation in

6 Abiola Makinwa & Tina Søreide, eds, *Structured Settlements for Corruption Offences: Towards Global Standards?* (London: IBA Anti-Corruption Committee: Structured Criminal Settlements Subcommittee, 2018), online: www.oecd.org/corruption/anti-bribery/IBA-Structured-Settlements-Report-2018.pdf.

7 *OECD Anti-Bribery Convention*, above note 4.

8 *Resolving Foreign Bribery Cases with Non-Trial Resolutions: Settlements and Non-Trial Agreements by Parties to the Anti-Bribery Convention* (Paris: OECD, 2019) at 13 [*OECD Study*], online: www.oecd.org/corruption/Resolving-Foreign-Bribery-Cases-with-Non-Trial-Resolutions.htm.

9 Many countries have debarment laws or policies, as noted in United Kingdom, House of Lords, Select Committee on the Bribery Act 2010, *The Bribery Act 2010: Post-legislative Scrutiny* (HL Paper 303) (March 2019) at para 248.

Canada of a non-trial resolution mechanism (admittedly, and unfortunately for the cause, while it was facing a charge of foreign bribery).[10]

With transnational criminal law having expanded to include transnational organizational criminality, and most corporate crime prosecutions resolved through negotiated deals, there has also been a significant transnational diffusion of prosecutorial practice. The recent introduction of a Canadian remediation agreement regime provides an example,[11] with the prospects for its use inspired by a lengthy record of US practice that has led to innovations in both France and Britain, which find resonance in the Canadian approach (as discussed below).[12] Cooperation between the authorities in all three states is not only supporting the suppression of the corporate commission of serious economic crime, but these cross-border links also lead to the cross-pollination of ideas for avoiding the risks and costs of lengthy trials. In addition, the remediation agreement, more widely known as a deferred prosecution agreement or DPA, has itself become a transnational tool in the fight against corruption. For example, the failure of Airbus SE to prevent an extensive bribery scheme across multiple jurisdictions was resolved in 2020 by the use of a coordinated trio of such agreements, resulting in the corporate payment of a record-breaking financial sanction of €3.6 billion (US$4 billion).[13]

Within Canada, however, the best-known example of a deferred prosecution agreement is likely that reached between US prosecutors and Huawei Technologies executive Meng Wanzhou in September 2021.[14] At

---

10 Discussed in Joanna Harrington, "Providing for Victim Redress Within the Legislative Scheme for Tackling Foreign Corruption" (2020) 43:1 *Dalhousie Law Journal* 245 at 245–50 [Harrington 2020]. As noted at 248, SNC-Lavalin had publicly taken the position that "companies in other jurisdictions, such as the United States and the United Kingdom, benefit from a different approach that has been effectively used in the public interest to resolve similar matters."

11 See *Criminal Code*, above note 1, Part XXII.1 ("Remediation Agreements").

12 On the evolution of US policy and its extension to matters of foreign corruption, see Mike Koehler, "Measuring the Impact of Non-prosecution and Deferred Prosecution Agreements on Foreign Corrupt Practices Act Enforcement" (2015) 49:2 *UC Davis Law Review* 497 at 501–2.

13 Laurence Frost, Iain Withers & Chris Prentice, "Record $4 Billion Airbus Fine Draws Line Under 'Pervasive' Bribery" Reuters (31 January 2020), online: www.reuters.com/article/us-airbus-probe-france-idUSKBN1ZU1X4.

14 United States, Department of Justice, US Attorney's Office, Eastern District of New York, Media Release, "Huawei CFO Wanzhou Meng Admits to Misleading Global Financial Institution: Meng Enters into Deferred Prosecution Agreement

the time, Ms. Meng was Canada's most famous detainee, having been under house arrest in Vancouver for almost three years following a US request for her extradition to stand trial on fraud charges arising from misrepresentations of Huawei's business dealings in Iran. The case attracted extensive media coverage, with Meng being not only the chief financial officer of China's largest and most successful company, but also the daughter of its founder. It also led to a major rift in Canada–China relations, with the Chinese government announcing the detention, ostensibly for spying, of two Canadian nationals, both named Michael, shortly after Meng's arrest. Once an agreement was reached to defer and eventually drop the charges, the extradition proceedings in Canada were brought to an end,[15] and Meng returned immediately to China.[16] A few hours later, China announced the release of the two Canadians, each having spent more than a thousand days in prison. The timing did nothing to dispel the belief that China had engaged in hostage diplomacy to secure a desired result.[17]

While the negotiated settlement of criminal charges is possible in Canada, the type of deal that Meng secured is not legally available. The law on remediation agreements in Canada limits their availability to companies, with this limitation reflective of an overarching debate as to the extent to which individuals should be held accountable for corporate crimes. By contrast, in the United States, the attempted prosecution of Meng is likely viewed as a digression from the main event in light

to Resolve Fraud Charges" (24 September 2021), online: www.justice.gov/usao-edny/pr/huawei-cfo-wanzhou-meng-admits-misleading-global-financial-institution. For a reliable account of the chronology of events, see "Huawei's Meng Wanzhou Released to China After Entering into Deferred Prosecution Agreement with U.S. Justice Department" (2022) 116:1 *American Journal of International Law* 184 ["Huawei's Meng Wanzhou Released"].

15 Canada, Department of Justice, Media Release, "Statement: Extradition in Canada" (24 September 2021), online: www.canada.ca/en/department-justice/news/2021/09/statement-from-the-department-of-justice-canada.html.

16 "Huawei's Meng Wanzhou Flies Back to China After Deal with US" *BBC News* (25 September 2021), online: www.bbc.com/news/world-us-canada-58682998.

17 Amanda Coletta, "Canada's 'Two Michaels' Back Home After More Than 1,000 Days Imprisoned in China as Huawei's Meng Cuts Deal with U.S." *Washington Post* (25 September 2021), online: www.washingtonpost.com/world/2021/09/24/canada-two-michaels-china-huawei/. Although overlooked in the Canadian media coverage focusing on the two Michaels, two American citizens, Cynthia and Victor Liu, were also prevented from leaving China. See further "Huawei's Meng Wanzhou Released," above note 14 at 184, 185.

of US claims that Huawei's global reach and its susceptibility to Chinese government interference present a serious national security threat.[18] Indeed, the deferred prosecution agreement with Meng makes clear that Huawei, and two of its subsidiaries, continue to face charges before the US courts in New York and Washington, supplemented by additional charges alleging the stealing of trade secrets from US technology companies.[19]

The remainder of this chapter consists of four parts. Section B examines the basis for corporate criminal liability, while Section C considers the resolution of corporate criminal cases through the use of alternative-to-prosecution agreements. I then discuss Canada's recent embrace of the use of corporate diversion agreements to resolve such cases, before commenting on their future transnational potential for the coordinated resolution of multi-jurisdictional cases of corporate criminality. I close with reference to the transnational development of international standards so as to ensure that the negotiated settlement of serious corporate criminality serves the public interest.[20]

B. ADDRESSING CORPORATE WRONGDOING

By design, the corporate form of business organization aims to protect its members, the shareholders, from personal liability for a corporation's wrongs. As a separate legal entity, and artificial legal person, the corporation is liable for its actions and financial obligations; its shareholders are not. Limited liability enables investors to limit their investment risk to the number of shares they hold, with the corporation's very purpose having

18 See further, Ana Swanson, "U.S. Delivers Another Blow to Huawei with New Tech Restrictions" *New York Times* (15 May 2020), online: www.nytimes.com/2020/05/15/business/economy/commerce-department-huawei.html.

19 United States, Department of Justice, Office of Public Affairs, Media Release, "Chinese Telecommunications Conglomerate Huawei and Subsidiaries Charged in Racketeering Conspiracy and Conspiracy to Steal Trade Secrets" (13 February 2020), online: www.justice.gov/opa/pr/chinese-telecommunications-conglomerate-huawei-and-subsidiaries-charged-racketeering; *United States of America v Huawei Technologies Co, Ltd*, Superseding Indictment, Case 18-CR-457-AMD (13 February 2020) (EDNY), online: www.justice.gov/opa/press-release/file/1248961/download.

20 On the need for international standards, see Radha Ivory & Tina Søreide, "The International Endorsement of Corporate Settlements in Foreign Bribery Cases" (2020) 69:4 *International & Comparative Law Quarterly* 945 and Tina Søreide & Abiola Makinwa, eds, *Negotiated Settlements in Bribery Cases: A Principled Approach* (Cheltenham, UK: Edward Elgar, 2020).

been identified as one of maximizing shareholder value. This focus on shareholder primacy is a relatively recent phenomenon, gaining strength over the past sixty years,[21] although efforts are underway to secure greater recognition for the wider impact and economic benefit of the corporation within society. Such efforts include express statements to recast a corporation's purpose so as to put the interests of customers, employees, suppliers, and communities on par with investors,[22] with a strong research case having been made for adopting corporate governance frameworks that recognize the interests of both shareholders and stakeholders.[23] The corporate social responsibility agenda,[24] and the linkages made between business and human rights,[25] also further the call for addressing the wider societal dimensions of corporate activity. Law too plays a role, from the obvious areas of corporate law, securities regulation, and taxation, to such varied fields as competition law, employment law, environmental law, and occupational health and safety law, as well as the law of negligence and civil litigation. Within this mix, there is also a role for criminal law, although the corporate form for doing business provides no special

21 See further, Leonardo Davoudi, Christopher McKenna & Rowena Olegario, "The Historical Role of the Corporation in Society" (2018) 6(s1) *Journal of the British Academy* 17.

22 Support for this position from the chief executive officers of 181 major US companies can be found in the revised "Statement on the Purpose of a Corporation" (Washington, DC: Business Roundtable, 2019), online: https://opportunity.businessroundtable.org/ourcommitment. See also the World Economic Forum's "Davos Manifesto 2020" identifying the universal purpose of a company as being "to engage all its stakeholders in shared and sustained value creation" (2 December 2019), online: www.weforum.org/agenda/2019/12/davos-manifesto-2020-the-universal-purpose-of-a-company-in-the-fourth-industrial-revolution.

23 See the conclusions of the British Academy's "Future of the Corporation" research project in *Principles for Purposeful Business: How to Deliver the Framework for the Future of the Corporation* (London: British Academy, 2019), online: www.thebritishacademy.ac.uk/documents/224/future-of-the-corporation-principles-purposeful-business.pdf. See also R. Edward Freeman, *Strategic Management: A Stakeholder Approach*, 2d ed (Cambridge: Cambridge University Press, 2010).

24 See, generally, Andrew Crane et al, eds, *The Oxford Handbook of Corporate Social Responsibility* (Oxford: Oxford University Press, 2008).

25 See, generally, Surya Deva & David Birchall, eds, *Research Handbook on Human Rights and Business* (Cheltenham, UK: Edward Elgar, 2020). See also the *United Nations Guiding Principles on Business and Human Rights*, endorsed by the UN Human Rights Council in 2011: UN Doc A/HRC/RES/17/4 (6 July 2011).

immunity from criminal proceedings for a corporation's officers, directors, and senior management employees.

It is clearly a truism that crimes are committed by humans. Nevertheless, some national legal systems, including Canada's, do provide for some form of corporate criminal liability, with the traditional area of conceptual difficulty being the need to establish the requisite mental element because a corporation, being an abstraction, has no mind of its own.[26] To meet this need, a legal fiction was invented that attributes an agent's state of mind to that of the corporation so as to provide a basis for corporate criminal liability so long as the agent occupies such a position in the organization or in its activities that they serve as its directing mind.[27] Known in English law as the identification theory or doctrine, this route for establishing corporate criminal *mens rea* through the acts or omissions of a director, officer, or senior manager was also embraced in Canada, receiving express judicial endorsement from the highest court in 1985.[28] The directing mind, being the ego or brain of the corporation, is generally also guilty of a criminal offence.[29]

A different path was taken in the United States. There, a vicarious liability approach, derived from the doctrine of *respondeat superior* (Latin for "let the master answer"), provided a basis for corporate criminal liability for the wrongful acts of all employees, managerial or otherwise.[30] This casting of a wider net, however, carries the risk of over-criminalization, with the acts of a low-level employee acting against corporate policy potentially grounding corporate culpability. On the other hand, the need for proof that a senior corporate executive had the intent necessary to commit a particular offence makes it difficult to lay charges against large-scale, decentralized corporations where a lax culture and deficiencies in internal controls serve to embolden lower-level employees to commit crimes.

The attributes of the British and US approaches have each had an influence on Canadian law, with the limitations of the identification

26 *Lennard's Carrying Co v Asiatic Petroleum Co*, [1915] AC 705 at 713 (HL), Viscount Haldane.

27 *Canadian Dredge & Dock Co v The Queen*, [1985] 1 SCR 662 at 675 and 691.

28 *Ibid* at 682–85.

29 *Ibid* at 685–86, citing Glanville Williams, *Textbook of Criminal Law* (London: Stevens & Sons, 1978).

30 *Ibid* at 686, citing *New York Central and Hudson River Railway Co v United States*, 212 US 481 (1909).

doctrine leading advocates for law reform to call for a greater focus on organizational liability.[31] Statutory change in 2003 later enabled criminal liability to be established through the failure of oversight at the senior level.[32] As a result, corporate criminal liability in Canada is no longer dependent on a directing mind, with the law able to locate a *mens reas* within an aggregation of fault from an organization's senior officers, and a wider range of representatives of the company able to provide the *actus reus*.

Reform also brought the development of specific sentencing principles to be applied when dealing with a corporate offender. Section 718.21 of the *Criminal Code* requires the sentencing judge to take into consideration a list of ten additional factors when imposing a sentence on an organization, including "any advantage realized by the organization as a result of the offence" and "the impact that the sentence would have on the economic viability of the organization and the continued employment of its employees."[33] Since corporations cannot do prison time, a monetary fine is the obvious sentence to be imposed, to be set at a level that reflects the gravity of the offence and serves to deter others from engaging in the illegal activity. A corporation may also be required to atone for its crimes through the making of restitution and the establishment of new policies, standards, and procedures to reduce the likelihood of repeat offending. Probation orders can be used to impose these requirements on corporate offenders, accompanied by communication, implementation, and compliance-monitoring obligations.[34] Public shaming orders are also an option for corporate offenders, with section 732.1(3.1)(f) of the *Code* enabling a court to compel the corporate provision of information to the public about the offence, the sentence imposed, and any measures it is taking to reduce the likelihood of a subsequent offence, including the publicizing of new policies, standards, and procedures.

However, not every person alleged to have committed an offence need be prosecuted, whether human or corporate, with there being a role for alternative measures, plea deals, and negotiated settlements, particularly

31 See further Jennifer A. Quaid, "The Assessment of Corporate Criminal Liability on the Basis of Corporate Identity: An Analysis" (1998) 43:4 *McGill Law Journal* 67.

32 *An Act to Amend the Criminal Code (Criminal Liability of Organizations)*, SC 2003, c 21.

33 See *Criminal Code*, above note 1, s 718.21(a), (d).

34 *Ibid*, s 732.1(3.1).

given the public cost of undertaking complex, lengthy trials.[35] Here too one can draw on examples from other fields of law, including environmental law, where corporate accountability for wrongdoing may be secured through an alternative to prosecution known as Environmental Protection Alternative Measures (EPAMs).[36] EPAMs provide for the negotiated imposition of measures or tasks to be carried out by a defendant for the protection of the environment in return for the eventual dropping of the charges and the avoidance of a criminal record. Compliance is monitored, and with the agreement being a public document, it can be made available for review by stakeholders. Competition law provides another example, where the disclosure of wrongdoing and the provision of cooperation with an investigation may result in a grant of immunity from prosecution or a recommendation to be given lenient treatment.[37] Leniency agreements are also used in criminal law, where cooperation with authorities to address wrongdoing has long been recognized as a mitigating factor in sentencing, regardless of whether the cooperator is cast as a snitch, turncoat, or whistleblower.

C. SECURING RESOLUTION THROUGH ALTERNATIVE-TO-PROSECUTION AGREEMENTS

Another form of alternative measure to address the corporate commission of serious, but non-violent, economic crime is a deferred prosecution or non-prosecution agreement.[38] Widely associated with a practice that has developed in the United States, these agreements "occupy an important middle ground between declining prosecutions and obtaining the conviction of a corporation," as the US Department of Justice notes in its current

35 Indeed, there may be some reluctance on the part of authorities to bring criminal charges against corporations, as distinct from individuals, because of the resources required for both investigating and prosecuting corporate crime.

36 *Canadian Environmental Protection Act, 1999*, SC 1999, c 33, ss 295–309. I have also discussed elsewhere how the federal Environmental Damages Fund provides a model for redirecting fines and penalties to support projects of general societal benefit: see Harrington 2020, above note 10 at 276–78.

37 See Canada, Competition Bureau, *Immunity and Leniency Programs Under the Competition Act* (15 March 2019), online: www.competitionbureau.gc.ca/eic/site/cb-bc.nsf/eng/04391.html.

38 On the various forms of non-trial resolutions, see *OECD Study*, above note 8, c 2.

reference guide for prosecuting attorneys.[39] They are a contractual measure, available as a matter of policy, but only at the discretion of a prosecutor. Acceptance of their use allows a prosecutor to negotiate a deal with an accused corporation that will require the carrying out of a specified program of reform and rehabilitation in return for the waiver or stay of the criminal charges, often upon proof of compliance with the agreement's terms. They also allow prosecutors to take into account the collateral consequences of a corporate criminal trial and conviction, including the possibly substantial consequences for the corporation's employees, investors, pensioners, and customers, "many of whom may," in the words of the US Department of Justice, "depending on the size and nature of the corporation and their role in its operations, have played no role in the criminal conduct, been unaware of it, have been unable to prevent it, or have been victimized by it."[40]

In essence, these alternative-to-prosecution agreements serve as a form of diversion program for corporate offenders, akin to programs that divert young offenders and those with addictions and mental health illnesses away from a traditional prosecution and trial. Indeed, the origins of the deferred prosecution agreement lie with the juvenile courts of the United States in the early 1900s, which pioneered the processing of juvenile offenders charged with minor offences in ways that avoided a criminal conviction.[41] Ninety years later, the idea arose to extend this approach to corporations, with ten to twelve agreements reached in the 1990s, although their use did not become a mainstay of US prosecutorial practice until the 2000s.[42] These agreements typically include obligations

39 United States, Department of Justice, *Justice Manual*, Title 9: Criminal, §§9-28.200: General Considerations of Corporate Liability (revised November 2015) [*Justice Manual*], online: www.justice.gov/jm/justice-manual.

40 *Ibid* at §§9-28.1100: Collateral Consequences.

41 Credit is often given to the Chicago Boys' Court in 1914. See Benjamin M. Greenblum, "What Happens to a Prosecution Deferred? Judicial Oversight of Corporate Deferred Prosecution Agreements" (2005) 105:6 *Columbia Law Review* 1863 at 1866.

42 Peter Spivack & Sujit Ramn, "Regulating the 'New Regulators': Current Trends in Deferred Prosecution Agreements" (2008) 45:2 *American Criminal Law Review* 159 at 164. Data on US federal organizational prosecutions, including deferred prosecution and non-prosecution agreements, can be obtained from the Corporate Prosecution Registry, a joint project of the Legal Data Lab at the University of Virginia School of Law and the Duke University School of Law, online: https://corporate-prosecution-registry.com. See also Brandon L. Garrett, *Too Big to Jail: How Prosecutors Compromise with Corporations* (Cambridge, MA: Harvard University Press, 2014).

of disclosure and acceptance of responsibility, cooperation with law enforcement authorities, and the payment of significant fines, as well as the reform of a corporation's business practices, all with a view to securing significant change so as to promote compliance with the law and prevent recidivism. In return, the intended prosecution can be held in abeyance until after an agreed period of monitoring demonstrates to the prosecutorial authority that the corporation has earned the dismissal of the criminal charges. It must be noted, however, that regardless of the ultimate corporate disposition, individual wrongdoers remain a point of focus for US prosecutors, with their reference guide expressly recognizing that "[b]ecause a corporation can only act through individuals, [the] imposition of individual criminal liability may provide the strongest deterrent against future corporate wrongdoing."[43]

Other states have since been influenced by the US example, introducing their own version of a deferred prosecution agreement to address the corporate commission of economic crimes. However, unlike the United States, which relies on a policy-based regime driven by the discretion of a prosecutor or a Securities and Exchange Commission official, other states show an alternative trend is emerging in favour of a statute-based regime with the added requirement of judicial oversight to address transparency and public interest accountability concerns. A key focal point for this second model is the jurisdiction of England and Wales, where the use of deferred prosecution agreements to address the corporate commission of economic crimes was introduced in 2014.[44] English law (though not Scots law, nor the law of Northern Ireland) makes the option of a deferred prosecution agreement available in corporate criminal matters, but only with the authorization of the director of public prosecutions or the director of the Serious Fraud Office, and only for companies, partnerships, and unincorporated associations, never individuals. As they do in the United States, these agreements serve to avoid the expense and effort of a complex and confusing trial, but an English deferred prosecution agreement, unlike a US one, cannot be concluded without the supervision of a judge, who must be convinced that such an agreement is "in the interests of justice" and that its terms are "fair, reasonable and proportionate."[45] To

43 *Justice Manual*, above note 39 at §§9-29.210: Focus on Individual Wrongdoers.

44 *Crimes and Courts Act 2013* (UK), c 22, Schedule 17, brought into force by *Crimes and Courts Act 2013 (Commencement No 8) Order 2014* (UK), SI 2014/258.

45 *Ibid*, Schedule 17, ss 7(1), 8(1), 10(2).

date, twelve such agreements have been negotiated by the Serious Fraud Office,[46] all with court approval, with the result that the English model has since attracted interest in Australia and Ireland,[47] as well as in Singapore.[48]

In late 2016,[49] France also introduced a similar alternative-to-prosecution option, known as a *convention judiciaire d'intérêt public* (judicial public interest agreement) or CJIP.[50] Like its English cousin, the French measure is a statute-based transactional tool, available, initially, to prosecutors dealing with legal persons implicated in acts of corruption and influence peddling, both active and passive, as well as tax evasion and money laundering, but then extended in late 2020 to include environmental crimes and other specialized criminal matters.[51] As with other deferred prosecution agreements, the French CJIP provides for the imposition of a series of requirements upon a corporation in return for the avoidance of a criminal conviction, including an obligation to pay a fine proportionate to the benefits derived from the crime, and where victims can be identified, an obligation to pay reparations.[52] A CJIP can also require a company to implement a corporate compliance program under the control of the French Anti-corruption Agency (*l'Agence française anticorruption*

46 Full details can be found on the website of the Serious Fraud Office, online: www.sfo.gov.uk.

47 After comparing the US and UK models, Ireland's Law Reform Commission recommended the latter because it is statutory-based, imposes limits on prosecutorial discretion, and provides for judicial oversight: *Report: Regulatory Powers and Corporate Offences: Volume 1: Regulatory Powers* (Dublin: Law Reform Commission, 2018), ch 5 at 219–80. For Australia, see *Public Consultation: Proposed Model for a Deferred Prosecution Agreement Scheme in Australia* (Canberra: Attorney-General's Department, 2017).

48 *Criminal Justice Reform Act 2018* (Singapore), No 19 of 2018, s 35 (inserting a new Part VIIA into the Criminal Procedure Code to provide for deferred prosecution agreements), online: https://sso.agc.gov.sg/Acts-Supp/19-2018.

49 *Loi n° 2016-1691 du 9 décembre 2016 relative à la transparence, à la lutte contre la corruption et à la modernisation de la vie économique* (Sapin II), online: www.legifrance.gouv.fr/loda/id/JORFTEXT000033558528/.

50 See generally, Gouvernement de la République Française, Ministère de la Justice, "La convention judiciaire d'intérêt public" (undated), online: www.justice.gouv.fr/publications-10047/cjip-13002.

51 *Loi n° 2020-1672 du 24 décembre 2020 relative au Parquet européen, à la justice environnementale et à la justice pénale spécialisée*, online: www.legifrance.gouv.fr/loda/id/LEGIARTI000042743877/.

52 *Code de procédure pénale* (France), art 41-1-2(I), online: www.legifrance.gouv.fr/codes/article_lc/LEGIARTI000039278942.

or AFA), which has since promulgated a common set of guidelines with the National Financial Prosecutor (*Le Procureur de la République financier*), available in both English and French.[53] As in England and Wales, the negotiated text of a CJIP must also receive judicial approval.[54] The AFA's website indicates that sixteen such agreements have been reached between 2017 and 2022.[55]

D. CROSSING THE POND: CORPORATE DIVERSION AGREEMENTS COME TO CANADA

Canada is also a follower of the English model. Canadian law embraced the discretionary use of deferred prosecutions agreements to tackle the corporate commission of serious economic crimes in 2018. Pitched as an addition to an array of existing tools,[56] the pre-enactment public consultation process led to largely positive expressions of support,[57] and within days of its completion[58] the federal government had introduced amendments to the *Criminal Code* to provide what is known in Canadian law as a remediation agreement, or *accord de réparation* in French. Because the amendments were included in a 582-page omnibus budget bill[59] — making them also a matter of confidence — scant parliamentary time was allotted for scrutinizing the details, and likely deliberately so.[60] A search

53 *Guidelines on the Implementation of the Convention Judiciaire d'Intérêt Public*, signed 26 June 2019, online: www.agence-francaise-anticorruption.gouv.fr/files/files/EN_Lignes_directrices_CJIP_revAFA%20Final%20(002).pdf.

54 *Code de procédure pénale*, above note 52, art 41-1-2(II).

55 Gouvernement de la République Française, Agence française anticorruption, "La convention judiciaire d'intérêt public" (undated), online: www.agence-francaise-anticorruption.gouv.fr/fr/convention-judiciaire-dinteret-public.

56 See *Expanding Canada's Toolkit to Address Corporate Wrongdoing: Discussion Paper for Public Consultation: Deferred Prosecution Agreement Stream* (Ottawa: Government of Canada, 2017).

57 See further, *Expanding Canada's Toolkit to Address Corporate Wrongdoing: What We Heard* (Ottawa: Government of Canada, 2018) [*What We Heard*].

58 The swiftness of which attracted comment in Canada, Office of the Conflict of Interest and Ethics Commissioner, *Trudeau II Report* (Ottawa: OCIEC, 2019) at para 41 [*Trudeau II Report*].

59 Bill C-74, *An Act to Implement Certain Provisions of the Budget Tabled in Parliament on February 27, 2018 and Other Measures*, later enacted as *Budget Implementation Act, 2018, No 1*, SC 2018, c 12, s 404.

60 Witnesses interviewed by the federal ethics commissioner "were of the view that non-fiscal items are typically included in a federal bill to expedite passage through

of the parliamentary record shows only four instances in the House of Commons and Senate when the remediation agreement provisions were discussed during the budget bill debates, with the most notable being a Finance Committee meeting at which the lead civil servant with responsibility for the proposed regime provided an overview and answered questions.[61] The budget bill was passed in June 2018, and the new provisions, now constituting Part XXII.1 of the *Criminal Code*, entered into force on 21 September 2018.[62] Five months later, the House of Commons Justice Committee would undertake a fuller discussion of the new regime but only as part of an inquiry into conversations between a former attorney general and the prime minister's office concerning corruption charges then faced by the Canadian engineering and construction company, the SNC-Lavalin Group.[63]

At its core, Part XXII.1 expands the sentencing options available to address the corporate commission of specified criminal offences of an economic nature, such as bribery, theft, and fraud.[64] It provides an alternative to prosecution for corporations willing to implement an agreed set of corrective measures in return for a stay of the criminal charges. The use of the language of remediation, rather than deferred prosecution, is a made-in-Canada addition to the body of practice in other jurisdictions, with this terminology presumably chosen to convey a focus on rehabilitation rather than on punishment.[65] To that end, a purpose clause was also included within the legislative scheme, identifying no less than six objectives for the

---

Parliament": *Trudeau II Report*, above note 58 at para 41. Another option was available in the form of Bill C-75, *An Act to Amend the Criminal Code, the Youth Criminal Justice Act and other Acts*, which received royal assent on 21 June 2019, a year after the budget bill.

61 Canada, Parliament, House of Commons, Standing Committee on Finance, *Evidence*, 42-1, No 154 (8 May 2018) at 21:25 (Ann Sheppard, Senior Counsel, Criminal Law Policy Section, Department of Justice) [*Ann Sheppard Committee Evidence*].

62 *Budget Implementation Act, 2018, No 1*, above note 59, s 409.

63 Canada, Parliament, House of Commons, Standing Committee on Justice and Human Rights, *Remediation Agreements, The Shawcross Doctrine and the Discussions between the Office of the Attorney General and Government Colleagues*, 42-1, Meetings 132, 133, 135, 137, 138 (21 February 2019, 25 February 2019, 27 February 2019 & 6 March 2019). On the charges brought against SNC-Lavalin, see Harrington 2020, above note 10 at 246–50.

64 The specified offences are listed in a schedule to *Criminal Code*, above note 1, Part XXII.1.

65 See also *What We Heard*, above note 57 at 14.

new regime.[66] These aims include the denouncement of wrongdoing and the provision of reparations for harm done — being the general purposes for sentencing those convicted of crimes in Canadian law[67] — as well as the promotion of a compliance culture and the voluntary disclosure of wrongdoing. The scheme also expressly aims "to reduce the negative consequences of the wrongdoing for persons — employees, customers, pensioners, and others — who did not engage in the wrongdoing," while also aiming to hold responsible those individuals within the corporation who did so engage.[68]

It must be emphasized, however, that there is no legal right to a remediation agreement, with even the invitation to begin negotiations governed by the exercise of prosecutorial discretion.[69] A public interest test governs the exercise of that discretion, with the law mandating various factors to be taken into account, including the nature and severity of the crimes, the degree of involvement of senior officers in the wrongdoing, and the actions taken in response, including the termination of those involved and efforts made to remedy the harm caused.[70] Any record of previous wrongdoing must also be considered, with the director of public prosecutions having stated publicly that remediation agreements will not be granted to repeat offenders, while acknowledging that this is not the case in the United States and Britain.[71]

Negotiated only in cases where there is a reasonable prospect of conviction,[72] and then only with the attorney general's consent,[73] the resulting remediation agreement must contain a statement of the facts related to the

66 *Criminal Code*, above note 1, s 715.31.

67 *Ibid*, s 718(a), (e).

68 *Ibid*, s 715.31(f).

69 As intended by the drafters (see *Ann Sheppard Committee Evidence*, above note 61) and later judicially confirmed (see *SNC-Lavalin Group Inc v Canada (Public Prosecution Service)*, 2019 FC 282 [*SNC-Lavalin Group*]).

70 See *Criminal Code*, above note 1, ss 715.32(1)(c) & 715.32(2). See also "Guideline of the Director Issued under Section 3(3)(c) of the *Director of Public Prosecutions Act*" (23 January 2020) published as s 3.21 of the *Public Prosecution Service of Canada Deskbook*, online: https://www.ppsc-sppc.gc.ca/eng/pub/fpsd-sfpg/fps-sfp/tpd/d-g-eng.pdf.

71 See Robert Fife, "No Deal Offered to SNC Due to Severity of Charges: Prosecutor" *Globe and Mail* (Ontario edition) (28 February 2020) A1.

72 *Criminal Code*, above note 1, s 715.32(1)(a).

73 *Ibid*, s 715.32(1)(d). The guideline issued by the Director of Public Prosecutions, above note 70, indicates that the assessment of the reasonable prospect of

offence, an admission of responsibility, and an indication of the penalty to be paid, as well as obligations to cooperate and assist in any investigation, prosecution, or other proceeding, including possibly foreign proceedings, such as the prosecution of any individuals involved in the crimes.[74] The agreement may also require the corporation to address specific deficiencies and improve internal control procedures and employee training programs, and might also add a requirement to accept independent ongoing monitoring.[75] If the corporation meets the terms of the remediation agreement, the prosecutor will apply for a court order indicating successful completion.[76] If the corporation breaches a term of the remediation agreement, the criminal proceedings could be recommenced,[77] although provision is also made for varying the terms of an approved remediation agreement.[78]

As is the case in England and Wales, and in France, remediation agreements are not secret deals concluded without the benefit of independent judicial oversight. Indeed, for a remediation agreement to take effect in Canada, a judge must be satisfied that "the agreement is in the public interest" and that its terms are "fair, reasonable and proportionate to the gravity of the offence."[79] The scheme also presumes that a court-approved remediation agreement will be made public "as soon as practicable,"[80] although the strength of this presumption has not, as yet, been tested. A court may, however, decide not to publish a remediation agreement if there is a need to protect the identities of victims,[81] with victims owed a duty to be informed when the negotiation of such agreements commence.[82] Victims' interests also receive attention at the judicial approval stage, as the court is required to consider any reparations made to victims and the content of any victim or community impact statements.[83] A victim surcharge for each offence to which the agreement applies is also to be

conviction is made before the consent is sought, with the attorney general delegating the authorization power to the deputy director of public prosecutions.

74 *Ibid*, s 715.34(1).

75 *Ibid*, s 715.34(3).

76 *Ibid*, s 715.4.

77 *Ibid*, s 715.39.

78 *Ibid*, s 715.38.

79 *Ibid*, s 715.37(6).

80 *Ibid*, s 715.42.

81 *Ibid*, s 715.42(3)(b).

82 *Ibid*, s 715.36.

83 *Ibid*, s 715.37(3).

paid by the corporation (an exception is provided for offences relating to the bribery of foreign public officials).[84]

In early 2020, the RCMP made known that there may be at least two cases of alleged foreign corruption that could lead to the first remediation agreements being presented for judicial approval in Canada.[85] Then, in September 2021, Quebec's chief prosecutor made known that it was open to negotiating a remediation agreement with SNC-Lavalin, this time in relation to fraud and forgery charges arising from a Montreal bridge refurbishment project.[86] In May 2022, Canada's first remediation agreement was concluded with two of SNC-Lavalin's entities as a result of these negotiations, with the deal involving the payment of a fine of C$29.6 million.[87]

Nevertheless, the judgment concerning SNC-Lavalin's earlier unsuccessful efforts to force the director of public prosecutions to enter into negotiations regarding offences in Libya remains the leading case.[88] Ultimately, the charges in that case were settled by a negotiated plea deal, involving a guilty plea to a charge of fraud by an SNC-Lavalin construction division that had not been active since 2015, and the dropping of all charges against the parent company.[89] The plea deal also contained elements similar to those found in a deferred prosecution agreement, notably the payment of a significant fine of C$280 million and the acceptance of a three-year probation order requiring SNC-Lavalin to hire an independent consulting firm to monitor the company's compliance and ethics program, and publish its reports on the company's website. The prosecution was also

---

84 *Ibid*, s 715.34(1)(h). For criticism of victim surcharges in the corruption of foreign public officials' context, see Harrington 2018, above note 4 at 135–36.

85 Daniel Leblanc, "RCMP Investigations Could Lead to First Test of Deferred Prosecution Agreements" *Globe and Mail* (Ontario edition) (15 January 2020) A7.

86 Nicolas Van Praet, "Prosecutors Look to Avoid Trial for SNC-Lavalin with Offer to Make Deal" *Globe and Mail* (27 September 2021) A1.

87 Nicholas Van Praet, "SNC-Lavalin Strikes Deal With Prosecutors in Fraud Case" *Globe and Mail* (Ontario edition) (7 May 2022) A5.

88 *SNC-Lavalin Group*, above note 69.

89 SNC-Lavalin, Media Release, "SNC-Lavalin Group Settles Federal Charges" (18 December 2019), online: www.snclavalin.com/en/media/press-releases/2019/18-12-2019. See also Kamila Hinkson, "SNC-Lavalin Pleads Guilty to Fraud for Past Work in Libya, Will Pay $280M Fine," *CBC News* (18 December 2019), online: www.cbc.ca/news/canada/montreal/snc-lavalin-trading-court-libya-charges-1.5400542; Nicolas Van Praet et al, "SNC-Lavalin Pleads Guilty to Fraud" *Globe and Mail* (Ontario edition) (19 December 2019) A1.

successful in its efforts to establish individual criminal culpability, with the former senior SNC-Lavalin executive in charge of the construction division, Sami Bebawi, found guilty of fraud, bribery of a foreign public official, and laundering charges in relation to activities in Libya.[90] The Crown's star witness in this case was Riadh Ben Aïssa, another former SNC-Lavalin executive, who had been jailed on Swiss charges of bribery, money laundering, and corruption (Switzerland having been the location in which the transfer of funds took place to execute the Libyan scheme).[91] Cooperation between the RCMP and the Swiss authorities had helped secure the guilty plea from Ben Aïssa.[92]

E. SECURING TRANSNATIONAL DEALS THROUGH TRANSNATIONAL COOPERATION

With the field of transnational criminal law having its roots in law enforcement, and the securing of inter-state cooperation between police and prosecuting authorities,[93] it is not surprising that Canadian authorities have cooperated with authorities in other jurisdictions to secure accountability for the commission of serious crimes. To date, however, this cooperation has taken place as and when the need arises, often at the investigative stage, and at times in support of efforts to secure a resolution elsewhere. There have also been difficulties, of which the foreign bribery case of Griffiths Energy International provides a notable example.[94] After negotiating a guilty plea deal with the corporate defendant for paying bribes to secure oil concessions in Chad, a separate proceeding was

---

90 Jonathan Montpetit, "Former SNC-Lavalin Executive Found Guilty on Libya Corruption Charges" *CBC News* (15 December 2019), online: www.cbc.ca/news/canada/montreal/sami-bebawi-snc-lavalin-1.5397115; Nicholas Van Praet, "Former SNC Executive Guilty of Corruption" *Globe and Mail* (Ontario edition), A1. See also *Bebawi c R*, 2020 QCCA 1397.

91 Nicolas Van Praet & Graeme Hamilton, "Libyan Fixer Faces Justice: Ex-SNC Executive Guilty" *National Post* (2 October 2014) A1.

92 Paul Waldie, "Arrest Deepens SNC Intrigue; Former Executive Held in Switzerland as Part of Corruption Probe That Prompted Montreal RCMP Raid" *Globe and Mail* (30 April 2012) A1; Greg McArthur & Sophie Cousineau, "RCMP Affidavit Outlines Trail of Alleged Bribes" *Globe and Mail* (26 January 2013) A4.

93 See, generally, Neil Boister, Sabine Gless & Florian Jeßberger, eds, *Histories of Transnational Criminal Law* (Oxford: Oxford University Press, 2021).

94 *R v Griffiths Energy International Inc*, [2013] AJ No 12 (QB).

initiated to seize the shares in the company that had formed the bribe; those shares having been made more valuable by the very plea deal that saved the company.[95] This separate forfeiture proceeding was later withdrawn, with the Canadian authorities refusing to disclose the reasons for withdrawal to both the US and UK authorities without the signing of a non-disclosure agreement.[96] After the corporate defendant paid the negotiated penalty of C$10.35 million, the company was later bought by the Anglo-Swiss resources giant Glencore for £807 million given the value of its oil concessions in Chad. The shares that had been provided as a bribe were now worth an estimated £22 million.[97] When the share certificates released by the Canadian authorities were surrendered to the stock transfer agent handling the company's acquisition, the US and UK authorities worked together to secure the seizure of the funds through the UK courts.[98] The Serious Fraud Office later directed that the funds it recovered in what it called the Chad Oil case be used in development projects that "will benefit the poorest in Chad."[99] One could conclude that Canada had dropped the ball, but perhaps a decision had been made internally to yield the floor in support of the more assertive actions of other prosecuting authorities. Eventually, in May 2021, the US Department of Justice unsealed its indictment against Chad's former ambassador and its deputy chief of mission for their role in the bribery scheme and for using the US financial system to launder the bribes.[100]

In future, complex multi-jurisdictional cases of transnational corporate criminality may be best resolved by the simultaneous and coordinated use of negotiated settlements put forward by multiple prosecuting

95 As discussed in Harrington 2018, above note 4 at 126–28.

96 *Ibid* at 130–31.

97 *Ibid* at 128.

98 *Serious Fraud Office v Saleh*, [2015] EWHC 2119 (QB). See also *Saleh v Director of the Serious Fraud Office*, [2017] EWCA Civ 18, and *Serious Fraud Office v Saleh*, [2018] EWHC 1012 (QB).

99 United Kingdom, Serious Fraud Office, Media Release, "SFO Recovers £4.4m from Corrupt Diplomats in 'Chad Oil' Share Deal" (22 March 2018), online: www.sfo.gov.uk/2018/03/22/sfo-recovers-4-4m-from-corrupt-diplomats-in-chad-oil-share-deal.

100 United States, Department of Justice, Office of Public Affairs, Media Release, "Charges Unsealed Against Former Chadian Diplomats to the U.S. Charged in Connection with International Bribery and Money Laundering Scheme" (24 May 2021), online: www.justice.gov/opa/pr/charges-unsealed-against-former-chadian-diplomats-us-charged-connection-international-bribery.

authorities. A coordinated multi-jurisdictional settlement may offer the best chance of securing corporate accountability for criminal conduct that takes place beyond the reach of any one enforcement agency. The coordinated resolution of multi-jurisdictional cases may also provide finality for corporate defendants, create efficiencies for prosecutors, and distribute the financial penalties to be paid across several participating jurisdictions.[101] Building on the pioneering work of Germany and the United States in securing the coordinated resolution of the Siemens AG bribery scandal in 2008,[102] the utility of negotiating coordinated multi-jurisdictional agreements is now best illustrated by the recent settlement with Airbus SE.

In early 2020, it became public that a coordinated effort between prosecuting authorities in the United Kingdom, the United States, and France had resulted in the conclusion of a record-breaking trio of deferred prosecution agreements with the global aerospace company Airbus SE, a Dutch and French domiciled company, registered in the Netherlands.[103] Under these agreements, Airbus agreed to disgorge profits and pay fines and costs in the amounts of €991 million in the United Kingdom, €2.08 billion in France, and €525 million in the United States, for a total sum of €3.6 billion, in resolution of allegations of bribery to secure contracts for its civilian and military aircraft. Airbus admitted its culpability, after the investigation efforts of multiple agencies revealed that the criminal activity had taken place over many years, in multiple countries. The UK and French authorities worked together, operating a joint investigation in parallel with US efforts. In negotiating the diversion agreements, each state took responsibility for a number of geographical areas, with the UK's Serious Fraud Office focusing on bribery offences in Malaysia, Sri Lanka, Taiwan, Indonesia, and Ghana, the French *Parquet National Financier* focusing on corruption and bribery offences in China, Colombia, Nepal,

101 See *OECD Study*, above note 8 at 37.

102 United States, Department of Justice, Media Release, "Siemens AG and Three Subsidiaries Plead Guilty to Foreign Corrupt Practices Act Violations and Agree to Pay $450 Million in Combined Criminal Fines: Coordinated Enforcement Actions by DOJ, SEC and German Authorities Result in Penalties of $1.6 Billion" (15 December 2008), online: www.justice.gov/archive/opa/pr/2008/December/08-crm-1105.html.

103 United Kingdom, Serious Fraud Office, Media Release, "SFO Enters into €991m Deferred Prosecution Agreement with Airbus as Part of a €3.6bn Global Resolution" (31 January 2020), online: www.sfo.gov.uk/2020/01/31/sfo-enters-into-e991m-deferred-prosecution-agreement-with-airbus-as-part-of-a-e3-6bn-global-resolution.

South Korea, the United Arab Emirates, Saudi Arabia, Taiwan, and Russia, and the US Department of Justice focusing on bribery and corruption offences in China, alongside a US Department of State investigation concerning civil violations of the US International Traffic in Arms Regulations which resulted in an additional agreement.[104] Transnational cooperation, and the use of a tool gaining transnational traction to address transnational corporate criminality, thus led to financial penalties of a scale that must surely serve as a deterrent, with the sums paid in the UK deal alone being "more than double the total of fines paid in respect of all criminal conduct in England and Wales in 2018."[105]

The Airbus resolution further suggests that no case — and no corporation — is too large for a negotiated deal, with Airbus SE being one of the two largest manufacturers of passenger aircraft in the world (the other being Boeing).[106] And yet, while the Airbus agreements pave a way forward for the use of multi-jurisdictional negotiated settlements and the cross-jurisdictional sharing of information in cases of transnational corporate criminality, there remains concern as to how best to secure associated individual accountability for the same criminal conduct. As the likely repository of material relevant for the purposes of prosecuting the individuals involved in the bribery scheme, Airbus was required to, and did, cooperate fully with the British and French joint investigation,[107] and at the time of the diversion agreements there were ongoing investigations concerning a number of individual suspects in various countries. However, as the UK judge noted in her decision of approval concerning

---

104 *Serious Fraud Office v Airbus SE*, Case No U20200108, Judgment of 31 January 2020 (Southwark Crown Court) at paras 2–3, online: www.judiciary.uk/wp-content/uploads/2020/01/Director-of-the-Serious-Fraud-Office-v-Airbus-SE-1.pdf [*Airbus SE*]. See also US Department of Justice, Office of Public Affairs, Media Release, "Airbus Agrees to Pay Over $3.9 Billion in Global Penalties to Resolve Foreign Bribery and ITAR Case" (31 January 2020), online: www.justice.gov/opa/pr/airbus-agrees-pay-over-39-billion-global-penalties-resolve-foreign-bribery-and-itar-case.

105 *Ibid* at para 1, Dame Victoria Sharp, President of the Queen's Bench Division of the Royal Courts of Justice.

106 Airbus had self-reported revenues of €64 billion, and a workforce of 134,000, in 2018: Airbus, Media Release, "Airbus Reaches Agreements with French, U.K. and U.S. Authorities" (31 January 2020), online: www.airbus.com/newsroom/press-releases/en/2020/01/airbus-reaches-agreements-with-french-uk-and-us-authorities.html.

107 Its efforts are listed in detail as part of the judicial assessment of the interests of justice: *Airbus SE*, above note 104 at para 74.

the UK agreement, some of these individuals were "based in jurisdictions where there are human rights concerns, and the death penalty exists for corruption"; a penalty that she acknowledged is contrary to the UK's international human rights treaty obligations.[108] By May 2021, the ongoing investigations being carried out by the Serious Fraud Office had been abandoned,[109] raising once again the criticism that it is easier to negotiate deals with corporations than hold their senior executives accountable.

The decision to take no further action against the individual suspects coincided with the collapse of a Serious Fraud Office effort to bring two former Serco executives to trial, following the conclusion of a deferred prosecution agreement with the company.[110] It was also reminiscent of the Serious Fraud Office's decision to abandon efforts to hold individuals responsible following the conclusion of deferred prosecution agreements with Rolls-Royce and GlaxoSmithKline.[111] As yet, no individual has been successfully prosecuted in a British case involving a deferred prosecution agreement, leading to calls from civil society for an "urgent review" to understand why.[112] However, even in the United States, with its lengthier record of experience with alternative-to-prosecution agreements, there remains no guarantee that a negotiated resolution for a company will be accompanied or followed by the prosecution of individual employees, let alone a company's top executives.[113] Further research is needed as to

108 *Ibid* at para 13.

109 Kristin Ridley, "UK Prosecutor Ends Investigation into Airbus Individuals—Sources" *Reuters* (4 May 2021), online: www.reuters.com/business/aerospace-defense/uk-prosecutor-ends-investigation-into-airbus-individuals-sources-2021-05-04.

110 Jasper Jolly, "Trial of Former Serco Executives Collapses as SFO Fails to Disclose Evidence" *Guardian* (26 April 2021), online: www.theguardian.com/business/2021/apr/26/serco-trial-collapses-as-serious-office-fails-to-disclose-evidence. Charges of fraud and false accounting had been avoided by a Serco subsidiary through the conclusion of a deferred prosecution agreement, with the charges arising from a scheme to defraud the Ministry of Justice by inflating costs in contracts for the provision of electronic monitoring services for prisoners.

111 United Kingdom, Serious Fraud Office, Media Release, "SFO Closes GlaxoSmithKline Investigation and Investigation into Rolls-Royce Individuals" (22 February 2019), online: www.sfo.gov.uk/2019/02/22/sfo-closes-glaxosmithkline-investigation-and-investigation-into-rolls-royce-individuals.

112 *Ibid.*

113 For journalistic coverage of the issue, see Jesse Eisinger, *The Chickenshit Club: Why the Justice Department Fails to Prosecute Executives* (New York: Simon and Schuster, 2017).

the reasons why. The complexity of transnational economic crimes — in which individuals of various ranks may play a part at various times — suggests the need for a strategy focused on organizational responsibility to secure at least some individual accountability for these crimes.

F. CONCLUSION

Transnational criminal law supports the efforts of national authorities to criminalize and suppress the commission of serious cross-border crimes, including crimes committed by corporations. It also encourages the transnational diffusion of prosecutorial practices, in addition to innovations, with cross-border influences having also played a role in establishing the conceptual basis for corporate criminal liability as well as our understanding of the sentencing options available. These options include the use of negotiated settlements and non-trial resolutions, with practices that were first developed in the United States, and then later refined in Britain and France, now finding support in Canada with the creation of a remediation agreements regime. In future, complex multi-jurisdictional cases of transnational corporate criminality may well be best resolved by the coordinated use of negotiated agreements with multiple authorities to secure a full accounting for the crimes. There remains, however, the need for the transnational development of an agreed set of standards to ensure that the negotiation of cross-border corporate criminality continues to serve the public interest, since various prosecutorial authorities have adopted their own localized codes of practices. The recent adoption of the new "2021 Anti-Bribery Recommendation" to supplement the *OECD Anti-Bribery Convention*[114] with a set of principles on the use of non-trial resolutions in foreign bribery cases will likely assist,[115] but the associated question of how best to secure individual criminal accountability for the same criminal conduct likely remains the most difficult aspect to tackle.

---

114 *OECD Anti-Bribery Convention*, above note 4.

115 *Recommendation of the Council for Further Combating Bribery of Foreign Public Officials in International Business Transactions*, adopted by the OECD Council on 25 November 2021, OECD/LEGAL/0378 (2022), online: legalinstruments.oecd.org/en/instruments/OECD-LEGAL-0378.

fifteen

The Long Arm of Canadian Price-Fixing Law? Canadian Jurisdiction Over Foreign Price-Fixing Conspiracies

W. MICHAEL G. OSBORNE*

A. INTRODUCTION

Global price-fixing conspiracies have been a focus of antitrust enforcement for the last twenty-five years or so, with the United States Department of Justice leading the charge. Global cartels typically involve meetings between representatives of the major players in the affected industry, often under cover of a sham (or even real) trade association. In some cases, such as the lysine conspiracy,[1] the conspirators fixed prices on a state-by-state basis;[2] in others, such as the auto-parts conspiracies,[3] they rigged bids for particular automakers.

---

* Michael Osborne, MStJ FCIArb, practises competition law and commercial litigation at Cozen O'Connor in Toronto.

1 An international conspiracy to fix prices for lysine, an animal feed additive. The conspiracy was prosecuted in both Canada and the United States. In Canada, it netted C$19.6 million in fines. It was also the subject of the Hollywood movie *The Informant*.

2 Scott D. Hammond, "Caught in the Act: Inside an International Cartel" Presentation to the OECD Competition Committee, Working Party No. 3, Public Prosecutors Program (18 October 2005), online: www.justice.gov/atr/speech/caught-act-inside-international-cartel.

3 The auto-parts conspiracies were a series of international conspiracies to fix prices for various auto parts. They were prosecuted in both Canada and the United States, resulting in fines of more than C$86 million in Canada alone.

These conspiracies have the potential to raise prices around the world, not just for the products whose price is fixed, but for downstream products as well. The overcharge exacted by the conspirators may (or may not) be passed on by each participant in the value and distribution chains, and so ripple through the entire economy, potentially affecting nearly every business and every consumer.

The problem is that these conspiracies often take place between foreign executives of foreign corporations meeting in foreign jurisdictions. Leaving aside practical difficulties of investigating conduct abroad, these foreign conspiracies raise the question of whether the competition authorities and courts in any given state have jurisdiction.

The United States famously takes "long arm" jurisdiction over "foreign conduct that was meant to produce and did in fact produce some substantial effect in the United States."[4] The European Union follows a similar policy. It applies its competition laws to cartels that are implemented in the EU—even if that implementation consists merely of a sale within the EU.[5]

In Canada, the Competition Bureau and the Public Prosecution Service of Canada (PPSC) have long taken the position that cartels that occur entirely outside Canada can be prosecuted in Canada if the cartel has an effect in Canada. The effect need not be direct; it seems that even an indirect effect on the price of downstream products will do. This policy has largely been successful: beginning with the lysine conspiracy in 1998, they have obtained guilty pleas and nearly C$300 million in fines relating to international conspiracies, more than five times the total fines for domestic conspiracies during the same period (C$56 million). Canada's plaintiff class action bar has pursued foreign conspiracies even more aggressively, collecting massive settlements even where the Bureau declined to investigate.

Despite these massive fines and settlements, it remains an open question whether the *Competition Act*'s[6] conspiracy provisions even apply to price-fixing conspiracies formed outside Canada. This is because Canadian criminal law traditionally takes a territorial, and not an effects-based,

4 *Hartford Fire Ins Co v California*, 509 US 764 at 796.

5 *Judgment of the Court of Justice of 27 September 1988, Ahlström v Commission* ("Wood Pulp"), C-89/85, C-104/85, C-114/85, C-116/85, C-117/85, C-125/85, C-126/85, C-127/85, C-128/85, and C-129/85, [1988] ECLI:EU:C:1988:447 at paras 16 & 17; *Judgment of the General Court of 25 March 1999, Gencor v Commission,* T-102/96, [1999] ECLI:EU:T:1999:65, para 87.

6 RSC 1985, c C-34 [*Competition Act* or *Act*].

approach to jurisdiction. This principle is embodied in section 6(2) of the *Criminal Code*, which provides that no one shall be convicted of an offence that was "committed outside Canada."[7]

I argue here that Canadian courts cannot take jurisdiction over foreign price fixing based solely on its effects in Canada. The question must always be whether the offence (usually a breach of the *Competition Act*'s conspiracy provision, section 45) took place outside Canada. This involves looking at where there is a real and substantial connection between the conduct and Canada. That connection will exist where the cartel involved fixing prices *in Canada*, but not where fixing prices elsewhere had an indirect effect in Canada.

B. CARTEL OFFENCES IN CANADA

Canada's competition legislation, the *Competition Act*,[8] contains a number of cartel-type offences. The most important are conspiracy (section 45), foreign directives (section 46), and big rigging (section 47). These offences are discussed below, followed by a discussion about the enforcement mechanisms under the *Competition Act*.

1) Conspiracy (Section 45)

Section 45 has long been the principal anti-cartel provision in the *Competition Act* (and its predecessor, the *Combines Investigation Act*). It is also the most commonly used provision in international conspiracy investigations.

Until 2010, section 45 created an offence of conspiracy to lessen competition "unduly." In 2010, "old section 45" was replaced with an entirely new offence of conspiring to fix prices, allocate markets, or restrict output. The chief difference between the two provisions is that old section 45 required showing that the conspiracy would lessen competition unduly if implemented, whereas new section 45 contains a *per se* prohibition on certain types of agreements between competitors.

7 *Criminal Code*, RSC 1985, c C-46, s 6(2).

8 *Competition Act*, above note 6.

a) Old Section 45

Old section 45 prohibited a variety of conspiracies or agreements, including agreements to limit production unduly, enhance prices unreasonably, or "otherwise restrain or injure competition unduly."[9] Three features of this offence are important from the standpoint of assessing jurisdictional issues.

The first is that the offence is complete upon the entering into of the agreement.[10] While it is necessary that the agreement would have the effect of unduly lessening competition, there was no need for the parties to implement it, or for the Crown to prove that competition was in fact unduly lessened. As a result, any implementation of a conspiracy in Canada is not part of the *actus reus* of the offence.

The second is that the offence required showing that harm to competition — the undue lessening — would result were the agreement to be implemented. The provision thus contemplated some likely effect as a precondition for liability.

The third feature is the exemption for conspiracies that relate only to the export of products from Canada, found in section 45(5). This provision is relevant to comity-based arguments.

b) New Section 45

In 2010, a completely new approach to agreements between competitors came into force. The old section 45 was replaced with a new provision containing a *per se* ban on agreements between competitors to fix prices, allocate markets, or restrict output. At the same time, a new civil provision (section 90.1) now permits the Competition Tribunal to prohibit other agreements between competitors that substantially lessen or prevent competition.

New section 45 is fundamentally different from old section 45. Old section 45 focused on the likely effect of agreements, that is, an undue lessening of competition. New section 45 prohibits certain types of agreements between competitors without regard to their effect. The focus is on the parties to the agreement (competitors) and the object of the agreement (price fixing, etc.).

---

9 *Competition Act*, above note 6, s 45 (as it stood before SC 2009, c 2, s 410).

10 *Container Materials Ltd v the King*, [1942] SCR 147; *R v Howard Smith Paper Mills Ltd*, [1957] SCR 403; *R v Aetna Insurance Co* (1977), 75 DLR (3d) 332 (SCC).

The new offence is complete upon the making of a prohibited agreement. Implementation of the conspiracy forms no part of the offence: "The section 45 offence resides in the agreement itself, not in carrying it out by overt acts."[11] Nor do anti-competitive effects form part of the offence. The elimination of the undue lessening element means that the "existence of actual or likely anti-competitive effects is no longer relevant."[12]

This aspect of new section 45 can be contrasted with its civil analogue, section 90.1. Section 90.1 permits the Competition Tribunal to prohibit an agreement between competitors where it finds that the agreement substantially lessens or prevents competition in a market, or is likely to do so. The focus in section 90.1 is on the effects of the agreement, not the object of the agreement.

New section 45 maintains the export conspiracy exemption in section 45(5). The new provision also preserves the regulated conduct defence in section 45(7). This provision is designed to allow federal and provincial legislatures to permit or even mandate price fixing in certain industries.

2) Foreign Directives (Sections 46 and 82(1)(b))

Section 46 creates an offence of implementing in Canada a foreign conspiracy that "if entered into in Canada would have been in contravention of section 45." The offence is an absolute liability offence; a corporation that implements a conspiracy in Canada commits the offence even if it was unaware of the conspiracy. The provision applies only to corporations.

Section 82(1)(b) fulfills a similar function, using similar language. It permits the Competition Tribunal to make an order prohibiting the implementation of a conspiracy "entered into outside Canada that, if entered into Canada, would have been in contravention of section 45." Arguably, these provisions provide a signal that Parliament recognized that section 45 does not have extraterritorial reach.

3) Bid-Rigging (Section 47)

The *Competition Act*'s bid-rigging provision prohibits three kinds of agreements between persons submitting bids: the submission of bids that are arrived at by arrangement or agreement, agreements not to submit a bid,

---

11 *Jensen v Samsung Electronics Co Ltd*, 2021 FC 1185 at para 103 [*Jensen*].

12 *Ibid* at para 96.

and agreements to withdraw a bid that has been submitted. In each case, the conduct is only an offence if the person calling for bids is not told of the arrangement.

There is no analogue in this provision to the export exemption found in section 45, nor is there a foreign directives offence for bid-rigging that occurs outside Canada.

4) Enforcement of Cartel Provisions

The Competition Bureau, led by the Commissioner of Competition, is charged with investigating suspected breaches of the criminal provisions of the *Competition Act*. Canada's federal prosecution service, the PPSC, generally prosecutes criminal offences under the *Competition Act*.[13]

Breaches of criminal provisions of the *Competition Act* give rise to civil causes of action in two ways. First, section 36 creates a statutory cause of action to recover damages caused by breaches of these criminal provisions. Second, breaches of the criminal provisions of the Act can also supply the unlawful conduct element in the tort of civil conspiracy.[14] In both cases, to succeed in an action based on a breach of a criminal provision of the Act, a plaintiff must prove all of the elements of the offence, that is, both the *actus reus* and the *mens rea*.[15]

C. ASSERTING EFFECTS-BASED JURISDICTION

The question of whether foreign conspirators commit an offence in Canada under sections 45 or 47 if the conspiracy has an effect on the market in Canada has yet to be determined. As discussed below, both prosecutors and private action plaintiffs rely on an effects-based approach, so far, successfully.

1) The Competition Bureau's Effects-Based Approach

Neither the Competition Bureau nor the PPSC have articulated a position about the basis for Canada to take jurisdiction over price-fixing

13 Provincial prosecutors can, and occasionally do, prosecute charges under the *Act*, above note 6.

14 *Pioneer Corp v Godfrey*, 2019 SCC 42.

15 *Ibid*; *Jensen*, above note 11 at para 97.

conspiracies entered into outside Canada. Nevertheless, it seems clear that they are applying an effects-based jurisdiction test. As the Bureau stated in 2017, "no matter where illegal agreements are conducted, if they affect Canadian consumers, the Bureau will not hesitate to take action."[16]

The Bureau takes the position that indirect effects are sufficient to found jurisdiction in Canada. This includes not just situations where the cartelized product itself reaches Canada through a distribution chain, but also where the cartelized product is incorporated into a downstream product that ultimately reaches Canada.[17]

The Bureau's emphasis on downstream effects is apparent from cases in which the Bureau has not asserted jurisdiction. For example, in 2016, the Bureau and the US Department of Justice's Antitrust Division agreed that one of the auto-parts defendants, Nishikawa Rubber Co. Ltd., should be dealt with in the United States and not in Canada. Nishikawa had participated in rigging bids for body-sealing products sold to automakers in both the United States and Canada. However, a "significant percentage" of the vehicles made in Canada were exported to the United States. The Antitrust Division included both US and Canadian sales in calculating the fine.[18]

2) Effects-Based Jurisdiction in *Competition Act* Private Actions

Foreign defendants have challenged jurisdiction in several section 36 private actions premised on breaches of section 45 of the *Competition Act*. Except in one case, these motions have failed on the basis that it was not plain and obvious that Canada could not take jurisdiction.

---

16 Canada, Competition Bureau, Press Release, "Mitsubishi Electric to Pay $13.4 Million for Rigging Bids for Car Parts" (25 April 2017) online: www.canada.ca/en/competition-bureau/news/2017/04/mitsubishi_electrictopay134millionforrigging-bidsforcarparts.html.

17 Canada, Competition Bureau, *Immunity and Leniency Programs under the Competition Act* (Ottawa: Competition Bureau, 2018), online: www.competitionbureau.gc.ca/eic/site/cb-bc.nsf/eng/04391.html at paras 18 and 125 [*Immunity and Leniency Bulletin*].

18 Canada, Competition Bureau, Press Release, "Unprecedented Cooperation with US Antitrust Enforcement Authority Leads to Major Cartel Crackdown" (20 July 2016), online: www.canada.ca/en/competition-bureau/news/2016/07/unprecedented-cooperation-with-us-antitrust-enforcement-authority-leads-to-major-cartel-crackdown.html.

None of these decisions establishes that section 45 (old or new) criminalizes price-fixing conspiracies formed entirely outside Canada, but only that it is not plain and obvious that it does not. None of these decisions considers section 6(2) of the *Criminal Code*. For the most part, they approach the jurisdictional issue from a purely tort law perspective, without considering the principles governing the predicate criminal offence.

a) *VitaPharm*

The most important of these decisions was the first, in *VitaPharm*.[19] Four defendants challenged the jurisdiction of the Ontario court over class actions alleging price fixing of vitamins. They did this even though two of them had pleaded guilty in Canada to offences under (old) section 45 and had admitted in the criminal proceeding that at least one of the conspiracy meetings occurred in Toronto.

In Ontario, Cumming J held that he had jurisdiction. It was arguable that a price-fixing conspiracy entered into outside Canada that raises prices in Canada gives rise to liability in Canada, he held, noting that the "language of s. 45 is not directed only to those conspiracies entered into within Canada."[20] Nor did section 46 limit the scope of section 45; rather, it "creates an offence for persons beyond those who are not co-conspirators but knowingly implement in whole or in part in Canada any directive for the purpose of giving effect to a conspiracy."[21]

The plaintiffs had also pleaded the tort of civil conspiracy. There was a good arguable case that a conspiracy to fix prices in Canada is a tort committed in Canada, because the "relevant inquiry must include an analysis as to the actual provisions of the agreement, which allegedly provide for price-fixing in respect of products sold to and within Canada."[22] Justice Cumming did not address the fact that the tort relied on the same predicate offence as the section 36 action, which meant that pleading the tort was no answer to the jurisdictional issue.

One of the defendants also challenged jurisdiction in British Columbia, unsuccessfully. That decision does not address section 45 at all, even though the case was based on a breach of that provision. Rather, the court

19 *VitaPharm Canada Ltd v F Hoffmann-La Roche Ltd* (2002), 20 CPC (5th) 351 (Ont SC) [*VitaPharm*].

20 *Ibid* at para 59.

21 *Ibid* at para 60.

22 *Ibid* at para 62.

considered only the common law tort of conspiracy. The tort of conspiracy requires damage to be actionable; and where that damage occurs in British Columbia, the tort occurs in British Columbia.[23]

b) Cases After *VitaPharm*

Cases decided since *VitPharm* tend to rely on *VitaPharm*. In *Fairhurst v Anglo American PLC*, for example, courts in British Columbia held that they had jurisdiction because the claim alleged that the defendants caused harm in British Columbia, which meant that the tort was committed there, and the restitutionary obligations arose there.[24] Both the Supreme Court and the Court of Appeal focused entirely on jurisdiction over torts. They did not consider whether conduct occurring outside Canada could breach section 45.

The Supreme Court of Canada had occasion to consider jurisdictional issues in *Sun-Rype*, one of the decisions in the indirect purchaser trilogy.[25] The jurisdictional issue was not central, as the court denied certification on other grounds. Justice Rothstein, writing for the majority, concluded that it was not plain and obvious that Canadian courts have no jurisdiction.

c) Lithium-Ion Batteries

The first, and so far, only, successful challenge to jurisdiction was brought in Ontario by two related defendants (NEC Corporation and NEC Tokin Corporation) in *Shah*,[26] a case alleging price fixing of lithium-ion batteries. Justice Perell found that NEC was not carrying on business in Ontario, that it was not reasonably foreseeable that lithium-ion batteries manufactured by NEC would reach Ontario through normal channels of trade, and that the plaintiffs had not established a good arguable case that NEC was a party to a conspiracy committed in Ontario. Consequently, the Ontario courts had no jurisdiction over the claim against NEC.

The plaintiffs had argued that none of this mattered, because NEC's co-conspirators did have sales into Ontario, and all tortfeasors are jointly liable. Justice Perell accepted that the tort of conspiracy is committed in

23 *Nutreco Canada Inc v F Hoffmann-La Roche*, 2001 BCSC 1146.

24 *Fairhurst v Anglo American PLC*, 2011 BCSC 705, aff'd 2012 BCCA 257.

25 *Sun-Rype Products Ltd v Archer Daniels Midland Co*, 2013 SCC 58. The other two cases in the trilogy are *Pro-Sys Consultants Ltd v Microsoft Corporation*, 2013 SCC 57, and *Infineon Technologies AG v Option consommateurs*, 2013 SCC 59.

26 *Shah v LG Chem, Ltd*, 2015 ONSC 2628 [*Shah*].

the jurisdiction where the damage from the conspiracy is suffered. But he rejected the notion that the Ontario court has jurisdiction *simpliciter* over a foreign co-conspirator who does not have any causal connection to the damage in Ontario. Unless NEC did something anywhere in the world that caused damage in Ontario, Ontario courts have no jurisdiction. For there to be joint liability in Ontario, he held, each co-conspirator must have done "an act or omission in furtherance of the conspiracy that causes damage to occur in Ontario."[27]

Shah was narrowed in a case alleging that roll-on/roll-off (RORO) marine shippers conspired to fix prices for transporting vehicles, causing British Columbia consumers to pay higher prices for vehicles.[28] While the BC Court of Appeal agreed with Perell J that "a defendant does not commit the tort of conspiracy in a jurisdiction if they do not do anything which is causally connected to the harm allegedly suffered in that jurisdiction,"[29] it distinguished *Shah* on the ground that NEC had denied participation in the conspiracy, whereas the RORO defendants had not. The court took jurisdiction because the tort of conspiracy is committed where the damage is suffered.[30] Once again, the court confined its analysis to the tort of conspiracy, without considering whether a price-fixing conspiracy conducted entirely outside Canada is an offence under section 45.

It is also questionable whether Perell J's reasoning in *Shah* would be accepted today in light of the Supreme Court of Canada's holding in *Pioneer Corp v Godfrey*[31] that umbrella purchasers can sue for damages caused by price fixing. Umbrella purchasers are those purchasers who buy the cartelized product made by firms that are *not* part of the cartel. The theory is that the overcharge exacted by the cartel members leads to non-members being able to charge higher prices, because "a rising tide lifts all boats."[32] On the same theory, a cartel member that had no sales into Canada would still make possible the higher prices charged by other cartel members, and even non-cartel members, for their sales into Canada. This might supply the causal connection sought by Perell J.

27 *Ibid* at para 109.

28 *Ewert v Höegh Autoliners AS*, 2020 BCCA 181.

29 *Ibid* at para 76.

30 *Ibid* at para 77.

31 *Pioneer Corp v Godfrey*, above note 14.

32 *Ibid* at para 59.

3) Effects-Based Jurisdiction in Section 90.1 Proceedings

In *HarperCollins*,[33] the Competition Tribunal took jurisdiction over a conspiracy by foreign publishers of e-books to raise prices in an application under the *Competition Act*'s civil provision dealing with agreements that harm competition (section 90.1).

The Tribunal held that it was not plain and obvious that section 90.1 could not be applied to agreements formed outside Canada. Tribunal chair Gascon J noted that there is no language in section 90.1 confining it to agreements reached in Canada; nor is there any analogue to sections 46 or 83 for section 90.1. Justice Gascon also pointed to a key difference between sections 45 and 90.1: section 45 is a *per se* offence that does not require proof of any anticompetitive effects, whereas proof of anticompetitive harm — a substantial lessening or prevention of competition — is an intrinsic component of section 90.1.[34]

Justice Gascon held that the "existence of anti-competitive effects in Canada attributable to the impugned agreement"[35] established a real and substantial connection with Canada sufficient to give the Tribunal jurisdiction.

D. CAN CANADIAN COURTS TAKE JURISDICTION OVER CARTELS BASED SOLELY ON EFFECTS?

As noted above, some states have adopted effects-based jurisdiction for some offences. In those cases, courts take criminal jurisdiction over conduct done abroad whose effects are felt at home. This is the basis upon which the United States and the European Union exercise long-arm jurisdiction in competition law matters, and the ground upon which the Competition Bureau, the PPSC, and Canadian plaintiffs also rely. While there is no formal barrier at international law to Canada taking effects-based jurisdiction, Canada follows the territorial principle in criminal matters. This principle is codified in section 6(2) of the *Criminal Code*, which provides that "no person shall be convicted … of an offence

33 *Commissioner of Competition v HarperCollins Publishers LLC*, 2017 Comp Trib 10 [*HarperCollins*].

34 *Ibid* at para 104. See also Michael Osborne, "Ebooks: 4 Settlements and 1 Application" *The Litigator* (30 January 2017), online: www.thelitigator.ca/2017/01/ebooks-4-settlements-and-1-application/.

35 *HarperCollins*, above note 33 at para 150.

committed outside Canada." As subsections (1) and (3) provide, "offence" here refers to any offence created by an Act of Parliament, which thus includes offences under the *Competition Act*.

The question therefore must be whether this provision allows Canadian courts to take jurisdiction over price fixing that occurs entirely outside Canada based solely on its effects in Canada, whether direct or indirect. As discussed below, the cases do not support the conclusion that they can do so.

1) The Real and Substantial Connection Test

In *Libman v R*,[36] La Forest J articulated what has come to be known as the "real and substantial connection" test for territorial jurisdiction:

> All that is necessary to make an offence subject to the jurisdiction of our courts is that a significant portion of the activities constituting that offence took place in Canada. As it is put by modern academics, it is sufficient that there be a "real and substantial link" between an offence and this country, a test well known in public and private international law.[37]

There are two ways to read this passage. It can be read as requiring that "a significant portion of the activities constituting that offence took place in Canada" for a Canadian court to take jurisdiction. In other words, for there to be a "real and substantial link," something must have been done in Canada. This reading is consistent with section 6(2). But the real and substantial connection test can also be read as a free-standing test, in which case it is not necessary that any of the activities constituting the offence take place in Canada. On this reading, the real and substantial connection test effectively replaces section 6(2).

Cartel cases highlight this tension because, in some cases at least, it is possible to argue that none of the activities constituting the offence occurred in Canada.

Several passages in *Libman* seem to suggest that La Forest J did intend to replace section 6(2) with this new test. He cites Professor Hall for the proposition that legislation is not needed, because the courts had "defined the manner in which the doctrine of territoriality applied, and the

36 *Libman v The Queen*, [1985] 2 SCR 178 [*Libman*]. See also chapters 3 and 4 in this volume.

37 *Libman*, *ibid* at para 74.

test proposed simply amounts to a revival of the earlier way of formulating the principle."[38] But Hall was writing in England, where criminal law has not been codified. Judges there could continue to develop criminal law, including the law on jurisdiction. This is not open to a Canadian court, because criminal law is codified in Canada. The fact that a statute codifies judge-made common law does not change the cardinal constitutional principle that courts have no power to amend legislation.

In order to respect that cardinal principle, the *Libman* test must be kept anchored to section 6(2). The question must always be whether the offence took place outside Canada; the real and substantial connection test is a way of determining whether that is the case.

Libman does stand for the proposition that the concept of where an offence is committed may not be entirely contiguous with where its elements occurred. Justice La Forest was careful to speak of the "activities constituting the offence" and not the elements of the offence in formulating his approach.

Thus the fact that Libman obtained the fruits of the transaction in Canada was "relevant in considering whether a transaction falls outside Canadian territory," even though "it may not in strictness constitute part of the offence."[39] Libman had defrauded residents of the United States from a boiler room in Toronto. The money was sent to Costa Rica, where Libman went to collect it and bring it back to Canada. He was charged with fraud, which involves defrauding a person of any property, money, or valuable security, by deceit, falsehood, or other fraudulent means.[40] This offence is complete when the victim is deprived of money by fraud; Libman's eventual receipt of the money was not a necessary element. But his receipt of the fruits of his fraud were of the essence of his scheme. In that sense, it was very much "part of the activities constituting the offence."

2) Does *Libman* Support Effects-Based Jurisdiction?

Throughout *Libman*, La Forest J emphasized that Canadian courts have never applied the territorial principle rigidly. He anchored much of his analysis in comity, going so far as to state that the "outer limits of the test

38 *Ibid* at para 74.

39 *Ibid* at para 71.

40 *Criminal Code*, above note 7, s 338(1).

may, however, well be coterminous with the requirements of international comity."[41] He pointed to Canada's "legitimate interest in prosecuting persons for activities that take place abroad but have an unlawful consequence" in Canada.[42]

Despite passages in *Libman* that tend to support the idea of effects-based jurisdiction, it is problematic to interpret it as holding that Canadian courts can take jurisdiction over an offence committed outside Canada based solely on effects in Canada. *Libman* itself was not decided based on effects; it was decided based on Libman's activities in Canada. None of the cases cited by La Forest J involve Canadian courts taking jurisdiction solely on the basis of effects.

Justice La Forest refers to *Re Hanes and the Queen*[43] as a case in which a Canadian court took jurisdiction over an offence consisting of acts committed abroad that had adverse effects in Canada. *Hanes* is not an effects case, however. It is a case in which an essential element of the offence (deprivation) occurred *in Canada*. Hanes was charged with fraud, the same offence as Libman. He had obtained a credit card from a Canadian bank, went to California, and charged money on the card, all as part of a scheme to defraud the bank. The basis for Southey J's decision is that the offence had been committed in Canada because Hanes had intended that the Canadian bank pay the merchants in California.

3) Cases After *Libman*

In *R c Ouellette*,[44] Béliveau J held that section 6(2) of the *Criminal Code* precluded adopting the effects test. This is because the term "committed" ("*commise*" in French) has a technical sense in criminal law: it cannot refer only to the effects of the offence.[45] He concluded that at least one essential *element* of the offence must be *connected* ("*rattaché*") to Canada.

In that case, there was. Ouellette and his girlfriend were on vacation in the Dominican Republic. They quarrelled. Ouellette struck his girlfriend, who fell and lost consciousness. She was returned to Quebec,

41 *Libman*, above note 36 at para 76.

42 *Ibid* at para 67.

43 *Re Hanes and the Queen* (1982), 69 CCC (2d) 420 (Ont HCJ).

44 *R c Ouellette*, [1997] AQ No 4076 (SC).

45 *Ibid* at para 96.

where she died a few days later. Because she died in Canada, and death is what distinguishes manslaughter from assault, the offence was not committed outside Canada, Béliveau J held.

Another case that might appear to be an effects case is *R v Dos Santos*.[46] A Portuguese fishing-boat captain directed his sailors to set nets inside the 200-mile Canadian fishing zone, which was prohibited. He was convicted of fishing inside the limit. The court noted that Canada has a direct concern over the actions of persons outside the 200-mile limit when those actions harm conservation and management within the limit. The basis of the decision, however, is that while the offence was planned outside Canada, its culmination occurred inside the limit.

4) Taking Jurisdiction Over Offences Committed Outside Canada?

The *Karigar* and *Barra* cases may at first glance appear to be a case of courts applying the real and substantial connection test in isolation from section 6(2) and taking jurisdiction over offences committed outside Canada. Closer examination shows, however, that there was a connection between Canada and an essential element of the offence.

Nazir Karigar, Robert Barra, and Shailesh Govindia were charged under the *Corruption of Foreign Public Officials Act* (*CFPOA*)[47] with a conspiracy to bribe officials from Air India and the Indian government in order to obtain a contract for an Ottawa company. Section 3 of that Act makes it a crime to bribe a foreign public official in order to obtain or retain an advantage in the course of business. Because the provision includes the act of agreeing to give or offer a bribe, it incorporates an offence of conspiracy to offer a bribe.[48] The three men were charged with the conspiracy version of the offence.

The difficulty was that this conspiracy seems to have been conducted entirely outside Canada. Today, the *CFPOA* contains a deeming provision that makes it an offence in Canada for Canadians to commit an offence

46 *R v Dos Santos*, [1992] NJ No 34 (SCTD).
47 *Corruption of Foreign Public Officials Act*, SC 1998, c 34 [*CFPOA*].
48 *R v Karigar*, 2013 ONSC 5199 at para 28 [*Karigar* ONSC].

under the *CFPOA* outside Canada.[49] That provision had not been enacted at the time of the offence, however.

Ontario Superior Court Justice Hackland rejected Karigar's argument that the bulk of the elements of the offence must be grounded in Canada for territorial jurisdiction to be made out. He stated that the "substantial connection test is not limited to the essential elements of the offence,"[50] adding that one cannot segregate the bribery from the rest of the transaction.

It was primarily the transaction that created the real and substantial connection. Karigar, a Canadian businessman, acted as an agent for a Canadian company in attempting to obtain a contract with Air India through bribery. Had the contract been awarded, much of the work would have been done in Ottawa.[51]

Justice Hackland added that taking jurisdiction would not offend international comity. To the contrary, Canada was required under the *OECD Anti-Bribery Convention*[52] to enforce its provisions against bribing foreign public officials.[53]

Karigar appealed. The Court of Appeal upheld the conviction,[54] characterizing Karigar's jurisdictional argument as an attempt to "resurrect the concept that the *Libman* test requires the court to determine whether the essential elements of the offence took place in Canada."[55] Feldman JA emphasized that La Forest J did not confine the analysis to acts that are strictly part of the offence, but rather looked to all relevant facts that take place in Canada.

Barra and Govindia were tried several years later. Their jurisdictional challenge met with a similar fate, for essentially the same reasons. Echoing *Libman*, the trial judge held that the *CFPOA* "would be lame if it did not

---

49 *CFPOA*, above note 47, s 5. This provision also contains an international double jeopardy provision that allows a person to plead *autrefois acquit* and *autrefois convict* based on a trial outside of Canada.

50 *Karigar* ONSC, above note 48 at para 39.

51 *Ibid* at para 40.

52 *Convention on Combating Bribery of Foreign Public Officials in International Business Transactions,* 17 December 1997, OECD Doc DAFFE/ IME/BR(97)20 (1997), 37 ILM 1 (1998), Can TS 1999 No 23 (entered into force 15 February 1999, ratified by Canada 7 December 1998).

53 *Karigar* ONSC, above note 48 at 41.

54 *R v Karigar*, 2017 ONCA 576 [*Karigar* ONCA].

55 *Ibid* at 27.

apply to a situation where members of senior management of a Canadian company" meet outside Canada to "agree to pay bribes to foreign officials to obtain a contract for the Canadian company."[56] In affirming that decision, the Court of Appeal focused on Canada's legitimate interest in prosecuting the offence, holding that the "in Canada" facts give this country a legitimate interest in prosecuting the offence.[57]

Interestingly, none of the four decisions in these cases discusses, much less cites, section 6(2) of the *Criminal Code*.[58] They treat the real and substantial connection test as having entirely supplanted the legislative provision.

The four decisions all rely heavily on the fact that the bribery was for the benefit of a Canadian company as being the principal connecting factor, even while acknowledging that this fact may not have been strictly part of the offence. All four decisions seem to have missed the fact that the benefit is very much a part of the offence. Section 3 of the *CFPOA* requires that the bribery be "in order to obtain or retain an advantage in the course of business." The locus of the "advantage in the course of business" in these cases was in Canada.

Consequently, notwithstanding the apparent willingness of the Ontario courts to take jurisdiction over offences committed outside Canada in these cases, in fact they did not.

5) Comity and Conspiracy

Comity suffuses La Forest J's reasoning in *Libman*. He saw the territorial rule as having been developed "to respond to two practical considerations, first, that a country has generally little direct concern for the actions of malefactors abroad; and second, that other states may legitimately take umbrage if a country attempts to regulate matters taking place wholly or substantially within their territories."[59] He noted that section 6(2) "expresses the territorial principle in a manner that rather reflects its purpose. That provision does not say that criminal law is confined to Canadian territory; it says rather that no person 'shall be convicted in Canada for an offence

56 *R v Barra*, 2018 ONSC 2659, at para 30.

57 *R v Barra*, 2021 ONCA 568 at para 55.

58 Feldman JA does make a passing reference to the provision, by way of background to *Libman*: *Karigar* ONCA, above note 54 at para 25.

59 *Libman*, above note 36 at para 65.

committed outside of Canada.'"[60] He added that Canada has an interest in "prosecuting persons for activities that take place abroad but have unlawful consequences here," and that "another nation could not easily say" that protecting the Canadian public in this way offends the dictates of comity.[61]

Canada certainly has an interest in defending its markets and consumers from distortions caused by price fixing, whether by domestic or by foreign cartels. In *R v Maxzone*, Crampton CJ of the Federal Court described price fixing as "analogous to fraud and theft," which represents "nothing less than an assault on our open market economy."[62]

All of this is true, but the offences in the *Competition Act* are not "real crimes"; they are regulatory offences. They are not by their very nature criminal and deserving of sanction. Price fixing is only a criminal offence in Canada because the *Competition Act* makes it so, not because it is "generally regarded as by its very nature criminal and worthy of criminal sanction," but for "strictly instrumental reasons," to achieve "desirable economic goals."[63] At common law, price fixing is not unlawful.[64]

New section 45 explicitly preserves a loophole allowing Parliament and provincial legislatures to permit price-fixing behaviour through statute (the regulated conduct defence in section 45(7)). Large parts of Canada's agricultural sector are effectively cartelized, by legislative fiat, through supply management. Producers of milk (the largest of these cartels) jointly set prices through milk marketing boards. These cartels are just as much, if not more, of an assault on the market and consumers as unlawful price fixing. According to OECD calculations, transfers from consumers to producers was an astounding C$61.5 billion for supply-managed products from 2000 to 2020, or just over C$2.9 billion on average each year. Almost 90 percent of this overcharge was paid for milk: C$53 billion, or more than C$2.5 billion every year.[65] The total fines and class action settlements during this same period are less than one year's worth of this wealth transfer.

---

60 *Ibid* at para 66.

61 *Ibid* at para 67.

62 *R v Maxzone Auto Parts (Canada) Corp*, 2012 FC 1117 at para 54.

63 *Thomson Newspapers Ltd v Canada (Director of Investigation and Research, Restrictive Trade Practices Commission)*, [1990] 1 SCR 425 at para 133; *R v Wholesale Travel Group Inc*, [1991] 3 SCR 145 at para 35.

64 *Mogul Steamship Company, Limited v McGregor, Gow & Co*, [1892] AC 25; *Norris v United States of America*, [2008] UKHL 16.

65 OECD, *PSE Database for Canada* (6 June 2021), online: www.oecd-ilibrary.org/agriculture-and-food/data/agricultural-support-estimates/reference-tables_

Canada also tolerates, and arguably even actively supports, export cartels, through the export cartel exception in section 45(5). One well-known example is the potash cartel. When Australian mining company BHP Billiton proposed to buy Potash Corporation of Saskatchewan in 2010, the Saskatchewan government actively opposed the takeover, in part because it might mean the end of the export cartel that Potash Corporation participated in, and the federal government ultimately blocked it under the *Investment Canada Act*. A report commissioned by the Saskatchewan government from the Conference Board of Canada expressed the concern that the acquirer might choose to "ignore market disciplines and compete for market share through higher volumes and lower prices" (although it thought it unlikely that BHP Billiton would do this).[66] In 2012, the chair of the OECD Competition Committee, Frédéric Jenny, estimated that this cartel cost India C$1.183 billion annually, and China, about US$500 million.[67] So much for comity.

Although today the Competition Bureau cooperates with US competition authorities on criminal matters, Canada still has statutes enacted to counteract overly aggressive extraterritorial enforcement by other countries of their competition laws. For example, the *Foreign Extraterritorial Measures Act* allows the attorney general to block orders for production of documents from foreign courts, and to block the enforcement of a foreign judgment under an antitrust law where Canadian interests in relation to international trade or commerce might be adversely affected.[68]

Nor can it be said that there is a global consensus that price fixing should be dealt with through criminal sanction. Outside of North America, most states historically prohibited price fixing through civil, rather than criminal, penalties. The European Union, for example, imposes fines

---

538bf42b-en.

66 Michael Grant, Michael Burt & Lin Ai, *Saskatchewan in the Spotlight: Acquisition of Potash Corporation of Saskatchewan Inc — Risks and Opportunities* (Ottawa: Conference Board of Canada, 2020).

67 Frederic Jenny, "Price Instability and Competition Law: The Case of the Potash Cartel" (OECD Global Forum on Trade and Competition, 2012), online: www.oecd.org/competition/globalforum/49737333.pdf.

68 *Foreign Extraterritorial Measures Act*, RSC 1985, c F-29. This statute has been little used. There are two extant orders made under the Act, one in relation to US sanctions against Cuba, in 1992, and more recently to counteract potential effects of US "Buy America" provisions on facilities leased by Alaska at the Port of Prince Rupert, in 2014.

on cartel members through an administrative, not criminal, regime. That said, several other countries have introduced criminal sanctions for cartel behaviours, including, for example, the United Kingdom, Ireland, Israel, Mexico, Brazil, Chile, Australia, Japan, and South Korea.

In short, there is no consensus, either within Canada or internationally, that price fixing is always wrong, or that it should be treated as a crime. Courts cannot blithely assume that other states will not take umbrage at an assumption of criminal jurisdiction by Canada over conduct that occurs on their territories.

E. ARE FOREIGN PRICE-FIXING CONSPIRACIES OFFENCES IN CANADA?

If Canadian courts cannot take jurisdiction over foreign conspiracies based solely on their effects in Canada, does this mean that these conspiracies cannot be prosecuted in Canada, and that legislative reform is needed? As argued below, Canadian courts can exercise jurisdiction over foreign conspiracies where it can fairly be said that the cartelists agreed outside Canada to fix prices, allocate markets, or restrict output *in Canada*. Drawing the line in this way will limit which foreign conspiracies can be prosecuted, because increases in prices for downstream products that end up in Canada would not be a sufficient basis to take jurisdiction.

1) Statutory Signals

Although section 45 is silent as to its reach, two other provisions in the *Competition Act* signal that Parliament recognized that section 45 could not always reach price-fixing conspiracies that occur outside Canada.

The first is section 46. Section 46 makes it an offence for a corporation that carries on business in Canada to implement a directive from outside Canada that is "for the purpose of giving effect to a conspiracy, combination, agreement or arrangement entered into outside Canada that, if entered into in Canada, would have been in contravention of section 45." The second provision, section 83(2), contains identical language. It allows the Competition Tribunal to prohibit a person in Canada from implementing a directive from outside Canada whose purpose is to implement a conspiracy "entered into outside Canada that, if entered into in Canada, would have been in contravention of section 45."

This language suggests that a conspiracy entered into outside Canada does not contravene section 45. The language ("entered into outside Canada") tracks the language of section 6(2) of the *Criminal Code* ("committed outside Canada").

In *VitaPharm*, Cumming J disagreed with the suggestion that section 46 imposes limiting language on section 45.[69] That misses the point, however. The purpose of section 46 is not to limit section 45, but to make it possible for Canada to reach those who implement a conspiracy when the conspirators themselves are beyond reach.[70]

In *HarperCollins*, Gascon J recognized that section 46's function of expanding liability did not prevent it being a signal that section 45 may be limited to conspiracies entered into in Canada:

> As drafted, section 46 therefore ends up having two dimensions. It serves both to expand section 45 to corporations carrying on business in Canada which implement a conspiracy entered into outside Canada, and to suggest that section 45 may be limited to conspiracies, agreements and arrangements entered into in Canada. Section 83 contains similar wording.[71]

2) The Conspiracies Rule

Conspiracies have long been a special case from a jurisdictional standpoint. It is tempting, but incorrect, to assume that section 45 conspiracies are the same as other kinds of conspiracies.

At common law, a conspiracy is deemed to occur where its intended effects are felt.[72] This principle has been codified in the *Criminal Code* conspiracy offence since 1976. Section 465(4) deems a conspiracy entered into outside Canada, to commit an offence in Canada, to have been entered into in Canada. The same principle applies to the tort of conspiracy.[73] Courts dealing with jurisdiction in private actions alleging a breach of section 45 seem to have assumed, without giving the issue much consideration, that the same principle would apply to section 45.

69 *VitaPharm*, above note 19 at para 60.
70 *HarperCollins*, above note 33 at para 91.
71 *Ibid.*
72 *R v Reilly*, [1982] 3 All ER 27 (CA); *DPP v Doot*, [1973] 1 All ER 940 (HL).
73 *British Columbia v Imperial Tobacco Canada Ltd*, 2006 BCCA 398 at para 41.

The problem with this assumption is that there is a key difference between a section 45 conspiracy and other types of conspiracy. The crime of conspiracy to commit an offence is a form of secondary criminal liability. The conspiracy is unlawful because of unlawfulness of the predicate offence. For example, if a gang conspires to commit a theft, then all are liable, not just the person who actually commits the theft. The conspiracy offence expands liability for the offence to those who participated in its planning. It is also available if the authorities interrupt the plot before the crime can be committed. The same is true, in my view, of the unlawful means branch of the tort of conspiracy: it takes its tortious character from the unlawful means employed. It expands liability to include not just the person who committed the unlawful conduct, but also those who participated in its planning.

Thus, what criminal and tortious conspiracy have in common is that they involve secondary liability for some predicate unlawful conduct. They are conspiracies to do something unlawful. When the conspirators agree in one place to do something unlawful in another place, it makes sense to prosecute the offence in the targeted jurisdiction.

By contrast, the liability for a section 45 offence is primary. The source of the unlawful character of section 45 conspiracies is *not* some predicate offence or unlawful act. Section 45 prohibits agreements among competitors to fix prices, allocate markets, or restrict outputs. Unlike theft, decisions on prices, markets, and production levels by one firm, on its own, are not only lawful, but expected. A section 45 conspiracy is *not* an agreement to commit an offence. Rather, the agreement itself is the crime; section 45 makes it unlawful for competitors to do jointly what they could lawfully do separately.

Nor is section 45 a mechanism for expanding the scope of liability beyond those who actually commit an unlawful act to those who plan it. Participants in a section 45 conspiracy commit the unlawful act itself. Because of this difference, section 45 cannot be analyzed as though it were the same as the crime or tort of conspiracy. Rather, the analysis must focus on the nature of the section 45 offence itself. This is discussed below.

3) Object of the Agreement

The agreements prohibited by section 45 do have an object that must be proven, namely fixing prices, allocating markets, or restricting output. This is similar to the "in order to obtain or retain an advantage in the course of business" requirement in section 3 of the *CFPOA*. There is nothing unlawful in obtaining an advantage in the course of business, just as there is nothing unlawful in a firm setting prices on its own. If the fact that the advantage is obtained in Canada is sufficient to ground an offence under section 3 of the *CFPOA* in Canada, then it is equally arguable that a conspiracy whose object is to fix prices, allocate markets, or restrict output *in Canada* gives rise to an offence in Canada under section 45, regardless of where the conspiracy was formed.

It is obvious that if executives of Canadian companies were to decamp to a foreign locale to conspire to fix prices *in Canada*, they should be prosecuted here, since the object of their agreement was to fix prices *in Canada*. But what of the case where executives of foreign companies fix prices outside Canada? When can it be said that they are fixing prices *in Canada*?

It is helpful to examine how a cartel can affect prices in Canada. There are essentially four scenarios.

1) Fixing prices for Canada: The cartel might fix prices in Canada by explicitly adopting prices for the Canadian market, or by rigging bids for customers located in Canada. In this scenario, it is logical to assert that the cartel has agreed to fix prices in Canada or rigged bids *in Canada*, and that the offence did not take place outside Canada.
2) Fixing prices for geographic regions that include Canada: The cartel might fix prices in Canada by fixing prices for geographic markets that include Canada (such as North America), or by rigging bids pursuant to a call for tenders that includes product for Canada. In this scenario, it is arguable that the cartel agreed to fix prices in Canada or rigged bids in Canada, and that the offence did not take place outside Canada, but this connection is less direct than in the first scenario.
3) Fixing prices for distributors outside Canada: The cartel might fix prices for their sales to distributors or other resellers outside Canada, who then sell the cartelized product into Canada. In this scenario, we cannot maintain a legal fiction that the conduct occurred in Canada. One might argue that it is foreseeable by the cartelists that the cartelized product would find its way into Canada through normal trade channels. But the fact remains that the cartel is not fixing prices in Canada; it is fixing prices for sales that occur outside Canada.

Any effect in Canada is dependent on the pricing decisions of others (whether to pass on or absorb the overcharge).

4) Fixing prices for manufacturers outside Canada: The cartel might fix prices or rig bids for firms located outside Canada that incorporate the cartelized product into other products, and these downstream products might then be sold into Canada either by the manufacturer itself or through a distributor. In this scenario, the impact in Canada is at two removes (or more) from the cartel. That impact is dependent on decisions by the manufacturer and distributors to pass on or absorb the overcharge. It is impossible to say that the cartelists agreed to fix prices or rig bids *in Canada.*

In the first two scenarios, the cartelists can be said to be fixing prices, allocating markets, or restricting output *in Canada*, even though they may not be themselves in Canada. There is thus a basis to say that the offence did not occur outside Canada, since the object of the agreement — an element of section 45 — is closely connected to Canada. By the same token, where the effect in Canada is indirect, through a distributor reselling the cartelized product, or doubly so, through a manufacturer including the cartelized product in a downstream product, it cannot be said that conspirators have agreed to fix prices *in Canada*. In those cases, the better view is that the conspirators have not contravened section 45.

4) Competitors in Canada

New section 45 only prohibits agreements between *competitors*. Whether the parties to a price-fixing conspiracy must be competitors or potential competitors *in Canada* for there to be an offence has yet to be determined.

Were Canada to take jurisdiction over foreign conspiracies based solely on their effects in Canada, and even indirect effects, then it would not make sense to require that the conspirators be competitors in Canada. After all, the goal would be to protect the Canadian economy from the damage caused by price fixing. But, as argued above, applying a purely effects-based jurisdiction where the conspirators cannot be said to have conspired to fix prices *in Canada* is not consistent with section 6(2) of the *Criminal Code*.

If section 45 is confined to cases where the parties have agreed to fix prices for products they sell in Canada, either by addressing the Canadian market specifically, or by including Canada within the ambit of the agreement, then the problem goes away. Since the conspirators are selling in Canada, they are competitors in Canada. It is not necessary for a firm to have a presence in Canada to be a competitor here.

But what if the conspiracy involves a market allocation agreement pursuant to which one firm agrees not to enter the Canadian market? The object of the conspiracy would clearly be to allocate markets in Canada (the entire Canadian market), but would the firm that is not present as a competitor in Canada be a potential competitor? The answer to that question must be found in section 45(8), which extends the notion of "competitor" to include a "person who it is reasonable to believe would be likely" to be a competitor but for the conspiracy. Thus, it must be reasonable to believe that the firm that does not compete in Canada would do so but for the agreement.

F. CONCLUSION

I have argued above that section 6(2) establishes a line between foreign price-fixing conspiracies that can be prosecuted in Canada and those that cannot, based on whether the agreement can be said to be an agreement to fix prices, allocate markets, or restrict output *in Canada*. This will be limited to situations where the cartel members either fixed prices for their sales to Canada or included prices for their sales to Canada in a larger geographic region over which they fixed prices. Both of these situations involve direct sales of the cartelized product into Canada.

Where, however, the cartel members do not have the Canadian market within their contemplation, or where their sales to Canada are indirect, it cannot be said that they fixed prices *in Canada*, and there is thus no offence under section 45 in Canada.

No amendment to the *Competition Act* would be required for a court to draw this line. Of course, the question of whether, and to what extent, section 45 captures foreign price-fixing conspiracies has yet to be litigated in either criminal or civil proceedings. Nor is it likely that it ever will be. To date, there has been no contested prosecution of a foreign cartel. Most potential foreign corporate criminal defendants have no need to contest jurisdiction, because they cannot be served outside Canada. By the simple expedient of refusing to appear in Canada voluntarily to answer charges, corporations can avoid being prosecuted. While Canada could seek extradition of foreign executives of cartelists, the number of states from which Canada could seek extradition is somewhat limited (because price fixing is not treated as a criminal offence in much of the world, and thus the double criminality rule could not be met).

Of course, foreign corporate cartelists cannot avoid damages actions with the same ease. To date, however, no action alleging an international price-fixing conspiracy has gone to trial; all have settled. Courts are reluctant to rule on an issue like this at the certification stage (and plaintiffs keep their pleadings vague as to where the conspiracy occurred). Once the action is certified as a class action, the defendants are practically "compelled to pay a settlement to the plaintiff."[74]

At some point, the extent of section 45's extraterritorial reach needs to be decided. While the present state of uncertainty is profitable for the Canadian treasury and class action plaintiff law firms, it is not good for Canadian competition law to have such an important question remain unanswered. If the courts will not do it, then it may be that section 45 should be amended to make clear in what situations a price-fixing conspiracy entered into abroad will be an offence in Canada.

74 *Atlantic Lottery Corp Inc v Babstock*, 2020 SCC 19, quoting J.M. Martin, "Waiver of Tort: An Historical and Practical Study" (2012) 52 *Canadian Business Law Journal* 473 at 476.

V

COMMODITY CRIMES

sixteen

International Trafficking of Cultural Property: An Overview and the Canadian Perspective

KATHRYN ZEDDE*

A. INTRODUCTION

Over the past fifty years, trafficking in cultural property has evolved from being perceived primarily as a cultural or moral issue in the wake of theft and looting during World War II, to being acknowledged by the United Nations as a significant and growing transnational crime,[1] and more recently as a source of terrorism financing.[2] While accurate statistics on the global magnitude of this traffic cannot be reliably compiled,

* Master of Arts (Middle Eastern Archaeology), University of London (UK). Senior Analyst and Manager (Ret'd), Heritage Policy and Legislation, Government of Canada and Past Chair, UNESCO Intergovernmental Committee for Promoting the Return of Cultural Property to its Countries of Origin or its Restitution in Case of Illicit Appropriation (ICPRCP).

1 ECOSOC Resolution 2004/34 and the Eleventh UN Congress on Crime Prevention and Criminal Justice, Bangkok, 18–25 April 2005: Report prepared by the Secretariat, ch I, resolution 1; subsequently endorsed in UNGA Resolution 60/177 (16 December 2005) and contained in the annex thereto. See also: Arianna Visconti, "The Illicit Trade in Cultural Objects: From Marginalization to the Current Surge in Attention by Transnational Criminal Policymakers" in Neil Boister et al, eds, *Histories of Transnational Criminal Law* (Oxford: Oxford University Press, 2021) for a general historical overview.

2 UNSC Resolutions 2199 (2015), 2322 (2016), and 2347 (2017).

estimates have placed its value as high as US$7 billion annually[3] and UN resolutions consistently refer to the involvement of organized criminal groups. Aside from its value and links to other forms of criminal activity such as money laundering, trafficking in cultural property has prompted action by the international community because of its long-term damage to humanity and cultural identity. As the two primary UNESCO conventions protecting movable cultural property state, cultural property constitutes one of the basic elements of civilization and national culture,[4] and "damage to cultural property belonging to any people means damage to the cultural heritage of all mankind, since each people makes its contribution to the culture of the world."[5]

This chapter will provide an overview of the international legal regime that has developed to deal with the traffic in cultural property, with emphasis on the transnational criminal suppression aspects. A definitional and descriptive introduction to the trade will be followed by a review of the most relevant international law instruments. The chapter will conclude with an examination of the Canadian perspective, including relevant domestic legislation, caselaw, and some insights into Canada's participation in the development of international law norms.

B. "CULTURAL PROPERTY" AND ITS TRAFFICKING

There is no universally accepted definition of "cultural property,"[6] nor is it defined in Canadian law. International conventions protecting cultural objects contain definitions for their purposes, generally including a broad range of object types, from natural history specimens and fossils to scientific and technological objects, antiquities, Indigenous material, art, and archival documents and books. The primary instrument focusing on the

3 UNODC, UNESCO & World Tourism Organization, "Be a Responsible Traveler," online: https://beresponsibletraveller.org.

4 *Convention on the Means of Prohibiting and Preventing the Illicit Import, Export and Transfer of Ownership of Cultural Property*, (1970) 823 UNTS 231 [*1970 Convention*].

5 *Convention for the Protection of Cultural Property in the Event of Armed Conflict*, (1954) 249 UNTS 215 [1954 Hague Convention], Preamble.

6 For further discussion of definitional challenges and other issues see: Arianna Visconti, "Cultural property trafficking" in Neil Boister & Robert J. Currie, eds, *Routledge Handbook of Transnational Criminal Law* (New York: Routledge, 2015).

fight against trafficking, the *1970 Convention*, also requires that cultural property be designated as "important" by States Parties.[7]

Similarly, domestic laws differ in the range of objects they protect. Canadian cultural property legislation does not define cultural property, but a regulation to it describing eight categories of objects requiring export permits[8] is referenced as being Canada's designation for the purposes of the *1970 Convention*.[9]

Overall, definitions suggest that cultural property may be understood as movable objects determined to have a degree of social, historical, scientific, or artistic importance that has resulted in states enacting legal measures to protect the property in the public interest. Importance may be from a universal, national, regional, or local perspective and is subjective. It may be inherent, as in art, or it may be acquired: through age, context, or association. An old pen is just an old pen, but if it was used by Abraham Lincoln to write the Gettysburg address, it becomes culturally important property.

For border control or law enforcement, this is the first challenge that sets trafficking in cultural property apart from other forms of trafficking. Upon discovery, it is not always immediately evident, or possible to determine, whether an object is cultural property, and whether it is genuine or fake. As with other forms of trafficking, cultural property may also be disguised to prevent its discovery, and sophisticated criminal methods may mean that scientific analysis is required but not always be readily available to law enforcement.

For example, in 1985, among two groups of material seized by Canadian customs authorities, fifty-nine ceramic pieces were released as modern replicas and therefore not subject to cultural property import prohibitions. The remaining material was confirmed to have been illegally exported from Peru, and subsequently returned to the Peruvian government. Following further investigation and international cooperation among law enforcement, however, the fifty-nine objects were re-seized and re-examined by archaeologists at the University of Calgary. The majority were eventually determined to be genuine pre-Columbian antiquities physically altered to appear as modern replicas. False bases had been added and stamped or incised with markings suggesting the vessels were souvenirs, or a thin

7 *1970 Convention*, above note 4, art 1.

8 *Canadian Cultural Property Export Control List*, CRC, c 448 [*CCPECL*].

9 *Cultural Property Export and Import Act*, RSC 1985, c C-51, s 38 [*CPEIA*].

layer of clay applied to mask cracks or other indications of age.[10] The international cultural property literature contains many similar stories.[11]

In addition to the challenge of identifying cultural property is that of identifying when its cross-border movement amounts to trafficking. Cultural property may be legally bought and sold, transported, imported, and exported. If human beings are discovered in a shipping container, it is clear that a crime has taken place, but if an ancient Roman sculpture is in a container, it may be entirely licit. Whether international trade in cultural property is illicit depends on various considerations: where the property is from, how it came to be in its current location, and whether its export or import is controlled or prohibited by any domestic laws—within or outside the context of an international treaty.

Unlike trafficking in firearms or persons, both of which are defined in protocols to the United Nations *Convention against Transnational Organized Crime* (*UNTOC*),[12] there is no similar definition of trafficking in cultural property. There is also a range of views on what constitutes the licit and illicit markets in it. Some scholars reject illegal export under the laws of a state as a component of the illicit market, on the basis that the domestic export laws of one country need not have weight in other jurisdictions.[13] Others have offered somewhat disingenuous arguments suggesting that sales of contested items cannot be unlawful if their original removal was undertaken by local individuals.[14] There appears to be wider acceptance that any trade in cultural property that has been stolen, or taken from

10 Department of Canadian Heritage, "Canada Returns Seized Heritage Artifacts to Peru," Government of Canada press release, 2000, online: https://web.archive.org/web/20040901074741/http://www.canadianheritage.gc.ca/newsroom/news_e.cfm?Action=Display&code=ONR004E.

11 Two of the most well-known cases involved smuggled Egyptian antiquities doctored to look like fakes that resulted in 1997 in the conviction and imprisonment in England of Jonathan Tokeley-Parry and that of his American business partner, dealer Frederick Schultz, in 2002. See *R v Tokeley-Parry*, [1999] Criminal Law Reports (UK) 578, and *United States v Schultz*, 333 F2d 393 (2d Cir 2003).

12 *United Nations Convention against Transnational Organized Crime*, (2000) 2225 UNTS 209 [*UNTOC*].

13 John Henry Merryman, "A Licit International Trade in Cultural Objects" in Martine Briat & Judith A. Freedberg, eds, *Legal Aspects of International Trade in Art* (The Hague: Kluwer Law International, 1996).

14 Scott Reyburn, "Disputed African Artifacts Sell at Auction" *New York Times* (29 June 2020), online: www.newyorktimes.com/2020/06/29/arts/design/christies-african-art-auction.html.

its context (usually, but not exclusively, archaeological) without proper documentation, should be considered illicit. At one end of the spectrum, some source countries (those that have lost and continue to lose significant quantities of heritage material) reject altogether the idea of any licit market. At the other end are individuals who maintain that any control over the trade in cultural property is based on an outdated idea of cultural nationalism and that there is now only "universal culture"— an idea criticized in turn by others as cultural imperialism masquerading as "cultural internationalism."[15]

Canadian cultural property law does not define trafficking, but prohibits a range of transactions, and in its support for broad resolutions at fora such as the United Nations General Assembly (UNGA) and the Economic and Social Council (ECOSOC), Canada has taken (in contrast to the more restrictive approaches described above) a generous public policy approach to the issue. For present purposes, then, and reflecting Canada's longstanding approach, "trafficking in cultural property" refers to the trade in stolen or looted (illegally removed from its context) cultural property, or to the trade in any cultural property imported or exported contrary to the domestic laws of a state or its international treaty obligations (such as export of cultural property from an occupied territory).

Identifying instances of trafficking presents further challenges. Thefts are not always reported, due to embarrassment over security failures, or because owners are keen to maintain confidentiality about their collections. Identifying stolen items may be made more difficult by poor documentation or the failure to share information with agencies such as INTERPOL that maintain databases of stolen cultural property. Identifying instances of looted material is even more difficult, particularly given that trafficked items rarely travel directly from source to market.

It is necessary, first of all, to identify the object and the modern state in which it may have been found, to determine which state holds jurisdiction and whether its removal from context or its export took place in violation of a domestic law. On purely stylistic grounds, identification can be difficult given that ancient cultural boundaries seldom correspond to those of modern states; the ancient Khmer empire, for example, traversed what is now Cambodia and Thailand, and ancient Roman antiquities may

15 Steven Vincent, "Who Owns Art?" *Art & Auction* (January 1995) at 80–85. See also Steven Vincent, "The War on Collecting" *Art & Auction* (February 1999) at 32–39.

be unearthed anywhere from North Africa to the British Isles. Laws and treaties are seldom retroactive in their application, so it is often necessary to determine when removal from context or export took place to conclude whether such actions were illegal. This will depend in turn on when domestic laws came into force and what range of actions and cultural property they regulate. Ancient tombs may have been looted in antiquity, predating laws protecting them; some domestic laws cover only a narrow range of cultural property such as antiquities, excluding Indigenous material or fossils—both of which are subject to looting. And finally, even when instances of trafficking are identified, they may not be pursued and prosecuted if their source country or their country of interception is not party to an international agreement that establishes mutual obligations.

C. THE INTERNATIONAL LAW AND CRIMINAL JUSTICE RESPONSE

In an attempt to combat international trafficking in cultural property, states have established a range of measures individually and collectively through intergovernmental and non-governmental organizations. As Stefano Manacorda has rightly observed, those measures had for some time been weighted more toward civil and administrative sanctions than criminal law responses;[16] this imbalance has in recent years been lessened somewhat by additional developments. Success can be hampered by how conventions, when not self-executing, are (or are not) implemented in domestic law. Indeed, some contend that this disconnect is a major factor fuelling the illicit market in cultural property.[17]

1) The 1954 Hague Convention and Protocols

Any situation involving the breakdown of societal structures, governments, and law enforcement, whether as a result of natural or man-made disasters

16 Stefano Manacorda, "Criminal Law Protection of Cultural Heritage: An International Perspective" in Stefano Manacorda & Duncan Chappell, eds, *Crime in the Art and Antiquities World: Illegal Trafficking in Cultural Property* (New York: Springer, 2011).

17 Evelien Campfens, "Whose Cultural Objects? Introducing Heritage Title for Cross-Border Cultural Property Claims" (2020) 67:2 *Netherlands International Law Review* 257.

or armed conflict, establishes fertile ground for theft, looting, and trafficking of cultural property, usually expanding on pre-existing criminal activity.

The 1954 Hague Convention[18] and its 1954 First Protocol[19] were the international community's response to widespread destruction, looting, and theft of cultural property during World War II. The 1999 Second Protocol[20] was added, in part, as a response to direct targeting of cultural property during more recent ethnically based non-international conflicts such as that in the former Yugoslavia. It applies to both international conflicts and conflicts not of an international character. These instruments are considered part of international humanitarian law[21] and echo general principles enshrined in the 1977 Additional Protocols to the 1949 Geneva Conventions.[22] Violation of certain of their provisions can be considered war crimes.

With respect to trafficking, it is the Protocols that contain relevant provisions. The First Protocol requires States Parties that are occupying powers to prevent export of cultural property from occupied territory.[23] If any such exported property subsequently enters the territory of another State Party, it must take it into safekeeping and return it at the end of hostilities.[24]

The lack of specific provisions dealing with criminal responsibility and jurisdiction in the 1954 Hague Convention and First Protocol was one the issues that led to development of the Second Protocol. Theft, pillage, and misappropriation of cultural property are among the "serious violations" of the Second Protocol and article 15.2 therein requires States Parties to establish such acts as criminal offences. In doing so, States Parties are to "comply with general principles of law and international law, including the rules extending individual criminal responsibility to persons other than those

18 1954 Hague Convention, above note 5.

19 *Protocol for the Protection of Cultural Property in the Event of Armed Conflict*, (1954) 249 UNTS 358 [First Protocol].

20 *Second Protocol to the Hague Convention of 1954 for the Protection of Cultural Property in the Event of Armed Conflict*, (1999) 2253 UNTS 172 [Second Protocol].

21 See the International Committee of the Red Cross Treaties, States Parties and Commentaries database online: https://ihl-databases.icrc.org/ihl.

22 *Protocol Additional to the Geneva Conventions of 12 August 1949, and Relating to the Protection of Victims of Non-International Armed Conflicts*, (1977) 1125 UNTS 609, art 16.

23 First Protocol, above note 19, art 1.

24 *Ibid*, arts 2 & 3.

who directly commit the act." They are also required to establish extraterritorial jurisdiction over the offences.[25] However, these acts are excluded from the list of violations that are to be established as extraditable offences.[26]

Building on provisions in the First Protocol, article 9 of the Second Protocol requires States Parties that are an occupying force to prohibit and prevent

- Illicit export, other removal, or transfer of ownership of cultural property
- Archaeological excavations unless strictly required to safeguard, record, or preserve cultural property
- Alteration to, or change of use of, cultural property, which is intended to conceal or destroy cultural, historical, or scientific evidence, all of which are or can be components of trafficking

Illicit export, other removal, or transfer of ownership of cultural property from occupied territory is included under "other violations" in article 21, and States Parties are required to establish legislative, administrative, or disciplinary measures to suppress such acts. Article 1 defines "illicit" as meaning "under compulsion or otherwise in violation of the applicable rules of the domestic law of the occupied territory in question or of international law."

2) The *1970 Convention*

The *1970 Convention* deals exclusively with trafficking in cultural property. It suffers the same lack of provisions on jurisdiction and comprehensive enforcement as the Hague Convention.

Articles 2 and 3 of the *1970 Convention* create sweeping prohibitions against illicit import, export, and transfer of ownership of cultural property, and very general requirements that States Parties take steps to remove their causes, stop current practices, and make reparations. The *1970 Convention* details capacity-building and regulatory measures such as export certificates,[27] promotes education and public awareness to promote safeguarding of cultural property and to deter illicit activities,[28] and prescribes

25 Second Protocol, above note 20, art 16.1.

26 *Ibid*, art 18.1.

27 *1970 Convention*, above note 4, arts 5 & 6.

28 *Ibid*, art 10b.

control of the market and dealers.[29] A significant emphasis is placed on recovery and return of cultural property that has been lost through trafficking. The *1970 Convention* includes an obligation to impose penalties or administrative sanctions for only two acts: export of cultural property without a required export certificate,[30] and importation of cultural property stolen from a museum or a religious or secular public monument or similar institution.[31]

In contrast to the Hague regime, then, the approach taken in the *1970 Convention* emphasizes measures to prevent trafficking in cultural property, and international cooperation to intercept and return items lost through the illicit trade. But sanctions, where they are mentioned, may be either penal or administrative, with — unsurprisingly in an instrument negotiated between source and market states — qualifying language such as "as appropriate for each country"[32] and "consistent with the laws of each state"[33] that provides significant leeway to States Parties.

The Hague instruments and the *1970 Convention* adopt different approaches to trafficking. The Hague Convention and Protocols, apart from preparatory measures to be undertaken in peacetime, apply exclusively to conditions of conflict and occupation. Violations potentially constitute war crimes, and trafficking is more likely to be accompanied by violence and loss of life. On that basis, the Second Protocol's emphasis on criminal responsibility and jurisdiction is altogether appropriate.

The *1970 Convention*, in contrast, applies at all times (i.e., during both peacetime and conflict), emphasizes international cooperation, and takes a more holistic approach to fighting trafficking, perhaps suggesting that criminal justice tools may have a limited utility to combat this type of international traffic. An examination of certain characteristics of the phenomenon of trafficking in cultural property can help illustrate this.

While the chain of theft from a public or private collection begins with criminals, looting of undocumented cultural property from its context commonly involves local individuals whose primary activity is not crime: they are often members of impoverished communities for whom cultural property has little meaning apart from its monetary value. They

29 *Ibid*, art 10a.

30 *Ibid*, art 6b.

31 *Ibid*, art 7b.

32 *Ibid*, art 5.

33 *Ibid*, art 13.

are not the participants in the chain of actors who realize huge profits, and their involvement in trafficking cannot be divorced from their overall socio-economic circumstances. Seen through this lens, provisions of the *1970 Convention* requiring measures to increase public awareness and appreciation of cultural property and its protection are important.[34] A poor farmer who has found an antiquity may sell it only once, but if they understand that its retention, either *in situ* in an interpreted cultural site, or in a local museum, may result in employment and a better financial return in the long run, they may be more likely to help preserve it than sell it on the illicit market.

Similarly, while criminal sanctions may have some effect as a deterrent (though for criminal organizations, the resulting penalties may simply be regarded as the cost of doing business), they do not speak directly to remedying the actual damage that trafficking inflicts. With or without punishment of perpetrators, only return of cultural property lost through trafficking can remedy the societal damage done, either in whole (in cases of theft) or in part. In cases of looting where knowledge that might have resulted from appropriate removal cannot be fully recovered, an object's proper preservation, documentation, and public access may nevertheless be assured. If one sees that remedy as the ultimate defeat of trafficking, the emphasis placed on recovery and return, rather than criminal sanctions, in the *1970 Convention* is easily understood.

And finally, as is likely the case with all trafficking, demand-side market pressure plays a significant role in trafficking in cultural property and requires attention in strategies to combat it. The role of the market was well illustrated in a 1990 study by the Government of Canada on the level and nature of looting of Canada's archaeological heritage. It revealed low levels of looting in areas such as the Prairies, where the material likely to be found, such as stone arrowheads, holds little interest on the international market. In contrast, it showed that cultural property on Canada's West Coast, such as Indigenous material located in above-ground graves,

34 For a further discussion on the limitations of criminal law responses see: Arianna Visconti, "The Illicit Trade in Cultural Objects: From Marginalization to the Current Surge in Attention by Transnational Criminal Policymakers" in Neil Boister et al, eds, *Histories of Transnational Criminal Law* (Oxford: Oxford University Press, 2021) C16 P37-38.

which was, and is, highly sought after on the international art market, was the subject of a high level of looting.[35]

Although collectors figure highly in fueling the illicit market, the trafficking chain seldom ends with them, and they may, in any case, be good faith purchasers who, despite due diligence, unknowingly purchase trafficked items. In certain countries, including Canada, collectors often collect with the ultimate intent of donating the cultural property to museums and galleries for a tax benefit. It is therefore easy to see the relevance and potential benefit of provisions in the *1970 Convention* that advocate increased transparency in the dealer community, compensation for good faith purchasers, and measures to prevent museums from acquiring trafficked items. The latter could include changes to cultural property charitable tax regimes in Canada and elsewhere — an option for further action against trafficking that has had little attention but could be instrumental in changing the behaviour of collectors.

3) Civil Law and Further Criminal Justice Measures

Parts of the international community — particularly source countries — remain dissatisfied with aspects of the *1970 Convention*, and this has prompted additional measures. First, at the request of UNESCO, to better address matters related to private law, and in an attempt to grapple with differences in private law such as those between civil and common law states, the International Institute for the Unification of Private Law (UNIDROIT) developed the 1995 *UNIDROIT Convention on Stolen or Illegally Exported Cultural Objects*.[36] It expands on issues related to acquisition of cultural property that is determined to have been stolen or illegally exported, focusing on facilitating its return. It addresses limitation periods for claims, due diligence, compensation for good faith purchasers, and return and restitution. Notable from a Canadian perspective, it explicitly provides for the return to Indigenous communities of illegally exported items made by them for traditional or ritual use, and the significant

35 *Research on Looting of Canada's Archaeological Heritage* (2001) (unpublished). Prepared by Jacques Whitford Environment Ltd. for the Department of Canadian Heritage. Copy on file, Heritage Policy and Programs Directorate, Department of Canadian Heritage.

36 *UNIDROIT Convention on Stolen or Illegally Exported Cultural Objects*, (1995) 2421 UNTS 457.

impairment of such use is one of the grounds requiring an order for return by courts or other competent authorities in States Parties.[37]

Second, source countries have continued to seek strengthened approaches to enforcement. Those states advocating revisions to the *1970 Convention*, or the addition of a protocol to it, have so far been rebuffed, and have turned to the *UNTOC* and the UN Office on Drugs and Crime (UNDOC). As a compromise to those who sought a cultural property trafficking protocol to the *UNTOC*, and pursuant to a request by the UN General Assembly,[38] expert and intergovernmental meetings from 2011 to 2014 drafted a set of non-binding guidelines for criminal justice responses to the issue. Canada participated in the intergovernmental meetings. The *International Guidelines for Crime Prevention and Criminal Justice Responses with Respect to Trafficking in Cultural Property and Other Related Offences* were adopted by the UNGA in December 2014.[39] They are intended as a tool for use by states in the development and strengthening of policies, strategies, legislation, and cooperation mechanisms in the fight against trafficking in cultural property. In places, when discussing crime prevention, the *Guidelines* arguably stray into UNESCO's mandate, and as such overlap rather than complement provisions of the *1970 Convention*. Put simply, UNESCO's mandate and actions focus on trafficking primarily from the perspective of protection of the cultural property, preventing trafficking, and the return of trafficked items, whereas UNDOC's focus is or arguably should be on the suppression and prosecution of the crime itself.

The *Guidelines* are an advancement in multilateral efforts to combat trafficking from a criminal justice perspective, but they contain several provisions that Canada found problematic during drafting. Details of those provisions, and Canada's perspective, are discussed in the final part of this chapter.

A more recent development is the 2017 *Council of Europe Convention on Offences Relating to Cultural Property*.[40] The *CoE Convention* may be ratified by any state, not just members of the Council of Europe (CoE).

37 For a comprehensive analysis, see "UNIDROIT Convention on Stolen or Illegally Exported Cultural Objects: Explanatory Report" (2001) 3 *Uniform Law Review* 476.

38 UNGA Res 66/180 (2011).

39 *International Guidelines for Crime Prevention and Criminal Justice Responses with Respect to Trafficking in Cultural Property and Other Related Offences*, UNGA Res 69/196 (2014).

40 Council of Europe, *Convention on Offences Relating to Cultural Property*, CETS No 221 (2017) [2017 *CoE Convention*].

It mirrors the scope of the UN *Guidelines* and incorporates many of them into a binding treaty, but goes further. In addition to the expected range of offences (theft, unlawful excavation, illegal export and import) covered in other instruments, it requires States Parties to criminalize additional acts, such as falsifying or tampering with documents in order to conceal illicit provenance,[41] and aiding or abetting any of the criminal acts specified in the *CoE Convention*.[42]

It is particularly worth noting that the *CoE Convention* adds a criminal justice element absent in previous instruments that, without actually using the term, is clearly aimed at the role corruption plays in the trafficking chain in some countries. It requires States Parties, in determining the sanctions to be applied for convictions, to consider as aggravating circumstances instances in which the offence was committed by those "abusing trust placed in them as professionals,"[43] or in which the offence was committed by a public official tasked with the conservation or protection of cultural property.[44] In a nod to the role of organized crime, aggravating circumstances are also to include whether an offence was committed "in the framework of a criminal organization."[45]

The *CoE Convention* represents a significant step forward in expanding the toolkit available to states in fighting trafficking in cultural property. It remains to be seen how many will take advantage of the opportunity it presents to strengthen the criminal law aspects of that fight.[46]

D. THE CANADIAN PERSPECTIVE

1) Implementation

Canada is a State Party to the *1970 Convention* and to the Hague Convention and both of its Protocols; it has publicly endorsed the 1995

41 *Ibid*, art 9.

42 *Ibid*, art 11.

43 *Ibid*, art 15a.

44 *Ibid*, art 15b.

45 *Ibid*, art 15c.

46 The 2017 *CoE Convention* came into force on 1 April 2022. As of 25 January 2023, eleven CoE Member States had signed the Convention but only five of those states had ratified it. As of the same date, one non-Member of the CoE (Mexico) had ratified the Convention. The Russian Federation had signed the Convention in 2018 while a CoE Member State, but that signature is considered to have been suspended as of 16 March 2022 when Russia was expelled from the CoE.

UNIDROIT Convention but has not joined it. The Government of Canada has not taken a formal position on the 2017 *CoE Convention.*

The *1970 Convention* is implemented in Canadian law primarily through the *Cultural Property Export and Import Act* (*CPEIA*),[47] which came into force in 1977. Constitutionally, jurisdiction over archaeological and fossil resources on non-federal lands is vested in the provinces, so certain aspects of the *Convention* concerning those categories of cultural property fall under provincial heritage legislation.

The Hague instruments are implemented primarily through three statutes: the *CPEIA*, the *Crimes Against Humanity and War Crimes Act* (*CAHWCA*)[48] and the *Criminal Code.*[49] Aspects related to military conduct fall under the *National Defence Act* and its Code of Service Discipline.[50]

The *CPEIA* approaches trafficking through import control, and export control using permits. No cultural property is prohibited for export, most does not require a permit, and no permit may be permanently refused. A limited range of cultural property requiring a permit for export is specified in the *Canadian Cultural Property Export Control List*,[51] a regulation under the *CPEIA*. Temporary permits and certain permanent export permits are issued immediately; permits for permanent export of nationally significant items are either issued on review or after a delay that allows an opportunity for purchase by Canadian public institutions.

This regime differs considerably from those in certain source countries where virtually any export of cultural property is prohibited unless for temporary exhibition or conservation or study purposes or, as is the case in Egypt,[52] for exchange with foreign museums or similar institutions. Canada is among those countries taking pragmatic approaches to fighting trafficking by recognizing that no state will ever have sufficient resources to protect or preserve every item of its heritage, or to successfully prevent all exports. Instead, in Canada and like-minded countries such as the United Kingdom and the People's Republic of China (PRC), export

---

47 *CPEIA*, above note 9.

48 *Crimes Against Humanity and War Crimes Act*, SC, 2000, c 24 [*CAHWCA*].

49 *Criminal Code*, RSC 1985, c C-46 [*Criminal Code*].

50 *National Defence Act*, RSC 1985, c N-5.

51 *CCPECL*, above note 8.

52 *Concerning the Issuance of Antiquities' Protection Law*, Law No 117 (1983), UNESCO Database of National Cultural Heritage Laws, English translation called "Law on the protection of Antiquities" in database.

control is limited to a range of items based on their cultural importance. Some may be freely exported, others require a permit, and in the case of countries like the PRC or Australia, a very limited range are prohibited from export. These policies accept that an international market exists and will continue to exist. While trafficking may be curtailed, it likely cannot be eliminated altogether, and limited resources are best focused on the cultural property that is most important.

Legitimate exporters understand that Canada's cultural property export laws present minimal obstacles, and as a result the regime enjoys a high level of compliance. There have only been a small number of convictions for illegal export.[53] Although, as already noted, certain types of Canadian cultural property are sought by the market (licit and illicit), Canada is not generally considered a major source country for trafficking.

There is no indication that Canada is a major market either, yet the approach to import control in the *CPEIA* is arguably among the most faithful to the spirit of the *1970 Convention* of any party to that treaty. It prohibits the import of any cultural property illegally exported from any state with which Canada has a relevant agreement (such as the *1970 Convention*), provided that illegal export took place after the agreement's coming into force in Canada and the other state (whichever is later). There is also a provision for a civil action for recovery that allows return of the property to the state from which it was illegally exported, whether or not charges have been brought against the importer. Charges and returns may also take place under the *Customs Act*.[54]

2) Caselaw

While advantageous from the point of view of a country seeking to recover its cultural property, this approach presents certain evidentiary challenges to Canadian law enforcement. The standard of evidence required for conviction for illegal import under the *CPEIA* was established in *R v Heller*,[55] concerning the import to Canada of an ancient Nigerian sculpture. *Heller* established that, to secure a conviction for illegal import or attempted illegal import under section 43 of the *CPEIA*, the Crown must prove several facts. First, based on the definitions in section 37(1) of the *CPEIA*,

53 All but one of those convictions involved fossils.

54 *Customs Act*, RSC 1985, c 1 (2nd Supp).

55 *R v Heller, Zango and Kassam*, 1983 CanLII 4627 (AB PC) [*Heller*].

the property must have been exported from a "reciprocating state," that is, a state that is party to either a bilateral cultural property agreement with Canada, or party to a multilateral cultural property agreement to which Canada is also a party. The property must be "foreign cultural property," meaning that it has been specifically designated by the reciprocating state as being of importance for archaeology, prehistory, history, literature, art, or science, as per the definition in the *1970 Convention*. Finally, the illegal export from the reciprocating state and import into Canada must have occurred after the coming into force of the aforementioned agreement in Canada. Ultimately *Heller* did not proceed to trial because there was evidence that the sculpture was already outside Nigeria in 1977, a year before the *1970 Convention* came into force in Canada in 1978.

As already noted, it can be a challenge to prove from which modern state illegal export occurred, and therefore to demonstrate that the object is from a reciprocating state. It can also be very difficult to establish when the illegal export occurred, and therefore that it took place after the date when an agreement existed with Canada. Official translations of the foreign export law must be available, and it must be sufficiently clear to show that the object falls under its provisions, in order to demonstrate that the object is foreign cultural property within the meaning of the *CPEIA*. These challenges contrast somewhat with the fact that the civil action for recovery under the *CPEIA* is based on the balance of probabilities, rather than on the beyond a reasonable doubt standard required for conviction of the strict liability offence of illegal import. Accordingly, it is not surprising that Canada has, to date, returned more than 21,000 items of cultural property to fourteen States Parties to the *1970 Convention*,[56] but has sought and secured convictions only twice.[57]

The *CPEIA* does not expressly prohibit import of cultural property stolen from a museum or monument, despite this being an obligation under the *1970 Convention*. Drafters may have reasoned it unnecessary, assuming that all such property would be considered illegally exported anyway. However, it is easier to demonstrate that an object has been stolen (through its inclusion in an inventory, theft report, etc.) than to meet the

56 The list of returns is posted by the Department of Canadian Heritage, online: www.canada.ca/en/canadian-heritage/services/import-cultural-property/returns.html.

57 *R v Roger Cornelius Russell Yorke*, 1996 CanLII 5380 (NS SC) [*Yorke*], and *R v Kelly Dean Claude*, 2002 Saskatchewan Provincial Court, Regina, docket 46704753 (unreported).

evidentiary challenges related to illegal export or import. It would also be useful where foreign laws cover export only of antiquities — modern art, after all, is also subject to theft and trafficking — or do not explicitly control export of cultural property at all, as is the case in the United States. The *CPEIA*, which has not been comprehensively updated since its passage in 1977, could be strengthened by an amendment to address this gap.

The *CPEIA* also lacks provisions regulating the domestic trade. As jurisdiction over such property matters (unless the material in question is designated a controlled substance for the purposes of public health and safety) is vested with the provinces, it would appear to be beyond federal constitutional power to legislate in this regard.

While Canada has had a measure of success in deterring illegal export and in returning trafficked foreign cultural property, there is little caselaw demonstrating interpretation of the *CPEIA* by the courts, particularly with respect to import. In that regard, in addition to *Heller*, the other landmark case is *R v Yorke*.[58]

Roger Yorke was charged with illegally importing more than 400 ancient Bolivian textiles between January 1980 and February 1986. He had been a business associate in Bolivia of an American dealer who, at the time Yorke was charged, was also under a US grand jury investigation pursuant to a request by the Bolivian government for return of cultural property. The items imported by Yorke were his share of the inventory of their dissolved partnership and had originally been obtained through local intermediaries. Ancient Peruvian textiles were also seized, but Peruvian legislation at the time was deemed too vague to allow prosecution under the *CPEIA*, so the case proceeded to trial on the Bolivian material alone. The proceedings, including decisions and appeals, took eight years, ending in 1996 with a conviction of Yorke; a subsequent appeal to the Nova Scotia Court of Appeal was unsuccessful,[59] and leave to appeal to the Supreme Court of Canada was denied in 1998. Yorke was fined C$10,000 and given two years' probation; the textiles were subsequently returned to the Government of Bolivia.

The case is informative from a variety of perspectives. While its initial stages consisted of decisions, motions, and appeals related to the search

58 *Yorke*, above note 57, and *R v Yorke*, 1998 CanLII 58 (NS CA).

59 *Ibid.*

warrant and seizure, it went on to test a number of substantive issues related to whether the *CPEIA*

- Created an offence that is outside the territorial jurisdiction of the court (Yorke submitted that in order to prove elements of the offence, the Canadian court was required to prosecute the offence of illegal export from Bolivia)
- Violated section 7 of the *Canadian Charter of Rights and Freedoms*[60] by reason of vagueness, focusing specifically on the issues of fair notice and sufficient clarity of the law
- Violated section 7 *Charter* rights by not meeting a minimum constitutionally required element of *mens rea* of the accused, in that sections 37(2) and 43 create an absolute liability offence

The court rejected these arguments. In his 1996 judgment, Anderson J also rejected arguments that the relevant Bolivian law did not conform to the *1970 Convention* or the *CPEIA* and that the Crown had failed beyond a reasonable doubt to establish the Bolivian provenance and age of the textiles, and therefore that they met the *CPEIA* definition of foreign cultural property.

Comprehensive discussion of fair notice (formal and substantive) in the decision on the 1998 appeal is worth noting. Among several issues considered therein was that of due diligence. Both parties in the case agreed that the *CPEIA*'s prohibitions constitute regulatory offences; the court observed that as with other such offences, there is a duty on importers to be familiar with rules of the regulated activity. Given his long professional involvement with South American textiles, it was therefore deemed reasonable for Yorke to have known about the *CPEIA*'s import controls and how they related to Bolivian textiles. But the judgment also suggests that the standard of due diligence might be applied to an "ordinary traveller" differently than to "a person whose business is the trading in and importation of cultural property."[61]

Caselaw concerning export violations of the *CPEIA* has been more straightforward, but an example of note is *R v Groulx*,[62] which the Crown won on appeal after an initial judgment had found that controlled cultural

60 *Canadian Charter of Rights and Freedoms*, Part I of the *Constitution Act, 1982*, being Schedule B to the *Canada Act 1982* (UK), 1982, c 11 [*Charter*].

61 *R v Yorke*, above note 58.

62 *R v Groulx*, 2004 CanLII 35502 (QC CS).

property leaving Canada temporarily did not constitute an export, and that no permit under the *CPEIA* was required, despite the *CPEIA* containing specific provisions for temporary export permits.

3) Contemporary Developments: Further Implementation and International Negotiation

As already noted, the *1970 Convention*, and the *CPEIA* as its implementing statute, cover trafficking in cultural property during both peacetime and armed conflict and occupation. However, additional legislative steps were required to ensure full implementation of the Hague Protocols in order for Canada to accede to them in 2005. Passage of the *Crimes Against Humanity and War Crimes Act* had established the required jurisdiction to prosecute violations of the Hague Convention and both Protocols as war crimes, based on the definitions of "war crime" and "conventional international law" therein. However, given the lack of caselaw interpreting the *CAHWCA*, it was unclear whether all violations of both Protocols—including those related to trafficking—would be recognized as grievous enough to constitute war crimes, or whether cultural property offences would only be prosecuted if associated with other more serious acts such as those involving loss of life. The Second Protocol itself differentiates between "serious violations" and "other violations." And while theft, pillage, and misappropriation of cultural property are among those serious violations, again, it was unclear whether all such acts would be prosecuted as war crimes under the *CAHWCA*.

As a result, amendments were made to the *CPEIA* and *Criminal Code*.[63] The *CPEIA* now prohibits export of objects meeting the 1954 Hague Convention definition of cultural property from an occupied territory of a State Party to the Second Protocol,[64] and establishes extraterritorial jurisdiction over such acts when committed by a Canadian citizen, a permanent resident of Canada, or a stateless person ordinarily residing in Canada.[65] The act is an offence whether or not the cultural property comes to Canada.

63 Bill S-37, *An Act to Amend the Criminal Code and the Cultural Property Export and Import Act*, SC 2005, c 40.

64 It is only the Second Protocol, not the 1954 Hague Convention or First Protocol, that requires the establishment of such jurisdiction and creation of an offence.

65 *CPEIA*, above note 9, s 36.1(3).

The *CPEIA* was also amended to allow a civil action for recovery of cultural property located in Canada after being exported from an occupied territory of a State Party to the 1954 Hague Convention and either of its Protocols, as had already existed for illegally imported cultural property. The Protocols do not require states to prohibit the import of such items, presumably to better facilitate their interception and return.

Amendments made to the *Criminal Code* went further than required by the Protocols. For five existing property offences in the *Code* (theft, fraudulent concealment, fraud, robbery, mischief/vandalism, and arson), extraterritorial jurisdiction is now established over the categories of persons described above, with the only condition being that the property affected is cultural property that is sufficiently important to meet the definition in article 1 of the Hague Convention.[66] The act need not take place in a state that is party to the Hague instruments, nor during armed conflict or occupation.

While this approach was taken for reasons of policy and practicality, the resulting effect is to significantly strengthen Canada's role in the international protection of cultural property and the fight against trafficking in it. Provided that the property meets the Hague definition, any Canadian citizen, permanent resident, or stateless person residing in Canada who commits those acts against cultural property (or conspires or attempts them or is an accessory after the fact to them or counsels in relation to them) anywhere in the world at any time is committing an offence under the *Criminal Code* and can be prosecuted in a Canadian court. There appear to have been no prosecutions of the offences to date.

A final note on Canada's legislation is that penalties for the above-described offences in the *CPEIA* and *Criminal Code* meet the threshold to be considered serious crimes under the *UNTOC*, namely that they allow for a maximum imprisonment of at least four years.[67] The maximum custodial sentence for offences under the *CPEIA* is five years; for the relevant offences in the *Code*, it is ten years. Conviction for a war crime under the *CAHWCA*, which could include acts related to trafficking in cultural property, carries a maximum penalty of life imprisonment.

Canada has enjoyed success in returning cultural property that has been subject to trafficking; it has not moved to join additional multilateral

66 *Criminal Code*, above note 49, s 7(2.01) & (2.02).

67 *UNTOC*, above note 12, art 2(b).

instruments such as the 1995 or 2017 *Conventions*, nor has it advocated changes to existing instruments or the introduction of new measures. But, as already noted, source countries have continued to seek new criminal justice approaches that Canada cannot wholly support.

The differences surfaced during negotiations on the UN *Guidelines* and some of the concepts in question are now enshrined in the 2017 *CoE Convention*.[68] Input received from states[69] on draft versions of the *Guidelines* shows Canadian opposition to the following five proposals, among others. All but one survived into the final version adopted by the UNGA.

- **Guideline 19**[70] proposes that states infer a perpetrator's knowledge of the illicit provenance of an item when it has been registered in a publicly accessible database for stolen, illicitly excavated, etc. cultural property. In Canada's view, this suggested a strict liability offence whereby a person could be found guilty of a crime if they failed to exercise a specific form of due diligence. Canada did not support this guideline as drafted, arguing that a failure to exercise due diligence does not necessarily indicate prior knowledge or criminal intent, and should be distinguished from the more general duty to exercise reasonable care in ascertaining the status of cultural property. It was due only to the addition of a qualifying phrase that states consider such a measure "in a way not contradictory to their fundamental legal principles" that Canada was able to avoid blocking consensus.
- **Guideline 26**[71] introduces a concept that is increasingly advocated by source countries: assuming that all cultural property on the market is there unlawfully unless the possessor can demonstrate otherwise. Canada viewed this as a reversal of the burden of proof that rests

68 2017 *CoE Convention*, above note 40.

69 CCPCJ, *Updated Compendium of Comments from Member* States, UN Doc E/CN.15/2013/CRP.7/Rev.1 (4 December 2013).

70 "States should consider making it possible, in a way not contradictory to their fundamental legal principles, to infer a perpetrator's knowledge that an object has been reported as trafficked, illicitly exported or imported, stolen, looted, illicitly excavated or illicitly traded, on the basis of objective factual circumstances, including when the cultural property is registered as such in a publicly accessible database."

71 "States should consider, in a way not contradictory to their fundamental legal principles, the possibility of requiring that the alleged offender, the owner or the holder (if different) demonstrate the lawful origin of cultural property liable to seizure or confiscation for trafficking or related offences."

with the state to prove that an offence has occurred, and counter to the presumption of innocence that is not only a fundamental characteristic of Canada's legal system and included in the *Charter*,[72] but is also enshrined in the *Universal Declaration of Human Rights*[73] and the UN *International Covenant on Civil and Political Rights*.[74] Canada could not support this guideline as drafted, but joined consensus with the addition of the same qualifying phrase employed in Guideline 19.

- **Guideline 32**[75] proposes that states establish extraterritorial jurisdiction over the offences described in the *Guidelines* that are related to trafficking in cultural property. While it has established such jurisdiction for specific acts against cultural property, Canada's position was that it is best restricted to the context of implementation of binding treaties. It was only with the addition of the qualifier "should consider" that Canada was able to join consensus on the point.
- While it did not survive the drafting stage, it is worth noting, as a window into the perspectives of source countries, that a proposal was made that states establish jurisdiction over offences committed outside their territories where the cultural property in question "belongs to their heritage."[76] Canada criticized this as both impractical—one wonders whether, for example, Italy would claim that all cultural property related to the Roman empire "belongs to its heritage"—and unacceptable, as implying that states retain a legal interest in cultural property originating within their borders even after it has been (legally) purchased and exported.

---

72 *Charter*, above note 60, s 11(d).

73 *Universal Declaration of Human Rights*, UNGA Res 217A(III) (1948), art 11.1.

74 *International Covenant on Civil and Political Rights*, (1966) 999 UNTS 171, art 14.2.

75 "States should consider establishing their jurisdiction over the above-mentioned criminal offences when such offences are committed within their territory or when committed outside their territory by one of their nationals, in a manner consistent with the principles of sovereign equality, the territorial integrity of States and non-intervention in the domestic affairs of other States, as enshrined in the Charter of the United Nations and the Organized Crime Convention."

76 See "Comments by the Republic of Turkey on the Draft Guidelines," UNODC/CCPCJ/EG.1/2014/CRP.1 (15 January 2014) at 4, draft Guideline 39: "States should consider establishing their jurisdiction over the aforementioned criminal offences, if committed abroad, when they impinge on a cultural property that belongs to their cultural heritage or is subject to enhanced protection."

- **Guideline 36**[77] and two subsequent guidelines propose making specific acts against cultural property extraditable offences. Canada opposed this on the basis that it was inconsistent with modern approaches that make conduct extraditable based on the severity of a potential sentence (rather than the name of the offence) and suggested that if states made the crimes sufficiently serious, this guideline's objective would be achieved without setting a new precedent. Again, use of the qualifier "should consider" meant that Canada could avoid blocking consensus.

An observer might question why Canada would take the trouble to comment in such detail on issues such as those above, given that the *Guidelines* are non-binding, and given that their language allows states to simply disregard concepts they disagree with. The answer is that even non-binding "soft law" instruments are normative in nature, in that they seek to establish norms for the conduct of states, and thus can contribute to the development of customary international law. They can also evolve into binding instruments when states feel that they are not being followed. Once certain principles are accepted at the soft law stage, it can be difficult for states to reject them when drafting a later binding instrument. Recall that the development of the *Guidelines* was in large part a concession to states who were seeking a cultural property protocol to the *UNTOC*; Canada's strategy to go on record as being unable to accept certain concepts would allow it to more easily justify its continued opposition to them if efforts to develop a protocol to the *UNTOC* were to gain traction in the future.

E. CONCLUSION

The future may yet hold more challenges for Canada. Much of the current legal discourse continues to centre not on fighting trafficking, but on the means to recover material already lost, particularly during the colonial period. One legal scholar contends that an obligation to return such material now constitutes customary international law and proposes a new convention with 275 years' retroactivity,[78] while another advocates a new

77 "States should consider making the crimes against cultural property enumerated in guideline 16 extraditable offences."

78 Geoffrey Robertson, QC, *Who Owns History? Elgin's Loot and the Case for Returning Plundered Treasure* (London: Biteback Publishing, 2019) at 217–48.

concept of "heritage title" as a means to negotiate recovery of trafficked cultural property.[79] And finally, the implications for cultural property law in Canada, and indeed globally, of relevant aspects of the *UN Declaration on the Rights of Indigenous Peoples*[80] have yet to be seen.

79 Campfens, above note 17.

80 *UN Declaration on the Rights of Indigenous Peoples*, UNGA Res 61/295 (2007). Article 11.2: "States shall provide redress through effective mechanisms, which may include restitution, developed in conjunction with indigenous peoples, with respect to their cultural, intellectual, religious and spiritual property taken without their free, prior and informed consent or in violation of their laws, traditions and customs."

seventeen

From Opium to Fentanyl: Drug Smuggling, Canada, and Enforcement Challenges

STEPHEN SCHNEIDER*

A. INTRODUCTION

Smuggling that crosses national borders has come to epitomize transnational crime, while organized drug smuggling has come to epitomize transnational organized crime. With that said, smuggling is inextricably tied to numerous other organized crimes. As Kleemans writes, "many profitable criminal activities boil down to international smuggling activities — drug trafficking, smuggling illegal immigrants, human trafficking for sexual exploitation, arms trafficking, trafficking in stolen vehicles."[1]

Transnational smuggling has also helped expose the significant limitations of transnational law enforcement, given that criminal laws and justice systems are confined within the boundaries of individual nation-states. Notwithstanding UN-brokered international conventions that have forged criminal justice standards among Member States to address the smuggling and trafficking of drugs and people, there appears to be little appetite among most countries to enact a system of binding transnational laws and enforcement agencies, due to concerns they will compromise a nation's sovereignty.

---

* Professor, Department of Criminology, St. Mary's University.

1 Edward R. Kleemans, "Theoretical Perspectives on Organized Crime" in Letizia Paoli, ed, *The Oxford Handbook of Organized Crime* (Oxford: Oxford University Press, 2014) 32 at 47 [*Oxford Handbook*].

The purpose of this essay is to examine transnational drug smuggling affecting Canada as a case study for the inherent enforcement challenges that many countries face in combatting crimes that cross their national borders. Canada is a signatory to relevant United Nations conventions, has specific offences concerning drug smuggling, as well as federal agencies dedicated to border enforcement and criminal investigations. However, these criminal justice policies, institutions, and processes have had little lasting impact on the scope of drug smuggling into and out of this country.

Indeed, all available metrics indicate that the problem has progressively worsened throughout the post–World War II period: the volume of drugs smuggled across Canadian borders has soared, the payloads of individual shipments have progressively become larger, and there is a wider variety of drugs being illegally brought into the country.[2] The production of marijuana and synthetic drugs in Canada means it is now an exporter of illicit substances, while federal enforcement agencies must guard against the illegal importation of chemicals used in the domestic production of methamphetamine and MDMA (ecstasy). The introduction of the synthetic opioid fentanyl into the black market has helped feed a larger public health crisis stemming from the abuse of both licit and illicit opioids.[3]

---

2 Mia Dauvergne, *Trends in Police-Reported Drug Offences in Canada* (Ottawa: Statistics Canada, Canadian Centre for Justice Statistics, 2019); Stephen Schneider, *Canadian Organized Crime* (Toronto: Canadian Scholars Press, 2018) [Schneider 2018]; Public Safety Canada, *2019 Law Enforcement Roundtable on Drugs* (2019), online: www.publicsafety.gc.ca/cnt/rsrcs/pblctns/2019-lw-nfrcmnt-rndtbl-drgs/index-en.aspx; CBSA, *Canada Border Services Agency Seizures* (2021), online: www.cbsa-asfc.gc.ca/security-securite/seizure-saisie-eng.html.

3 According to Health Canada, there were 22,828 apparent opioid toxicity deaths in Canada between January 2016 and March 2021. There were 1,772 apparent opioid toxicity deaths between January and March 2021 (approximately twenty deaths per day), representing a 65 percent increase compared to January to March 2020 (1,073 deaths). Since the onset of the COVID-19 pandemic, 6,946 apparent opioid toxicity deaths occurred (April 2020 to March 2021), representing an 88 percent increase over the same period prior to the pandemic (April 2019 to March 2020: 3,691 deaths). "Numerous factors have likely contributed to a worsening of the overdose crisis, including the increasingly toxic drug supply, increased feelings of isolation, stress and anxiety and limited availability or accessibility of services for people who use drugs." Special Advisory Committee on the Epidemic of Opioid Overdoses, *Opioid- and Stimulant-Related Harms in Canada* (2021), online: https://health-infobase.canada.ca/substance-related-harms/opioids-stimulants.

The near futility of enforcement in this country is underscored when one considers myriad conditions inherent in Canada that make it so vulnerable to smuggling: the widespread demand for illicit drugs; the involvement of (transnational) organized crime groups; thousands of miles of largely unguarded coastline; the country's lengthy undefended border with the United States (the global vortex of the illegal drug trade); well-established smuggling routes and infrastructure; inadequate border enforcement resources; Canada's dependence upon legal international trade (which is adroitly exploited by smugglers), and our growing economic and cultural ties to China (a global source of illegal drugs, precursor chemicals, and counterfeit goods).

This essay begins with a historical overview of drug smuggling into and out of Canada, which is meant to illuminate how this criminal problem has long responded to and fed into the country's (illicit) economy and its (vice) culture. This history includes a description of some significant milestones as well as key factors that have precipitated the advent or increase of a particular drug smuggling problem. The next section dissects this history and recent developments by identifying salient features of drug smuggling involving Canada; in particular, the type of illegal drugs imported and exported, source countries, smuggling conveyances, official and unofficial ports of entry used, and the criminal groups involved. This section is followed by an accounting of the many factors that make Canada highly vulnerable to both inbound and outbound drug smuggling. A brief description and analysis of enforcement efforts targeting drug smuggling, including relevant federal criminal statutes, is then provided. The essay concludes that the war on drugs, with its emphasis on supply-side enforcement that relies on border inspections and interdiction, has been a failure, and alternative measures must be considered to limit the harms of illegal drugs on Canadian society.

B. HISTORY OF DRUG SMUGGLING AFFECTING CANADA AND RECENT TRENDS

I have argued elsewhere that "smuggling is the most historically rooted, persistent, and widespread form of organized non-compliance perpetrated by Canadians."[4] Canada's history of smuggling dates to its colonial days

4 Schneider 2018, above note 2 at 15.

when prohibitive tariffs imposed by Great Britain promoted widespread contraband markets for tea and other imported necessities of colonial life. According to Chambliss, the stifling taxes would become an economic noose around commerce in the British colonies and, as a result, "smuggling activities promoted an institutionalization of crime in the colonies in order to ensure their commercial survival."[5] Following Confederation, high taxes on legal consumer products implemented by the Dominion government enlarged organized smuggling to include tobacco products, liquor, motor fuels, car parts, jewellery, gems, and blue jeans, much of which was illegally imported from the United States.

Opium had been introduced into North America as early as the 1850s, and was imported and sold legally. This would change beginning in 1865 when a 50 percent tariff on opium imported into the colony of British Columbia was imposed,[6] prompting its widespread smuggling into British Columbia. By the 1870s, Chinese merchants had opened factories in Victoria and the Lower Mainland to convert raw gum opium into a smokable form. In 1890, when the US Congress imposed its own prohibitive tariffs on opium and morphine imports, the smokable opium manufactured in British Columbia began to be smuggled across the US border.[7]

The criminalization of non-medicinal opiates in Canada in 1908[8] meant that for the first time in this country, a narcotic was now regulated by criminal law, ushering in a new era of smuggling that focused on illegal drugs. By the end of World War I, demand for opiates spiked, due to the return of many soldiers who had become addicted to morphine in Europe. Beginning in the 1920s, Montreal would become a central conduit through which opium from Southwest Asia, as well as heroin and black-market morphine from Europe, were illegally imported into Canada via passenger ships for domestic consumption or transshipment to New York City. Vancouver was also established as a major port of entry for opium and heroin from Southeast Asia and a transshipment point for

5 William Chambliss, "Piracy and Other Crimes of War," *Nathanson Centre Newsletter*, Winter 2005, 12.

6 *An Ordinance to amend the Duties of Customs*, SBC 1865, c 3.

7 Stephen Schneider, *Iced: The Story of Organized Crime in Canada* (Toronto: Harper Collins Canada, 2016) [Schneider, *Iced*] at 97–98; Anthony Chan, *Gold Mountain: The Chinese in the New World* (Vancouver: New Star Books, 1983) at 76; "Opium Smuggling" *Manitoba Morning Free Press* (11 January 1893) at 1.

8 *Opium Act*, SC 1908, c 50.

other illicit markets in the Pacific Northwest of the United States, the Prairie provinces, and as far east as Toronto. Heroin from Mexico was also being smuggled into Canada via American land border crossings.[9]

At the start of the 1940s, Italian Mafia groups in the United States and Canada became the main illegal importers and wholesalers of heroin from Europe. Their source was the world's biggest heroin producers at the time: *L'Union Corse*, a criminal syndicate made up of French nationals who hailed from the island of Corsica and processed much of the heroin in Marseilles. Montreal was one of the main entry points for heroin entering North America due to its inviting seaports, Quebec's cultural, commercial, and linguistic ties to the French Corsicans, the subservience of the crime groups in the province to New York City's Mafia families, as well as Montreal's proximity to New York City and their numerous commercial transportation links.[10] One of the legacies of the so-called French Connection was that it gave Canada and Canadian mobsters a pivotal role in the heroin trade in North America while further pulling the country's criminal underworld into the orbit of the American *La Cosa Nostra*.[11]

In 1971, the Nixon administration persuaded Turkey to ban the cultivation of opium and pressured French authorities to crack down on the extensive heroin-processing plants in Marseilles. The result was a reorganization of global heroin trafficking: Turkey was replaced as the chief supplier of opium by the Golden Triangle of Thailand, Myanmar, and Laos. Vancouver would now become a major gateway for a highly potent variety

9 RCMP, *Report of the Royal Canadian Mounted Police for the Year Ended September 30, 1921* (Ottawa: F.A. Acland); National Archives of Canada, *Records of the Royal Canadian Mounted Police*, RG 18, vol 3167, File No G494-1; National Archives of Canada, *Records of the Royal Canadian Mounted Police*, RG 18, vol 3291, File No 1922-HQ-189-Q-1 (Opium and Narcotic Drug Act—General—Miscellaneous Reports. Document cited: RCMP "E" Division report re: Opium and Narcotic Drug Act dated 20 May 1922); "All Boats from Asia Bring in Illicit Drugs" *Vancouver Daily World* (16 January 1922) 1. "Chinese Says Police Sold Opium to Him" *Vancouver Sun* (24 November 1923) 3.

10 William E. Mann, *Some Aspects of Organized Crime in Canada: A Preliminary Review* (Toronto: Social Science Publishers, 1968) at 176; Jean-Pierre Charbonneau, *The Canadian Connection: An Exposé on the Mafia in Canada and Its International Ramifications* (Montreal: Optimum Pub Co, 1976) at 45–48; McClellan Committee, "Organized Crime and Illicit Traffic in Narcotics" in Francis Ianni & Elizabeth Reuss-Ianni, eds, *The Crime Society: Organized Crime and Corruption in America* (New York: New American Library, 1976) at 186.

11 Schneider, *Iced*, above note 7.

of heroin known as "China White," which was arriving via the local marine port, airport, and mail.[12] By the end of the decade, Criminal Intelligence Services Canada (CISC) was reporting there were "six major heroin trafficking organizations in existence in the Vancouver area, all of which are involved at the 'importing' level."[13]

As the psychedelic drug era emerged in North America in the 1960s, illegal drug consumption skyrocketed and a variety of illegal drugs was now being imported into and exported from Canada and the United States. The smuggling of marijuana into Canada increased significantly while outlaw motorcycle gangs, in particular the Hells Angels, the Outlaws, and Satan's Choice in Ontario and Quebec, began manufacturing synthetic drugs, many of which were smuggled into the United States. Among the chemical drugs produced in Canada were methamphetamine, phencyclidine powder (PCP), Lysergic acid diethylamide (LSD), and a sedative made up of diazepam, commonly referred to by the brand name Valium but marketed illegally in the American Midwest as "Canadian Blue." This era was noteworthy for several reasons: it introduced illegal drugs that were entirely chemical in substance, it established Canada as a major producer and exporter of synthetic drugs, and it signalled a new role for outlaw motorcycle gangs as drug producers, smugglers, and traffickers.[14]

The most substantial development in the drug smuggling and trafficking world in the 1970s was the rise in the demand for, and trafficking of, cocaine. By the end of the decade through to the late 1990s, the Colombian-based Medellin and Cali cartels were the foremost importers into Canada, supplying their own distribution cells and other cocaine-trafficking wholesalers, most notably the Hells Angels and the Montreal Mafia.[15] Cocaine was first imported from Colombia into Canada in small quantities by airline passengers. By the late 1980s, the Medellin Cartel was flying single-engine planes into remote airstrips in New Brunswick and Quebec

12 "Illegal Immigrants and Drug Smuggling" *Washington Post* (13 May 1973) 12; RCMP, *Drug Situation in Canada 1999* (Ottawa: RCMP, 2000) at 5.

13 CISC, *Annual Report on Organized Crime in Canada, 1979* (1979) at 12.

14 President's Commission on Organized Crime, *America's Habit. Drug Abuse, Drug Trafficking, & Organized Crime* (Washington, DC: United States Government Printing Office, 1986) at 67; John Schenk & John Kesser, "Born-to-Raise-Hell Inc." *Maclean's* (22 August 1977) at 30; RCMP and Drug Enforcement Administration, *Outlaw Motorcycle Gangs and the Drug Trade* (Ottawa: RCMP & DEA, 1986).

15 RCMP, *RCMP National Drug Intelligence Estimate 1984/85* (Ottawa: RCMP, 1986).

with hundreds of kilograms onboard.[16] The Cali Cartel used large mother ships that anchored in international waters and then offloaded hundreds, and sometimes thousands, of kilos of the drug into smaller speedboats, which would offload along the unprotected coastline.[17] By the start of the new millennium, the two cartels had imploded and the cocaine supply became more diversified; much of the cocaine coming into Canada was now being transported directly from Colombia or via transit countries in South America and the Caribbean through shipping containers arriving at marine ports in Montreal, Halifax, or Vancouver. When Mexican groups began to dominate the global cocaine supply, a far greater share began entering Canada via the United States, through official land-border entry points aboard commercial tractor-trailers.[18]

During the late 1980s, domestic marijuana growing operations began to proliferate in British Columbia, and soon the amount of high-potency pot being produced domestically exploded. Not only did Canada become self-sufficient in cannabis, but it was also now exporting large quantities to the United States, where it fetched a much higher price.[19] Despite the 2018 legalization of marijuana for recreational use in Canada, there continues to be illegal grow operations that supply both domestic and foreign black markets. The US *Narcotics Control Strategy Report* for 2021 indicates that after Canada legalized cannabis for non-medical purposes in 2018, "there was a surge in US seizures of cannabis in transit from Canada to the United States."[20]

---

16 Peter Edwards, *The Big Sting. The True Story of the Canadian Who Betrayed Colombia's Drug Barons* (Toronto: Key Porter Books, 1991); Schneider, *Iced*, above note 7 at 507–12.

17 RCMP, *Drug Situation in Canada 1999* (Ottawa: RCMP, Criminal Analysis Branch, Criminal Intelligence Directorate, Organized Crime Analysis Section, 2000).

18 Andrew Hogan & Douglas Century, *Hunting El Chapo: The Inside Story of the American Lawman Who Captured the World's Most-Wanted Drug Lord* (New York: HarperCollins, 2018); CISC, *Public Report on Organized Crime in Canada* (Ottawa: CISC, 2019).

19 United States Drug Enforcement Administration, "BC Bud: Growth of the Canadian Marijuana Trade," *Drug Intelligence Brief* (Washington, DC: DEA, 2000); White House Office of National Drug Control Policy, *National Drug Control Strategy* (Washington, DC: The White House, 2004) at 43; RCMP, *Report of the Illicit Drug Situation in Canada—2009* (Ottawa: RCMP, 2009) at 17.

20 United States Department of State, International Narcotics Control Strategy Report Volume I, Drug and Chemical Control (Washington, DC: United States Department of State, Bureau for International Narcotics and Law Enforcement Affairs, 2021) at 108–9 [*Narcotics Control Strategy*].

The 1990s also heralded a boom in synthetic drug production in Canada — in particular, MDMA and the highly addictive "crystal meth." Driven in part by Chinese criminal networks and outlaw biker gangs, Canada became a major producer and exporter of both. "The continuing rise in domestic Ecstasy production has given Canada an increased role as a source country in both the domestic and international markets," the RCMP wrote in its 2005 drug intelligence report. This has resulted in "escalated cross-border MDMA trafficking from Canada to the United States and overseas smuggling of MDMA and methamphetamine, particularly to Japan and Australia."[21]

Canadian border officials on the West Coast now had to be on the lookout for the thousands of gallons of precursor chemicals from China being legally and illegally imported through Vancouver's marine ports. At the same time, American border officials were on guard at land crossings against the deluge of synthetic drugs being exported southbound.[22]

By 2010, a growing opiate epidemic was gripping Canada and the United States, fueled in part by a growing supply of black-market fentanyl. The majority of the illegal fentanyl entering Canada is in powdered form and comes primarily from China, through the Port of Vancouver.[23] The powder is processed into pill form, primarily in Greater Vancouver, for domestic consumption and export. Seizures of illegal fentanyl pills by US Customs and Border Protection officials at the Canadian border increased to more than twenty-six kilograms in 2020, up from a mere three kilograms in 2019.[24]

One of the more recent developments in the international drug trade is the arrival of cyber-trafficking through the anonymous and heavily encrypted dark web. Even though online illicit markets represent only a tiny fraction of the global drug trade, Broséus et al depict them as a "revolution and a criminal evolution" in drug trafficking given their worldwide reach, the anonymity they provide, the vast array of illegal drugs and other goods offered, and the end to physical interactions between transacting

21 RCMP, *Drug Situation Report, 2005* (Ottawa: RCMP, 2006), online: https://publications.gc.ca/collections/collection_2013/grc-rcmp/PS61-14-2005-eng.pdf at 11–12.

22 National Drug Intelligence Center, *National Drug Threat Assessment 2010* (U.S. Department of Justice, 2012).

23 CISC, *Public Report on Organized Crime in Canada* (Ottawa: Criminal Intelligence Service Canada, 2020) at 2.

24 *Narcotics Control Strategy*, above note 20 at 79.

parties (which in theory reduces conflict and violence).[25] Fentanyl and methamphetamine trafficking networks in Canada are known to sell through the dark web.[26] Online illicit markets are similar to legitimate ones like Amazon or eBay in many ways, one of which is the use of postal services and private couriers to transport goods to purchasers. This has meant there has been an increase in the smuggling of heroin, fentanyl pills, and methamphetamine into Canada from foreign sources through Canada Post.[27]

C. KEY TRAITS OF DRUG SMUGGLING AFFECTING CANADA

Canada is vulnerable to both inbound and outbound drug smuggling, while also serving as a transit country for certain illegal substances. The illicit drugs smuggled into Canada include opium, heroin, marijuana, cocaine, hashish, ketamine, and a range of synthetic drugs (methamphetamine, MDMA, gamma-hydroxybutyrate, and fentanyl). As noted, Canada also has a history of being an exporter of illicit drugs that result from domestic production. Overwhelmingly, the export market for these illicit products has been the United States. According to the 2021 US *International Narcotics Control Strategy Report*, "In 2020, transnational criminal organizations trafficked cocaine, heroin, methamphetamine, synthetic drugs, and counterfeit prescription drugs to Canada for domestic consumption, some of which transited the United States" while Canada also remains "a primary source of synthetic drugs, cannabis, and MDMA (ecstasy) trafficked to the United States."[28]

In recent years, Canadian-produced synthetic drugs have been shipped to Australia, New Zealand, Japan, and the Philippines. Canada has also been a transshipment point in the global drug trade most notably for Southwest Asian heroin transiting through Montreal to New York City,

25 Julian Broséus et al, "Studying Illicit Drug Trafficking on Darknet Markets: Structure and Organisation from a Canadian Perspective" (2016) 264 *Forensic Science International* 7 at 8.

26 CISC, *Public Report on Organized Crime in Canada* (Ottawa: Criminal Intelligence Service Canada, 2020) at 2.

27 Public Safety Canada, *2019 Law Enforcement Roundtable on Drugs* (Ottawa: Public Safety Canada) at 4.

28 *Narcotics Control Strategy*, above note 20 at 108.

for Southeast Asian heroin going through Vancouver for the US West Coast, and for cocaine from Mexico, which is ultimately destined for other Pacific Rim countries.[29] Toronto's Pearson International Airport has also been identified as a departure point for cocaine being smuggled to the United Kingdom.[30]

The countries and regions of the world that constitute the sources for illicit drugs smuggled into Canada are dictated by the type of drug, although the source countries have varied over the years. Since the 1970s, the Golden Triangle of Thailand, Myanmar, and Laos has been the main source of heroin for Canada. Colombia has long been the world's primary producer of cocaine, and shipments to Canada either come directly from there or arrive via transit countries in South America or the West Indies. More recently cocaine arrives from Mexico via the United States.[31]

Most hashish is imported into Canada from the Middle East and Southwest Asian countries, in particular, Lebanon, Pakistan, Afghanistan, and Morocco. When synthetic drugs such as MDMA or methamphetamine first became popular in the 1990s, they were imported into Canada from Europe or Israel. Today, Canada is largely self-sufficient in these synthetic drugs, and imports have dropped off considerably, although methamphetamine is smuggled from Mexico into the United States and Canada.[32] Much of the fentanyl smuggled into Canada comes from China, although a smaller amount is also exported from Mexico. The table below provides a summary of illegal drugs seized by the Canada Border Services Agency (CBSA) for fiscal years 2017–18 to 2020–21 (measured in kilos).

---

29 Kyra Gurney, "Canada Drug Trafficking Groups Expanding Mexico Ties" *InSight Crime* (12 September 2014), online: https://insightcrime.org/news/analysis/canada-drug-trafficking-groups-expanding-mexico-ties/; Australian Crime Commission, *Illicit Drug Data Report* (Canberra: ACC, 2013) at 105.

30 RCMP, "RCMP and UK's National Crime Agency Collaborate to Make Further Arrests in International Cocaine Smuggling Ring" News release on Cision, 15 November 2013, online: https://www.newswire.ca/news-releases/rcmp-and-uks-national-crime-agency-collaborate-to-make-further-arrests-in-international-cocaine-smuggling-ring-513250901.html.

31 UNODC, *World Drug Report, 2019* (New York: United Nations, 2019).

32 CISC, *Public Report on Organized Crime in Canada* (Ottawa: CISC, 2019); Chris Dalby, "Sinaloa Cartel Places Unwanted Surprise Inside New Ford Cars" *InSight Crime* (1 March 2019), online: https://insightcrime.org/news/brief/sinaloa-cartel-unwanted-surprise-ford-cars/.

TABLE 17.1 CBSA PROHIBITED AND CONTROLLED DRUG SEIZURES (KG/YEAR)

	2017–18	2018–19	2019–20	2020–21
Cannabis products[33]	497	1,708	4,322	11,177
Hashish	949	729	24	10
Cocaine/crack[34]	2,860	1,429	1,304	1,215
Heroin	189	119	178	78
Fentanyl	15	5	3	7.4
Other opioids[35]	321	358	991	1,161
Other narcotics, drugs & chemicals	15,901	12,770	27,122	24,463

SOURCE: Canada Border Services Agency (2021). Canada Border Services Agency Seizures, www.cbsa-asfc.gc.ca/security-securite/seizure-saisie-eng.html

Canadian entry points for drug smuggling have varied over the years. Cocaine, marijuana, and hashish have been smuggled across unguarded land border points shared with the United States or landed along coastal shorelines. However, the vast majority of drugs smuggled into Canada enters through official ports of entry, whether these are land border crossings, marine container ports, international airports, or via Canada Post or courier services. The largest payloads are brought in via marine containers (through marine ports) and tractor-trailer trucks (through official land border crossings). The use of marine containers for smuggling into Canada took off in the 1990s when Canadian criminal groups such as the Montreal Mafia, the Hells Angels, and Montreal's West End Gang began directly coordinating their own shipments of cocaine from suppliers in Colombia or hashish from Pakistan. To be profitable, both cocaine and hashish must be shipped in large quantities, which are accommodated by marine containers.[36] As one RCMP officer observed following a large

33 The "Cannabis products" category consists of dried and fresh cannabis, cannabis seeds, solids, non-solids, concentrates, and synthetic cannabis. These numbers include both declared cannabis forfeited to the CBSA and undeclared cannabis seized by the CBSA.

34 Includes coca leaves, coca paste, cocaine, and crack cocaine.

35 Includes opium, methadone, morphine, and morphine base.

36 RCMP, *Report of the Illicit Drug Situation in Canada—2009* (Ottawa: RCMP, Criminal Analysis Branch, Criminal Intelligence Directorate, Organized Crime Analysis Section, 2009).

bust at the Port of Montreal, marine containers are essential to hashish smuggling into Canada "because it's hard to hide 4,000 pounds of hash in the trunk of a car."[37]

The marine container ports of Montreal and Halifax are major conduits for cocaine and hashish entering the country, while the Port of Vancouver is an entry point for cocaine and the main channel for the illegal entry of fentanyl and precursor chemicals used in the domestic production of synthetic drugs. The busiest official land border crossing for cocaine imports is the Ambassador Bridge that connects Detroit to Windsor (uncoincidentally, the busiest border crossing for legitimate commercial traffic between the two countries).[38]

Heroin is frequently transported via the airlines, either through air cargo or hidden in the suitcases of passengers on commercial flights. The latter smuggling technique relies on numerous nondescript couriers, often women, who take circuitous routes to Canada from source countries.[39] International airports in Toronto and Montreal are frequent entry points for Southwest Asian heroin smuggled into Canada.

The criminalization of many drugs combined with their popularity among the consuming public has attracted the involvement of well-organized criminal groups and networks in both smuggling and wholesaling. Paoli, Spapens, and Fijnaut write, "the trafficking of illegal narcotics and other psychoactive drugs is considered one of the prototypical activities of organised crime and is a matter of serious concern worldwide."[40] The logistics of large-scale (transnational) drug trafficking necessitates some level of organization given the many phases, processes, and activities involved, including cultivation, refinement, transportation, storage, wholesaling, retail distribution, corruption, security, and money laundering.

Some of the biggest transnational drug trafficking organizations and networks, based in Canada and other countries, have been responsible for

37 Catherine Solyom, "Drug Dealers as Busy as Ever" *Montreal Gazette* (9 August 2002) A1.

38 Jeremiah Rodriguez, "Canadian Trucker Arrested in Suspected $6M Cocaine Smuggling Bust" *CTV News* (10 September 2019), online: www.ctvnews.ca/canada/canadian-trucker-arrested-in-suspected-6m-cocaine-smuggling-bust-1.4586364.

39 CBSA, "CBSA Intercepts Over 22 Kilograms of Suspected Heroin at the Toronto Pearson International Airport" News release (27 May 2013), online: http://cbsa-asfc.gc.ca/media/prosecutions-poursuites/tcr/2013-04-08-eng.html.

40 Letizia Paoli, Torine Spapens & Cyrille Fijnaut, "Drug Trafficking" in Fiona Brookman et al, eds, *Handbook on Crime* (Portland, OR: Willan Publishing, 2010) at 626.

the ongoing and sizeable drug smuggling into the country. The Montreal Mafia was central to heroin smuggling into North America from the 1940s to the 1970s, and also financed cocaine and hashish imports from the 1980s onward. The Hells Angels are active in smuggling cocaine and hashish into the country through land border crossings and marine ports.[41] Some of the initial chapters of the Hells Angels established in Canada were in port cities (Montreal, Vancouver, and Halifax), the outermost flanks in their coast-to-coast web of chapters that was constructed as a national drug pipeline.[42] Chinese criminal networks in Canada are prolific importers of cocaine, heroin, fentanyl, and precursor chemicals used in the domestic production of synthetic drugs.[43]

During the 1980s and 1990s, both the Medellin and Cali cartels from Colombia established cells in Canada to facilitate cocaine importation and wholesaling. "These groups view Canada as a trans-shipment point for cocaine destined for the United States, as well as an expanding market in its own right."[44] Mexican cocaine trafficking groups such as the Sinaloa Cartel have long exported to Canada, but it has only been in the last few years that they began inserting operatives here to coordinate the importation and distribution of cocaine and other drugs, thereby eliminating the Canadian importing and wholesaling intermediaries.[45] A 2013 article in the RCMP *Gazette* magazine notes, "the roles of those individuals within Canada are very much those of gatekeepers, involved in the importation and distribution of cocaine, as well as logistics and money laundering/currency movement."[46]

41 CISC, *Public Report on Organized Crime in Canad*a (Ottawa: CISC, 2019).

42 RCMP & Drug Enforcement Administration, *Outlaw Motorcycle Gangs and the Drug Trade* (Ottawa: RCMP & DEA, 1986) at 18–19 and 21.

43 CISC, *Public Report on Organized Crime in Canada* (Ottawa: CISC, 2019); Sam Cooper, *Wilful Blindness: How a Criminal Network of Narcos, Tycoons and CCP Agents Infiltrated the West* (Montreal; Toronto: Optimum Publishing International, 2021).

44 Canadian Association of Chiefs of Police, *Organized Crime Committee Report, 1992* (Ottawa: CACP, 1992) at 64–65.

45 Hogan & Century, above note 18 at 138; Daniel Renaud, "Les cartels mexicains ont leurs gérants au Québec" *La Presse* (28 March 2019), online: www.lapresse.ca/actualites/justice-et-faits-divers/201903/28/01-5219865-les-cartels-mexicains-ont-leurs-gerants-au-quebec.php.

46 Rick Penney, "The Evolving Nature of Organized Crime" (2013) 75:1 RCMP *Gazette* 22.

Research into international drug smuggling operations summarized by Decker and Pyrooz suggests that transport and distribution are not carried out by vertically structured hierarchical transnational organizations. Instead, the transnational drug trade is "horizontally organized" involving "discrete cells" of independent operators at different levels of the international supply chain, from the production in a source country to the retail, street-level distribution.[47] Established Canadian crime groups such as the Hells Angels, the Mafia, and West End Gang in Quebec and the 'Ndrangheta in Ontario purchase cocaine from Colombian and Mexican suppliers but may use independent brokers as intermediaries. CISC has identified what it calls key facilitators in the drug trade such as "brokers involved in the methamphetamine market, either as precursor chemical diverters or importers" as well as "brokers involved in cocaine importation."[48]

D. CONDITIONS THAT MAKE CANADA VULNERABLE TO SMUGGLING

Arguably, there is no other country that has as many traits that make it vulnerable to smuggling as Canada. First, is the high level of demand among Canadians for drugs (and other contraband) illegally transported into the country (not to mention demand outside our borders for illicit products produced in and exported from Canada). A high level of public demand translates into a highly profitable underground industry, attracting numerous criminal entrepreneurs and groups, which "exist largely to profit from providing illicit goods and services in public demand or providing legal goods and services in an illicit manner."[49] In Colombia, a kilogram of pure cocaine hydrochloride can be purchased for around C$5,000. Once it is in Canada, the same kilogram can be wholesaled for anywhere between C$25,000 and C$50,000 a kilo. In their book on Mexico's Sinaloa Cartel, Hogan and Century explain how profits from cocaine

47 Scott Decker & David Pyrooz, "Gangs: Another Form of Organized Crime?" in Letizia Paoli, ed, *The Oxford Handbook of Organized Crime* (Oxford, New York: Oxford University Press, 2014) 270 at 279.

48 CISC, *Public Report on Organized Crime in Canada* (Ottawa: Criminal Intelligence Service Canada, 2020) at 4.

49 James Finckenauer, "Problems of Definition: What Is Organized Crime?" (2005) 8:3 *Trends in Organized Crime* 63 at 81–82.

trafficking were higher in Canada than in the United States. "It was a straightforward price-point issue: retail cocaine on the streets of Los Angeles or Chicago sold for $25,000 per kilo, while in major Canadian cities it sold for upwards of $35,000 per kilo."[50]

Geography and topography also play roles in Canada's vulnerability to smuggling. The illegal transport of goods into Canada is enabled by the more than 240,000 kilometres of coastline, along three oceans, most of which are insufficiently guarded. Having coastlines along both the Pacific and Atlantic Oceans means that smugglers have marine access to drug source countries in South America, Asia, Europe, and the Middle East.

The nature and scope of smuggling into and out of Canada are also significantly affected by its proximity to the United States and the shared border of 9,000 kilometres. The United States is a major supplier or transit country to Canada for cocaine, marijuana, and methamphetamine (not to mention tobacco products and firearms smuggled into the country). The US also constitutes the largest consumer market for marijuana and synthetic drugs produced in Canada. Smuggling routes are well established along the Canada–US border, with some dating back to the eighteenth century. With that said, railways, highways, and marine shipments that use inter-modal connections are the most prevalent forms of drug smuggling between the two countries given the direct connections they provide between Canadian official ports of entry, such as container ports, and American cities. Canada also has a large concentration of its population living within a short distance of the US border, which provides a convenient marketplace for inbound smuggled goods as well as a sympathetic and skilled labour pool from which to draw smugglers.

The Canada–US border is also marked by a unique geopolitical feature that has created the most porous point along the international boundary: the Akwesasne/St. Regis reserve of the Mohawk Nation. The 14,000-acre reserve traverses five jurisdictions — Canada, the United States, Ontario, Quebec, and New York State — and agreements have been negotiated with federal, state, and provincial governments that uphold the right of the Mohawk people to freely cross the border that cuts through the reserve without having to report to border protection agencies or pay duties on goods brought across the border. This geopolitical anomaly has been thoroughly exploited through the rampant smuggling of drugs, cigarettes,

50 Hogan & Century, above note 18 at 138–39.

weapons, and people. The Akwesasne reserve has attracted the attention of numerous criminal groups, turning it into what the Mackenzie Institute calls the "Klondike of Organized Crime."[51] As a Mohawk Grand Chief once opined, "On their maps, the gangsters put a pin at Akwesasne, and said, 'This is where it's easiest to cross.'"[52]

As discussed, the presence of (transnational) organized crime groups and networks in Canada has increased the country's vulnerability to both inbound and outbound smuggling of drugs at both unofficial and official ports of entry. Organized crime groups are known to use corruption and internal conspiracies at official ports of entry to help ensure the unfettered import and export of drugs and other contraband. In its 1998 annual report on organized crime, the CISC writes, criminal organizations are "firmly entrenched in all major Canadian seaports," the purpose of which is to facilitate smuggling (and cargo theft).[53] This entrenchment is achieved through the infiltration of the labour force at marine ports, whether this is the placement of members and associates of organized crime groups as dock workers, the corruption and intimidation of other dock workers, or the infiltration of unions that represent dock workers.[54] A 2010 report by the CBSA asserts that the Mafia and Hells Angels "have exerted the most significant criminal influence at major Canadian marine ports" and are "in key positions — longshoremen, equipment operators, foremen and truck drivers."[55]

Canada's vulnerability to smuggling also derives from its deep integration into the global economy and dependence upon international trade. The sheer volume of imports and exports to and from the country provides an ideal opportunity to hide drugs and other contraband. Smugglers readily take advantage of legitimate international trade in that much of the drugs entering Canada are intermingled with shipments of legal goods, in

---

51 "Long Fall of the Mohawk Warriors" *Mackenzie Institute*, 1996, online: www.mackenzieinstitute.com.

52 Tom Fennel, "The Human Smugglers" *Maclean's* (22 November 1999) at 18.

53 CISC, *Annual Report on Organized Crime in Canada, 1998* (Ottawa: CISC, 1998) at 13.

54 Canada, Parliament, Senate, Standing Senate Committee on National Security and Defence, *Canadian Security Guide Book: An Update of Security Problems in Search of Solutions* (Ottawa: Standing Senate on National Security and Defence, 2007); Kim Bolan, "How Hells Angels and Criminal Gangs Came to Control Much of the Vancouver Docks" *National Post* (9 May 2015), online: https://nationalpost.com/news/metro-vancouver-docks-special-investigation-768024.

55 *Ibid.*

marine containers, tractor-trailers, and air cargo. Finite CBSA resources mean only a small proportion of these conveyances are ever inspected, while inter-modal connections for freight help expedite the efficient distribution of illegal drugs to other provinces, states, and cities in North America.

E. SMUGGLING ENFORCEMENT CHALLENGES

Another significant factor accounting for the vibrant smuggling trade affecting Canada is the relative shortage of enforcement resources. As mentioned, the sheer amount of coastline, land border, and airspace enveloping Canada make it almost impossible to sufficiently guard the country's flanks.

Protecting the border from smuggling falls into what is called supply-side enforcement, which refers to measures undertaken by criminal justice agencies to limit the supply of illegal goods through detection and interdiction. There are two main ways that criminal justice agencies carry this out. The first is through border-control agencies that guard against the illegal importation of drugs, other contraband, and even illegal immigrants. The second is through the investigation function which includes the seizure of harmful goods for evidentiary purposes and to reduce supply to black markets.

Supply-side enforcement at Canada's borders is the shared responsibility of two federal law enforcement agencies: the CBSA, which is mandated to detect and interdict prohibited and controlled goods at official ports of entry, and the RCMP, which has law enforcement authority over all other locations along Canada's borders. The RCMP is also the federal agency responsible for inland investigations into contraventions against the *Customs Act*[56] and the *Controlled Drugs and Substances Act* (*CDSA*).[57]

The *Customs Act* is the principal legislation enforcing the smuggling of contraband and drugs into Canada. Part VI details specific enforcement provisions, including the powers of CBSA officers to search individuals and vehicles coming into Canada and to seize any items that may contravene the *Customs Act* or any act of Parliament that "prohibits, controls or regulates the importation or exportation of goods."[58] The *CDSA* proscribes

56 *Customs Act*, RSC 1985, c 1 (2d Supp) [*Customs Act*].

57 *Controlled Drugs and Substances Act*, SC 1996, c 19 [*CDSA*].

58 *Customs Act*, above note 56, s 101.

the possession, use, manufacture, importation, and trafficking of both prohibited drugs (those that are illegal) and controlled drugs (those that are legal but are subject to restrictions on their distribution and use — in particular, prescription drugs). Section 6 also includes specific offences for the import and export of controlled and prohibited substances. Amendments have been made recently to the *CDSA* that recognize Canada's growing stature as a synthetic drug source country by creating offences related to the unauthorized importation of precursor chemicals[59] and devices (in particular, pill presses)[60] which are used in the production of synthetic drugs.

Measures have also been put in place to specifically address smuggling across the Canada–US border. The most notable initiative is the Integrated Border Enforcement Teams (IBETs), which target cross-border criminal activity between the two countries and include the CBSA, the RCMP, US Customs and Border Protection, the US Coast Guard, and the US Immigration and Customs Enforcement. One IBET initiative is the Shiprider program, in which the RCMP and the US Coast Guard "work together to seamlessly enforce the law on both sides of the border in shared waterways." This includes placing Canadian and American "law enforcement officers on a single patrol vessel," combining law enforcement resources, and providing "the operational flexibility required to interdict suspect vessels across jurisdictions, removing the international maritime boundary as a barrier to law enforcement."[61]

In 2020, the United States and Canada signed the bilateral Joint Action Plan to Combat Opioids, which is "designed to strengthen cross-border cooperation and find effective approaches to addressing the opioid overdose crisis across three working groups covering law enforcement, border security, and health." Among the border security-related mandates of these working groups are measures "to share intelligence to better understand cross-border drug trafficking," to "strengthen the capacity of border services personnel to detect and interdict fentanyl, its related substances, and other synthetic opioids illegally crossing our

---

59 *CDSA*, above note 57, s 7.1 (1).

60 *Ibid*, s 46.3.

61 RCMP, *2014–15 Departmental Performance Report* (Ottawa: Minister of Public Safety and Emergency Preparedness, 2015) at 25.

borders" and to "formalize Canada–US coordination to target opioids and other illegal drugs shipped through the mail."[62]

Bilateral agreements have also been consummated to address perhaps the most urgent smuggling issue that has emerged in Canada in recent years: the illegal importation of fentanyl from China. In 2017, RCMP Chief Superintendent Andris Zarins informed the Senate Legal and Constitutional Affairs Committee that the RCMP had renewed a memorandum of understanding with the Chinese Ministry of Public Security to strengthen "cooperation on crime prevention and criminal investigations involving illegal drugs, tri-national crime, and smuggling. China has committed to cooperate with Canada and other international partners to disrupt the export of fentanyl, including classifying a number of fentanyl analogues as controlled substances under Chinese law and investigating leads provided by Canadian law enforcement."[63]

Despite these initiatives, federal enforcement in Canada is continually hampered by a lack of resources; while Canada has the second-largest landmass of any country, it is rather small in terms of population, which means there is an insufficient taxation basis to adequately fund the public border protection resources necessary to guard these thousands of kilometres of coastline and border. The RCMP has gone so far as to complain in a 2019 financial report that its federal enforcement mandate has "been constrained by government-wide spending reduction exercises which have resulted in significant financial pressures"[64] and "without new funding" and "sufficient technology, tools, and information systems, there is a risk that Federal Policing may not be able to meet critical operational requirements."[65] In short, there is a considerable lack of enforcement

62 "Steering Committee Meeting of the Canada–U.S. Joint Action Plan on Opioids 2021," Public Safety Canada, updated 12 July 2021, online: www.publicsafety.gc.ca/cnt/rsrcs/pblctns/2021-jnt-ctn-pds/index-en.aspx.

63 Canada, Parliament, Senate, Standing Senate Committee on Legal and Constitutional Affairs, *Proceedings* "Bill C-37, An Act to amend the Controlled Drugs and Substances Act and to make related amendments to other acts," No 25 (30 March 2017), 42nd Parliament, 1st Session.

64 "Quarterly Financial Report—For the Period Ending December 31, 2019," RCMP, last modified February 26, 2020, online: www.rcmp-grc.gc.ca/en/quarterly-financial-report-the-period-ending-december-31-2019.

65 "Royal Canadian Mounted Police 2020–2021 Departmental Plan," RCMP, last modified 10 March 2020, online: www.rcmp-grc.gc.ca/en/royal-canadian-mounted-police-2020-2021-departmental-plan#A2.

resources for both official and unofficial ports of entry, especially given the scope of both legal and illegal goods entering and exiting the country. It has long been estimated that less than one percent of marine shipping containers are screened for drugs at Canadian ports.[66]

Federal smuggling enforcement is also faced with the resilience, opportunism, and adaptability of well-organized smugglers. A review of federal anti-smuggling initiatives in Canada produced in 2000 indicated they "[do] not appear to have had a strong deterrent effect on organized smuggling in general." Instead, "the impact on smuggling groups can more accurately be characterized as one of displacement. Indeed, history shows that early successes in organized crime enforcement are often followed by diminishing returns as groups become more adaptive and sophisticated."[67] A summary of a 2019 roundtable on illegal drugs convened by Public Safety Canada documents how "criminal enterprises are using increasingly advanced methods to produce, smuggle, and traffic illicit substances." Organized crime groups and criminal entrepreneurs "adapt to detection and interdiction efforts and develop alternative transportation and concealment methods. Consequently, drug enforcement efforts in both Canada and the United States must continuously evolve."[68]

Transnational criminal operations have also capitalized on the primacy of territorial sovereignty for nation-states and how this undermines transnational law enforcement. While some organized criminal conspiracies transcend national borders, most law enforcement in Canada is carried out at the municipal level. Even those federal law enforcement agencies that have national jurisdiction— the RCMP and CBSA—are limited in conducting international investigations and gathering evidence in other countries. International cooperation and coordination among law enforcement agencies, while steadily improving, pales in comparison to the nature and scope of the international networking and cooperation that

66 Erin Ubels & Sean Boynton, "Deltaport's Lack of Police Means Less Than 1 per cent of Containers Get Checked, Officials Say" *Global News* (12 September 2019), online: https://globalnews.ca/news/5892137/deltaport-no-police/.

67 Stephen Schneider, "Contraband Smuggling and Its Enforcement in Canada: An Evaluation of the Canadian Anti-Smuggling Initiative" (2001) 6:2 *Trends in Organized Crime* 3.

68 Public Safety Canada, *2019 Law Enforcement Roundtable on Drugs* (Ottawa: Public Safety Canada, 2019) at 5.

exists among organized criminal actors.[69] The legal means that are available to law enforcement to facilitate international enforcement—such as extradition or mutual legal assistance treaties—can take months and even years to expedite. Meanwhile, organized criminal actors do not require any of this legal apparatus to forge international connections.

Challenges facing smuggling enforcement must also be placed within the larger context of the failures of supply-side drug enforcement. The lightning rod for discontent over traditional smuggling enforcement is the much-criticized "war on drugs" and its preoccupation with interdiction and supply reduction. While drug enforcement has won a few battles, the war on drugs has effectively been lost or, at the very most, is at a stalemate.[70] Paoli argues that drug enforcement "may have helped keep the US drug market relatively 'disorganized' but has failed to reach its main goal of reducing drug availability."[71] More concerning is the growing evidence that the supply of many recreational drugs and their purity levels have increased while prices have dropped.[72] The uninterrupted introduction of new types of illegal street drugs (crack cocaine, crystal meth, bath salts, ecstasy, synthetic marijuana, fentanyl, etc.) is another indicator of how reliance on supply-side enforcement has failed to curtail entrepreneurially opportunistic drug trafficking.

Accusations have been made that Canadian policies regarding illegal drugs have been too heavily dictated by definitions, values, and policies of the United States. Wheatley writes that the *UN Convention against Transnational Organized Crime*[73] was most influenced by and reflective of

---

69 Felia Allum & Stan Gilmour, "Introduction" in Felia Allum & Stan Gilmour, eds, *Routledge Handbook of Transnational Organized Crime* (London, New York: Routledge, 2012) at 1; Andrea Di Nicola, "Trafficking in Persons and Smuggling of Migrants" in Philip Reichel & Jay Albanese, eds, *Handbook of Transnational Crime and Justice*, 2d ed (Los Angeles: Sage Publications, 2014) at 143.

70 Kyle Grayson, "Discourse, Identity, and the U.S. 'War on Drugs'" in Margaret Beare, ed, *Critical Reflections on Transnational Organized Crime, Money Laundering, and Corruption* (Toronto: University of Toronto Press, 2003) 145 at 147.

71 Letizia Paoli, "Introduction" in *Oxford Handbook*, above note 1 at 1.

72 Dan Werb et al, "The Temporal Relationship Between Drug Supply Indicators: An Audit of International Government Surveillance Systems" (2013) 3 *British Medical Journal Open* 1; and see UNODC, above note 31.

73 *United Nations Convention against Transnational Organized Crime*, (2000) 2225 UNTS 275 [*UNTOC*].

American and Italian experiences with the Mafia.[74] Some see the UN *Convention Against Illicit Traffic in Narcotic Drugs and Psychotropic Substances*,[75] with its unyielding stance on the prohibition and criminal enforcement of recreational drugs, as nothing more than an extension of the US war on drugs.[76] As Carrapiço notes, "The US's growing perception of its domestic narcotic situation as a war on drugs gradually established itself as an important element of the country's foreign policy, which in turn rapidly became part of the international agenda."[77] Central to this agenda is pressuring other countries to sign extradition treaties, implement made-in-America criminal justice policies, accept US law enforcement agents on their soil, and submit to crop eradication programs.[78]

F. CONCLUSION

Since at least the early part of the twentieth century, smuggling and drug trafficking affecting Canada have been inextricably intertwined. While Canada has long been perceived as a destination for illegal drugs produced elsewhere, this ignores the international role it plays in the production and export of high-grade marijuana and synthetic drugs, as well as its position as a transit country for cocaine or synthetic drugs produced in other countries.

Despite criminal laws and supporting enforcement resources at the border and inland, there are few expectations that drug smuggling will be reined in any time soon. This is due to the inherent characteristics of Canada that promote the smuggling and trafficking of illicit substances, combined with significant enforcement limitations.

Illegal drug smuggling, trafficking, and consumption have perhaps reached their most threatening apogee in recent years with the introduction of fentanyl. This narcotic has come to encapsulate drug trafficking

---

74 Joseph Wheatley, "Transnational Organized Crime: A Survey of Laws, Policies and International Conventions, in Allum & Gilmour, above note 69 at 65.

75 *United Nations Convention Against Illicit Traffic in Narcotic Drugs and Psychotropic Substances*, (1988) 1582 UNTS 95.

76 Petrus van Duyne & Mark Nelemans, "Transnational Organized Crime: Thinking in and out of Plato's Cave" in Allum & Gilmour, above note 69 at 36.

77 Helena Carrapiço, "Transnational Organized Crime as a Security Concept" in Allum & Gilmour, above note 69 at 24.

78 *UNTOC*, above note 73 at 152.

affecting Canada: the smuggling of an illegal substance (in the form of powdered fentanyl), its domestic production (in the form of pills), the domestic trafficking of the drug, as well as its export to other countries. The ample supply of fentanyl in (both powdered and tablet form) also highlights the immense challenges and failures of supply-side law enforcement in controlling this problem.

The current opioid crisis, the unsatiated demand for illicit drugs generally, and the enervating limitations of supply-side enforcement have heightened calls for alternatives to the war on drugs. Despite the many harms that organized crimes and criminal offenders inflict, Canadians have a symbiotic relationship with drug smugglers and traffickers by readily consuming illegal goods and services to satisfy their many vices. As long as demand for illicit drugs exists in Canada, there will be a supply from both domestic and international sources.

VI

INTER-STATE COOPERATION *and* ENFORCEMENT

eighteen

Human Rights Considerations in Extradition

FRÉDÉRIC MÉGRET*

A. INTRODUCTION

Extradition is traditionally conceived as an inter-state process designed to deal with the problem of fugitives. It is only relatively recently that human rights concerns have come to the foreground.[1] This is particularly the case in Canada where the *Charter*[2] has arguably significantly transformed the framing of extradition, albeit with occasionally limited practical impact.

The constraints that weigh on the desirability of extradition are multifaceted. States are evidently interested in enforcing their laws and asserting their criminal jurisdiction, and so have a strong interest in addressing the problem of fugitives. There are also certain inbuilt international limitations to any extradition scheme. States can only expect other states to accept their extradition requests to the extent that they are willing to honour similar requests. This is the basic *quid pro quo* of international law. States that do not comply with their extradition treaty

* Full Professor and Dawson Scholar, Co-director Centre for Human Rights and Legal Pluralism, Faculty of Law, McGill University. Thanks to Isabella Spano for her invaluable assistance.

1 John Dugard & Christine Van den Wyngaert, "Reconciling Extradition with Human Rights" (1998) 92:2 *American Journal of International Law* 187.

2 *Canadian Charter of Rights and Freedoms*, Part I of the *Constitution Act, 1982*, being Schedule B to the *Canada Act 1982* (UK), 1982, c 11 [*Charter*].

obligations will also find that their treaty partners will be disinclined to respect theirs. In other words, states' interest in extradition is based on their own, homegrown interest in securing custody over criminal suspects abroad, reinforced by the necessarily reciprocal nature of international treaty arrangements. To make matters more complicated, extradition regimes have increasingly been mandated through international law. This turn to international law occurs especially in relation to what one might broadly characterize as transnational or supranational crimes (a reality spectacularly illustrated by simplified regimes of surrender to international criminal tribunals, but also in efforts to deal with terrorism). These domestic and international factors suggest that, all other things being equal, states have a strong interest in implementation of and compliance with extradition obligations.

At the same time, there is no denying that extradition implicates human and *Charter* rights. It threatens those who are targeted with both forced removal from Canadian territory and prosecution (as well as, possibly, punishment) in a foreign land. This sort of judicial uprooting has severe consequences on all aspects of persons' lives, implicating, for example, sections 2, 6, or 7. Just as it has often been said that the *Charter* has profoundly reshaped criminal justice in Canada in general, it has also had an impact on extradition proceedings, which are a complex and unique mix of executive discretion, judicial scrutiny, and international comity.

This chapter first describes the basic conceptual framework wherein *Charter* and human rights claims in relation to extradition arise in Canada. It then looks more specifically at the sort of rights concerns that arise at various stages of the extradition process.

B. THE BASIC FRAMEWORK

1) The Constitutional Equation

Extradition is based on principles of comity and mutual cooperation that are central to international law as well as to Canadian foreign policy. The Canadian government freely negotiates and ratifies extradition treaties, susceptible to a range of limitations often associated with treaty-making in Canada, including limited involvement of Parliament or the provinces. It is important to stress that in complying with its extradition obligations, Canada is not doing other states' bidding, but participating in the very "pressing and substantial Canadian objectives"[3] of "protecting the public against crime, bringing fugitives to justice, and ensuring, through international cooperation, that national boundaries do not serve as a means of escape from the rule of law."[4] This idea that Canada should not become a "safe haven" is ultimately, aside from comity, a policy based on Canadian social protection.

The government is accordingly eager to comply with its extradition obligations, in a context where extradition treaties are marked by a profound degree of reciprocity. Failure by Canada to honour its extradition obligations would undoubtedly have an impact on its ability to request compliance from treaty partners. Whatever reticence Canada may occasionally have about extraditing certain individuals (particularly, but not only, Canadian citizens) tends to be compensated for by the symmetrical desire to ensure the extradition of persons wanted by the Canadian justice system. The importance of the executive in concluding international treaties concerning extradition is reflected in the considerable role that is given to the minister of justice (hereinafter the minister) in the decision to ultimately surrender a person sought.

The courts, in turn, have a somewhat limited role marked by a considerable degree of deference to executive discretion. At the committal level, an extradition judge is involved whose decisions are open to appeal, but whose competence extends mostly to formal compliance with the terms of the *Extradition Act*.[5] At the surrender level, the decision is mostly the minister's to make, and although it is susceptible to judicial review under the *Charter*,[6] courts have also tended to defer quite significantly to the minister.

The Supreme Court has held that the ability of Canada to honour its international treaty obligations is a "pressing and substantial" need in terms of section 1 of the *Charter*.[7] Canadian *Charter* law should, as it were, take the international system as it finds it. Moreover, given the largely political nature of the surrender decision, the minister "has superior expertise in international relations and foreign affairs" and therefore "is in the

3 *MM v United States of America*, 2015 SCC 62 [*MM*].

4 *Sriskandarajah v United States of America*, 2012 SCC 70 at para 10 [*Sriskandarajah*].

5 *Extradition Act*, SC 1999, c 18 [*Extradition Act*].

6 *United States of America v Ferras*, 2006 SCC 33 [*Ferras*].

7 See *Sriskandarajah*, above note 4.

best position to determine whether the factors, taken as a whole, tilt the balance for or against extradition."[8] Consequently, court interference with that discretion should be limited to exceptional cases "of real substance" and operate with "the utmost circumspection"[9] in a context where courts cannot simply substitute their views for that of the executive.[10]

In practice, Canadian courts seem to have struck down only a small minority of cases submitted to them for judicial review. That said, the last few decades have been marked by increasingly bold assertions of the applicability of *Charter* guarantees to extradition proceedings. It is largely recognized that the minister's authority to order the surrender of a person whose extradition is sought, which is regulated by section 40(1) of the *Extradition Act*, must be exercised in accordance with the *Charter*. A surrender order clearly affects a person's liberty and security, and so can only be limited in accordance with principles of fundamental justice. Courts have applied a standard of review of extradition decisions of reasonableness such that, on the basis of the relevant facts, the minister can be found to have rendered a defensible conclusion.[11]

Part of the difficulty is, in fact, that extradition exists somewhere at the intersection of the executive and the judicial, both in Canada and often in partner states. Just as the Canadian judiciary needs to find the right balance between asserting *Charter* protections and deferring to executive authority, the Canadian government itself needs to tread carefully in its dealings with foreign governments. Another difficulty is the extraterritorial application of rights protections. The applicability of *Charter* guarantees to matters of extradition is rooted, first, in the fact that the *Charter* applies to all within Canada. Those whose extradition is sought are, by definition, on Canadian territory. Second, it derives from the fact that the *Charter*'s realm is less territorial than it is governance-based, perhaps as befits a fundamentally constitutional instrument. Section 32, in particular, anticipates that the *Charter* applies to "the Parliament and government of Canada." Third, it is based on a recognition that "individuals who choose to commit an offence in a foreign jurisdiction generally must accept the

8 *India v Badesha*, 2017 SCC 44 at para 39 [*Badesha*].

9 *Argentina v Mellino*, [1987] 1 SCR 536 at 353, La Forest J [*Mellino*].

10 *Canada (Minister of Citizenship and Immigration) v Vavilov*, 2019 SCC 65 at paras 105–14.

11 *Lake v Canada (Minister of Justice)*, 2008 SCC 23 at paras 34 and 41.

local law, procedure and punishments which the foreign state applies to its own residents."[12]

International law has played a somewhat ambiguous role. Canada is bound both by treaties with extradition components (including multilateral ones for certain supranational and transnational offences) and international human rights treaties such as the *ICCPR*[13] or the *CAT*[14] that may pull in different directions. Canadian courts have occasionally referred to international human rights developments to reinforce interpretations of the *Charter*, as in the case of extradition to a state that has the death penalty (discussed below). Moreover, litigants who did not find a favourable outcome before Canadian courts have occasionally gone to international human rights bodies.[15] Nonetheless, by and large Canada's international human rights obligations have remained in the background, notably as a result of Canada's dualist character.

2) Pluralism in Criminal Justice

Canadian public opinion and media have occasionally been aghast at the treatment of individuals, particularly Canadian nationals, whose extradition is sought. This was notably the case in the long, winding *Diab* case, which saw an Ottawa professor accused of participation in a terrorist attack in Paris that had occurred decades earlier.[16] Without going into the details, some criticisms of the French judicial system in that case were well taken, whilst others may reflect cultural misunderstandings about a different justice system. For example, the lack of emphasis on sworn statements is explained in the inquisitorial tradition by the reliance put on an investigating magistrate. The problem often arises when practices that make sense within an overall system have to be evaluated via extradition in another system that is naturally wary of them.

---

12 *Mellino*, above note 9.

13 *International Covenant on Civil and Political Rights* (1966), 999 UNTS 171.

14 *United Nations Convention against Torture and other Cruel, Inhuman and Degrading Treatment or Punishment* (1984), 1465 UNTS 85, Can TS 1987 No 36 [*CAT*].

15 William A. Schabas, "Soering's Legacy: The Human Rights Committee and the Judicial Committee of the Privy Council Take a Walk Down Death Row" (1994) 43:4 *International & Comparative Law Quarterly* 913.

16 Alex Neve, "The Hassan Diab Case: Injustice Expands, Need for Redress and Reform Deepens" (2021) 5 *PKI Global Justice Journal* 4.

Certainly, for every Canadian prosecuted on the basis of what may be unfamiliar and less-than-ideal foreign standards, there will be foreigners who are prosecuted on the basis of equally unfamiliar and less-than-ideal Canadian standards. It is not as if Canada itself has always scrupulously respected the right to a fair trial (delays come to mind as a significant structural problem). The reality of extradition is that

> while premised on our conceptions of what is fundamentally just, [it] must accommodate differences between our system of criminal justice and the systems in place in reciprocating states.... [B]eyond ... basic conditions precedent of reciprocity, much diversity is, of necessity, tolerated.[17]

Clearly other legal systems are not required to conform to a Canadian standard of justice, let alone "mirror" it.[18]

The basic presumption of extradition law, therefore, is that it is an imperfect system to ensure cooperation between criminal justice systems that are significantly and legitimately different. Negative consequences for rights stand to be limited from the very outset, in that extradition treaties have so far only been concluded by Canada with states that can be deemed to protect broadly fair trial standards (although efforts at negotiating an extradition treaty with China have created concerns from human rights groups, as has the existing extradition treaty with India). This reflects "a certain level of confidence in the administration of justice in that country, even if the system may be different from ours, with different priorities and disparate punishments."[19] This is the philosophy that has traditionally militated for significant deference to other legal systems. It is what led, for example, to the adoption of the *Extradition Act* in 1999, and, for example, a more liberal admissibility of hearsay in committal hearings, even though such evidence was *a priori* anathema to the common law tradition.[20]

As La Forest J put it, "The judicial process in a foreign country must not be subjected to finicky evaluations against the rules governing the

17 *Kindler v Canada (Minister of Justice)*, [1991] 2 SCR 779, McLachlin J at 844 [*Kindler*].

18 *United States of America v Barbu*, 2010 ONCA 891 at para 43.

19 *United States v Hillis*, 2021 ONCA 447 at para 101 [*Hillis*].

20 Anne Warner La Forest, "The Balance Between Liberty and Comity in the Evidentiary Requirements Applicable to Extradition Proceedings" (2002) 28:1 *Queen's Law Journal* 95.

legal process in this country."[21] Deference to other systems is also a consequence of the fact that they may be experiencing different penal crises (for example, the drug problem may be cause for greater social alarm in the United States), have adopted laws democratically, and adhere to different philosophies of social protection.[22] The Supreme Court has been at pains to emphasize that it is not evaluating the rights compatibility of foreign legal systems *per se* as much as how those foreign legal systems would be perceived in Canada at the moment of extradition. Comity commands that a certain horizontal margin of appreciation be granted to other states with which the Canadian executive has decided extradition agreements would be beneficial.

By the same token, the rise of *Charter* protections, as well as increasingly salient international human rights standards, have provided a more incontrovertible and universally defensible yardstick by which to evaluate occasional domestic deviations — spectacularly illustrated, as will be seen below, in the case of the death penalty. Evaluating the criminal justice practices of a foreign state has long ceased to be barred by a rule of non-inquiry, and Canada might feel confident that, in evaluating *Charter* rights transnationally, it is not so much imposing local standards as holding foreign states up to often common international commitments.

The Supreme Court has in principle recognized that Canada is required to engage in a human rights appraisal of the criminal justice system of the requesting state for the purposes of surrender.[23] The standard to find that a foreign practice too significantly departs from Canada's own constitutional tradition is, however, a high one. In *Schmidt*, the Supreme Court found that section 7's principles of fundamental justice will be violated if the extradition "shocks the conscience," where the "conscience" is understood as that of Canadians.[24] In *Kindler*, the Court spoke of an outcome being "simply unacceptable to right-thinking Canadians."[25] As Baudouin JA put it, "The issue is not to extol the virtues of our own system (much more liberal, it goes without saying), nor to put on trial the American system (very repressive), but only to decide whether the law and the

21 *Canada v Schmidt*, [1987] 1 SCR 500 at para 48 [*Schmidt*].

22 See, for example, Baudouin JA's dissenting opinion in *Jamieson v Canada (Justice)*, (1994), 93 CCC (3d) 265 (QC CA) [*Jamieson*].

23 *Badesha*, above note 8.

24 *Schmidt*, above note 21.

25 *Kindler*, above note 17.

justice system which will be applied to the person who will be extradited are unacceptable to our conscience."[26]

Presumably, Canadians have a certain understanding that foreign criminal justice systems operate differently than Canada's, allowing for a degree of pluralism. Especially within a broad family of liberal legal systems, traditions may vary somewhat even as many key facets of the criminal law and justice system remain commensurable. Moreover, Canadians might be expected to weigh whatever differences exist against the broader goals and benefits of extradition. By the same token, there may be cases where extradition would offend "the Canadian sense of what is fair, right and just, bearing in mind the nature of the offence and the penalty, the foreign justice system and considerations of comity and security."[27]

The kind of balance that courts are asked to strike between deference to pluralism internationally and adherence to fundamental rights standards at home is reminiscent of a similar attention to "the margin of appreciation"[28] in the international human rights regime and the difficulty of allowing for local variation whilst maintaining a sense of red lines.

C. TYPES OF RIGHTS CONCERNS

1) Rights Concerns at the Committal Stage

A number of rights concerns arise already at the *authority to proceed* and *judicial committal* stages, given the potential deprivation of liberty involved. It is worth noting that states may have politically motivated reasons to ask for extradition, raising the danger that Canada will unwittingly be enlisted in an enterprise of transnational repression.[29] The tendency of states like the United States to extend their criminal jurisdiction extraterritorially,[30] or like China to aggressively pursue economic criminals, suggests that the rights implications of being extradited at all (independently of conditions

26 *Jamieson*, above note 22 at 268–70.

27 *Kindler*, above note 17 at para 176.

28 Andreas Follesdal & Nino Tsereteli, "The Margin of Appreciation in Europe and Beyond" (2016) 20:8 *The International Journal of Human Rights* 1055–57.

29 Nicola Langille & Frédéric Mégret, "Red Notices and Transnational Police Practices" in Mikkel Jarle Christensen & Ron Levi, eds, *International Practices of Criminal Justice: Social and Legal Perspectives* (Abingdon-on-Thames: Routledge, 2017) at 108.

30 Paul Arnell & Alan Reid, "Hackers Beware: The Cautionary Story of Gary McKinnon" (2009) 18:1 *Information & Communications Technology Law* 1.

in the requesting state) can be serious. This would militate ideally for a culture of caution about the good faith of states requesting extradition, trusted international partners with broadly compatible legal systems though they may be.

Extradition law may already objectively protect rights even though that was not particularly the original intent. For example, the old dual criminality requirement or the requirement in the *Extradition Act* to the effect that the offence could result in a jail sentence of two years or more in Canada[31] is not always justified on human rights grounds. *De facto*, however, the dual criminality requirement ought to protect individuals from extradition for behaviour which is not of such a nature as to be criminal or of a sufficient degree of gravity in Canada. Similarly, the principle of specialty ensures that individuals may only be prosecuted for the offence for which they were extradited, providing a further layer of protection.

By the same token, dual criminality is understood as not requiring a formal match between offences, so much as a basic correspondence of the *essence* of the conduct at stake.[32] This raised a degree of skepticism in the Meng Wanzhou case, for example, where extradition was sought for fraud—which obviously exists in Canadian criminal law—but specifically in relation to US sanctions against Iran that had no equivalent in Canada.[33] In effect, a failure to appreciate the significant differences that may exist between nominally "equivalent" offences may lead to extradition for behaviour that would have been unlikely to lead to a conviction in Canada, notably if one takes into account available defences.[34] This relativizes the sense that the *Extradition Act* provides much protection by requiring the existence of an equivalent offence in Canada.

The committal hearing is itself, at least theoretically, a protection for those sought, in that it is functionally equivalent to a preliminary inquiry. It involves an assessment of the evidence presented in a record of the case (ROC) against the person sought for extradition, a document that has been certified by the requesting state as in conformity with its own laws of evidence collection. The ROC is presumed reliable, but its tendency to do

31 *Extradition Act*, above note 5, s 3.

32 *Canada (Justice) v Fischbacher*, 2009 SCC 46 [*Fischbacher*].

33 That argument was nonetheless eventually rejected. See *United States of America v Meng*, 2020 BCSC 785 [*Meng*].

34 *MM c Ministre de la Justice du Canada*, 2019 QCCA 683, leave denied 2019 CanLII 96496.

away with admissibility requirements tends to launder the evidence-collection practices of other countries. The cursory and selective character of the evidence presented by foreign states, as well as that the ROC may not contain sworn statements or *viva voce* evidence, has been criticized, notably in the wake of the *Diab* case. However, the Supreme Court has found that the test for committal is merely "whether or not there is any evidence upon which a reasonable jury properly instructed could return a verdict of guilty."[35]

It is true that the person sought may challenge evidence, and that an extradition judge may engage in a limited weighing to determine whether there is a plausible case, thus providing a meaningful judicial process.[36] The courts, however, have generally been unwilling to go beyond an examination of whether the evidence on its face might lead to a verdict of guilty (which, very exceptionally, it might not when the requesting state omits key evidence). *A fortiori*, they have clearly resisted being drawn into a discussion of the facts, their possible legal characterizations, the availability of defences, or the past history of a case.[37] Extradition judges may not deny committal, at any rate, "simply because the case appears to the extradition judge to be weak or unlikely to succeed at trial."[38] The extradition hearing is not a mini-trial in Canada (in which, for example, the presumption of innocence would apply) and even judges who were clearly unimpressed by the evidence before them have felt that they had no choice but to order committal.[39]

In fact, neither guilt nor innocence are per se supposed to be part of the extradition hearing. The Crown has no obligation to disclose exculpatory evidence, and judges have been receptive to the notion that the primary goal is to promote international comity with Canada's extradition partners. The only possibility is for defence to challenge committal on the basis that the ROC is defective or manifestly unreliable, which courts almost never contemplate. Challenging extradition at the committal stage thus remains difficult, since one must find a way to specifically

35 *United States of America v Shephard*, [1977] 2 SCR 1067 at 1080.

36 See *Ferras* above note 6.

37 See *MM* above note 3; see also, for example, *United States of America v Wilcox*, 2015 BCCA 39 [*Wilcox*].

38 *United States of America v Prudenza (sub nom Anderson)*, 2007 ONCA 84 at para 28 [*Anderson*].

39 *Ibid.*

impugn the reliability of the evidence provided by the requesting state as worthy of complete rejection. Robert Currie has described "rebutting the presumption of reliability" as "not only a difficult hill to scale but an impossible one,"[40] especially in a context where the government seems *ab initio* highly committed to expediting extradition and committal judges resigned to rubber stamping what is presented to them.

It is worth noting that the subsequent acquittal of someone in the state to which they were extradited does not necessarily make the extradition process retrospectively illegitimate. The threshold for committal to extradition is much lower than the threshold to find someone culpable under most systems of liberal criminal justice. Prosecutors routinely bring charges only to lose cases, having failed to meet the exceptionally high threshold of proof beyond a reasonable doubt. That this happens in other states, just as it does in Canada, should not come as a surprise, and may in fact be seen as evidence of the proper operation of criminal justice. Nonetheless, the considerable disruption to life and rights involved in an extradition may retrospectively be appreciated differently if it turns out that individuals have been extradited on the basis of what were all along very weak cases.

An extradition judge may grant *Charter* relief where a breach relates directly to the relevant issues at the committal stage,[41] notably "in the rare case where misconduct by the requesting state reaches directly into the Canadian judicial process and irremediably taints the fairness of the extradition proceedings or so undermines the integrity of the Canadian judicial process that no remedy short of stay of proceedings will be adequate to protect the repute of the administration of justice."[42] A rare case of abuse of process is *Cobb*, where a US prosecutor had stated publicly that the person sought would become "the boyfriend of a very bad man" if he resisted extradition.[43] The extradition judge found that "no right-thinking Canadian would endorse the use of a threat of homosexual rape as a means of persuading Canadian residents to abandon their rights to a full extradition hearing" and the Supreme Court upheld the stay he imposed.[44]

40 Robert J. Currie, "Wrongful Extradition: Reforming the Committal Phase of Canada's Extradition Law" (2021) 44:6 *Manitoba Law Review* 1 at 23.

41 See *Extradition Act*, above note 5, s 25.

42 *United States of America v Wong*, 2017 BCCA 109 para 18 [*Wong*].

43 *United States of America v Cobb*, 2001 SCC 19.

44 *Ibid* at para 14.

Abuses of process, however, will most often not be that clear, and the burden of proof lies on the person making the allegation. The person sought is entitled to further disclosure from the requesting state,[45] when a violation of the *Charter* is alleged, if the claim has an "air of reality" and therefore is not mere "wishful thinking," conjecture, speculation, or a "fishing expedition."[46] The process is therefore quite protective of the requesting state in a context where "misconduct allegations directed at foreign authorities are very serious because they impugn the motives and actions of a neighboring and friendly power with whom Canada has an extradition treaty."[47] Individuals who have ascribed nefarious intentions to the requesting state that could be explained by a range of innocent factors have typically failed to meet the air-of-reality test, let alone proved an abuse of process.[48]

2) Rights Concerns at the Surrender Stage

In addition to the grounds for ordering committal, rights protections under the *Charter* extend to the broad consequences of a surrender. The minister's decision to surrender is subject to potential judicial review. It is worth noting that the courts have consistently held that extradition by itself is not a violation of the section 6 right to remain in Canada, and Canada quite freely extradites Canadian nationals. Although it may be a *prima facie* infringement of that right, and the authorities "ought to direct their minds to whether prosecution would be equally effective in Canada," extradition will often be justifiable under section 1. This has also not prevented extradition in cases where the crimes were committed wholly in Canada, the persons sought had not set foot in the requesting country, and they could conceivably have been tried in Canada.[49]

Aside from section 6, it is in fact mostly section 7 that has been relevant in assessing the *Charter* compatibility of extradition requests. Moreover, section 44(1)(a) of the *Extradition Act* anticipates that surrender may be

45 *United States of America v Kwok*, 2001 SCC 18.

46 *R v Larosa*, [2002] 166 CCC (3d) 49 at para 76 (Ont CA).

47 *United States of America v Feimuth*, 2004 BCSC 154 at para 56.

48 *Martin v Canada (Minister of Justice)*, 2017 BCCA 220 [*Martin*]. See also *États-Unis Mexicains c Boily*, 2005 QCCA 599.

49 *United States of America v Cotroni; United States of America v El Zein*, [1989] 1 SCR 1469.

refused if, in light of all the circumstances, the surrender would be "unjust or oppressive." In practice, what "shocks the conscience" or is "simply unacceptable" has proven to be a difficult standard to pin down. The courts have noted that "the judge must avoid imposing his or her own subjective views on the matter, and seek rather to objectively assess the attitudes of Canadians on the issue."[50] At the same time, as the Supreme Court put it in *Burns*, "the phrase 'shocks the conscience' and equivalent expressions are not to be taken out of context or equated to opinion polls" and are "not intended to signal an abdication by judges of their constitutional responsibilities in matters involving fundamental principles of justice."[51]

The standard of judicial review is the largely procedural one of whether the minister applied the correct legal tests.[52] The exercise is presented as one of weighing *Charter* rights against the many factors favouring extradition. An even more deferential test is accorded the application to the facts where the standard of judicial review is normally one "at the extreme legislative end of the continuum of administrative decision-making."[53]

3) Punishments

Canadian courts have been unwilling to conclude that particular forms of punishment could be subject to review under section 12 of the *Charter* on "cruel and unusual punishment," which proscribes sentences that are "grossly disproportionate" to the offence committed, as such. This would come too close to applying Canadian standards extraterritorially to punishments that are foreign in essence. What is squarely within Canada's jurisdiction, however, is the decision to surrender someone and its implications under section 7. Section 12 nonetheless has a tendency to come through the back door as "informing" the evaluation of section 7.[54]

---

50 *Kindler*, above note 17 at 850.

51 *United States v Burns*, 2001 SCC 7 at para 67 [*Burns*].

52 However, it has also been argued by some courts that where disposition of *Charter* questions is concerned, the appropriate standard of decision is that of correctness. See *Canada (Minister of Justice) v Stewart*, [1998] 131 CCC (3d) 423 at para 17 (BCCA).

53 *Idziak v Canada (Minister of Justice)*, [1992] 3 SCR 631 at 659.

54 As opposed to being a relevant factor in assessing a s 12 violation. See *R v Lloyd*, 2016 SCC 13 at paras 40, 47.

a) The Death Penalty

Clearly, extraditing someone to a state where they would be subjected to torture would violate section 7. The very nature of certain punishments might "sufficiently violate our sense of fundamental justice as to tilt the balance against extradition."[55] Examples given by the Supreme Court in *Burns* include "stoning to death individuals taken in adultery, or lopping off the hands of a thief."[56] Section 7 is also *a priori* implicated when individuals are extradited to states where they may be subjected to the death penalty. But are all extraditions to the death penalty *violations* of section 7? This now largely resolved question preoccupied Canadian courts throughout the 1990s, with a considerable degree of initial variation.

The initial position of the Supreme Court in the 1991 *USA v Kindler* case was that the death penalty did not shock the conscience of Canadians, and so extradition could proceed.[57] Deterring fugitives from fleeing to Canada as a perceived safe haven was a compelling social goal. Moreover, the Court did not find a unified norm internationally that would incite it to consider the death penalty shocking. Very soon after, in the quite similar *Reference Re Ng* case,[58] the Court confirmed that there was no *Charter* violation. This did, however, put Canada in an awkward position, particularly in relation to its international commitments as a, by then, solidly abolitionist state. It is true that the continuous support of a significant part of Canadian public opinion for the death penalty — notwithstanding its abolition — suggested that its existence and imposition elsewhere might not shock the conscience. It is worth noting that the UNHRC itself, which heard a petition from Kindler two years later, found no violation by Canada of its obligations under the *ICCPR*.[59]

The mood had significantly changed by the time the case of *USA v Burns* was heard some ten years later, leading to a dramatic reversal. The minister of justice had again not sought assurances that the death penalty would not be imposed, even though he was allowed to under the US–Canada extradition treaty. Unanimously, the Supreme Court found that extraditing to the death penalty violated principles of fundamental justice. In reaching that conclusion, the Court was by 2001 much more

55 *Burns*, above note 51 at para 69.
56 *Ibid.*
57 *Kindler*, above note 17.
58 *Reference Re Ng Extradition (Can)*, [1991] 2 SCR 858.
59 *Kindler v Canada* (1993), Comm No 470/1991, UN Doc CCPR/C/48/D/470/1991.

willing to invoke arguments from the general register against the death penalty, such as the risk of a miscarriage of justice and the irreversibility of the punishment. Moreover, the Court found that opposition to the death penalty had solidified from a political preference into a Canadian social value. The Court also pointed to the entrenchment of an anti-death penalty norm in international law, no doubt a high point in the use of international law in Canadian jurisprudence. Interestingly, the UNHRC, hearing a similar (deportation-related) petition soon after, also changed its own jurisprudence, finding that the failure to seek assurances was a violation of Canada's international commitments.[60]

b) Prison Sentences

The relative certainty that has emerged around the issue of the death penalty has not been replicated when it comes to other, possibly harsh forms of punishment.[61] Canadian courts have been more reluctant to find that even considerably more severe prison sentences than those anticipated in Canada would alone violate section 7.[62] Although disparity "is a factor to be considered,"[63] it also clearly reflects that different legal systems may judge similar behaviour to be more or less reprehensible. Many of the cases on the issue have arisen in relation to the United States, where notoriously harsh punishments, notably mandatory minimum sentencing, create a significant disparity with Canada's comparatively more benign regime. Canadian courts have generally been disinclined to consider that mandatory sentences that would be undesirable or even unconstitutional in Canada would shock the conscience. This included, for example, a foreign sentence of twenty-six to 108 years' imprisonment, as opposed to a Canadian sentence of forty-five days to ten years for sexual interference;[64] or twenty-one to twenty-seven years for sexual exploitation of minors as opposed to six months to ten years in Canada.[65] The possibility that

60 *Judge v Canada* (2003), Comm No 829/1998, UN Doc CCPR/C/78/D/829/1998.
61 *Kindler*, above note 17 per La Forest J at 837.
62 *Hillis*, above note 19 at para 76.
63 *Fischbacher*, above note 32 at para 54; *MM*, above note 3 at paras 115–20.
64 *Wilcox*, above note 37.
65 *Wong*, above note 42.

a highly significant disparity would justify refusing a surrender remains theoretically possible,[66] but has become largely moot.

Particularly in relation to the United States, Canadian courts have also been remarkably unwilling to strike down surrender decisions in cases of harsh or mandatory sentencing. Neither a mandatory sentence of minimum twenty to thirty years for trafficking ten ounces of a mixture containing cocaine,[67] or a mandatory minimum of twenty years for dealing in hard drugs, or ten years for marijuana,[68] or, for that matter, mandatory life sentences without the possibility of parole[69] (even though such a sentence falls closest to a sort of death sentence)[70] have been found to shock the conscience. In the latter case this is despite an international trend, visible in the extradition practices of other states, against "life is life" sentences.[71] The same is true where conditions of detention are harsh. Although the concern with solitary confinement notably did feature prominently in the public criticism of the *Diab* case, courts have not found that the mere possibility of segregated imprisonment, which is "a necessary reality in both Canadian and United States correctional institutions,"[72] renders a decision to surrender unconstitutional.[73] However, evolutions in Canada's own sentencing practices are likely to have repercussions on how the legality of extradition is conceived as well. For example, the finding by the Supreme Court that life without parole is a section 7 breach that

66 For example, a twenty- to thirty-year sentence for possession of a single marijuana cigarette might shock the conscience of the community; see *Jamieson*, above note 22.

67 *Ibid.*

68 See *United States of America v K (JH)*, [2002] 165 CCC (3d) 449 (Ont CA); see also *Whitley v United States of America*, [1994] 20 OR (3d) 794 (CA).

69 See *United States v Qumsyeh*, 2015 ONCA 551; see, also, *United States v Muhammad 'Isa*, 2014 ABCA 256.

70 See Joanna Harrington, "Canadian Legal Values, Extradition, and Life Imprisonment Without Parole" *Constitutional Studies* (14 August 2014), online: www.constitutionalstudies.ca/2014/08/guest-post-professor-joanna-harrington-on-canadian-legal-values-extradition-and-life-imprisonment-without-parole/.

71 Dirk van Zyl Smit, Pete Weatherby & Simon Creighton, "Whole Life Sentences and the Tide of European Jurisprudence: What Is to Be Done?" (2014) 14:1 *Human Rights Law Review* 59.

72 *Martin*, above note 48 at para 27.

73 This is despite a clear trend internationally to consider that solitary confinement may by itself be a form of inhuman or degrading treatment. See Anna Conley, "Torture in US Jails and Prisons: An Analysis of Solitary Confinement Under International Law" (2013) 7:4 *ICL Journal* 415.

cannot be saved by section 1[74] means that it would be exceedingly difficult henceforth to extradite in such cases.

c) Particular Categories of Offenders

Relatively more success has been achieved in relation to particular categories of offenders. For example, with young offenders the minister must be satisfied that the persons sought will obtain due consideration of age and diminished moral capacity. Life imprisonment without parole may shock the conscience, although this does not mean that "the requesting state must have a system in place for young offenders that mirrors Canadian law's focus on rehabilitation and reintegration."[75]

One area where a chasm, perhaps predictably, has emerged in terms of fairness between Canada and its extradition partners is in relation to Indigenous offenders. As is well known, Canadian sentencing law has made significant strides in recent years, notably leading to the finding in *R v Gladue*,[76] that sentencing should take into account a convicted person's Indigenous background. To this day, such an accommodation has not been replicated in any other criminal justice system, and so the question arises as to how it should play out in an extradition context.

Canadian courts have made it clear that, though the extension of *Gladue* principles beyond sentencing remains challenging,[77] the minister is required to take into account the Indigenous status of a person threatened with extradition in order to avoid perpetuating the systemic discrimination and disadvantage Indigenous persons have experienced in the judicial and correctional systems.[78] In other words, the test of whether extradition would be unjust, oppressive, or contrary to the principles of fundamental justice must take into account a person's Indigenous heritage assessment.[79] Specifically, the question is how far the minister should be satisfied that the state soliciting extradition will in some form be able to accommodate these Canadian demands, given that foreign states for the most part (with

---

74 *R v Bissonnette*, 2022 SCC 23.

75 *Doyle Fowler c Canada (Minister of Justice)*, 2013 QCCA 1001 at para 45 [*Doyle Fowler*].

76 *R v Gladue*, [1999] 1 SCR 688.

77 Andrew Flavelle Martin, "Gladue at Twenty: Gladue Principles in the Professional Discipline of Indigenous Lawyers" (2020) 4:1 *Lakehead Law Journal* 20–49.

78 *United States v Leonard*, 2012 ONCA 622 [*Leonard*].

79 *Martin*, above note 48 at para 43.

the arguable exception of the United States)[80] do not partake in Canada's specific legacies of Indigenous racism and discrimination (although they may partake in similar legacies).

In *Martin*, the Court noted that the absence of a "codified recognition of the need to sentence Aboriginal offenders differently" is not a barrier to extradition. It is however a relevant factor.[81] In *Sheck*, the Court of Appeal for British Columbia found that the minister had failed to properly take into account the appellant's Indigenous heritage, even though he had received general information that Sheck's Indigenous status would be considered in the US criminal justice system.[82] There was no evidence that a US court would actually be required to take it into account, or that it would take judicial notice of Canada's history of mistreatment of its Indigenous communities.

Also relevant in the minister's decision was any significant disparity. The minister should compare not only the corresponding offence in Canada *in abstracto*, but the likely sentence an offender with an Indigenous background would receive.[83] This, then, often serves to reveal a gross disparity, as was the case in *Leonard* (fifteen to nineteen years in the United States, versus short custodial sentence in Canada) or *Sheck* (two to four years in Canada, compared to nineteen to twenty-seven years in the United States). Conditions of detention also matter. For example, in the *Martin* case, the Court upheld the minister's finding that a Métis offender who would likely be incarcerated close to his family and his spiritual practices would be adequately accommodated.[84]

Another factor that has affected evaluations of whether extradition ought to proceed is the best interests of children affected by the removal of their parent from the jurisdiction.[85] The obligation to consider such factors lies squarely with the minister. The interest of children must "be considered in light of other important legal principles and the facts of the individual case" and may, in fact, be "subordinated to other concerns in

---

80 Larry French, "Aboriginal Antecedents and Contemporary Practices of Restorative Justice: Canada and United States Comparisons" (2014) 25:3 *Indigenous Policy Journal*, online: http://indigenouspolicy.org/index.php/ipj/article/view/289.

81 *Martin*, above note 48 at para 30.

82 *Sheck v Canada (Minister of Justice)*, 2019 BCCA 364 [*Sheck*].

83 *Anderson*, above note 38 at para 27.

84 *Martin*, above note 48 at para 30.

85 *MM*, above note 3 at para 144.

appropriate contexts."[86] The best interest of the child is "a recognized legal principle but not a principle of fundamental justice"[87] and it has rarely sufficed to prevent extradition. However, it is a concern that is magnified where Indigenous persons are concerned, given legacies of separating Indigenous children from their parents, and one the minister should specifically consider.[88]

d) Fairness of the Trial

Just as Canada is required largely to defer to foreign states when it comes to punishment, so it is equally required in matters of due process, which is even harder to compare in a context of significant variation between procedural traditions. This militates toward "trusting the courts in the foreign country to give the fugitive a fair trial, including such matters as giving proper weight to the evidence and adequate consideration of available defences and the dictates of due process generally."[89] For example, the Supreme Court found in *Schmidt* that sending someone to a legal system that does not abide by the presumption of innocence does not shock the conscience. As La Forest J put it:

> A judicial process is not … fundamentally unjust — indeed it may in its practical workings be as just as ours — because it functions on the basis of an investigatory system without a presumption of innocence or, generally, because its procedural or evidentiary safeguards have none of the rigours of our system.[90]

Nonetheless, there have been cases where a complete lack of due process will suffice to defeat extradition, although extreme circumstances are required to rebut the assumption that Canada's extradition partners will grant a fair trial. In the *Pacificador* case, the individual sought was a Philippine national who successfully claimed that he would face charges before a kangaroo court, and the Court of Appeal set aside the minister's surrender order on such grounds.[91] The case of Leonard Peltier, who was

86 *Ibid* at para 26.
87 *Carruthers v Canada (Minister of Justice)*, 2019 ABCA 490 at para 28.
88 *Sheck*, above note 82.
89 *Schmidt*, above note 21 at para 51.
90 *Ibid* at 522–23.
91 *Canada (Minister of Justice) v Pacificador* (2002), 60 OR (3d) 685 (CA), leave refused [2002] SCCA No 390 [*Pacificador*].

extradited to the United States on the basis of what may well have been FBI misconduct, is sometimes mentioned as a problematic extradition from a rights perspective, in light of the risk of wrongful conviction.[92] Excessive delays have also been blamed in the context of Canada's relationship with some extradition partners such as France.

e) Level of Risk and Minimization

In the above, the risks of punishment or unfair trial were presented as is. In reality, however, the question is how likely the person is to suffer from such a violation. Even take the case of torture: it is always conceivable that someone would be tortured upon being extradited, but that does not mean it is likely. No state in the world is totally immune from torture. *Any* danger of torture, however remote, cannot be a reason for otherwise ignoring clear treaty obligations to extradite. By necessity, therefore, a decision to surrender must involve a weighing of the level of risk. The Supreme Court has spoken, in relation to torture, of a "serious" or "substantial" risk.[93]

In practice, this will involve considering how likely a particular rights violation is to occur. In the case of mandatory sentencing, Proulx JA considered that Michigan state laws would not have given any grounds to depart from a mandatory minimum sentence.[94] In *Pacificador*, the Court of Appeal considered that many of Pacificador's co-accused had been imprisoned without bail for years, and concluded that it was unlikely that he would receive more favourable treatment.[95] In some cases, the courts will have the benefit of decisions in similar cases, or even of decisions regarding accomplices, that will shed light on the treatment that a person whose extradition is sought might expect.[96] Having said that, an element of uncertainty seems almost unavoidable, even in relation to trusted states with legal cultures largely compatible with Canada's, as was the case of France in the *Diab* case. Neither Canadian courts nor the Canadian executive can anticipate in advance where a trial is headed, nor would it be justifiable for them to speculate about the mere possibility of dysfunction.

92 Dianne L. Martin, "Extradition, The Charter and Due Process: Is Procedural Fairness Enough?" (2002) 16:1 *The Supreme Court Law Review* 6.

93 See, for example, *Suresh v Canada (Minister of Citizenship and Immigration)*, 2002 SCC 1 at paras 78, 119; see, also, *Badesha*, above note 8 at para 23.

94 *Jamieson v Directeur du Centre de Prevention Parthenais*, [1992] RJQ 561 at 571 (CA), Proulx JA, dissenting.

95 *Pacificador*, above note 91.

96 *Doyle Fowler*, above note 75 at para 60.

One way in which risk may be mitigated, however, is through the minister securing assurances from the requesting state. Assurances provide a useful way to avoid the problem of significant incompatibility between criminal justice systems. A requesting state that reneges on assurances exposes itself to the risk that Canada will no longer accept such assurances and will decline to extradite to it. Simply obtaining assurances is not enough, however; the assurances must address the risk they seek to mitigate, and courts may intervene if assurances are unreasonably and uncritically accepted.[97] By the same token, there may be limits to the sorts of assurances that the minister may request from other states and, in particular, assurances as to the type of charges to be laid may be seen as an inappropriate interference in another state's judicial system.[98] Some assurances are more complex than agreement not to seek the death penalty: giving assurances of a fair trial may require a more complete overhauling of judicial institutions than is reasonable to expect.

D. CONCLUSION

The visibility of *Charter* rights in the context of extradition litigation should not mislead one as to its true impact. The vast majority of appeals from committal and judicial reviews of ministerial decisions to surrender are unsuccessful, with the notable exception of extradition to the death penalty. The system is undeniably one that leans heavily toward extradition. This results from a combination of factors: extradition treaties that the Canadian government feels strongly it needs to comply with; a heavy reliance on the good faith of the requesting state; and a high level of judicial deference.

But this picture needs to be nuanced by a realization that this lack of success in challenging extradition may simply mean that the minister has largely internalized *Charter* constraints when it comes to surrender decisions. As many as 40 percent of extradition requests each year do not lead to extradition.[99] It may also be the case that many extradition requests are, in fact, legitimate and fair, notwithstanding that unfair ones do not

97 *Badesha*, above note 8 at paras 37–40.

98 *Wilcox*, above note 37 at para 50.

99 Justice Canada, "Extradition Fact Sheet — Statistics on Requests from the United States" (29 November 2013), online: www.justice.gc.ca/eng/cj-jp/emla-eej/stat.html. (29 November 2013).

garner much attention. The vast majority of extradition cases in Canada concern the United States, a state which, for all its penal differences, is considered a close and trustworthy partner.[100]

Nonetheless, the sheer hybridity of extradition as a legal object makes it difficult to apprehend, and creates ongoing dilemmas. If states lean too heavily in the direction of international cooperation (otherwise a global and domestic public good) they may be blind to the real effects extradition has on rights of persons within their jurisdiction; if they lean too heavily on the side of protecting rights, they risk hegemonically imposing their preferences on others, and undermining the very basis of extradition systems.

The debate is further complicated by the need for both international cooperation and respect for human rights, as the two policy pillars of extradition, to be reframed in terms of each other: international cooperation to punish crimes, whether transnational or supranational, certainly does much in principle to remedy impunity, and thus provide human rights remedies to victims. This is hardly a blank cheque to violate the rights of the accused, but it is not neutral in the overall rights equation. This was spectacularly illustrated in the long *Mugesera* saga in Quebec, involving a Rwandan accused of participation in genocide whose extradition was seen both as a way of validating Canada's commitment to fighting genocide, and as a very real risk to his individual rights.[101]

In this context, high profile *causes célèbres*, whatever their specific merits, do not necessarily make for sound policy. An extradition relationship is not defined only by the worst cases to which it gives rise (*Meng* in relation to the United States, *Diab* in relation to France), although such cases certainly disclose a measure of what may go wrong in a particular relationship. Moreover, the focus on a few unfortunate extradition cases involving botched prosecutions and difficult-to-translate procedural features should not obfuscate a continuous stream of extraditions to the US to face often much harsher punishment that feeds into the prison–industrial complex there.

100 See Gary Botting, *Extradition between Canada and the United States* (Ardsley, NY: Transnational, 2005).

101 *Mugesera v Canada (Minister of Citizenship and Immigration)*, 2005 SCC 40.

The problem may be less with foreign legal systems than with an executive culture that often finds state agents, from the RCMP to the minister via Justice Canada's International Assistance Group, appearing keener to honour foreign demands than to shield Canadians. Paradoxically, however, there may be room for further executive interventions to shield persons in Canada from extradition in cases where their rights are at risk. Denial of surrender on humanitarian or diplomatic grounds by the minister of justice might serve more often than it has as an ultimate safety valve, although obviously that regime is not a way to mend a broken extradition relationship, and is too discretionary to make a systemic difference.

Finally, it seems that courts' evolving notions of what shocks the conscience, in line with dynamic evolutions in international human rights law, might provide a more suitable degree of protection. Just as Canadian courts have shown a tremendous evolution over time in relation to the death penalty, it may be that, in the future, harsh mandatory sentences that bear no relation to the punishment that would be meted for the same offence in Canada will come to be seen as shocking the conscience. It remains difficult, however, to break courts' stupor in the presence of executive discretion. It has been suggested in this context that *Charter* issues should be decided by the extradition judge at the committal stage in the first place, or on appeal before the minister exercises discretion, rather than being left to a subsequent judicial review which very rarely succeeds.[102] The committal stage itself is ripe for reform in a context where it has been allowed to degenerate into little more than an administrative exercise, and where a higher degree of transparency, adversarialism, and disclosure would go a long way toward halting extradition requests that are manifestly unjust.[103] As Canada seeks to reconcile the occasionally conflicting goals of international cooperation and *Charter* rights, it is high time that the persistent anomaly that is extradition in the constitutional landscape be normalized.

102 See the reasons of McEachern CJ in *United States of America v Burns*, [1997] 116 CCC (3d) 524 at paras 76–79 (BCCA).

103 Robert J. Currie, *Changing Canada's Extradition Laws: The Halifax Colloquium's Proposals for Law Reform* (2021), online: https://cpij-pcji.ca/changing-canadas-extradition-laws-the-halifax-colloquiums-proposals-for-law-reform.

nineteen

Disguised Extradition Through Deportation as an Abuse of Process

JEFFREY G. JOHNSTON*

A. INTRODUCTION

Extradition and immigration serve distinct, yet sometimes complementary objectives. A person wanted for prosecution in another state might be extradited or deported. Either way, from an extradition perspective, the person will have to answer to the criminal justice system of that state while, from an immigration standpoint, the removal of the person from Canada is conducive to the public good. There is nothing abusive about this outcome. It is only when immigration proceedings are used to deliberately circumvent the extradition process that these proceedings or related extradition proceedings are vulnerable to attack on abuse of process grounds.

Unfortunately, this form of "disguised extradition" is often distorted in an attempt to stretch its application to factual scenarios it was never intended to capture. The morphing of this concept has engendered unwarranted concerns in cases where extradition and immigration proceedings overlap and resulted in avoidable legal uncertainty for Canadian courts required to adjudicate this issue.

* Jeffrey G. Johnston, BA (Hons) (Western Ontario), LLB (Victoria), MSt (Dist) (International Human Rights Law) (Oxon), General Counsel, Department of Justice Canada, and part-time Professor, Faculty of Common Law, University of Ottawa. The views expressed in this paper are those of the writer and all errors remain his.

This paper seeks to clarify this area of Canadian extradition law. It will analyze the law of disguised extradition through deportation with the aim of exposing the myths surrounding its application. The paper will seek to separate fact from fiction in explaining the narrow circumstances in which extradition proceedings can be stayed as an abuse of process based on disguised extradition owing to preceding or parallel immigration proceedings.

B. THE HISTORY OF DISGUISED EXTRADITION AS AN ABUSE OF PROCESS

Disguised extradition originated in criminal cases in which authorities in the prosecuting jurisdiction employed extrajudicial means to return an accused from another state to stand trial. Historically, these means typically involved the forcible abduction of the accused across state borders. While this paper will focus on manipulating immigration proceedings to achieve the purposes of extradition, this practice is objectionable for many of the same underlying reasons. In 1964, O'Higgins described this abuse of the deportation power in these terms:

> By this term [disguised extradition] we mean to refer to cases to which the use of a power, with which it has been vested for another and different purpose, the state may give effect to a request for the surrender of a fugitive criminal which it is not otherwise lawfully authorised to do. Thus State A by exercising the authority given to it by its municipal law to deport aliens may surrender an alien to his national state which has requested his surrender for trial or punishment.[1]

This form of disguised extradition takes place when a state relies "on its immigration procedures such as exclusion, deportation and removal to affect the transfer of an individual to the custody of another state for the purpose of punishment."[2] For example, disguised extradition through deportation occurs "where the evidence is not strong enough for extradition and the authorities of both countries collude together through

1 Paul O'Higgins, "Disguised Extradition: The Soblen Case" (1964) 27:5 *Modern Law Review* 521 at 522.

2 Margaret L. Satterthwaite, "The Legal Regime Governing Transfer of Persons in the Fight against Terrorism" in Larissa van den Herik & Nico Schrijver, eds, *Counter-Terrorism Strategies in a Fragmented International Legal Order: Meeting the Challenges* (New York: Cambridge University Press, 2013) at 8.

deportation to achieve indirectly what they could not achieve through extradition."[3]

The consequences to an accused in this situation are significant. In being deported, the individual does not benefit from the legal protections afforded a person sought in extradition proceedings. These protections include the guarantee of specialty, barring the prosecuting state from trying the person for offences other than those for which the person was surrendered, or the availability of diplomatic assurances as conditions for extradition, such as a condition that the death penalty will not be sought or imposed in the case of an accused wanted for capital crimes.[4]

In 1992, Cowling explained the legal implications of a state improperly exercising its deportation powers to achieve the objectives of extradition as follows:

> The expelling state should not concern itself with the destination of the deportee, nor should deportation be preceded by a request from another state. Thus, if a supposed act of deportation was initiated by a request from another state ... to the effect that an alien should be deported to that state with the ultimate objective of his standing trial, this would constitute a clear case of disguised extradition. And in such a case the domestic courts of the receiving state ... should grant relief to such an offender on the basis that his presence before the courts is irregular.[5]

In Canada, the leading case of disguised extradition through deportation is *United States of America v Tollman*.[6] However, before turning to consider the Canadian experience, the international jurisprudence that has informed the domestic caselaw will be canvassed.

The most significant case on disguised extradition is *Regina v Horseferry Road Magistrates' Court, ex parte Bennett*.[7] Mr. Bennett, a New Zealand citizen, was apprehended in South Africa on the pretense of deporting him to his native New Zealand. This was a ruse, as British and South

---

3 *Bembenek v Canada (Minister of Employment and Immigration)* (1991), 69 CCC (3d) 34 at 49 (Ont Ct (Gen Div)) [*Bembenek*].

4 *Shepherd v Canada (Minister of Employment and Immigration)* (1989), Imm LR (2d) 9 at 2 (Ont HCJ), aff'd (1989), 70 OR (2d) 765 (CA) [*Shepherd*].

5 Michael G. Cowling, "Unmasking Disguised Extradition — Some Glimmer of Hope" (1992) 109:2 *South African Law Journal* 241 at 254.

6 *United States of America v Tollman* (2006), 212 CCC (3d) 511 (Ont SCJ) [*Tollman*].

7 *R v Horseferry Road Magistrates' Court, Ex parte Bennett*, [1994] 1 AC 42 (HL) [*Bennett*].

African authorities had colluded to return him to the United Kingdom to face prosecution, to avoid having to seek his extradition. Mr. Bennett was arrested in South Africa under the guise of being deported to New Zealand, but instead was returned to the United Kingdom on a flight destined for New Zealand which transited London, England, where, upon his arrival, he was arrested by British authorities.

The House of Lords found that, in deliberately circumventing the extradition process, British authorities had denied Mr. Bennett the protections afforded him under that process. It noted that extradition is not only meant to "ensure that criminals are returned from one country to another but also to protect the rights of those who are accused of crimes by the requesting country."[8] The House of Lords concluded that the trial court had the discretion to stay the prosecution based on the manner by which Mr. Bennett was brought before the court. It stated: "The High Court in the exercise of its supervisory jurisdiction has power to inquire into the circumstances by which a person has been brought within the jurisdiction and if satisfied that it was in disregard of extradition procedures it may stay the prosecution and order the release of the accused."[9]

Bennett stands in sharp contrast to the decision of the English Court of Appeals almost thirty years earlier in *Soblen*.[10] In that case, the United States requested Dr. Soblen's return from Israel, where he fled while on bail, pending the outcome of his conviction appeal for espionage offences. At the time, there was no extradition treaty between Israel and the United States. Dr. Soblen was deported from Israel to the United States on a flight chartered by the Israeli government that transited the United Kingdom. A US marshal was also on board the flight.

As the plane prepared to land in London, Dr. Soblen stabbed himself. British immigration authorities boarded the plane intending to serve a now unconscious Dr. Soblen with papers barring him entry into the United Kingdom. While he was detained in a hospital in London, the British Home Secretary ordered the Israeli carrier, El Al, to remove Dr. Soblen to the United States. The Israeli government refused to obey this

8 *Ibid* at para 105.

9 *Ibid.*

10 *R v Governor of Brixton Prison, ex parte Soblen*, [1962] 3 WLR 1154 (CA) [*Soblen*].

order as being contrary to Israeli law.[11] The Home Secretary then ordered Dr. Soblen's deportation to the United States. Dr. Soblen challenged the deportation order, claiming that it was an attempt to effect his illegal extradition.

The Court of Appeals rejected this argument. It concluded that there was no evidence that the deportation order was being used for an ulterior purpose or had been issued in bad faith. Quite the opposite, the Court found that there was "reasonable ground on which the Home Secretary could consider the applicant's presence [in the United Kingdom] ... was not conducive to the public good"[12] to support Dr. Soblen's valid deportation. Although Lord Denning noted that "the Crown cannot and must not surrender a fugitive criminal to another country at its request except in accordance with the Extradition Acts duly fulfilled,"[13] he was alone in recognizing this principle.

The Constitutional Court of South Africa in *Mohamed*[14] and the New Zealand Court of Appeal in *Hartley*[15] have both arrived at similar outcomes to *Bennett* in holding that illegal attempts to bypass extradition can have legal consequences for the states involved.

Mr. Mohamed was wanted in New York for prosecution for the bombing of the American embassy in Tanzania. He was located in Cape Town by South African immigration authorities who handed him over to FBI agents stationed there. After interrogating Mr. Mohamed, the agents planned to remove him to the United States to stand trial. In challenging his removal, Mr. Mohamed alleged that this conduct was unlawful as supporting his disguised extradition. In response, South African authorities argued that he was in South Africa illegally and that he could be deported to the United States as an illegal immigrant.

In considering these opposing positions, the Constitutional Court distinguished between the differing nature of deportation and extradition, noting that

---

11 O'Higgins opines that the Israeli government's position presumably reflected its tacit awareness that Israeli participation in Dr. Soblen's return to the United States would amount to its involvement in his unlawful extradition. O'Higgins, above note 1 at 534.

12 *Soblen*, above note 10 at 1181.

13 *Ibid* at 661B.

14 *Mohamed v President of the Republic of South Africa*, Judgment, Constitutional Court of South Africa, No. CCT 17/01, 28 May 2001 [*Mohamed*].

15 *R v Hartley*, [1978] 2 NZLR 199 (CA) [*Hartley*].

> [t]he purposes may … coincide where an illegal alien is deported to another country which wants to put him on trial for having committed a criminal offence the prosecution of which falls within the jurisdiction of its courts.
>
> Deportation is usually a unilateral act while extradition is consensual. Different procedures are prescribed for deportation and extradition, and those differences may be material in specific cases, particularly where the legality of the expulsion is challenged.[16]

The Court concluded that this distinction was irrelevant, as neither process was lawfully followed in Mr. Mohamed's case, particularly in light of his facing the prospect of the death penalty if returned to the United States. The Court noted that, were he properly the subject of an extradition request, this could be addressed by South African authorities obtaining a death penalty assurance from US authorities as a condition of his extradition.

Mr. Hartley, who was wanted in New Zealand for murder, was returned there from Australia based merely on the request of the New Zealand police to the Australian police to have him arrested in Australia and placed on a plane back to New Zealand. Justice Woodhouse, in concluding that the judiciary could not countenance this state conduct, explained:

> There are explicit statutory directions that surround the extradition procedure. The procedure is widely known. It is frequently used by the police in the performance of their duty. For the protection of the public the statute rightly demands the sanction of recognised court processes before any person who is thought to be a fugitive offender can properly be surrendered from one country to another. And in our opinion there can be no possible question here of the court turning a blind eye to action of the New Zealand police which has deliberately ignored those imperative requirements of the statute.… [T]his must never become an area where it will be sufficient to consider that the end has justified the means.[17]

The decisions in *Bennett*, *Mohamed*, and *Hartley* marked a turning point in the evolution of the law of extradition in the modern era. Prior to these cases, the predominant view, and that espoused by prosecuting

16 *Mohamed*, above note 14 at paras 42–43.

17 *Hartley*, above note 15 at 216–17.

courts in particular, was that the manner by which an accused was returned to face prosecution was not of concern to the trial court.[18] Provided the accused was lawfully detained on valid criminal charges, circumventing the lawful process of extradition did not affect the domestic criminal proceedings. This doctrine, usually termed *male captus, bene detentus*, stands for the the principle "that a court may exercise jurisdiction over an accused person regardless of how that person has come into the jurisdiction of the court."[19]

While this issue has yet to be adjudicated in Canada, it is fair to predict that a Canadian court would be inclined to adopt the *Bennett* approach over the *male captus, bene detentus* approach, as evidenced by the decision in *Purdy v Canada (Attorney General)*.[20] In that case, benign luring by Canadian authorities that circumvented Mr. Purdy's lawful ability to resist extradition to the prosecuting jurisdiction triggered the application of the *Charter*.

Mr. Purdy, a Canadian citizen residing in Vancouver, was the subject of money laundering charges in Florida stemming from a joint FBI–RCMP

18 See, for example: *Ker v Illinois*, 119 US 436 (1886), in which the majority of the US Supreme Court held that the trial court had jurisdiction to prosecute Mr. Ker for fraud offences, notwithstanding that he was kidnapped and brought back to the United States from Peru by a private investigator hired by the defrauded American bank; *Attorney-General of the Government of Israel v Eichmann* (Israel Sup Ct 1962), (1968) 36 *International Law Reports* 277 (English translation) in which the Israeli Supreme Court held that the abduction of Dr. Eichmann from Argentina to Israel by Israeli secret agents to stand trial for war crimes did not deprive the trial court of jurisdiction to prosecute him; *United States v Alvarez-Machain*, 504 US 655 (1992) in which the majority of the US Supreme Court held that the trial court's jurisdiction to prosecute Dr. Machain, a Mexican national, for his alleged involvement in the kidnapping, torture, and murder of a Drug Enforcement Administration agent was not affected by Dr. Machain's abduction from Mexico to the United States by a private American citizen hired by the DEA; and *Prosecutor v Dragan Nikolic*, Case No IT-94-2-PT, Decision on Defence Motion Challenging the Exercise of Jurisdiction by the Tribunal (9 October 2002) [*Nikolic TC*], confirmed on appeal, (IT-94-2-AR73), Decision on Interlocutory Appeal Concerning Legality of Arrest, (5 June 2003) in which both levels of court at the International Criminal Tribunal for the former Yugoslavia held that Mr. Nikolic's kidnapping in Serbia and Montenegro to stand trial for war crimes did not deprive the Trial Chamber of jurisdiction to prosecute him based on the gravity of the offences involved.

19 *Nikolic TC*, *ibid* at para 70.

20 *Purdy v Canada (Attorney General)* (2003), 175 CCC (3d) 306 (BCSC) [*Purdy BCSC*], aff'd *Purdy v Canada (Attorney General)* (2003), 177 CCC (3d) 438 (BCCA) [*Purdy BCCA*].

investigation. He was lured to the United States by an undercover RCMP officer on the pretense of attending a meeting to further the money laundering activity. Upon his arrival in New York, Mr. Purdy was taken into custody by the FBI on a sealed arrest warrant. As part of his defence to the charges in the United States, Mr. Purdy successfully applied to a British Columbia judge for disclosure of material in relation to RCMP involvement in the investigation.

Even though there were no Canadian charges, the chambers judge ordered this disclosure. The Court held that "if the ordinary extradition process had not been circumvented by the inducement of Mr. Purdy to travel to the U.S.A.... he would have been entitled to disclosure, at least from the Canadian authorities, of information they had in their possession pertaining to their part in the investigation."[21] It found that Mr. Purdy was entitled to disclosure as a remedy for the infringement of his constitutional right to make full answer and defence to the US charges as a Canadian whose freedom was "placed in jeopardy by the actions of Canadian legal authorities conducting a joint investigation with U.S. agencies, in Canada."[22]

The British Columbia Court of Appeal, in upholding this decision, held that the luring involving Canadian authorities served as an "expedient" which "avoided extradition."[23] The Court of Appeal concluded that this "ruse employed by the police to by-pass extradition"[24] and "effect the respondent's arrest in the U.S.... provided a sufficient peg on which to hang the petition"[25] for *Charter* relief in the form of the disclosure order.

C. THE CANADIAN EXPERIENCE OF DISGUISED EXTRADITION THROUGH DEPORTATION

The Canadian jurisprudence can be divided into two categories: disguised extradition claims in immigration proceedings and disguised extradition claims in extradition proceedings. Those cases in the extradition context can be further divided into cases from two time periods: the pre-*Tollman* and post-*Tollman* eras.

---

21 *Purdy BCSC*, *ibid* at para 23.

22 *Ibid* at para 25.

23 *Purdy BCCA*, above note 20 at para 8.

24 *Ibid* at para 20.

25 *Ibid* at para 15.

1) Disguised Extradition Claims in Immigration Proceedings

Canadian courts first considered the argument of disguised extradition in a series of immigration cases starting with the decision of the Supreme Court of Canada in *Moore*.[26] Mr. Moore, a US citizen wanted for offences in the United States, entered Canada illegally from Panama using a false Canadian passport. He was arrested by Canadian immigration authorities two days after his arrival as he waited to board a plane back to Panama. The Minister of Citizenship and Immigration initiated inadmissibility proceedings to have him deported to the United States. Mr. Moore argued that he was voluntarily prepared to return to Panama, and that the decision to deport him to the United States was a disguised extradition.

In upholding the deportation order, the Court found that it had issued for a valid immigration purpose based on Mr. Moore's criminality in the United States. The Court did, however, endorse the following statement of English law from the *Soblen* decision as applying to allegations of disguised extradition in Canada: "[T]he onus of proving that a deportation order valid on its face is in fact a sham, or not made *bona fide*, is on the party who alleges it, 'however difficult it may be for him to discharge the onus.'"[27] To discharge this onus, it held that "it is necessary to hold that the Minister did not genuinely consider it in the public interest"[28] to seek the non-citizen's removal by way of immigration proceedings.

Moore thus established that an applicant advancing a disguised extradition claim is faced with the daunting task of demonstrating that the immigration proceedings were a sham initiated to achieve the objectives of extradition. In the absence of such evidence, the decision to expel a foreign national from Canada based on serious criminality in another state will tend to be viewed as a legitimate exercise of the deportation power. As the Supreme Court of Canada has stated in the extradition context, "[t]he Government has the right and duty to keep out and to expel aliens from this country if it considers it advisable to do so. This right ... exists independently of extradition."[29]

26 *Moore v Canada (Minister of Manpower and Immigration)*, [1968] SCR 839 [*Moore*].

27 *Ibid* at 843, citing *Soblen*, above note 10.

28 *Ibid.*

29 *Kindler v Canada (Minister of Justice)*, [1991] 2 SCR 779 at 834.

Following *Moore*, the Federal and Ontario courts considered disguised extradition claims in four seminal immigration cases: *Kindler*,[30] *Shepherd*, *Bembenek*, and *Halm*.[31] Mr. Kindler was found guilty of first-degree murder, conspiracy to commit murder, and kidnapping in Philadelphia. The jury recommended the death penalty. Before the imposition of sentence, Mr. Kindler escaped from prison and entered Canada illegally. After the RCMP was alerted to his presence in Canada by the FBI, Mr. Kindler was arrested in Quebec and removal proceedings were initiated to deport him back to the United States.

In resisting deportation, Mr. Kindler raised a claim of disguised extradition. In considering this claim, Rouleau J, as he then was, observed that deportation and extradition may legitimately achieve the same end result:

> [W]here deportation is ordered to the State of embarkation of the national State, the description "disguised extradition" is really a conclusion drawn by those who assert it as being the intent of the deporting authorities. While the motive of restoring a criminal to a competent jurisdiction may indeed be paramount in the intention of the deporting State, it may also in many cases be a genuine coincidence that deportation has this result.[32]

The Federal Court in *Kindler* concluded that the fact that the RCMP were advised of Mr. Kindler's presence in Canada by the FBI and that the two police agencies cooperated in locating and apprehending him was not evidence of abusive conduct. To succeed, Mr. Kindler was required to meet the higher standard of demonstrating that the immigration proceedings were a sham initiated for the real purpose of removing him to the United States to face prosecution. The Court found that Mr. Kindler had failed to discharge this "heavy onus" in concluding that "[t]here were reasonable grounds for the immigration authorities to conclude that the Petitioner's continued presence in Canada would not be conducive to the public good."[33]

Mr. Shepherd, a US citizen charged with murder and rape in the United States, escaped custody and fled to Canada. A decade later, he was

30 *Kindler v Minister of Employment and Immigration*, [1985] 1 FC 676 (QL) [*Kindler*].

31 *Halm v Canada (Minister of Employment and Immigration)*, [1996] 1 FC 547 [*Halm*].

32 *Kindler*, above note 30.

33 *Ibid.*

discovered by Canadian immigration authorities and ordered deported. In appealing his deportation order, Mr. Shepherd alleged that the immigration proceedings were intended to return him to the United States to stand trial. The trial judge rejected this argument. In upholding this decision, the Ontario Court of Appeal identified six key principles to distinguish between a legitimate deportation and a disguised extradition:

1) If the purpose is to deport a person because the person's presence in Canada is not conducive to the public good, that is a legitimate exercise of the deportation power.
2) If the purpose is to surrender a person as a fugitive criminal to a state because it has asked for the person's return, that is not a legitimate exercise of the deportation power.
3) It is open to the courts to inquire whether the immigration purpose of the government was lawful or otherwise.
4) The onus is on the party alleging an unlawful exercise of the deportation power. It is a heavy onus.
5) To succeed, it would be necessary to hold that the Minister of Citizenship and Immigration did not genuinely consider it in the public interest to expel the person in question.
6) The adoption of the *Charter* has not lessened the onus.

Applying these principles, the Court of Appeal concluded that immigration authorities were acting in the public interest in seeking to expel Mr. Shepherd, notwithstanding that US authorities had publicly indicated their interest in having him returned.

While serving a life sentence for murder, Ms. Bembenek escaped from custody in the United States and entered Canada. She was apprehended by immigration authorities who sought to deport her for serious criminality due to her murder conviction. Ms. Bembenek alleged that the immigration proceedings were a disguised extradition. She contended that she was arrested by Canadian immigration officials at the request of US authorities to deport her from Canada to the United States for the enforcement of her sentence.

The Ontario Court of Justice rejected this argument. Justice Campbell found that Ms. Bembenek faced "a very heavy onus" to be able to demonstrate that the immigration proceedings had an ulterior motive. The Court concluded that she had failed to show that the proceedings were undertaken in bad faith:

> In testing the question of bad faith, it is necessary to decide first whether there is an apparently legitimate reason for the immigration officials to seek deportation, and secondly, what would be gained from deportation rather than extradition.
>
> The mere presence in Canada of an escaped American convict under life sentence for murder provides an obviously legitimate reason for deportation. This is clearly not the classic case of disguised extradition because there is an obvious evidentiary basis for both deportation and extradition, and deportation is not being used after the failure of extradition through lack of evidence.[34]

The Court in *Bembenek* found that there was nothing improper in Canadian immigration officials communicating with US authorities, and that this assistance and cooperation were not capable on their own of supporting the inference that the immigration proceedings were a disguised extradition.

Finally, in *Halm*, the Federal Court again considered a claim of disguised extradition as part of a challenge to the decision to deport Mr. Halm for serious criminality after he fled to Canada from the United States while on bail pending an appeal of his conviction for criminal offences. Mr. Halm claimed that the decision to seek his deportation rather than his extradition was due to the fact that he could not be extradited for the offences in the United States because the alleged conduct did not meet the requirement of double criminality.

Justice Rothstein, as he then was, rejected the disguised extradition argument. In so doing, he endorsed the six principles recognized by the Ontario Court of Appeal in *Shepherd*. The Court stated that it would only be in an "extremely rare case" that a disguised extradition claim would succeed, such as where there is clear evidence of bad faith demonstrating that the immigration proceedings were a sham. The Court found that there was nothing improper in Canadian immigration officials communicating with US authorities. It also found that bad faith could not be inferred from the fact that the United States wanted Mr. Halm returned. There was also nothing improper about the conduct of US authorities in delaying in seeking his extradition while the immigration proceedings were ongoing. Finally, the Court held that Mr. Halm's deportation was supported by a legitimate immigration objective, since "Canada is free to

34 *Bembenek*, above note 3 at 25.

initiate and carry out effective deportation proceedings in respect of an alien that Canada does not wish to remain in this country."[35]

2) Disguised Extradition Claims in Extradition Proceedings Pre-*Tollman*

The first Canadian extradition case to consider disguised extradition was *United States of America v Quintin*.[36] Mr. Quintin and Ms. Westphal were wanted in the United States for prosecution and the enforcement of a sentence. Prior to the commencement of extradition proceedings, they were the subject of immigration proceedings seeking their removal from Canada to the United States. They applied to stay the extradition proceedings alleging that the decision of US authorities to defer seeking their extradition while the immigration proceedings were ongoing, and the attempt by Canadian officials to deport them, constituted an abuse of process. Justice Dambrot declined to embark on a *Charter* hearing into the disguised extradition claim, finding that there was no evidentiary foundation to support the allegation.

In concluding that there was no "air of reality" to the contention that the immigration proceedings were a sham, the Court in *Quintin*, drawing heavily on the immigration jurisprudence considering disguised extradition, made the following findings:

1) There is nothing wrong with the Canadian government, in cooperation with the government of the United States, seeking to return a US citizen who is present in Canada and who is facing serious charges in the United States by immigration or extradition proceedings, whichever is most expeditious.
2) The disguised extradition argument is an allegation of bad faith which depends on evidence that the immigration proceedings where a sham.
3) Immigration proceedings will not amount to a disguised extradition if they are in pursuit of the obvious and legitimate duty of discouraging US citizens charged with serious offences from using Canada as a safe haven.
4) Canada–US cooperation, and the deferring of extradition proceedings while immigration proceedings are ongoing, even if that gives

35 *Halm*, above note 31 at para 31.

36 *United States of America v Quintin* (2000), 73 CRR (2d) 237 (Ont SCJ) [*Quintin*].

US authorities some tactical advantage, are perfectly proper, and provide no support for the claim that the immigration proceedings were a sham.

5) There is nothing wrong in the activation of extradition proceedings when a person sought is unexpectedly granted judicial interim release in immigration proceedings.

3) *Tollman*: The Perfect Storm

Tollman represented the perfect storm for disguised extradition through deportation. As Molloy J stated in staying the extradition proceedings, "[i]t is only in an exceptional case that extradition proceedings will be stayed as an abuse of process. This is such a case."[37] In *Tollman*, there were four different aspects to the abuse based on misconduct by US and Canadian authorities that the court found formed part of an "overall scheme to get Mr. Tollman into U.S. custody without having to use extradition proceedings."[38]

First, US prosecuting authorities engineered Mr. Tollman's fugitive status. Despite knowing Mr. Tollman's whereabouts in London, England, and being familiar with the British extradition process, US prosecuting authorities did not seek his extradition from the United Kingdom, nor did they unseal the US charges and arrange for him to turn himself in through his New York lawyer. Instead, they waited until they knew he was travelling abroad for business to arrange for his apprehension at his destination, Toronto, Canada. The court found that there was "overwhelming" evidence that the US prosecutor was "determined … to seek Mr. Tollman's arrest outside his home jurisdiction."[39] In orchestrating his arrest in another state where he was "not ordinarily resident"[40] and did not have family or employment ties or other supports, US authorities had engaged in a deliberate tactic designed to place "considerable pressure" on

37 *Tollman*, above note 6 at para 1.

38 *Ibid* at para 37.

39 *Ibid* at para 48.

40 Thereby placing him in a reverse onus situation in seeking his release on bail pursuant to s 19 of the *Extradition Act*, SC 1999, c 18 and s 516(6)(b) of the *Criminal Code*, RSC 1985, c C-46.

Mr. Tollman "to abandon his rights and surrender to the jurisdiction of the United States to stand trial."[41]

Second, the conduct of US and Canadian authorities amounted to disguised extradition. US prosecuting authorities initially did not make an extradition request through the normal and required channels. Instead, the US prosecutor alerted Canadian immigration authorities to Mr. Tollman's travel to Canada, and requested that they arrest him and deport him to the United States relying on the American charges. More troubling still was that Canadian immigration authorities acted on this request. Justice Molloy held that there was "substantial evidence that in the planning stages senior Canadian immigration personnel gave assurances that Mr. Tollman would be detained, deported and summarily passed over to US authorities at the border so that US authorities could proceed with their prosecution against him."[42] In the meantime, American authorities, rather than taking steps to seek his extradition, were arranging "to be at the border ... waiting to receive Mr. Tollman into their custody."[43]

Third, Canadian authorities acted improperly in failing to comply with the Immigration and Refugee Board's (IRB) order granting Mr. Tollman judicial interim release. After Mr. Tollman was ordered released by the IRB, and despite perfecting his bail, Canadian immigration authorities delayed his release. In the interim, US authorities made an extradition request for Mr. Tollman's provisional arrest. Justice Molloy found the "troubling and unexplained" timing of these events "suspicious," as they had the effect of facilitating Mr. Tollman's arrest on an extradition warrant while he was still in custody on the immigration matter. The court found it an "astonishing coincidence" that the "refusal by a CBSA official to honour an order of the IRB ... fortuitously" coincided with "US authorities ... making an urgent request for a provisional arrest warrant under the *Extradition Act*."[44]

Finally, Canadian extradition authorities acted improperly in obtaining the provisional arrest warrant in failing to comply with the duty of candour that applies to *ex parte* applications. The court found that the material filed in support of the application "was misleading in many respects and many material facts were either not disclosed or were

41 *Tollman*, above note 6 at para 32.

42 *Ibid* at para 85.

43 *Ibid* at para 83.

44 *Ibid* at para 98.

buried in attachments and not referred to in the main affidavit."[45] For example, the supporting affidavit indicated that Mr. Tollman possessed multiple passports, when he had already surrendered these passports, which comprised a grand total of two, as part of his immigration bail. The court characterized this as a "strategic omission" designed to suggest that Mr. Tollman was a flight risk by not disclosing "that he did not have access to either of his passports."[46] The affidavit also stated that Mr. Tollman told Canadian immigration authorities that he was not aware of the US charges against him, but omitted the salient fact that he could not have known about the charges, since they were under seal.

The court concluded that what transpired in Mr. Tollman's case was a clear abuse of process warranting a stay of the extradition proceedings. It found that "[t]he actions taken by the United States against Gavin Tollman in this country speak loudly of a deliberate plan to engineer the return of Mr. Tollman to the United States … without having to go through … an extradition proceeding."[47] In reaching this conclusion, Molloy J held that "US authorities sought to avoid the extradition process altogether" and that "Canadian immigration authorities agreed to assist the United States as requested"[48] in the absence of a "legitimate Canadian immigration concern about Mr. Tollman."[49] To the contrary, the court found that the "sole purpose of the proposed Canadian action was to assist the United States in prosecuting Mr. Tollman, which is a clear example of using the immigration system to effect a disguised extradition."[50] The court further found that "Canadian legal processes were manipulated in an attempt to get Mr. Tollman into US custody to face charges without the safeguards of an extradition proceeding."[51] In concluding that this misconduct amounted to an abuse of process warranting a stay, the court accepted "Mr. Tollman's contention that the United States deliberately set out to thwart the Canadian extradition process and to deny him the protections afforded to him under our legislation."[52]

45 *Ibid* at para 10.
46 *Ibid* at para 138.
47 *Ibid* at para 120.
48 *Ibid* at para 6.
49 *Ibid* at para 123.
50 *Ibid* at para 127.
51 *Ibid* at para 146.
52 *Ibid* at para 13.

In arriving at this conclusion in *Tollman*, the court endorsed the following principles: first, in deciding whether conduct supports disguised extradition, the issue is not whether a person sought could legitimately be deported from Canada to a requesting state pursuant to section 36(1)(c) of the *Immigration and Refugee Protection Act*[53] based on serious criminality in the other state, but rather whether this discretionary power was exercised for a valid immigration purpose.

Second, where the immigration power is improperly invoked "to remove a foreign national to another country for the purpose of enabling that foreign state to prosecute him or her," this conduct is objectionable since "[i]t is an abuse of process to exercise a statutory power for a reason that is unrelated to the purpose for which that power was granted."[54]

Third, the allegation of abuse of process based on disguised extradition imposes a "heavy burden" on the person sought who bears the onus of establishing this allegation on a balance of probabilities, relying on either direct or circumstantial evidence of improper motive or intent.

Fourth, unlike the discretionary nature of removal proceedings in the immigration context, extradition is a mandatory process governed by the *Extradition Act* and the relevant extradition arrangement between Canada and the requesting state. Taken together, the *Act* and the applicable treaty mandate that an extradition request must be made of the Minister of Justice, must be executed in accordance with the laws of the requested state (including any legal remedies availed the person sought under these laws), and must be transmitted through diplomatic channels.

Fifth, there is no barrier to Canadian immigration authorities deporting a foreign national to a prosecuting jurisdiction, provided this decision is made for a legitimate immigration purpose. However, if a requesting state enlists the assistance of Canadian immigration authorities to return an accused to face prosecution and these authorities act on this request in the absence of a valid immigration objective, as occurred in *Tollman*, this will be improper and abusive as circumventing the lawful process of extradition and the safeguards built into that process.

53 *Immigration and Refugee Protection Act*, SC 2001, c 27 [*IRPA*]. Section 36(1)(c) of *IRPA* provides: "A permanent resident or a foreign national is inadmissible on the grounds of serious criminality for committing an act outside Canada that is an offence where it was committed and that, if committed in Canada, would constitute an offence under an Act of Parliament punishable by a maximum term of imprisonment of at least 10 years."

54 *Tollman*, above note 6 at para 24.

4) Post-*Tollman*

Not surprisingly, in the wake of *Tollman*, disguised extradition claims have become commonplace. By and large, the generic argument advanced in these cases is invariably the same: where a person sought is the subject of preceding or parallel immigration proceedings, this is sufficient to support a finding of disguised extradition. This argument was not valid pre-*Tollman*, nor is it post-*Tollman*.

Tollman was first distinguished in *United States of America v Kissel*.[55] Mr. Kissel applied for a stay of extradition proceedings instituted after the commencement of immigration proceedings seeking his removal to the United States for serious criminality involving the same conduct. Relying on *Tollman*, he argued that this was a case of disguised extradition.

In dismissing the application, Beaulieu J articulated a number of additional principles governing the adjudication of claims of disguised extradition:

1) There is significant overlap between extradition and deportation, which is not, in and of itself, improper. Indeed, the end result of extradition, namely, the return of a person to a place where the person is wanted for prosecution, may be legitimately achieved through deportation, if the removal of that person from Canada is conducive to the public good.
2) The fact that there is practical overlap between the outcome of these two proceedings does not necessarily suggest that extradition proceedings, rather than deportation, should always be undertaken where a person is wanted by a state. In order to show impropriety, the applicant must bring enough evidence to show, or at least to strongly suggest, that the deportation proceedings were undertaken by Canadian authorities in bad faith and with an ulterior motive.
3) There is also nothing improper in US authorities making a tactical choice between deportation and extradition as long as Canadian authorities have a legitimate basis to pursue deportation.
4) Cooperation between Canadian and US authorities with respect to a certain individual who is sought for prosecution in the United States also does not, by itself, suggest bad faith or improper motive. Indeed, such communication and cooperation is necessary in order

55 *United States of America v Kissel*, [2006] OJ No 1868 (SCJ) [*Kissel*].

for Canadian authorities to successfully pursue the objectives of Canadian immigration law.

5) There is nothing improper about US authorities notifying Canadian authorities of the presence of a person wanted for criminal charges, thereby effectively initiating a process of investigation under Canadian immigration law.
6) Where either deportation or extradition are legitimately pursued, there is no violation of the individual's rights, unless the individual is able to demonstrate bad faith.

The court in *Kissel*, applying these principles, found that Mr. Kissel had failed to make out a case of disguised extradition for three reasons. First, he did not tender any convincing evidence that the deportation proceedings were undertaken in bad faith. Second, the communications and cooperation between US and Canadian authorities were legitimate. Third, even if it could be said that US authorities decided to pursue extradition because they believed that the immigration process would not go their way, there was nothing improper about this decision, as they were entitled to make any strategic choices that they wished, as long as the deportation proceedings were founded on a legitimate basis.

The post-*Tollman* cases also illustrate that Canadian immigration authorities are sometimes uncertain as to the legally permissible overlap between immigration and extradition proceedings. This legal uncertainty manifests itself in one of two ways. Immigration officials either fail to appreciate the legitimate intersection between the two proceedings, or improperly stray into matters reserved for extradition officials.

United States of America v Talashkova[56] is a good example of both. Ms. Talashkova, a Russian citizen, was wanted for prosecution in the United States for fraud and money laundering offences. She was detained by Canadian immigration authorities when she landed at Toronto Pearson International Airport as part of the flight crew on a Russian airliner. Immigration officials commenced inadmissibility proceedings against her for serious criminality based on the US charges. However, these proceedings were abandoned and Ms. Talashkova was permitted to leave Canada without an admissibility hearing. This decision was motivated in part by concerns over the public perception of immigration officers having

56 *United States of America v Talashkova*, [2013] OJ No 1283 (SCJ) [*Talashkova* Ont SCJ], aff'd *United States of America v Talashkova*, 2014 ONCA 74.

"improperly referenced extradition" in their notes and reports as part of the inadmissibility proceedings. Ms. Talashkova was then arrested on an extradition warrant as she was about to board a plane to return to Russia.

Ms. Talashkova applied to the extradition judge to stay the proceedings as an abuse of process alleging that "CBSA [Canada Border Security Agency] engaged in conduct that merged immigration and extradition ... which resulted in ... a disguised extradition."[57] She claimed, *inter alia*, that CBSA officials acted improperly and in bad faith: in delaying the immigration process to facilitate extradition; in seeking information from the United States in relation to extradition issues; in referencing extradition in the immigration documents and then redacting these references; in considering extradition as a factor in commencing the inadmissibility proceedings; and in failing to offer Ms. Talashkova an opportunity to leave the country.

Immigration officials acknowledged having inquired of the United States whether it would be seeking extradition in asking for information about the US charges, and admitted to referencing and then deleting references to extradition in their notes. The court found that, in making these inquiries, CBSA exceeded its mandate in asking about extradition. The court characterized the inquiries related to extradition as "improper" and "irrelevant" to CBSA's task, and concluded that this conduct could create the impression "that the Canadian immigration procedures were being used to facilitate extradition."[58]

However, the court was not persuaded that CBSA deliberately sought information about extradition in order to improperly use it in the immigration proceedings to facilitate extradition. The court reached this conclusion for three reasons. First, McMahon J found that CBSA had an ample evidentiary foundation to conclude that Ms. Talashkova was inadmissible to Canada based on her serious criminality in the United States. Second, the court pointed out that CBSA fully documented in its written report the fact that it had inquired into the possibility of extradition. Justice McMahon reasoned that it would be difficult to conclude that CBSA wished to use the immigration procedure to facilitate a disguised extradition where it recorded information in relation to extradition in its report. Finally, the only information about extradition that CBSA had

57 *Talashkova* Ont SCJ, *ibid* at para 2.

58 *Ibid* at paras 41–42.

in making the valid determination that Ms. Talashkova was inadmissible to Canada was the fact that the United States would not be seeking extradition.

The court nonetheless found that CBSA improperly considered the issue of extradition in making this determination. Justice McMahon was satisfied that CBSA's decision to consider the irrelevant factor of extradition was based on a lack of proper training and was not a deliberate attempt to use the immigration system as a disguised extradition. The court was still "very troubled" by this conduct, and emphasized that Canadian immigration officials should be trained to avoid seeking information about extradition, and to understand that extradition is not relevant to their role.

In rejecting the abuse of process claim, the court concluded that there was a valid immigration objective to the inadmissibility proceedings. The court accepted that the CBSA concerns and the related decision to allow Ms. Talashkova to leave Canada voluntarily were motivated by the perception or appearance of disguised extradition rather than as the result of any actual impropriety or bad faith conduct by Canadian immigration officials aimed at using the immigration process to facilitate extradition.

While the preponderance of immigration and extradition caselaw has rejected claims of disguised extradition through deportation, *Tollman* is not a complete outlier in this area. The case of *Poland v Bartoszewicz*[59] is the only other Canadian case in which a court has concluded that the commencement of inadmissibility proceedings based on serious criminality was not *bona fide*, and instead was intended to assist a foreign state in its efforts to advance a prosecution against an accused by having the person sought deported rather than extradited.

Mr. Bartoszewicz was wanted for prosecution in the Republic of Poland for fraud-related offences. Poland requested his extradition from Canada. Canadian authorities advised Polish authorities that Canada could not execute the request because, at that time, there was no extradition relationship between the two states. In providing this information, Canadian authorities asked if Poland consented to Canadian extradition authorities providing the extradition request to Canadian immigration authorities to pursue possible deportation proceedings against Mr. Bartoszewicz based on serious criminality. Poland gave its consent and indicated that it

59 *Poland v Bartoszewicz*, 2012 ONSC 250 [*Bartoszewicz*].

wished to have Mr. Bartoszewicz returned by extradition or deportation. The extradition package was forwarded to Citizenship and Immigration Canada (CIC) for its consideration. Poland also requested that Canadian authorities deport Mr. Bartoszewicz.

Although CIC had closed its file on Mr. Bartoszewicz, following receipt of the extradition material and the Polish deportation request, it commenced inadmissibility proceedings against him based on the Polish criminal charges. In the interim, Canada ratified the *United Nations Convention against Corruption*,[60] to which Poland was already a party, which imposes reciprocal extradition obligations on state parties.[61] Poland renewed its request for Mr. Bartoszewicz's extradition pursuant to *UNCAC*. The Canadian immigration proceedings against Mr. Bartoszewicz were withdrawn and Canadian authorities commenced extradition proceedings against him.

Mr. Bartoszewicz successfully applied to stay the extradition proceedings as an abuse of process on the basis that the immigration proceedings were a disguised extradition. In deciding this application, the court summarized the prevailing state of the law on this topic thus:

> A deportation proceeding which is proved to have been a disguised extradition has long been recognized as an abuse of process. This conclusion flows from rule of law considerations. The rule of law is a foundational principle of our democracy. Where the executive uses a proceeding, e.g., deportation, for a purpose for which it is not intended, e.g., extradition, this conduct is a violation of the rule of law and constitutes an abuse of process.
>
> The purposes of extradition and deportation are fundamentally different. Extradition is intended to advance the requesting state's interests. Canada's only interest is to comply with its treaty obligations and to ensure compliance with the requirements for extradition as agent of the requesting state. Deportation proceedings (technically an admissibility hearing which results in a removal order) are to protect Canada's national interests in removing, in accordance with our law, foreign nationals who are not entitled to be in Canada.[62]

60 *United Nations Convention against Corruption*, (2003) 2349 UNTS 41 [*UNCAC*].

61 *Ibid*, art 44.

62 *Bartoszewicz*, above note 59 at paras 19–20.

In granting the application for a stay, the court held that the sole purpose of the deportation proceedings was to assist Poland in obtaining the return of Mr. Bartoszewicz. The proceedings were not initiated for a valid immigration purpose because it was "conducive to the public good" to remove him from Canada. In reaching this conclusion, Backhouse J found that CIC had no interest in deporting Mr. Bartoszewicz until Poland became involved, and that the deportation proceedings were only commenced because that is what the Polish government wanted. The court further found that, but for Poland consenting to the extradition package being provided to Canadian immigration authorities and requesting Mr. Bartoszewicz's deportation, nothing would have been done to attempt deportation. The court noted in this regard that there was no evidence that the immigration proceedings were initiated in the public good in furtherance of Canada's national interests. Rather, the proceedings were only commenced to appease the Polish government.

The court found that this conclusion was bolstered by the absence of any explanation of why the extradition proceedings were not commenced once Canada ratified *UNCAC*, but only after the deportation proceedings were terminated in Mr. Bartoszewicz's favour. In staying the extradition proceedings, the court stated that the "cavalier manner" in which Mr. Bartoszewicz was treated as a result of the "commencement of meritless deportation proceedings intended to bring about his extradition" shocked both the conscience of the court and the Canadian public.[63]

D. CONCLUSION

As this paper has attempted to elucidate, there are sound legal and policy reasons for Canadian courts not sanctioning immigration proceedings initiated to achieve the objectives of extradition. At the end of the day, for this conduct to amount to an abuse of process justifying a stay of related extradition proceedings, a court must be satisfied on a balance of probabilities that the immigration proceedings were a sham and were initiated in bad faith to accomplish the purposes of extradition, as in *Tollman*. That immigration proceedings having a legitimate purpose complement the objectives of extradition will not rise to this level.

63 *Ibid* at para 57.

While the law in this area is now hopefully clear, it can be expected that disguised extradition-inspired arguments will continue to percolate in extradition cases wherever there is overlap between immigration and extradition proceedings. This is most recently illustrated in the extradition proceedings against Huawei executive Meng Wanzhou who, in resisting her extradition to the United States to stand trial for fraud-related offences, alleged that Canadian authorities colluded with US authorities to exercise Canadian immigration powers for extradition purposes.

Although Ms. Meng was successful in obtaining additional disclosure from Canadian immigration authorities on the basis that this abuse of process allegation possessed an "air of reality,"[64] the issue was ultimately not adjudicated, since the extradition proceedings were halted after the United States withdrew its extradition request as a result of Ms. Meng resolving the US charges against her. Needless to say, it is fair to predict that *Meng* will not be the last word on the topic of disguised extradition through deportation as an abuse of process.

64 *United States v Meng*, 2019 BCSC 2137.

twenty

Operation CARIBBE: A Case Study in Combatting Drug Trafficking on the High Seas

AMÉLIE AUBUT*

A. INTRODUCTION

Drug trafficking affects most states — if not all — in an intertwined manner.[1] Illicit drugs trafficked and consumed in Canada can be manufactured in one state and smuggled through several others before reaching Canadian soil.[2] The criminal organizations involved in drug trafficking are increasingly sophisticated and often put down roots in countries around the world.[3] Specifically relevant to this chapter is the significant threat drug trafficking constitutes to maritime security and international

* At the time of writing the author had been a legal officer in the Office of the Judge Advocate General of the Canadian Forces for nearly seven years. She holds a Civil Law degree from the University of Montréal, a Common Law degree from the University of Ottawa, and a Master's degree in International Law from the University of Cambridge. The views expressed in this chapter are the author's alone. They do not necessarily reflect, nor should they be taken to reflect, the views of the Government of Canada, the Department of National Defence, the Canadian Armed Forces or the Office of the Judge Advocate General.

1 Robert J. Currie & Joseph Rikhof, *International and Transnational Criminal Law*, 3d ed (Toronto: Irwin Law, 2020) at 439 and 479–80 [Currie & Rikhof]; *UNODC World Drug Report 2020* (2020), Booklet 1 at 34 [*World Drug Report 2020*].

2 *Ibid.*

3 *Ibid.*

stability.[4] It endangers safety and security at sea, international maritime transport, and local and global economies.[5]

Maritime transportation is the least common mode of transportation used by drug traffickers. However, it potentially has the greatest impact on drug supplies within national borders.[6] It reduces the possibility of detection and interception by law enforcement officials (because the seas are so vast), and permits drug traffickers to transport larger quantities than by air or land.[7] Furthermore, as noted by the UN Office on Drugs and Crime (UNODC), "[t]he COVID-19 pandemic may have accelerated existing trends of an increased use of sea and waterway routes for drug trafficking. Use of maritime and waterway routes was found to have increased in several regions and countries."[8]

The Secretary General of the United Nations recently stated that tackling drug trafficking remains an international responsibility.[9] The Commission on Narcotic Drugs has also repeatedly highlighted the importance of international cooperation to address cross-border trafficking.[10] This need for a coordinated response in the maritime sphere is increasingly important, as criminal organizations often turn to the high seas to avoid detection and interception, and use innovative methods (such as semi-submersible vessels) that are even more difficult to detect and intercept.[11]

---

4 *Report of the Secretary General on Oceans and the Law of the Sea* (2019), UN Doc A/74/350 at para 38 [*Oceans and the Law of the Sea Report*].

5 *Report of the Secretary General on Oceans and the Law of the Sea* (2014), UN Doc A/69/71/Add.1 at para 28.

6 UNODC, *World Drug Report* (2015) at 39.

7 *World Drug Report 2020*, above note 1 at 11–12; "Although maritime seizures constitute no more than 11 per cent of all cases across all drug categories globally, each maritime seizure was on average almost 30 times larger than seized consignments trafficked by air." Efthymios Papastavridis, "The Illicit Trafficking of Drugs" in David Joseph Attard et al, eds, *The IMLI Manual on International Maritime Law*, Vol III (Oxford: Oxford University Press, 2016) at 465 [Papastavridis].

8 UNODC, *World Drug Report 2021* (2021) Booklet 5 at 16 and 91 [*World Drug Report 2021*].

9 *Oceans and the Law of the Sea Report*, above note 4 at para 37.

10 *Ibid.* See also *World Drug Report 2020*, above note 1 at 34 and *World Drug Report 2021*, above note 8, Booklet 1 at 13 and 30.

11 Allyson Bennett, "That Sinking Feeling: Stateless Ships, Universal Jurisdiction, and the Drug Trafficking Vessel Interdiction Act" (2012) 37:2 *Yale Journal of International Law* 433 at 434 and 445 [Bennett].

Canada has been contributing to the international effort to tackle maritime drug trafficking for many years. Among other efforts, Operation CARIBBE constitutes Canada's participation in US-led counter-narcotics operations within the Caribbean Sea, the Gulf of Mexico, and the eastern Pacific Ocean. The purpose of this chapter is to consider Operation CARIBBE as a case study of a multinational effort to combat drug trafficking on the high seas. In the discussion that follows, I will canvass three issues: (1) the legal regimes governing maritime drug trafficking, (2) the US and Canadian responses to maritime drug trafficking, and (3) issues arising from these responses.

This chapter will focus only on drug trafficking occurring on the high seas, using the definition of *high seas* from the *United Nations Convention on the Law of the Sea* (*UNCLOS*): "[A]ll parts of the sea that are not included in the exclusive economic zone, in the territorial sea or in the internal waters of a State, or in the archipelagic waters of an archipelagic State."[12]

B. LEGAL REGIMES GOVERNING MARITIME DRUG TRAFFICKING

1) International Legal Regime

Various multilateral instruments and bilateral arrangements govern drug trafficking on the high seas. The two most relevant ones in the context of this chapter are *UNCLOS* and the *United Nations Convention Against Illicit Traffic in Narcotic Drugs and Psychotropic Substances*, also called the *Vienna Convention*.[13]

a) *UNCLOS*

Freedom of the high seas is a fundamental tenet under *UNCLOS*.[14] Article 92 states that "[t]he high seas are open to all States, whether coastal or

12 *United Nations Convention on the Law of the Sea*, (1982) 1833 UNTS 3, arts 86 and 92 [*UNCLOS*].

13 *United Nations Convention Against Illicit Traffic in Narcotic Drugs and Psychotropic Substances*, (1988) 1582 UNTS 95, Can TS 1990 No 42 [*Vienna Convention*]. For a more exhaustive examination of the legal regimes governing maritime drug trafficking, see Papastavridis, above note 7.

14 *UNCLOS* came into force in 1994 and was in force for Canada in 2003. It currently has 168 parties. See Government of Canada, "Law of the Sea: United Nations

land-locked."[15] However, this freedom is not unlimited. On the high seas, a vessel will generally fall under the exclusive jurisdiction of the state where the vessel is registered (the flag state).[16]

Regarding drug trafficking, article 108(1) provides that "[a]ll States shall cooperate in the suppression of illicit traffic in narcotic drugs and psychotropic substances engaged in by ships on the high seas contrary to international conventions."[17] The principle of exclusive jurisdiction is reiterated, in that only a state which has reasonable grounds for believing that a vessel flying *its* flag is engaged in illicit traffic may request cooperation of other States to suppress such traffic.[18] As one commentator has noted, *UNCLOS* "falls short of providing any enforcement mechanism to complement the obligation to cooperate."[19]

There is no right under *UNCLOS* to visit, board, or seize a foreign-registered vessel in case of reasonable grounds for suspecting that a vessel is engaged in illicit drug trafficking.[20] Drug trafficking is not a proscribed activity for which a right of visit by foreign ships is recognized.[21] Authority to take enforcement measures lies with the flag state unless otherwise provided for either by *ad hoc* consent or in multilateral instruments and bilateral arrangements.[22] Arguably, the only relevant legal justification for boarding suspected foreign drug-trafficking vessels under *UNCLOS* is the right of visit that exists in respect of vessels that are without nationality (flagless or stateless vessels).[23] The right of visit means that papers may be inspected and that a full search should only be initiated if suspicions remain.[24] However, it has been argued that "the right to visit

---

Convention," online: www.canada.ca/en/environment-climate-change/corporate/international-affairs/partnerships-organizations/law-sea-united-nations-convention.html.

15 *UNCLOS*, above note 12, art 87.

16 *Ibid*, art 92.

17 *Ibid*, art 108(1).

18 *Ibid*, art 108(2).

19 Papastavridis, above note 7 at 468.

20 Natalie Klein, *Maritime Security and the Law of the Sea* (Oxford: Oxford University Press, 2011) at 131.

21 *UNCLOS*, above note 12, art 110.

22 Douglas Guilfoyle, "The High Seas" in Donald R. Rothwell et al, eds, *The Oxford Handbook of the Law of the Sea* (Oxford: Oxford University Press, 2015) at 220.

23 *UNCLOS*, above note 12, art 110; Papastavridis, above note 7 at 468; *Medvedyev and Other v France*, no. 3394/03 ECHR (29 March 2010) at paras 85 and 87.

24 *UNCLOS*, above note 12, art 110(2).

stateless vessels does not *ipso jure* entail the right to seize the illicit cargo or exert any further enforcement jurisdiction over the persons on board the vessel."[25]

b) *Vienna Convention*[26]

The *Vienna Convention* is dedicated to tackling drug trafficking, including on the high seas. Article 3 prescribes certain drug trafficking offences that must be established under States Parties' domestic laws, and article 4 requires that States Parties establish jurisdiction over those offences, including when the offence is committed on board a vessel flying its flag. Unlike *UNCLOS*, the *Vienna Convention* specifically allows for the interception of a ship suspected of illicit drug trafficking by a State Party other than the flag state.[27] Article 17 sets up a procedure whereby a State Party may request authorization to board a vessel flying the flag of another State Party, search the vessel, and take appropriate action with respect to the vessel, persons, and cargo on board. However, here, too, the principle of exclusive flag-state jurisdiction remains key. The flag state's explicit authorization to board is required under the *Vienna Convention*. This authorization may be afforded on an *ad hoc* basis, or by means of separate bilateral or regional agreements or arrangements.[28] As noted by Professors Currie and Rikhof, this is, "at best, a weak provision, since nothing prevents any state from requesting permission to board, either under *UNCLOS* or general international law."[29]

In sum, in cases of drug trafficking on the high seas, the authority to take enforcement measures lies with the flag state unless that state has authorized another state to take enforcement actions. To analyze any given specific situation, reference can be made to myriad multilateral instruments and bilateral arrangements that govern.

---

25 Papastavridis, above note 7 at 468.

26 This Convention came into force in 1990 both internationally and for Canada. It currently has 191 parties.

27 *Vienna Convention*, above note 13, art 17(3).

28 *Ibid*, art 17(9).

29 Currie & Rikhof, above note 1 at 443.

2) National Regimes

a) Legal Regime of the United States

The United States is not a party to *UNCLOS*,[30] but is party to the *Vienna Convention*. The *Maritime Drug Law Enforcement Act* (*MDLEA*),[31] which goes further than the *Vienna Convention*, is the primary criminal statute that the US Coast Guard (USCG) utilizes in counter-drug operations.[32] This law—of which there is no Canadian equivalent—applies extraterritorially, and gives broad authority to make seizures of vessels on the high seas.[33] It criminalizes the manufacture, distribution, or possession of illicit drugs for the purpose of trafficking while onboard (1) a US-flagged vessel, (2) a stateless vessel, or (3) a foreign-flagged vessel, where the flag state consents or waives its objection to the enforcement of US law by the United States.[34]

Individuals charged with offences under the *MDLEA* may be tried in any US district court.[35] Challenges to the *MDLEA*'s jurisdictional provisions have been repeatedly dismissed by US courts. Most US courts have held that international law permits any state to subject stateless vessels on the high seas to its jurisdiction.[36] This issue is far from settled. Although many scholars disagree with the US position, the latter has some support in international law and scholarship.[37]

To facilitate the enforcement of the *MDLEA*, the USCG has concluded (as of 2020) forty-one "counter-drug bilateral agreements and operational procedures with partner nations [that] enable the Coast

30 Aaron J. Casavant, "In Defense of the U.S. Maritime Drug Law Enforcement Act: A Justification for the Law's Extraterritorial Reach" (2017) 8 *Harvard National Security Journal* 191. "Although the United States has not ratified *UNCLOS*, it considers the Convention's navigation and overflight articles as codifications of customary international law." *Ibid* at 203.

31 *Maritime Drug Law Enforcement Act*, 46 USC §70501 (West 2008) [*MDLEA*].

32 United States, Homeland Security, *Fiscal Year 2020 Report to Congress—Counter-Drug Operations* (2020) at 2 [*Report to Congress*].

33 *MDLEA*, above note 31, §§70502 & 70503.

34 *Ibid.*

35 *Ibid*, §70504.

36 Bennett, above note 11 at 443.

37 For a summary of the diverging views on this, see Brent Clute, "The Lawfulness of Canadian Interdiction of Stateless Vessels on the High Seas in Counter-Narcotics and Counter-Terrorism Operations" (unpublished master's thesis, 2014) at 52–60, online: www.cfc.forces.gc.ca/papers/csc/csc40/mds/clute.pdf.

Guard to: board suspect vessels, facilitate interdictions in territorial waters of partner nations, deter illicit activity in the littoral regions, and coordinate interdiction and apprehension operations."[38] Close to 60 percent of all USCG interdiction in the 2019 fiscal year involved the use of a bilateral agreement or an operational procedure.[39]

In 2008, Congress enacted the *Drug Trafficking Vessel Interdiction Act* (*DRVIA*)[40] to address issues encountered with the use of submersible vessels or semi-submersible vessels in drug trafficking operations. Crew members often sink these vessels before the arrival of the USCG, rendering prosecution of such cases difficult, since the evidence has been destroyed. Thus, the *DTVIA* made it a crime to "operate ... or embark ... in any submersible vessel or semi-submersible vessel that is without nationality and that is navigating or has navigated into, through, or from waters beyond the outer limit of the territorial sea of a single country ... with the intent to evade detection."[41]

The *DTVIA* represents quite a unique and far-reaching exercise of criminal jurisdiction. As noted by Professor Papastavridis, "[u]nlike other relevant laws, the *DTVIA* does not use a vessel's statelessness solely as a jurisdictional hook, but makes the operation of a stateless vessel a key component of the substantive crime it proscribes."[42] Accused persons have challenged the *DTVIA* on various grounds and US courts have upheld the Act for substantially the same reasons articulated in the courts' earlier cases affirming the validity of the *MDLEA*—resting on the basis, among others, that a vessel's status as stateless is sufficient to authorize the exercise of US jurisdiction.[43] In doing so, the courts have not drawn

38 An operational procedure is a process to facilitate law enforcement activity agreed to with a partner nation that is less formal than a bilateral agreement. See *Report to Congress*, above note 32 at 4.

39 *Ibid.*

40 *Drug Trafficking Vessel Interdiction Act*, 18 USCA §2285 (West 2011) [*DTVIA*].

41 *Ibid*, §2285(a).

42 Papastavridis, above note 7 at 469. See also, Bennett, above note 11 at 445: "the DTVIA has thereby blurred the line between exercising jurisdiction based on a vessel's status as stateless and treating the operation of a stateless vessel as if it were a universal crime."

43 Bennett, above note 11 at 445; for a discussion on this, see Ann Marie Brodarick, "High Seas, High Stakes: Jurisdiction over Stateless Vessels and an Excess of Congressional Power Under the Drug Trafficking Vessel Interdiction Act" (2012) 67:1 *University of Miami Law Review* 255 at 269 & 270; Papastavridis, above note 7 at 469 & 470.

the distinction between the *MDLEA* and the *DTVIA* highlighted by Professor Papastavridis.[44]

b) Canadian Legal Regime

Canada is a party to *UNCLOS* and the *Vienna Convention*. The *Oceans Act*[45] implements most of Canada's obligations under *UNCLOS*. The *Controlled Drugs and Substances Act* (*CDSA*)[46] and the *Criminal Code*[47] primarily implement Canada's obligations under the *Vienna Convention*. The *CDSA* contains no explicit provisions regarding questions of jurisdiction on the high seas, but the *Code* does. Section 477.1 of the *Code* provides for prescriptive jurisdiction over any criminal or federal regulatory offence on the high seas in the following circumstances: (1) on a Canadian-flagged vessel, (2) on a foreign-flagged vessel in the course of hot pursuit,[48] or (3) on a foreign-flagged vessel if a Canadian citizen is on board and is suspected of having committed an offence on the high seas.[49] Pursuant to section 477.2(3), the consent of the attorney general of Canada is required in order to prosecute in the two latter circumstances.

Enforcement jurisdiction is found under section 477.3 of the *Code*. Powers of arrest, entry, search, and seizure are extended to those acts or omissions occurring in the above-mentioned circumstances. Pursuant to section 477.3(2)(b), a justice or judge in any territorial division in Canada has jurisdiction to authorize an arrest, entry, search, seizure, and an investigation or other ancillary matter related to an offence referred to in

---

44 Bennett, above note 11 at 435.

45 *Oceans Act*, SC 1996, c 31; Currie & Rikhof, above note 1 at 88.

46 SC 1996, c 19; *R v Wookey*, 2013 ONCJ 83 at para 33; Currie & Rikhof, above note 1 at 445.

47 *Criminal Code*, RSC 1985, c C-46, s 745 [*Criminal Code* or *Code*].

48 The right of hot pursuit is found under article 111 of *UNCLOS*, above note 12.

49 Section 477.1 of the *Code*, above note 47, reads as follows:

> (c) that is committed outside Canada on board or by means of a ship registered or licensed, or for which an identification number has been issued, pursuant to any Act of Parliament;
> (d) that is committed outside Canada in the course of hot pursuit; or
> (e) that is committed outside the territory of any state by a Canadian citizen.

Prior to 1990, jurisdiction under the *Code* was limited to offences committed on the territorial sea of Canada or on internal waters between the territorial sea and the coast of Canada (RSC 1985, c-C46, s 477). The current version came in by way of *Code* amendments in 1990 (RSC 1990, c 44, s 15).

section 477.1 in the same manner as if the offence had been committed in that territorial division. These powers may be exercised at the *locus* of the offence or, in cases of hot pursuit, anywhere on the seas, other than a place that is part of the territorial sea of another state.[50] Per section 477.3(3), where the offence is alleged to have been committed on board a foreign vessel, the consent of the attorney general is required before exercising enforcement jurisdiction.

In sum, *the commencement of criminal proceedings* for drug-trafficking offences in Canadian courts against Canadians and non-Canadian citizens intercepted on the high seas is authorized. However, the consent of the attorney general will be required unless the individuals were intercepted on a Canadian-flagged vessel. *The power of arrest, entry, search, and seizure* on board Canadian-flagged vessels on the high seas is also authorized. For foreign-flagged vessels, it may be authorized by the attorney general in only two cases: (1) in the course of hot pursuit, or (2) where a Canadian citizen is onboard and is suspected of having committed an offence on the high seas.

Enforcement powers where a Canadian citizen is on board a foreign-flagged vessel and is suspected of having committed an offence on the high seas could potentially be far reaching.[51] Under the relevant provisions of the *Code*, there is no requirement to obtain authorization from the flag state before boarding a foreign-flagged vessel, as required per article 17 of the *Vienna Convention*. As discussed above, US law has imported the *Vienna Convention* requirement into its domestic law for foreign-flagged vessels.[52] The requirement to obtain the consent of the attorney general of Canada may be used for this purpose, that is, to ensure flag-state consent before exercising enforcement jurisdiction over a foreign-flagged vessel.[53]

---

50 *Ibid*, s 477.3(1).

51 For a discussion on the caselaw, see Andrew Brian Gough, "Canadian Criminal Jurisdiction over the Seas: Current State and Present and Future Sources for Expansion" (2008) 22:1 *Ocean Yearbook* 479 at 499 & 500. See also Clute, above note 37 at 93.

52 See above Section A(2)(a).

53 The requirement to obtain the consent of the attorney general dates back to at least 1953: *Criminal Code*, SC 1953–54, c 51, s 420. However, as discussed, at that time, the jurisdiction was more limited than it is today. See above note 49.

C. FROM THEORY TO PRACTICE: THE RESPONSE OF THE UNITED STATES AND CANADA

1) Operation MARTILLO

The United States has been seizing drugs on the high seas for decades. Operation MARTILLO, which was launched in 2012, is the US contribution to a multinational effort to detect and monitor suspect air and maritime drug activity in the Caribbean Sea, Gulf of Mexico, and the eastern Pacific. It is led by the USCG and includes US Navy and aircraft from US federal law enforcement agencies, and military and law enforcement units.[54] In total, fourteen states are participating in this operation: Belize, Canada, Colombia, Costa Rica, El Salvador, France, Guatemala, Honduras, the Netherlands, Nicaragua, Panama, Spain, United Kingdom, and the United States.[55]

The involvement of the US military is limited to providing indirect assistance to the USCG. This may be because of the *posse comitatus* doctrine prohibiting US military personnel from directly engaging in law enforcement activities. However, it has been argued that this doctrine does not apply to the US Navy.[56] As it currently stands, "[t]he use of LEDETs [USCG Law Enforcement Detachments] appears to be based on both the law enforcement institutional expertise inherent in the Coast Guard and continued uncertainty about the legal restrictions on the Navy acting independently on the high seas."[57]

In 2016, the USCG detained 585 suspected drug smugglers, and 80 percent of them were taken to the United States to face criminal charges, up from a third of detainees in 2012. In the twelve months that ended in September 2017, the Coast Guard captured more than 700 suspects.[58]

---

54 US Southern Command, "Campaign Martillo," online: www.southcom.mil/Media/Special-Coverage/Operation-Martillo [*MARTILLO*].

55 *Ibid.*

56 Mark P. Nevitt, "Unintended Consequences: The Posse Comitatus Act in the Modern Era" (2014) 36:1 *Cardozo Law Review* 119 at 123–24 [Nevitt]; Darin Reeves, "Detainee Rights and State Obligations: Charting the Shoals Facing the Royal Canadian Navy" (unpublished LLM thesis, Dalhousie University, 2014) at 63.

57 Nevitt, above note 56 at 144–45.

58 Seth Freed Wessler, "The Coast Guard's 'Floating Guantánamos'" *New York Times Magazine* (20 November 2017), online: www.nytimes.com/2017/11/20/magazine/the-coast-guards-floating-guantanamos.html [Wessler].

In terms of quantity seized, the US Department of Homeland Security stated in its 2020 Report to Congress that

> [i]n FY 2019, the Coast Guard removed 207.9 metric tons of cocaine and more than 63,000 pounds of marijuana from the [Western Hemisphere Transit Zone (WHTZ)].... During the past 4 years, the Coast Guard removed more than 816 metric tons of pure cocaine from the WHTZ.... The 207.9 metric tons of cocaine is valued at $6.14 billion.[59]

According to US officials, if more assets were made available, four times as much cocaine could be intercepted. It is also alleged that because of asset shortfalls, 74 percent of suspected maritime drug smuggling avoids detection and interdiction.[60]

2) Operation CARIBBE

Operation CARIBBE was launched in 2006 and is the Canadian Armed Forces' (CAF) contribution to Operation MARTILLO. Under Operation CARIBBE, CAF warships and aircraft deploy to the Gulf of Mexico, Caribbean Sea, and eastern Pacific Ocean to support the USCG mission to suppress drug trafficking on the high seas. A memorandum of understanding between the CAF and the USCG was signed in 2010 to organize the cooperation between the two as part of Operation MARTILLO/ Operation CARIBBE.[61] The CAF considers Memoradums of Understanding (MOUs) of this type non-legally binding, but note that they carry significant political and moral weight, and that the responsibilities reflected in MOUs are to be carried out in good faith.[62]

---

59 *Report to Congress*, above note 32 at 5.

60 Wessler, above note 58.

61 Memorandum of Understanding between the Canadian Forces and the United States Coast Guard concerning the embarkation of United States Coast Guard Law Enforcement Detachments and Observers on Canadian Forces Vessels and Aircraft to Suppress Illicit Traffic in the Joint Interagency Task Force South Joint Operating Area, 8 October 2010 (not publicly available). See also, Government of Canada, "Operation CARIBBE" (last modified 16 June 2021), online: www.canada.ca/en/department-national-defence/services/operations/military-operations/current-operations/operation-caribbe.html ["CARIBBE"].

62 Canada, Department of National Defence, *Defence Administrative Orders and Directives (DAOD) 7014-0, Memoranda of Understanding* (last modified 7 June 2017) at para 3.2, online: www.canada.ca/en/department-national-defence/corporate/

Under Operation CARIBBE, Canadian warships and aircraft find and track vessels of interest. USCG law enforcement teams onboard the CAF warships (which are paradigmatically Canadian-flagged vessels) approach suspect vessels using CAF small boats and intercept them. USCG teams then board and inspect the ship and cargo. If illicit drugs are found, then the persons onboard are detained by the USCG on the apprehended vessel until they and the drugs can be transferred to a USCG vessel and eventually delivered to the United States for prosecution.

The USCG has care and custody of those detained throughout the operation.[63] Nonetheless, CAF ships must on occasion temporarily bring detainees on board for reasons of safety of life at sea (SOLAS) as per Canada's international obligations.[64] During such occasions, detainees remain Persons Under Custody of the USCG until they can be transferred to a USCG ship.[65] From 2010 to 2018, eighteen detainees were transferred onto Canadian vessels for safety reasons during five of nineteen total expeditions. These detainees were transferred onto Canadian ships for short periods.[66]

CAF members and assets, like those of the US Navy, are not directly involved in law enforcement operations and the detention of vessels or persons. This indirect role for the CAF may stem from the legal basis for this operation, which will be discussed below (and which may limit the tasks that the CAF can undertake),[67] but it may also stem from the limitation in section 477.3 of the *Code* discussed above. Indeed, the USCG

---

policies-standards/defence-administrative-orders-directives/7000-series/7014/7014-0-memoranda-of-understanding.html.

63 Seth Wessler & Kristin Nelson, "U.S. Coast Guard Detentions of Drug Smugglers 'Violating International Law,' and Canada May Be Complicit" *CBC* (5 June 2018), online: www.cbc.ca/radio/thecurrent/coast-guard-detainees-canada-1.4673272 [Wessler & Nelson].

64 See the *International Convention for the Safety of Life At Sea*, (1974) 1184 UNTS 3, which stipulates the general obligation of the master of a ship to proceed where necessary to the assistance of a ship, aircraft, or survival craft in distress. See also, article 98 of *UNCLOS*, above note 12.

65 CARIBBE, above note 61.

66 See Rear-Admiral Santarpia's statement. "No Evidence Detainees Mistreated Aboard U.S. Coast Guard Ships, Canadian Military Says" *CBC* (6 October 2018), online: www.cbc.ca/radio/thecurrent/the-current-for-october-4-2018-1.4849068/no-evidence-detainees-mistreated-aboard-u-s-coast-guard-ships-canadian-military-says-1.4850363 ["No Evidence"].

67 See below Section C(1), discussion on s 273.6(2) of the *National Defence Act*, RSC 1985, c N-5 [*NDA*] and the Crown prerogative.

operation casts a much wider net and allows for enforcement operations on stateless vessels and foreign-flagged vessels under more expansive conditions than what is provided for under the *Code*.

According to the CAF, it has contributed to the disruption or seizure of approximately 105 tonnes of cocaine and more than 6.725 tonnes of marijuana over the past fifteen years.[68]

D. ISSUES ARISING FROM THE US AND CANADIAN RESPONSES

1) Policing the High Seas: The CAF's Job?

Operation CARIBBE raises interesting and rarely discussed questions regarding CAF operations—questions about the domestic legal authority under which an operation is authorized, and about the extent of the tasks that CAF soldiers may undertake in an operation. More specifically, in the context of Operation CARIBBE: What is the legal basis for this operation, and does it allow for the CAF to police the high seas?

Canada will seldom disclose the legal basis for CAF operations.[69] In the case of Operation CARIBBE, the Government has not produced any public statements or records to this effect. Nonetheless, there are two potential legal authorities for this operation.

First, it is possible that this operation was authorized under section 273.6(2) of the *National Defence Act*,[70] which states that the CAF may provide assistance in respect of any law enforcement matter under certain conditions:

> (2) The Governor in Council, or the Minister on the request of the Minister of Public Safety and Emergency Preparedness or any other Minister, may issue directions authorizing the Canadian Forces to provide assistance in respect of any law enforcement matter if the Governor in Council or the Minister, as the case may be, considers that
>
> (a) the assistance is in the national interest; and

68 "CARIBBE," above note 61; Wessler & Nelson, above note 63.

69 See Alexander J. Braden, "Decision Instruments of the Federal Cabinet: Legally Exercising the 'War Prerogative'" (2021) 3 *Journal of Commonwealth Law* 157 at 180–82 [Braden].

70 *NDA*, above note 67.

(b) the matter cannot be effectively dealt with except with the assistance of the Canadian Forces.

Section 273.6(2) raises a few issues in the context of Operation CARIBBE. For one, it has been suggested that section 273.6(2) only provides a source of authority for domestic operations.[71] However, there is nothing in section 276.3 of the *NDA* that limits its application to the territorial boundaries of Canada.[72] Notably, section 273.6(2) states that it applies to "any" law enforcement matters, and section 273.6(3) provides for the only exception to this section: it "does not apply in respect of assistance that is of a minor nature and limited to logistical, technical or administrative support."

Moreover, for section 273.6(2) to be the legal basis for this operation, the Governor in Council (GIC) or the minister of national defence must consider that Operation CARIBBE is in the national interest and that the matter cannot be effectively dealt with except with the assistance of the CAF. It is probably in the national interest to keep drugs off of Canadian streets, and to cut sources of financing to criminal organizations.[73] However, at this point there could be doubt as to whether maritime drug trafficking "cannot be effectively dealt with except with the assistance of" the CAF, given that there are fourteen states participating in the US-led operation and that, over a period of fifteen years, Canada has only contributed to the interdiction of half of the amount of cocaine that the United States has seized in a single year.[74]

Finally, section 273.6(2) only allows the CAF to provide *assistance* in respect of law enforcement matters. Where is the line between law enforcement and *assistance* to law enforcement? Arguably, under section

---

71 See for instance Braden, above note 69 at 160, n 12.

72 This issue was not discussed when the bills passed through the House and Senate (1998 enactment and 2004 amendment). See also Clute, above note 37 at 88.

73 As reported by the UNODC, "[f]or the North American market, cocaine is typically transported from Colombia to Mexico or Central America by sea and then onwards by land to the United States and Canada." UNODC, "Mexico, Central America and the Caribbean" (no date), online: www.unodc.org/unodc/en/drug-trafficking/mexico-central-america-and-the-caribbean.html; see also UNODC, *World Drug Report 2020*, Executive Summary (2020) at 8 & 9, online: wdr.unodc.org/wdr2020/en/exsum.html; see also Currie & Rikhof, above note 1 at 439.

74 See above Section C. Nonetheless, the bar is relatively low under s 273.6(2). It only requires that the GIC/minister *consider* that its twin requirements have been met, lending a more subjective analysis, and thereby providing more scope for a broad interpretation.

273.6(2), the CAF could not conduct drug interdiction operations on the high seas without the involvement of another government department or agency. What is less clear is whether allowing USCG operators to use CAF small boats to board vessels of interest, and housing detainees on board CAF vessels (in cases of SOLAS only), amounts to more than mere assistance.

Apart from section 273.6, Operation CARIBBE may alternatively have been authorized by the exercise of the Crown prerogative. However, the scope and limits of the Crown prerogative is not well delineated, as courts have only very rarely considered it.[75] While it is clearly within the scope of the prerogative to deploy CAF internationally to engage in armed conflict,[76] the case for assistance to foreign law enforcement agencies is less clear.[77]

Furthermore, the enactment of section 273.6(2) of the *NDA* may suggest that Parliament has now occupied that terrain, and that the prerogative has been displaced by legislation.[78] A court might conclude that section 273.6(2) applies to international operations, and that displacement by implication suffices.[79] Then, Operation CARIBBE could only have been legally authorized under section 273.6(2) of the *NDA*.

In conclusion, section 273.6(2) of the *NDA* and the Crown prerogative could both form the legal basis underpinning Operation CARIBBE. However, as shown above, reliance on each of these authorities has its own hurdles. These issues are complex, and could themselves form the basis of another entire chapter or law journal article. The purpose of raising them here is simply to highlight the legal complexity involved in the operations, and to demonstrate the type of thought process that one must follow in order to evaluate the lawfulness of CAF operations.

---

75 Braden, above note 69 at 163–65.

76 Craig Forcese, "The Executive, the Royal Prerogative and the Constitution" in Nathalie Des Rosiers et al, eds, *Oxford Handbook of the Canadian Constitution* (Oxford: Oxford University Press, 2017) at 161 [Forcese].

77 Clute, above note 37 at 90 & 91.

78 This issue was not discussed when the bills passed through the House and Senate. See above, note 72.

79 "The precise scope of this displacement by implication is remarkably opaque in Canadian law." Forcese, above note 76 at 158. See also Braden, above note 69 at 160, n 12. *Contra*: Philippe Lagassé, "Parliamentary and Judicial Ambivalence Toward Executive Prerogative Powers in Canada" (2012) 55:2 *Canadian Public Administration* 157 at 166–67.

2) Alleged Detainee Mistreatment by the USCG: Impact for Canada and CAF soldiers

On 20 November 2017, the *New York Times* (NYT) published an article entitled "The Coast Guard's Floating Guantanamo,"[80] alleging detainee mistreatment by the USCG in the context of Operation MARTILLO. It alleged that persons detained on USCG vessels were shackled on deck without protection from the elements for weeks and even months, that they were provided inadequate nutrition, experienced weight loss and were required to use buckets to relieve themselves without privacy. The article indicated that since individuals were not formally under arrest when the Coast Guard detained them on board USCG vessels, they were not read *Miranda* rights, not appointed lawyers, and not allowed to contact their consulates or their families. According to the NYT, "[i]t is as if their rights are in suspension during their capture at sea."[81]

The article referred to individuals who petitioned a US federal court to have their indictments dismissed for "outrageous government conduct." Although the judge dismissed the motion, he stated that he was troubled by detainees' accounts and noted that "[t]his is not to say that such treatment of detainees is condoned by this court. Far from it."[82]

The NYT interviewed Professor Efthymios Papastavridis, a maritime law scholar at Oxford University, who stated that "[i]n a European context, what the US does would not meet the standard .... It would have to be measured against human rights and due-process law and this would be unlikely to pass the test."[83]

The USCG denied any wrongdoing and maintained that all detainees were treated humanely and in accordance with the law. Furthermore, it stated that it patrolled six million square miles, which created "logistical and transportation challenges."[84]

On 6 June 2018, the Canadian Broadcasting Corporation (CBC) published an article reiterating the allegations of detainee mistreatment, and highlighting the implications of CAF involvement in the USCG

---

80 Wessler, above note 58; *United States v Cheme-Ibarra*, No 14CR3305, 2016 BL 488635 (DS Cal June 03, 2016) at 12.

81 *Ibid.*

82 *Ibid.*

83 *Ibid.*

84 *Ibid.*

operation.[85] The CBC reported that no allegations of mistreatment were made against CAF members. An individual who was brought on board a CAF vessel along with two others stated that he did not have any complaints about the treatment he and his companions received while on the CAF vessel. He said that they "were led to a tent and permitted to rest. They were provided a meal and allowed to walk the deck, under guard, to stretch their legs."[86] When he was transferred to the USCG vessel "his detention took a turn for the worse."[87] The man alleged that he was detained for seventeen days on a USCG vessel where he was chained to the deck, shackled almost all the time, not protected from the elements, and not allowed to contact an attorney or his family.[88]

Following these news articles, the CAF recognized that it "had a responsibility as part of the operation ... to make sure that the entire operation is conducted legally and ethically and [that it took] that responsibility very seriously."[89] It further stated that it "quickly took several steps to ensure that [its] mission continues to be carried out with integrity and consistent with the law, which included reviewing logs, incident reports and post-deployment reports."[90] It also conferred with its US counterparts and confirmed its "expectations regarding the treatment of suspected drug smugglers."[91] Furthermore, the CAF sent a Canadian naval officer to spend twenty days aboard a USCG boat to get a "first-hand view of how they conduct the operation."[92]

The CAF concluded that "[h]aving taken these steps, [it is] confident that no CAF members participating in Op CARIBBE have witnessed or been implicated in the mistreatment of suspected criminals, either on board Canadian vessels or those of [its] Allies."[93] The CAF "issued new direction to its commanding officers to make sure that they fully

85 See Wessler & Nelson, above note 63.
86 *Ibid.*
87 *Ibid.*
88 *Ibid.*
89 Rear-Admiral Brian Santarpia, interviewed by Anna Maria Tremonti, *The Current* CBC Radio, 4 October 2018, www.cbc.ca/radio/thecurrent/the-current-for-october-4-2018-1.4849068/thursday-october-4-2018-full-transcript-1.4850995#segment2.
90 Wessler & Nelson, above note 63.
91 *Ibid.*
92 "No Evidence," above note 66.
93 *Ibid.*

understand how long it's anticipated that suspected drug smugglers will be at sea."[94]

a) Impact for CAF Soldiers: Canadian Criminal Law

The discussion that follows is theoretical, as no allegations of mistreatment or knowledge of mistreatment by CAF members were made. There is no intention here to disparage the work ethic and integrity that CAF soldiers have demonstrated in the course of this operation. However, it is worth considering how the situation would be dealt with under Canadian criminal law if the NYT allegations were true, and if CAF members were aware of, or involved in — even indirectly — the mistreatment of detainees.

The allegations of mistreatment concern acts that occurred on USCG vessels and therefore outside Canada. This raises the question as to whether Canada could exercise criminal jurisdiction over CAF members, who remained on a CAF vessel,[95] for alleged acts that occurred on USCG vessels.

Such jurisdiction could likely be exercised, by virtue of the *Criminal Code* and of the *Code of Service Discipline*.[96] Under section 477.1(c) of the *Criminal Code*, any federal offence (including but not limited to *Code* offences) committed outside of Canada on board a Canadian-flagged vessel is deemed to have occurred in Canada. This provision is in line with Canada's obligations under international law, including *UNCLOS*, which requires states to exercise criminal jurisdiction over their flagged vessels.[97] Also, under section 477.1(e) Canada can exercise jurisdiction over any offence committed outside the territory of any state by a Canadian citizen, which would include conduct on the high seas by virtually every member of the CAF.

Under Canadian criminal law, the alleged USCG mistreatment, if proven, could amount to one of several criminal offences, including criminal negligence and assault.[98] Even if CAF members did not directly participate in the commission of an offence, on particular facts they could

94 *Ibid.*

95 There is no evidence that as part of Operation CARIBBE, CAF members embarked on USCG vessels for the purposes of transferring or observing detainees.

96 The Code of Service Discipline is part III of the *NDA*, above note 67, and is the basis of the CAF military justice system. Regarding jurisdiction, see Currie & Rikhof, above note 1 at 71.

97 *UNCLOS*, above note 12, arts 92 and 95.

98 *Code*, above note 47, ss 219, 221, 265, 268, and 465(1); *NDA*, above note 67, ss 72 and 128. See Craig Forcese, "Touching Torture with a Ten-Foot Pole: the Legality of

be accused of aiding or abetting its commission, or of conspiring with or counselling, a party to an offence, or being accessories after the fact.[99]

Moreover, quite apart from the *Code*, the CAF *Code of Service Discipline* provides that an act or omission that takes place outside Canada that would, if it had taken place in Canada, be punishable under Part VII of the *National Defence Act*, the *Code* or any other act of Parliament, is an offence.[100] This means that irrespective of section 477.1 of the *Code*, CAF members could be tried before a Canadian court martial or a civilian criminal court for offences that occurred on a CAF vessel (including *Code* offences).[101] There is thus no question that Canada could exercise jurisdiction over CAF members for participating in mistreatment, even where it was committed on a USCG vessel.[102]

b) Impact for Canada: Applying the *Charter of Rights and Freedoms*

With regard to the impact of the above-mentioned allegations for Canada, concerns about the legality of Canadian actions may also arise under the *Charter*.[103] Regardless of the legal basis for this operation,[104] both the exercise of statutory powers and of the Crown prerogative may be reviewed in

---

Canada's Approach to National Security Information Sharing with Human Rights Abusing States" (2014) 52:1 *Osgoode Hall Law Journal* 263 at 292–93 [Forcese 2014].

99 *Code*, above note 47, ss 21–23. For a discussion of the potentially available defence of obedience to superior orders, see *R v Finta*, [1994] 1 SCR 701. In relation to the alleged mistreatment detainees in Afghanistan by Afghan authorities, Michael Byers of the University of British Columbia and William Schabas, then of the Irish Centre for Human Rights, appealed to the prosecutor of the International Criminal Court to exercise jurisdiction over the matter and prosecute those responsible. Deborah Bayley, "Six Degrees of Separation: Canadian Accessory Liability in Afghan War Crimes" (2011) 20 *Dalhousie Journal of Legal Studies* 61 at 62–63.

100 *NDA*, above note 67, s 130(1)(b).

101 *Ibid*, ss 130(1)(b), 166, 173, and 273.

102 See, for example, *R v Semrau*, 2010 CM 4010, where Captain Semrau was tried and found guilty for offences committed in Afghanistan.

103 *Canadian Charter of Rights and Freedoms*, Part I of the *Constitution Act, 1982*, being Schedule B to the *Canada Act 1982* (UK), 1982, c 11, s 7 [*Charter*]. For more on extraterritorial application of the *Charter*, see Leah West, "Canadian ISIS Fighters and Supporters and the Irony of the *Khadr* Exception," in this volume.

104 See above, Section C(1).

accordance with the *Charter*.[105] The main issue here is whether the *Charter* would apply on a CAF or USCG vessel on the high seas.

i) On a USCG Vessel

The most pressing and complex issue in this case is whether the *Charter* would apply to actions of Canadian state officials extraterritorially. In other words, could detainees invoke *Charter* violations before a Canadian court for the alleged mistreatment by USCG personnel (with the implication or involvement[106] of Canadian state officials)[107] that occurred on a USCG vessel navigating on the high seas?

Of note, detainees intercepted by the USCG in the context of Operation CARIBBE are not brought into Canada to be arrested, detained, or charged. Furthermore, there is no allegation that Canadian citizens were among those detained by the USCG. Therefore, one might ask, how could these individuals challenge CAF conduct on *Charter* grounds before a Canadian court?

To answer this question, we must consider the methodology developed by the Supreme Court in *Hape* and *Khadr I* and *II*.[108] Customary international law and the principle of comity of nations generally prevent the *Charter* from applying to the actions of Canadian state officials operating outside of Canada. However, there are two exceptions to this principle:

(1) If the facts disclosed "an exception to the principle of sovereignty that would justify the application of the *Charter* to the extraterritorial activities of the state actor" (e.g., with the other State's consent) (*Hape* exception);[109] or

---

105 *Canada (Prime Minister) v Khadr*, 2010 SCC 3 at para 36 [*Khadr II*]; *Amnesty International Canada v Canada (Chief of the Defence Staff)*, 2008 FC 336 at paras 87–91; upheld on appeal, 2008 FCA 401 [*Amnesty*].

106 *R v Harrer*, [1995] 3 SCR 562 at para 12; *R v Hape*, 2007 SCC 26 at para 94 [*Hape*].

107 For instance, "[c]ourt records show that four suspected traffickers were picked up with the assistance of the Canadian Forces during [a] deployment. They were held by the Coast Guard for three weeks before they were brought to a U.S. court." See Seth Wessler, *The Current* CBC Radio, 6 June 2018, online: www.cbc.ca/radio/thecurrent/the-current-for-june-6-2018-1.4693817/wednesday-june-6-2018-full-episode-transcript-1.4695079#segment1.

108 *Hape*, above note 106; *Canada (Justice) v Khadr*, 2008 SCC 28 [*Khadr I*]; *Khadr II*, above note 105.

109 *Hape*, above note 106 at para 113.

(2) If the Canadian state officials had "participated in a process that was contrary to Canada's international human rights obligations" (*Khadr* exception).[110]

Unfortunately, this methodology has proven difficult to manage, leaving the law on this issue in an unsettled state. Further clarification from the Court would be beneficial to ensure legal certainty.[111]

In the meantime, in the context of Operation CARIBBE, this means that the *Charter* would not as a general rule apply on a USCG vessel, unless one of the two exceptions mentioned above were met. Since there is no evidence of US consent,[112] I will only assess the latter exception.[113]

Among Canada's international human rights obligations are the *Convention against Torture and Other Cruel and Inhuman or Degrading Treatment or Punishment* (*CAT*)[114] and the *International Covenant on Civil and Political Rights* (*ICCPR*).[115] The *CAT* requires parties not engage in or permit torture, and other cruel and inhuman or degrading treatment or punishment.[116] The *ICCPR*, similarly to the Canadian *Charter*, protects the right to life, the right to be free from cruel and inhuman treatment, and provides rights upon arrest and detention.[117]

---

110 *Khadr I* above note 108 at para 27. In *Khadr I*, the Supreme Court referred interchangeably to Canada's "international obligations" and Canada's "international human rights obligations." See paras 2, 3, 18–19, 24, 25, 26 & 27.

111 Currie & Rikhof, above note 1 at 623 and 631.

112 As with CAF vessels, USCG vessels fall under the exclusive jurisdiction of the flag state, in this case, the United States.

113 The Afghan Detainees case (here *Amnesty*, above note 105) had a somewhat similar factual underpinning to the allegations raised in the context of Operation CARIBBE. It involved allegations of detainee mistreatment in the context of CAF operations abroad by foreign armed forces. However, I will not discuss this case at length since "*Khadr 2010* [*Khadr I*] seems to render the result in *Afghan Detainees* a matter only of historical interest." Currie & Rikhof, above note 1 at 638.

114 *Convention against Torture and Other Cruel and Inhuman or Degrading Treatment or Punishment*, (1984) 1465 UNTS 85, Can TS 1987 No 36 [*CAT*]. Canada's obligations under the *CAT* were considered in the lower court's decision in *Khadr I*, but were not addressed by the Supreme Court. See Gib van Ert, "Torture and the Supreme Court of Canada" (2014) 65 *University of New Brunswick Law Journal* 21 at 34–35.

115 *International Covenant on Civil and Political Rights*, (1966), 999 UNTS 171 [*ICCPR*].

116 *CAT*, above note 114, arts 2 and 16.

117 *ICCPR*, above note 115, arts 6–10.

In practice, the threshold to find that a given process violates Canada's international human rights obligations is high.[118] In *Khadr I* and *II*, the Supreme Court's conclusion that Canada participated in a process that was contrary to Canada's international human rights obligations [119] relied on the fact that the US Supreme Court had found that the United States had violated US and international law.[120]

In the case of Operation CARIBBE, a Canadian court would need to assess the evidence with regard to the allegations of prolonged detention, shackling to the deck, inadequate nutrition, lack of privacy, and lack of protection from the elements in light of Canada's international human rights obligations referred to above. By contrast with *Khadr*, there is no pre-existing judgment recognizing that the USCG process violates US and international law. In the US case referred to above,[121] the court noted that the treatment of USCG detainees is "troubling, but … it does not rise to the level of outrageous government conduct sufficient to dismiss the indictment."[122]

A Canadian court would also need to consider whether Canada has *participated* in such a process. Here, the threshold appears to be relatively low. In *Khadr I*, making the product of the RCMP's interview of Mr. Khadr available to US authorities amounted to participation.[123] In the case of Operation CARIBBE, for the past fifteen years there has been a close coordination and cooperation between the CAF and the USCG to counter illicit drug trafficking in the Caribbean Sea, the Gulf of Mexico, and the eastern Pacific Ocean. CAF vessels have been authorized to embark USCG personnel, and, at times, USCG detainees as well.

---

118 See Benjamin Berger, "The Reach of Rights in the Security State: Reflections on *Khadr v Canada (Minister of Justice)*" (2010) 56 *Criminal Reports* (6th) 68; Kent Roach, "The Supreme Court at the Bar of Politics: The Afghan Detainees and Omar Khadr Cases" (2010) 28:1 *National Journal of Constitutional Law* 115 at 129.

119 In this case, Canada was said to have violated common article 3 of the four *Geneva Conventions* of 1949, which Canada ratified in 1965 (Can TS 1965 No 20), and has incorporated into Canadian law with the *Geneva Conventions Act*, RSC 1985, c G-3.

120 See *Khadr I*, above note 108 at para 25: "The right to challenge the legality of detention by *habeas corpus* is a fundamental right protected both by the *Charter* and by international treaties. It follows that participation in the Guantanamo Bay process which violates these international instruments would be contrary to Canada's binding international obligations."

121 See Section C(2).

122 *United States v Cheme-Ibarra*, above note 80 at 12.

123 *Khadr I*, above note 108 at para 27.

As indicated above, there is no evidence that Canadian citizens were among those detained by the USCG. Some lower court judgments suggest that the *Charter* does not apply extraterritorially to non-Canadian citizens.[124] However, there is no such limitation in the Supreme Court's jurisprudence or in the *Charter*, and there are strong reasons to doubt the validity of this interpretation.[125]

In the event that a Canadian court were to find that Canada had participated in a process that was contrary to its international human rights obligations, the *Charter* would apply extraterritorially to Canadian state officials for mistreatment that occurred on a USCG vessel. The court would then be required to assess whether *Charter* rights had been violated — likely to be the case since "contrary to international human rights obligations" is already made out; and if so, whether the breach was saved by section 1. The rights that could be invoked include the right not to be deprived of life, liberty, and security of the person except in accordance with principles of fundamental justice, the right to be free from arbitrary detention, the procedural rights applicable, and the protection against cruel and unusual punishment.[126]

ii) On a CAF Vessel

This question is theoretical as no allegations of mistreatment on CAF vessels were made,[127] but more easily answered. As stated above, CAF vessels are Canadian-flagged vessels that fall under the exclusive jurisdiction of Canada on the high seas.[128] The *Charter* could apply to actions of Canadian state officials on a CAF vessel operating on the high seas.[129] As noted by Professors Currie and Rikhof, "[t]his kind of example is consistent with

124 *Slahi v Canada (Justice)*, 2009 FC 160 at para 48; upheld on appeal, 2009 FCA 259; *Tabingo v Canada (Citizenship and Immigration)*, 2013 FC 277; *Amnesty*, above note 105 at paras 312–15.

125 In particular, section 7 rights are extended to "everyone," not only Canadian citizens. See: Forcese 2014, above note 98 at 296–97; Roach, above note 118 at 133–34; Currie & Rikhof, above note 1 at 622.

126 *Charter*, above note 103, ss 7, 9, 10, and 12. See for instance, *Amnesty*, above note 105, where the applicants claimed that their rights under ss 7, 10, and 12 of the *Charter* had been violated.

127 See above, Section C(2).

128 *UNCLOS*, above note 12, art 92.

129 Currie & Rikhof, above note 1 at 613.

international law . . . and does not truly qualify as an 'exception' [under the *Hape* exception]."[130]

USCG detainees could therefore claim that their *Charter* rights were violated by a Canadian state actor while they were on a CAF vessel, and that the breaches were not saved by article 1. Such claims would have to deal with the issue of *Charter* application to foreign nationals raised above[131] — though they would possibly be distinguishable on the basis that the detainees were on a ship under the exclusive jurisdiction of Canada, on the high seas.

E. CONCLUSION

This chapter sought to provide a solid understanding of the applicable international and domestic law governing Canadian maritime counter-drug operations, and a better appreciation of how these Canada–US operations are actually conducted at sea.

The case study of Operation CARIBBE sheds light on the complex legal framework and the unique problems that flow from using military personnel and equipment to achieve a deterrent effect on criminals outside of Canadian territory. It also suggests that the legal basis for the operation may not be as clear as the participants might hope. Finally, it highlights where and how Canada and Canadian military participants in this operation could be exposed to legal risks.

---

130 *Ibid.*

131 See above note 126.

twenty-one

The International Transfer of Sentenced Individuals to Canada: Procedure and Issues

ADELINA IFTENE & OLIVIA GENGE*

A. INTRODUCTION

The commission of a crime by the citizen of one state on the territory of another triggers several potential international and transnational responses. These actions include extradition,[1] deportation, and transfer of prisoners. Extradition sends the individual back to their country of origin for trial. Deportation, in relation to crime, often occurs after an individual has served their sentence in a foreign country. A prisoner transfer moves the individual, under sentence in a foreign country, to serve the remainder of their sentence in the country of citizenship.

The latter process has received far less attention in Canada than the first two. In fact, there is very little scholarship and commentary on the issues raised by the regulation and implementation of the transfer-of-prisoners framework.[2] Yet, this process affects the lives of hundreds of

---

* Adelina Iftene, Associate Professor and Coordinator of the JD Criminal Justice Program Schulich School of Law at Dalhousie University, and Olivia Genge, JD 2022, Schulich School of Law at Dalhousie University. Thank you to Liam Protheroe, JD 2022 Dalhousie and Faith Hwang, JD 2024 Dalhousie, for their thorough editing assistance and to Professor Rob Currie for his thoughtful comments and suggestions on the substance of this chapter.

1 See the chapters by Frédéric Mégret and Jeffrey Johnston in this book.

2 There is a dearth of scholarship on this issue. One author has written about this issue from a comparative perspective: Jamil Ddamulira Mujuzi, "The Supreme Court of

individuals and their families yearly, and interacts in complex ways with human rights, international, constitutional, criminal, and administrative laws. Internationally, the importance of this process has been recognized by the UN Office on Drugs and Crime (UNODC), which issued the *Handbook on the International Transfer of Sentenced Persons*.[3]

Canada is currently party to fifteen bilateral international treaties[4] and three multilateral agreements[5] that allow for the transfer of sentenced individuals back to their states of origin to serve the remainder of their

---

Canada and the Offender's Right to be Transferred to Serve His Sentence in Canada: Interpreting the International Transfer of Offenders Act in Light of Canada's National and International Human Rights Obligations" (2013) 6:2 *Baltic Journal of Law & Politics* 102; Jamil Ddamulira Mujuzi, "The Transfer of Offenders from Other Countries to Canada: Analysing Theory and Practice" (2014) 2:1 *Chinese Journal of Comparative Law* 120 [Mujuzi 2014]; Jamil Ddamulira Mujuzi, "The 'Best Interests of the Child' as a Factor in Allowing Foreigners with Criminal Records to Enter Canada and in Staying the Deportation of Foreign National Offenders from Canada" (2017) 13:1 *Acta Universitas Danubius* 162; Jamil Ddamulira Mujuzi, "Legal Pluralism and the Right to Family Life, and the Transfer of Offenders Who Are Nationals of African Countries, within Africa and to Africa" (2013) 45:3 *Journal of Legal Pluralism and Unofficial Law* 267 [Mujuzi 2013]. A handful of Canadian publications include case commentary related to transfer of prisoners in the broader context of national security and public international law: Yavar Hameed, "Unmasking the Public Interest in Discretionary National Security Decisions in Canada" (2014) 92:1 *Canadian Bar Review* 31 [Hameed]; Benjamin Oliphant, "Interpreting the Charter with International Law: Pitfalls & Principles" (2014) 19 *Appeal: Review of Current Law and Law Reform* 105; Gib van Ert, Greg J. Allen & Rebecca Robb, "Canadian Cases in Public International Law in 2013" [2013] 51 *Canadian Yearbook of International Law* 535 [van Ert, Allen & Robb 2013]; and Gib van Ert, Greg J. Allen & Rebecca Robb, "Canadian Cases in Public International Law in 2014" [2014] 52 *Canadian Yearbook of International Law* 535 [van Ert, Allen & Robb 2014].

3 UNODC, *Handbook on the International Transfer of Sentenced Persons* (United Nations, 2012) [UNODC].

4 These include treaties with Argentina, Barbados, Bolivia, Brazil, Cuba, Dominican Republic, Egypt, France, Mexico, Mongolia, Morocco, Peru, Thailand, the USA, and Venezuela. See Correctional Service Canada, "List of Countries Acceding a Bilateral Treaty with Canada" (last modified 9 April 2020) ["List of Countries Acceding a Bilateral Treaty with Canada"], online: www.csc-scc.gc.ca/international-transfers/004001-0004-eng.shtml.

5 *Convention on the Transfer of Sentenced Persons*, (1983) ETS No 112 (entered into force 1 July 1985); Canada, *Commonwealth Scheme for the Transfer of Offenders* (1990), online: travel.gc.ca/assistance/emergency-info/consular/framework/commonwealth; *Inter-American Convention on Serving Criminal Sentences Abroad*, OAS, 9 June 1993, OR OEA/Ser.P/XXIII.O.2/Doc.1205 (1993).

sentences. The *International Transfer of Offenders Act* (*ITOA*)[6] is the Canadian legislation created to implement these treaties and any *ad hoc* agreements that may arise between Canada and states with which Canada has not signed a bilateral or multilateral treaty. The minister of public safety and emergency preparedness (hereinafter the minister) is responsible for administering this Act, and the minister makes decisions on whether to grant or deny transfers by considering the factors listed in section 10 of the *ITOA*. Thus, the transfer of prisoners is governed in Canada by the relevant international treaty, the *ITOA*, and the other state's national legislation. International and national human rights regimes also need to be considered when interpreting the legislation.[7]

This chapter provides the reader with an understanding of the Canadian framework governing the transfer to Canada of Canadians serving a sentence abroad. It also identifies legal and policy gaps that should be considered and addressed for a more robust and fair process to be achieved. Section B will provide an overview of the legislative framework (including its purpose and transfer procedures) and an outline of the various conditions that must be fulfilled for the process to be set in motion. Special consideration will be given to the factors that inform the minister's decision to approve or deny a transfer, as well as the judicial review of these decisions. Section C will describe certain gaps in the process. For this discussion we used official statistics (which are only as recent as 2017) provided by the Correctional Service of Canada (CSC), the small amount of available commentary, and the judicially reviewed minister's decisions between 2004, when *ITOA* came into force, and 2020. The discussion is therefore limited due to the scarcity of available information, particularly the lack of up-to-date statistics and the inaccessibility of the ministerial transfer decisions that have not been judicially reviewed. Yet, even based on the sparse information available, it is clear that the prisoner transfer process is highly discretionary, is vulnerable to political influences, benefits from minimal scrutiny, and engages factors that do little to ensure the consistency of the process. We will conclude by noting that the gaps identified likely inhibit the achievement of the purposes of the *ITOA*.

6 *International Transfer of Offenders Act*, SC 2004, c 21 [*ITOA*].

7 For a general description of the legal instruments that may regulate the international transfer of prisoners see *UNODC*, above note 3 at 17–24.

B. LEGISLATIVE FRAMEWORK

1) Purposes and General Conditions for Transfer

The stated purposes of the *ITOA* are to enhance public safety, to uphold the administration of justice, and to contribute to the rehabilitation and reintegration of individuals into society. All of these are to be achieved by "enabling offenders to serve their sentences in the country of which they are citizens or nationals."[8]

The *ITOA*, as well as the various treaties it implements, set up certain conditions that must be met in order for a Canadian sentenced in a foreign country (the *sending state*) to be eligible for transfer to a Canadian prison. First, the offence of which the individual was convicted in the sending state must also be a crime in Canada (i.e., there must be dual criminality).[9] Second, the individual requesting the transfer must be a Canadian citizen.[10] The constitutionality of the citizenship requirement was challenged by a Canadian permanent resident in *Catenacci v Canada (Attorney General)*,[11] but the challenge was unsuccessful. Third, all criminal proceedings against the individual in the foreign state (i.e., the trial, sentencing, any appeals, and the period of time in which any further appeals could be filed) must have concluded or expired.[12] Thus, a Canadian who has committed a crime abroad will have been tried and sentenced in that country and in accordance with its laws.

In addition, various treaties may impose additional conditions that must also be met.[13] For instance, the treaty between Canada and the

8 *ITOA*, above note 6, s 3. These purposes are aligned with the goals set up for the transfer of prisoners generally in *UNODC*, above note 3 at 9–15.

9 *Ibid*, s 4.

10 *Ibid*, s 37.

11 *Catenacci v Canada (Attorney General)*, 2006 FC 539.

12 *ITOA*, above note 6, s 2.

13 *ITOA* does not specifically say that the terms of the treaty apply even if they are not explicitly laid out in the Act. However, the terms of the treaties are generally considered in the caselaw in conjunction with the provisions of the Act. Also, section 8(3) of the Act provides that "[t]he Minister or the relevant provincial authority, as the case may be, shall inform a foreign offender, and the Minister shall take all reasonable steps to inform a Canadian offender, of the substance of any treaty—or administrative arrangement entered into under section 31 or 32—that applies to them." It seems reasonable to conclude that the individual is entitled to know about the substance of applicable treaties because these will provide information regarding the circumstances under which they could or should be transferred, whether or not such information is included in the Act.

United States (the country which is the main sending state for transfers to Canada[14]), stipulates that the offence committed by the individual cannot be an immigration or military offence.[15] Also, in accordance with the same treaty, the individual must have at least six months left on the sentence to be served.[16] The six-month-bar rule was interpreted in *Chambers v Daou (Senior Manager, International Transfers Unit, Correctional Services)*[17] to mean that there must be six months left of an individual's foreign sentence in order for a transfer to be allowed.[18] (The event of a difference between the foreign sentence and the Canadian one is discussed in more detail in Section 3, below.)

2) The Transfer Decision-Making Process

Along with the requirements described above, all parties to a transfer must consent to it, including the individual, the relevant authorities of the foreign state, and Canada.[19] The Canadian authority that must consent to the transfer is the minister or its delegate.[20] If the person to be transferred is serving a sentence of fewer than two years, is a young person, has been found unfit to stand trial, or has been found not criminally responsible on account of mental disorder (NCR-MD), the consent of the provincial authority must also be sought (as the person will be transferred to a provincial institution).[21]

The minister, or the relevant provincial authority, and (generally, based on treaties) the relevant authority in the foreign state[22] have an obligation to inform incarcerated individuals who meet the conditions for transfer of the substance of the treaty, which includes the right to request to be

14 Correctional Service Canada, *International Transfers Annual Report 2016–2017* (no date, last modified 2 August 2018) at 3 [*International Transfers Annual Report 2016–2017*], online: www.csc-scc.gc.ca/international-transfers/092/004001-1004-en.pdf.

15 *Treaty between Canada and the United States of America on the Execution of Penal Sentences*, (1977) Can TS 1978 No 12, art II(c) (entered into force 19 July 1978) [*Treaty*].

16 *Ibid*, art II(d).

17 *Chambers v Daou (Senior Manager, International Transfers Unit, Correctional Services)*, 2014 BCSC 1284, rev'd in part 2015 BCCA 50.

18 See also van Ert, Allen & Robb 2014, above note 2 at 553–54.

19 *ITOA*, above note 6, s 8(1).

20 *Ibid*, ss 2, 6(1) & (2).

21 *Ibid*, ss 8 & 9, 32(2).

22 See, for example, *Treaty*, above note 15, art III.2.

transferred.[23] If interested, the individual must send a written request for transfer to initiate the process.[24] Though the procedure is not explicitly stated in the *ITOA*,[25] the written request is generally first reviewed by the sending state. If the sending state does not approve the transfer, the transfer process comes to a halt. As noted in *Divito v Canada (Minister of Public Safety and Emergency Preparedness)*,[26] which considered a mobility-rights claim under section 6(1) of the *Charter of Rights and Freedoms*,[27] an individual does not have a right to be transferred. One reason for this is that Canada does not have jurisdiction under international law to demand the transfer of its incarcerated nationals.[28]

If the sending state approves, however, it will forward the transfer request to the Canadian minister of public safety, who decides whether to approve or deny the transfer based on the factors listed in section 10 of the *ITOA*. The minister enjoys wide discretion under the *ITOA* in making this decision. This discretion has only increased since 2012 when the *ITOA* was last amended. Prior to 2012, the minister had to consider the listed factors, but the language has been changed such that now the minister *may* consider those factors.[29] The phrase "in the opinion of the Minister" has also been added before most factors to consider in determining whether to consent to the transfer.

The current version of the *ITOA* includes the factors from the pre-2012 version of the Act. Factors to be considered are whether, in the opinion of the minister: the individual's return to Canada will constitute a threat to the security of the country,[30] the individual is likely to continue to engage in criminal activity,[31] the individual left or remained outside Canada with the intention of abandoning Canada as a place of residence,[32] the foreign entity or prison system presents a serious threat to the offender's security

23 *ITOA*, above note 6, s 8(3).

24 *Ibid*, s 7.

25 Treaties may be explicit about this — see, for example, *Treaty*, above note 15, art III.3.

26 *Divito v Canada (Minister of Public Safety and Emergency Preparedness)*, 2013 SCC 47, aff'g 2011 FCA 39 [*Divito*].

27 *Canadian Charter of Rights and Freedoms*, Part I of the *Constitution Act, 1982*, being Schedule B to the *Canada Act* 1982 (UK), 1982, c 11 [*Charter*].

28 *Divito*, above note 26 at paras 40 and 44.

29 *ITOA*, above note 6, s 10(1).

30 *Ibid*, s 10(1)(a).

31 *Ibid*, s 10(1)(c).

32 *Ibid*, s 10(1)(d).

or human rights,[33] the offender has social or family ties in Canada,[34] and the offender will engage in terrorism or organized crime.[35] The Act also includes the following new factors: whether, in the minister's opinion, the offender's return to Canada will endanger public safety (including the safety of a victim, family member, or child);[36] the offender's health;[37] whether the offender has refused to participate in a rehabilitation or reintegration program;[38] whether the offender has accepted responsibility for the offence for which they have been convicted, including by acknowledging the harm done to victims and to the community;[39] the manner in which the offender will be supervised, after the transfer, while serving the sentence;[40] whether the offender has cooperated, or has undertaken to cooperate, with a law enforcement agency;[41] and any other factor the minister considers relevant.[42] The minister will also consider the recommendation provided by the CSC (the authority that administers the sentence in Canada), but will not be bound by it.[43] Again, the jurisprudence has been consistent on the fact that no Canadian imprisoned abroad has the right to be transferred to a Canadian prison. Just as the foreign state may refuse the transfer, so may Canada.[44] This will be further discussed in the next section.

While the minister enjoys great discretion, the decision must be reasonable and is reviewable in Federal Court. To that end, the minister's decision must be in writing and, when the application for transfer is denied, reasons must be given.[45] Jurisprudentially, these obligations have

33 *Ibid*, s 10(1)(e).
34 *Ibid*, s 10(1)(f).
35 *Ibid*, s 10(2).
36 *Ibid*, s 10(1)(b).
37 *Ibid*, s 10(1)(g).
38 *Ibid*, s 10(1)(h).
39 *Ibid*, s 10 (1)(i).
40 *Ibid*, s 10(1)(j).
41 *Ibid*, s 10(1)(k).
42 *Ibid*, s 10(1)(l).
43 *Goulet v Canada (Minister of Public Safety & Emergency Preparedness)*, 2012 FC 65 at paras 6–8 [*Goulet*] seems to suggest this.
44 *Dudas v Canada (Minister of Public Safety & Emergency Preparedness)*, 2010 FC 942 at para 30 [*Dudas*]; *Getkate v Canada (Minister of Public Safety & Emergency Preparedness)*, 2008 FC 965 at para 26 [*Getkate*].
45 *ITOA*, above note 6, s 11. See also *LeBon v Canada (Minister of Public Safety and Emergency Preparedness)*, 2012 FCA 132 at para 25, rev'g 2011 FC 1018 [*LeBon* (Decision 1)].

been framed as the minister's "duty to explain"[46] and as the minister's obligation to highlight what purposes and factors in section 10 were relied on in reaching the decision.[47] Absent such explanations, the Federal Court would not be able to review the reasonableness of the decision.[48]

The judicial review mechanism is a positive aspect of this process, especially when considering that other processes that may involve national security do not benefit from judicial oversight.[49] This also increases the transparency of the whole transfer process. Unlike ministerial decisions, judicial decisions are public and provide insight into how the minister exercised discretion, as well as what factors were invoked and why. While this is an area of law in which the Federal Court grants a high degree of deference to the minister, there have been somewhat frequent judicial interventions in the ministerial decisions.[50]

3) Administration of the Foreign Sentence in Canada

There are two main ways that countries deal with the administration of foreign sentences: conversion, and continued enforcement and adaptation. Conversion means that, upon transfer, the sentence is converted to whatever the receiving state would have assigned for the crime had it been responsible for sentencing. Continued enforcement and adaptation means that the sentence imposed by the foreign state is simply administered by the receiving state upon transfer, and only adapted if it is not in accordance with the laws of the receiving state.[51]

The *ITOA* has adopted the approach of continued enforcement and adaptation.[52] A sentence is adapted if it is inconsistent with Canadian law.[53] Sometimes, foreign sentences are longer than the maximum sentences for the equivalent crimes in Canada. If this is the case, the sentence will be adapted upon transfer such that the total length of the sentence is the

46 *Singh v Canada (Minister of Public Safety & Emergency Preparedness)*, 2011 FC 115 at para 19 [*Singh*].
47 *Dudas*, above note 44 at para 43.
48 *Goulet*, above note 43 at para 15.
49 For a discussion on this see Hameed, above note 2 at 38–39.
50 See Appendix for a list of judicial reviews and outcomes over the last twenty years.
51 Van Ert, Allen & Robb 2014, above note 2 at 552.
52 *ITOA*, above note 6, ss 13 & 14; *Khadr v Edmonton Institution*, 2014 ABCA 225 at para 31, aff'd 2015 SCC 26 [*Khadr*].
53 *ITOA*, above note 6, s 14.

length of the maximum sentence for the equivalent crime in Canada.[54] By contrast, the sentence cannot be increased upon transfer, even if the minimum Canadian sentence for a comparable crime is longer than the sentence received by the individual abroad.[55] Also, any period of supervised release imposed by the foreign state will be converted to a period of probation under Canadian law.[56]

Upon transfer, consistent with Canadian law, an individual will serve time in a provincial prison if sentenced to fewer than two years, or in a penitentiary (under CSC's authority) if sentenced to two years or more.[57] The *ITOA* provisions regarding sentencing are set up to ensure that parole eligibility prescribed to Canadians upon transfer are consistent with parole law in Canada. Once an individual has served either seven years or one third of the sentence (whichever comes first), they are eligible for full parole.[58] This calculation includes a consideration of any reduction in sentence, other than for time served after the sentence was imposed,[59] and seems to be based on the length of the individual's adapted sentence where applicable. Similarly, parole eligibility for murder is calculated in accordance with *ITOA* and the *Criminal Code*.[60] This makes sense given that in some foreign jurisdictions, like the United States, there are sentences of life without possibility of release, which do not exist in Canada. However, it is unclear how this provision can be squared with section 5(1) of the *ITOA*, which states that the sentence cannot be increased upon transfer. Given that, the United States aside, Canada has some of the longest periods of parole ineligibility for murder among comparable countries,[61] this may be an issue in the future. If an individual is eligible for parole before the date of transfer, based on the adapted Canadian sentence, then "the day of their transfer is deemed to be their day of eligibility."[62]

54 *Ibid.*

55 *Ibid*, s 5(1).

56 *Ibid*, s 16.

57 *Ibid*, s 21(a) & (b).

58 *Ibid*, s 23.

59 *Ibid*, s 22(1).

60 *Ibid*, s 24; *Criminal Code*, RSC 1985, c C-46.

61 Mary E. Campbell & David Cole, "Sentencing and Parole for Persons Convicted of Murder" in David Cole & Julian Roberts, eds, *Sentencing in Canada: Essays in Law, Policy, and Practice* (Toronto: Irwin Law, 2020) 183 at 187.

62 *ITOA*, above note 6, s 27.

4) Special Issues

The *ITOA* provides some special considerations and procedures for youth transfers, transfers of persons found either unfit to stand trial or NCR-MD, and transfers of those who have committed sexual offences. In Canada, youth and individuals deemed not criminally responsible fall under provincial authority; for these two categories, the consent of the province of custody is required, in addition to that of the minister.[63]

The Canadian *Youth Criminal Justice Act* (*YCJA*)[64] contains provisions limiting the sentences for young offenders based on crime and age group (twelve- to thirteen-year-olds are one group and fourteen- to seventeen-year-olds are another). If the foreign sentence is longer than the maximum provided by the *YCJA* for the relevant category, the foreign sentence will need to be adapted.[65] If the foreign sentence would have been a youth sentence if it had been imposed in Canada, and the individual is under the age of twenty upon transfer, or if the sentence would have been an adult sentence if it had been imposed in Canada and the individual is under the age of eighteen upon transfer, the person will be transferred to a youth correctional facility.[66] If the individual is more than twenty at the time of transfer, serving what would be a youth sentence had it been imposed in Canada, or more than eighteen and serving what would be an adult sentence of fewer than two years had it been imposed in Canada, they will be transferred to a provincial adult correctional facility.[67] Courts have confirmed that this is the case, regardless of the length of the sentence.[68] If more than eighteen and serving what would be an adult sentence of two years or more if it had been imposed in Canada, the individual will be transferred to a federal penitentiary.[69]

The administrative arrangements for the transfer of those NCR-MD or those unfit to stand trial are generally different from those for sentenced individuals, and they are regulated separately in bilateral, multilateral,

63 *Ibid*, ss 9(1) and 32(2).

64 *Youth Criminal Justice Act*, SC 2002, c 1 [*YCJA*].

65 *ITOA*, above note 6, s 17.

66 *Ibid*, ss 20(a)(i) and 20(b)(i).

67 *Ibid*, ss 20(a)(i) and 20(b)(ii).

68 *Khadr*, above note 52 at paras 121–22. See also van Ert, Allen & Robb 2014, above note 2 at 550–53.

69 *ITOA*, above note 6, s 20(b)(iii).

or *ad hoc* administrative agreements.[70] For this category, the Provincial Review Board will make a recommendation to the attorney general of the province as to whether consent to the transfer should be given, based on the factors listed under section 32(3)(a), (b), and (c) of the *ITOA*.[71] If transferred, the individual offender will generally be committed until the Review Board holds a hearing, between forty-five and ninety days after the transfer, for assessing whether a different order is needed.[72]

Finally, to transfer someone whose offence would be a designated sexual offence in Canada, in addition to the custodial sentence or committal order for those NCR-MD, compliance with the *Sex Offender Information Registration Act* (*SOIRA*),[73] including registration as a sex offender and any applicable conditions, is required.[74] These obligations begin on the day of the transfer.[75]

C. ISSUES IN THE REGULATION AND IMPLEMENTATION OF TRANSFERS

1) A Politically Fuelled Process?

The only sources of numeric information on the application of the *ITOA* and the outcome of the ministerial decision-making process are the CSC's International Transfers Annual Reports.[76] Between 2004 and 31 March 2014 (so largely under the previous version of the *ITOA*) there were 2,542 applications for transfer to Canada, out of which 1,214 were denied by one state or the other.[77] The Canadian minister rendered a total of 1,274 decisions, out of which 967 (or 76 percent) were approved.[78] A third of these applications were approved in the 2004–06 period under a Liberal

70 *Ibid*, s 31.

71 *Ibid*, s 32(3).

72 *Ibid*, s 34(2) & (3).

73 *Sex Offender Information Registration Act*, SC 2004, c 10 [*SOIRA*].

74 *ITOA*, above note 6, s 36.1.

75 *Ibid*, s 36.2(1).

76 Correctional Service Canada, *International Transfers 2013–2014 Annual Report* (no date, last modified 20 May 2015) [*International Transfers Annual Report 2013–2014*], online: www.csc-scc.gc.ca/004/001/092/004001-1003-eng.pdf; *International Transfers Annual Report 2016–2017*, above note 14.

77 *International Transfers Annual Report 2013–2014*, *ibid* at 4.

78 *Ibid* at 5–6.

minister (McLellan).[79] Under Minister McLellan, the rate of approval was 98–100 percent.[80] Under the subsequent Conservative ministers, the rate of approval dropped as low as 27 percent, with the average being 65–75 percent approval, depending on the year.[81] No major legislative, policy, or societal changes had occurred during that time that could explain the difference. Also, there is no evidence of an increase in security concerns coinciding with the period of increased denials.[82]

In 2012–13, under the Conservative government, the *ITOA* was amended to further increase the discretion of the minister to deny a transfer request. One would have expected to see a growth in the number of denied transfers with the passing of the amendments. However, starting in 2014, there was a significant drop in the number of rejected applications. In fact, between 2014–17 (the last years for which statistics are currently available), the rate of denied applications went back to that of the pre-2006 era of 1–4 percent.[83] This period coincides with the return to power of the Liberal Party.

In conjunction with the issues raised by some of the factors listed in the *ITOA*, as well as by the problems identified by the Federal Court in judicial review decisions (both of which are discussed in following sections), this fluctuation in numbers raises significant red flags regarding the arbitrariness of the transfer decision-making process. As other commentators have noted, it is of concern that a process clearly created to help ensure the safe reintegration and rehabilitation of individuals seems to be driven by political ideology more than anything else and may lead to "an unfair or discriminatory exercise of discretionary authority."[84]

2) Public-Safety Related Factors in the Decision-Making Process

The most common factors relied on by the minister to deny transfer applications were that the individual's return to Canada constitutes a threat to the security of the country under section 10(1)(a) of the *ITOA* (30

---

79 *Ibid.*

80 *Ibid.*

81 *Ibid.*

82 Hameed, above note 2 at 38.

83 *International Transfers Annual Report 2016–2017*, above note 14 at 6.

84 Hameed, above note 2 at 31.

percent of denials between 2004–14[85] and 32 percent between 2012–17[86]), and that the individual will, after the transfer, commit a terrorism offence or criminal organization offence under section 10(2)(a) of the *ITOA* (40 percent in 2004–14[87] and 32 percent in 2012–17[88]). It is not immediately clear what "threat to the security of Canada" means. Decisions that have relied on the threat to security have often been found unreasonable by the Federal Court due to insufficient evidence to establish such a threat.[89] The factor has been invoked less often with the passage of time, especially once courts interpreted security as having the very precise meaning of "threats of general terrorism and warfare against Canada or threats to the security of Canadians *en masse*,"[90] and not simply that "the applicant poses a general threat to Canadians."[91]

The "public safety" factor was added to section 10(1)(b) through the 2012 *ITOA* amendments, but was relied upon regularly in ministerial decisions long before that, as illustrated by the numbers above. It is not clear how public safety is distinguishable from some other *ITOA* factors, including whether the individual is likely to continue to engage in criminal activity after the transfer (section 10(1)(c)), and whether the individual will, after the transfer, commit a terrorism offence or criminal organization offence (section 10(2)(a)). Based on those decisions that have been judicially reviewed, it seems that these factors have often been used interchangeably. In particular, cases referencing the likelihood of someone engaging in criminal activity or organized crime will also engage with public safety and national security.[92]

Similarly, while the Federal Court distinguished between national security and public safety in *Getkate v Canada (Minister of Public Safety & Emergency Preparedness)*,[93] the minister clearly did not make this distinction

---

85 *International Transfers Annual Report 2013–2014*, above note 76 at 6.

86 *International Transfers Annual Report 2016–2017*, above note 14 at 6–7.

87 *International Transfers Annual Report 2013–2014*, above note 76 at 6.

88 *International Transfers Annual Report 2016–2017*, above note 14 at 6–7.

89 *Goulet*, above note 43; *Getkate*, above note 44; *Grant v Canada (Public Safety and Emergency Preparedness)*, 2010 FC 958 [*Grant*]; *Carrera v Canada (Minister of Public Safety)*, 2013 FC 798, aff'd 2013 FCA 277 [*Carrera*].

90 *Getkate*, above note 44 at para 41.

91 *Ibid.*

92 See, for example, *Grant*, above note 89; *Holmes v Canada (Minister of Public Safety and Emergency Preparedness)*, 2011 FC 112 [*Holmes*].

93 *Getkate*, above note 44.

for a long period of time.[94] (Ministers must now make this distinction.) Before *Getkate*, the minister argued that someone with a prior record or someone convicted of sexual offences was a security threat, while after *Getkate*, the minister posited that drug offences were a threat to national security.[95]

The arguments given by ministers for denying prisoner transfer based on public safety and national security illustrates the lack of robust meaning attributable to these factors, which allows room for each minister to apply them as they see fit. Public safety and national security often appear to have been used as a catch-all that cover everything not included under other factors, and that can easily ground any denial decision (given that the applicants are people with prior criminal histories and who have often been engaged in serious crimes).[96] As one commentator noted:

> The malleability of the "public interest" to suit the political agenda of the government of the day in a manner inconsistent with the rule of law and the will of Parliament reveals the arbitrary character of the definition of public safety in relation to international prisoner transfers.[97]

The likelihood of recidivism and engaging in organized crime has been heavily relied on (in conjunction with other vague notions of public safety concerns) in decisions that were judicially reviewed.[98] The minister has often been criticized by courts for giving primacy to this one factor (especially in cases of drug-related offences), without any evidence to support it beyond the type of offence itself, in what are often formulaic decisions.[99] Notably, in *LeBon v Canada (Minister of Public Safety and*

94 Hameed, above note 2 at 41.

95 *Grant*, above note 89 at paras 3 and 17.

96 On this see Hameed, above note 2 at 40.

97 *Ibid* at 38.

98 For a discussion on how and when the minister has used this factor in his decisions, and how courts have engaged with it see Mujuzi 2014, above note 2 at 142–46.

99 See, for example, *Dudas*, above note 44; *Curtis v Canada (Minister of Public Safety and Emergency Preparedness)*, 2010 FC 943 [*Curtis*]; *Tangorra v Canada (Minister of Public Safety and Emergency Preparedness)*, 2011 FC 1433 [*Tangorra*]; *Carrera*, above note 89 at para 24. *LeBon* (Decision 1), above note 45; *Vatani v Canada (Minister of Public Safety and Emergency Preparedness)*, 2011 FC 114; *Singh*, above note 46; *Downey v Canada (Minister of Public Safety and Emergency Preparedness)*, 2011 FC 116; *Balili v Canada (Minister of Public Safety and Emergency Preparedness)*, 2011 FC 396; *Randhawa v Canada (Minister of Public Safety and Emergency Preparedness)*, 2011 FC 625 [*Randhawa*]; *Yu v Canada (Minister of Public Safety and Emergency*

Emergency Preparedness), the court directed the minster to re-evaluate his application decision and provide reasons why he believed LeBon was a public safety risk, likely to engage in organized crime.[100] In particular, the minister was asked why these factors outweigh all the factors in favour of the transfer.[101] Despite these directions from the court, the minister's resulting redetermination was essentially a reworded version of his initial decision.[102] In response to this, the Federal Court, in an unprecedented decision, exercised its remedial power under section 18.1(3) of the *Federal Court Act* and ordered the transfer of the individual.[103] The Federal Court of Appeal upheld the decision and ordered that the minister abide by the court's decision.[104]

Beyond the confusion regarding their meaning, scope, and application, it is unclear how section 10 factors, such as engagement in a criminal organization, public safety, and engagement in criminal activity, advance the goals of the legislation. First, the legislative concern regarding such criminal engagements presumably refers to the period of time *after* the individual is released from custody. One would assume that Parliament does not question the ability of the federal or provincial systems to prevent the criminal activity *while* individuals are in their custody.[105] If it does, that raises a whole different set of problems beyond transfer of prisoners. Second, if the legislative concern indeed pertains to the engagement in criminal activity *after* release from custody, how will a denial of transfer prevent that? If the individual is only a Canadian national, they will most likely be deported to Canada upon release.[106] If the person has dual citizenship, they might not be deported, but they could voluntarily return

Preparedness), 2011 FC 819 [*Yu*]; *Del Vecchio v Canada (Minister of Public Safety and Emergency Preparedness)*, 2011 FC 1135; *Villano v Canada (Minister of Public Safety and Emergency Preparedness)*, 2011 FC 1434 [*Villano*]; *Goulet*, above note 43.

100 *LeBon* (Decision 1), above note 45 at para 21.

101 *Ibid.*

102 *LeBon v Canada (Minister of Public Safety & Emergency Preparedness)*, 2012 FC 1500 at para 13 [*LeBon* (Decision 2)].

103 *Ibid.*

104 *LeBon v Canada (Minister of Public Safety & Emergency Preparedness)*, 2013 FCA 55, aff'g 2012 FC 1500 [*LeBon CA*].

105 However, see *Lau v Canada (Minister of Public Safety and Emergency Preparedness)*, 2015 FCA 28, where the minister's decision was found reasonable because the minister had grounds to be concerned about the individual escaping custody, which made him a threat to public safety while in prison.

106 Mujuzi 2014, above note 2 at 148.

to Canada after serving the sentence. Intuitively, one would think that, if criminal engagement is a concern, then returning the person to the country where there are family relationships and close cultural kinship, while allowing for various targeted programs and interventions in custody, would best serve the goal of diminishing recidivism risks. This very fact was noted as an important crime prevention and law enforcement benefit of transfers by the UNODC in its handbook.[107]

The only situation in which the issue of criminal engagement after release could be different upon transfer is that in which, once transferred to Canada, the sentence is adapted and the individual is released earlier or is not under supervision upon release. Early or unsupervised release is possible every time the foreign sentence is higher than the maximum allowed in Canada for a comparable offence. For instance, in *Markevich v Canada (Minister of Public Safety and Emergency Preparedness)*,[108] the court, upon a second judicial review of a ministerial decision for the same case, stated that "the Minister did address factors more clearly linked to the Act in denying the request," and noted he "found that *it was not in the interests of or consistent with the goal of the administration of justice to have Markevich forego the rehabilitative purpose of the 3 years of supervised release which would occur if he were transferred to a Canadian prison*."[109] The reason that Markevich would not have been required to serve three years of supervised release upon transfer to Canada is because his sentence would have been adapted to be consistent with Canadian law, and the adapted sentence would not have included a period of supervised release.

This issue appeared in at least two other cases. In *Scheiring v Canada (Public Safety and Emergency Preparedness)*,[110] the minister held that the applicant, who was convicted of distribution of child pornography, would endanger public safety if transferred. However, not only was there minimal evidence presented by the minister regarding such a risk,[111] but also, upon transfer, the applicant would have automatically had to follow the *SOIRA* requirements. If he served his sentence in the United States and

107 *UNODC*, above note 3 at 13.

108 *Markevich v Canada (Minister of Public Safety and Emergency Preparedness)*, 2011 FC 113 [*Markevich*].

109 *Ibid* at para 8 [emphasis added].

110 *Scheiring v Canada (Public Safety and Emergency Preparedness)*, 2020 FC 651 [*Scheiring*].

111 *Ibid* at para 26.

then returned to Canada upon release, he would not.[112] Despite this, the minister held that upon "an overall examination of this factor, including the seriousness of the offence, the significantly large amount of child pornography images and videos found in Mr. Scheiring's possession, and *the fact that Mr. Scheiring would immediately be released upon transfer in Canada*, I conclude that Mr. Scheiring's return to Canada will endanger public safety, including the safety of the child."[113] In *Kozarov v Canada (Minister of Public Safety and Emergency Preparedness)*,[114] the minister did not specifically mention that the reason for denial was that the individual would be eligible for release for his drug-related offences much earlier in Canada than in the United States. However, he invoked public safety concerns that are otherwise difficult to explain given that, at the time of the transfer application, the United States had already communicated its decision to deport the applicant back to Canada upon his release.

To summarize, in the vast majority of cases in which various public safety factors are invoked, the concern appears to be misplaced. In most cases, this factor should be neutral, since the individual could eventually return (or be returned) to Canada anyway. In other cases, like *Scheiring*,[115] transferring to Canada may have, in fact, better served public safety, since the transfer in such situations allows for the individual to take relevant programs in Canadian prisons and it requires him to register as a sex offender under *SOIRA*. Finally, there are those cases in which the individual would indeed serve a less onerous sentence if transferred to Canada. However, it seems absurd to suggest that adapting a sentence to be consistent with Canadian maximum sentences and parole law somehow runs contrary to the administration of justice and endangers the public, hence serving as a reasonable justification for transfer denial. Would the implication not then be that Canadian laws are insufficient to protect the public?

112 *SOIRA*, above note 73.

113 *Scheiring*, above note 110 at para 20 [emphasis added].

114 *Kozarov v Canada (Minister of Public Safety and Emergency Preparedness)*, 2007 FC 866 [*Kozarov*].

115 *Scheiring*, above note 110. See also *Tosti v Canada (Minister of Public Safety and Emergency Preparedness)*, 2015 FC 747 at para 38.

3) Other Factors for Ministerial Consideration

"Social or family ties in Canada" is also a listed factor for consideration in transfer decisions.[116] In a small number of decisions (9 percent in 2004–14[117] and 4 percent in 2012–17[118]), the denial of the minister was based, in full or in part, on the individual's lack of social ties to Canada, or on the fact that the family did not want the individual to be transferred. This factor was often invoked in conjunction with section 10(1)(d) of the *ITOA*, "whether, in the Minister's opinion, the offender left or remained outside Canada with the intention of abandoning Canada as their place of permanent residence."[119] These two factors, when read together, could provide a justification for refusing a transfer. However, family or social ties have not been given strong consideration in approving transfers, even when the family has made supportive submissions.[120] While we do not have data on the number of transfers approved or denied without considerations of family ties, it also appears that at least some people whose transfers were denied had such ties. Based on the information available in the decisions judicially reviewed, this factor appears to become truly relevant only when it works against the individual's interest.[121]

"Whether the offender has refused to participate in a rehabilitation or reintegration program" in the foreign prison is a newer factor added in 2012.[122] It is unclear why refusal to engage in prison activities is deemed in and of itself as a negative factor. Given that the individual is a Canadian in a foreign prison, the programs offered may be culturally irrelevant to the needs of the individual.[123] This is particularly true for individuals who will be deported upon release. Prison programs are meant to prepare people for reintegration in a certain society. If the individual will be released to a society different than the one prepared for through prison programs, an

---

116 *ITOA*, above note 6, s 10(1)(f).

117 *International Transfers Annual Report 2013–2014*, above note 76 at 6.

118 *International Transfers Annual Report 2016–2017*, above note 14 at 6.

119 *Kozarov*, above note 114.

120 See, for example, *Holmes*, above note 92 at para 21; *Curtis*, above note 99; *Grant*, above note 89; *Randhawa*, above note 99; *Yu*, above note 99; *Tangorra*, above note 99; *Villano*, above note 99.

121 For a general discussion on transfer of prisoners and right to family life internationally and in Canada, see Mujuzi 2013, above note 2 at 272–85.

122 *ITOA*, above note 6, s 10(1)(h).

123 Mujuzi 2014, above note 2 at 150.

insistence on them taking those programs makes little sense. This concern may be less applicable where the foreign country is culturally similar to Canada, such as the United States. However, even then, programs that pertain to accessing resources in the community, banking, housing, social services, etc., will not be pertinent. In addition, depending on the foreign country, there may be logistical issues preventing the individual's meaningful engagement in programs, such as language barriers or a lack of available programming. All in all, if, as stated in *ITOA*, one of the main purposes of transfers is to contribute to the rehabilitation and reintegration of offenders,[124] and if, as UNODC notes, "sentenced persons who serve their sentences in their home countries can be rehabilitated, socialized, and reintegrated into the community better than anywhere else,"[125] it makes little sense to hang the transfer of a prisoner on whether they attended rehabilitative and reintegrative programs in the foreign country.

The factor listed under section 10(1)(i) of the *ITOA* is also newer and raises its own set of concerns, even if there are no reports of it having been relied on yet. Refusing the transfer of an individual for not taking responsibility for the offence[126] potentially increases the risk of, or at least compounds problems arising from, wrongful convictions. For instance, people may accept responsibility at trial or after being wrongfully found guilty (which would reduce their chances of ever being exonerated) in order to expedite the transfer process. Even in countries with strong judicial systems, wrongful convictions are a reality that cannot be ignored. The states with which Canada has transfer agreements[127] have varying degrees of procedural and substantive protections for accused people. The chances of wrongful convictions may be even higher in some of these countries. Thus, the concerns regarding people wrongly taking responsibility out of a desire to be transferred should not be dismissed lightly.

The residual consideration added in 2012 of "any other factor the Minister deems relevant"[128] has been used in nearly 1 percent of denials prior to 2017.[129] Even though the number of cases affected by residual considerations is not high based on the data available, the concern with this factor

124 *ITOA*, above note 6, s 3.

125 *UNODC*, above note 3 at 10.

126 *ITOA*, above note 6, s 10(1)(i).

127 CSC, "List of Countries Acceding a Bilateral Treaty with Canada," above note 4.

128 *ITOA*, above note 6, s 10(1)(l).

129 *International Transfers Annual Report 2016–2017*, above note 14 at 7.

should be obvious: it increases the discretion of the minister and makes the decisions even harder to review by courts. Given the fluctuation in approvals based on the party in power and the regular criticism of the courts regarding the formulaic application of the listed factors, a factor such as this that further widens the minister's discretion should not be seen as a welcome addition.

4) Mobility Rights Under the *Charter*: Did the Courts Get It Right?

In many cases in which an individual has applied for judicial review of the minister's decision to deny a transfer request, the question has also been raised as to whether section 8 of the *ITOA* (which stipulates that Canada must consent to the transfer) and section 10 of the *ITOA* (which provides the factors that may be considered by the minister) breach the applicant's section 6(1) *Charter* right to enter Canada.[130] Essentially, the argument advanced by counsel for the applicants in these cases has been that once the individual and the foreign state have consented to the transfer, Canadian authorities (i.e., the minister and the CSC) should not have the power to deny the transfer request, and doing so breaches the individual's mobility rights.[131] In other words, a Canadian applicant has the right to transfer. In all cases, the Federal Court found that there is no such right, and that the temporary restriction of mobility due to the foreign sentence does not breach section 6(1). Most cases note that the individual is responsible for this temporary restriction, or that there is freedom to return to Canada upon completion of the sentence.[132]

The only case to make it to the Supreme Court of Canada — and which is now the leading authority on this point — is *Divito.*[133] Justice Abella, writing for the majority of the Court, held that the impugned provisions of the *ITOA* do not engage the individual's section 6(1) rights. Justice Abella noted that mobility rights are rooted in international human rights, which grant some level of protection to Canadians.[134] However,

130 *ITOA*, above note 6, ss 8 and 10; *Charter*, above note 27, s 6(1).

131 For example, *Divito*, above note 26 at para 14.

132 *Kozarov*, above note 114; *Getkate*, above note 44 at para 26; *Dudas*, above note 44 at para 26; *Holmes*, above note 92 at para 21.

133 *Divito*, above note 26.

134 *Ibid* at paras 21–29.

she then proceeded to posit that granting an individual a right to transfer would infringe state sovereignty: Canada cannot require that other countries transfer their Canadian prisoners.[135] Also, the reason a prisoner can be transferred is by virtue of the treaties implemented by the *ITOA*, not because of an individually existing right. Hence, Canada cannot be forced to accept the transfer of its nationals, either.[136]

As other commentators have noted, this is not necessarily a valid argument. Canada can, through bilateral and multilateral treaties, require that the states it enters into agreements with transfer their prisoners to Canada (though of course, it cannot compel the transfer).[137] Also, the *ITOA* is simply the instrument through which the transfer occurs; it does not prove or disprove the existence of an independent right to transfer. The mechanism through which an existing right is implemented, however, could certainly be in breach of this right. In this case, the discretion given to the minister to consent (or not) could conceivably breach section 6(1). Indeed, the minority in *Divito* found that section 6(1) rights are in fact engaged but determined that the infringement was nonetheless justified under section 1 of the *Charter*.[138]

The result in *Divito* is ultimately unsatisfactory because the judgments are fragmented and the arguments are underdeveloped. There is a lack of substantial engagement both with international human rights and with mobility rights. In the words of van Ert et al, by not engaging with what it means to "be arbitrarily deprived of the right to enter his own country," Abella J and her colleagues "missed an opportunity to develop international mobility rights through a thoughtful, thorough consideration of the right to enter one's own country."[139] Thus, it is fair to conclude that, while the law seems settled, in that the discretion afforded to the minister does not breach section 6(1), it is not immediately clear if and why this interpretation of the *Charter* is correct.

135 *Ibid* at para 43.
136 *Ibid* at paras 47 & 48.
137 Van Ert, Allen & Robb 2013, above note 2 at 563.
138 *Divito*, above note 26 at paras 68–84.
139 Van Ert, Allen & Robb 2013, above note 2 at 565.

D. CONCLUSION: IS THE APPLICATION OF THE *ITOA* CONSISTENT WITH ITS GOALS?

The *ITOA* was created with the goals of upholding the administration of justice, enhancing public safety, and ensuring the reintegration and rehabilitation of individuals. There is an underlying understanding in this Act, as well as in the treaties it implements, that the best interest of the offender is generally to be as close as possible to family and support networks, to receive culturally appropriate programs, and to receive the type of post-release supervision that will allow reintegration into society. This is also likely the best strategy to enhance public safety, given that a Canadian national cannot be kept out of the country forever.

In this context and with these goals in mind, the situations in which a transfer application would warrant a refusal strikes us as very rare. The process and the factors that the minister is invited to consider are not conducive to the consistent fulfillment of these goals. Public safety and criminal activity are used as catch-alls to keep out those deemed undesirable, based on political ideologies and, possibly, financial considerations[140] (given that Canada would pay for the transfer of a Canadian[141]).

While there may be good reasons to reject a transfer request in specific circumstances, the framework as it currently stands allows for much more than that. The mostly unrestricted exercise of ministerial discretion has led to decisions that are hard to square with the goals of the legislation. Moreover, these are just those decisions that are available because they have been judicially reviewed and were found unreasonable by courts (see Appendix). For every decision that has been reviewed, there are many others that have never been challenged.[142] That is hardly a surprise; most people do not understand the process, and without legal representation it would be very difficult to challenge a ministerial decision. Representation for transfers is not covered by legal aid and many individuals cannot afford

140 This is speculative, but given the numerous cases discussed where there do not appear to be any reasons under the applicable factors for the application to be denied, and given the very broad ministerial discretion that allows for the implicit considerations of any other factors, one has to question to what extent financial matters affect the minister's decisions.

141 *Treaty*, above note 15, art III.4 and art IV.4.

142 If we compare the annual reports with the reported decisions, it is clear that the rate of denied transfers is higher than the number of decisions judicially reviewed.

it. Thus, there is no reason to believe that unchallenged decisions are any sounder than those that have been challenged. In addition, it is important to remember that even when courts have rejected a challenge, they have done so based on the deferential reasonableness standard, within the confines of the legislation that grants the minister wide discretion.[143] A denied challenge does not mean that the decision was correct and that it advanced the goals of the legislation: it simply means that the minister expressly relied on some factors listed in the *ITOA* and had some evidence of those factors.

Furthermore, the fact that so many of the challenged decisions are found unreasonable is telling regarding the extent of the issue; even in the context of the wide discretion granted by legislation, the ministers may be consistently abusing their powers. It is perhaps time to revisit the *ITOA* and reframe the process and the powers granted to the minister such that they accord with the goals of the legislation, with the best public safety practices, and with Canada's international and national human rights obligations to its nationals.

143 With one exception (*Scheiring*, above note 110) all cases reviewed in this chapter are pre-*Vavilov* (*Canada (Minister of Citizenship and Immigration) v Vavilov*, 2019 SCC 65), which tinkered with the reasonableness standard. It is too early to tell if *Vavilov* will have any serious impact on the judicial review of transfer application decisions.

APPENDIX: TRANSFER DECISIONS JUDICIALLY REVIEWED (2004–2020)

Reference	Judicial Review Granted or Denied?	Sentencing Country	Offence(s)
Van Vlymen v Canada (Solicitor General), 2004 FC 1054	Granted	US	• Bank robbery; • Bank robbery by use of a dangerous weapon
Catenacci v Canada (AG), 2006 FC 539	Denied	US	• Conspiracy to possess with intent to distribute cocaine
Kozarov v Canada (Minister of Public Safety and Emergency Preparedness), 2007 FC 866	Denied	US	• Conspiracy to possess with intent to distribute detectable amounts of cocaine, marijuana, and ecstasy
Getkate v Canada (Minister of Public Safety & Emergency Preparedness), 2008 FC 965	Granted	US	• Three counts of aggravated child molestation; • One count of child molestation
Dudas v Canada (Minister of Public Safety and Emergency Preparedness), 2010 FC 942	Granted	US	• One count of conspiracy to import marijuana
Curtis v Canada (Minister of Public Safety and Emergency Preparedness), 2010 FC 943	Granted	US	• One count of conspiring to possess with intent to distribute cocaine
Grant v Canada (Minister of Public Safety and Emergency Preparedness), 2010 FC 958	Denied	Costa Rica	• International drug trafficking
Holmes v Canada (Minister of Public Safety and Emergency Preparedness), 2011 FC 112	Denied	US	• Drug importation

Reference	Judicial Review Granted or Denied?	Sentencing Country	Offence(s)
Markevich v Canada (Minister of Public Safety and Emergency Preparedness), 2011 FC 113	Denied	US	• Attempted possession of a significant quantity of ecstasy
Vatani v Canada (Minister of Public Safety and Emergency Preparedness), 2011 FC 114	Granted	US	• Possession of cocaine
Singh v Canada (Minister of Public Safety and Emergency Preparedness), 2011 FC 115	Granted	US	• Importation of marijuana and ecstasy (in large quantities)
Downey v Canada (Minister of Public Safety and Emergency Preparedness), 2011 FC 116	Granted	US	• Conspiracy to import and distribute 100 kg or more of marijuana and hash oil
Balili v Canada (Minister of Public Safety and Emergency Preparedness), 2011 FC 396	Granted	US	• Conspiracy to import with intent to distribute 5 kg or more of cocaine
Duarte v Canada (Minister of Public Safety and Emergency Preparedness), 2011 FC 602	Denied	US	• Conspiracy to import with intent to distribute more than 5 kg of cocaine
Randhawa v Canada (Minister of Public Safety and Emergency Preparedness), 2011 FC 625	Granted	US	• Conspiracy to traffic narcotics
Tippett v Canada (Minister of Public Safety and Emergency Preparedness), 2011 FC 814	Denied	US	• Conspiracy to possess with intent to distribute cocaine
Yu v Canada (Minister of Public Safety and Emergency Preparedness), 2011 FC 819	Granted	US	• Conspiracy to import into the US in excess of 500 g of methamphetamine

Reference	Judicial Review Granted or Denied?	Sentencing Country	Offence(s)
Del Vecchio v Canada (Minister of Public Safety and Emergency Preparedness), 2011 FC 1135	Granted	US	• Conspiracy to distribute 30 kg of cocaine
Newberry v Canada (Minister of Public Safety and Emergency Preparedness), 2011 FC 1261	Denied	US	• Conspiracy to distribute more than 5 kg of cocaine
Tangorra v Canada (Minister of Public Safety and Emergency Preparedness), 2011 FC 1433	Granted	US	• Conspiracy to possess with intent to distribute MDMA
Villano v Canada (Minister of Public Safety and Emergency Preparedness), 2011 FC 1434	Granted	US	• Conspiracy to import MDMA
Goulet v Canada (Minister of Public Safety and Emergency Preparedness), 2012 FC 65	Granted	US	• Conspiracy to distribute in excess of 50 kg of marijuana; • Conspiracy to import in excess of 50 kg of marijuana
LeBon v Canada (Minister of Public Safety and Emergency Preparedness), 2012 FCA 132, rev'g 2011 FC 1018 (LeBon Decision 1)	Granted	US	• Possession with intent to distribute cocaine; • Improper entry into the United States by an alien
LeBon v Canada (Minister of Public Safety and Emergency Preparedness), 2012 FC 1500, aff'd 2013 FCA 55 (LeBon Decision 2)	Granted. Minister ordered to allow transfer.	US	• Possession with intent to distribute cocaine; • Improper entry into the United States by an alien

Reference	Judicial Review Granted or Denied?	Sentencing Country	Offence(s)
Carrera v Canada (Minister of Public Safety), 2013 FCA 277	Granted	US	• Conspiracy to distribute and possession with intent to distribute cocaine; • Attempt to distribute and possess with intent to distribute cocaine
Divito v Canada (Minister of Public Safety and Emergency Preparedness), 2013 SCC 47	Denied	US	• Conspiracy to possess over 30 kg of cocaine with intent to distribute
Bowden Institution v Khadr, 2015 SCC 26	Granted. Transfer from federal prison to provincial facility ordered	US (held in naval base in Cuba)	• Murder in violation of the law of war; • Attempted murder in violation of the law of war; • Conspiracy; • Providing material support for terrorism; • Spying
Lau v Canada (Minister of Public Safety and Emergency Preparedness), 2015 FCA 28	Denied	Australia	• Possession of commercial quantity of heroin; • Being knowingly concerned in importation of a commercial quantity of heroin
Chambers v Daou (Senior Manager, International Transfers Unit, Correctional Services), 2015 BCCA 50	Transfer occurred by virtue of a *habeas corpus* application	US	• One count of conspiracy to commit money laundering; • Four counts of money laundering
Tosti v Canada (Minister of Public Safety and Emergency Preparedness), 2015 FC 747	Granted	US	• Attempted enticement of a minor to engage in sexual activity
Scheiring v Canada (Public Safety and Emergency Preparedness), 2020 FC 651	Granted	US	• Possession and distribution of child pornography

twenty-two

Canadian Orders Can Compel Production of Data Controlled by US Companies

FRASER M. KELLY*

A. INTRODUCTION

Sometimes Canadian police can obtain a warrant to retrieve and use account passwords found in a Canadian's computer.[1] Doing so allows them to obtain Canadians' communications *content data*[2] wherever it may be stored. When that approach is unavailable, a request under the Canada–US Mutual Legal Assistance Treaty[3] must be sought to obtain the content

* General Counsel, Ministry of the Attorney General (Ontario) (retired). The views herein are those of the author alone and may not reflect the views of the Ministry of the Attorney General (Ontario).

1 In *R v Strong*, 2020 ONSC 7528 [*Strong*], the legality of this technique was upheld. There, a general warrant under s 487.01 of the *Criminal Code*, RSC 1985, c C-46 [*Code*] was obtained requiring a (non-accused) person to turn over an unlocked cellphone. The warrant permitted police to change the accused's Gmail password then access and download some of the accused's emails. The court held it was a "relatively simple solution for obtaining the sought-after data without engaging in the metaphysical exercise of determining where the data resides" (*Strong* at para 112). The court placed "little weight on the impact of the technique on Google," pointing out that purely domestic warrants "routinely authorize police to conduct covert entries by defeating alarm systems and/or locks. The technique here is essentially no different" (*Strong* at para 119).

2 *Content data*, for the purposes of this chapter, means information concerning the substance, purport, or meaning of a communication. This is the same definition adopted in the US *Stored Communications Act*, 18 US Code c 121 § 2510(8) [*SCA*].

3 *Treaty Between the Government of Canada and the Government of the United States of America on Mutual Legal Assistance in Criminal Matters*, (1985) Can TS 1990 No 19 [*MLAT*].

data because it is usually controlled by a US company that will not comply with a Canadian production order.[4] That is a problem. Canadian police and prosecutors live with a harsh truth, namely, that treaty requests are often impractical because they are too slow. The common refrain "Canadian police do not need production orders because they can *always* get the data by treaty" is the mantra of those lacking experience prosecuting criminal cases in Canada. That refrain is simply not true. The treaty route is not "always" available for practical reasons. Post-*Jordan*,[5] waiting for the data to arrive can become so problematic that forging on without even attempting to obtain all relevant evidence or data is often the safer course for the prosecution. In the insightful words of one court, it "seems reasonably clear that the *MLAT* provides a slow and uncertain mechanism of investigation."[6] In contrast, obtaining the data by a production order could be much faster than using the treaty (if companies comply) and afford better protection to Canadians than treaty requests, for two reasons. First, obtaining a production order requires Canadian police to provide reasonable grounds to a court—unlike treaty requests, which do not.[7] Second, Canadian defendants have a right to review the affidavit material filed to obtain a production order, but generally have no access to privileged state-to-state treaty requests or the affidavit material used to obtain a US warrant.

Unless US companies change how they respond to Canadian production orders, Canadian courts will eventually need to weigh in. Alternatively, Parliament could enact some form of data sovereignty laws[8] requiring businesses that receive Canadians' data to keep it within reach of Canadian judicial orders.

This chapter posits that Canadian jurists have jurisdiction to issue production orders for content data controlled by US companies. It also

4 A production order is issued under s 487.014*ff* of the *Code* and allows police to require persons (including corporate entities) that hold evidence to produce it.

5 In *R v Jordan*, 2016 SCC 27 [*Jordan*], the Supreme Court of Canada laid out its current approach on the right to be tried within a reasonable time under s 11(b) of the *Canadian Charter of Rights and Freedoms*, Part I of the *Constitution Act, 1982*, being Schedule B to the *Canada Act 1982* (UK), 1982, c 11 [*Charter*].

6 *British Columbia (Attorney General) v Brecknell*, 2018 BCCA 5 at para 57 [*Brecknell*].

7 *Schreiber v Canada (Attorney General)*, [1998] 1 SCR 841.

8 Data *sovereignty*, data *residency*, and data *localization* laws have been enacted in various forms by many countries globally. A comparative analysis of the nature of these regimes' breadth and scope is beyond the scope of this paper.

explains why the main arguments advanced for non-compliance are dubious at best. Last, it explains why "big data's" resistance on this issue makes data sovereignty laws the most prudent course going forward.

Before forging on, two broad issues bear mention. While the title of this chapter is self-explanatory, the ability of Canadian courts to reach Canadian data stored abroad is not solely a law enforcement problem. If Canadians' content data held by big US companies is beyond the reach of Canadian courts, that data is *also* beyond the reach of Canadian criminal defendants and many regulators, all of whom lack the ability to access the *MLAT* regime. There is a larger issue still, namely, whether companies who do business in Canada are *required* to obey domestic laws, which necessarily includes obeying Canadian court orders.

B. THE TREATY DOES NOT OBLIGE CANADA TO FIRST SEEK CONTENT DATA UNDER THAT REGIME

Determining the location of *tangible* items is usually straightforward so, for tangible items, *MLAT* is a good fit. Under article IV of the Canada–US treaty, there is an obligation to make a treaty request to seek documents and records or other articles "*known* to be located *in the territory* of the other Party."[9] In this age, intangible data flows across borders like the wind. As rightly noted by one scholar,[10] it is a fiction that all data is in the United States merely because it is accessible from a company that is physically present on US soil. The world's leading technology companies are transparent about how they function — *they* say that they use "*world-wide* networks of computer servers including servers located outside the United States."[11] What Canadians never know is where Canadian data is stored. Frankly, most users do not really *care*, provided their data is

9 *MLAT*, above note 3, art IV. Emphasis added.

10 Jennifer Daskal, "Whose Law Governs in a Borderless World?" National Constitution Centre (2017) [Daskal], online: https://constitutioncenter.org/digital-privacy/whose-law-governs-in-a-borderless-world. She argues that there are multiple reasons that "translation of the traditional rules governing searches and seizures to the world of digital evidence does not make good sense."

11 *Brief amici curiae of Technology Companies* (including Apple, Google, and Facebook) filed in the US Supreme Court in the *Microsoft (Ireland)* case. *Microsoft Corporation v United States of America*, 829 F3d 197 (2d Circ 2016), rehearing *en banc* denied, No 14-2985, 2017 WL 362765 (2d Circ Jan 24, 2017) at 1 [*Microsoft Ireland Amicus Brief*]. The same companies also use the even more amorphous term "cloud storage."

available to them when they want access to it. Canadians' data can be stored, split up, and copied or backed up in multiple storage facilities around the globe at the discretion of the US company that controls it, without notice to anyone.

Further, where data is to be found today may not be where it is tomorrow, because it can also be moved around the world any time for any reason — again without any user even knowing, let alone consenting. The user is oblivious and, importantly, so are Canadian authorities. The only thing Canadian authorities really know is that the US companies who control the data can find it and copy it when *they* want it from wherever on this planet they have decided to put it.

In short, often, if not usually, the treaty does not oblige Canada to make a treaty request up front because the location of intangible data is unknown — particularly when dealing with multinational companies.

C. *MLAT* IS TOO SLOW

By a very wide margin, most Canadian prosecutions proceed by summary conviction. That is important because they carry a presumptive eighteen-month *Jordan*[12] cap, after which a stay of proceedings becomes the most probable outcome.

In 2019, the US Department of Justice (DOJ) reported that the number of treaty requests for data that they were receiving had increased "dramatically" in recent years. They said they were having challenges "keeping up."[13] In Canada, police and prosecutors share the DOJ's pain, but from the other side of the fence. Social media data is relevant to criminal cases with increasing frequency. The *MLAT* process is too slow once one includes the entire relevant time frame — the time from when the drafting the *MLAT* request commences to the receipt of content data from US data companies (with an authentication affidavit).[14]

---

12 *Jordan*, above note 5.

13 US Department of Justice, *Promoting Public Safety Privacy and the Rule of Law Around the World: The Purpose and Impact of the CLOUD Act, White paper*, April 2019 [*White paper on the CLOUD Act*], online: www.justice.gov/CLOUDAct at 3.

14 In my experience, and based on anecdotal impressions from my practice, turnaround times for *MLAT* requests vary significantly depending on whom one asks and what time periods enter into that calculation. Defining the start and end times becomes important to get an accurate estimate. Estimates commonly do not include the

Launching the treaty request process increases the risk of a stay of proceedings based on unreasonable delay. There is little doubt that *MLAT* requests can be expedited in emergencies, however, the only factor that would change a routine case into an emergency is the passage of time associated with awaiting evidence (and authentication affidavits) to arrive pursuant to an *MLAT* request. Receiving data under the wire but late in the litigation process is no panacea either, because its receipt inevitably prompts an adjournment, putting the case in jeopardy for unreasonable delay.[15] Delaying arrests to await *MLAT* results is often unworkable, because safety issues often require immediate arrests. Sometimes the ability of police to obtain the data by *MLAT* before arrest is impossible for the simple reason that its existence is not known to investigators before the arrest occurs.

Jordan and the cases that followed have had an unintended consequence: most investigators tend to avoid *MLAT* completely whenever possible, and proceed to trial without even attempting to obtain the data stored abroad. If a fully informed court is the goal, the sluggishness of the *MLAT* process sometimes undermines the quality of criminal justice in Canada. Because production orders are more quickly sought and obtained, using them to obtain all relevant evidence would improve the current situation—but only if multinational companies comply.

---

police time required to draft the initial request, and the time taken in the inevitable back-and-forth to satisfy domestic and US authorities about the form and content of the request. Estimates commonly do not consider follow-up requests if the data delivered is deficient or incomplete in any way. In 2017, Daskal stated that the average turnaround time in the US was ten months. Daskal, above note 10. This US estimate varies from a Canadian estimate of four to five months—a calculation not factoring in the time needed to draft and redraft *MLAT* requests. The best source of the *real* timeline would be provincial Attorneys General and police.

15 As an example of a court looking unfavourably on delay associated with awaiting *MLAT* results, see *R v Kaulback*, 2017 CanLII 7095 (Nfld Prov Ct); reversed on appeal, 2018 NLCA 9, but at para 44 the Court of Appeal affirmed the lower court's analysis on the *MLAT* issue. Canadian prosecutors, the court explained, have an obligation to oversee the *MLAT* process "to ensure undue delay is avoided." Aside from expressing a concern, the reality is that Canadian prosecutors cannot *oversee* much—because they lack any ability to compel foreign governments or data companies to hurry up.

D. CANADA'S PRODUCTION ORDER SECTIONS WERE ENACTED TO ALLOW COLLECTION OF DATA STORED ABROAD

What is the territorial reach of a Canadian production order? According to the world's leading technology companies, US legislators *could* legally enact provisions "saying that its warrants apply extraterritorially."[16] It is difficult to disagree. The current wrinkle is that Canada did what leading technology companies said that the United States could have done, and those companies do not like it very much. Principles of comity and statutory interpretation have never barred states from passing "laws having extraterritorial operation" but they are presumed not to have done so absent "clear words *or necessary implication.*"[17]

Parliament intended production orders to collect data stored outside Canada. First, the territorial reach of "all court orders" is a matter of interpretation gleaned from "the language of the order *and the policies served by the order.*"[18] Further, Canada's production order sections are not penal provisions, so they are to be given a *liberal and purposive interpretation*—interpreted in a way that best achieves their intended purpose. The Supreme Court of Canada has explained that evidence-gathering provisions (and production orders are one form of those) are intended to provide mechanisms for investigators to "unearth and preserve *as much relevant evidence as possible.*"[19] The court in *Brecknell*,[20] discussed in more detail later, held that Parliament intended production orders to modernize police powers *in an internet age*, i.e., in relation to data. Given the nature of modern commerce, by *necessary implication* Canada's production order legislation must have extraterritorial reach.

Determining Parliament's intent is not difficult. Section 487.014 of the *Criminal Code* defines the prerequisites for a general production order.[21] It came into force in March 2015, replacing Canada's first production order

---

16 *Microsoft Ireland Amicus Brief*, above note 11 at 26.

17 *R v Hape*, 2007 SCC 26 at paras 47ff; *Society of Composers, Authors and Music Publishers of Canada v Canadian Association of Internet Service Providers*, 2004 SCC 45 at paras 54*ff.*

18 *R v Greco*, (2001), 159 CCC (3d) 146 at para 30 (Ont CA), Moldaver JA (as he then was), speaking for a unanimous court.

19 *CanadianOxy Chemicals Ltd v Canada (Attorney General)*, [1999] 1 SCR 743 at para 22.

20 *Brecknell*, above note 6.

21 Other specialized production orders are not fully explored because the focus here relates to *contents* of historical communications that fit within *Code* s 487.014.

section that was enacted in 2004.[22] The versions are nearly identical. A section 487.014 production order can issue when a judge is satisfied there are reasonable grounds to believe that an offence has been or will be committed, that the data in question will afford evidence in relation to that offence, and that the "data is in the person's custody or control." Two issues do not present much of a drafting hurdle, and can be addressed here briefly. First, "person" is defined expansively,[23] and includes corporations. Second, drawing on experience, and by reading companies' terms of service and privacy policies, affiants have little difficulty establishing reasonable grounds to believe content data exists and is possessed or controlled somewhere.[24]

That the 2004 production order legislation was re-enacted in largely the same terms in 2015 becomes more significant when one notes a Supreme Court of Canada decision released between those dates. Specifically, in 2008, the Supreme Court of Canada decided *Tele-mobile.*[25] The Court considered whether and when it was appropriate for judges to add a term to the production orders requiring the government to pay costs for compliance. Of note in this context are the Court's comments about the legislative intent of the 2004 production order section. Justice Abella cited the remarks of the secretary to the Minister of Justice at second reading, explaining the impetus for the original bill:

> Law enforcement agencies and crown prosecutors have been asking for a new investigative tool for some time and *with the proliferation of the Internet and the widespread adoption of new communications technologies*, the timing is right for this form of investigative tool.
>
> The production orders will solve a number of nagging issues for investigators including extraterritorial searches and timing issues. Under these new orders, persons who have possession or control of documents, data or information will have to produce that information whether it resides in Canada or abroad. Thus, as long as they have possession or control over the relevant information, they will be required to produce

22 *Code*, above note 1, s 487.012 in 2004.

23 See the definitions of "person" and "organization" in s 2 of *Code*.

24 Most terms of service explain that companies retain content of communications. Further, affiants are permitted to draw upon their experience in other cases as part of their grounds to obtain warrants and jurists are required to consider it, *R v Cunsolo*, 2008 CanLII 48640 at para 68.

25 *Tele-mobile Co v Ontario*, 2008 SCC 12.

it no matter where it is located. *This solves the problem that has in part been created by inexpensive overseas data warehousing.*[26]

Thus, in the shadow of the Supreme Court's dicta in 2008, Parliament declined to change the wording of the production order section in 2015, when the production order provisions were overhauled. In the unlikely event legislators were unaware that Canadian data was being stored abroad before 2004, the Supreme Court's dicta in *Telus* leaves no room to doubt that legislators knew about it in 2015. There seems little to suggest that Canada's production order power was intended to stop at the border, and much to support that it was intended to allow the capture of data stored abroad. Indeed, the production order sections would be drastically less useful without that ability.[27]

If one accepts that interpretation, the only remaining jurisdictional issue is whether companies controlling the data are "here," because a Canadian production order can only issue against an entity "in Canada."

E. VIRTUAL PRESENCE AND CORPORATE SEPARATENESS

1) Virtual Presence

Virtual presence is well recognized in Canada and in the United States. In the age of digital commerce, physical presence of a data controller may simplify the analysis, but it is not required. Companies, unlike people, can be in more than one place at one time. Any realistic examination of how US technology companies operate shows that they are virtually present *in Canada* in a pervasive way. Their apps are stored in millions of Canadians' electronic devices. US companies receive Canadians' data sent from devices located in Canada. They collect advertising revenue from thousands of Canadian businesses with whom they contract from afar, and purposely direct that advertising to millions of Canadians' devices.

Several authorities support the logical proposition that a Canadian court has jurisdiction to make an order against a foreign company that chooses to conduct business in Canada. Consider the following.

---

26 *Ibid* at para 40 [emphasis in original].

27 For example, most Canadians' health information is stored on servers located in the United States (Nova Scotia and British Columbia excepted). A strict territorial approach would lead to the absurd result that data would become unavailable to law enforcement from within Canada.

In *Google Inc v Equustek*,[28] the Supreme Court of Canada upheld an injunction (an order punishable by contempt for non-compliance) against Google Inc., the US corporation. Of note, Google Inc. did not challenge the lower court's determination that *in personam* and territorial jurisdiction were established "because Google carried on business in the province through its advertising and search operations."[29] In upholding the lower court's injunction, it appears the Supreme Court of Canada agreed.

In *Equustek* why did Google Inc. not challenge the Supreme Court of Canada's jurisdiction to make an order against it? Its position on this issue may have been influenced by its 2014 experience in Europe, in *Google (Spain)*.[30] In that case, a Spanish national brought an action against both the US parent Google Inc., and its subsidiary incorporated in Spain, Google (Spain). At issue was whether a European court could make an order compelling Google Inc. to de-index certain content from its search indices. The companies raised a jurisdictional argument: Google Inc. operated the search engine from the United States without any input from its Spanish subsidiary, putting it beyond the reach of European courts. The local subsidiary, Google (Spain), played a limited role in the global enterprise, merely promoting and selling advertising space that was offered and eventually displayed by the parent company.

The Court rejected the jurisdictional argument, finding jurisdiction to make an order against Google Inc. because there was an inextricable link between the two companies. The Court explained that Google (Spain)'s marketing of advertising was "the means of rendering the search engine at issue economically profitable" and Google Inc.'s ongoing practice of displaying advertisements provided Google (Spain) with a service or product to market.

Next, look to the US Supreme Court's 2018 decision in *South Dakota v Wayfair, Inc*,[31] an interstate tax case. At issue was whether Wayfair had any obligation to obey South Dakota's tax collection laws when Wayfair was not "in" South Dakota. While Wayfair shipped merchandise *to*

28 *Google Inc v Equustek Solutions Inc*, 2017 SCC 34.

29 *Ibid* at para 37.

30 *Google Spain SL and Google Inc v Agencia Española de Protección de Datos (AEPD) and Mario Costeja González*, Case C-131/12 (Official Case No), ECLI:EU:C:2014:317 (Neutral Citation), (European Court of Justice (Grand Chamber)), online: https://eur-lex.europa.eu/legal-content/EN/ALL/?uri=CELEX%3A62012CJ0131.

31 *South Dakota v Wayfair, Inc*, 138 S Ct 2089 (2018).

South Dakota to fill online orders, the company had no *physical* presence in South Dakota—no offices, no employees, no warehouse, no subsidiary. The Supreme Court recognized the significance of *virtual* presence, rejecting Wayfair's reliance on the traditional physical presence test. The Supreme Court changed the physical presence test because it was unsound. Specifically, the Court recognized that "virtual presence" (the Court's term) sufficed. The Court could not maintain the physical presence rule "that ignores these substantial virtual connections" any longer. Any rule that turned on a "physical presence test" for companies in a digital age was "unsound and incorrect." Justice Kennedy delivered the majority opinion of the court and noted:

> [I]t is not clear why a single employee or a single warehouse should create a substantial nexus while "physical" aspects of pervasive modern technology should not. For example, a company with a website accessible in South Dakota may be said to have a physical presence in the State via the customers' computers. A website may leave cookies saved to the customers' hard drives, or customers may download the company's app onto their phones.... The "dramatic technological and social changes" of our "increasingly interconnected economy" mean that buyers are "closer to most major retailers" than ever before—"regardless of how close or far the nearest storefront." Between targeted advertising and instant access to most consumers via any internet-enabled device, "a business may be present in a State in a meaningful way without" that presence "being physical in the traditional sense of the term."[32]

It would appear the US Department of Justice (DOJ) agrees that virtual presence in the US *can* require a company to obey *US* laws, including the *Stored Communications Act* (*SCA*).[33] In the US DOJ's white paper on the *CLOUD Act*, a series of questions are posed and answered, including whether a company located outside the United States that provides services inside the United States is subject to the terms and orders set out in the *SCA*. The salient part of the DOJ's answer is the following:

32 *Ibid* at 2095 [citations omitted].

33 *SCA*, above note 2.

> Whether a company providing services in US territory is subject to US jurisdiction is a highly fact-dependent analysis regarding whether the entity has sufficient contacts with the US to make the exercise of jurisdiction fundamentally fair. The more a company has purposefully availed itself of the privilege of conducting activities in the United States or purposefully directed its conduct into the US, the more likely a US court is to find that the company is subject to US jurisdiction.[34]

Closer to home, the British Columbia Court of Appeal's 2018 decision in *Brecknell* expressly held that virtual presence of a company in Canada permits a Canadian court to issue a Canadian production order against it. Physical presence is not required. In *Brecknell*, the court found that a production order for data held by Craigslist was lawful, even though Craigslist was an internet-based advertising company with no physical presence in Canada. The court noted that "[c]orporate persons can exist simultaneously in multiple jurisdictions. They can be simultaneously both here and there, to borrow a phrase."[35] Given the nature of its business, the court held that Craigslist had a "real and substantial connection" to Canada that was "sufficient to provide personal jurisdiction over Craigslist."[36]

Quite similarly to the US Supreme Court in *Wayfair*, the court in *Brecknell* found that in our "Internet era it is formalistic and artificial to draw a distinction between physical and virtual presence" and to do so would "defeat the purpose of the legislation and ignore the realities of modern electronic commerce."[37] The court explained that Parliament's legislative intent was to "modernize police powers to investigate Canadian crime that is increasingly occurring through the internet or about which evidence exists in an international world."[38] While enforcement issues could engage international principles, the better approach was to treat a production order as "more akin to a subpoena" than a search warrant permitting entry into a place and seizure of a tangible item.[39] The court in *Brecknell* noted that US courts have long held that US court orders

34 *White paper on the CLOUD Act*, above note 13 at 17.
35 *Brecknell*, above note 6 at para 35.
36 *Ibid* at para 37.
37 *Ibid* at para 40.
38 *Ibid* at para 46.
39 *Ibid* at para 47.

(subpoenas) can be served on subsidiaries present on US soil to compel production of data—including data held overseas.[40]

Brecknell also addressed three other issues: problems with service, problems with enforcement, and the significance of the availability of *MLAT* as an alternative means to obtain the data. The rulings on all three issues were essentially the same: they do not impact the jurisdiction to make the production order.[41] Provincial courts outside British Columbia have split on following *Brecknell*, but as of the date of writing one other appellate court has followed *Brecknell* in relation to virtual presence as a basis for jurisdiction.[42]

2) Corporate Separateness

Putting aside the virtual presence issue for a moment, there is a forest-for-the-trees issue here. Proving virtual presence should not be necessary most of the time. A court may never need to assess virtual presence when a US company has a subsidiary in Canada, because the existence of that subsidiary may constitute "physical presence"[43] *in addition to* virtual presence. A

40 *Ibid* at para 48. This includes using subpoenas to circumvent troublesome international treaties. See for example, *Re Sealed Case*, 932 F 3d 915 (DC Circ 2019) where the court upheld the legality of US authorities' use of subpoenas to obtain Chinese banking data from US subsidiaries rather than making a request through their Mutual Legal Assistance Agreement. US Department of Justice lawyers were convinced China's response to a treaty request would be sluggish or simply ignored. Relying on a number of authorities, the court noted that under US law entities "cannot refuse to provide data simply because it is abroad." *In re Marc Rich & Co*, 707 F.2d 663 (2d Cir 1983) at 667: A witness may not "resist the production of documents on the ground that the documents are located abroad"; "[A] federal court has the power to require the production of documents located in foreign countries if the court has *in personam* jurisdiction of the person in possession or control of the material." *United States v First National City Bank*, 396 F2d 897, 900-01 (2d Cir 1968).

41 *Brecknell*, above note 6 at paras 51–52, 53, and 58.

42 *In the Matter of an application to obtain a Production Order pursuant to section 487.014 of the Criminal Code of Canada, 2018*, 2018 CanLII 2369 (NL PC); *Re Application for a Production Order, s 487.014 of the Criminal Code*, 2019 ONCJ 775. In Ontario, in a case dealing with probation orders, it appears that enforceability to make an order is a distinct issue from the jurisdiction to make it. *Greco*, above note 18. And see *R v Love*, 2022 ABCA 269 applied in *Re textPlus Inc*, [2022] OJ No 4959 (SC) and *Re Service de Police de la Ville Montreal*, 2022 QCCS 3935 (SC).

43 For example, in *Re Application for Production Order*, 2020 NSPC 55, the court accepted that "virtual presence" as explained in *Brecknell*, was immaterial because Facebook Inc.

detailed factual record in an affidavit or in litigation would be required to establish the necessary foundation for such a finding. An example would be evidence showing that parents and subsidiaries have (accurately) represented to the world that they are one entity. Where physical presence is asserted, it would help courts to know if Canadian subsidiaries are incorporated separately in Canada, whether they are privately owned, and whether they are largely funded by the parent.

Other factors can affect whether claimed corporate separateness is really a myth: how subsidiary employees and executives are hired, who they report to, what Canadian executives say publicly about who they work for, how Canadian remuneration levels and bonuses are set, what the subsidiary actually does, or who oversees how the Canadian subsidiary runs. The fraud-based test for piercing the corporate veil developed to insulate the parent from flow-through liability in the civil context (addressed in more detail below) should be restricted to the context in which that test was formulated. As in European court decisions, notably *Google (Spain)* described earlier, Canada courts have jurisdiction over both the subsidiary and parent, because they are integral parts of each other.

As a related legal matter, Canadian courts may be called upon to revisit the presumption of corporate separateness in the context of production orders (as they did in *Google (Spain)*). In *Yaiguaje v Chevron*,[44] the majority of the Ontario Court of Appeal declined to revise its two-part test for piercing the corporate veil when the issue arises in the civil context. To pierce in civil cases requires "that (i) there is complete control of the subsidiary, such that the subsidiary is the 'mere puppet' of the parent corporation; and (ii) the subsidiary was incorporated for a fraudulent or improper purpose or used by the parent as a shell for improper activity."[45] In a minority opinion (but concurring with the result), Nordheimer JA explained why this two-part test "should not have its scope expanded beyond the situations from which it arose."[46] It remains to be seen how this test would be applied to a US parent company that adopts a policy of placing Canadians' communication data beyond the reach of its Canadian subsidiaries for commercial reasons, when it would be lawful under

"has a physical presence in Canada"—in Ontario—so it was "not necessary for this court to reckon with the sufficiency of *virtual presence*."

44 *Yaiguaje v Chevron Corp*, 2018 ONCA 472.

45 *Ibid* at para 66.

46 *Ibid* at para 94.

US law for its Canadian subsidiaries to have access to it. US companies cannot claim ignorance about the impact of conducting business in that manner. Such a policy can and does result in "the effective, if unintended, frustration of investigation into serious criminal conduct" in Canada.[47] Continuing to do so may constitute an *improper purpose* within the meaning of *Yaiguaje*.

F. THE *STORED COMMUNICATIONS ACT*

US companies say the *SCA*[48] poses a significant barrier to providing communications content data absent a US court order to do so. In the event a Canadian production order is issued for content data, the *SCA* may be advanced on an application for relief under section 487.0193(2) of the *Criminal Code*. That section provides an avenue for relief where the company demonstrates that compliance with the Canadian production order would be "unreasonable" or would result in disclosure of information "protected from disclosure by law."

In the context of a Canadian production order, three things must be considered. First, this type of defence is statute-barred in Canada. It was contemplated by Parliament and reflected in section 487.0196 of the *Criminal Code*:

> No one is excused from complying with an order made under any of sections 487.014 to 487.018 [production order sections] on the ground that the document that they are required to produce may tend to incriminate them *or subject them to a proceeding or penalty*. However, no document that an individual is required to prepare may be used or received in evidence against them in a criminal proceeding that is subsequently instituted against them, other than a prosecution for an offence under section 132, 136 or 137. [emphasis added]

Second, if one sees a production order as akin to a subpoena to deliver evidence in Canada, the decision in *Spencer*[49] becomes significant. In *Spencer*, the Supreme Court of Canada considered whether a witness could lawfully refuse to deliver *testimonial* evidence in Canada on the ground that

47 *Brecknell*, above note 6 at para 58.

48 *SCA*, above note 2 §§ 2701–12. See also § 2510 for the definitions that apply to those provisions.

49 *Spencer v The Queen*, [1985] 2 SCR 278.

doing so would contravene a Bahamian law. The Court was not receptive. To allow this refusal in the face of a valid subpoena, itself a Canadian order, would be to "permit a foreign country to frustrate the administration of justice in this country."[50] Like the Bahamian law in *Spencer*, the *SCA* is the law of another country. Based on *Spencer*, it seems unlikely Canadian courts would accept a claim that compliance would be in breach of the *SCA* as a valid reason for refusing to comply.

Third, even US courts have held that the *SCA* does not apply outside the United States. The case of *Zheng v Yahoo!*[51] is instructive. There, Zheng's lawsuit against Yahoo! Inc. (in the United States) was summarily dismissed. The claim was that a foreign subsidiary, Yahoo! (China), released personal data to the Chinese government. The American court held that the *SCA* had no application on the facts of the case because disclosure was made abroad (in China), even if Yahoo! (China) was a subsidiary and even if the communications passed through US servers. The court recognized the "longstanding principle of American law that legislation is presumed to apply only within the territorial jurisdiction of the United States unless the contrary affirmative intention of Congress is clearly expressed."[52] Nothing in the legislation or legislative history expressed or demonstrated Congress intended the *SCA* to have extraterritorial effect.

A wealth of US jurisprudence has held that US wiretap provisions also have no extraterritorial effect. In short, where a foreign subsidiary hands over data, the *SCA* is not engaged. *Zheng* provides authority for the following significant proposition: if the *SCA* does not apply to disclosures made in Canada, if Canadian subsidiaries were to hand over the data in response to a Canadian production order, doing so would not expose the US parent to any risks in the United States.[53] But there is more.

US data companies rely on sections 2701(a) and 2703(b) of the *SCA*, pointing to a general prohibition against disclosure of contents of

---

50 *Ibid* at para 5.

51 2009 US Dist. LEXIS 111886 [*Zheng*].

52 *Ibid* at page 5.

53 Under s 231.2 of the *Income Tax Act*, RSC 1985, c 1 (5th Supp), it appears that Canadian subsidiaries that have access to data located abroad "for business reasons" can be compelled by Canadian order to produce it. See *eBay Canada Ltd v Minister of National Revenue*, 2008 FCA 348. In those circumstances the data was both here and there. Extraterritorial application of the *Income Tax Act* was not a significant issue due to the terms of service that explained what would be disclosed on order from a non-US court—a term very similar to those of most large data holders.

communications except pursuant to US court orders. Compliance with a Canadian production order, they say, raises the possibility they will be charged with an offence,[54] or sued,[55] in the United States. Not so fast. It is *not* clear that compliance with a Canadian court order exposes the US data holder to any repercussions should they deliver up data. There are several reasons:

- First, content data can be shared with the consent of the originator or intended recipient or the subscriber.[56] What do users consent to? Terms of service and privacy policies make clear that users agree to the terms the company sets. Those terms usually explain content data is subject to court orders—including, if lawful, orders from courts outside the United States.[57]
- Second, under US law, US companies can insulate exposure by having policies that permit their Canadian subsidiary to produce the data if so minded. After all, content data *can* be made available to subsidiaries for two reasons. First, the *SCA* makes clear that content data can be lawfully shared with subsidiaries as "necessarily incident to the rendition of" their "service."[58] Upon reading terms of service and data privacy policies, large data companies explain to users that the data they collect includes the contents of communications. Further, users are told their data will be shared within their *group* of associated companies *globally*. Users agree to these terms.
- Third, in addition to and distinct from the principle in *Zheng v Yahoo!*, companies that collect data have a statutory defence in the unlikely event that a Canadian sued them under the *SCA*, or if they were charged under the *SCA* in the United States for delivering

54 *SCA*, above note 2 § 2701(a).

55 *Ibid*, § 2707(a).

56 *Ibid*, § 2702(b)(3).

57 For example, in July 2021, Facebook's data policy included: "We . . . share your information with law enforcement or others in response to a legal request (like a search warrant court order or subpoena) if we have a good faith belief that the law requires us to do so. *This may include responding to legal requests from jurisdictions outside the United States* when we have a good faith belief that the response is required by law in that jurisdiction, affects users in that jurisdiction and is consistent with internationally recognized standards" [emphasis added], online: www.facebook.com/policy.php.

58 *SCA*, above note 2 § 2702(b)(5). American data companies' services usually include advertising that is sold in Canada by Canadian salespeople to Canadian businesses. When purchased, that advertising is directed at Canadians.

up Canadians' content data in response to a Canadian production order. If they take the position that the *SCA* applies to disclosure of this data—then they would have the benefit of section 2707(e) of the *SCA*. It expressly provides a defence where there is "good faith reliance on a court order or statutory authorization." Note the section does not specify *US* court order. "Court order," used in 2707(e), is not defined in section 2510 or in section 2711, either. To the extent there is legislative ambiguity, it would favour the defendant company.[59]

In summary, Canadian legislation and jurisprudence suggest that citing the *SCA* in Canada will not relieve a data company from compliance with a Canadian production order. Besides, the assertion that the *SCA* is a clear and *absolute* bar to production is not accurate. The claim that US data companies could face civil or criminal consequences for complying with a Canadian production order to deliver Canadians' data is dubious, especially if the data is handed over by their Canadian subsidiaries (with whom their terms say they lawfully share the data they collect). On the remote chance they faced an *SCA* charge or lawsuit in the United States, they will have a defence under *Zheng* and under section 2707(e) of the *SCA*.

G. COMITY

Comity is but one factor Canadian courts are to consider before issuing orders having extraterritorial effects. It is a principle with limitations. Before determining whether a Canadian provision having extraterritorial effect is permissible, Canadian courts "must consider whether (and if so, *the extent to which*) the action in question has some impact *of significance*" abroad, and whether the act has any real impact upon a foreign company that has no real and substantial link to Canada.[60] For reasons explained above, it is suggested that US data companies have substantial links to Canada, and that production of Canadians' data under the *SCA* is lawful, so there is likely no impact upon the foreign companies abroad. Comity should not bar issuance.

59 The "rule of lenity requires ambiguous criminal laws to be interpreted in favor of the defendants subjected to them." *US v Santos*, 553 US 507 (2008) at 514.

60 *1068754 Alberta v Quebec*, 2019 SCC 37 at para 84 [emphasis added].

From the other side of the border, a mere conflict with US law does not mean the order is unenforceable. Comity requires US courts to take a more nuanced approach. They are to attempt to respect judicial acts of Canadian courts "having regard to both international duty and the rights of its own citizens or of others who are under the protection of its laws." Under US law, it is incorrect to suggest "that foreign judgments that are inconsistent with American law must be dismissed as unenforceable."[61] Where a Canadian production order compels the production of Canadians' data in relation to Canadian crime, no US citizens (including corporations) are affected. Comity should result in US courts upholding a Canadian production order for Canadian data in relation to Canadian crime.

H. *CLOUD ACT* EXECUTIVE AGREEMENTS — WILL THEY HELP?

In response to pending litigation (the *Microsoft Ireland* case[62]), the United States passed the *Clarifying Lawful Overseas Use of Data Act* (*CLOUD Act)* in 2018.[63] It amended the *SCA* in several ways, including a relaxation of the disclosure restrictions for content data pursuant to the terms of executive agreements the United States might negotiate with foreign governments. Where executive agreements are reached, US data companies could *choose* to comply with foreign orders for data, avoiding the need for the treaty process. The idea or hope is that *CLOUD Act* executive agreements would facilitate more expeditious access to content data. If there were an executive agreement, the non-US "order" could be treated as a "request" when received by US companies. They could then lawfully hand over the data. Currently, Canada and the United States do not have an executive agreement, and the only one that exists is not operational yet.[64] Still, if the US and Canada ever negotiate an executive agreement, there is ample room for pessimism about whether it will work as hoped.

61 *Yahoo! Inc v La Ligue contre Je racisme et J'antisemitisme*, 433 F3d 1199 at 1213–15 and 1239–41 (9th Circ En banc 2006).

62 *Microsoft Ireland Amicus Brief*, above note 11.

63 The *CLOUD Act* was part of the *Consolidated Appropriations Act*, 2018, PL 115-141, Division V, online: www.govinfo.gov/content/pkg/PLAW-115publ141/html/PLAW-115publ141.htm.

64 As of July 2021—three *years* after the *CLOUD Act* was passed, the US has just one executive agreement—with the UK, and it is still not operational.

To see why, one must understand what these agreements cannot and will never do. The US DOJ rightly pointed out that requests under the *CLOUD Act* executive agreements

1) Cannot contain terms mandating decryption of data
2) Do not impose any obligation on US data companies to comply
3) Do not purport to vest any foreign court (including Canadian courts) with jurisdiction to order US companies to do anything[65]

The upshot is that the only thing executive agreement requests will ever do is remove a legal impediment. Compliance remains at the discretion of the US company. We know this much with certainty: large US technology companies have a long and unrelenting track record of resisting law enforcement even when faced with circumstances in which corporeal citizens might be inclined to cooperate. The much-publicized 2015 mass shooting in San Bernardino provides one example, and there are others involving other companies.[66] In that case, Apple remained steadfast that it would not assist the FBI in bypassing the auto-lock security feature on the iPhone owned by the mass killer (despite a court order), even though they were "shocked and outraged by the deadly act of terrorism."[67] Privacy and precedent were Apple's publicly expressed concerns.

To gauge the likelihood that executive agreements *between governments* may change the persistent resistance *of data collection companies* requires assessing why US tech giants have remained so predictably uncooperative when they have had a choice. In part, the answer lies in the reality that they are publicly traded companies. Shareholder primacy is the driving principle. Boards manage corporations to maximize shareholder wealth. Maximizing wealth and *not* cooperating with law enforcement are related. The value of their product—often advertising—is directly tied to user numbers. How companies *are perceived* by users directly affects the bottom line. If a company is perceived as being too cooperative with law enforcement, and too lax with respect to protecting privacy, users will leave and revenue will decline. This profit/privacy correlation is not a mere

65 *White paper on the CLOUD Act*, above note 13 at 4–6.

66 By way of background, see "The Story So Far: Apple–FBI Battle Over San Bernardino Terror Attack Investigation: All the Details" *Los Angeles Times* (19 February 2016), online: www.latimes.com/business/technology/la-fi-tn-apple-fbi-20160219-htmlstory.html.

67 Apple's response to its customer base is online: www.apple.com/customer-letter/?form=MY01SV&OCID=MY01SV.

theory. It is express. For example, examine how Facebook (now Meta) expressed this correlation in its 2021 Security and Exchange Commission (SEC) Form 10-K filing:

- Facebook stated they "generate substantially all our revenue from selling advertising placements to marketers."
- Further, "any significant decrease in user ... engagement could render our products less attractive to ... marketers and developers, which is likely to have a material and adverse impact on our revenue."
- Facebook explained that many factors could negatively affect user engagement, including "decreases in user sentiment" due to "concerns relating to privacy" and "changes mandated by legislation, government and regulatory authorities, or litigation that adversely affect our products or users."
- "Our brands may also be negatively affected ... by perceived or actual efforts by governments to obtain access to user information for security-related purposes."[68]

Championing privacy and resisting law enforcement influences public perceptions. It also increases or maintains the customer base, and thereby affects revenue. Technology and software giants' unrelenting resistance to police and legislators' efforts to get access to user content data is predictable and likely to continue if Canada ever does enter a *CLOUD Act* executive agreement. That conclusion becomes inescapable once the situation is viewed through a profit-maximization lens. Because executive agreements leave compliance permissive, the million-dollar question in the boardroom will be this: how will users perceive the company once it is learned that it is handing law enforcement private data that it could lawfully keep private? There seems to be little reason to expect a seismic shift in the pattern of resistance that the world has witnessed from global tech companies in the past decade.

If a US–Canada executive agreement is unlikely to work, the continuing need for timely access to content data for criminal investigations means that data sovereignty laws are required. There is no other way. Even

68 A PDF version of this 10-K filing is available for download on Facebook's Investor Relations webpage, online: https://investor.fb.com/financials/default.aspx.

if orders against US companies can be obtained, they are unlikely to comply, and enforcement is ugly. Enforcement is addressed next.

I. ENFORCEMENT MEANS MORE THAN PROSECUTION

It would be preferable if access to Canadian content data could be achieved without any kind of litigation, including enforcement. Enforcement is problematic and should never arise if the issues addressed in this chapter are addressed legislatively.

If enforcement is truly to be considered, the question becomes what Canada can do when a foreign company refuses to comply with a Canadian court order. Launching a *Criminal Code* prosecution is extremely challenging for two reasons (at least). First, proof of the offence, as currently contemplated in the *Criminal Code*, might be impossible to obtain because, per section 22.2, the Canadian prosecution would need to establish beyond a reasonable doubt that a "senior officer," within the meaning of section 2 of the *Criminal Code*, was aware of the production order and directed non-compliance. Second, under section 487.0198, fines for non-compliance with a production order are capped at a mere C$250,000; such fines are effectively meaningless to giant corporations that collect data assuming they were inclined to pay a fine at all.[69]

To understand what could be done, an attitudinal shift is required. Foreign companies that operate in Canada and, as a policy, refuse to comply with Canadian court orders or adopt policies that frustrate Canadian law enforcement are choosing not to obey Canadian law. A corporeal foreigner would not be permitted entry to Canada if that person had demonstrated an ongoing practice of disobeying Canadian law. Property that person owned and used to engage in criminality would be seized. Accomplices to criminal behaviour would also be barred from entry. Translated to a corporate entity: corporate charters can be wound up and assets can be seized civilly. Taxes on Canadian commercial activity can be levied, and entry for employees can be tightened. The answer lies in Ottawa, not in the courts.

---

69 According to *Fortune*, Facebook's publicly reported 2020 revenue was US$86 billion. "Fortune 500: Meta Platforms," online: https://fortune.com/company/facebook/fortune500/. To understand the scale, consider the maximum C$250,000 fine to a company with revenue of US$86 billion is as if a Canadian with a yearly income of $100,000 received a 23-cent fine.

In short, in the face of non-compliance, Canada can do a lot more than laying a charge; but none of this should be necessary because there is another solution that can be (and should be) accomplished domestically, one more likely to work than *CLOUD Act* executive agreements. The fix is in the form of six areas for legislative reform:

1) Enact data sovereignty legislation that compels companies doing business in Canada to store Canadian communication content data in Canada (or at least to store it in a place accessible to Canadian entities). Doing so removes all jurisdictional questions about the reach of Canadian orders.
2) Legislation must clarify that corporate separateness principles apply differently in the context of court orders to produce data than they do in relation to flow-through civil liability.
3) Legislation must clarify what constitutes service upon subsidiaries and companies that are virtually present in Canada. Currently, tech companies commonly insist the only way they will consider themselves served is if law enforcement officers upload copies of court orders to the US parent company online.[70]
4) Amend the non-compliance offence legislation (or amend section 22.2 of the *Criminal Code)* such that it no longer requires proof of the mental state of a senior officer in a multinational company before a company can be prosecuted for ignoring a Canadian production order.
5) Amend section 487.0198 of the *Criminal Code* to increase the penalty for non-compliance.
6) Amend other federal legislation to increase Canada's ability to tax and seize assets, and wind up corporations that habitually do business in Canada without complying with Canadian court orders.

J. CONCLUSION

The reach of Canadian production orders includes data stored abroad if the entity that controls it is present in Canada. Foreign companies

70 Without domestic laws that better define what constitutes service, big tech companies act more like countries, unilaterally deciding the issue for themselves. The idea that big tech companies function more like countries is attributed to Mark Zuckerberg, CEO and co-founder of Facebook (now Meta). See Jennifer Daskal, "Borders and Bits" (2018) 71:1 *Vanderbilt Law Review* 179 at 181–82.

that control Canadians' data are commonly both virtually and physically present in Canada. Right now, US companies could choose to comply or choose to allow their Canadian subsidiaries to comply with Canadian production orders for Canadian communication content data without any civil or criminal exposure in the United States. So far, they will not comply. This being so, Canadian data sovereignty laws should be created, and enforcement provisions should be bolstered. It would not be a radical development on the world stage or domestically. Law enforcement access to Canadians' data would be subject to judicial and legislative oversight—just as are bank records, phone records, health records, etc.—and to the overarching protection of section 8 of the *Charter* against unreasonable search and seizure. And the cause of effective law enforcement and timely criminal justice would be better served.

Table of Cases

Table of Instruments

Index

T after a page number indicates a table.

About the Editor

Robert J. Currie, KC, is Distinguished Research Professor at the Schulich School of Law at Dalhousie University, where he teaches international, transnational, Canadian and comparative criminal law; public international law; international advocacy; evidence; civil procedure; and law and technology. He studied at both St Francis Xavier University and the Norman Paterson School of International Affairs at Carleton University, and has degrees in law from Dalhousie and the University of Edinburgh. A member of the Nova Scotia Bar since 2000, Professor Currie has practiced both civil litigation and criminal law, and has appeared before all levels of court in Nova Scotia, as well as before the Federal Court.

Professor Currie has authored, co-authored, or co-edited numerous books, articles, and comments in the area of international and transnational criminal law, and his work has been cited by numerous Canadian courts, including the Supreme Court of Canada. He acts as a consultant and advisor for both government and private clients in criminal matters with transnational aspects. An award-winning teacher, he is often called upon to provide CLE and judicial education for the practising bar. He is a former president of the Law Reform Commission of Nova Scotia, a member of the board of directors of the International Society for the Reform of Criminal Law (ISRCL), and a member of the Canadian Task Force Against Global Corruption.

FSC
www.fsc.org
MIX
Papier | Fördert gute Waldnutzung
FSC® C083411

Kolibri 360 GmbH
Ferdinand-Jühlke-Straße 7
99095 Erfurt, Deutschland
produktsicherheit@kolibri360.de